A LITTLE MATTER OF GENOCIDE

Holocaust and Denial in the Americas
1492 to the Present

Other Books by Ward Churchill

Authored:

Fantasies of the Master Race:
Literature, Cinema and the Colonization of
American Indians (1992)

Struggle for the Land:
Indigenous Resistance to Genocide, Ecocide
and Expropriation in Contemporary North America (1993)

Indians Are Us?
Culture and Genocide in Native North America (1994)

Since Predator Came:
Notes from the Struggle for American Indian Liberation (1995)

From a Native Son:
Selected Essays in Indigenism, 1985–1995 (1996)

Pacifism as Pathology;
Observations on an American Pseudopraxis (1997)

Coauthored:

Culture versus Economism:
Essays on Marxism in the Multicultural Arena
with Elisabeth R. Lloyd (1984)

Agents of Repression:
The FBI's Secret Wars Against the Black Panther Party
and the American Indian Movement
with Jim Vander Wall (1988)

The COINTELPRO Papers:
Documents from the FBI's Secret Wars
Against Dissent in the United States
with Jim Vander Wall (1990)

Edited:

Marxism and Native Americans (1983)
Critical Issues in Native North America (2 vols., 1989–90)

Coedited:

Cages of Steel:
The Politics of Imprisonment in the United States
with J.J. Vander Wall (1992)

A LITTLE MATTER OF GENOCIDE

Holocaust and Denial in the Americas
1492 to the Present

BY WARD CHURCHILL

CITY LIGHTS BOOKS
SAN FRANCISCO

Cover design by Rex Ray
Book design by Elaine Katzenberger
Typography by Harvest Graphics

Library of Congress Cataloging-in-Publication Data

Churchill, Ward.
    A little matter of genocide : holocaust and denial in the Americas, 1492 to the
present / by Ward Churchill.
        p.   cm.
    Includes bibliographical references and index.
    ISBN 0–87286–323–9
    1. Indians, Treatment of—North America—History.   2. Indians of North
America—Government relations.   3. Indians of North America—Government policy.
4. Genocide—North America—History.   5. United States—Race relations.   6. North
America—Politics and government.
I. Title.
E91.C47   1997
970.004'97—dc20

          96–9668
          CIP

City Lights Books are available to bookstores through our primary distributor: Subterranean
Company, P.O. Box 160, 265 S. 5th Street, Monroe, OR 97456. Tel.: (541)-847-5274.
Toll-free orders (800)-274-7826. Fax: (541)-847-6018. Our books are also available through
library jobbers and regional distributors. For personal orders and catalogs, please write
to City Lights Books, 261 Columbus Avenue, San Francisco, CA 94133 or visit us at
http://www.citylights.com.

CITY LIGHTS BOOKS are edited by Lawrence Ferlinghetti and Nancy J. Peters and
published at the City Lights Bookstore, 261 Columbus Avenue, San Francisco, CA 94133.

ACKNOWLEDGEMENTS

Although none of them is responsible for any errors or biases appearing in my work, a number of people have been particularly constructive in shaping my thinking on the matter of genocide. Aside from those whose writings have been most influential — Raphaël Lemkin, Jean Paul Sartre, Leo Kuper, and Richard Drinnon — they include in a more direct and conversational sense Milner Ball, David Barsamian, Jimmie Durham, Richard A. Falk, T. Moana Jackson, Glenn T. Morris, David E. Stannard, George Tinker, Haunani-Kay Trask, and Sharon H. Venne. By way of negative inspiration, I suppose Yehuda Bauer, Steven T. Katz, and their colleagues are also deserving of special recognition in this regard.

Several others have been quite helpful in terms of preparing various portions of the manuscripts. These include Heather Davis, who chased down more than a few cites, and Leah Kelly, who undertook the daunting task of compiling both the bibliography and the index. Elaine Katzenberger of City Lights not only provided consistently superb editing of a project which mutated steadily, as most of mine do, into something more than it started out to be, she provided continuous encouragement during periods when it had begun to seem endless. I would also like to thank Pam Colorado for the poem used as a foreword, David Stannard for his preface, and Rex Ray for the fine cover.

A debt of gratitude is also owed to those who provided me with much needed personal support during a time when my mind was too deeply mired in the ugliest subject matter imaginable. At the head of the list is of course my wife, Leah, and my wider family, both Allens and Kellys. Sustenance was also gained from interactions with my people, the United Keetoowah Band of Cherokees, with the members of the American Indian Movement of Colorado, the Dark Night Collective, and my colleagues and students, most especially Rick Butler, in the Department of Ethnic Studies at the University of Colorado/Boulder.

Two essays — "Deconstructing the Columbus Myth" and "Genocide in the Americas" — are borrowed from my 1995 *Since Predator Came*. Appreciation is due to Aigis Publications for permission to reprint. Thanks also to the various journals, especially *Z Magazine* and *Peace Review,* in which earlier versions of some of these materials first appeared.

for Raphaël Lemkin (1901–1959)

and for genocide's many millions of victims
down through the ages

All my life, I've had to listen to rhetoric about the United States being a model of freedom and democracy, the most uniquely enlightened and humanitarian country in history, a "nation of laws" which, unlike others, has never pursued policies of conquest and aggression. I'm sure you've heard it before. It's official "truth" in the United States It's what is taught to school children, and it's the line peddled to the general public. Well, I've got a hot news flash for everybody here. It's a lie. The whole thing's a lie, and it always has been. Leaving aside the obvious points which could be raised to disprove it by Blacks and Chicanos and Asian immigrants right here in North America — not to mention the Mexicans, the Nicaraguans, the Guatemalans, the Puerto Ricans, the Hawaiians, the Filipinos, the Samoans, the Tamarros of Guam, the Marshall Islanders, the Koreans, the Vietnamese, the Cubans, the Dominicans, the Grenadans, the Libyans, the Panamanians, the Iraqis, and a few dozen other peoples out there who've suffered American invasions and occupations first hand — there's *a little matter of genocide* that's got to be taken into account right here at home. I'm talking about the genocide which has been perpetrated against American Indians, a genocide that began the instant the first of Europe's boat people washed up on the beach of Turtle Island, a genocide that's continuing right now, at this moment. Against Indians, there's not a law the United States hasn't broken, not a Crime Against Humanity it hasn't committed, and it's still going on.

—Russell Means
American Indian Movement
October 12, 1992

CONTENTS

What Every Indian Knows

by Pam Colorado

Auschwitz ovens
burn bright
in America
twenty-four million
perished in the flame
    Nazi
        not a people
        but
        a way of life
Trail of Tears Humans
ends in Oklahoma
           an Indian name for
           Red Earth

Redder still
soaked in blood
of two hundred
removed tribes
the ovens burn bright
in America
Ancestral ashes
sweep the nation
carried in
        Prevailing winds
Survivors know
        the oven door stands wide
    and some like mouse
        cat crazed and frenzied
        turn
        and run into the jaws

at night
the cat calls softly
to the resting
us

WARD Churchill is a man looking for trouble. Of course, anyone familiar with his voluminous writings during the past two decades—on subjects such as racism in American film and literature, New Age spiritual hucksterism and counterfeit Indians, U.S. government death squads, the damage done to indigenous peoples by the forces of capitalism *and* marxism, and a great deal more—know that Churchill quite audaciously has been courting (and finding) trouble for some time now. But with *A Little Matter of Genocide* he is certain to bring on the enmity of an entirely new and particularly vitriolic collection of critics. And this is a shame because the sentiments of his new book are extraordinarily compassionate and humanitarian, while its overall argument is eminently fair, deliberative, and reasonable.

But debates on the subject of genocide are rarely hospitable to fair, deliberative, or reasoned discourse. And I am not speaking here only of writings by the well-known neo-fascist crackpots and cranks who attempt to deny the reality or the magnitude of the Holocaust. Beyond them, there are those who apply the word "genocide" so indiscriminately—claiming, for example, that legalized abortion in the United States has resulted in fetal genocide—that the term begins to lose any meaning at all. On the other hand, there are those who attempt to seize the word as their own private property and narrow its meaning to a single case—in asserting, for instance, that the only "true" genocide in the history of the world was that perpetrated by the Nazis against Jews—thus trivializing the sufferings of many other terribly damaged groups of people in both the present and the past.

In both of these cases the arguments almost invariably are advanced with a noisy ferocity that attempts to drown out opposing voices or to shame them into silence. Thus, those who disagree with the contention that abortion is genocide are labeled as murderers, or at least accomplices in murder. Similarly, those, including some of the most eminent scholars in the world today, who contend that the Nazi attempt to exterminate the Jews was not a unique event in world history are dismissed as anti-Semites or Holocaust deniers.[1]

It should not be surprising to discover that in both of these cases the driving force behind them is what religion scholar Richard L. Rubenstein calls "religio-mythic" traditions.[2] But if it is the zealotry of spiritual dogma that gives them internal power, both of these arguments also benefit from close linkages with secular political ideologies. I will not dwell on, or further pursue here, the obvious connections between the religious and political agendas of those who claim to see a fetal holocaust as a consequence of women being granted the right to terminate unwanted pregnancies. But the political and religious linkage that is at the heart of what has become conventional public wisdom on the uniqueness of Jewish suffering during the Holocaust does deserve a few words more, in part because that linkage is less well known, in part because of the great damage that it does to victimized people everywhere, and in part because this is certain to be the key source of criticism that will be leveled at *A Little Matter of Genocide*.

Ethnocentrism is one of the most common characteristics of human groups and, as often as not, it is fairly harmless. It simply makes sense that individual groups would consider their ideas, their cultures, their religions or aesthetic standards, and so on, to be either superior to others, or at least in certain ways to be preferential or noteworthy in comparison with other groups. Group histories are no different. Both the accomplishments and the sufferings of one's own people, as distinct from others, are the standard fare of historical chronicles the world over. That these accounts are often at least in part fictitious should come as no surprise, and in fact the ubiquitousness of the so-called "invention of tradition" in many cultures has become a topic of intense scholarly interest of late.[3]

Seen in this light, the fiction that Jewish suffering under the Nazis is wholly incomparable with the suffering of any other people at any other time is quite understandable. After all, the horrors endured by Jews at the hands of the Nazis were indeed monumental—and neither Ward Churchill nor I would suggest that the mass murder of Jews that occurred under Hitler was one whit less than what has been known and described for years by the greatest Jewish historians of the Holocaust. But it is essential that we recognize that Jews as a people, and Israel as a nation, are no less given to ethnocentric historical accounts than is any other human group.

More than a decade before mobilization for the Holocaust began in Germany, a Ukranian Jewish immigrant to Palestine named Yitzhak Lamdan published a poem entitled "Masada," recounting the heroic resolve of the

Jewish defenders of the mountain fortress Masada against assault by Roman forces in 73 A.D. In a recent study, "The Recovery of Masada," Barry Schwartz, Yael Zerubavel, and Bernice Barnett have shown that, although the story of Masada "was one of the least significant and least successful events in ancient Jewish history," unknown to most Jews prior to the 1920s and not even mentioned in the Talmud or the Midrash or in any other sacred text, following the publication of Lamdan's poem in 1927 the story of Masada became one of constant retelling and emotional commemoration by Jews in the Zionist movement. Indeed, in the 1950s and 1960s, as Israeli journalist Tom Segev has noted, "Masada, the symbol of Hebrew rebellion and pride, was the object of pilgrimage for Israeli youngsters; soldiers scaled its sharp cliffs to swear fealty to the army and to receive their first rifles."[4]

The resurrection of the story of Masada clearly functioned to energize a people in struggle—at first, in the 1920s, with the effort to launch the Zionist movement, and continuing through the 1960s, as Israel perceived itself to be fighting for nothing less than survival. As George Steiner has written, in words chosen by Schwartz, Zerubavel, and Barnett to serve as an epigraph for their essay: "A society requires antecedents. Where these are not naturally at hand, where a community is new or reassembled after a long interval of dispersal or subjection, a necessary past tense to the grammar of being is created by intellectual and emotional fiat." But, important as the story of Masada and Lamdan's poem once were to Israel and its supporters, that poem, once a prominent part of the curriculum, is in fact no longer routinely used in Israeli school textbooks.[5] It is no longer necessary. Times have changed.

But remembering the Holocaust does remain necessary—as it should. So, apparently, do claims for the historically unrivaled magnitude of Jewish suffering during the Holocaust—which should not. Indeed, so insistent is Israel on retaining its "official story" of the Holocaust that for decades now some of the most outstanding works of scholarship on Jewish history and politics—including volumes by Hannah Arendt and even Raul Hilberg's monumental study, *The Destruction of the European Jews* —have not been translated into Hebrew. The reason: they critically discuss the behavior of certain Jews in Europe during the years of Nazi rule, and such criticism cannot be tolerated in the Israeli theocracy. As Segev notes, in Israel today the Holocaust, by one measure at least, has an even higher status than religion, since the maximum legal penalty for denying the existence of God is one year in prison, while the punishment for denying the existence of the Holocaust is up to five years' imprisonment.[6]

Nor can the existence of *other* genocides be acknowledged by Israeli officialdom. Thus, the government of Israel has banned from Israeli television a documentary film on the early twentieth-century Turkish genocide against the Armenians, and it has prohibited the Israeli Education Ministry from introducing the story of the Armenian genocide into high school curricula. Moreover, in the United States, Israeli officials of the Foreign Office have joined hands with the government of Turkey in blocking Congressional efforts to acknowledge the Armenian genocide with an official Armenian day of remembrance.[7]

Thus, what began as an understandable and admirable effort to "never forget" has evolved into official Israeli policy to undermine the efforts of others to have their own historical victimhood acknowledged. Yet, in the world of scholarship, there exists a strange paradox: while some of the most prominent opponents of this state-sponsored exclusivist agenda are Israeli scholars such as Israel Charny, the head of Jerusalem's Institute on the Holocaust and Genocide, the majority of the most prominent proponents of Holocaust exclusivism are Jewish American writers.

The chauvinistic motivations of this latter group are too transparent and psychologically self-evident to bother discussing here, but they have long been on display regarding extremist positions on other Israeli issues, while the burden has often fallen on Israeli scholars themselves to offer the necessary correctives.[8] And just as the Turkish government now openly (and self-servingly) supports the claim that only Jews have suffered true genocide—while the Israeli government accommodatingly denies the existence of the Turkish genocide against the Armenians—so too does a similar propagandistic *quid pro quo* operate in the United States.

As Ward Churchill and others have overwhelmingly documented, the European conquest of the New World, including the U.S. government's destruction of its own indigenous peoples, was the most massive interrelated sequence of genocides in the history of the world. Over the course of four centuries—from Columbus's first landing on Hispaniola in the fall of 1492 to the U.S. Army's massacre of innocent Indian men, women, and children at Wounded Knee in the winter of 1891—tens of millions of the Western Hemisphere's native people were consumed in a holocaust of mass violence that, in locale after locale, *typically* destroyed 90–95 percent and more of the indigenous inhabitants.[9]

Historians and politicians once liked to boast of the slaughter of Indians that characterized the European and Euro-American conquest of North America. Thus, the most celebrated American historian of his time, Francis

Parkman, described the Indian as "man, wolf, and devil all in one," and as "deserving" of the extermination that was proceeding apace as he wrote. And President Theodore Roosevelt happily called the U.S. military's grisly mass murder and ritual dismemberment of hundreds of Indian women and children at Sand Creek in Colorado "as righteous and beneficial a deed as ever took place on the frontier."[10]

In the post-Nazi era, however, gloating over genocide has fallen out of vogue. In its place are discussions of the sad "inevitability" of the native peoples' destruction, of the "unintentionally" unleashed European diseases that are said to have done all the damage, and of the kind efforts of the European invaders to find a "middle ground" of accommodation and understanding between themselves and the Indians—generosities fated to fail, alas, because of the Indian leaders' alleged inability to "control" their warriors.[11] It has been quite an intellectual pirouette to behold: from proudly taking credit for mass murder to blaming the victim—from open celebration of genocide to genocide denial—in just a few short generations.

In this climate, with American scholars and politicians now adamantly denying that there is any blood on their forebears' visibly dripping hands, the claim of certain Jewish scholars and their acolytes that the Nazi killing of Jews was unprecedented and unique falls on welcoming ears. As Edward Herman and Noam Chomsky observe in their book *Manufacturing Consent:* "A propaganda system will consistently portray people abused in enemy states as *worthy* victims, whereas those treated with equal or greater severity by its own government or clients will be *unworthy.*"[12]

Herman and Chomsky illustrate this observation by comparing the lavish attention heaped by the U.S. mass media on the murder of a priest by Polish police in 1984 (a worthy victim killed by the agents of an enemy state) with the almost nonexistent coverage afforded the murders of priests in U.S. client states in Latin America (unworthy victims killed by the agents of American allies). Later in that same volume they similarly compare the American response to genocide in Cambodia (horror—since the Cambodian government was our enemy, thereby making its victims worthy) with the U.S. reaction to the simultaneous genocide in East Timor (silence—since Indonesia, the perpetrator of the genocide, is our friend, thereby making its victims unworthy).

This, of course, is precisely the same dynamic involved in the treatment by American scholars, politicians, and journalists regarding Jewish victimhood in the Holocaust and the European and Euro-American genocide against the indigenous peoples of the Americas. The Jews were killed by the government that today epitomizes the very idea of evil, Nazi Germany, thereby making Jews today the ultimate "worthy" victims (although not sufficiently worthy at the time to prevent the United States and Britain from ignoring and suppressing efforts that would have rescued countless Jews from the gas chambers).[13] On the other hand, the native peoples of the Americas were killed by our very own forebears (those of us who are white, at least), thus making them the ultimate "unworthy" victims.

It should hardly be surprising, then, to learn of the U.S. government's major support for the United States Holocaust Memorial Museum—whose former executive director attempted to exclude from the museum's exhibits any mention of Nazi victims other than Jews—while the very seat of the American government is located in a part of the country where the indigenous peoples were once openly hunted and slaughtered into extinction. Of course, there is no talk of a Holocaust Memorial Museum for them.

Like the unholy alliance between Israel and Turkey, in the United States an equally unholy alliance prevails. Here, the partners are the governmental and intellectual protectors of the American image, and the home-grown purveyors of the idea that Jewish suffering under Nazi rule was incomparable with that of any other people at any other time or place. As with Israel and Turkey, it is a brutal alliance of benefit to both parties.

Only the victims of other genocides suffer. Genocides long past—and officially denied—whose few survivors huddle in poverty and broken health (far and away the worst poverty and the worst health of any group of people in the United States) on reservations and in ghettoes in the forgotten backwaters of American life. And genocides ongoing—also officially denied—where American client states liquidate inconvenient indigenous people with impunity, so long as such states remain within the U.S. protective orbit.

So it is a good thing that Ward Churchill, with this book, *A Little Matter of Genocide,* has decided once again to go looking for trouble. He will get plenty of it. But it is only because of trouble-makers like him that the deadened conscience of this nation might some day begin to stir. May his kind multiply.

David E. Stannard
Honolulu
May 1997

1. See, for instance, Deborah Lipstadt, *Denying the Holocaust: The Growing Assault on Truth and Memory* (New York: Free Press, 1993), pp. 212–15, where, as Churchill points out, anyone who disagrees with her extreme exceptionalism regarding the Holocaust is placed in a catchall category embracing straightforward Holocaust "deniers" and what she calls "not yet deniers," ranging from out-and-out anti-Semites to the allegedly even more insidious "relativists" (including essentially all comparative historians of genocide and the Holocaust) who are said to be "the equivalent of David Duke without his robes."

2. See Richard L. Rubenstein, "Religion and the Uniqueness of the Holocaust," in *Is the Holocaust Unique? Perspectives on Comparative Genocide,* ed. Alan S. Rosenbaum (Boulder: Westview Press, 1996), pp. 11–18.

3. The classic work, and the one that started it all, is *The Invention of Tradition,* ed. Eric Hobsbawm and Terence Ranger (Cambridge: Cambridge University Press, 1983).

4. Barry Schwartz, Yael Zerubavel, and Bernice M. Barnett, "The Recovery of Masada: A Study in Collective Memory," *The Sociological Quarterly,* 27 (1986), 147–64; Tom Segev, *The Seventh Million: The Israelis and the Holocaust* (New York: Hill & Wang, 1993), p. 516.

5. Schwartz, et al, "Recovery of Masada," pp. 147, 158.

6. See Segev, *Seventh Million,* pp. 464–65.

7. Yossi Klein Halevi, "The Forgotten Genocide," *Jerusalem Report,* 6 (June 1995), pp. 20–21; Judith Miller, *One, by One, by One: Facing the Holocaust* (New York: Simon & Schuster, 1990), p. 259; Edward T. Linenthal, *Preserving Memory: The Struggle to Create America's Holocaust Museum* (New York: Viking Press, 1995), pp. 238–39. I have previously discussed these and related matters in my "Uniqueness and Denial: The Politics of Genocide Scholarship," in Rosenbaum, ed., *Is the Holocaust Unique?,* esp. pp. 195–96.

8. One well known example of this phenomenon a number of years ago involved the publication of *From Time Immemorial: The Origins of the Arab-Jewish Conflict Over Palestine,* by Joan Peters. This was a book that justified Israel's twentieth-century colonization of Palestine by, in effect, arguing that the Palestinian people were a fabrication—that is, that prior to the rise of Zionism, during the late Ottoman and early British periods, Palestine was a barren land, essentially absent of Arab populations other than a few wandering Bedouin tribes. Peters's book thus echoes the founding (and equally false) myths of the United States and South Africa, that European settlement occurred on unoccupied and unimproved "virgin land." While most Jewish American reviewers were falling all over themselves to celebrate Peters's claims, one of the most prominent criticisms of *From Time Immemorial* was the work of the Israeli scholar Yehoshua Porath, who pointed out that the volume was built upon the selective manipulation of old and discredited sources of extreme Zionist provenance—and sources that no self-respecting Israeli scholar would be associated with today. See Yehoshua Porath, "Mrs. Peters's Palestine," *The New York Review of Books* (January 16, 1986), pp. 36–39.

9. See David E. Stannard, *American Holocaust: The Conquest of the New World* (New York: Oxford University Press, 1992).

10. Francis Parkman, *The Conspiracy of Pontiac and the Indian War After the Conquest of Canada* (New York: Charles Scribner's Sons, 1915), Volume One, pp. ix, 48. Roosevelt is quoted in Thomas G. Dyer, *Theodore Roosevelt and the Idea of Race* (Baton Rouge: Louisiana State University Press, 1980), p. 79.

11. An instructive example of such victim-blaming, among many, is Richard White's *The Middle Ground: Indians, Empires and Republics in the Great Lakes Region, 1650–1815* (Cambridge: Cambridge University Press, 1991).

12. Edward S. Herman and Noam Chomsky, *Manufacturing Consent: The Political Economy of the Mass Media* (New York: Pantheon Books, 1988), p. 37.

13. On the latter point, see David S. Wyman, *The Abandonment of the Jews: America and the Holocaust, 1941–1945* (New York: Pantheon Books, 1984).

ENCOUNTERING THE AMERICAN HOLOCAUST
The Politics of Affirmation and Denial

> The bigger the lie, the greater the likelihood that it will be believed.
> — Adolf Hitler

DURING the four centuries spanning the time between 1492, when Christopher Columbus first set foot on the "New World" of a Caribbean beach, and 1892, when the U.S. Census Bureau concluded that there were fewer than a quarter-million indigenous people surviving within the country's claimed boundaries, a hemispheric population estimated to have been as great as 125 million was reduced by something over 90 percent. The people had died in their millions of being hacked apart with axes and swords, burned alive and trampled under horses, hunted as game and fed to dogs, shot, beaten, stabbed, scalped for bounty, hanged on meathooks and thrown over the sides of ships at sea, worked to death as slave laborers, intentionally starved and frozen to death during a multitude of forced marches and internments, and, in an unknown number of instances, deliberately infected with epidemic diseases.[1]

Today, every one of these practices is continued, when deemed expedient by the settler population(s) which have "restocked" the native landbase with themselves, in various locales throughout the Americas. In areas where the indigenous population remains so small or has become so assimilated that it no longer poses a "threat" to the new order which has usurped and subsumed it, it is kept that way through carefully calibrated policies of impoverishment and dispersal, indoctrination and compulsory sterilization. Insofar as native peoples retain lands in these latter regions, it is used as a convenient dumping ground for the toxic industrial waste by-products of the dominant society. The situation is now so acute, and so apparently irreversible, that several major scientific organizations have recommended the terrain be declared "sacrifices" to the interests of national comfort and prosperity. That these

1

places are inhabited by what thus become sacrificial *peoples* is left politely unstated. So, too, are most of the costs borne by the victims which are of benefit to their victimizers.[2]

It was not always that way. Through most of the history of what has happened, the perpetrators, from aristocrats like Jeffrey Amherst to the lowliest private in his army, from the highest elected officials to the humblest of farmers, openly described America's indigenous peoples as vermin, launched literally hundreds of campaigns to effect their extermination, and then reveled in the carnage which resulted. Martial glory was attained by more than a few officers who proudly boasted in later years of having instructed their troops, when attacking essentially defenseless native communities, to "kill and scalp all, little and big [because] nits make lice." The body parts taken by soldiers in such slaughters remain prized possessions, discretely handed down as trophies through the generations of all too many American families.[*] Thus occurred what even dishonest commentators have acknowledged as being "very probably the greatest demographic disaster in history."[3]

Today we discover, while perusing the texts of orthodox scholarship, that much of this never happened, or, to the extent that some things must be at least partially admitted, was "tragic," "unavoidable," and "unintended." The decimated natives were peculiarly responsible for their own demise, having never bothered to develop immunities to the host of pathogens unleashed among them by the ever-increasing numbers of "Old World settlers" swarming to their shores. In North America, where the practice of denial is most accomplished, successive waves of historians and anthropologists harnessed themselves to the common task of advancing the pretense that the aboriginal population of the continent was but a small fraction of its real number. Thus, the deaths of people who never existed need not be explained, nor can there be serious questions as to the original ownership of territory which was uninhabited until the settlers came. The formal term is *territorium rez nullius:* land vacant and therefore open to whomever might wish to claim it.[4]

In the relatively rare instances where even this complex of denial and evasion is insufficient—the 1864 Sand Creek Massacre and its 1890 counter-

---

[*]In 1991, the American Indian Movement of Colorado removed two Cheyenne scalps from the mantle of a ski lodge in the Rocky Mountains, where the proprietor displayed them for the edification of guests. The man expressed surprise, "never having had any complaints before," that Indians might be upset by such "relics," which he said had been taken by his great-grandfather, a trooper who participated in the 1864 Sand Creek Massacre, and had been "handed down in the family" ever since. Such stories are, unfortunately, not at all uncommon.

2

part at Wounded Knee, for example, are too well known to be simply "disappeared"—orthodoxy frames its discourse in terms of madmen and anomaly. Overall, the nomenclature and emphasis employed is designed to turn the tables entirely. We hear only of "Indian wars," never of "settlers' wars." It is as if the natives, always "warlike" and "aggressive," had invaded and laid waste to London or Castile rather than engaging in desperate and always futile efforts to repel the hordes of "pioneers" and "peaceful settlers" overrunning their homelands—often quite illegally, even in their own terms—from sea to shining sea. It is the kind of historiography one might have expected of nazi academics a century after a German victory in World War II: "When the Poles, led by sullen Jewish chiefs, savagely attacked our innocent troops west of Warsaw in 1939, murdering thousands, we were forced to respond by… "[5]

All citizens of the United States (and, to a somewhat lesser extent, Canada) are subjected to indoctrination to this perspective through the elementary and secondary school systems. The outlook they obtain there is substantially reinforced on television, in the "news" media (both print and electronic), in popular literature, and in the well over 2,000 films Hollywood and its Canadian counterparts have produced on such themes during the past seventy years. For those with both means and inclination, higher education builds upon this groundwork, not only through a fleshing out of those nuanced inventories of theory and psuedofact by which "experts" are defined, but psychologically and emotionally as well. Such is the manner in which those interconnecting webs of mythic interpretation and social value known as hegemony are always woven.[6]

Reproduction, evolution, and perfection of any hegemonic structure is inevitable, left to its own devices. Ultimately, what emerges is a sense of triumphalism among the dominant population which is so seamless, pervasive, and pronounced that previously inadmissible facts can begin to be reintegrated with the record, reconciled to and incorporated into the prevailing mythology. Certain aspects of what was done to the first peoples of the Americas, it is now conceded—not just "aberrations" like Sand Creek, but even a few *policies*—may have been "excessive" (as in, "too much of a good thing"). They "went too far" and were therefore "errors" (as in, "We didn't really mean it"). To that extent, but no more, they were "unfortunate," even "dismal" (but never criminally reprehensible).[7]

The falsity of such limited expressions of regret (as in, "Oops!") and accompanying pretenses of sociocultural humility (as in, "We all make mis-

3

takes") are, moreover, invariably belied by the assertions that immediately follow such admissions. While there are many variations, they all go in substance to the premise, presented as a foregone conclusion, that, "*however* unfortunate and regrettable the past, it has all worked out for the best" for victim and victimizer alike, given the superlative nature of the civilization we now mutually inhabit. This new—and supposedly vastly superior—mode of existence was created, so the story goes, solely on the basis of obliterating the "squalid, brutish inhumanity" of the old.[8] In this way denial of past realities is used as the crux for imposing an equally firm denial of the present. The voices of our hypothetical postvictory nazi pundits ring through, loud and clear.

Denying the American Holocaust

The American holocaust was and remains unparalleled, both in terms of its magnitude and the degree to which its goals were met, and in terms of the extent to which its ferocity was sustained over time by not one but several participating groups. The ideological matrix of its denial is also among the most well developed of any genocide—or, more accurately, series of genocides—for which a significant amount of information is readily available (i.e., copious official and unofficial primary records of the processes, explicit statements of intent by perpetrators, published philosophical justifications of the results, and so on).[9] In other words, denial is manifested in more-or-less equal parts at all points on the ideological compass of the dominant society. Am I exaggerating? Being "hyperbolic," "strident," or "shrill" (to borrow the most common terms employed by deniers to dismiss such points without responding to them)?*

It would be useful to assess recently stated positions on the matter at each stop along the orthodox political spectrum. Here, we may begin on the right, where we might presume ourselves most likely to encounter reaction and denial. Undisappointed in our expectations, we find then-director of the National Endowment for the Humanities Lynne Cheney, in collaboration with the United States Senate, preparing for the 1992 Columbus quincentenniary by refusing to fund any film production which proposed to use the

---

*After five solid years of delivering public lectures in this subject area, I can testify that these descriptors—along with the accusation that one is "angry" and/or "emotional"—are used every time, both in Q & A sessions following talks and in such press coverage as may result. Never, in my experience, have those employing such terms attempted to do so in the context of addressing what was actually said. I am thus convinced that the mode of delivery is irrelevant in terms of generating such responses.

word "genocide," even in passing, to explain the subsequent liquidation of America's indigenous population. They were joined by then-Secretary of Education William Bennett, who thundered—in a manner worthy of Oswald Spengler—that popularization of such "distortions of history" would signify an undermining of "the Western cultural tradition which has made this great nation what it is today."[10] Such sentiments, which have been ascendant in the United States (and Canada) since 1980, have of course been amply represented in the media. For example:

> Charles Krauthammer, one of *Time* magazine's regular political columnists, used an entire column [on May 27, 1991] to lambaste as "politically correct" opportunists anyone who dared express regret over the killing of millions of innocent people and the destruction of entire ancient cultures in the Americas. What happened in the wake of the European invasion was only what has always characterized human history, Krauthammer claimed, citing the Norman conquest of Britain as an apt (though actually absurd) comparison. "The real question is," he noted, "what eventually grew on this bloodied soil?" For, regardless of the level of destruction and mass murder that was visited upon the indigenous peoples of the Western Hemisphere, it was, in retrospect, entirely justified because in the process it wiped out such alleged barbarisms as the communally based Inca society (which really was only a "beehive," Krauthammer said) and gave the world "a culture of liberty that endowed the individual human being with dignity and sovereignty."[11]

From here, one could anticipate a follow-up column which would explain why, irrespective of the estimated 50 million lives consumed by nazism, its existence should be celebrated rather than condemned. After all, the nazis were responsible for introducing "our civilization" to, among many other things, the wonders of expressways, jet aircraft, missile technologies, synfuels, methamphetamines, the Volkswagen, and the basis for today's genetic engineering. In the process, moreover, nazism managed to permanently eradicate the "insect-like" Jewish culture of Poland and—perhaps most miraculous of all—forced an unprecedented degree of collaboration among Western democracies, the formation of the United Nations, and thus the eventual "New World Order" proclaimed by George Bush (with all the obvious benefits to human dignity, liberty, and sovereignty this has to offer).[12]

Moving leftward, to liberalism, we might expect things to improve at least marginally. What we encounter instead is the denunciation by historian J.H. Elliott in the *New York Review of Books* of what he describes as the "indiscriminate use [of the term] genocide" in depicting the fate of America's indigenous peoples because it carries such "powerful contemporary freight" as to "impede rather than assist genuine understanding" of what happened (he does not bother to explain further). This "wisdom" couples readily to that of noted ethnohistorian James Axtell, who assures us that it is time we "stop flogging ourselves" over "largely imaginary" questions of genocide, a word he habitually situates in quotes wherever American Indians are concerned. Axtell's view, in turn, fits in neatly with that of Arthur Schlesinger, Jr., who, using the pages of *The Atlantic* for the purpose, not only repeats Krauthammer's argument but surpasses it. [13]

> Schlesinger…was not content to build his case on the purported shortcomings of the ancient societies of the Americas. No, he gazed into his crystal ball and asserted…that without the European conquests and slaughter at least some New World societies today would be sufficiently unpleasant places to live so as to make acceptable the centuries of genocide that were carried out against the native people of the entire Western Hemisphere.[14]

As for left radicals, consider the long-standing postulations of the Revolutionary Communist Party U.S.A., published nearly a decade before the quincentenniary, that the precolumbian population of North America was about half that admitted at the time by even the thoroughly reactionary Smithsonian Institution, that the people were so "primitive" that they were forced to regularly consume their own fecal matter in order to survive, and that only European conquest and colonization had lifted them from their state of perpetual degradation to the level of rudimentary humanity.[15] Nor do socialists deviate appreciably from such naziesque diatribes, a matter evidenced by columnist Christopher Hitchens, writing in a purportedly "dissident" weekly, *The Nation,* on October 19, 1992.

> To Hitchens, anyone refusing to join him in celebrating with "great vim and gusto" the annihilation of the native peoples of the Americas was (in his words) self-hating, ridiculous, ignorant, and sinister. People who regard critically the genocide that was carried out in America's past, Hitchens continued, are simply reactionary, since such grossly inhuman atrocities "happen to be the way history is made." And thus "to complain about [them] is as empty as complaint about climactic, geological or tectonic shift." Moreover, he added, such violence is worth glorifying since it more often than not has been for the long-term betterment of mankind—as in the United States today, where the extermination of [American Indians] has brought about "a nearly boundless epoch of opportunity and innovation."[16]

The same holds true of Euroamerica's supposedly most radical strain, anarchism (or "antiauthoritarianism," as it more often fancies itself these days). Witness self-professed "anarchist's anarchist" Bob Black, author of two books and frequent contributor to such titles as *Anarchy,* addressing native activists as "Taunto" and "Shitting Bull," telling them to "stop whining" about a genocide they "never experienced," and asserting that he has "as much right to this land as any of you, maybe more." Not to be outdone, the more prominent John Zerzan makes the utterly bizarre insinuation that, whatever happened to them, native people have no complaint since they themselves were "guilty" of having "colonized" plantlife in their precolumbian fields.[17]

Sieg heil. Distinctions in perspective between right, center, left, and extreme left in the United States are quite literally nonexistent on the question of the genocide of indigenous peoples. From all four vantage points, the historical reality is simultaneously denied, justified, and in most cases celebrated. But preposterous as some of the argumentation has become, all of it is outstripped by a substantial component of zionism which contends not only that the American holocaust never happened, but that *no* "true" genocide has ever occurred, other than the Holocaust suffered by the Jews at the hands of the nazis during the first half of the 1940s. In their frenzy to validate the "uniqueness" of their own people's experience, the exclusivism asserted by adherents to this outlook — and they have proven extraordinarily potent in their promotion of it — extends even to the Gypsies, who were subjected to the very same nazi extermination program as they. In kind with the sort of vulgar name-calling practiced by Black, Hitchens, and the RCP, proponents of Jewish exclusivism consistently label anyone referring to a genocide other than their own as an "antisemite."[18]

Affirming the American Holocaust

There have, to be sure, been exceptions to this apparently homogeneous sensibility. Beginning in 1968, the American Indian Movement, for example, following the definition attending Raphaël Lemkin's coinage of the term in 1944, and the legal description of the crime which was adopted by the United Nations in 1948, began to apply the concept of genocide with some precision to American history. AIM was quickly joined in its usage of the term by allied groups within the Black and Chicano liberation movements, the Puerto Rican independence movement, portions of the antiwar movement and at least some elements of the (non-marxist) New Left. By the early 1970s, liberation movements abroad, both in Europe and throughout the Third World, adopted the term with specific reference to the historical devastation of indigenous American societies.[19]

7

In terms of scholarship, there have also been those who have broken decisively with orthodoxy. Among them have been Carl O. Sauer, Woodrow W. Borah, Sherburn F. Cook, Leslie B. Simpson, Henry F. Dobyns, Noble David Cook, Russell Thornton, and, all of whom laboriously excavated the data necessary to reveal the true size of the native population of 1492, both hemispherically and regionally, and entered into the process of honestly describing the means by which it was reduced to almost nothing. Others—notably Richard Drinnon, Francis Jennings, David Stannard, Rupert and Jeanette Henry Costo, Robert F. Heizer, Tzvetan Todorov, Eduardo Galeano, Robert Davis, Mark Zannis, Kirkpatrick Sale, John Grier Varner and Jeanette Johnson Varner, Ann F. Ramenofsky, Lynwood Carranco, Estle Beard, and David Svaldi—have undertaken the effort to document, refine, and amplify these themes in admirable fashion. Because of their work, upon which I rely quite heavily, the veil behind which the American holocaust has been masked for so long has started to slip away.[20]

A Little Matter of Genocide

A Little Matter of Genocide, an admittedly sarcastic title provoked by the sort of insistent trivialization described earlier, is intended to contribute to this unmasking. This is not to say that it purports to offer some new body of factual information about the genocide of America's indigenous peoples. Instead, it attempts to present a comprehensive overview of what is already known, bringing several data streams together between two covers for the first time to provide what I hope represents something of the "Big Picture." More important than this synthesizing effort, the book seeks to contextualize the American holocaust through direct comparison to other genocides—most especially the nazi Holocaust—to an extent not previously undertaken on such a scale.[21]

From there, it is possible to advance a definitional typology of genocide which should prove useful in facilitating the analytical apprehension of all holocausts, not only as they've occurred in the past, but as they are unfolding in the present and will likely come about in the future. From there as well, it is possible to offer a concrete illustration, subject to all manner of replication and variation, of how such a conceptualization of genocide can be applied in the "real world" as an integral component of direct-action strategies designed to stop, or at least blunt, genocidal processes. In other words, a primary underlying objective of *A Little Matter of Genocide* is to assist in the forging of a viable countergenocidal praxis.[22]

Structurally, the body of the book follows a certain progression, leading from definitional considerations through informational array and back again. A pair of overlapping essays, "Assaults on Truth and Memory" and "Lie for Lie," are used to open. This is mainly for purposes of framing the matter of holocaust denial, first by examining its best known element, "revisionist" denial of the nazi Holocaust, and then by comparing the techniques used by proponents of Jewish exclusivism in presenting their doctrine of "uniqueness" to those of the neonazi revisionists. In the second essay, emphasis is placed on the manner in which exclusivism has subverted the very definition of genocide to its own ends, while exploring the hegemonic functions of doing so. In the process of these investigations, every effort is made to restore non-Jewish victims of the Holocaust to their rightful place within it, so that the nazi genocide can be appreciated for what it really was.

With the true scope of what happened in eastern Europe under nazism revealed, and thus available for use as a reference point, we take up the historical realities of the American holocaust. This is approached with three essays—"Deconstructing the Columbus Myth," Genocide in the Americas," and "Nits Make Lice"—arranged chronologically, according to the historical juncture at which the genocidal process in the geographic area under consideration commenced. Hence, the first essay is devoted to the Caribbean Basin, the second to Iberoamerica, and the third to North America. The last two of the three essays trace the pattern of genocide within their respective regions up to the present moment. The first, however, breaks off in roughly 1540, since by that point the extermination of the indigenous population of the Caribbean was virtually complete.

We turn next, in "Cold War Impacts on Native North America," to the examination of a specifically contemporary phenomenon, the lethal contamination by transient industry of the landbase to which native people are constricted in North America and the consequent declaration of their residual territories as "National Sacrifice Areas." In this interrogation of the linkage between targeted ecocide and collateral genocide, we follow AIM leader Russell Means' 1980 prognosis that declaring Indian reservations to be sacrifice areas equates to sacrificing the indigenous residents themselves. The essay also explores to some extent the question of "spillover" of the by-products of certain industrial processes, intended for containment within reservation boundaries, into the habitat of the non-indigenous population.

By this point, all the essential information has been deployed which seems necessary to allow a fruitful examination of the formal relationship of the United States to the United Nations' legal prohibition against genocide. "The United States and the Genocide Convention" explores why America, alone among the member-states of the United Nations, took forty years to offer even a pretense of ratifying this most fundamental element of international human rights law, and how the exemptions from compliance it sought to provide itself in the instrument of ratification invalidated the Convention's original intent. In effect, the United States—in perfectly Hitlerian fashion—remains to this day outside the law, claiming to transcend mere international legality on its own authority, still refusing to accept the idea that refraining from genocidal activity is not an "abridgment of [its] sovereignty."

The last essay, "Defining the Unthinkable," again follows from everything which has come before. As its title implies, the piece attempts to provide a complete and workable delineation of the term's meaning(s), and to provide illustrations, many of them already discussed in some detail by this juncture, of its various gradients and nuances. Throughout the exposition, we will remain consistent with the definitional criteria worked out by Raphaël Lemkin when he established the concept of genocide—and drafted the international Convention outlawing it—under the presumption that there is no valid basis for conforming it to the preferences or convenience of one or another set of perpetrators (e.g., the U.S. and former Soviet governments) or special-interest groups (e.g., Jewish exclusivists). The result should prove to be something of a precision tool for application to both legal and more purely analytical contexts.

Throughout the book, I have gone out of my way to provide what Noam Chomsky has called "rich footnotes."[23] The reasons for this are several, and devolve not merely upon the usual scholarly fetish with indicating familiarity with "the literature." I *do* believe that when making many of the points I've sought to make, and with the bluntness which typically marks my work, one is well-advised to be thorough in revealing the basis upon which they rest. I also believe it is a matter not just of courtesy, but of ethics, to make proper attribution to those upon whose ideas and research one relies. Most importantly, I want those who read this book to be able to interrogate what I've said, to challenge it and consequently to build on it. The most expedient means to this end is the provision of copious annotation, citing sources both pro and con.

Finally, the obvious should be stated: this is a collection of essays. Hence, unlike most book chapters, each piece was constructed to stand on its own. An inevitable result is that there is a certain amount of repetition from essay to essay—greater here, lesser there—as each strives to establish the context in which its particular point or points will be made. It is, of course, possible to classify this as sheer redundancy, a problem inherent to all such collections (and more than a few booklength treatments as well). In this case, however, I will perhaps be forgiven for suggesting that repetition might be viewed in a more positive light, as what exponents of Freirian pedagogy have termed "recursiveness."[24] In any event, I am of the opinion that, since much of what follows has been said so little, it is worth saying some of it more than once.

Questions of Motive

All of this leaves open the question of my motives in undertaking yet another book centering in the genocide of American Indians, or what it is that I hope motivates people to read it. Let me say that, although I readily admit to bearing an abstract allegiance to them, I am not prompted by primarily academic concerns (as in "The Quest for Truth"). Nor, frankly, do I anticipate that *A Little Matter of Genocide* will be favorably received by most academic specialists in its subject area or related disciplines. The positions it advances are far too uncomfortably contrary to theirs for it to find much acceptance in that quarter.

To put it plainly, my goals are unequivocally political. Ironically, it is Deborah Lipstadt, a firm denier of the American holocaust, who, in the process of decrying neonazism's denial of her own people's Holocaust, has most aptly summed up my own reasoning. "The general public tends to accord victims of genocide a certain moral authority. . . . If you devictimize a people you strip them of their moral authority."[25] As an American Indian, as a twenty-year member of the American Indian Movement, and simply as a human being imbued with the conscience and consciousness of such, I believe that American Indians, demonstrably one of the most victimized groups in the history of humanity, are entitled to every ounce of moral authority we can get. My first purpose is, and always has been, to meet my responsibilities of helping deliver that to which my people is due.

At another level, the agenda is rather broader. As Roger Smith, Erik Markusen, and Robert Jay Lifton have pointed out, the denial of *any* genocide contributes to "a false consciousness which can have the most dire reverberations," underpinning a "deadly psychohistorical dynamic in which unopposed genocide begets new genocides."[26] The recent and/or ongoing slaughters in places like Rwanda, Bosnia, and East Timor should be proof enough of that. Assuming that we do not actively embrace such carnage, or believe we can slough it off with banalities about "human nature," we are obligated to find ways and means of stopping it. Here, an insight offered by Frank Chalk and Kurt Jonassohn seems quite germane.

> The major reason for doing comparative research on genocides is the hope of pre-venting them in the future. Such prevention will present difficult applied problems, but first it must be based on an understanding of the social situations and the social struc-tures and the processes that are likely to lead to genocides. Only by acquiring such knowledge can we begin to predict the likely occurrence of genocides and direct our efforts toward prevention.[27]

Or, to use Isador Wallimann's and Michael N. Dobkowski's formulation, "Any worthwhile activism with regard to genocide will have to be radically different from other human rights efforts. In order to be of help to the poten-tial victims, it will have to focus solely on prevention… [To] prevent such lethal crimes, we would have to be able to predict their occurrence—some-thing that our present state of knowledge does not yet permit. Thus, any efforts at preventing future genocides will have to start with research capable of yielding predictive indicators that would then allow concerted efforts at prevention."[28] With this, I doubt there can be much disagreement, even among those who would deny the nazi Holocaust or claim that it was unique. Since there can be no serious question that *A Little Matter of Genocide* goes very much in the direction indicated, it should be of interest to anyone opposed to the notions of genocide being sometimes a good thing, at least in "certain instances," or that is somehow a "normative human condition."* It is, I think, an absolutely essential book for anyone sharing my own commitment, not just to opposing genocide but to ending it.

---

*If I had a dollar for every time a member of the American professorate had responded in this fashion to my public lectures, at least indirectly and especially with the latter contrivance, I would buy back the hemisphere.

Notes

1. The estimated population range is 112 million to 125 million in 1492; Henry F. Dobyns, "Estimating Aboriginal American Population: An Appraisal of Techniques with a New Hemispheric Estimate," *Current Anthropology,* No. 7, 1966. According to the 1890 federal census, referenced here, the "aboriginal population" in the U.S. portion of North America had been reduced to 248,253; U.S. Bureau of the Census, *Report on Indians Taxed and Indians Not Taxed in the United States (except Alaska) at the Eleventh U.S. Census: 1890* (Washington, D.C.: U.S. Government Printing Office, 1894). The actual nadir was reached around 1900, when the Census Bureau counted only 237,196 surviving Indians; U.S. Bureau of the Census, *Fifteenth Census of the United States, 1930: The Indian Population of the United States and Alaska* (Washington, D.C.: U.S. Government Printing Office, 1937). On causes of death, see generally, David E. Stannard, *American Holocaust: Columbus and the Conquest of the New World* (New York: Oxford University Press, 1992).

2. On impoverishment, see, e.g., U.S. Department of Health, Education and Welfare, *Chart Series Book* (Washington, D.C.: Public Health Service, 1988); on dispersal, see Donald L. Fixico, *Termination and Relocation: Federal Indian Policy, 1945–1960* (Albuquerque: University of New Mexico Press, 1986); on indoctrination, see David Wallace Adams, *Education for Extinction: American Indians and the Boarding School Experience, 1875–1928* (Lawrence: University Press of Kansas, 1995); on sterilization, see Janet Larson, "And Then There Were None: IHS Sterilization Practices," *Christian Century,* No. 94, Jan. 26, 1976; Bill Wagner, "Lo, the Poor and Sterilized Indian," *America,* No. 136, Jan. 29, 1977; Brint Dillingham, "Indian Women and IHS Sterilization Practices," *American Indian Journal,* Vol. 3, No. 1, Jan. 1977. On national sacrifice areas, see Federal Energy Administration, Office of Strategic Analysis, *Project Independence: A Summary* (Washington, D.C.: U.S. Department of Energy, 1974).

3. See, generally, Richard Drinnon, *Facing West: The Metaphysics of Indian Hating and Empire Building* (Minneapolis: University of Minnesota Press, 1980). The order to "kill them all" is attributed to Col. John M. Chivington, commander of the 3rd Colorado Volunteer Cavalry; quoted in Stan Hoig, *The Sand Creek Massacre* (Norman: University of Oklahoma Press, 1961) p. 192. The closing quote is taken from Steven T. Katz, *The Holocaust in Historical Context, Vol. 1: The Holocaust and Mass Death Before the Modern Age* (New York: Oxford University Press, 1992) p. 20.

4. See, e.g., James Axtell, *Beyond 1492: Encounters in Colonial North America* (New York: Oxford University Press, 1992) pp. 261–3. For the best overview of how the "books were cooked," see Francis Jennings, *The Invasion of America: Indians, Colonialism and the Cant of Conquest* (Chapel Hill: University of North Carolina Press, 1975) pp. 15–31. Overall, see Robert A. Williams, Jr., *The American Indian in Western Legal Thought: The Discourses of Conquest* (New York: Oxford University Press, 1990).

5. A computer search reveals more than 500 titles including the term "Indian War" or "Wars," but none devoted to "settlers' wars." See, e.g., John Tebbel and Keith Jennison, *The American Indian Wars* (New York: Harper & Row, 1960); T. Harry Williams, *The History of America's Wars from 1745 to 1918* (Baton Rouge: Louisiana State University, 1981); Edwin P. Hoyt, *America's Wars and Military Incursions* (New York: McGraw-Hill, 1987).

6. See, generally, Ralph Friar and Natasha Friar, *"The Only Good Indian…" The Hollywood Gospel* (New York: Drama Book Specialists, 1972); Raymond William Stedman, *Shadows of the Indian: Stereotypes in American Culture* (Norman: University of Oklahoma Press, 1982); Ward Churchill, *Fantasies of the Master Race: Literature, Cinema and the Colonization of American Indians* (Monroe, ME: Common Courage Press, 1992). The statement about hegemony is intended in the Gramscian sense; see Walter L. Adamson, *Hegemony and Revolution: A Study of Antonio Gramsci's Political and Cultural Theory* (Berkeley: University of California Press, 1980); Alastair Davidson, *Antonio Gramsci: Towards an Intellectual Biography* (London/Atlantic Highlands, NJ: Merlin Press/Humanities Press, 1977).

7. An unabashed exposition of the sentiments at issue will be found in J.M. Roberts, *The Triumph of the West* (London: British Broadcasting Corporation, 1985). Articulations of the "need" for such intellectual reinforcement of the status quo abound; see, e.g., Arthur M. Schlesinger, Jr., *The Disuniting of America: Reflections on a Multicultural Society* (New York: W.W. Norton, 1992). For useful discussion of the problem and strategies to transcend it, see Edward Said, "The Politics of Knowledge," in Paul Berman, ed., *Debating P.C.: The Controversy Over Political Correctness on College Campuses* (New York: Laurel, 1992). See also, Wilcomb E. Washburn, "Land Claims in the Mainstream of Indian/White Land History," in Imre Sutton, ed., *Irredeemable America: The Indians' Estate and Land Claims* (Albuquerque: University of New

Mexico Press, 1985); "Distinguishing History from Moral Philosophy and Public Advocacy," in Calvin Martin, ed., *The American Indian and the Problem of History* (New York: Oxford University Press, 1987). More broadly, see Patricia Nelson Limerick, *The Legacy of Conquest: The Unbroken Past of the American West* (New York: W.W. Norton, 1987); Edward Lazarus, *Black Hills, White Justice: The Sioux Nation versus The United States, 1775 to the Present* (New York: HarperCollins, 1991).

8. For a heavy dose of such characterization, see James E. Clifton, ed., *The Invented Indian: Cultural Fictions and Government Policies* (New Brunswick, NJ: Transaction Books, 1990). Also see *Time, Newsweek,* and other mass-circulation periodicals, 1991–92, inclusive.

9. For a series of apt comparisons of holocausts, see Frank Chalk and Kurt Jonassohn, eds., *The History and Sociology of Genocide: Analyses and Case Studies* (New Haven, CT: Yale University Press, 1990). Excellent analysis of the implications of a parallel example will be found in Roger W. Smith, Eric Markusen, and Robert Jay Lifton, "Professional Ethics and Denial of the Armenian Genocide," *Holocaust and Genocide Studies,* No. 9, 1995.

10. "Our civilization" is being "brought low by the forces of ignorance, irrationality and intimidation"; quoted in Jack McCurdy, "Bennett Calls Stanford Curriculum Revision Capitulation to Pressure," *Chronicle of Higher Education,* April 27, 1988. The parallels in both logic and rhetoric to those of Spengler, a hero of the nazis, is striking. On Spengler, see Oswald Spengler, *Der Untergang des Abendlandes, Welthistorische und Wirklichkeit* (Münich: C.H. Beck'sche Verlagsbuchhandlung, 1896); published in English translation as *The Decline of the West* (New York: Alfred A. Knopf, 1926).

11. David E. Stannard, "The Politics of Holocaust Scholarship: Uniqueness as Denial," in Alan S. Rosenbaum, ed., *Is the Holocaust Unique? Perspectives on Comparative Genocide* (Boulder, CO: Westview Press, 1996) p. 165.

12. This actually comes fairly close to the arguments presented in contemporary neonazi literature; see, e.g., Christof Friedrich and Eric Thompson, *The Hitler We Loved and Why* (Reedy, WV: White Power Publications, 1978).

13. *New York Review of Books,* June 24, 1993. J.H. Elliott is author of such epic apologia as *The Old World and the New, 1492–1650* (Cambridge, MA: Cambridge University Press, 1970). Axtell, *op. cit.,* p. 263.

14. Stannard, "The Politics of Holocaust Scholarship," *op. cit.,* pp. 165–6; Schlesinger's *Atlantic* piece ran in the September 1992 issue, timed to appear just a month before the Columbian quincentennial.

15. The RCP, "Searching for a Second Harvest," in Ward Churchill, ed., *Marxism and Native Americans* (Boston: South End Press, 1983).

16. Stannard, "The Politics of Holocaust Scholarship," *op. cit.,* p. 166.

17. Although Black's deep-seated racism is an underlying current in much of his published work, it *really* bubbles forth from what he takes to be the privacy of unsolicited personal correspondence, numerous examples of which the author maintains on file. The quotes employed are taken therefrom. Readers are referred to his *Friendly Fire* (Brooklyn, NY: Autonomedia, 1992) and *The Abolition of Work and Other Essays* (Port Townsend, WA: Loompanics, n.d.). See also John Zerzan, *Future Primitive and Other Essays* (Brooklyn, NY: Autonomedia, 1994).

18. With the publication of the first massive volume of his projected three-volume study, *The Holocaust in Historical Context (op. cit.),* Steven T. Katz has probably become the leading exponent of this view; for a more succinct rendering, see his "The Uniqueness of the Holocaust: The Historical Dimension," in Rosenbaum, *op. cit.* He is followed closely by Yehuda Bauer, the previously reigning "dean" of such distortion; see, e.g., Bauer's *The Holocaust in Historical Perspective* (Seattle: University of Washington Press, 1978). Other heavy-hitters include Elie Wiesel, Lucy Dawidowicz, Leni Yahil, Yisrael Gutman, Robert Marrus, Deborah Lipstadt, and Martin Gilbert; see the first two essays in this book. Also, see Lucy Dawidowicz, *The Holocaust and the Historians* (Cambridge: Harvard University Press, 1981) pp. 10–11.

19. On AIM, see Peter Matthiessen, *In the Spirit of Crazy Horse* (New York: Viking, [2nd. ed.] 1991). On tie-ins with other liberation movements, see Rex Weyler, *Blood of the Land: The U.S. Government and Corporate War Against the American Indian Movement* (Philadelphia: New Society Publishers, [2nd. ed.] 1992).

20. See, e.g., Carl O. Sauer, *Sixteenth Century North America* (Berkeley: University of California Press, 1971); Woodrow W. Borah and Sherburn F. Cook, *The Aboriginal Population of Mexico on the Eve of the Spanish Conquest* (Berkeley: University of California Press, 1963); Sherburn F. Cook, *The Conflict*

Between the California Indians and White Civilization (Berkeley: University of California Press, 1976); Sherburn F. Cook and Leslie B. Simpson, *The Population of Central Mexico in the Sixteenth Century* (Berkeley: University of California Press, 1948); Henry F. Dobyns, *Their Numbers Become Thinned: Native American Population Dynamics in Eastern North America* (Knoxville: University of Tennessee Press, 1983); Noble David Cook, *Demographic Collapse: Indian Peru, 1520–1620* (Cambridge: Cambridge University Press, 1981); Russell Thornton, *American Indian Holocaust and Survival: A Population History Since 1492* (Norman: University of Oklahoma Press, 1987); Robert H. Jackson, *Indian Population Decline: The Missions of Northwestern New Spain, 1687–1840* (Albuquerque: University of New Mexico Press, 1995); Drinnon, *op. cit.*; Jennings, *op. cit.*; Stannard, *American Holocaust, op. cit.*; Rupert Costo and Jeanette Henry Costo, *The California Missions: A Legacy of Genocide* (San Francisco: Indian Historian Press, 1987); Robert F. Heizer, *They Were Only Diggers: A Collection of Articles from California Newspapers, 1851–1866, on Indian and White Relations* (Ramona, CA: Ballena Press, 1974), revised and republished under the title *The Destruction of California Indians* (Lincoln: University of Nebraska Press, 1993); Tzvetan Todorov, *The Conquest of America: The Question of the Other* (New York: HarperPerennial, 1984); Eduardo Galeano, *The Open Veins of Latin America: Five Centuries of the Pillage of a Continent* (New York: Monthly Review Press, 1973); Robert Davis and Mark Zannis, *The Genocide Machine in Canada: The Pacification of the North* (Montréal: Black Rose Books, 1973); Kirkpatrick Sale, *The Conquest of Paradise: Christopher Columbus and the Columbian Legacy* (New York: Alfred A. Knopf, 1990); John Grier Varner and Jeanette Johnson Varner, *The Dogs of Conquest* (Norman: University of Oklahoma Press, 1983); Ann F. Ramenofsky, *Vectors of Death: The Archaeology of European Contact* (Albuquerque: University of New Mexico Press, 1987); Lynwood Carranco and Estle Beard, *Genocide and Vendetta: The Round Valley Wars of Northern California* (Norman: University of Oklahoma Press, 1981); David Svaldi, *Sand Creek and the Rhetoric of Extermination: A Case Study in Indian-White Relations* (Lanham, MD: University Press of America, 1989). Exposition on the intended meaning of stripping away the veil will be found in J.G. Merquior, *The Veil and the Mask: Essays on Culture and Ideology* (London: Routledge & Keegan Paul, 1979).

21. Stannard in particular, in *American Holocaust, op. cit.*, and also in "The Politics of Holocaust Scholarship," *op. cit.* covers a great deal of ground in this direction. *A Little Matter of Genocide* should be seen as consciously building on his accomplishments. My present effort is also meant to extend the avenues opened up in several of my own earlier books, notably *Struggle for the Land: Indigenous Resistance to Genocide, Ecocide and Expropriation in Contemporary North America* (Monroe, ME: Common Courage Press, 1993); *Indians Are US? Culture and Genocide in Native North America* (Monroe, ME: Common Courage Press, 1994); and *Since Predator Came: Notes from the Struggle for American Indian Liberation* (Littleton, CO: Aigis, 1995).

22. Although it differs sharply with each of them in some respects, the book is meant to be linked to such recent efforts as Chalk and Jonassohn's *The History and Sociology of Genocide (op. cit.)*, Leo Kuper's *Genocide: Its Political Use in the Twentieth Century* (New Haven, CT: Yale University Press, 1981), Isidor Wallimann and Michael N. Dobkowski's *Genocide in the Modern Age: Etiology and Case Studies of Mass Death* (Westport, CT: Greenwood Press, 1987), and George Andreopoulos' *Genocide: Conceptual and Historical Dimensions* (Philadelphia: University of Pennsylvania Press, 1994). Philosophical and methodological discussion of praxis will not be undertaken herein. Those interested in such matters should be advised that I subscribe generally to the formulations of Gramsci and the *young* Lukács; for further elaboration, see my "Marxist Theory of Culture: A Cross-Cultural Critique," in Ward Churchill and Elisabeth R. Lloyd, *Culture versus Economism: Essays on Marxism in the Multicultural Arena* (Denver: Fourth World Center for Study of Indigenous Law and Politics, University of Colorado, [2nd. ed.] 1989) or Richard Kilminster, *Praxis and Method: A Sociological Dialogue with Lukács, Gramsci and the Early Frankfurt School* (London: Routledge & Keegan Paul, 1979).

23. See the remarks on annotation in Noam Chomsky, *Class Warfare: Interviews with David Barsamian* (Monroe, ME: Common Courage Press, 1996).

24. See, e.g., Paulo Freire, *Education for Critical Consciousness* (New York: Continuum, 1982).

25. Lipstadt, *op. cit.*, pp. 7–8.

26. Smith, Markuson and Lifton, *op. cit.*, p. 16.

27. Chalk and Johansson, *op. cit.*, p. 32.

28. Wallimann and Dobkowski, *op. cit.*, p. 18.

Slit trench filled with bodies at
Nordhaven, 1945.
Photo: U.S. Army Signal Corps

Slit trench filled with bodies at
Wounded Knee, 1890.
Photo: U.S. Army

Soviet POWs loaded aboard wagon en route to mass burial, 1942. Photo: Bildarchiv Preussischer Kulturbesitz, Berlin

Lakota POWs loaded aboard wagon en route to mass burial, 1890. Photo: U.S. Army

ASSAULTS ON TRUTH AND MEMORY
Holocaust Denial in Context

> Where scholars deny genocide, in the face of decisive evidence that it has occurred, they contribute to a false consciousness that can have the most dire reverberations. Their message in effect is: [genocide] requires no confrontation, no reflection, but should be ignored, glossed over. In this way scholars lend their considerable authority to the acceptance of this ultimate human crime. More than that, they encourage—indeed invite—a repetition of that crime from virtually any source in the immediate or distant future. By closing their minds to the truth, that is, scholars contribute to the deadly psychohistorical dynamic in which unopposed genocide begets new genocides.
>
> —Roger W. Smith, Eric Markusen, and Robert Jay Lifton
> "Professional Ethics and Denial of the Armenian Genocide"

OF all the intellectual monstrosities arising during the course of the late twentieth century, one of the most vicious and factually indefensible has been that "school of historical revisionism" known as "Holocaust denial." Its proponents purport to have "proven" that the systematic nazi extermination of somewhere between five and six million Jews did not occur. Such genocidal dimensions were never really part of the nazi character, they argue. Rather, the whole idea of a Holocaust perpetrated by the Third Reich is instead a colossal and sustained "propaganda myth" contrived for purposes of gaining moral advantage by Germany's politicomilitary adversaries, in combination with an amorphous "International Jewish Conspiracy," during and after the Second World War.

Probably the first purveyor of such tripe was Paul Rassinier, a former French communist party member turned virulent anticommunist *cum* nazi apologist, who published his seminal work on the topic, *Le Passage de la Ligne* [*Crossing the Line*], in 1948.[1] His position can be reduced to a simple duality: first, that much of that for which the nazis are accused accrues from "the natural tendency of its victims to exaggerate"; second, that to the extent atrocities happened at all in the nazi death camps, they were more the responsibility of the victims themselves—who, Rassinier claimed, had been placed "in charge" by their SS keepers—than of the SS or nazism more generally.

Rassinier's themes were quickly picked up by pro–nazi/antisemitic figures in the United States, men such as the evangelical "Christian" publicist W.D. Herrstrom (*Bible News Flashes*), white supremacist publisher James Madole (*National Renaissance Bulletin*), open national socialists like George Lincoln Rockwell and Gerald L.K. Smith (*The Cross and the Flag*), and eminent Smith College historian Harry Elmer Barnes. The latter, with the release of his *The Struggle Against Historical Blackout* in 1947, can be said to have set down the ideological/theoretical framework within which Rassinier, Smith, Herrstrom, and their ilk could pretend to at least marginal "scholarly" credibility.*

By the late 1950s, the emerging "field" of Holocaust denial in the United States had produced its first genuine "academic specialist," Austin J. App, a professor of English literature at the University of Scranton and, later, at LaSalle College. App's tactic was to place Rassinier's form of "logical" denial on a tentatively "scientific" footing, developing an obfuscatory "statistical profile" of pre- and postwar European demography through which conventional estimates of six million Jewish victims of nazi exterminators might be challenged as "grossly inflated." This, in turn, was linked to a polemic against German indemnification of surviving Jews in which Germany was presented as the "real victim" of the "Myth of the Final Solution."[2]

During the second half of the 1960s, and throughout the '70s, App's sort of "scholarship" began to take hold on North America's extreme right, and, increasingly, to cross-pollinate with European strains of itself. In the United States, 1969 saw the anonymous release of *The Myth of the Six*

---

*Barnes was considered a first-rank historian during the interwar period, becoming a full professor at Smith by the age of thirty and serving a stint in the '30s as editor of *Foreign Affairs*. His self-published tome attempting to exculpate Hitler and nazism for starting World War II was reprinted nine times between 1947 and 1952. During the 1960s, others of his works—for example, *The Genesis of the World War: An Introduction to the Problem of War Guilt* (New York: 1929; reprinted under the title *Who Started World War I?* by the Institute for Historical Review in 1983)—still served as required history texts at such elite institutions as Harvard and Columbia. Ample testimony to the significance of Barnes' thinking for U.S. Holocaust deniers may be found in the introduction by "Lewis Brandon" (one of the many aliases used by William David McCalden, founding director of the Institute for Historical Review) to a single-volume compilation, *The Barnes Trilogy: Three Revisionist Booklets by Harry Elmer Barnes, Historian, Sociologist, Criminologist, Economist* (Torrance, CA: Institute for Historical, 1979). That he never truly lost his appeal in more mainstream academic quarters is evidenced in Justus D. Doenecke, "Harry Elmer Barnes: Prophet of a Usable Past," *History Teacher*, February 1975.

Million, a book actually written by a Harvard-trained history professor named David Leslie Hoggan,[3] published by Willis Carto, founder of the neonazi Liberty Lobby and owner of the openly fascist Noontide Press, and introduced by E.L. Anderson, a contributing editor for what was then Carto's main periodical publication, *American Mercury*.[*] In England, Richard Verrall (a.k.a. Richard Harwood), leader of the British National Front and publisher of a neonazi tabloid, *Spearhead*, followed suit with the of 1974 publication of a booklet entitled, *Did Six Million Really Die?*[4]

A couple of years later in the United States, an MIT/University of Minnesota graduate named Arthur R. Butz, employed at the time as a professor of electrical engineering at Northwestern University, moved things forward by publishing *The Hoax of the Twentieth Century: The Case Against the Presumed Extermination of European Jewry*.[5] In this book, it is argued on a supposedly technical basis that the mass gassings and cremations of Jews and others documented during the Nuremberg Trial as having taken place at locations like Auschwitz (Oswieçim) and Treblinka "simply could not have occurred," given "the rather obvious technological limitations" of the equipment used.[6] At this point, it is fair to say that all the cornerstones for a comprehensive "rebuttal" of the Holocaust as a historical fact had been laid.

Advent of the Institute for Historical Review

In 1978, the various international strands of Holocaust denial began to be consolidated under the rubric of a Los Angeles-based entity called the Institute for Historical Review (IHR), funded by Willis Carto and headed by a former British National Front officer named William David McCalden.[†] In

---

[*] Anonymous, *The Myth of the Six Million* (Los Angeles: Noontide Press, 1969). In the introduction, Anderson describes the author as a college professor who had completed his manuscript by 1960, only to have it "suppressed" for nine years by "the zionist-controlled American publishing industry." It was necessary to protect the author's identity, Anderson claimed, so that he would not be summarily fired from his university position. Hoggan filed suit for public recognition of his authorship in late 1969; he has suffered no discernible professional consequences. The book contained as an appendix a collection of five articles which had appeared in *American Mercury* during 1967 and '68. These included a piece by Austin App entitled "The Elusive Six Million," Harry Elmer Barnes' "Zionist Fraud," Leo Heinman's "The Jews That Aren't," Teressa Hendry's "Was Anne Frank's Diary a Hoax?", a biographical sketch of Paul Rassinier by Herbert C. Roseman, and a glowing review of Rassinier's *Debunking the Holocaust Myth* by Barnes.

[†] In 1981, McCalden—whose many pseudonyms include Lewis Brandon, Sondra Ross, David Berg, Julius Finklestein, and David Stanford—resigned his position as Director of the IHR, due to a dispute with Willis Carto. He was replaced by Tom Marcellus, who presumably came closer to a knee-jerk embrace of Carto's outlook, set forth in a 1950 book by Notre Dame Law School graduate Francis Parker Yockey, dedicated to Adolf Hitler and entitled *Imperium: The Philosophy of History and Politics*

addition to unrestricted access to what had become Carto's own primary periodical publication, *The Spotlight*, and to the Noontide Press, his book-publishing concern, the IHR quickly established its own "academic" organ, *The Journal of Historical Review*, and a book-publishing operation under its own imprimatur. Moreover, in 1979, it initiated a series of "scholarly conferences"—known as International Revisionist Conventions—to bring together and coordinate the activities of deniers the world over.*

One of the IHR's first moves was to utilize the mass media to place Holocaust denial squarely before the public by issuing an "open challenge to peddlers of the Holocaust hoax." A $50,000 reward was offered to "anyone able to prove, through the offering of tangible evidence, that a single Jew was ever gassed by the government of the Third Reich."[7] Although it was later established that the challenge constituted fraud—it having been demonstrated to a court's satisfaction that the IHR never seriously intended to pay the proffered award[†]—it had accomplished its objective: seemingly serious

---

(Los Angeles: Noontide Press, [reprint] 1992). In 1960, Yockey committed suicide by cyanide while in jail awaiting trial on charges of possessing false passports. His last known visitor was Willis Carto; see John C. Olbert, "Yockey: Profile of an American Hitler," *The Investigator*, October 1984. In 1979, Carto acknowledged under oath that he subscribed to the fervently pro-nazi tenets advanced by Yockey; see William F. Buckley, Jr., "The Liberty Lobby and the Carto Network of Hate," *ADL Facts*, Vol. 27, No. 2, Winter 1982.

*For example, in addition to such U.S. mainstays as Harry Elmer Barnes and Arthur Butz, the IHR's initial editorial board included Ditleib Felderer, allegedly an Austrian Jew living in Sweden, who produces *Jewish Information Bulletin*, a crudely antisemitic publication reminiscent of nazi propagandist Julius Streicher's notorious *Der Stürmer*. In 1983, Felderer was sentenced to ten months' imprisonment for "dissemination of hate material," to wit: the mailing of locks of hair and lumps of fat—along with a note asking if they could identify the remains—to leaders of the European Jewish community. Also on the board was Robert Faurisson, a Frenchman and former professor of literature at the University of Lyon, whose specialization is "semiotics" (i.e., he now claims to "deconstruct" official documents and other texts related to the Holocaust). Faurisson became something of an international celebrity in 1981 when he was able to convince no less a figure than Noam Chomsky to defend his "right" to publish denials that the nazis had utilized gas chambers in exterminating Jews; see Noam Chomsky, "The Faurisson Affair: His Right to Say It," *The Nation*, February 28, 1981; "Freedom of Expression? Absolutely," *The Village Voice*, July 1, 1981; "The Commissars of Literature," *The New Statesman*, August 14, 1981.

† *Mel Mermelstein v. Institute for Historical Review, et al.*, Superior Court for the State of California, Civ. No. 356542, July 1985 (filed in February 1981). In addition to having to pay the plaintiff, an Auschwitz survivor, the sum of $90,000—the amount of the award, plus $40,000 for "pain and suffering" inflicted upon Mermelstein and all other Holocaust survivors—the IHR and associated entities were also required to officially recant as part of the resolution to the case; see "Statement of Record and Letter of Apology to Mel Mermelstein," signed by Elizabeth and Willis Carto, as well as representatives of the IHR, Legion for the Survival of Freedom, Noontide Press, and Liberty Lobby, dated July 24, 1985. In August 1986, Willis Carto filed suit against Mermelstein for "defamation," an action which was withdrawn a year-and-a-half later. Mermelstein has responded by filing a second suit naming Carto and his Legion for the Survival of Freedom as defendants, this time for malicious

questions concerning the historical fact of nazi Judeocide had been raised in the public consciousness.

These were concretized to a considerable extent during the 1980s via the case of Ernst Zundel, a German immigrant to Canada and ardent nazi, who was charged by Crown Counsel with instigating social and racial intolerance through his publishing house, Samisdat Press.* During his first trial, in which the IHR arranged for him to be represented by attorney Douglas Christie[†] and otherwise assisted by an "expert" witness, French Holocaust denier Robert Faurisson, Zundel was convicted and sentenced to serve fifteen months in prison. He was then able to win an appeal on procedural grounds and was retried in 1988.[8]

During the second trial, Christie and Faurisson brought in yet another expert, prominent British denier David Irving.[‡] Between the three, a strategy was hatched—presumably under a variation of the theory that it could

---

prosecution. The case (*Mel Mermelstein v. Legion for the Survival of Freedom, et al.*, filed May 4, 1992) remains in litigation as of this writing, but seems likely to be settled in the plaintiff's favor. It is unlikely to impair Carto's operations, however, as his Liberty Lobby recently received a $75 million bequest from the granddaughter of all-American inventor Thomas Alva Edison.

* Zundel is himself the author of two books, one of them written under a "coauthor" pseudonym; see Christof Friedrich and Eric Thompson, *The Hitler We Loved and Why* (Reedy, WV: White Power Publications, 1978) and Ernst Zundel, *UFOs: Nazi Secret Weapons?* (Toronto: Samisdat Publications, 1982). Although the reach of Samisdat at that point encompassed all of Canada and nearly 30,000 "subscribers" in the United States, its main distribution target was West Germany; a 1980 government report in the latter concluded that about a hundred shipments of Samisdat books, recordings, and nazi paraphernalia were entering the country each year; in 1981, a German police crackdown on neonazi groups revealed hundreds of caches of weapons, explosives, and Samisdat products; see Leonidas E. Hill, "The Trial of Ernst Zundel: Revisionism and the Law in Canada," *Simon Wiesenthal Annual,* 1989.

† Christie's specialty has been the defense of nazi war criminals, deniers, and neonazis in Canada. He achieved a certain notoriety in the mid-'80s, when he defended Jim Keegstra, an Alberta school teacher who had spent fourteen years indoctrinating his students, among other things, with the ideas that a secret Jewish conspiracy called the "Illuminati" had fomented all manner of societal maladies since 1700, and that the Holocaust was a hoax; see Kirk Makin, "Douglas Christie, Counsel for the Defense," *Ontario Lawyers Weekly,* March 29, 1985. Also see Alan T. Davies, "The Queen Versus James Keegstra: Reflections on Christian Antisemitism in Canada," *American Journal of Theology and Philosophy,* Vol. 9, Nos. 1–2, January–May 1988. Probably the leading North American proponent of the Illuminati idea over the past twenty years has been former leftist ideologue Lyndon LaRouche; see Dennis King, *Lyndon LaRouche and the New American Fascism* (New York: Doubleday, 1989). For an exercise in the theory itself, see Milton William Cooper, *Behold a Pale Horse* (Sedona, AZ: Light Technology, 1991).

‡ Irving, who heads a British political party he describes as being "moderate fascist" in orientation, displays a portrait of Hitler on the wall above his desk, has described a pilgrimage to the Führer's mountaintop retreat as a "spiritual experience," has publicly advocated that Deputy Führer Rudolf Hess should be awarded a posthumous Nobel Peace Prize, and has devoted his life to exonerating Hitler of all criminal acts committed by his regime; see Deborah Lipstadt, *Denying the Holocaust: The Growing Assault on Truth and Memory* (New York: The Free Press, 1993) p. 161.

be established that "the truth is the best defense"—wherein the thesis advanced by Arthur Butz would be "scientifically" corroborated. For this purpose, they retained the services of Fred A. Leuchter, reputedly "an engineer, skilled in the functioning of gas chambers," who, as a consultant to prison administrations across the United States, "specialized in constructing and installing execution apparatus."[9] Shortly, having been dispatched to Auschwitz/Birkenau and Majdanek on "site visits," Leuchter submitted a detailed report holding that it was "chemically and physically impossible for the Germans to have conducted gassings" in those camps.[10]

Although it was quickly established in court that Leuchter lacked even the most rudimentary engineering credentials—his sole degree turned out to be a B.A. in history from Boston University*—his "findings" had already caused something of an international media sensation.[11] Although these were debunked almost as rapidly as their author,[12] with the result that Zundel was convicted and sentenced to serve nine months in jail,[13] the IHR immediately launched an intensive campaign to capitalize on the popular first impression it had achieved.

For this, the institute relied primarily on the talents of a California-based publicist named Bradley Smith who packaged and promoted Leuchter's discredited material as if it were the very essence of "scientific research"—or at least a tenable "point of view," intrinsically worthy of inclusion in the academic agenda—while concentrating his energy on obtaining ad space trumpeting this notion in campus newspapers across the country.[14] Hence, by 1992, it was observable that the IHR had managed to shift the sordid fabrications comprising Holocaust denial from the outermost lunatic fringe of social discourse into the vastly more legitimate arenas of First Amendment debate and scholarly dialogue.[15]

Although there is a marked tendency in mainstream circles to scoff at the potential public impact of the "progress" made by the IHR and its

---

* As a result, Alabama Assistant Attorney General Ed Carnes issued a memo on July 20, 1990, to all capital punishment states. In it, Carnes not only challenged Leuchter's credentials, he accused the "engineer of death" of running a shake-down racket in which states were obliged either to acquire Leuchter's devices—$200,000 for a gas chamber, $100,000 for a portable "death van" unit, $85,000 for a gallows, $35,000 for an electric chair, $30,000 for a lethal injection system—or find him testifying as an expert witness for the condemned. At about the same time, Leuchter's home state of Massachusetts brought charges against him for illegally practicing engineering without a license. The matter was resolved in June 1991, when Leuchter signed a consent agreement admitting that he had fraudulently presented himself as an engineer and promising not to do so in the future; see "Consent Agreement," *Commonwealth of Massachusetts v. Fred A. Leuchter, Jr.*, July 11, 1991.

cohorts since 1978 in their increasingly sophisticated marketing of "bad history," numerous indicators suggest the effect has already been substantial.[16] A 1991 Gallup poll, for example, indicated that nearly 40 percent of adult Austrians expressed "doubts" as to whether a European Holocaust of the magnitude depicted in standard histories occurred during World War II; a substantial portion questioned whether anything truly definable as genocide happened at all.[17] This, among a population which, in 1950, evidenced nearly universal acceptance of the historical realities involved.*

In Italy, a similar poll conducted during 1992 revealed that close to 10 percent of the adult population had become "convinced" that the Holocaust is a myth; another quarter thought the matter was "overstated."[18] Similar circumstances seem to prevail in England, France, Germany, and Canada.[19] In most cases, the extent and degree of societal skepticism expressed regarding the Holocaust can be correlated fairly well to a marked resurgence of nazi-style extreme rightwing racism over the past fifteen years, all of it acted out with mounting fervor in the "real world."[20]

A Firm Rebuttal

In 1993, Deborah Lipstadt, Dorot Chair in Modern Jewish and Holocaust Studies at Emory University, produced what is probably the first comprehensive public effort at rejoining the rising tide of Holocaust denial.[21] Her book, *Denying the Holocaust: The Growing Assault on Truth and Memory* is thus a milestone of sorts, trying as it does not only to rebut the deniers' arguments point-by-point, but to place their activities in the broader sociopolitical panorama which gives them potency.[22]

Of necessity, the weight of Lipstadt's presentation rests on providing the information that thoroughly debunks the sort of intentional disinformation by which deniers have adorned themselves with a veneer of superficial plausibility. For example, with regard to Paul Rassinier's contention, subsequently developed by Barnes and App, that the number of Jewish victims of nazi

---

* There are no comprehensive polls on the matter in the United States. The situation must therefore be assessed anecdotally, as with Holocaust denier David Duke's electoral popularity in Louisiana, where he first won a seat in the state legislature, then carried a majority of the white vote in a bid for the governorship; *New Orleans Times-Picayune*, Aug. 26, 1990. Another indicator is the obvious popularity of syndicated columnist and aspiring presidential candidate Patrick J. Buchanan, who has repeatedly denied aspects of the Holocaust; Jacob Weisberg, "The Heresies of Pat Buchanan," *New Republic*, Oct. 22, 1990. Even movie actor Robert Mitchum has weighed in, expressing doubts as to whether the Jewish genocide ever occurred, in an interview in *Esquire*, Feb. 1983.

genocide was deliberately inflated by zionists in order to "swindle" an insupportably high level of reparations from the postwar West German government,[23] she goes directly to the 1951 source documents in which Israeli officials pressed their claims.

> The government of Israel is not in a position to obtain and present a complete statement of all Jewish property taken or looted by the Germans, and said to total more than $6 thousand million. It can only compute its claim on the basis of total expenditures already made and the expenditure still needed for the integration of Jewish immigrants from Nazi-dominated countries. The number of these immigrants is estimated at some 500,000, which means a total expenditure of $1.5 thousand million.[24]

The author then proceeds to state the obvious: "It hardly seems necessary to point out that the money the state received was based on the cost of resettling survivors, had Israel wanted to increase the amount of reparations it obtained from Germany it would have been in its interest to argue that fewer than six million had been killed and that more had managed to flee to Israel."[25] She then exposes the assorted pontifications of Barnes as the uninterrupted string of lies and obfuscations they actually are.[*] Turning next to App, she demolishes the tautological and statistical sleights-of-hand by which he purportedly demonstrated that genocide was never part of the nazi agenda.[26]

With these mainly polemical opponents out of the way, Lipstadt moves on to the more recent psuedoscientific postulations of others, such as Butz, Faurisson, and Leuchter. Here, largely because of the sheer extent and solidity of the technical literature available, she is devastating.[27] By the time she is finished, the author has utterly dismembered every known variation of such shopworn revisionist themes as Zyklon-B being a chemical appropriate only for delousing rather than extermination of human beings, the gas chambers at Auschwitz and elsewhere being "ill designed" to serve the purpose

---

[*] This is as opposed to the apologia offered by Robert LeFevre, Dean of Ramparts College, for Barnes' scholarship when the latter's "The Public Stake in Revisionism" was published in *Rampart Journal* during the summer of 1967. At one point in this essay, Barnes offers a description of the task of the SS *Einsatzgruppen* (mobile extermination teams) — groups which systematically slaughtered approximately a million Jews and Gypsies in the U.S.S.R. between 1941 and '43 — as "battling guerrillas." At another point, he refers to the "doings, real or imagined, at Auschwitz." In his introduction to the issue, LeFevre excused such matters as being born of "understandable frustration," which was "unfortunate, although it can be forgiven." On the realities at issue, see Yitzhak Arad, Shmuel Krakowski, and Schmuel Spector, eds., *The Einsatzgruppen Reports: Selections from the Nazi Death Squads' Campaign Against the Jews in Occupied Territories of the Soviet Union, July 1941–January 1943* (New York: Holocaust Library, 1989).

ascribed to them, and the crematoria at such facilities being "inadequate" to handle the volume of corpses "allegedly" run through them.[*]

In framing her responses, Lipstadt does a further great service by setting out a sort of typology of Holocaust revisionism. Not everyone involved, she maintains, is as crude as the outright deniers. Others might be better understood as "minimizers"; that is, those who engage in a range of sophistries designed to make the magnitude of the Holocaust appear less than it was.[28] From there, by carefully mixing known facts with their fictions, the latter group advances false sets of moral comparisons—e.g., the nazi extermination center at Auschwitz was "really no different" than the concentration camps at Dauchau (false);[29] *and* Dauchau wasn't all that different from the camp at Manzanar in which Japanese Americans were interned by the U.S. government during the war (true);[30] *therefore* the nazi treatment of *Untermenschen* was "no worse than" that accorded by the United States to its "Jap" minority (false)—which the author rightly describes as being "immoral equivalencies."[31]

The trick to a proper understanding of Holocaust revisionism, Lipstadt points out, is in seeing how these somewhat different elements interact in a mutually supportive fashion. This leads her to examine not only the main flow of Holocaust denial and minimization, but its antecedents and certain of its contemporary counterparts. The former brings about an exploration of post–World War I "Germanofilic" revisionism, not only on the part of the young Harry Elmer Barnes but also a number of other academic luminaries like Sidney B. Fay and Charles A. Beard.[32] These are treated in combination with such antisemitic/pro-nazi champions of interwar isolationism as North Dakota Republican Senator Gerald P. Nye, Washington's Democratic Senator Homer T. Bone, California Republican Senator Hiram W. Johnson, Mississippi's Democratic Congressman John E. Rankin, aviation hero Charles A. Lindbergh, and industrialist Henry Ford.[33]

> Barnes's work [in particular] won a broad popular audience in the United States and abroad…[He] used his World War I revisionism to propound the isolationist cause. Even before World War II had ended he was challenging the official version of its his-

---

[*]To stay with the Auschwitz example, there were five crematoria, each of which could accommodate well upwards of 200 corpses per day. Working at an average aggregate rate of 1,350 corpses per day, or about 493,000 per year, the crematoria at this death camp could have disposed of more than 1,725,000 of the roughly two million victims attributed to it during the 3.5 years it was operational. This does not count the very large number of corpses known to have been buried in mass graves, cremated on huge funeral pyres, and so on.

tory. He was part of a small group of isolationists who tried to resurrect the movement's reputation and to sully Roosevelt's. They were funded by prewar isolationists, including Charles Lindbergh and Henry Ford.[34]

This context was as indispensable to the birth and eventual maturation of Holocaust minimization and denial as the more recent actions and pronouncements of established and highly visible political figures are to its increasing acceptability. Salient in this regard was U.S. President Ronald Reagan's 1986 official "gesture of reconciliation" with Germany's nazi past, laying a commemorative wreath near the graves of SS troops in Bitburg.[35] Reagan informed the press that he would be unwilling to make a similar gesture at the site of a death camp because Germans "have a guilt feeling that's been imposed upon them and I just don't think it's necessary."[36] This, taken in combination with syndicated columns questioning orthodox Holocaust historiography by former Reagan press chief *cum* presidential candidate Patrick J. Buchanan,[37] should remove any mystery as to how an unabashed white supremacist and outright denier like David Duke might have been deemed a reasonable addition to the state legislature by Louisiana voters in the late 1980s.[38]

The same sort of dynamic is evident in France, where President François Mitterand ostentatiously conducted a wreath-laying ceremony at the grave of Marshal Philippe Pétain, head of the collaborationist World War II Vichy government which, among many other offenses — he was convicted of treason by a French court in 1945 — assisted the nazis in rounding up Jews for deportation and extermination.[39] Mitterand's symbolic but official forgiveness of Pétain's criminality is reflected in an across-the-board refusal of French lower courts to accept indictments of former Vichy officials charged with complicity and/or direct participation in all manner of wartime German atrocities. To date, despite an abundant record in this regard, no French citizen has ever been tried, much less convicted or punished, for perpetrating crimes against humanity.[40]

A similar phenomenon has been manifested in Germany, as is evidenced in the quasi-official renderings of such reactionary nationalist historians as Hellmut Diwald, Andreas Hillgruber, and Michael Stürmer. Diwald, in his 1978 *Geschichte der Deutschen* [*History of the Germans*], attempted to establish a genuinely immoral equivalency when he argued that the displacement of Germans from eastern Europe at the end of the Second World War constituted a crime "on par with" those perpetrated by the nazis against the Jews, Poles, Slovenes, Ukrainians, and many others.[41] Hillgruber followed up in 1986 with *Zweierlei Untergang: Die Zerschlagung des deutschen Reiches und das Ende des europäischen Judentums* [*Two Kinds of Downfall: The Shattering of the German Reich and the End of European Jewry*], a narrower but more refined argument to much the same effect.[42] Such "interpretations" underpinned open calls by Stürmer—Chancellor Helmut Kohl's historical adviser at the time of Bitburg—for a more general rewriting of history to "alleviate Germany's obsessive guilt" over the Holocaust, thereby facilitating "a rebirth of German pride and patriotism."[43]

It is to these much more diffuse, institutionalized, and ubiquitous symptomologies of denial, rather than the blatant crudities of Rassinier and Butz, that we must address ourselves, Lipstadt contends, if we are ever to rid ourselves of the hideous implications represented by the deniers themselves. "If Holocaust denial has demonstrated anything," she observes, "it is the fragility of memory, truth, reason, and history."[44] The object, of course, is to affirm and reinforce each of these as natural societal barriers against repetition of that which is being denied and forgotten. "When we witness assaults on truth," she says, "our response must be strong, though neither polemical nor emotional. We must educate the broader public and academe about this threat and its historical and ideological roots. We must expose these people for what they are," most especially when they—like Reagan, Mitterand, Kohl, and the intellectuals in their service—occupy positions of elite authority.[45]

Degeneration

Had *Denying the Holocaust* ended there, or, more accurately, had it been constrained to encompass only the material summarized above, it would be an altogether good and useful book. Unfortunately, Lipstadt incorporates a subtext into her final chapter which undoes quite a lot of the good she might otherwise have accomplished. Moreover, she does so with a heavy overload of precisely the distortion, polemicism, and emotion-laden prose she herself condemns.

The problem emerges most clearly when, in conjunction with her rebuttal of German conservative historians, she takes up the work of Ernst Nolte, a neoliberal known mainly for his masterly historical/philosophical analysis of fascism, published during the early 1960s.[46] At issue is the evolution of Nolte's handling of the Holocaust in and since the 1976 publication of his *Deutschland und der kalte Krieg* [*Germany and the Cold War*]. He has been increasingly prone to an "historicization" of nazi genocide by contrasting and comparing it to other phenomena, including the Turkish extermination of Armenians in 1918, the Stalinist program against Ukrainians during the 1930s, the American performance in Vietnam during the 1960s and early 1970s, and the Khmer Rouge "autogenocide" of the mid-'70s.[47]

Although Nolte's motivations are highly problematic—as well as his attribution of motivations to some of the historical figures he treats (e.g., Hitler, Stalin, and Pol Pot)—this has been critiqued rather severely by the prominent left social philosopher Jürgen Habermas, in a series of essays which ushered in the so-called *Historikerstreit* ["historians' controversy"] of 1986 in Germany.[48] It is telling that Lipstadt offers not so much as an oblique reference to Habermas or his arguments.[49] This is because she is not especially concerned in Nolte's case with debunking a minimization or denial of the Holocaust at all.[50] Indeed, she acknowledges that he not only affirms its occurrence, but that it occurred in its full dimension.[51] What she has in mind instead is to use Nolte as a vehicle upon which to attack comparative methods, per se.

This is accomplished via an uninterrupted transition from Lipstadt's solid denunciations of Diwald's, Hillgruber's, and Stürmer's spurious attempts to equate German suffering under the Soviets with that of the Jews under nazism, to her purported rebuttal of Nolte's much broader sets of comparisons.[52] As the first three men's comparisons are not only inaccurate but immoral, so too are Nolte's and, by extension, comparison by *anyone* of *any* phenomenon to the Holocaust. *All* efforts to contextualize the Holocaust— "relativizing" it—are by definition as reprehensible as denial itself in Lipstadt's scheme of things.

> These historians are not crypto-deniers, but the results of the work are the same: the blurring of boundaries between fact and fiction... Ultimately the relativists contribute to the fostering of what I call the "yes, but" syndrome... Yes, there was a Holocaust, but it was essentially no different than an array of other conflagrations in which innocents were massacred. The question that logically follows from this is, Why, then, do we "only" hear about the Holocaust? For the deniers and many others who are "not yet" deniers, the answer to this final question is obvious: because of the power of the Jews. "Yes, but" is a response that falls into the gray area between outright denial and relativism. In certain respects it is more insidious than outright denial because it nurtures a form of pseudohistory whose motives are difficult to identify. *It is the equivalent of David Duke without his robes* (emphasis added).[53]

This, from a woman who claims to reject "immoral equivalencies." The wild sweep of her brush not only smears Nolte with the same tar as Hillgruber and Diwald—or Paul Rassinier and David Irving, for that matter—but also such *decisively* anti-nazi historians as Joachim Fest, who have defended Nolte's comparativist methods while disagreeing with many of his conclusions.[54] By the same token, the splatters extend without nuance or distinction to a host of emphatically progressive scholars like David Stannard, Ian Hancock, and Vahakn Dadrian, each of whom has argued the case that one or more other peoples has suffered a genocide comparable to that experienced by the Jews without attempting to diminish the gravity and significance of the Holocaust in the least (if anything, they endeavor to reinforce its importance as a historical benchmark).[55] Even Jewish scholars like Israel Charny and Richard Rubinstein, and nazi-hunter Simon Wiesenthal, who acknowledge similarities between the nazi genocide and those undergone by Armenians, Poles, Gypsies, American Indians, and others, are necessarily encompassed within Lipstadt's astonishing definition of neonazi scholarship.[56]

What has happened is that, in her project's final pages, the author has subtly substituted one agenda for another. Without pause or notification, she shifts from the entirely worthy objective of systematically exposing, confronting, and repudiating those who deny the existence of the Holocaust to a far more dubious attempt to confirm the nazi genocide of European Jewry as something absolutely singular, a process without parallel in all of human history.[57] There is a tremendous difference between the two propositions, yet Lipstadt bends every effort to make them appear synonymous. In effect, any "failure" to concede the intrinsic "phenomenological uniqueness" of the Holocaust is to be guilty of denying it altogether.[58]

Ultimately, only the Truth of the exclusivity of the Holocaust remains unscathed.[59] The fundamental and deliberate distortiveness of Lipstadt's formulation speaks for itself. It is a lie, or complex of lies, consciously and maliciously uttered, lies of a type which readily conform in their magnitude and intent to those of the very deniers Lipstadt has devoted the bulk of her text to combatting. In the end, *Denying the Holocaust* is thereby reduced to an exercise in holocaust denial.

Uniqueness as Denial

Nowhere is Lipstadt's allegiance to the kind of duplicitous argumentation employed by deniers more obvious than when, during her polemic against Ernst Nolte, she "explains" why the mass internment of Japanese-Americans by the United States in 1942 is different in kind, not just from outright extermination programs but from nazism's policy as a whole:

In [an] attempt at immoral equivalence, Nolte contends that just as the American internment of Japanese Americans was justified by the attack on Pearl Harbor, so too was the Nazi "internment" of European Jews. In making this comparison Nolte ignores the fact that, however wrong, racist, and unconstitutional the U.S. internment of the *Japanese* (emphasis added), the Jews had not bombed Nazi cities or attacked German forces in 1939. Even his use of the term *internment* to describe what the Germans did to the Jews whitewashes historical reality.[60]

Actually, what Nolte argues is that neither example is more justified than the other, a very different position from that of which he is accused.[61] Secondly, Lipstadt's conversion of Japanese-Americans into "Japanese" from one sentence to the next is illuminating. Plainly, the misrepresentation—magically transforming a racially defined group of American citizens into subjects of a hostile foreign power—is vital to her position. Equally plainly, an identical notion— that the Jews comprised a foreign and racially hostile element within German society—was a crux of Hitlerian ideology.[62] The nazis held, falsely, that Jews thus comprised an inherent "Fifth Column" within German-held territory, a myth duly adopted by David Irving and other deniers to justify Jewish internment (but not extermination, since they claim it did not occur).[*] The United States, for exactly similar reasons, contended that Japanese-Americans constituted a comparably subversive element, a glaring untruth Lipstadt seconds without hesitancy or equivocation.[63] In any event, "internment" is a word which sanitizes the experiences of *both* the Japanese-Americans and the Jews.[64]

Whatever Nolte's shortcomings, and they are many, it is Lipstadt who is ignoring facts here, forming a methodological symmetry with the deniers. The same may be said with respect to her cavalier dismissals of any possibility for legitimate comparison between the Jewish experience under the nazis and that of other peoples slaughtered as a matter of state policy during the twentieth century. Take "the brutal Armenian tragedy" of 1918, in which well upwards of a million people were killed and millions more

---

[*] The ridiculous idea of "Jewish Fifth Columnism" is complicated by the fact that, unlike Japanese-Americans vis-à-vis the United States, there was active Jewish participation in partisan operations against Germany from 1939 onward. It is true that zionist leader Chaim Weizman announced in September of that year that Jews would fight with those countries allied against the Reich. How extensively this was or even could have been acted upon is unclear. The consensus has been that Jewish engagement in armed struggle was "meager"; see, e.g., Lucy S. Dawidowicz, *The War Against the Jews, 1933–1945* (New York: Holt, Rinehart & Winston, 1975) p. 371. More recently, however, at least some prominent zionist scholars have begun to claim that Jews comprised the veritable backbone of partisan groups in many areas; see, e.g., Yehuda Bauer, "Jewish Resistance and Passivity in the Face of the Holocaust," in François Furet, ed., *Unanswered Questions: Nazi Germany and the Genocide of the Jews* (New York: Schocken Books, 1989).

subjected to a "ruthless Turkish policy of expulsion and resettlement." This was "horrendous," Lipstadt informs us, "but it was not part of a process of total annihilation of an entire people," so it is not comparable to the Holocaust.[*]

This "yes, but" conclusion is immediately followed by others. The "barbaric" Khmer Rouge extermination campaign in Cambodia? It was "conducted as part of a brutalizing war" in which "imagined collaborators"—a million of them?—were "subdued and eliminated."[65] What the nazis did to the Jews, unlike what the Khmer Rouge did to the Cambodians, was "gratuitous." Besides, Cambodia is a backward kind of place, not "a prosperous, advanced, industrial nation at the height of its power" like Germany, so the fate of its population apparently doesn't count.[66] Hence, it is obviously "immoral" to compare the Khmer Rouge genocide to that perpetrated by nazism.

The Soviet "collectivization" of the 1930s, in which millions of people were deliberately starved to death as a matter of developmental economic policy, is depicted as being "arbitrary" rather than "targeted [on] a particular group."[67] This will undoubtedly come as a great surprise and comfort to the Ukrainians who see themselves as having been very much targeted by the Soviets, about five of the seven million estimated deaths by starvation during the winter of 1931–32 alone having accrued from their ranks.[68] It will likely prove even more startling to the Kazakhs, who were totally obliterated.[69] And, since "no citizen of the Soviet Union assumed that deportation and death were inevitable consequences of his or her ethnic origins," no legitimate comparison of Stalinist "terror" to the Holocaust is possible.[70] To suggest otherwise, much less to argue the point, is to become "David Duke without his robes" or, at best, guilty of "an unconscious reflection of anti-Semitic attitudes."[71]

Such historical misrepresentations of other peoples' suffering aside, the essential claim to uniqueness for the Holocaust put forth by Lipstadt and those sharing her view, is lodged in a double fallacy. The first half of this duality is the assertion that, under the nazis, "*every single one* of millions of targeted Jews was to be murdered. Eradication was to be total" (emphasis in the

---

[*] Lipstadt, *Denying the Holocaust, op. cit.*, p. 212. It is worth noting that she underpins her assessment of the Armenian genocide with no citations whatever. Her colleague Steven T. Katz, however, who offers a virtually identical argument, has been known to rely upon the work of notorious Turkish deniers, even when they've been exposed as "full-blown revisionists" and more accurate sources are readily available; see, e.g., Katz's "The Uniqueness of the Holocaust: The Historical Dimension," in Rosenbaum, *Is the Holocaust Unique?, op. cit.*

original).[72] This was true, according to senior Holocaust scholar Yehuda Bauer of the Hebrew University in Jerusalem, not just with respect to German or even European Jewry, but worldwide, because nazism set out in a "pseudo-religious" and "pseudo-messianic" fashion to extirpate Jews on a "*global, universal, even cosmic*" scale (emphasis in the original).[73] As Cornell University professor Steven T. Katz frames things, "the Nazi racial imperative [was] that *all* Jews must die, and that they must die here and now."[74] And, Bauer concludes elsewhere, "total physical annihilation...is what *happened* to the Jews (emphasis added)."[75]

These characterizations of nazi intent and its impact upon its victims couples readily to the second part of the dualism: nothing meeting this description of the Holocaust has ever happened to anyone else, anywhere, at any time. "To date," says Bauer, "this has happened once, to the Jews under Nazism."[76] "The fate of the Jews under National Socialism was [therefore] unique," historian Lucy Dawidowicz continues.[77] This is because, as Michael Marrus puts it in his book, *The Holocaust in History*, in cases like that of the Armenians, the "killing was far from universal."[78] Or, as Yehuda Bauer is wont to wrap things up, in every other recorded instance of wholesale and systematic population eradication, "the destruction was not complete."[79]

The problem is that neither half of this tidy whole is true. Rhetoric notwithstanding, there is no evidence at all that any nazi leader, Hitler included, ever manifested a serious belief that it would actually be possible to liquidate every Jew on the planet.[*] Indeed, there is ambiguity in the record as to whether the total physical annihilation of European Jewry itself was actually a fixed policy objective.[†] What is revealed instead is a rather erratic

---

[*] Some scholars—e.g., Leni Yahil, *The Holocaust: The Fate of European Jewry, 1933–1945* (New York: Oxford University Press, 1990) p. 313—have attempted to use a passage from the Wannsee Protocol of January 20, 1942, as "documentary evidence of a plan to exterminate Jews worldwide." The language in question authorizes Reichsführer SS Heinrich Himmler to effect the "final solution of the Jewish problem...without regard to geographic borders." This "proof" is disingenuously offered, however, since it has been deliberately decontextualized to create the desired impression. Placing the sentence in which the phrase appears back in its proper context—that is, following two sentences making explicit reference to *European* Jews—makes it clear that the only borders at issue are those of Europe; David E. Stannard, "The Politics of Holocaust Scholarship: Uniqueness as Denial," in Rosenbaum, *Is the Holocaust Unique?, op. cit.*, p. 206. For the text of the Wannsee Protocol itself, see John Mendelsohn and Donald S. Detwiler, eds., *The Holocaust: Selected Documents in Eighteen Volumes* (New York: Garland, 1982) pp. 22–5.

[†] From 1933 until 1941, nazi efforts to make their territory *Judenrein* [Jew-free] devolved on coerced individual immigration and exploration of the possibilities of mass expulsion first to Palestine, then Madagascar, and finally, after 1939, into the newly conquered General Government area of Poland;

and contradictory hodgepodge of anti-Jewish policies which, as late as mid-1944, included an apparently genuine offer by the SS to trade a million Jews to the Western allies in exchange for 10,000 trucks to be used in Germany's war against the Soviets.* Contrary to Bauer's irrational contention of a "cosmic" and unparalleled total extermination, approximately two-thirds of the global Jewish population survived the Holocaust, as did about a third of the Jews of Europe.[80]

This in no way diminishes nazi culpability or Jewish suffering. There can be no question that nazism's program for creating a *Judenrein Lebensraum* [Jew-free living space] for "Aryans" entailed a substantial reduction in the size of the European Jewish population, thoroughgoing dislocation/expulsion of survivors, and a virtually total elimination of Jewish cultural existence within the German sphere of influence.[81] Nor can there be any serious question as to whether the nazis were *willing* in the end to kill every Jew who came within their grasp, *if* that's what was required to achieve the goal. *All* of this, beyond doubt, qualifies as genocide,[82] but it is not the uniquely obsessive drive to achieve a complete biological liquidation of Jewry attributed to the Holocaust by "scholars" like Yehuda Bauer, Steven Katz, and Deborah Lipstadt.

The experience of the Jewish people under nazism is unique only in the sense that all such phenomena exhibit unique characteristics. Genocide, as the nazis practiced it, was never something suffered exclusively by Jews,

---

see, e.g., Philip Friedman, "The Lublin Reservation and the Madagascar Plan: Two Aspects of Nazi Jewish Policy During the Second World War," *YIVO Annual of Jewish Social Studies*, 1953. This has led as reputable a scholar as Christopher R. Browning, among many others, to conclude that the "practice of Nazi Jewish policy until 1941 does not support the thesis of a long-held, fixed intention to murder the European Jews"; *The Fateful Months: Essays on the Emergence of the Final Solution* (New York: Holmes & Meier, 1985) pp. 8–38. Those who would nonetheless assert the opposite—most recently Lehman College professor John Weiss in his *Ideology of Death: Why the Holocaust Happened in Germany* (Chicago: Ivan R. Dee, 1996) p. 329—are reduced to arguing with utter implausibility that the nazi plan was first to deport the Jews to Madagascar, subsequently conquer the island, then proceed with the extermination they'd planned all along.

*This is detailed by none other than Yehuda Bauer, in his *Jews for Sale? Nazi-Jewish Negotiations, 1933–1945* (New Haven: Yale University Press, 1994). Bauer, of course, realizes that such facts cannot be squared with his own often hyperbolic insistence that "complete biological eradication of the Jews" was an unwavering, indeed "pseudo-messianic," goal of nazism from 1933 onward. Hence, at page 252, he attempts to finesse the problem in the same manner as Weiss by advancing the preposterous assertion that in the summer of 1944, with their armies everywhere in an incipient state of collapse, "the Nazis [still] expected to win the war, and if they did, they might finally 'solve' the 'Jewish question' by total annihilation; any Jews who might escape momentarily would in the end be caught and killed."

nor were the nazis singularly guilty of its practice.[83] In attempting to make it appear otherwise—and thus to claim the status of an "unparalleled" victimization ("accumulating moral capital," as exclusivist Edward Alexander has put it)[*]—proponents of uniqueness have engaged in holocaust denial on the grand scale, not only with respect to the Armenians, Ukrainians, and Cambodians, but as regards scores of other instances of genocide, both historical and contemporary. By doing so, they have contributed to the invisibility of the victims of this hideous multiplicity of processes in exactly the same way the Jewish victims of nazism have often been rendered invisible even by those whose work falls well short of outright Holocaust denial.[84] To this extent, Lipstadt and her colleagues have greatly surpassed anything attempted by Rassinier and his ilk. Those who would deny the Holocaust, after all, focus their distortions upon one target. Those who deny all holocausts other than that of the Jews have the same effect upon many.

Reclaiming the Invisible Victims

The costs of these systematic assaults on truth and memory have often been high for those whose suffering is correspondingly downgraded or shunted into historical oblivion. This concerns not only the victims of the many genocides occurring outside the framework of nazism, but also the non-Jews targeted for elimination within the Holocaust itself. Consider, for example, the example of the Sinti and Roma peoples (Gypsies, also called "Romani"), whom Lipstadt doesn't deign to accord so much as mention in her book. Her omission is no doubt due to an across-the-board and steadfast refusal by the Jewish scholarly, social, and political establishments over the past fifty years to even admit the Gypsies were part of the Holocaust, a circumstance manifested most strikingly in their virtual exclusion from the United States Holocaust Memorial Museum in Washington, D.C.[†]

---

[*] Alexander asserts "a Jewish claim to a specific suffering that was of the 'highest,' the most distinguished grade available" and worries that, if other genocides are acknowledged, the victims will be in a position to "steal the Holocaust" and thereby "plunder the moral capital which the Jewish people unwittingly accumulated"; Edward Alexander, *The Holocaust and the War of Ideas* (New Brunswick, NJ: Transaction, 1994) p. 195; "Stealing the Holocaust," *Midstream*, Nov. 1980. A good overview of these sentiments at play will be found in Jacob Neusner, *Stranger at Home: "The Holocaust," Zionism and American Judaism* (Chicago: University of Chicago Press, 1981).

[†] When it was proposed that there might be room in the museum's council for a Gypsy representative, its executive director, the Rabbi Seymour Siegel, rejected the suggestion as "cockamamie"; Edward T. Linenthal, *Preserving Memory: The Struggle to Create America's Holocaust Museum* (New York: Viking, 1995) pp. 242–3.

In their zeal to prevent what they call a "dilution" or "de-Judaization" of the Holocaust,[*] Jewish exclusivists have habitually employed every device known to deniers to depict the *Porrajmos* (as the Holocaust is known in the Romani language; the Hebrew equivalent is *Shoah*) as having been something "fundamentally different" from the Holocaust itself. The first technique has been to consistently minimize Gypsy fatalities. Lucy Dawidowicz, for instance, when she mentions them at all, is prone to repeating the standard mythology that, "of about one million Gypsies in the countries that fell under German control, nearly a quarter of them were murdered."[†] The point being made is that, while Gypsy suffering was no doubt "unendurable," it was proportionately far less than that of the Jews.[85]

Actually, as more accurate — or honest — demographic studies reveal, the Gypsy population of German-occupied Europe likely came to somewhere around *two* million in 1939.[86] Of these, it was known at least thirty years ago that between 500,000 and 750,000 died in camps such as Buchenwald, Neuengamme, Bergen-Belsen, Belzec, Chelmno, Majdanek, Sobibór, and Auschwitz.[‡] More recent research shows that there were as many as a million more Gypsies exterminated when the tolls taken by the *Einsatzgruppen*, antipartisan operations in eastern Europe, and actions by nazi satellite forces are factored in.[§] One reason for this ambiguity in terms of

---

[*] The terms were used by Yehuda Bauer in his denunciation of Jimmy Carter for exhibiting "unconscious antisemitism" when the U.S. President committed the offense of mentioning in a speech that others besides Jews had died in the Holocaust; "Whose Holocaust?" *op. cit.*, p. 45.

[†] Dawidowicz omits the Gypsies altogether in her ostensibly comprehensive history of the Holocaust, aptly titled, *War Against the Jews, op. cit.* She makes the statement quoted in *The Holocaust and the Historians, op. cit.*, p. 11. The same data are reiterated endlessly by other Jewish exclusivists, e.g., Martin Gilbert in his own massive history of the Holocaust, predictably subtitled "A History of the Jews of Europe During the Second World War," *op. cit.*, p. 824. These are also the data displayed at the U.S. Holocaust Memorial Museum. It should be noted that Gilbert, in his foreword to Carry Supple's *From Prejudice to Genocide: Learning About the Holocaust* (Stoke-on-Trent: Trentham Books, 1993), a text used to expose and orient schoolchildren in England, totally "disappears" Gypsies from their awareness by describing the Holocaust exclusively in terms of an "attempt by the Nazis to destroy all the Jews of Europe between 1941 and 1945."

[‡] Louis Pawells and Jacques Bergier, *Le Matin des Magiciens* (Paris: Editions Gallimard, 1960) p. 430; published in English translation as *The Morning of the Magicians* (New York: Stein and Day, 1963). In the most recent book on the subject, Donald Kendrick's *Gypsies Under the Swastika* (Hartfield: Hertfordshire University Press, 1995), a figure of 200,000 dead is advanced. Kendrick notes, however, that the idea of a nazi program of genocide against Gypsies as well as Jews is "very sensitive." He therefore selected the absolute "lowest possible number" in hopes that conservatism might forestall criticism. He readily concedes that the actual number of Gypsy dead could be "very much higher."

[§] "The Gypsies outside the Reich were massacred at many places... In the *Generalgouvernement* alone, 150 sites of Gypsy massacres are known... Unlike the Jews...Gypsies were not included in national census data. Therefore it is an impossible task to find the actual number of Gypsy victims in Poland,

how many Gypsies died at the hands of the nazis, leaving aside the gross undercounting of their initial population, is that their executioners not infrequently tallied their dead in with the numbers of Jews killed (thus somewhat inflating estimations of the Jewish count while diminishing that of the Sinti and Roma).* In sum, it is plain that the proportional loss of the Gypsies during the Holocaust was at least as great as that of the Jews, and quite probably greater.[87]

Be that as it may, exclusivists still contend that the Gypsies stand apart from the Holocaust because, unlike the Jews, they were "not marked for complete annihilation."[88] According to Richard Breitman, "The Nazis are not known to have spoken of the Final Solution of the Polish problem or the Gypsy problem."[89] Or, as Yehuda Bauer put it in his three-page entry on "Gypsies" in the *Encyclopedia of the Holocaust*—that's all the space the Sinti and Roma are accorded in this 2,000-page work, "[The] fate of the Gypsies was in line with Nazi thought as a whole; Gypsies were not Jews, and therefore there was no need to kill them all."[90]

Keeping in mind the likelihood that there was always a less-than-perfect mesh between the rhetoric and realities of nazi exterminationism in all cases, *including* that of the Jews, the distinctions drawn here bear scrutiny. As we shall see with respect to the Poles, such claims are of dubious validity. As concerns the Gypsies, they amount to a bold-faced lie. This is readily evidenced by Himmler's "Decree for Basic Regulations to Resolve the Gypsy Question as Required by the Nature of Race" of December 8, 1938, which initiated preparations for the "*complete extermination* of the Sinti and Romani" (emphasis added).[91] Shortly after this, in February 1939, a brief was circu-

---

Yugoslavia, White Ruthenia and the Ukraine, the lands that probably had the greatest number of victims"; State Museum of Auschwitz-Birkenau, *Memorial Book: The Gypsies of Auschwitz-Birkenau* (Munich: K.G. Saur, 1993) p. 2; C. Tyler, "Gypsy President," *Financial Times*, March 26, 1994; Susan Strandberg, "Researcher Claims Thousands of Gypsies Exterminated by Czechs," *Decorah Journal*, May 5, 1994; Jiří Lípam "The Fate of the Gypsies in Czechoslovakia Under Nazi Domination," in Berenbaum, *A Mosaic of Victims, op. cit.*, pp. 207–15; Brenda Davis Lutz and James M. Lutz, "Gypsies as Victims of the Holocaust," *Holocaust and Genocide Studies*, No. 9, 1995.

*"The count of half a million dead Sinti and Roma murdered between 1939 and 1945 is too low to be tenable; for example in the Soviet Union many of the Romani dead were listed under non-specific labels such as *Liquidierungsübrigen* [remainder to be liquidated], 'hangers-on' and 'partisans'... The final number of the dead Sinti and Roma may never be determined. We do not know how many were brought into the concentration camps; not every concentration camp produced [this kind of] statistical material"; Ulrich König, *Sinti und Roma unter dem Nationalsozialismus* (Bochum: Brockmeyer Verlah, 1989) pp. 129–33. Also see Ian Hancock, "Responses to the *Porrajmos:* The Romani Holocaust," in Rosenbaum, *Is the Holocaust Unique?, op. cit.*, p. 49.

lated by Johannes Behrendt of the nazi Office of Racial Hygiene in which it was stated that "all Gypsies should be treated as hereditarily sick; the only solution is elimination. The aim should be the elimination without hesitation of this defective population."* Hitler himself is reported to have verbally ordered "the liquidation of all Jews, Gypsies and communist political functionaries in the entire Soviet Union" as early as June 1940.[92] A year later, Obergruppenführer Reinhard Heydrich, head of the Reich Main Security Office, followed up by instructing his *Einsatzcommandos* to "kill all Jews, Gypsies and mental patients" in the conquered areas of the East.[93]

> Heydrich, who had been entrusted with the "final solution of the Jewish question" on 31st July 1941, shortly after the German invasion of the U.S.S.R., also included the Gypsies in his "final solution"... The senior SS officer and Chief of Police for the East, Dr. Landgraf, in Riga, informed Rosenberg's Reich Commissioner for the East, Lohse, of the inclusion of the Gypsies in the "final solution." Thereupon, Lohse gave the order, on 24th December 1941, that the Gypsies "should be given the same treatment as the Jews."[94]

At about the same time, "Adolf Eichmann made the recommendation that the 'Gypsy Question' be solved simultaneously with the 'Jewish Question'... Himmler signed the order dispatching Germany's Sinti and Roma to Auschwitz on 16th December 1942. The 'Final Solution' of the 'Gypsy Question' had begun" at virtually the same moment it can be said to have really gotten underway for the Jews.[95] Indeed, Gypsies were automatically subject to whatever policies applied to Jews during the entire period of the Final Solution, pursuant to a directive issued by Himmler on December 24, 1941 (i.e., four months prior to the Wannsee Conference which set the full-fledged extermination program in motion).[96] Hence, there is no defensible way the fate of the Gypsies can be distinguished from that of the Jews.

Jewish exclusivists have nonetheless attempted to do so with the verbatim regurgitation of the nazi fable that Gypsies were killed en masse, not on specifically racial grounds, but because *as a group* they were "asocials"

---

*Quoted in Hancock, "Responses to the *Porrajmos*," *op. cit.*, p. 43. This placed the Gypsies, as a racially defined group, within the nazi conception of *Lebensunwertes Leben* [life unworthy of life] initially formalized in the "Law for the Prevention of Hereditarily Diseased Offspring" of July 14, 1933. While this earlier law called only for the involuntary sterilization of those targeted—400,000 people were ultimately subjected to this genocidal "treatment"—it was quietly amended to include euthanasia in 1939; Robert Jay Lifton, *The Nazi Doctors: Medical Killing and the Psychology of Genocide* (New York: Basic Books, 1986); Arthur L. Caplan, ed., *When Medicine Went Mad: Bioethics and the Holocaust* (Totowa, NJ: Humana Press, 1992). For pre-nazi German pseudoscientific/philosophical background, see Karl Binding and Alfred Hoche, *Die Freigabe der Vernichtung Lebensunwerten Lebens* (Leipzig: Felix Meiner, 1920).

(criminals).* And, as if this blatantly racist derogation weren't bad enough, the Rabbi Seymour Siegel, a former professor of ethics at the Jewish Theological Seminary and at the time executive director of the U.S. Holocaust Memorial Council, compounded the affront by using the pages of the *Washington Post* to publicly cast doubt as to whether Gypsies can even make a legitimate claim to comprising a distinct people.[97]

Predictably, Yehuda Bauer, no stranger to self-contradiction, presumes to have the last word not once, but twice. First, completely ignoring the 1935 Nuremberg Laws, which defined Gypsies in precisely the same racial terms as Jews, he states that "the Gypsies were not murdered for racial reasons, but as so-called asocials…nor was their destruction complete."† Then, barely two pages later, he reverses field entirely, arguing that the Sinti and Romani were privileged over Jews—and were thus separate from the "true" Holocaust—because a tiny category of "racially safe" Gypsies were temporarily exempted from death.‡ Besides trying to have it both ways, it is as if this leading champion of exclusivism were unaware of the roughly 6,000 Karait Jews who were permanently spared in accordance with nazism's bizarre racial logic.[98]

---

* See, e.g., Dawidowicz, *The Holocaust and the Historians, op. cit.*, p. 10. Actually, Gypsies and Jews were viewed in very much the same way, even as biologically related: "In medieval Europe they were thought to be a race formed by the intermarriage of Jews and non-Jewish vagabonds, a mongrel people sharing responsibility for the death of Christ. Like Jews, Gypsies were shunned as homeless wanderers and possessors of satanic and occult powers. In modern times Gypsies were thought to be racially impure, unnatural kidnappers and disease-carriers, even cannibals. Hunted like game in Eastern Europe, they were often hanged just because they were Gypsies"; Weiss, *Ideology of Death, op. cit.*, pp. 327–8. For exploration of precisely the same volatile mixture of mythic ingredients vis-à-vis Jews, see Cohn, *Warrant for Genocide, op. cit.*

†Bauer, "Whose Holocaust?" *op. cit.* The relevant language reads, "In Europe only Jews and Gypsies are of foreign blood"; quoted in Weiss, *Ideology of Death, op. cit.*, p. 328, who goes on to observe that, "By 1942, death was the penalty for anyone known to have Gypsy blood, and even some found serving in the army were sent to death camps." Meanwhile, under the Nuremberg Laws, the Gypsies, like the Jews, were made noncitizens, prohibited from intermarrying or propagating with persons outside their racial group, subjected to compulsory sterilization, denied the right to practice a profession and otherwise disemployed, and increasingly stripped of whatever property they possessed; Erika Thurner, "Nazi Policy Against the Gypsies," unpublished paper presented at the U.S. Holocaust Memorial Council Conference on Other Victims, Washington, D.C., Mar. 1987; Sybil Milton, "Nazi Policies Towards Roma and Sinti, 1933–1945," *Journal of the Gypsy Lore Society*, Vol. 2, No. 1, 5th Series, 1992.

‡Bauer, "Whose Holocaust?" *op. cit.* This was an idea put forth by Heinrich Himmler in 1941 that a few dozen "pure" Gypsies be culled out for purposes of establishing an experimental "zoo." The proposal was quashed by Martin Bormann, head of the Nazi Party Chancellery, in 1942 and was thereafter abandoned. Bauer nonetheless uses Himmler's nonpolicy as a pretext to return repeatedly to the theme of Gypsy "privilege"; see, e.g., his and Yitzak Mais' contribution to Berenbaum, *The World Must Know, op. cit.*, p. 51.

To be fair, there *are* differences between the Jewish and Gypsy experiences under nazism. The racial classification of Gypsies was much more stringent and rigidly adhered to than that pertaining to Jews.[99] By 1938, if any two of an individual's eight great-grandparents were proven to be Gypsy "by blood," even in part, he or she was formally categorized as such. This is twice as strict as the criteria used by the nazis to define Jewishness.[100] Had the standards of "racial identity" applied to Jews been employed with regard to the Sinti and Roma, nine-tenths of Germany's 1939 Gypsy population would have survived the Holocaust.[101]

All during the 1930s, while Gypsies as well as Jews were subjected to increasingly draconian racial oppression, first in Germany, then in Austria and Czechoslovakia, a certain amount of international outrage was expressed on behalf of the Jews.[102] Foreign diplomatic and business pressure was exerted, resulting in an at least partial and transient alleviation in Jewish circumstances, and facilitating Jewish emigration to a small degree (150,000 left by 1938).[103] From then until the collapse of the Third Reich, the nazis displayed a periodic willingness to broker Jewish lives for a variety of reasons, and diplomats like Sweden's Count Folke Bernadotte made efforts to effect their rescue.[104] *None* of this applies to the Sinti and Roma.

The Western democracies have been harshly—and properly—criticized for their failure to intervene more forcefully to prevent the genocide of the Jews, not even to the extent of allowing greater numbers of Jewish refugees to find sanctuary within their borders.[105] The fact is, however, that nothing at all was done to save the Gypsies from their identical fate, and in this connection international Jewish organizations have no better record than do the governments of the United States, Great Britain, and Canada.[106] As researcher Ian Hancock describes the results:

> It is an eerie and disheartening feeling to pick up [reference books like *Encyclopedia of the Third Reich*] and find the attempted genocide of one's people written completely out of the historical record. Perhaps worse, in the English-language translation of at least one book, that by Lujan Dobroszycki of *The Chronicle of the Lodz Ghetto*, the entire reference to the liquidation of the Gypsy camp there (entry number 22 for April 29 and 30, 1942, in the original work) has been deleted deliberately. I have been told, but have not yet verified, that translations of other works on the Holocaust have also had entries on the Roma and Sinti removed. Furthermore, I do not want to read references to the United States Holocaust Memorial Museum in the national press and learn only that it is a monument to "the plight of European Jews," as the *New York Times* told its readers on December 23, 1993. I want to be able to watch epics such as *Schindler's List*

and learn that Gypsies were a central part of the Holocaust, too; or other films, such as *Escape from Sobibór*, a Polish camp where, according to Kommandant Franz Stangl in his memoirs, thousands of Roma and Sinti were murdered, and not hear the word "Gypsy" except once, and then only as the name of somebody's dog.[107]

Or to take an even more poignant example:

National Public Radio (NPR) in Washington, D.C. covered extensively the fiftieth anniversary of Auschwitz-Birkenau on January 26, 1995, but Gypsies were never once mentioned, despite being well represented at the commemoration. In its closing report on NPR's "Weekend Edition" on January 28, Michael Goldfarb described how "candles were placed along the tracks that delivered Jews and Poles to their death." But it was little wonder the Gypsies weren't mentioned; they were not allowed to participate in the candle ceremony. An article on the Auschwitz commemoration that appeared in the British press (though not the U.S. press) included a group of Roma staring mournfully through a wire fence, with a caption reading "Cold-shouldered: Gypsies, whose ancestors were among Auschwitz victims, are forced to watch the ceremony from outside the compound." In a speech given at that ceremony, Elie Wiesel said that the Jewish people "were singled out for destruction during the Holocaust."[108]

The attitudes underlying such gestures are manifested, not merely in Jewish exclusivism's sustained and concerted effort to expunge the *Porrajmos* from history, but, more concretely, through its ongoing silence concerning the present resurgence of nazi-like anti-Gypsy sentiments and activities in Europe. In 1992, the government of the newly unified German Republic negotiated a deal in which it paid more than a hundred million deutsche marks to Romania—notoriously hostile to Gypsies—in exchange for that cash-poor country's acceptance of the bulk of Germany's Sinti/Roma population (a smaller side deal is being arranged with Poland to receive the rest).[109] Summary deportations began during the fall of 1993, with more than 20,000 people expelled to date, for no other reason than that they are Gypsies.[110] Their reception upon arrival? A December 1993 news story sums it up very well:

An orgy of mob lynching and house-burning with police collaboration has turned into something more sinister for Romania's hated Gypsies: the beginnings of a nationwide campaign of terror launched by groups modeling themselves on the Ku Klux Klan… "We are many, and very determined. We will skin the Gypsies soon. We will take their eyeballs out, smash their teeth, and cut off their noses. The first will be hanged."[111]

The German government had every reason to know this would be the case well before it began deportations. The depth and virulence of Romania's anti-Gypsy sentiment was hardly an historical mystery. Moreover, a leader of the Romanian fascist movement, directly descended from the Arrow Cross formations which avidly embraced nazi racial policies during World War II, had openly announced what would happen nearly six months earlier: "Our war against the Gypsies will start in the fall. Until then, preparations will be made to obtain arms; first we are going to acquire chemical sprays. We will not spare minors either."[112]

No accurate count of how many Gypsies have been killed, tortured, maimed, or otherwise physically abused in Romania is currently available (unconfirmed reports run into the hundreds). What *is* known is that there has been a veritable news blackout on the topic, and that reaction from those elements of the Jewish establishment which profess to serve as the "world's conscience" on such matters has been tepid at best.[113] No serious protest arose from that quarter, not even when Romani leaders, hoping to avoid what they knew was in store, took a large delegation of their people during the spring of 1993 to seek sanctuary in the Neuengamme concentration camp where their fathers and mothers were murdered a generation earlier. Certainly, no Jewish human rights activists came forth to stand with them as an act of solidarity.*

As usual, it was Yehuda Bauer who produced what was perhaps the best articulation of exclusivist sentiment on the matter. As early as 1990, he was publicly complaining that such desperate attempts by Gypsies to end the condition of invisibility he himself had been so instrumental in imposing upon them was coming into "competition" with the kind of undeviating focus on "radical anti-Semitism" he'd spent his life trying to engender.[114] No better illustration of what the distinguished Princeton historian of the Holocaust Arno J. Mayer has described as the "exaggerated self-centeredness" of Jewish exclusivism and its "egregious forgetting of the larger whole and all of the other victims" can be imagined.[115]

Recovering the Holocaust

There should be no need to go into such detail in rejoining exclusivist denials of the genocides perpetrated against Slavic peoples within the over-

---

*The author, as a representative of the American Indian Movement, was present for a period with these hundreds of people—including many elders and young children—who were stranded for weeks along an asphalt road outside Neuengamme after the German government deployed guards to keep them out of the unused concentration camp. Their primary support accrued from German radicals. Tangible support from Jewish organizations was conspicuously absent.

all framework of the Holocaust. However, a tracing of the general contours seems appropriate, beginning with the familiar assertion that "they were treated differently from the Jews, and none were marked out for total annihilation."[116] As Lucy Dawidowicz puts it, "It has been said that the Germans ...planned to exterminate the Poles and Russians on racial grounds since, according to Hitler's racial doctrine, Slavs were believed to be subhumans [*Untermenschen*]. But no evidence exists that a plan to murder the Slavs was ever contemplated or developed."[117]

There is both a grain of truth and a bucketful of falsity imbedded in these statements. In other words, it is true that Slavs were not named in the *Endlösung* [Final Solution] sketched out for Gypsies and Jews during the 1942 Wannsee conference.[*] This clearly suggests that the last two groups were given a certain priority in terms of the completion of their "special handling," but it is not at all to say that Slavs weren't "marked out" to suffer essentially the same fate in the end. Presumably, the final phases of the nazis' anti-Slavic campaigns would have gotten underway once those directed against the much smaller Jewish and Gypsy populations had been wrapped up.[†] In any event, the idea that "no plan [for Slavic extermination] was ever contemplated or developed" is quite simply false.

As is abundantly documented, the Hitlerian vision of *Lebensraumpolitik*

---

*A problem with Wannsee is that there is no documentary evidence that Hitler ordered the conference, ever approved the conclusions arrived at, or that he was even necessarily aware of it; Gerald Fleming, *Hitler and the Final Solution* (Berkeley: University of California Press, 1982). Contra David Irving's cynical use of these facts to argue that the Führer must therefore be presumed innocent of participation in the Holocaust (*Hitler's War* [New York: Viking, 1977]), responsible historians and other analysts exercise reasonable judgment in asserting that he not only participated, but was the critical element in it.
† Granted, this requires a certain amount of reading into the record. However, an exactly similar exercise in common sense is required when imputing intent with respect to the destruction of Jews and Gypsies. For example, the words "killing," "extermination," etc., are used nowhere in the Wannsee Protocol, generally considered the crucial authorizing document for the "final solution of the Jewish [and Gypsy] question." Indeed, as late as September 21, 1939—that is, as Poland was being overrun— Reinhard Heydrich explicitly defined the "ultimate goal" of nazi Jewish policy to his subordinates as bringing about a total *emigration* of the Jews via the *Generalgouvernement* to Madagascar. Might this not be what is meant by the term, *Endlösung*? The documentary record leaves little basis for any other conclusion. One must interpolate, based on subsequent nazi *practice*, to arrive at an understanding that this is what is meant by terms such as "treated accordingly," or Adolf Eichmann's use of the term "special handling" to signify mass murder. As analyst Christopher Browning has observed, "There are no written records of what took place among Hitler, Himmler, and Heydrich concerning the Final Solution, and none of them survived to testify after the war. Therefore, the decision-making process at the center must be reconstructed by the historian, who extrapolates from events, documents, and testimony originating outside the inner circle"; Browning, *The Fateful Months, op. cit.*, pp. 13–4. The same principles and procedures apply to understanding the campaigns against the Slavs.

—the conquest of vast expanses of Slavic territory in eastern Europe for "resettlement" by a tremendously enlarged Germanic population—entailed a carefully calculated policy of eliminating resident Slavs.[118] In the U.S.S.R. alone, this planned "depopulation" was expressly designed to reduce those within the intended area of German colonization from about 75 million to no more than 30 million.[119] This sizable "residue" was to be maintained for an unspecified period to serve as an expendable slave labor pool to build the infrastructure required to support what the nazis deemed "Aryan" living standards.[120] The 45 million human beings constituting the difference between the existing population and its projected diminishment were to be dispensed with through a combination of massive expulsion—"drive them eastward"—and a variety of killing programs.[121]

Plans for more westerly Slavic peoples like the Poles, Slovenes, and Serbs were even worse (or at any rate set on a faster track). As early as *Mein Kampf,* Hitler unambiguously announced that they, like the Jews, were to be entirely exterminated.* For the Poles at least, this was to be accomplished in a series of stages, which seems likely to have been intended as a model for similarly phased eradication of the Ukrainians and other peoples to the east: immediately upon conquest, the Poles would be "decapitated" (i.e., their social, political, and intellectual leadership would be annihilated, *en toto*); second, the mass of the population would be physically relocated in whatever configuration best served the interests of the German economy; third, the Poles would be placed on starvation rations and worked to death.[122] Whether or not there would have been a fourth and "final" phase à la Auschwitz, the results, both practical and intended, are identical.

Unlike the Gypsies and Jews, the Slavs were mostly organized in a way

---

*As Heinrich Himmler put it, "all Poles will disappear from the world... It is essential that the great German people should consider it as a major task to destroy all Poles"; Hans Frank, nazi administrator of the *Generalgouvernement* area of occupied Poland, took it as his "special mission" to "finish off the Poles"; Hitler himself instructed his military commanders to order their troops to "kill without mercy all men, women, and children of Polish descent or language. Only in this way can we obtain the living space we need"; quoted in Richard C. Lukas, "The Polish Experience during the Holocaust," in Berenbaum, *A Mosaic of Victims, op. cit.,* pp. 88–95. This is entirely in keeping with the oft-enunciated Hitlerian notion of "Germanizing" Slavic territories to the east. "Hitler's conception of genocide is based not on cultural but on biological patterns. He believes that '*Germanization* can only be carried out with *soil* and never with *men*'... With respect to the Poles particularly, Hitler expressed the view that it is their soil alone which *can and should be profitably Germanized*"; Lemkin, *Axis Rule, op. cit.,* pp. 81–2 (he is quoting *Mein Kampf,* pp. 588, 590). On the Serbs, see Louis Adamic, *My Native Land* (New York: Harper and Brothers, 1943). Overall, see Hermann Rauschning, *The Voice of Destruction* (New York: G.P. Putnam's Sons, 1940).

lending itself to military resistance.[*] Consequently, planning for their decimation necessarily factored in attrition through military confrontation.[123] Insofar as German methods in the East, in sharp contrast to those employed against non-Slavic western opponents, always devolved upon the concept of "a war of annihilation,"[124] the extraordinarily high death rates suffered by Soviet prisoners of war are not really separable from the extermination plan as a whole.[†] Similarly, according to SS Gruppenführer Eric von dem Bach-Zelewski, who commanded antipartisan operations in eastern Europe, the manner in which such warfare was waged was consciously aimed not just at suppressing guerrilla activities, but to help "achieve Himmler's goal of reducing the Slavic population to 30 million."[‡]

> Available evidence suggests that the principle victims in the partisan-Nazi confrontations were the civilian population. Thus, for example, when 9,902 partisans were killed or executed between August and November 1942, at the same time the Germans executed 14,257 civilians whom they suspected of aiding the partisans... A Polish scholar, Ryszard Torzecki, views the mass extermination of civilian population as the greatest drama of the Ukraine during World War II. According to him there were 250 sites of mass extermination of Ukrainian people together with detention camps in which thousands of people perished... In a great many cases, mass murder was related to partisan warfare. H. Kuhnrich estimated that as a result of the antipartisan war 5,909,225 people were killed. Since the Ukraine was the center of partisan activity, it was there that the greatest losses occurred. According to Kuhnrich some 4.5 million people, both fighters and civilians, lost their lives in the Ukraine, as did 1,409,225 in Byelorussia.[125]

---

[*] "The Jews, of course, were an absolutely powerless minority in Europe. They numbered about 500,000 in Germany, 300,000 in France, 200,000 in the Netherlands and Belgium combined, and even in Poland they were a minority of 3.3 million, or 10 percent of the population. Including the U.S.S.R., there were about 8 million [actually, nine] Jews among a European population of 500 million, scattered, without a government, without cohesion or identity or purpose...so armed resistance [was impossible] for most Jews during the Holocaust"; Bauer, "Jewish Resistance and Passivity," op. cit., pp. 236–7.

[†] Of a total of approximately 5.7 million Soviet POWs, at least 3.3 million—57 percent—died in captivity. By comparison, of 231,000 British and American POWs, 8,348—3.6 percent—died; Christian Streit, "The Fate of Soviet Prisoners of War," in Berenbaum, A Mosaic of Victims, op. cit., p. 142. Also see Szymon Datner, Crimes Against POWs: Responsibility of the Wehrmacht (Warsaw: Zachodnia Agencja Prasowa, 1964) esp. pp. 218–27.

[‡] Quoted in Nazi Conspiracy and Aggression, Vol. 6, op. cit., p. 427. Ignoring such explicit statements by the perpetrators, proponents of uniqueness habitually argue that the victims of German antipartisan operations are still somehow "different" than those of the Holocaust. Among other things, this begs the fact that they count Jewish victims of nazi antipartisanism into the Holocaust total. Moreover, their argument for excluding Slavs is in this case identical to that used by certain deniers to disqualify more than a million Jewish fatalities from being considered the result of genocide. One contention is no more absurd than the other.

Certainly, these slaughtered civilians should be included in the total of those taken by nazi extermination policies, not labeled as "war deaths."* And, if the standard practice of including the deaths of Jewish partisan fighters in the total of six million Jews claimed by the Holocaust were applied equally to Slavs, then plainly the bodycount of partisans should be as well.[126] And again, since the Jews killed by Bach-Zelewski's SS men during the 1943 Warsaw ghetto uprising are rightly included among the Jewish victims of the Holocaust, so too should the masses of civilian Slavs liquidated during the German seizures of cities like Kiev, Kharkov, Sebastopol, and Mink be tallied.† When the totals of those deliberately worked to death, who died of exposure during the process of being driven eastward under any and all conditions, who were intentionally starved to death, and who perished in epidemics which spread like wildfire because of a calculated nazi policy of denying vaccines, the true dimensions of the genocide of the Slavs begins to emerge.‡

Between 1939 and 1945, Poland, the first Slavic nation to fall to the Germans, suffered 6,028,000 nonmilitary deaths, about a 22 percent population reduction (three million of the Polish dead were Jews, and another

---

* With regard to Slavs, Dawidowicz, for example, is careful to segregate Soviet civilian losses from "air raids and bombardments" as well as "reprisals for continuing guerrilla warfare" from extermination per se. Jews killed during air raids, bombardments, and the like are, however, tabulated into the toll of the Holocaust; *The Holocaust and the Historians, op. cit.*, pp. 6–7.

† Hunczak observes that by the time "the Germans were cleared from Ukrainian territory more than 700 cities and towns, representing 42 percent of all urban centers devastated by the war in the entire U.S.S.R., and more than 28,000 villages had been destroyed... The fate of Kiev epitomizes the tragedy of [a] city population of 900,000. By 1945, as the result of the extermination of 195,000 people and deportation to Germany of another 100,000, the city had a population of 186,000 [the balance having fled eastward]"; Hunczak, "The Ukranian Losses During WWII," *op. cit.*, pp. 122, 124.

‡ In *The Holocaust and Historians* (*op. cit.*, p. 6) Dawidowicz—again following the practice used by Holocaust deniers to minimize the number of genocide-induced Jewish fatalities—somehow segregates deaths caused by "starvation and disease" among Slavic civilians from the fate of the Jews. This is customary among exclusivists, despite the fact that the 1942–44 Ukrainian depopulation resulted from a policy explicitly intended to reduce the number of Slavs within German-controlled territory. Vaccines against epidemic diseases, and treatment for those who contracted them, were deliberately withheld from Slavs for the same reason; Office of United States Chief of Counsel for Prosecution of Axis Criminality, *Nazi Conspiracy and Aggression, Vol. 2* (Washington, D.C.: U.S. Government Printing Office, 1946) p. 904. Of course, Jewish deaths by starvation and disease—about 1.6 million of the 3.1 million in the camps, and some 800,000 outside (a total of 2.4 million) according to Arno J. Mayer and others—*are* incorporated by Dawidowicz and her colleagues into the aggregate number of Jews consumed by the Holocaust. It is not that these deaths shouldn't be included in the Jewish total (they obviously should), but the double standard is unmistakable; Mayer, *Why Did the Heavens Not Darken? op. cit.*, pp. 365, 402; Yisrael Gutman, "Auschwitz—An Overview," in Yisrael Gutman and Michael Berenbaum, eds., *Anatomy of the Auschwitz Death Camp* (Bloomington: Indiana University Press in association with the United States Holocaust Memorial Museum, 1994) p. 27. Also see Hilberg, *The Destruction of the European Jews, op. cit.*

200,000 or so Gypsies, so the Slavic reduction would come to about 14 percent). Virtually every member of the Polish intelligentsia was murdered.[127] In
Yugoslavia, some 1.2 million civilians, or 9 percent of the population, were
killed between 1941 and 1945 (this is aside from approximately 300,000 military casualties suffered by the Yugoslavs).[128] Impacts in other non–Soviet areas
of eastern Europe—e.g., Slovakia and the Protectorate of Bohemia and
Moravia—were less substantial, although nonetheless severe.[129]

The U.S.S.R. suffered by far the highest number of fatalities. By May
10, 1943, the Germans had taken 5,405,616 Soviet military prisoners; of
these, around 3.5 million were starved, frozen, shot, gassed, hanged, killed by
unchecked epidemic, or simply worked to death.[*] Another 5 million people
were deported to Germany as slave laborers—2.2 million from the Ukraine
alone—where an estimated 3 million died as a result of the intentionally
abysmal conditions to which they were subjected.[†] By the time the Germans
were finally driven completely out of the Ukraine in 1944, its prewar population of almost 42 million had been reduced to 27.4 million, a difference of
14.5 million. Of these, at least 7 million were dead.[130] Overall, the Soviet
Union lost, at a minimum, 11 million civilians to nazi extermination measures.[‡] The real total may run as high as 15 million, to which must be added
the 3.5 million exterminated prisoners of war, and perhaps as many as a million troops who were simply executed by Wehrmacht and Waffen SS units
rather than being taken prisoner in the first place.[131]

A gross estimate of the results of nazi genocide against the Slavs thus
comes to somewhere between 15.5 and 19.5 million in the U.S.S.R.,
between 19.7 and 23.9 million when the Poles, Slovenes, Serbs, and others

---

[*] Another comparison: during the same period, mortality among German prisoners held by the Soviets
came to about 1.2 million of 3.25 million taken, or 36 percent. This is horrendous, but considerably
lower than the 57 percent rate pertaining to Soviet troops held by Germany; Streit, "The Fate of
Soviet Prisoners of War," *op. cit.*, p. 142.

[†] "Hitler's occupation forces transported more than five million Soviet citizens into slavery in Germany
to work in the labor camps. The Germans forced Soviet civilians into slavery in Germany not only to
fill their insufficient labor needs, but also as a way to deplete the Soviet population… The Germans
were determined to destroy a significant part of our population and to that end they knew no limits.
They used various methods… Their principle means of destroying the civilian population as well as
prisoners of war was systematic mass murder: they starved people to death, let them freeze or die of
epidemics, and subjected them to many other tortures"; Kumanev, "The German Occupation
Regime," *op. cit.*, p. 139.

[‡] Kumanev (ibid., p. 140) gives four million as the minimum for the Ukraine, 2.5 million for Byelo-
russia, and 1.7 million for other territories, a total of 8.2 million for the U.S.S.R. as a whole. However,
he omits those lost through deportation as slave laborers, and acknowledges that his numbers are not
"final or exact."

are added in. As Simon Wiesenthal, himself a survivor of Auschwitz, long ago observed, "the Holocaust was not only a matter of the killing of six million Jews. It involved the killing of eleven million people, six million of whom were Jews."[132] Wiesenthal spoke on the basis of what was then the best available evidence. Today, some fifty years later, the only correction to be made to his statement lies in the fact that we now know his estimate of eleven million was far too low. The true human costs of nazi genocide came to 26 million or more, six million of whom were Jews, a million or more of whom were Gypsies, and the rest mostly Slavs. Only with these facts clearly in mind can we say that we have apprehended the full scope of the Holocaust, and have thereby positioned ourselves to begin to appreciate its real implications.

Uncovering the Hidden Holocausts

University of Hawaii historian David Stannard has summed up the means by which exclusivists attempt to avert such understanding. "Uniqueness advocates *begin* by defining genocide (or the Holocaust or the *Shoah*) in terms of what they already believe to be experiences undergone only by Jews. After much laborious research it is then 'discovered'—*mirabile dictu*—that the Jewish experience was unique. If, however, critics point out after a time that those experiences are not in fact unique, *other* allegedly unique experiences are invented and proclaimed. If not *numbers* killed, how about *percentage* of population destroyed? If not *efficiency* or *method* of killing, how about perpetrator *intentionality* (emphasis in original)?"[133] It is as Stephen Jay Gould has said of another group of intellectual charlatans, "They began with conclusions, peered through their facts, and came back in a circle to the same conclusions."[134] As Stannard has concluded, this is not scholarship, it is sophistry.[135]

To put it another way, as Gould does, it is "advocacy masquerading as objectivity."[136] The connection being made is important insofar as Gould is describing the academic edifice of nineteenth-century scientific racism which provided the foundation for the very nazi racial theories under which the Jews of the Holocaust suffered and died.[137] Given that Deborah Lipstadt, Yehuda Bauer, Steven Katz, Lucy Dawidowicz, and other exclusivists are of a people which has recently experienced genocide, the natural inclination is to align with them against those like Paul Rassinier, Austin App, Robert Faurisson, and Arthur Butz who would absolve the perpetrators. Yet, one cannot.

One cannot, because it is no better for Lipstadt to "neglect" to mention that the Gypsies were subjected to the same mode of extermination as the

Jews—or for Dawidowicz and Bauer to contrive arguments that they weren't—than it is for Rassinier to deliberately minimize the number of Jewish victims of nazism or for Butz to deny the Holocaust altogether. One cannot, because there is nothing more redeeming about Katz's smug dismissal of the applicability of the term "genocide" to any group other than his own than there is about Robert Faurisson's contention that no Jews were ever gassed. One cannot, because Yehuda Bauer's *The Holocaust in Historical Perspective,* Steven Katz's *The Holocaust in Historical Context,* and Lucy Dawidowicz's *The Holocaust and the Historians* are really only variations of Arthur Butz's *The Hoax of the Twentieth Century* written in reverse. All of them, equally, are conscious exercises in the destruction of truth and memory.

Deniers of the Holocaust must, of course, be confronted, exposed for what they are, and driven into the permanent oblivion they so richly deserve. But so too must those who choose to deny holocausts more generally, and who shape their work accordingly. Deborah Lipstadt rightly expresses outrage and concern that Holocaust deniers like Bradley Smith have begun to make inroads on college campuses during the 1990s. She remains absolutely silent, however, about the implications of the fact that she and scores of other holocaust deniers have held professorial positions for decades, increasingly branding anyone challenging their manipulations of logic and evidence an "antisemite" or a "neonazi," and frequently positioning themselves to determine who is hired and tenured in the bargain.* The situation is little different in principle than if, in the converse, members of the Institute for Historical Review were similarly ensconced (which they are not, and, with the exceptions of App and Harry Elmer Barnes early on, never have been).[138]

Viewed on balance, then, the holocaust deniers of Jewish exclusivism represent a proportionately greater and more insidious threat to understanding than do the Holocaust deniers of the IHR variety. This is all the more true insofar as the mythology peddled by exclusivists dovetails perfectly with the institutionalized denials of genocides in their own histories put forth by the governments of the United States, Great Britain, France, Turkey, Indonesia, and many others. Indeed, Lucy Dawidowicz has sweepingly accused those suggesting that the U.S. transatlantic slave trade was genocidal—or, by extension, that U.S. extermination campaigns against American

---

*An interesting variation on this theme has been the propensity of exclusivists like Lipstadt to attempt to discredit those who support Palestinian rights vis-à-vis Israel as being, on that basis alone, "antisemitic." This, despite the fact that the Palestinians are a Semitic people.

Indians were the same—not only of antisemitism but of "a vicious anti-Americanism."[139] She is equally straightforward in her efforts to contain "the genocidal mentality" within the framework of uniquely German character-istics.* Steven Katz and James Axtell, the reigning dean of American histori-cal apologism, have taken to virtually regurgitating one another's distortive polemics without attribution.†

Plainly, if we are to recover the meaning of the Holocaust in all its dimensions, according it the respect to which it is surely due and finding within it the explanatory power it can surely yield, it is vital that we con-front, expose, and dismiss these "dogmatists who seek to reify and sacralize" it, converting it into a shallow and sanctimonious parody of its own signifi-cance.[140] Only in this way can we hope arrive at the "universality" called for by Michael Berenbaum, executive director of the U.S. Holocaust Memorial Museum, when he suggested that the "Holocaust can become a symbolic orienting event in human history that can prevent recurrence."[141] Undoubtedly, this was what the executive director of the Institute on the Holocaust and Genocide in Jerusalem, Israel Charny, had in mind when he

---

*Davidowicz, *The Holocaust and Historians, op. cit.*, p. 61. This is in response to a rather reasonable suggestion by the German historian Hans Rothfels that, "In many respects National Socialism can be considered as the final summit of an extreme consequence of the secularization movement of the nineteenth century"; *The German Opposition to Hitler: An Appraisal* (Chicago: Henry Regnery, 1962). She rejects any such formulation since it situates the social dynamics culminating in nazism in a context broader than anything specifically German, and therefore necessarily encompasses the victimization of peoples other than Jews. In the process, of course, she lets everyone but the Germans off the hook and denies all genocides other than that of European Jewry. For the term cited, see Robert Jay Lifton and Robert Markusen, *The Genocidal Mentality: Nazi Holocaust and the Nuclear Threat* (New York: Basic Books, 1988).

†Although neither cites the other in these connections, Katz argues for an extremely narrow redefinition of genocide—deliberately misrepresenting Raphaël Lemkin in the process (see "Lie for Lie," in this volume)—which he believes (wrongly) applies only to the Jewish experience of the Holocaust; *The Holocaust in Historical Context, Vol. 1, op. cit.*, pp. 125–39. Axtell trots out precisely the same construction, as if it *were* the operant definition, in order to deny that genocide is a concept applicable to the destruction of American Indian peoples; James Axtell, *After Columbus: Essays in the Ethnohistory of Colonial North America* (New York: Oxford University Press, 1988) p. 44; *Beyond 1492: Encounters in Colonial North America* (New York: Oxford, 1992) p. 261. Conversely, Axtell claims that the massive death suffered by American Indians from disease, starvation, exposure, and the like was "entirely unintended" and thus not genocidal; *Beyond 1492*, pp. 236–8, 262–3; most clearly in set-piece lectures delivered during the run-up to the 1992 Columbian Quincentennial (e.g., talk at the University of Florida, April 1, 1991; tape on file). Katz parrots exactly the same falsehood, almost verbatim, in asserting the uniqueness of the Holocaust; *The Holocaust in Historical Context*, p. 20: "[The] depopulation of the New World, for all its terror and death, was a largely *unintended* tragedy, a tragedy that occurred despite the sincere and indisputable desire of the Europeans to keep the Indian population alive… Nature, not malice, was the main cause of the massive, incomprehensible devastation (emphasis in the original)."

denounced "the leaders and 'high priests' of different cultures who insist on the uniqueness, primacy, superiority, or greater significance of the specific genocide of their people,"[142] elsewhere adding that:

> I object very strongly to the efforts to name the genocide of any one people as the single, ultimate event, or as the most important event against which all other tragedies of genocidal mass death are to be tested and found wanting... For me, the passion to exclude this or that mass killing from the universe of genocide, as well as the intense competition to establish the exclusive "superiority" or unique form of any one genocide, ends up creating a fetishistic atmosphere in which the masses of bodies that are not to be qualified for the definition of genocide are dumped into a conceptual black hole, where they are forgotten.[143]

In restoring the Gypsies and Slavic peoples to the Holocaust itself, where they've always belonged, we not only exhume them from the black hole into which they've been dumped in their millions by Jewish exclusivism and neonazism alike, we establish ourselves both methodologically and psychologically to remember other things as well. Not only was the Armenian holocaust a "true" genocide, the marked lack of response to it by the Western democracies was used by Adolf Hitler to reassure his cabinet that there would be no undue consequences if Germany were to perpetrate its own genocide(s).* Not only were Stalin's policies in the Ukraine a genuine holocaust, the methods by which it was carried out were surely incorporated into Germany's *Generalplan Ost* just a few years later.[144] Not only was the Spanish policy of conscripting entire native populations into forced labor throughout the Caribbean, as well as much of South and Central America holocaustal, it served as a prototype for nazi policies in eastern Europe.[145] Not only were U.S. "clearing" operations directed against the indigenous peoples of North America genocidal in every sense, they unquestionably served as a conceptual/practical mooring to which the whole Hitlerian rendering of *Lebensraumpolitik* was tied.†

In every instance, the particularities of these prior genocides—each of them unique unto themselves—serve to inform our understanding of the

---

* "The analogies between the Armenian genocide and the Holocaust teach a number of moral lessons. For example, Hitler used the world's indifference to Armenian suffering to silence cabinet opposition to his plans for the Poles. The Armenian genocide assured Hitler that negative consequences would not greet his actions"; Berenbaum, "The Uniqueness and Universality of the Holocaust," *op. cit.*, p. 34.
† "Neither Spain nor Britain should be the models of German expansion, but the Nordics of North America, who had ruthlessly pushed aside an inferior race to win for themselves soil and territory for the future"; Rich, *Hitler's War Aims, op. cit.*, p. 8.

Holocaust. Reciprocally, the actualities of the Holocaust serve to illuminate the nature of these earlier holocausts. No less does the procedure apply to the manner in which we approach genocides occurring since 1945, those in Katanga, Biafra, Bangladesh, Indochina, Paraguay, Guatemala, Indonesia, Rwanda, Bosnia, and on and on.* Our task is—*must* be—to fit *all* the various pieces together in such a way as to obtain at last a comprehension of the whole. There is no other means available to us. We must truly "think of the unthinkable," seriously and without proprietary interest, if ever we are to put an end to the "human cancer" which has spread increasingly throughout our collective organism over the past five centuries.[146] To this end, denial in *any* form is anathema.

---

*Citations relevant to each of these examples and more are provided in the following essay. It is worth noting, however, the exclusivist response, as represented by Steven Katz, to the idea the two very recent examples might be considered genocides. "Steven Katz, ever obsessed with his Jewish uniqueness *idée fixe*, has crassly dismissed the killing in Bosnia as a mere 'population transfer supported by violence' and has described the massive slaughter of up to a million people in Rwanda as 'not genocidal' but simply a struggle for 'tribal domination' "; Stannard, "The Politics of Genocide Scholarship," *op. cit.*, p. 191. For the full context of Katz's remarks, see Liz McMillen, "The Uniqueness of the Holocaust," *Chronicle of Higher Education*, June 22, 1994.

Notes

1. Rassinier's several short but highly influential tracts on the subject, published between 1948 and 1966, are compiled in a single volume entitled *Debunking the Holocaust Myth: A Study of the Nazi Concentration Camps and the Alleged Extermination of European Jewry* (Torrance, CA: Institute for Historical Review, 1978). For a good sample of the contemporaneous scholarly literature he sought to undermine, see Gerald Reitlinger, *The Final Solution: The Attempt to Exterminate the Jews of Europe, 1939–1945* (New York: Beechhurst Press, 1953).

2. The crux of App's various arguments are contained in two volumes; see *The Six Million Swindle: Blackmailing the German People for Hard Marks with Fabricated Corpses* (Tacoma Park, MD: Boniface Press, 1973), and *A Straight Look at the Third Reich: Hitler and National Socialism, How Right? How Wrong?* (Tacoma Park, MD: Boniface Press, 1974). As he put it on p. 2 of the former, "Talmudists have from the beginning used the six million swindle to blackmail West Germany into 'atoning' with twenty billion dollars of indemnities to Israel." The actual figure paid Israel was $110 million; see *Documents Relating to the Agreement Between the Government of Israel and the Government of the Federal Republic of Germany* (Jerusalem: Israeli Ministry of Foreign Affairs, 1953).

3. Hoggan's 1955 dissertation—a revision of which was later published as a book entitled *The Forced War: When Peaceful Revision Failed* (Heidelberg: Herbert Grabert, 1961; reprinted by Noontide Press, 1989)—concluded that Poland and England, rather than Germany, precipitated Word War II. On the basis of this work, he was awarded a faculty position in history at the University of California/Berkeley.

4. Richard Harwood (Richard Verrall), *Did Six Million Really Die? The Truth at Last* (Richmond Surrey: Historical Review Press, 1974). It was claimed—falsely, in this case—that the author was a professor at the University of London. On the National Front and Verrall's role in it, see M. Walker, *National Front* (London: Fontana, 1977).

5. Arthur R. Butz, *The Hoax of the Twentieth Century: The Case Against the Presumed Extermination of European Jewry* (Torrance, CA: Institute for Historical Review, 1976). The title is a deliberate play upon that of the infamous "philosophical" tract by chief nazi ideologist Alfried Rosenberg, *Der Mythus des 20. Jahrhunderts* (*The Myth of the Twentieth Century*), published in Munich in 1930; see Robert Cecil, *The Myth of the Master Race: Alfred Rosenberg and Nazi Ideology* (New York: Dodd, Meade & Co., 1972).

6. Other deniers quickly incorporated Butz's "groundbreaking" work into their own; see, for example, Robert Faurisson, "The Problem of Gas Chambers," *Journal of Historical Review*, Summer 1980.

7. See "Letter of IHR to All Interested Parties Intending to Claim $50,000 Reward," Institute for Historical Review, Torrance, CA, n.d.

8. Alan Davies, "A Tale of Two Trials: Antisemitism in Canada," *Holocaust and Genocide Studies*, Vol. 4, 1989.

9. Robert Faurisson was originally referred to Leuchter by William Armantrout, warden of the Missouri State Prison.

10. Frederick A. Leuchter, *The Leuchter Report: An Engineering Report on the Alleged Execution Gas Chambers at Auschwitz, Birkenau, and Madjanek, Poland*, submitted in the case of *Her Majesty the Queen vs. Ernst Zundel*, District Court of Ontario, 1988. The report was published in Canada by Zundel's Samisdat Press, and in England, with an introduction by David Irving, under the title *The End of the Line: The Leuchter Report —The First Forensic Examination of Auschwitz* (London: Focal Point Publications, 1989). Excerpts were also published as "Inside the Auschwitz 'Gas Chambers'," *Journal of Historical Review*, Summer 1989.

11. Charles R. Allen, Jr., "The Role of the Media in the Leuchter Matter: Hyping a Holocaust Denier," in Shelly Shapiro, ed., *Truth Prevails: The End of the "Leuchter Report"* (Albany, NY: Holocaust Education Project, 1990).

12. Jean-Claude Pressac, "The Deficiencies and Inconsistencies of 'The Leuchter Report'," in Shapiro, *op. cit.* Also see his *Auschwitz: Technique and Operation of the Gas Chambers* (New York: Holmes & Meier, 1989).

13. Manuel Prutschi, "The Zundel Affair," in Alan Davies, ed., *Antisemitism in Canada* (Rexdale, Ontario: John Wiley & Sons, 1992). It should be noted that Zundel again appealed and, on August 27, 1992, the Canadian Supreme Court vacated his conviction, declaring the law under which he was found guilty to be unconstitutional.

14. The crux of the IHR pitch is contained in Smith's article, "The Holocaust Story: How Much Is False? The Case for Open Debate," run as a full page ad, in Northwestern University's student paper, *The Daily Northwestern*, on April 4, 1991. It is probably instructive to note that Northwestern is Arthur Butz's home institution and that its campus paper was the first to accept Smith's material.

15. Kathleen M. Sullivan, "The First Amendment Wars," *The New Republic*, September 28, 1991; Carlos C. Huerta, "Revisionism, Free Speech and the Campus," *Midstream*, April 1992; Nat Hentoff, "An Ad That Offends: Who's On First?" *The Progressive*, May 12, 1992.

16. Carl N. Degler, "Bad History," *Commentary*, June 1981; Marvin Perry, "Denying the Holocaust: History as Myth and Delusion," *Encore American and Worldwide News*, September 1981.

17. Fritz Karmasin, *Austrian Attitudes Towards Jews, Israel and the Holocaust* (New York: American Jewish Committee, 1992).

18. Reported by the *Jewish Telegraphic Agency*, November 2, 1992. Comparable data has been obtained in Brazil, Mexico, Chile, Argentina, Peru, New Zealand, and Australia; Deborah Lipstadt, *Denying the Holocaust: The Growing Assault on Truth and Memory* (New York: The Free Press, 1993) pp. 12–13.

19. On England, see Colin Holms, "Historical Revisionism in Britain: The Politics of History," in *Trends in Historical Revisionism: History as Political Device* (London: Macmillan, 1985); on France, see Frederick Brown, "French Amnesia," *Harpers*, December 1981; on Germany, see Charles Maier, *The Unmasterable Past: History, Holocaust and German National Identity* (Cambridge: Cambridge University Press, 1988); on Canada, see Gabriel Weimann and Conrad Winn, *Hate on Trial: The Zundel Affair, the Media, and Public Opinion in Canada* (Oakland, Ontario: Mosaic Press, 1986).

20. As examples: on the United States, see Kevin Flynn and Gary Gerhardt, *The Silent Brotherhood: Inside America's Racist Underground* (New York: The Free Press, 1989); on Germany, see Michael Schmidt, *The New Reich: Violent Extremism in Unified Germany and Beyond* (New York: Pantheon Books, 1993); on Canada, see Stanley R. Barrett, *Is God a Racist? The Right Wing in Canada* (Toronto: University of Toronto Press, 1987).

21. To date, rejoinders have assumed essay rather than book form, and have therefore been both limited in scope and relatively inaccessible; see, as examples, Arnold Forster, "The Ultimate Cruelty," *ADL Bulletin*, June 1959; Gita Sereny, "The Men Who Whitewash Hitler," *The New Statesman*, November 1979; and Yehuda Bauer, " 'Revisionism'—The Repudiation of the Holocaust and Its Historical Significance," in Yisrael Gutman and Gideon Grief, eds., *The Historiography of the Holocaust Period* (Jerusalem: Hebrew University Monographs, 1988).

22. A preliminary effort at achieving Lipstadt's result can be found in Gill Seidel, *The Holocaust Denial: Antisemitism, Racism and the New Right* (Leeds, 1986). Another good, albeit abbreviated, treatment will be found in C.C. Aronsfeld, *The Text of the Holocaust: A Study of the Nazis' Extermination Propaganda, 1919–1945* (Marblehead, MA: Micah, 1985). Since these essays were written, other book-length rebuttals have appeared; see Pierre Vidal-Naquet, *Assassins of Memory: Essays on the Denial of the Holocaust* (New York: Columbia University Press, 1992); Kenneth Stern, *Holocaust Denial* (New York: American Jewish Committee, 1994). The Anti-Defamation League of B'nai Brith have also produced a sort of "who's who of Holocaust denial" entitled *Hitler's Apologists: The Anti-Semitic Propaganda of Holocaust "Revisionism"* (New York: ADL, 1993).

23. In order to "make Germany an ever-lasting milk cow for Israel," zionism had manufactured the "Holocaust hoax" to force "Germany to pay Israel sums calculated on the basis of 6,000,000 dead," at least 80 percent of whom "were very much alive at the end of the war"; Rassinier, *Debunking the Holocaust Myth, op. cit.*, pp. 214, 224.

24. Israeli Ministry of Foreign Affairs, *op. cit.*, pp. 1–9. Also see the March 14, 1951 statement of Israeli Minister of Foreign Affairs Moshe Sharett to the Knesset, that "the demand for reparation has been calculated according to the burden that the people of Israel and Jewish organizations throughout the world have taken upon themselves in financing the rehabilitation and the absorption of a half a million survivors of the Holocaust who have settled or will settle in Israel"; Nana Sagi, *German Reparations: A History of the Negotiations* (Jerusalem: Hebrew University, 1980) p. 55. Also see Nicholas Balabkins, *West German Reparations to Israel* (New Brunswick, NJ: Rutgers University Press, 1971).

25. Lipstadt, *Denying the Holocaust, op. cit.*, p. 57.

26. Indeed, on pages 92–3, she is able to link App's 1949 argument that even estimates of about

1.5 million Jewish fatalities under the Third Reich were "too high" directly to assertions made by the nazis themselves. Consider, for instance, the postwar claim advanced by nazi foreign service officer Peter Kleist—published in his *Auch Du Warst Dabei!* (Heidelberg: Wehr and Wissen, 1952)—that the exact number of dead Jews was 1,277, 212; quoted in Aronsfeld, *The Text of the Holocaust, op. cit.*, p. 53. It is instructive that both Kleist and App went to great lengths to "reveal" that even these deaths resulted, not from extermination per se, but from liquidation of Jews who acted as "guerrillas and fifth columnists," as well as inadvertent "by-products of wartime conditions" such as starvation and disease.

27. She relies primarily on the data compiled and presented in Pressac, *Auschwitz, op. cit.*

28. Particularly at issue are a series of articles and essays by Harry Elmer Barnes, including the above-noted "Public Stake in Revisionism," "Revisionism: A Key to Peace," *Rampart Journal*, Spring 1966; "Zionist Fraud," *American Mercury*, Fall 1968; and "Revisionism and the Promotion of Peace," *Journal of Historical Review*, Spring 1982.

29. For a cogent examination of the vast distinction between concentration camps and extermination centers, see Lucy S. Dawidowicz, *The War Against the Jews, 1933–1945* (New York: Holt, Rinehart & Winston, 1975) esp. Chapter 7, "The Annihilation Camps: Kingdom of Death."

30. On the realities of the Japanese American internment, and apt comparison of the relevant U.S. facilities to Dauchau, see Richard Drinnon, *Keeper of Concentration Camps: Dillon S. Myer and American Racism* (Berkeley: University of California Press, 1987).

31. Lipstadt, *Denying the Holocaust, op. cit.*, p. 85.

32. Especially at issue is Barnes' *The Genesis of the World War, op. cit.*; Sidney B. Fay, "New Light on the Origins of the World War," *American Historical Review*, Vol. 25, 1920; and Charles Beard, "Heroes and Villains of the World War," *Current History*, Vol. 24, 1926.

33. A good overview may be found in Wayne S. Cole, *Roosevelt and the Isolationists, 1932–1945* (Lincoln: University of Nebraska Press, 1983); also see his *Charles A. Lindbergh and the Battle Against American Intervention in World War II* (New York: Doubleday, 1974). Rankin was a particularly vicious piece of work; see Edward S. Shapiro, "Antisemitism, Mississippi Style," in David Gerber, ed., *Antisemitism in American History* (Urbana/Chicago: University of Illinois Press, 1986).

34. Lipstadt, *Denying the Holocaust, op. cit.*, p. 68. It should be noted that Ford had been doing rather more than this. During the 1930s, he had, for example, underwritten U.S. publication of two of nazism's most virulently antisemitic tracts, *The Protocols of the Elders of Zion* and *The International Jew: The World's Foremost Problem*. Both books are currently in circulation due to regular reprintings by Noontide Press; George Johnson, *Architects of Fear: Conspiracy Theories and Paranoia in American Politics* (Boston: Beacon, 1983) pp. 111–4. A thorough assessment of the effects of people's being duped into believing in the legitimacy of the utterly fabricated *Protocols* may be found in Norman Cohn, *Warrant for Genocide: The Myth of Jewish World-Conspiracy and the Protocols of the Elders of Zion* (New York: Harper & Row, 1969).

35. For various viewpoints on the meaning of Reagan's conduct, see Geoffrey Hartman, ed., *Bitburg in Moral and Political Perspective* (Bloomington: University Press of Indiana, 1986); also see Ilya Levkov, ed., *Bitburg and Beyond: Encounters in American, German, and Jewish History* (New York: Shapolsky, 1987).

36. Quoted in Deborah E. Lipstadt, "The Bitburg Controversy," in David Singer, ed., *The American Jewish Yearbook, 1987* (New York: American Jewish Committee, 1987) p. 22.

37. See Jacob Weisburg, "The Heresies of Pat Buchanan," *The New Republic*, October 22, 1990.

38. Duke, a former member of the American Nazi Party and Imperial Wizard of the Ku Klux Klan, ran a "literary merchandising concern" specializing in titles such as *The Holy Book of Adolf Hitler, The International Jew, The Protocols of the Elders of Zion,* and *The Hitler We Loved and Why* throughout the '80s. In 1988, he was elected to the Louisiana state legislature, and used his office as an outlet for his bookselling enterprise. In 1990, he captured 40 percent of the vote in a bid to enter the U.S. Senate. In 1991, he received nearly 700,000 votes in a gubernatorial bid. In 1992, he declared himself a presidential candidate. See Jason Berry, "Duke's Disguise," *New York Times*, October 16, 1991.

39. Lipstadt, *Denying the Holocaust, op. cit.*, p. 216. For background, see Michael R. Marrus and Robert O. Paxton, *Vichy France and the Jews* (New York: Basic Books, 1981).

40. *Jewish Daily Telegraph*, Dec. 2, 1992.

41. Hellmut Diwald, *Geschichte der Deutschen* (Frankfurt a.M.: Suhrkamp, 1978). It should be noted

that denier Richard Verrall, in a letter to the *New Statesman* (Sept. 21, 1979), publicly lumped Diwald's book in with those of Butz and Faurisson as "carrying on the work of Paul Rassinier."

42. Andreas Hillgruber, *Zweierlei Untergang: Die Zerschlagung des deutschen Reiches und das Ende des europäischen Judentums* (Berlin: Corso bei Siedler, 1986).

43. See, e.g., Michael Stürmer, "Weder verdrängen noch bewältigen. Gesischte und Gegenwartsbewusstein der Deutschen," *Schweizer Monatschefte*, No. 66, Sept. 1986. In a 1987 interview, Kohl indicated that he considered the inculcation of precisely this type of "historical consciousness" among the German public to be a "major accomplishment" of his first term in office; James M. Markham, "Election Eve Talk with Kohl: Sure of Victory and All Smiles," *New York Times*, Jan. 21, 1987. For context, see Peter Schneider, "Hitler's Shadow: On Being a Self-Conscious German," *Harper's Magazine*, Sept. 1987.

44. Lipstadt, *Denying the Holocaust, op. cit.*, p. 216.

45. Ibid., p. 222.

46. Ernst Nolte, *Der Fascismus in seiner Epoche* (Munich: Piper, 1963), published in English as *Three Faces of Fascism: Action Française, Italian Fascism, National Socialism* (New York: Holt, Rinehart & Winston, 1966).

47. Ernst Nolte, *Deutschland und der kalte Krieg* (Munich: Piper, 1976); *Marxismus und Industrielle Revolution* (Stuttgart: Klett-Cotta, 1983); *Der europäische Bürgerkrieg, 1917–1945* [*The European Civil War, 1917–1945*](Berlin: Corso bei Siedler, 1987).

48. Jürgen Habermas, "Neoconservative Cultural Criticism in the United States and West Germany: An Intellectual Movement in Two Political Cultures," *Telos*, No. 56, 1983; reprinted in Richard J. Bernstein, ed., *Habermas and Modernity* (Cambridge: MIT Press, 1985); "Eine Art Schwadensabwicklung. Die apologetischen Tendenzen in der deutschen Zeitgeschichtsschreibung" ["One sort of compensation: Apologetic trends in German historiography"], *Die Zeit*, July 11, 1986. On the *Historikerstreit*, see Charles S. Maier, *The Unmasterable Past: History, Holocaust, and German National Identity* (Cambridge: Harvard University Press, 1988).

49. There can be no question that Lipstadt is aware of Habermas' critique insofar as she relies heavily on Maier, ibid., whose book centers on it.

50. She does say that Nolte "comes dangerously close to validating the deniers" in his *The European Civil War, op. cit.*; Lipstadt, *Denying the Holocaust, op. cit.*, p. 214.

51. Ibid.

52. Ibid., pp. 210–6.

53. Ibid., p. 215.

54. Ibid., p. 211. Fest's main offense seems to have been publishing a photo of a pile of human skulls accruing from the Khmer Rouge slaughter of over a million Cambodians during the 1970s in conjunction with an article entitled "Die geschuldete Erinnerung. Zur Kontroverse über die Unvergleichbarkeit der nationalsozialistischen Massenverbrechen" ["Indebted memory: Concerning the controversy about the incomparability of National Socialist crimes"], *Frankfurter Allgemeine Zeitung*, Aug, 29, 1986. For his interpretive differences with Nolte, which are pronounced, see Fest's *The Face of the Third Reich* (New York: Pantheon, 1970).

55. See, e.g., David E. Stannard, *American Holocaust: Columbus and the Conquest of the New World* (New York: Oxford University Press, 1992); Ian Hancock, "Responses to the *Porrajmos*: The Romani Holocaust," in Alan S. Rosenbaum, ed., *Is The Holocaust Unique? Perspectives on Comparative Genocide* (Boulder, CO: Westview Press, 1996); Vahakn N. Dadrian, *History of the Armenian Genocide: Ethnic Conflict from the Balkans to Anatolia to the Caucasus* (Providence, RI: Berghahn, 1995).

56. See, e.g., Israel Charny, *How Can We Commit the Unthinkable? Genocide, the Human Cancer* (Boulder, CO: Westview Press, 1982); Richard Rubenstein, *The Cunning of History: The Holocaust and the American Future* (New York: Harper & Row, 1978); on Wiesenthal's view, see Michael Berenbaum, "The Uniqueness and Universality of the Holocaust," in Michael Berenbaum, ed., *A Mosaic of Victims: Non-Jews Persecuted and Murdered by the Nazis* (New York: New York University Press, 1990) pp. 20–3; on Wiesenthal's nazi-hunting activities, a vocation to which he has devoted himself since 1945, see his *Justice, Not Vengeance: Recollections* (New York: Grove Weidenfeld, 1989).

57. The idea that the Holocaust is so unique as to "stand outside history," of course, does not originate with Deborah Lipstadt. Rather, its initial formulation is generally attributed to Elie Wiesel; see

Gerd Korman, "The Holocaust in Historical Writing," *Societas*, Vol. 2, No. 3, 1972.

58. For by far the most comprehensive attempt to explain the supposed phenomenological uniqueness of the Holocaust, see Steven T. Katz, *The Holocaust in Historical Context, Vol. I: The Holocaust and Mass Death Before the Modern Age* (New York: Oxford University Press, 1992); the massive study is projected to include another two volumes, which are to include further amplification and refinement of this notion.

59. "Relativism" only "*sounds…*more legitimate than outright denial" (emphasis added); Lipstadt, *Denying the Holocaust, op. cit.*, p. 215.

60. Ibid. pp. 213–4.

61. Ernst Nolte, "Between Myth and Revisionism," in H.W. Koch, ed., *Aspects of the Third Reich* (London: Allen & Unwin, 1985). The argument is in keeping with Nolte's overall method, always present in his work, of making "horizontal comparisons" as a strategy of achieving historicization; Maier, *op. cit.*, p. 18. Lipstadt consistently distorts the particulars of Nolte's positions, often without citation, as an expedient to making her "case."

62. Even the most cursory reading of *Mein Kampf* will reveal this. For in-depth analysis, see Michael Burleigh and Wolfgang Wipperman, *The Racial State: Germany, 1933–1945* (Cambridge: Cambridge University Press, 1991).

63. No less than J. Edgar Hoover, head of the FBI (America's counterpart to the Gestapo, according to President Harry Truman), confirmed *at the time* that Japanese-Americans were by no means a threat to U.S. national security; Curt Gentry, *Secrecy and Power: The Life of J. Edgar Hoover* (New York: The Free Press, 1987) p. 250. Overall, see Richard Drinnon, *Keeper of Concentration Camps: Dillon S. Myer and American Racism* (Berkeley: University of California Press, 1987).

64. Lane Ryo Hirabayashi, *Inside an American Concentration Camp: Japanese American Resistance at Poston, Arizona* (Tucson: University of Arizona Press, 1995).

65. Lipstadt, *Denying the Holocaust, op. cit.*, p. 212. This is *exactly* the argument advanced by Arthur Butz and others to place the operations of the *Einsatzgruppen* "in perspective."

66. Ibid. Lipstadt is quoting Richard Evans, *In Hitler's Shadow: West German Historians and the Attempt to Escape from the Nazi Past* (New York: Alfred A. Knopf, 1989) p. 87. The implicit discounting by both authors of human life in the Third World is remarkable.

67. Lipstadt, *Denying the Holocaust, op. cit.*, p. 212. Actually, she is carefully confusing the Stalinist collectivization/development programs with programs of sociopolitical repression in precisely the same manner as Holocaust deniers create deliberate ambiguity by interchanging concentration camps like Dauchau (sociopolitical repression) with death camps like Auschwitz (extermination). For details on the collectivization, see Robert Conquest, *The Harvest of Sorrow: Soviet Collectivization and the Terror Famine* (New York: Oxford University Press, 1986). On the much more arbitrary and non-ethnically focused political terror, see Conquest's *The Great Terror: Stalin's Purge of the Thirties* (New York: Macmillan, 1968). The differences between the two processes are obvious.

68. Total fatalities by starvation for the decade may have run as high as eleven million; Conquest, *Harvest of Sorrow, op. cit.*, pp. 299–307. Also see Roman Serbyn and Bohdan Krawchenko, eds., *Famine in the Ukraine, 1932–1933* (Edmonton: Canadian Institute for Ukrainian Studies, University of Alberta, 1986).

69. Conquest, *Harvest of Sorrow, op. cit.*, pp. 189–98.

70. Lipstadt, *Denying the Holocaust, op. cit.*, p. 212.

71. The first quote is from Lipstadt, already cited. The second is taken from Yehuda Bauer, "Whose Holocaust?" *Midstream*, Vol. 26, No. 9, Nov. 1980, p. 45.

72. Lipstadt, *Denying the Holocaust, op. cit.*, p. 213. She is quoting Michael Marrus, *The Holocaust in History* (Hanover, NH: Brandeis University Press and the University Press of New England, 1987) p. 24.

73. Yehuda Bauer, "Is the Holocaust Explicable?" in Yehuda Bauer, et al., eds., *Remembering for the Future, Vol. 2: Working Papers and Addenda* (Oxford: Pergamon Press, 1989) p. 1970.

74. Katz, *The Holocaust in Historical Context, Vol. 1, op. cit.*, p. 580.

75. Yehuda Bauer, "Holocaust and Genocide: Some Comparisons," in Peter Hayes, ed., *Lessons and Legacies: The Meaning of the Holocaust in a Changing World* (Evanston, IL: Northwestern University Press, 1991) p. 40.

76. Yehuda Bauer, *The Holocaust in Historical Perspective* (Seattle: University of Washington Press, 1978) p. 38.

77. Lucy S. Dawidowicz, *The Holocaust and the Historians* (Cambridge: Harvard University Press, 1981) p. 11.

78. Marrus, *The Holocaust in History,, op. cit.*, pp. 21–2.

79. Bauer, "Whose Holocaust?" *op. cit.*, p. 45.

80. What may be the most careful assessment of Jewish survival rates will be found in Hilberg, *The Destruction of the European Jews, op. cit.*, pp. 1047–8, 1220.

81. Hence, "for all practical purposes the Jewish question had been solved" by November 1944, despite the fact that a third of Jews of Europe remained alive; ibid., pp. 980–1.

82. In other words, the actualities of nazism's anti-Jewish programs and policies readily conform to the definition of genocide coined by Polish jurist Raphaël Lemkin in 1944, as well as the legal criteria elaborated by the United Nations in the Convention on the Punishment of the Crime of Genocide (1948); Raphaël Lemkin, *Axis Rule in Occupied Europe: Laws of Occupation, Analysis of Government, Proposals for Redress* (Washington, D.C.: Carnegie Endowment for International Peace, 1944) p. 79; Ian Brownlie, ed., *Basic Documents on Human Rights* (Oxford: Clarendon Press, [3rd. ed.] 1988) pp. 31–4.

83. For fuller discussion, see Isador Walliman and Michael N. Dobkowski, eds., *Genocide and the Modern Age: Etiology and Case Studies of Mass Death* (Westport, CT: Greenwood Press, 1987); George J. Andreopoulos, ed., *Genocide: Conceptual and Historical Dimensions* (Philadelphia: University of Pennsylvania Press, 1994).

84. For discussion, see Dawidowicz, *The Holocaust and the Historians, op. cit.* (esp. the section entitled "The Invisible Jews" in chap. 2) pp. 22–42.

85. Dawidowicz, *The Holocaust and the Historians, op. cit.*, pp. 13–4. Gilbert (*The Holocaust, op. cit.*), makes the same point with the same numbers.

86. Ian Hancock, "'Uniqueness' of the Victims: Gypsies, Jews, and the Holocaust," *Without Prejudice*, Vol. 1, No. 2, 1988.

87. Overall attrition of 65 percent—rather than the 25 percent allowed by Dawidowicz, Gilbert, and their cohorts—is a very conservative estimate; Ian Hancock, "Uniqueness, Gypsies, and Jews," in Bauer, et al., *Remembering for the Future, Vol. 2, op. cit.*, pp. 2017–25. Also see Sybil Milton, "The Context of the Holocaust," *German Studies Review*, Vol. 13, No. 2, 1990.

88. Michael Berenbaum, *The World Must Know: The History of the Holocaust as Told in the United States Holocaust Memorial Museum* (Boston: Little, Brown, 1993) p. 2. Interestingly, a special 1985 report commissioned by the U.S. Holocaust Memorial Museum, which Berenbaum directs, reached the opposite conclusion and deployed considerable data to support its findings. The document, by Gabrielle Tyrnauer and entitled *The Fate of the Gypsies During the Holocaust*, was immediately restricted from public access.

89. Richard Breitman, *Architect of Genocide: Himmler and the Final Solution* (Hanover, NH: University Press of New England, 1991) p. 20.

90. Yisrael Gutman, ed., *Encyclopedia of the Holocaust* (New York: Macmillan, 1990). Steven T. Katz is also among those who explicitly deny that the Gypsies were targeted for the same treatment as Jews; *The Holocaust in Historical Context, Vol. 1, op. cit.*, p. 25.

91. *Memorial Book, op. cit.*, p. xiv.

92. Breitman, *Architect of Genocide, op. cit.*, p. 164.

93. Benno Muller-Hill, *Murderous Science: Elimination by Scientific Selection of Jews, Gypsies and Others, 1933–1945* (Oxford: Oxford University Press, 1988) p. 59.

94. Ibid., pp. 58–9.

95. Burleigh and Wipperman, *The Racial State, op. cit.*, p. 125.

96. Hancock, "Responses to the *Porrajmos*," *op. cit.*, p. 51.

97. Lloyd Grove, "Lament the Gypsies: 40 Years after Auschwitz, Petitioning for a Place," *Washington Post*, July 21, 1984.

98. Yahil, *op. cit.*, p. 273. According to Donald Kendrick and Grattan Puxton, "Certain classes of Jews with mixed parentage were retained in the armed forces throughout the war," and were also thereby consciously exempted from extermination; *The Destiny of Europe's Gypsies* (London: Sussex University Press, Chatto & Heinemann, 1972) p. 82.

99. "Analysis of blood groups, haptoglobin phenotypes, and HLA types establish Gypsies as a distinct racial group with origins in the Punjab region of India. Also supporting this is the worldwide Gypsy language, Romani, which is quite similar to Hindi"; J.D. Thomas, et al., "Disease, Lifestyle, and Consanguinity in 58 American Gypsies," *Lancet* 8555, August 15, 1977. Also see, R. Patai and J. Patai-Wing, *The Myth of the Jewish Race* (Detroit: Wayne State University Press, 1989).

100. Kendrick and Puxton, *Destiny of Europe's Gypsies, op. cit.*, p. 68.

101. Annegret Ehmann, "A Short History of the Discrimination and Persecution of the European Gypsies and Their Fate Under Nazi Rule," unpublished paper presented as a lecture to the Institute of Contemporary Jewry, Hebrew University, Jan. 27, 1981, p. 10. Also see Sybil Milton, "The Racial Context of the Holocaust," *Social Education*, February 1991.

102. See, e.g., Ralph W. Barnes, "The Shame of Nuremberg," *New York Times*, Sept. 15, 1935; not a word is said about the Gypsies. The same is true of a similar story featured prominently in *The Times* of London on September 17. The bias is consistent for all major news outlets throughout the decade.

103. Gilbert, *The Holocaust, op. cit.*, p. 78; Dalia Ofer, *Escaping the Holocaust* (New York: Oxford University Press, 1990).

104. Bauer, *Jews for Sale?, op. cit.*; Edwin Black, *The Transfer Agreement* (New York: Macmillan 1984); Henry L. Feingold, *The Politics of Rescue* (New Brunswick, NJ: Rutgers University Press, 1970).

105. Arthur D, Morse, *While Six Million Died: A Chronicle of American Apathy* (New York: Random House, 1968); David S. Wyman, *The Abandonment of the Jews: America and the Holocaust, 1941–1945* (New York: Pantheon, 1984); Irving Abella and Harold Troper, *None Is Too Many: Canada and the Jews of Europe, 1933–1948* (New York: Random House, 1982). There is not so much as an index entry on Gypsies in any of these rather detailed studies.

106. Short of reviewing the entire copious record of official pronouncements by organizations such as the World Jewish Congress during the period 1941–1945, an assessment can be made from works such as Walter Laqueur's *The Terrible Secret: Suppression of the Truth About Hitler's "Final Solution"* (Boston: Little, Brown, 1981) which ably summarize the Jewish organizations' efforts to draw official Western attention to the dimensions of the Holocaust. Plainly, their depictions of what Laqueur calls "the most terrible crime in human history" was (and remains) couched exclusively in terms of Jewish victimization. The Gypsies were never mentioned at the time,

107. Hancock, "Responses to the *Porrajmos,*" *op. cit.*, p. 59. This cinematic issue raised is not accidental or inadvertent. On p. 57, Hancock quotes James Michael Holmes of Phoenix International Productions to the effect that, in 1995, two Hollywood studios declined to consider a remake of the highly successful 1947 film *The Golden Earrings*, about Gypsy victims of nazism. In both cases, the reason stated was that it would be "inappropriate" to make a movie about the Holocaust which did not focus attention on the fate of the Jews.

108. Ibid., p. 60. The reference is to Margaret Stapinska, "Faceless, Stateless, Endless Victims," *Yorkshire Post*, Jan. 28, 1995.

109. Steven Kinzer, "Germany Cracks Down: Gypsies Come First," *New York Times*, Sept. 27, 1992; *Situation der Roma in Europa und Deutschland seit der Widervereinigung* (Hamburg: Roma National Congress, May 1993). For background on the attitudes of Poles toward Gypsies, see Jerzy Fickowski, *The Gypsies in Poland* (Warsaw: Interpress, 1989).

110. Stannard, "The Politics of Holocaust Scholarship," *op. cit.*, p. 170.

111. Louise Branson, "Romanian Gypsies Being Terrorized," *San Francisco Chronicle*, Dec. 19, 1993.

112. Quoted in Sangor Balogh, "Following in the Footsteps of the Ku Klux Klan: Anti-Gypsy Organization in Romania," *Nemzetközi Cigány Szövetség Bulletin*, No. 5, 1993.

113. Harvey Meyerhoff, "Council Decries Germany's Treatment of Gypsies," *U.S. Holocaust Memorial Council Newsletter*, Winter issue, 1992–1993.

114. Yehuda Bauer, "Continuing Ferment in Eastern Europe," *SICSA Report*, Vol. 4, Nos. 1/2, 1990. It should be noted that this was during a period when "no incidents of antisemitic violence" were listed in the *1990 Country Report on Human Rights* for all of Europe.

115. Arno J. Mayer, *Why Did the Heavens Not Darken? The "Final Solution" in History* (New York: Pantheon, 1990). pp. 6, 17.

116. Katz, *The Holocaust in Historical Context, Vol. 1, op. cit.*, p. 25.

117. Dawidowicz, *The Holocaust and the Historians, op cit.*, p. 10.

118. This includes the famous memorandum prepared by Hitler's adjutant, Col. Friedrich Hössbach, summarizing a high-level conference conducted on November 5, 1937, during which the Führer outlined his plans in great detail; *Trial of the Major War Criminals before the International Military Tribunal, Vol. 25* (Nuremberg: International Military Tribunal, 1947–1949) pp. 402–13. Overall, see Robert Koehl, *RKFDV: German Resettlement and Population Policy, 1939–1945* (Cambridge: Harvard University Press, 1957); Ihor Kamensky, *Secret Nazi Plans for Eastern Europe: A Study of Lebensraum Policies* (New York: Bookman Associates, 1961); Norman Rich, *Hitler's War Aims: Ideology, the Nazi State, and the Course of Expansion* (New York: W.W. Norton, 1973).

119. Systematic "depopulation" of a targeted group is, by definition, genocide; see Lemkin's *Axis Rule in Occupied Europe (op. cit.)*. On nazi depopulation plan objectives, see, e.g., Alexander Dallin, *German Rule in Occupied Russia, 1941–1945: A Study in Occupation Policies* (New York: Macmillan, 1957) esp. p. 278.

120. The overall scheme was committed to writing under the title "Generalplan Ost" (General Plan East) in early 1942; Ibid., p. 282; "Der Generalplan Ost," *Viertjahrshefte fuer Zeitgeschichte*, No. 6 (1958), No. 1 (1960).

121. Office of United States Chief of Counsel for Prosecution of Axis Criminality, *Nazi Conspiracy and Aggression, Vol. 6* (Washington, D.C.: U.S. Government Printing Office, 1946) p. 427.

122. *Nazi Conspiracy and Aggression, Vol. 6, op. cit.*, p. 435; Lukas, *Forgotten Holocaust, op. cit.*, p. 90.

123. These come within the scope of "Fall Barbarossa," the plan for the invasion of the Soviet Union. See, e.g., the so-called "Oldenburg Protocol" of March 29, 1941; Fieldmarshall Wilhelm Keitel's May 13, 1941, memorandum entitled "On the Military Jurisdiction in the Region of 'Barbarossa' and on Special Military Powers"; and the directive "Twelve Commandments for German Behavior in the East and for Treatment of Russians" of June 1, 1941; all in *Nazi Conspiracy and Aggression, Vol. 6, op. cit.*

124. "Appearing on March 30, 1941, at a meeting of his top brass, Hitler said that when one talks about war with the U.S.S.R., 'one is talking about annihilation' "; quoted in Georgily A. Kumanev, "The German Occupation Regime on Occupied Territory in the U.S.S.R. (1941–1944)," in Berenbaum, *A Mosaic of Victims, op. cit.*, p. 130. There are many comparable examples; see generally, Rich, *Hitler's War Aims, op. cit.*

125. Taras Hunczak, "The Ukrainian Losses During World War II," in Berenbaum, *A Mosaic of Victims, op. cit.*, p. 119.

126. Bauer, "Jewish Resistance and Passivity," *op. cit.*; Yisrael Gutman, "The Armed Struggle of Jews in Nazi-Occupied Countries," in Yahil, *op. cit.*, pp. 457–98; Reubin Ainsztein, *Jewish Resistance in Nazi-Occupied Eastern Europe* (New York: Barnes & Noble, 1974); Lucien Steinberg, *The Jews Against Hitler (Not Like a Lamb)* (London: Gordon & Cremonesi, 1978); Isaiah Trunk, *Jewish Responses to Nazi Persecution* (New York: Scarborough Books, 1982).

127. Jan Szafranski, "Poland's Losses in World War II," in Roman Nurowski, ed., *1939–1945: War Losses in Poland* (Pozán: Wydawnictwo Zachodnie, 1960) esp. pp. 44–9; Central Commission for the Investigation of German Crimes in Poland, *German War Crimes in Poland* (Warsaw: State Publishing House, 1947). Overall, see Richard C. Lukas, *Forgotten Holocaust: The Poles Under German Occupation, 1939–1944* (Lexington: University of Kentucky Press, 1986). Dawidowicz contends that the Poles are seeking to "appropriate" the Holocaust; *The Holocaust and the Historians, op. cit.*, pp. 88–124.

128. Dawidowicz notes that these were "mainly victims of German reprisals for the continuing guerrilla warfare that the Yugoslavs conducted during the German occupation"; Ibid., p. 7. For details on the realities underlying this bland statement, see Paul Helm, *The German Struggle Against Yugoslav Guerillas in World War II: German Counter-Insurgency in Yugoslavia, 1941–1943* (Boulder,CO: East European Monographs, 1979).

129. Lemkin, *Axis Rule, op. cit.*, pp. 138, 143. Also see Randolph Braham, *The Politics of Genocide: The Holocaust in Hungary*, 2 Vols. (New York: Columbia University Press, 1981).

130. Hunczak, "The Ukrainian Losses During WWII," *op. cit.*, p. 124; Bodhan Krawchenko, "Soviet Ukraine under Nazi Occupation, 1941–1944," in Y. Boshyk, ed., *Ukraine During World War II: History and Aftermath* (Edmonton: Canadian Institute for Ukrainian Studies, University of Alberta, 1986).

131. On the routine execution of Soviet troops attempting to surrender, see George H. Stein, *The*

Waffen SS: Hitler's Elite Guard at War, 1939–1945 (Ithaca, NY: Cornell University Press, 1966); Peter Neumann, *The Black March: The Personal Story of an SS Man* (New York: Bantam, 1958).

132. Wiesenthal has been making such statements since shortly after the war. I am paraphrasing a paraphrase contained in Berenbaum, "The Uniqueness and Universality of the Holocaust," *op. cit.*, pp. 20–1.

133. Stannard, "The Politics of Holocaust Scholarship," *op. cit.*, p. 190.

134. Stephen Jay Gould, *The Mismeasure of Man* (New York: W.W. Norton, 1981) p. 85.

135. Stannard, "The Politics of Holocaust Scholarship," *op. cit.*, p. 185.

136. Gould, *Mismeasure of Man, op. cit.*, p. 85.

137. Aside from Gould's fine study, the best books on the topic are probably Samuel L. Chorover's *From Genesis to Genocide* (Cambridge: MIT Press, 1979) and William Stanton's *The Leopard's Spots: Scientific Attitudes on Race in America, 1815–1859* (Chicago: University of Chicago Press, 1960). Also see Stefan Kühn, *The Nazi Connection: Eugenics, American Racism, and German National Socialism* (New York: Oxford University Press, 1994).

138. App and Barnes were members of the professorate in relevant disciplines. Arthur Butz's professorship in electrical engineering hardly places him in a position to determine who teaches in the area of genocide studies, or from what perspective.

139. Dawidowicz, *The Holocaust and the Historians, op. cit.*, p. 17.

140. Mayer, *Why Did the Heavens Not Darken?, op. cit.*, p. 6.

141. Berenbaum, "The Uniqueness and Universality of the Holocaust," *op. cit.*, p. 34.

142. Israel W. Charny, *Genocide: A Critical Bibliographical Review* (London: Mansell, 1988) p. xxiv.

143. Israel W. Charny, "Toward a Generic Definition of Genocide," in Andreopoulos, *op. cit.*, p. 72.

144. Conquest, *Harvest of Sorrow, op. cit.*; Commission on the Ukrainian Famine, *Investigation of the Ukrainian Famine, 1932–1933: Report to Congress* (Washington, D.C.: U.S. Government Printing Office, 1988).

145. See, e.g., Juan A. Villamarin and Judith E. Villamarin, *Indian Labor in Colonial Spanish America* (Newark: University of Delaware Press, 1975); William L. Sherman, *Native Forced Labor in Sixteenth Century Central America* (Lincoln: University of Nebraska Press, 1979).

146. The phraseology accrues from Israel Charny's *How Can We Commit the Unthinkable?, op cit.*

LIE FOR LIE

Linkages Between Holocaust Deniers and Proponents of the "Uniqueness of the Jewish Experience in World War II"

> To claim that the Holocaust was unique can only imply that attempts to anni-
> hilate other national or cultural groups are not to be considered genocide, thus
> diminishing the gravity and moral implications of any genocide anywhere,
> any time. It also implies that the Jews have a monopoly on genocide, that no
> matter what misfortune befalls another people, it cannot be as serious or even
> in the same category as the Holocaust.
>
> —Pierre Papazian
> "A 'Unique Uniqueness'?"

ONE of the more unsavory phenomena marking the postwar intellectual environment has been the rise of a pseudoscholarly "historical revisionism" in which the nazi genocide of Europe's Jews is minimized or denied altogether. The main practicioners of this ugly craft have been united not only by their virulent antisemitism but by a patent willingness to distort or falsify the factual record upon which they supposedly base their conclusions.[1] As a consequence, they have been quite properly excluded from legitimate academic discourse, their adherents sometimes jailed in countries like Germany, Austria, France, and Canada.[2]

All of this is reasonably well known. Far less recognized is the fact that the ugly enterprise of Holocaust denial has a flip side—indeed, a mirror image —which is equally objectionable but which has been anything but marginalized by the academy, popular media, or the public at large. This is the view advanced by a much larger group of writers that the nazi genocide not only happened, but that it 1) is the only such occurrence in all of human history and 2) that it somehow happened uniquely and exclusively to its Jewish victims.[3]

In other words, no previous attempt to obliterate an entire people— not Cortés's butchery of an estimated 20,000 Mexicas (Aztecs) per day, ultimately putting to the sword more than 300,000 as he set his men to systematically reducing all evidence of their civilization to rubble;[4] not the Spanish system of forced labor (*encomiendo*) under which entire American Indian populations were worked to death;[5] not the transatlantic slave trade which cost millions of African lives, depopulating vast expanses of the "Dark Continent";[6] not the Virginia Colony's extermination of the Powhatans during the 1620s nor the Puritans' campaign to utterly eradicate the Pequots in Massachusetts a decade later;[7] not Lord Jeffrey Amherst's 1763 instruction that his subordinates use smallpox to "extirpate" the Ottawas nor the U.S. Army's replication of the tactic against the Mandans in 1836;[8] not the 1864 orders of both civil and military authorities in Colorado for the total extermination of Cheyennes and Arapahoes nor the actual extermination of entire aboriginal populations in Tasmania and Newfoundland;[9] not the 1918 Turkish slaughter of well over a million Armenians;[10] not the charnel houses of Indonesia, Katanga, and Biafra in the 1960s nor those of Bangladesh and Burundi in the 1970s;[11] not Cambodia under the Khmer Rouge nor even the more current horrors in East Timor, Bosnia, and Rwanda.[12] *Nothing* qualifies as being "truly" genocidal except the Holocaust, or *Shoah*, as it is known in the Jewish tradition.[13]

Moreover, of those who suffered at the hands of the nazis themselves, none but Jews experienced "actual" genocide. This remains true, argue proponents of the exclusivist position, whether reference is made to the Polish intelligentsia, a target group which was almost totally annihilated as part of the German program to cause the national entity of Poland to disappear forever,[14] or the calculated reduction of the Slavic populations of the western U.S.S.R. by perhaps 15 million to make way for "Germanic resettlement" of their territories (the Soviets suffered some 27 million fatalities overall).[15] It holds true even with respect to the fate of the Sinti and Romani (Gypsies), exterminated in the same proportion and in the same death camps as the Jews and as an equally integral aspect of Hitlerian "racial hygiene."[16]

The performance is truly astonishing, outstripping that of the neonazis. Whereas the latter content themselves with denying the authenticity of a single genocidal process, exclusivists deny, categorically and out of hand, the validity of myriad genocides. Yet, unlike the neonazis, those holding to the postulates of Jewish exclusivism are not only treated as being academically credible but are accorded a distinctly preferential treatment among the arbiters of scholarly integrity.

Embracing a Lie

An excellent topical example of what is at issue is described in a recent article by Christopher Shea in the *Chronicle of Higher Education* concerning the controversy attending preparation of a Westview Press collection, *Is the Holocaust Unique? Perspectives in Comparative Genocide*, a book which was supposed to be a free and open exchange between those holding to exclusivist principles and scholars expressing comparativist views.[17] As Shea observes, the problem devolves upon the fact that volume editor Alan S. Rosenbaum provided advance copies of all submissions to one contributor—and *only* one—Cornell University professor Steven T. Katz, author of the massive three-volume *Holocaust in Historical Context* and a leading advocate of exclusivism in its pure form.[18]

Upon reviewing what some comparativists had to say with respect to his own work, Katz whipped off a laundry list of changes and deletions he wanted to see made to their critiques. Rosenbaum in turn fronted these "suggestions" as if they were his own. Only when the editor accidentally faxed a memo intended for Katz to one of the more trenchant critics, historian David E. Stannard, was the subterfuge revealed (the missive outlined various contributors' compliance with Katz's secret manipulations). After a series of meetings with the publisher and its lawyers, most of the essays were returned to their original form—a matter Katz, apparently waxing indignant at having been caught, calls "a disgraceful business"—and the book was sent to press.[19]

One would think that such unethical behavior on the part of the book's major exclusivist contributor and its editor would tend to speak for themselves, offering statements which extend well beyond the immediate circumstance. Shea, however, turns completely away from these implications of the evidence, quoting Katz to the effect that the problem is lodged not in the documented sleaziness of his own actions but rather in *Stannard's* conduct, which he describes as lacking in "honorable" comportment, "[scholarly] ethics" and "morality." Meanwhile, he is allowed to rail—without comment from Shea—against "academic name calling." On the basis of this glaringly gratuitous and self-contradictory set of assertions, the *Chronicle* writer blandly reestablishes a proverbial "level playing field," dubbing the positions represented by the two men as merely "competing claims."[20]

If anything, the article ends up subtly aligned with Katz. Ultimately, it is Stannard's analysis of exclusivism—rather than Katz's own none-too-gentle assaults upon the work of literally hundreds of scholars as diverse as

Hannah Arendt, Ernst Nolte, and Stannard himself—which is saddled with the adjective "scorching."[21] The word choice, superficially benign, actually resonates quite well with the kind of vernacular employed by such official gatekeepers of the status quo as Lynne Cheney and William Bennett during the run-up to the 1992 Columbian Quincentenniary—"shrill," "exaggerated," "hyperbolic," "biased," "irresponsible," and so on—to denigrate and dismiss challengers to orthodox historiography of the Americas.[22]

Needless to say, the *Chronicle* would have handled things a bit differently had the "bitter squabble" been between David Stannard and a Holocaust denier like, say, Arthur Butz, author of *The Hoax of the Twentieth Century: The Case Against the Presumed Extermination of European Jewry*.[23] In the unlikely event that Butz were even allowed to air his squalid propaganda in the paper's noble pages, it would inevitably be contextualized in such a way as to ensure that readers understood it constituted a matrix of essential untruth. Under no circumstances can it be envisioned that the *Chronicle of Higher Education* would accord an Arthur Butz a scholarly integrity equal to that of a David Stannard (or just about anyone else, for that matter).

When it comes to a far more grandiose denier of genocide like Steven Katz, however, all bets are off. Stannard's and Katz's positions are presented in carefully weighted fashion as being opposing "opinions" of equal validity and legitimacy. No suggestion is made that one thesis might be inherently truer or falser than the other. It is as if the *Chronicle*'s editors had somehow forgotten—or never learned—one cardinal distinction: a lie is a lie, *not* an opinion, a "perspective," an "interpretation," an "outlook," or a "point of view." The principle is no less applicable to Steven Katz than it is to Arthur Butz. Yet the treatment accorded the two is as different as is reasonable to imagine.

The Lie Revealed

The question presents itself, to be sure, as to whether it is a fair and accurate characterization to contend that Holocaust exclusivists are cut of the same cloth as Holocaust deniers. Do the former, like the latter, really twist the record to fit preordained and ideologically defined conclusions? Do they deliberately misquote their sources, omit and often suppress contrary data, or orchestrate fabricated "facts" as a means of "proving" their case? And do they, as a matter of course, seek to defend not only their "truth" but the methodological improprieties underlying it with viciously *ad hominem* attacks upon all who might challenge them? The answer to each query is an unequivocal yes.

Here, one encounters such an amazing welter of possible illustrations that they threaten instantly to become overwhelming. These accrue not just from Katz's voluminous work, but from that of virtually all of his colleagues.[24] However, it would be well—for the sake of both simplicity and consistency—to stick with Steven Katz, and to constrain analysis to a pair of basic propositions lodged in *The Holocaust in Historical Context*, his most definitive work.[25] The first point for examination will be the manner in which Katz deals with the very concept of genocide, as it was first articulated by the Polish jurist Raphaël Lemkin in 1944. From there, we may proceed to consider his subsequent handling of the definitional criteria of the crime as they are codified in the 1948 United Nations Convention on Prevention and Punishment of the Crime of Genocide.

The Concept of Genocide

In seeking to explain the origin of the term, Katz remarks rather casually that "the neologism *genocide* was coined by Raphaël Lemkin to describe what was happening to the Jews of Europe during World War II–no then-existing term being, in his view, adequate."[26] This probably sounds plausible to anyone who has never read Lemkin's seminal *Axis Rule in Occupied Europe*, a category which would encompass almost everybody.[27] The problem is that Katz's single-sentence summary bears not the remotest connection to what Lemkin actually said. To the contrary, something on the order of 90 percent of what is presented to explain the meaning of genocide in *Axis Rule* concerns what was happening to groups *other than* Jews. The following passage, describing the nazi practice of genocide in Luxembourg is indicative:

> The Grand Duchy of Luxembourg has been for centuries bilingual (French and German). Nevertheless, the Chief of the German Civil Administration on August 6, 1940, issued an order in which he stated that "the language of Luxembourg is, and always has been, German... The German language shall be the exclusive official language," as well as the language of commercial life. All names of streets and localities were made German. Luxembourgers having non-German first names were required to assume in lieu thereof the corresponding German first name, or, if that were impossible, to select a German first name. Nationals of Luxembourg having a family name of German origin which later had been given a foreign or non-German form were required to resume the original German form. If the person involved did not apply for a change of name before February 15, 1941, the occupant himself conferred a German name upon him... An order was issued in Luxembourg concerning legitimation of illegitimate children, in which it is declared that an illegitimate child shall, in relation

to its mother or her relatives, have the legal status of a legitimate child. Although this provision does not expressly mention German fathers, one may infer by comparison with other genocide laws issued by the occupant that the order had as a goal the procreation of children by German fathers.[28]

This is what Lemkin had to say about nazi genocide in Luxembourg, and it's *all* he had to say. There is no indication whatever that he was motivated by a desire to "describe what was happening to the Jews of Europe during World War II." Jews not only remain unmentioned, none of what is offered here as evidence of nazi genocide pertained to them in any way. Indeed, the procreation of Jewish children by German fathers was flatly prohibited under nazi law.[29] Nor is the presentation on genocide in Luxembourg anomalous. Lemkin's remarks concerning other occupied countries—the Protectorate of Bohemia and Moravia, Norway, and the U.S.S.R., as examples—yield very similar results.[30] In instances where the treatment of Jews is directly addressed, it is all but invariably done in combination with policies afflicting other peoples such as the Slovakians, Serbians, and Croatians.[31]

None of this is to say that Lemkin was unaware of or unconcerned with the fate of Europe's Jews (he was both aware and very concerned). But it *is* to say that he perceived what was happening to the Jews as part of a much broader genocidal whole in which entire national and ethnic cultures were being destroyed by various means as part of the nazi master plan to impose the German national pattern on the whole of Europe.

> Genocide has two phases: one, destruction of the national pattern of the oppressed group; the other, the imposition of the national pattern of the oppressor. This imposition, in turn, may be made upon the oppressed population which is allowed to remain, or upon the territory alone, after removal of the population and colonization of the area by the oppressor's own nationals.[32]

In Chapter IX of *Axis Rule*, which is devoted entirely to explication of the concept of genocide, there are sections devoted to each of the main means by which Lemkin saw it being accomplished by the nazis: politically, socially, economically, biologically, physically, religiously, and morally. There is no section devoted specifically to what was happening to the Jews, nor does their fate define the content of any other section, including those focusing on biological and physical genocide. On the contrary, the author's emphasis throughout is on what was being done to the *Slavic* peoples —Czechs, Poles, and so on—of eastern Europe.[33]

Katz attempts to finesse this in two ways. First, in a footnote he tries to hedge his conscious and deliberate misrepresentation of the motives under-girding *Axis Rule* by suggesting that Lemkin was confused as to his own meaning: "He [Lemkin] appears to have held that Nazi behavior vis-à-vis a number of other groups approached, if not actually replicated, Nazi anti-Jewish activity and, therefore, should also be identified as genocide."[34] Secondly, in another footnote, he pretends that Lemkin actually intended to arrive at a completely different definition of genocide than that which appears in *Axis Rule*, but that he lacked sufficient information to do so: "I make bold to suggest that Raphaël Lemkin may well have formulated a def-inition of genocide closer (if not exactly like) mine had he been writing after the end of World War II when it became clear what Hitler's Judeocidal intentions were. Working in 1942–43, Lemkin was still unable to see the entire uncompromising, totalistic assault for what it was."[35]

Both caveats are extremely and intentionally distortive. The truth is that Lemkin was quite aware of the nature of the assault upon the Jews. Quoting *Mein Kampf*, he observes that, "Some groups [e.g., the Gypsies]—like the Jews —are to be destroyed completely."[36] Elsewhere, he goes into some detail: "The rounding up of the Jews in all occupied countries and deporting them to Poland for physical extermination is also one of the main tasks of the Gestapo and SS units. The Chief of the Gestapo in Poland, Krüger, who was killed by Polish patriots, organized the liquidation of the ghettos in Polish towns, with the physical annihilation of half a million inhabitants of the Warsaw ghetto. He also built up the technical apparatus of mass-murder [including] death by gas in special chambers."[37] At another point, Lemkin cites an American Jewish Congress report indicating that 1,702,500 Jews had been exterminated as of mid-1943, and quotes from a United Nations Joint Declaration of the same year condemning "this bestial policy of cold-blooded extermination."[38]

> From all the occupied countries Jews are being transported in conditions of appalling horror and brutality to Eastern Europe. In Poland, which has been made the principal Nazi slaughterhouse, the ghettos established by the German invader are being system-atically emptied of all Jews except a few highly skilled workers required for war indus-tries. None of those taken away are ever heard from again. The able-bodied are slowly worked to death in labor camps. The infirm are left to die of exposure and starvation or are deliberately massacred in mass executions.[39]

Axis Rule contains a number of similar passages. To assert that Raphaël Lemkin lacked the database necessary to define genocide in terms of the Jewish experience under the nazis, despite his own inclinations, is thus at best absurd. The fact that he meant something altogether different is abundantly evidenced in the fact that, unlike Katzian exclusivists, he proceeds immediately from quoting *Mein Kampf* on the Jews to a second quotation, this one to the effect that the Poles, too, were slated for eventual total extermination (Lemkin also places the Slovenes and Serbs in this category, based upon careful analysis).[40] Even more to the point, Lemkin makes it absolutely clear from the outset that his concept of genocide was never meant to pertain exclusively to direct killing, this being but one means to the end of destroying the *identity* of targeted groups.

> Generally speaking, genocide does not necessarily mean the immediate destruction of a nation, except when accomplished by mass killings of all members of a nation. It is intended rather to signify a coordinated plan of different actions aiming at the destruction of essential foundations of the life of national groups, with the aim of annihilating the groups themselves [even if all individuals within the dissolved group physically survive]. The objectives of such a plan would be a disintegration of political and social institutions, of culture, language, national feelings, religion, and the economic existence of national groups, and the destruction of personal security, liberty, health, dignity, and even the lives of the individuals belonging to such groups. Genocide is directed at the national group as an entity, and the actions involved are directed at individuals, not in their individual capacity, but as members of the national group.[41]

This is Raphaël Lemkin's definition of genocide. It is a far cry from—indeed, antithetical to—the vulgarization popularized by Jewish exclusivists that "genocide means to eradicate a gene pool."* Nor is it closer to the more refined Katzian version of the same crude notion, that genocide is simply "the actualization of the intent, however successfully carried out, to murder in its totality any national, ethnic, racial, religious, political, social, gender, or economic group, as these groups are defined by the perpetrator, by whatever means."[42] Katz's bald appropriation of Lemkin's name as a means of creating the appearance of legitimacy for an idea diametrically opposed to what was advanced in *Axis Rule* is thus an exercise in intellectual duplicity of the most fundamental kind, a performance worthy of the worst of the Holocaust deniers.

---

*This notion derives from a misperception, sometimes accidental, sometimes intentional, that the "gen" in genocide refers to "genes." In actuality, as Lemkin states at p. 79, it derives from the Greek word *genos*, meaning "type" (or, in the human context, "tribe" or "race"). When combined with the Latin word *cide* (killing), it yields the idea of group eradication. Plainly, there is nothing in Lemkin's formulation which requires the killing of all individual human group members to bring about the phenomenon described. For further discussion, see Israel W. Charny, ed., *Toward the Understanding and Prevention of Genocide: Proceedings of the International Conference on the Holocaust and Genocide* (Boulder, CO: Westview Press, 1984).

The Genocide Convention

The second article of the United Nations' 1948 convention on genocide specifies five different categories of action which constitute the crime when applied "with intent to destroy, in whole or in part, a national, ethnical, racial or religious group, as such." Following Lemkin, the U.N. saw to it that only one of these criteria involved direct killing. The others concern the systematic infliction of physical or psychological harm on group members, creating other conditions leading to group destruction, compulsory sterilization of group members, and the systematic transfer of children from the targeted group to the targeting group.[43] Some of these clearly apply to what happened to the Jews at the hands of the nazis. Equally obviously, others do not.

Katz duly enumerates these various criteria, and then spends a page and a half (properly) exploring the question of intent.[44] He next turns to other "problematic issues" and devotes a paragraph to pointing out (correctly) that the U.N. definition deviates from Lemkin's original formulation by omitting political and economic aggregates from the types of group which might be subjected to genocide.[45] These are "restored" before he goes on to make his "own" contribution, adding the category of gender (also correctly).* Then, with a couple of pages safely insulating readers from his verbatim regurgitation of the law, he takes up the question of the "degree of destruction" necessary for any given process to truly be considered a genocide.

On its face, the question is both logical and appropriate. Under Katz's

---

*Katz, *The Holocaust in Historical Context, op. cit.*, p. 127. Katz's addition of the gender category appears enlightened at first glance, but is actually another subterfuge insofar as he uses it primarily as a convenient hedge against the implications of European witchburning in the Middle Ages. By pegging the tally of female witches killed against the total population of European *women*, as he does at pp. 504–5, he is able to arrive at the statistically insignificant impact of 1/27 of 1 percent. With this, he easily rebuts proponents of the concept of "gynocide" like Andrea Dworkin (*Woman Hating* [New York: Dutton, 1974]) and Mary Daly (*Gyn/Ecology: The Metaethics of Radical Feminism* [Boston: Beacon Press, 1978]), describing the phenomenon as "misogynist...but hardly genocidal." If, in the alternative, he had been compelled, absent his new gender criteria, to assess witchburning in the context of their being an essential part of the leadership of non-Christian (pagan, "tribal") religious groups marked for eradication—which is, of course, what they were—and thus to consider their fate in conjunction with that of their male counterparts, his trivialization of witchburning's impact would have been impossible. Most pagan traditions in Europe have, after all, been rendered extinct as a result; see, e.g., Robin Lane Fox, *Pagans and Christians* (San Francisco: HarperCollins, 1986). Equally telling, since he was opting to "open up" the definition of genocide by adding possible target groups, is that Katz neglected to include the mentally and physically impaired, all of whom were formally marked for complete extermination under nazi euthanasia programs; see Stefan Kühl, *The Nazi Connection, op. cit.*; Robert Jay Lifton, *The Nazi Doctors: Medical Killing and the Psychology of Genocide* (New York: Basic Books, 1986) pp. 45–144.

handling, however, attention is diverted entirely to concerns with the scale of killing and conditions under which it occurs. Somehow, little matters like using sterilization as a means to bring about group extinction never come up.[*] Hence, by the time he finishes his "discussion" several pages later, the five categories of genocidal activity elaborated in law have been magically reduced to one. From there, it is a relatively straightforward matter to create the misimpression that his own definition of genocide not only conforms to the "spirit" of the Genocide Convention—even strengthens its utility—when in fact it completely voids 80 percent of the instrument.

And what of the resultant missing elements? Katz manages the question in an interesting fashion a bit later in his book. They belong under the heading of "cultural" rather than "physical" genocide, he opines, along with all the rest of Lemkin's original definition of the crime (how, exactly, sterilization becomes a cultural rather than physical phenomenon is left a bit mysterious). In practice, only the Katzian construction of physical genocide—direct killing accompanied by an express intent to murder every single individual within a targeted group—qualifies as genocide at all. Everything else is something else, for which appropriate statutory prohibitions should probably be enacted.[†]

While doing at least as much violence to the U.N. definition of genocide as he does to Lemkin's, all the while posturing himself as being consistent with the intent of both, Katz positions himself and his exclusivist cohorts to twist the whole of history to their own ends. The record of Jewish suffering

---

[*] This seems singularly odd, since the Jews as a group were slated by the nazis for sterilization during the 1930s, and many were subjected to ugly experiments—radiation, drugs and surgical techniques—for purposes of perfecting mass-sterilization techniques; *The Nazi Connection, op. cit.*, pp. 51–3, 58, 126, n. 62; *The Nazi Doctors, op. cit.*, pp. 22–44. The reason underlying this "oversight" undoubtedly resides in the fact that, as a group, homosexuals—another group falling under Katz's new gender category—were marked for universal sterilization by the nazis; Richard Plant, *The Pink Triangle: The Nazi War Against Homosexuals* (New York: New Republic/Henry Holt, 1986). By utterly ignoring sterilization as a technique of genocide, even in the erroneously restrictive sense of eradicating gene pools, Katz is able to restrict his consideration of antigay policies to killing programs directed against them in medieval times. Astonishingly, he is thereby able to arrive at not only the conclusion that homosexuals were never subjected to genocide, but that they actually experienced "nonoppression"; *The Holocaust in Historical Context, op. cit.*, pp. 514–24.

[†] "Cultural Genocide: What the Holocaust Is Not," ibid., pp. 139–46. It is worth noting that Katz readily concedes at p. 139 that "cultural genocide is an all-too-well-known historical category. The history of civilization is literally littered with attempts to eliminate various determinate sociopolitical (and religious) identities." In effect, were he to stick with Lemkin's and/or the legal definitions of genocide, rather than manufacturing one of his own, the Holocaust would be anything but unique.

is "adjusted" to conform uniquely to the Katzian formula.* That of all others is deformed to the extent that they fall outside it.[†] In its fully perfected form, exclusivism is thereby intended to become an hegemony, a seamless, self-validating and virtually unassailable mythic system in the Gramscian sense.[46]

To this end, exclusivism lays claim not just to holding an outright monopoly on scholarly correctitude while advancing its blatant distortions, it claims to do so by absolute moral right. Any comparison of the experience of another people to that of the Jews under Hitler represents, in the words of Deborah Lipstadt, both "the most vile sort of anti-Semitism" and the attempt to establish an "immoral equivalency."[47] While there may be no qualitative distinction between the two, it seems fair to observe that the project of Holocaust deniers is far less ambitious and, to that extent at least, quantitatively less demonstrative of sheer sophistry than that of Holocaust exclusivists like Lipstadt and Steven Katz.

Exclusivist Motivations

The factors motivating exclusivists to conduct themselves as they do have been analyzed elsewhere. They concern the agenda of establishing a "truth" which serves to compel permanent maintenance of the privileged political status of Israel, the Jewish state established on Arab land in 1947 as an act of international atonement for the Holocaust;[‡] to forge a secular reinforcement, based in the myth of unique suffering, of Judaism's theological belief in itself as comprising a "special" or "chosen" people, entitled to all the

---

*Examples of this in Katz's work are legion, but the most breathtaking example is that of Yehuda Bauer, completely ignoring the fact that about one-third of Europe's Jews survived the Holocaust, and over two-thirds worldwide, asserts that "total physical annihilation...is what *happened* to the Jews" (emphasis added); "Holocaust and Genocide: Some Comparisons," in Peter Hayes, ed., *Lessons and Legacies: The Meaning of the Holocaust in a Changing World* (Evanston, IL: Northwestern University Press) p. 40.

†A good illustration is Katz's "The Pequot War Reconsidered" (*New England Quarterly*, No. 64, 1991) in which he argues that at most, the Indians suffered "*cultural* genocide [since] the number killed probably totaled less than half the tribe (emphasis in the original)." But, then again, perhaps it totaled a little more: say, two-thirds. Either way, the killing was done in the context of a stated intent by the killers to exterminate *all* Pequots, placing it well within even Katz's own definition of genocide; *Facing West, op. cit.*

‡As Zygmunt Bauman has observed, Israel deploys the *Shoah* as "the certificate of its political legitimacy, a safe-conduct pass for its past and future policies, and above all as the advance payment for the injustices it might commit"; *Modernity and the Holocaust* (Cambridge: Polity Press, 1989) p. ix. It has been so from the outset, as is evidenced by the declaration of the first conference of Jewish survivors in Germany during July 1945, demanding "the immediate establishment of a Jewish state in Palestine"; quoted in Yahil, *The Holocaust, op. cit.*, p. 660.

prerogatives of such;[48] and to construct a conceptual screen behind which to hide the realities of Israel's ongoing genocide against the Palestinian population whose rights and property were usurped in its very creation.[49]

What prompts the intellectual status quo of much of the rest of the world to buy into such a thoroughly dishonest enterprise is less immediately evident. Although the particulars of motivation undoubtedly vary somewhat from place to place, group to group, or even from individual to individual, it seems likely that, overall, there is a perverse confluence of interests involved. Insofar as the academic elites of other countries accept the claims of Holocaust exclusivism at face value, they are presented with an automatic exemption from having to come to grips with the implications that they are themselves bound up, not just in the legacy of multitudinous genocides past, but also in avoiding for the most part their obligations to confront and put a stop to their societies' perpetration of genocides present.[50] Instead, they can entitle themselves to continue conjuring the endless triumphalist fantasies— themselves smacking of genocidal intent—that have shaped the Western canon for centuries.[51] As James Axtell, emergent dean of American "ethno-historians," has rather crudely framed it:

> The...problem with "genocide" as a description of, or even analogy to, the post-Columbian loss of Indian life is that the moral onus it tries to place on European colonists, equating them with the Nazi S.S., is largely misdirected and inappropriate... [We] make a hash of our historical judgements because we continue to feel guilty about the real or imagined sins of our fathers and forefathers and people to whom we have no relation whatsoever: Despite the result to universalizing labels such as "Imperialism" and "Colonialism," most of the battles of the sixteenth and seventeenth centuries are behind us... [We] can stop flogging ourselves with our "imperialistic" origins and tarring ourselves with the broad brush of "genocide." As a huge nation of law and order and increasingly refined sensibility, *we* are not guilty of murdering Indian women and babies, of branding slaves on the forehead, or of claiming any real estate in the world we happen to fancy.[52]

"We should recognize," Axtell sums up, "that to condemn every aggressive military, religious or economic action in the past is to question some of the fundaments of Western society, past and present."[53] One can readily imagine a German historian/apologist advancing an exactly similar argument a century or two after a World War II nazi victory (indeed, more than a few began making it less than 50 years after Germany's *defeat*).[54] To this, the best response probably remains that penned by Raphaël Lemkin at the end of World War II: "The entire problem of genocide needs to be dealt with as a whole; it is too important to be left for piecemeal discussion and solution in the future. Many hope there will be no more wars, but we dare not rely on mere hopes for protection against genocidal practices by ruthless conquerors... Moreover, we should not overlook the fact that genocide is a problem not only of war but of peace... That being the case, all countries must be concerned about such a problem, not only because of humanitarian, but also because of practical reasons affecting the interests of every country."[55] And, one might add, of all people.

It should go without saying that to combat and eliminate any sociopolitical phenomenon—most especially one bearing the malignantly functional utility of genocide—it is first necessary to understand it for what is. Exclusivism does nothing to promote development of genuine and constructive insights in this regard. Instead, it virtually precludes them. What seems most vitally necessary as an alternative and antidote to exclusivism is, as genocide scholar Vahakn Dadrian has so aptly put it, the kind of research and analysis that allows us to "discern patterns" in genocidal behavior.[56] Ultimately, this is the only means by which we may finally be enabled to apprehend genocides before rather than as or after they transpire, positioning ourselves at last to prevent them from happening.[57] To accomplish this, we clearly need far more, not fewer, serious comparative studies.

Notes

1. See, e.g., Paul Rassinier, *Debunking the Holocaust Myth: A Study of the Nazi Concentration Camps and the Alleged Extermination of European Jewry* (Torrance, CA: Institute for Historical Review, 1978); Harry Elmer Barnes, *The Barnes Trilogy: Three Revisionist Booklets by Harry Elmer Barnes, Historian, Sociologist, Criminologist, Economist* (Torrance, CA: Institute for Historical Review, 1979); Austin App, *The Six Million Swindle: Blackmailing the German People for Hard Marks with Fabricated Corpses* (Tacoma Park, MD: Noontide Press, 1974); David Leslie Hoggan, *The Myth of the Six Million* (Tacoma Park, MD: Noontide Press, 1969); Richard Harwood, *Did Six Million Really Die? The Truth at Last* (Richmond Surrey: Historical Review Press, 1974); David Irving, *Hitler's War* (London and New York: Macmillan, 1977); Arthur R. Butz, *The Hoax of the Twentieth Century: The Case Against the Presumed Extermination of European Jewry* (Torrance, CA: Institute for Historical Review, 1976); Robert Faurisson, "The Problem of Gas Chambers," *Journal of Historical Review*, Summer 1980.

2. Deborah Lipstadt, *Denying the Holocaust: The Growing Assault on Truth and Memory* (New York: Free Press, 1993) pp. 1102, 14, 141, 157–70, 219–22; Pierre Vidal-Niquet, *Assassins of Memory: Essays on the Denial of the Holocaust* (New York: Columbia University Press, 1992).

3. There are, as is demonstrated in note 24 below, numerous examples in the literature of works arriving at this conclusion. One excellent example is George M. Kren and Leon Rappoport, *The Holocaust and the Crisis of Human Behavior* (New York: Holmes & Meier, 1980).

4. Bernal Díaz del Castillo, *The Discovery and Conquest of Mexico, 1517–1521* (London: George Routledge & Sons, 1928); Miguel Leon-Portilla, ed., *The Broken Spears: The Aztec Account of the Discovery of Mexico* (Boston: Beacon Press, 1962).

5. Juan A. Villamarin and Judith E. Villamarin, *Indian Labor in Mainland Colonial Spanish America* (Newark, DL: University of Delaware Press, 1975); William L. Sherman, *Native Forced Labor in Sixteenth Century Central America* (Lincoln: University of Nebraska Press, 1979).

6. Basil Davidson, *The African Slave Trade* (Boston: Little, Brown, [revised ed.] 1980); Joseph E. Inikori and Stanley L. Engerman, eds., *The Atlantic Slave Trade: Effects on Economies, Societies, and Peoples, in Africa, the Americas, and Europe* (Durham: Duke University Press, 1992).

7. James Axtell, "The Rise and Fall of the Powhatan Empire," in his *After Columbus: Essays in the Ethnohistory of North America* (New York: Oxford University Press, 1988); Richard Drinnon, *Facing West: The Metaphysics of Indian Hating and Empire Building* (Minneapolis: University of Minnesota Press, 1980) pp. 35–45.

8. On Amherst, see E. Wagner Stearn and Allen E. Stearn, *The Effects of Smallpox on the Destiny of the American Indian* (Boston: Bruce Humphries, 1945) pp. 44–5; on the Mandans, see Russell Thornton, *American Indian Holocaust and Survival: A Population History Since 1492* (Norman: University of Oklahoma Press, 1987) pp. 94–6.

9. David Svaldi, *Sand Creek and the Rhetoric of Extermination: A Case Study in Indian-White Relations* (Lanham, MD: University Press of America, 1989); Lyndall Ryan, *The Aboriginal Tasmanians* (St. Lucia: University of Queensland Press, 1981); L.F.S. Upton, "The Extermination of the Beothuks of Newfoundland," *Canadian Historical Review*, No. 58, 1977.

10. Richard G. Hovannisian, ed., *The Armenian Genocide in Perspective* (New Brunswick, NJ: Transaction Books, 1986); *The Armenian Genocide: History, Politics, Ethics* (New York: St. Martin's Press, 1992).

11. Deirdre Griswold, *Indonesia: The Bloodbath That Was* (New York: World View, 1975); Jules Gerard-Libois, *Katanga Secession* (Madison: University of Wisconsin Press, 1966); Peter Schwab, ed., *Biafra* (New York: Facts on File, 1971); Kalyan Yatindra, *Genocide in Bangladesh* (Bombay: Orient Longman, 1972); René Lemarchand and David Martin, *Selective Genocide in Burundi* (London: Minority Rights Group Report No. 20, 1974).

12. Michael Vickery, *Cambodia, 1975–1982* (London: Allen & Unwin, 1984); John G. Taylor, *Indonesia's Forgotten War: The Hidden History of East Timor* (London: Zed Books, 1991); Ed Vulliamy, "Middle Managers of Genocide," *The Nation*, June 10, 1996; Gérard Prunier, *The Rwanda Crisis: History of a Genocide* (New York: Columbia University Press, 1995).

13. For implications, see George Steiner, "The Long Life of Metaphor: A Theological-Metaphysical Approach to the *Shoah*," in Asher Cohen, et al., eds., *Comprehending the Holocaust: Historical Research* (New York: Peter Lang, 1988).

14. Richard C. Lukas, *Forgotten Holocaust: The Poles Under German Occupation, 1939–1944* (Lexington: University of Kentucky Press, 1986).

15. Although he sets the death toll rather lower, based on preliminary data, one of the best explications of what was done in the U.S.S.R. remains Alexander Dallin's *German Rule in Russia, 1941–1945: A Study of Occupation Policies* (New York: St. Martin's Press, 1957).

16. Nazi law actually held the Sinti and Romani to far stricter biological standards than it did the Jews for purposes of determining who was to die. See Donald Kenrick and Grattan Puxon, *The Destiny of Europe's Gypsies* (New York: Basic Books, 1972) pp. 67, 85; Angus Fraser, *The Gypsies* (Oxford: Blackwell, 1992) p. 260. Also see Benno Müller-Hill, *Murderous Science: Elimination by Scientific Selection of Jews, Gypsies, and Others, 1933–1945* (New York: Oxford University Press, 1988).

17. Christopher Shea, "Debating the Uniqueness of the Holocaust," *Chronicle of Higher Education*, May 31, 1996; Alan S. Rosenbaum, *Is the Holocaust Unique? Perspectives in Comparative Genocide* (Boulder, CO: Westview Press, 1996).

18. Steven T. Katz, *The Holocaust in Historical Context, Vol. 1: The Holocaust and Mass Death Before the Modern Age* (New York: Oxford University Press, 1994). The 702-page tome is projected to be followed by two more equally ponderous volumes by the end of the decade.

19. Shea, *op. cit.* Stannard, a professor in the American Studies Department at the University of Hawaii/Manoa, is author of *American Holocaust: Columbus and the Conquest of the New World* (New York: Oxford University Press, 1992).

20. Shea, "Debating the Uniqueness," *op. cit.*

21. Ibid. For Katz on Arendt, see *Holocaust in Historical Context, op. cit.*, pp. 49–50, 54, 398; on Nolte, pp. 23–6, 54; on Stannard, p. 18.

22. Examples abound. For a succinct overview, see Paul Berman, ed., *Debating P.C.: The Controversy Over Political Correctness on College Campuses* (New York: Laurel Books, 1992).

23. Butz, *The Hoax of the Twentieth Century, op. cit.*

24. Whatever disagreements they share among them—and these are many—George M. Kren, Leon Rappoport, Deborah Lipstadt, Seymore Drescher, Barbara B. Green, Asher Cohen, Zev Garber and Bruce Zuckerman, Philip Friedman, Dennis Prager and Joseph Telushkin, Yehuda Bauer, Anthony Polonsky, John Roth and Michael Berenbaum, Sebastian Haffner, Gerd Korman, Raul Hilberg, Irving Abrahamson, Elie Wiesel, Michael R. Marrus, Lucy Dawidowicz, Léon Poliakov, Edward Alexander, Martin Gilbert, Henry Feingold, Arthur A. Cohen, Saul Friedländer, Nathan Rotenstreich, Helen Fein, Alice and A. Roy Eckhardt, Tal Uriel, Gerald Reitlinger, Jacob Robinson, Arad Yitzak, Alan Rosenberg, Leni Yahil, Emil Fackenheim, Menachem Rosensaft, Israel Gutman, and the entire establishment of the American Holocaust Memorial Museum are salient in this respect. See, e.g., Kren and Rappoport, *op. cit.*; Lipstadt, *op. cit.*; Drescher and Green in Rosenbaum, *op. cit.*; Asher Cohen, et al., *op. cit.*; Zev Garber and Bruce Zuckerman, "Why Do We Call the Holocaust 'The Holocaust'? An Inquiry Into the Psychology of Labels," *Modern Judaism*, Vol. 9, No. 2, 1989; Philip Friedman, *Roads to Extinction: Essays on the Holocaust* (New York & Philadelphia: Jewish Publication Society of America, 1980); Dennis Prager and Joseph Telushkin, *Why the Jews? The Reason for Antisemitism* (New York: Simon and Schuster, 1983); Yehuda Bauer, *The Holocaust in Historical Perspective* (Seattle: University of Washington Press, 1978) and *A History of the Holocaust* (New York: Franklin Watts, 1982); Anthony Polonsky, "Introduction" to Michael Burleigh and Wolfgang Wipperman, *The Racial State: Germany, 1933–45* (Cambridge: Cambridge University Press, 1991); John Roth and Michael Berenbaum, *Holocaust: Religious and Philosophical Implications* (New York: Paragon House, 1989); Gerd Korman, "The Holocaust in Historical Writing," *Societas*, Vol. 2, No. 3, 1972; Raul Hilberg, *The Destruction of the European Jews* (New York: Holmes and Meier, [3rd ed.] 1985); Irving Abrahamson, ed., *Against Silence: The Voice and Vision of Elie Wiesel* (New York: Holocaust Society, 1985) esp. Vol III, p. 314; Michael R. Marrus, *The Holocaust in History* (Hanover, NH: Brandeis University Press and University Press of New England, 1987); Sebastian Haffner, *The Meaning of Hitler* (New York: Macmillan, 1979); Lucy S. Dawidowicz, *The War Against the Jews, 1933–1945* (New York: Holt, Rinehart and Winston, 1975); *The Holocaust and the Historians* (Cambridge: Harvard University Press, 1981) and "The Holocaust was Unique in Intent, Scope, and Effect," *Center Magazine*, July–August 1981; Léon Poliakov, *Harvest of Hate: The Nazi Program for the Destruction of the Jews of Europe* (Syracuse, NY: Syracuse University Press, 1954); Edward Alexander, *The Holocaust and the War of Ideas* (New Brunswick, NJ:

Transaction, 1994) and "Stealing the Holocaust," *Midstream*, November 1980; Martin Gilbert, *The Holocaust: A History of the Jews of Europe During the Second World War* (New York: Henry Holt, 1985); Henry Feingold, "How Unique Is the Holocaust?" in Alex Grobman and Daniel Landes, eds., *Genocide: Critical Issues of the Holocaust* (Los Angeles: Rossell, 1983); Arthur A. Cohen, *The Tremendium: A Theological Interpretation of the Holocaust* (New York: Holmes & Meier, 1981); Saul Friedländer, "On the Possibility of the Holocaust: An Approach to Historical Synthesis," in Yehuda Bauer and Nathan Rosenstreich, eds., *The Holocaust as Historical Experience* (New York: Quadrangle, 1981); Helen Fein, *Accounting for Genocide: National Responses and Jewish Victimization during the Holocaust* (New York: Free Press, 1979). Alice and A. Roy Eckhardt, "The Holocaust and the Enigma of Uniqueness: A Philosophical Effort at Practical Clarification," *Annals of the American Academy of Political and Social Science*, No. 45, July 1980; Tal Uriel, "On the Study of the Holocaust and Genocide," *Yad Vashem Studies*, No. 13, 1979; Gerald Reitlinger, *The Final Solution: The Attempt to Exterminate the Jews of Europe* (New York: Barnes, 1971); Jacob Robinson, *And the Crooked Shall Be Made Straight: The Eichmann Trial, the Jewish Catastrophe, and Hannah Arendt's Narrative* (New York: Macmillan, 1965); Arad Yitzak, *Belzec, Sobibór, Treblinka: The Operation Reinhart Death Camps* (Bloomington: Indiana University Press, 1987); Alan Rosenberg, "Was the Holocaust Unique? A Peculiar Question," in Isador Walliman and Michael N. Dobkowski, eds., *Genocide and the Modern Age: Etiology and Case Studies of Mass Death* (New York: Greenwood Press, 1987) and "An Assault on Western Values," *Dimension*, Spring 1985; Leni Yahil, *The Holocaust: The Fate of European Jewry, 1932–1945* (New York: Oxford University Press, 1990); Emil Fackenheim, *To Mend the World: Foundations of Future Jewish Thought* (New York: Holmes & Meier, 1982) and "Forward" in Yehuda Bauer, *The Jewish Emergence from Powerlessness* (London: Macmillan, 1979); Menachem Rosensaft, "The Holocaust: History as Aberration," *Midstream*, May 1977; Israel Gutman, ed., *Encyclopedia of the Holocaust* (New York: Macmillan, 1990); Michael Berenbaum, *The World Must Know: The History of the Holocaust as Told by the American Holocaust Memorial Museum* (Boston: Little, Brown, 1993). Also see Liz McMillen, "The Uniqueness of the Holocaust," *Chronicle of Higher Education*, June 22, 1994.

The fact that everyone included in the list above is Jewish is not to suggest that there are not Jewish Holocaust scholars who oppose exclusivism, many of them strongly. Among the more prominent individuals and works have been the following: Hannah Arendt, *The Origins of Totalitarianism* (Cleveland: World, [2nd ed.] 1958) and *Eichmann in Jerusalem: A Report on the Banality of Evil* (New York: Penguin, 1964); Irving Louis Horowitz, *Taking Lives: Genocide and State Power* (New Brunswick, NJ: Transaction, [3rd ed.] 1982); Israel Charny, *How Can We Commit the Unthinkable? Genocide, the Human Cancer* (Boulder: Westview Press, 1982); Richard Rubenstein, *The Cunning of History: The Holocaust and the American Future* (New York: Harper & Row, 1978) and *The Age of Triage: Fear and Hope in an Overcrowded World* (Boston: Beacon Press, 1983); Pierre Papazian, "A 'Unique Uniqueness'?" *Midstream*, Vol. 30, No. 4, April 1984; Jacob Neusner, *Stranger at Home: "The Holocaust," Zionism and American Judaism* (Chicago: University of Chicago Press, 1981); Leo Kuper, *Genocide: Its Political Uses in the Twentieth Century* (New Haven, CT: Yale University Press, 1981); Michael Berenbaum, *A Mosaic of Victims: Non-Jews Persecuted and Murdered by the Nazis* (New York: New York University Press, 1990). Noam Chomsky would also certainly fit the mold, although he's not addressed the topic directly. Interestingly, Elie Wiesel, a career exclusivist before and after, joins the ranks of comparativists at least by virtue of his concession during the mid-1970s that Paraguay's contemporaneous extermination of the Aché Indians was genocide; "Now We Know," in Richard Arens, ed., *Genocide in Paraguay* (Philadelphia: Temple University Press, 1976).

25. Katz's other significant efforts in this connection include "The 'Unique' Intentionality of the Holocaust," *Modern Judaism*, Vol. 1, No. 2, September 1981; and *Post-Holocaust Dialogues: Critical Studies in Modern Jewish Thought* (New York: New York University Press, 1983).

26. *Holocaust in Historical Context, op. cit.*, p. 129. It should be noted that precisely this misrepresentation of Lemkin has been generally picked up by many varieties of denier, including those with no discernable interest in otherwise promoting Jewish interests; see, e.g., James Axtell, *Beyond 1492: Encounters in Colonial North America* (New York: Oxford University Press, 1992) p. 261: "As you know, the word was coined in 1944 to describe the infamous Nazi attempts to annihilate the Jews…"

27. Raphaël Lemkin, *Axis Rule in Occupied Europe: Laws of Occupation, Analysis of Government, Proposals for Redress* (Washington, D.C.: Carnegie Endowment for International Peace, 1944).

28. Ibid., pp. 196–7.

29. Under "Blood Protection" provisions of the so-called "Nuremberg Laws," effected by the nazis in September 1935, Jews were expressly forbidden, under pain of severe criminal penalty, to intermarry or procreate with "Aryans" and vice versa; Stefan Kühl, *The Nazi Connection: Eugenics, American Racism, and German National Socialism* (New York: Oxford University Press, 1994) pp. 97–8.

30. *Axis Rule in Europe, op. cit.*, pp. 138–9, 213, 236–7.

31. Ibid., pp. 143, 249, 260–1.

32. Ibid., p. 79.

33. Ibid., pp. 79–98.

34. *The Holocaust in Historical Context, op. cit.*, p. 129, n.14.

35. Ibid., pp. 129–30, n. 15.

36. *Axis Rule in Europe, op. cit.*, p. 81.

37. Ibid., pp. 21–2.

38. Ibid., p. 89. Lemkin's citation is from *Hitler's Ten-Year War Against the Jews* (New York: Institute of Jewish Affairs of the American Jewish Congress, World Jewish Congress, 1943) p. 307.

39. *Axis Rule in Occupied Europe, op. cit.*, p. 89. The source quoted is a Joint Declaration of the United Nations dated December 17, 1942; reprinted in *The United Nations Review*, Vol. III, No. 1, 1943, p. 1.

40. *Axis Rule in Occupied Europe, op. cit.*, p. 82.

41. Ibid., p. 79.

42. *The Holocaust in Historical Context, op. cit.*, p. 131. Axtell (*Beyond 1492, op. cit.*, p. 261) again trots right along: "The latest and most inclusive definition of *genocide* is simply 'a form of one-sided *mass* killing in which a *state* or other authority intends to destroy a group, as a group and membership in it are defined by the *perpetrator*' (emphasis in the original)."

43. The complete text of the convention will be found in Ian Brownlie, ed., *Basic Documents on Human Rights* (Oxford: Clarendon Press, [3rd ed.] 1988) pp. 31–4. For background and analysis, see Jeffrey Gayner, "The Genocide Treaty," *Journal of Social and Political Studies*, No. 2, Winter 1977.

44. *The Holocaust in Historical Context, op. cit.*, pp. 125–7.

45. The Soviets, primarily because of the manner in which Stalinism had dealt with such aggregates during its consolidation of power and crash industrialization of the U.S.S.R., blocked inclusion of these group categories in the convention; see, e.g., Nikolai Dekker and Andrei Lebed, eds., *Genocide in the U.S.S.R.: Studies in Group Destruction* (New York: Scarecrow Press, 1958); Robert Conquest, *The Nation Killers: The Soviet Deportation of Nationalities* (New York: Macmillan, 1970); Walter Dishnyck, *Fifty Years Ago: The Famine Holocaust in the Ukraine* (New York and Toronto: World Congress of Free Ukrainians, 1980); Lyman H. Letgers, "The Soviet Gulag: Is It Genocidal?" in *Toward the Understanding and Prevention of Genocide, op. cit.*

46. See, e.g., Walter L. Adamson, *Hegemony and Revolution: A Study of Antonio Gramsci's Political and Cultural Theory* (Berkeley: University of California Press, 1980).

47. *Denying the Holocaust, op. cit.*, pp. 212–5. Such treatment is not reserved exclusively for gentiles. Hannah Arendt, to name a prominent Jewish example, was subjected to extraordinary vilification— widely described as a "self-hating Jewess," among many less polite epithets—after writing her decisively nonexclusivist *Eichmann in Jerusalem (op. cit.)*. For the best overview, see Dwight Mcdonald, "Hannah Arendt and the Jewish Establishment," in his *Discrimination: Essays and Afterthoughts* (New York: Grossman, 1974).

48. John Murray Cuddly, "The Holocaust: The Latent Issue in the Uniqueness Debate," in Philip F. Gallagher, ed., *Christians, Jews and Other Worlds: Patterns of Conflict and Accommodation* (Lanham, MD: University Press of America, 1988).

49. See, e.g., Michael Palumbo, *The Palestinian Catastrophe: The 1948 Expulsion of a People from their Homeland* (London: Faber & Faber, 1987); Noam Chomsky, *The Fateful Triangle: The United States, Israel and the Palestinians* (Boston: South End Press, 1983). Marc H. Ellis, *Beyond Innocence and Redemption: Confronting the Holocaust and Israeli Power* (New York: Harper & Row, 1990); Edward Said, *The Question of Palestine* (New York: Vintage 1992).

50. The dynamic more broadly at issue is handled exceedingly well by Roger W. Smith, Eric Markusen, and Robert Jay Lifton in "Professional Ethics and the Denial of the Armenian Genocide," *Holocaust and Genocide Studies*, No. 9, 1995.

51. See generally, Martin Carnoy, *Education as Cultural Imperialism* (New York: David McKay, 1974); Henry A. Giroux, *Ideology, Culture and the Process of Schooling* (Philadelphia: Temple University Press, 1981); Page Smith, *Killing the Spirit: Higher Education in America* (New York: Penguin, 1990).

52. Axtell, *Beyond 1492, op. cit.*, pp. 262–3.

53. Ibid., pp. 231–2.

54. See, e.g., Charles S. Maier, *The Unmasterable Past: History, Holocaust, and German National Identity* (Cambridge: Harvard University Press, 1988).

55. *Axis Rule in Europe, op. cit.*, pp. 92–3.

56. Quoted in Shea, "Debating the Uniqueness," *op. cit.*

57. This is precisely the perspective guiding some of the best of the extant comparative volumes. See, e.g., *Toward the Understanding and Prevention of Genocide, op. cit.*; *Genocide and the Modern Age, op. cit.*; Leo Kuper, *The Prevention of Genocide* (New Haven, CT: Yale University Press, 1985); Frank Chalk and Kurt Jonassohn, *The History and Sociology of Genocide: Analyses and Case Studies* (New Haven: Yale University Press, 1990); Israel W. Charny, *Genocide: A Critical Bibliography* (New York and London: Facts on File/Mansell, 1988).

DECONSTRUCTING THE COLUMBUS MYTH

Was the "Great Discoverer" Italian or Spanish, Nazi or Jew?

> Christopher Columbus was a genuine titan, a hero of history
> and of the human spirit...To denigrate Columbus is to deni-
> grate what is worthy in human history and in us all.
>
> —Jeffrey Hart
> *National Review*

IT is perhaps fair to say that our story opens at Alfred University where, during the fall of 1990, I served as distinguished scholar of American Indian Studies for a program funded by the National Endowment for the Humanities. Insofar as I was something of a curiosity in that primarily Euroamerican-staffed and -attended institution, situated as it is within an area populated primarily by white folk, it followed naturally that I quickly became a magnet for local journalists seeking to inject a bit of color into their columns and commentaries. Given our temporal proximity to the much-heralded quincentennial celebration of Christopher Columbus' "discovery" of a "New World" and its inhabitants, and that I am construed as being in some part a direct descendant of those inhabitants, they were wont to query me as to my sentiments concerning the accomplishments of the Admiral of the Ocean Sea.

My response, at least in its short version, was (and remains) that celebration of Columbus and the European conquest of the Western Hemisphere he set off is greatly analogous to celebration of the glories of nazism and Heinrich Himmler. Publication of this remark in local news-papers around Rochester, New York caused me to receive, among other things, a deluge of lengthy and vociferously framed letters of protest, two of which are worthy of remark.

The first of these was sent by a colleague at the university, an exchange faculty member from Germany, who informed me that while the human costs begat by Columbus' navigational experiment were "tragic and quite regrettable," comparisons between him and the Reichsführer SS were nonetheless unfounded. The distinction between Himmler and Columbus, his argument went, resided not only in differences in "the magnitude of the genocidal events in which each was involved," but the *ways* in which they were involved. Himmler, he said, was enmeshed as "a high-ranking and responsible official in the liquidation of entire human groups" as "a matter of formal state policy" guided by an explicitly "racialist" ideology. Furthermore, the enterprise Himmler created as the instrument of his genocidal ambitions incorporated, deliberately and intentionally, considerable economic benefit to the state in whose service he acted. None of this pertained to Columbus, the good professor concluded, because the "Great Discoverer" was ultimately "little more than a gifted seaman," an individual who unwittingly set in motion processes over which he had little or no control, in which he played no direct part, and which might well have been beyond his imagination. My juxtaposition of the two men, he contended, therefore tended to "diminish understanding of the unique degree of evil" which should be associated with Himmler and ultimately precluded "proper historical understandings of the Nazi phenomenon."

The second letter came from a member of the Jewish Defense League in Rochester. His argument ran that, unlike Columbus (whom he described as "little more than a bit player, without genuine authority or even much of a role, in the actual process of European civilization in the New World which his discovery made possible"), Himmler was a "responsible official in a formal state policy of exterminating an entire human group for both racial and economic reasons," and on a scale "unparalleled in all history." My analogy between the two, he said, served to "diminish public respect for the singular nature of the Jewish experience at the hands of the Nazis," as well as popular understanding of "the unique historical significance of the Holocaust." Finally, he added, undoubtedly as a crushing capstone to his position, "It is a measure of your anti-semitism that you compare Himmler to Columbus" because "Columbus was, of course, himself a Jew."

I must confess the last assertion struck me first, and only partly because I'd never before heard claims that Christopher Columbus was of Jewish ethnicity. "What possible difference could this make?" I asked in my letter of reply. "If Himmler himself were shown to have been of Jewish extraction, would it then suddenly become antisemitic to condemn him for the genocide he perpetrated against Jews, Gypsies, Slavs and others? Would his historical crimes then suddenly be unmentionable or even 'okay'?" To put it another way, I continued, "Simply because Meyer Lansky, Dutch Schultz, Bugsy Siegel, and Lepke were all Jewish 'by blood,' is it a gesture of anti-semitism to refer to them as gangsters? Is it your contention that an individual's Jewish ethnicity somehow confers exemption from negative classification or criticism of his/her conduct? What *are* you saying?" The question of Columbus' possible Jewishness nonetheless remained intriguing, not because I held it to be especially important in its own right, but because I was (and am still) mystified as to why any ethnic group, especially one which has suffered genocide, might be avid to lay claim either to the man or to his legacy. I promised myself to investigate the matter further.

A Mythic Symbiosis

Meanwhile, I was captivated by certain commonalities of argument inherent to the positions advanced by my correspondents. Both men exhibited a near-total ignorance of the actualities of Columbus' career, and neither one demonstrated any desire to correct the situation. Indeed, in their mutual need to separate the topic of their preoccupation from rational scrutiny, they appeared to have conceptually joined hands in a function composed more of faith than fact. It seems that the whole notion of the "uniqueness of the Holocaust" serves both psychic and political purposes for Jew and German alike. The two groups are bound to one another in a truly symbiotic relationship founded in the mythic exclusivity of their experience: one half of the equation simply completes the other in a perverse sort of collaboration, with the result that each enjoys a tangible benefit.

For Jews, at least those who have adopted the zionist perspective, a "unique historical suffering" under nazism translates into fulfillment of a biblical prophecy that they are "the chosen," entitled by virtue of their destiny of special persecution to assume a rarified status among the remainder of humanity. To this end, zionist scholars such as Yehuda Bauer and Elie Wiesel have labored long and mightily, defining genocide in terms exclusively related to the forms it assumed under nazism.[1] Conversely, they have coined terms such as "ethnocide" to encompass the fates inflicted upon other peoples throughout history.[2] Such semantics have served, not as tools of understanding, but as an expedient means of arbitrarily differentiating the experience of their people—both qualitatively and quantitatively—from that of any other. To approach things in any other fashion would, it must be admitted, tend to undercut ideas like the "moral right" of the Israeli settler state to impose itself directly atop the Palestinian Arab homeland.

For Germans to embrace a corresponding "unique historical guilt" because of what was done to the Jews during the 1940s, is to permanently absolve themselves of guilt concerning what they may be doing *now*. No matter how ugly things may become in contemporary German society, or so the reasoning goes, it can *always* be (and is) argued that there has been a marked improvement over the "singular evil which was nazism." Anything other than outright nazification is, by definition, "different," "better" and therefore "acceptable" ("Bad as they are, things could always be worse"). Business as usual—which is to say assertions of racial supremacy, domination and exploitation of "inferior" groups, and most of the rest of the nazi agenda —is thereby free to continue in a manner essentially unhampered by serious stirrings of guilt among the German public *so long as it does not adopt the literal trappings of nazism*. Participating for profit and with gusto in the deliberate starvation of much of the Third World is no particular problem if one is careful not to goose-step while one does it.

By extension, insofar as Germany is often seen (and usually sees itself) as exemplifying the crowning achievements of "Western Civilization," the same principle covers all European and Euro-derived societies. No matter what they do, it is never "really" what it seems unless it was done in precisely the fashion the nazis did it. Consequently, the nazi master plan of displacing or reducing by extermination the population of the western U.S.S.R. and replacing it with settlers of "biologically superior German breeding stock" is roundly (and rightly) condemned as ghastly and inhuman. Meanwhile, people holding this view of nazi ambitions tend overwhelmingly to see consolidation and maintenance of Euro-dominated settler states in places like Australia, New Zealand, South Africa, Argentina, the United States, and Canada as "basically okay," or even as "progress." The "distinction" allowing this psychological phenomenon is that each of these states went about the intentional displacement and extermination of native populations, and their replacement, in a manner that was different in its particulars from that employed by nazis attempting to accomplish exactly the same thing. Such technical differentiation is then magnified and used as a sort of all purpose veil behind which almost anything can be hidden, so long as it is not openly adorned with a swastika.

Given the psychological, sociocultural, and political imperatives involved, neither correspondent, whether German or Jew, felt constrained to examine the factual basis of my analogy between Himmler and Columbus before denying the plausibility or appropriateness of the comparison. To the contrary, since the paradigm of their mutual understanding embodies the *a priori* presumption that there *must be no such analogy,* factual investigation is precluded from their posturing. It follows that any dissent on the "methods" involved in their arriving at their conclusions, never mind introduction of countervailing evidence, must be denied out of hand with accusations of "overstatement," "shoddy scholarship," "stridency," and/or "antisemitism." To this litany have lately been added such new variations as "white bashing," "ethnic McCarthyism," "purveyor of political correctitude," and any other epithet deemed helpful in keeping a "canon of knowledge" fraught with distortion, deception, and outright fraud from being "diluted."[3]

Columbus as Protonazi

It is time to delve into the substance of my remark that Columbus and Himmler, nazi *Lebensraumpolitik* and the "settlement of the New World" bear more than casual resemblance to one another. It is not, as my two correspondents wished to believe, because of his "discovery." This does not mean that if this were "all" he had done he would be somehow innocent of what resulted from his find, no more than is the scientist who makes a career of accepting military funding to develop weapons in any way "blameless" when they are subsequently used against human targets. Columbus did not sally forth upon the Atlantic for reasons of "neutral science" or altruism. He went, as his own diaries, reports, and letters make clear, fully expecting to encounter wealth belonging to others. It was his stated purpose to seize this wealth, by whatever means necessary and available, in order to enrich both his sponsors and himself.[4] Plainly, he prefigured, both in design and intent, what came next. To this extent, he not only symbolizes the process of conquest and genocide which eventually consumed the indigenous peoples of America, but bears the personal responsibility of having participated in it. Still, if this were all there was to it, I might be inclined to dismiss him as a mere thug rather than branding him a counterpart to Himmler.

The 1492 "voyage of discovery" is, however, hardly all that is at issue. In 1493 Columbus returned with an invasion force of seventeen ships, appointed at his own request by the Spanish Crown to install himself as "viceroy and governor of [the Caribbean islands] and the mainland" of America, a position he held until 1500.[5] Setting up shop on the large island he called Española (today Haiti and the Dominican Republic), he promptly instituted policies of slavery (*encomiendo*) and systematic extermination against the native Taino population.[6] Columbus' programs reduced Taino numbers from as many as eight million at the outset of his regime to about three million in 1496.[7] Only 100,000 were left by the time of the governor's departure in 1500. His policies, however, remained, with the result that by 1514 the Spanish census of the island showed barely 22,000 Indians still alive. In 1542, only two hundred were recorded.[8] Thereafter, they were considered extinct, as were Indians throughout the Caribbean Basin, an aggregate population which totalled more than fifteen million at the point the Columbian adventure began.[9]

This constitutes an attrition of population *in real numbers* every bit as great as the toll of twelve to fifteen million—about half of them Jewish— most commonly attributed to Himmler's slaughter mills. Moreover, the proportion of the indigenous Caribbean population destroyed by the Spanish in a single generation is, no matter how the figures are twisted, far greater than the 75 percent of European Jews usually said to have been exterminated by the nazis.[10] Worst of all, these data apply *only* to the Caribbean Basin; the process of genocide in the Americas was only just beginning at the point such statistics become operant, not ending, as it did upon the fall of the Third Reich. All told, it is probable that more than one hundred million native people were "eliminated" in the course of Europe's ongoing "civilization" of the western hemisphere.[11]

It has long been asserted by "responsible scholars" that the decimation of American Indians which accompanied the European invasion resulted primarily from disease rather than direct killing or conscious policy.[12] There is a certain truth to this, although starvation may have proven just as lethal in the end. It must be borne in mind when considering such facts that a considerable portion of those who perished in the nazi death camps died, not as the victims of bullets and gas, but from starvation, as well as epidemics of typhus, dysentery, and the like. Their keepers, who could not be said to have killed these people directly, were nonetheless found to have been culpable in their deaths by deliberately imposing the conditions which led to the proliferation of starvation and disease among them.[13] Certainly, the same can be said of Columbus' regime, under which the original residents were, as a first order of business, permanently dispossessed of their abundant cultivated fields while being converted into chattel, ultimately to be worked to death for the wealth and "glory" of Spain.[14]

Nor should more direct means of extermination be relegated to incidental status. As the matter is framed by Kirkpatrick Sale in his book, *The Conquest of Paradise:*

> The tribute system, instituted by the Governor sometime in 1495, was a simple and brutal way of fulfilling the Spanish lust for gold while acknowledging the Spanish distaste for labor. Every Taino over the age of fourteen had to supply the rulers with a hawk's bell of gold every three months (or, in gold-deficient areas, twenty-five pounds of spun cotton); those who did were given a token to wear around their necks as proof that they had made their payment; those who did not were, as [Columbus' brother, Fernando] says discreetly, "punished"—by having their hands cut off, as [the priest, Bartolomé de] Las Casas says less discreetly, and left to bleed to death.[15]

It is entirely likely that upwards of 10,000 Indians were killed in this fashion on Española alone, as a matter of policy, during Columbus' tenure as governor. Las Casas' *Brevísima relación,* among other contemporaneous sources, is also replete with accounts of Spanish colonists (*hidalgos*) hanging Tainos *en masse,* roasting them on spits or burning them at the stake (often a dozen or more at a time), hacking their children into pieces to be used as dog food and so forth, all of it to instill in the natives a "proper attitude of respect" toward their Spanish "superiors."

> [The Spaniards] made bets as to who would slit a man in two, or cut off his head at one blow; or they opened up his bowels. They tore the babes from their mother's breast by their feet and dashed their heads against the rocks...They spitted the bodies of other babes, together with their mothers and all who were before them, on their swords.[16]

No SS trooper could be expected to comport himself with a more unrelenting viciousness. And there is more. All of this was coupled to wholesale and persistent massacres:

> A Spaniard...suddenly drew his sword. Then the whole hundred drew theirs and began to rip open the bellies, to cut and kill [a group of Tainos assembled for this purpose] —men, women, children and old folk, all of whom were seated, off guard and frightened... And within two credos, not a man of them there remains alive. The Spaniards enter the large house nearby, for this was happening at its door, and in the same way, with cuts and stabs, began to kill as many as were found there, so that a stream of blood was running, as if a great number of cows had perished.[17]

Elsewhere, Las Casas went on to recount how:

> In this time, the greatest outrages and slaughterings of people were perpetrated, whole villages being depopulated...The Indians saw that without any offense on their part they were despoiled of their kingdoms, their lands and liberties and of their lives, their wives, and homes. As they saw themselves each day perishing by the cruel and inhuman treatment of the Spaniards, crushed to earth by the horses, cut in pieces by swords, eaten and torn by dogs, many buried alive and suffering all kinds of exquisite tortures [many surrendered to their fate, while the survivors] fled to the mountains [to starve].[18]

The butchery continued until there were no Tainos left to butcher. One might well ask how a group of human beings, even those like the Spaniards of Columbus' day, maddened in a collective lust for wealth and prestige, might come to treat another with such unrestrained ferocity over a sustained period. The answer, or some substantial portion of it, must lie in the fact that the Indians were considered by the Spanish to be *Untermenschen,* subhumans. That this was the conventional view is borne out beyond all question in the recorded debates between Las Casas and the nobleman, Juan Ginés de Sepúlveda, who argued for the majority of Spaniards that American Indians, like African blacks and other "lower animals," lacked "souls." The Spaniards, consequently, bore in Sepúlveda's estimation a holy obligation to enslave and destroy them wherever they might be encountered.[19] The eugenics theories of nazi "philosopher" Alfried Rosenberg, to which Heinrich Himmler more or less subscribed, elaborated the mission of the SS in very much the same terms.[20] It was upon such profoundly racist ideas that Christopher Columbus grounded his policies as the first governor of the new Spanish empire in America.[21]

In the end, all practical distinctions between Columbus and Himmler —at least those not accounted for by differences in available technology and extent of sociomilitary organization—evaporate upon close inspection. They are cut of the same cloth, fulfilling precisely the same function and for exactly the same reasons, each in his own time and place. If there is one differentiation which may be valid, it is that while the specific enterprise Himmler represented ultimately failed and is now universally condemned, that represented by Columbus did not and is not. Instead, as Sale has observed, the model for colonialism and concomitant genocide Columbus pioneered during his reign as governor of Española was to prove his "most enduring legacy," carried on "by the conquistadors in their invasions of Mexico, Peru, and La Florida."[22] The Columbian process is ongoing, as is witnessed by the fact that, today, his legacy is celebrated far and wide.

The Emblematic European

This leaves open the question as to whom, exactly, the horror which was Columbus rightly "belongs." There are, as it turns out, no shortage of contenders for the mantle of the man and his "accomplishments." It would be well to examine the nature of at least the major claims in order to appreciate the extent of the mad scramble which has been undertaken by various peoples to associate themselves with what was delineated in the preceding section. One cannot avoid the suspicion that the spectacle bespeaks much of the Eurocentric character.

Was Columbus Italian?

The popular wisdom has always maintained that Christopher Columbus was born in Genoa, a city-state in what is now called Italy. Were this simply a historical truth, it might be accepted as just one more uncomfortable fact of life for the Italian people, who are—or should be—still trying to live down what their country did to the Libyans and Ethiopians during the prelude to World War II. There is much evidence, however, militating against Columbus' supposed Genoese origin. For instance, although such records were kept at the time, there is no record of his birth in that locale. Nor is there reference to his having been born or raised there in any of his own written work, including his personal correspondence. For that matter, there is no indication that he either wrote or spoke any dialect which might be associated with Genoa, or even the Tuscan language which forms the basis of modern Italian. His own writings—not excluding letters penned to Genoese friends and the Banco di San Grigorio, one of his financiers in that city—were uniformly articulated in Castilian, with a bit of Portuguese and Latin mixed in.[23] Moreover, while several variations of his name were popularly applied to him during his lifetime, none of them was drawn from a dialect which might be considered Italian. He himself, in the only known instance in which he rendered his own full name, utilized the Greek *Xρõual de Colón*.[24] Still, Genoa, Italy, and those of Italian descent elsewhere in the world (Italoamericans, most loudly of all) have mounted an unceasing clamor during the twentieth century, insisting he *must* be theirs. Genoa itself invested considerable resources into "resolving" the question during the 1920s, ultimately printing a 288-page book assembling an array of depositions and other documents—all of them authenticated—attesting that Columbus was indeed Genoese. Published in 1931, the volume, entitled *Christopher*

Columbus: Documents and Proofs of His Genoese Origin, presents what is still the best circumstantial case as to Columbus' ethnic identity.[25]

Spanish?

Counterclaims concerning Columbus' supposed Iberian origin are also long-standing and have at times been pressed rather vociferously. These center primarily in the established facts that he spent the bulk of his adult life in service to Spain, was fluent in both written and spoken Castilian, and that his mistress, Beatriz Enríquez de Arana, was Spanish.[26] During the 1920s, these elements of the case were bolstered by an assortment of "archival documents" allegedly proving conclusively that Columbus was a Spaniard from cradle to grave. In 1928, however, the Spanish Academy determined that these documents had been forged by parties overly eager to establish Spain's exclusive claim to the Columbian legacy. Since then, Spanish chauvinists have had to content themselves with arguments that the Discoverer is theirs by virtue of employment and nationality, if not by birth. An excellent summary of the various Spanish contentions may be found in Enrique de Gandia's *Historia de Cristóbal Colón: analisis crítico,* first published in 1942.[27]

Portuguese?

Portuguese participation in the fray has been less pronounced, but follows basically the same course—*sans* forged documents—as that of the Spanish. Columbus, the argument goes, was plainly conversant in the language and his wife, Felipa Moniz Perestrello, is known to have been Portuguese. Further, the first point at which his whereabouts can be accurately determined, was in service to Portugal, plying that country's slave trade along Africa's west coast for a period of four years. Reputedly, he was also co-proprietor of a book and map shop in Lisbon and/or Madeira for a time, and once sailed to Iceland on a voyage commissioned by the Portuguese Crown. Portugal's desire to extend a serious claim to Spain's Admiral of the Ocean Sea seems to be gathering at least some momentum, as is witnessed in Manuel Luciano de Silva's 1989 book, *Columbus Was 100% Portuguese.*[28]

Jewish?

The idea that Columbus might have been a Spanish Jew is perhaps best known for having appeared in Simon Wiesenthal's *Sails of Hope* in 1973.[29] Therein, it is contended that the future governor of Española hid his ethnicity because of the mass expulsion of Jews from Spain ordered by King Ferdinand of Aragon on March 30, 1492 (the decree was executed on August 2 of the same year). Because of this rampant antisemitism, the Great Navigator's true identity has remained shrouded in mystery, lost to the historical record. Interestingly, given the tenacity with which at least some sectors of the Jewish community have latched on to it, this notion is not at all Jewish in origin. Rather, it was initially developed as a speculation in a 1913 article, "Columbus a Spaniard and a Jew?" published by Henry Vignaud in the *American History Review*.[30] It was then advanced by Salvador de Madariaga in his unsympathetic 1939 biography, *Christopher Columbus*. Madariaga's most persuasive argument, at least to himself, seems to have been that Columbus' "great love of gold" proved his "Jewishness."[31] This theme was resuscitated in Brother Nectario María's *Juan Colón Was a Spanish Jew* in 1971.[32] Next, we will probably be told that *The Merchant of Venice* was an accurate depiction of medieval Jewish life, after all. And, from there, that the International Jewish Bolshevik Banking Conspiracy really exists, and has since the days of the Illuminati takeover of the Masonic Orders. One hopes the JDL doesn't rally to defense of these "interpretations" of history as readily as it jumped aboard the "Columbus as Jew" bandwagon.[33]

Other Contenders

By conservative count, there are at present 253 books and articles devoted specifically to the question of Columbus' origin and national/ethnic identity. Another 300-odd essays or full volumes address the same questions to some extent while pursuing other matters.[34] Claims to his character, and some imagined luster therefrom, have been extended not only by the four countries already discussed, but by Corsica, Greece, Chios, Majorca, Aragon, Galicia, France, and Poland.[35]

In the final analysis, it is patently clear that we really have no idea who Columbus was, where he came from, or where he spent his formative years. It may be that he was indeed born in Genoa, perhaps of some "degree of Jewish blood," brought up in Portugal, and ultimately nationalized as a citizen of Spain, Province of Aragon. Perhaps he also spent portions of his childhood being educated in Greek and Latin while residing in Corsica, Majorca, Chios, or all three. Maybe he had grandparents who had immigrated from what is now Poland and France. It *is* possible that each of the parties now vying for a "piece of the action" in his regard are to some extent correct in their claims. And, to the same extent, it is true that he was actually *of* none of them in the sense that they mean it. He stands, by this definition, not as an Italian, Spaniard, Portuguese or Jew, but as the penultimate European of his age, the emblematic personality of all that Europe was, had been, and would become in the course of its subsequent expansion across the face of the earth.

As a symbol, then, Christopher Columbus vastly transcends himself. He stands before the bar of history and humanity, culpable not only for his deeds on Española, but, in spirit at least, for the carnage and cultural obliteration which attended the conquests of Mexico and Peru during the 1500s. He stands as exemplar of the massacre of Pequots at Mystic in 1637, and of Lord Jeffrey Amherst's calculated distribution of smallpox-laden blankets to the members of Pontiac's confederacy a century and a half later. His spirit informed the policies of John Evans and John Chivington as they set out to exterminate the Cheyennes in Colorado during 1864, and it road with the 7th U.S. Cavalry to Wounded Knee in December of 1890. It guided Alfredo Stroessner's machete-wielding butchers as they strove to eradicate the Aché people of Paraguay during the 1970s, and applauds the policies of Brazil toward the Jivaro, Yanomami, and other Amazon Basin peoples at the present moment.

And, the ghost of Columbus stood with the British in their wars against the Zulus and various Arab nations, with the United States against the "Moros" of the Philippines, the French against the peoples of Algeria and Indochina, the Belgians in the Congo, the Dutch in Indonesia. He was there for the Opium Wars and the "secret" bombing of Cambodia, for the systematic slaughter of the indigenous peoples of California during the nineteenth century and of the Mayans in Guatemala during the 1980s. And, yes, he was very much present in the corridors of nazi power, present among the guards and commandants at Sobibór and Treblinka, and within the ranks of the *Einsatzgruppen* on the Eastern Front. The Third Reich was, after all, never so much a deviation from as it was a crystallization of the dominant themes—racial supremacism, conquest, and genocide—of the European culture Columbus so ably exemplifies. Nazism was never unique: it was instead only one of an endless succession of "New World Orders" set in motion by "the Discovery." It was neither more nor less detestable than the order imposed by Christopher Columbus upon Española; 1493 or 1943, they are part of the same irreducible whole.

The Specter of Hannibal Lecter

At this juncture, the entire planet is locked, figuratively, in a room with the sociocultural equivalent of Hannibal Lecter. An individual of consummate taste and refinement, imbued with indelible grace and charm, he distracts his victims with the brilliance of his intellect, even while honing his blade. He is thus able to dine alone upon their livers, his feast invariably candlelit, accompanied by lofty music and a fine wine. Over and over the ritual is repeated, always hidden, always denied in order that it may be continued. So perfect is Lecter's pathology that, from the depths of his scorn for the inferiors upon whom he feeds, he advances himself as their sage and therapist, he who is incomparably endowed with the ability to explain their innermost meanings, he professes to be their savior. His success depends upon being embraced and exalted by those upon whom he preys. Ultimately, so long as Lecter is able to retain his mask of omnipotent gentility, he can never be stopped. The spirit of Hannibal Lecter is thus at the core of an expansionist European "civilization" which has reached out to engulf the planet.

In coming to grips with Lecter, it is of no useful purpose to engage in sympathetic biography, to chronicle the nuances of his childhood and catalogue his many and varied achievements, whether real or imagined. The recounting of such information is at best diversionary, allowing him to remain at large just that much longer. More often, it inadvertently serves to perfect his mask, enabling him not only to maintain his enterprise, but to pursue it with ever more arrogance and efficiency. At worst, the biographer is aware of the intrinsic evil lurking beneath the subject's veneer of civility, but—because of morbid fascination and a desire to participate vicariously—deliberately obfuscates the truth in order that his homicidal activities may continue unchecked. The biographer thus reveals not only a willing complicity in the subject's crimes, but a virulent pathology of his or her own. Such is and has always been the relationship of "responsible scholarship" to expansionist Europe and its derivative societies.

The sole legitimate function of information compiled about Lecter is to unmask him and thereby lead to his apprehension. The purpose of apprehension is not to visit retribution upon the psychopath—he is, after all, by definition mentally ill and consequently not in control of his more lethal impulses—but to put an end to his activities. It is even theoretically possible that, once he is disempowered, he can be cured. The point, however, is to understand what he is and what he does well enough to stop him from doing it. This is the role which must be assumed by scholarship vis-à-vis Eurosupremacy, if scholarship itself is to have any positive and constructive meaning. Scholarship is *never* "neutral" or "objective"; it *always* works either for the psychopath or against him, to mystify sociocultural reality or to decode it, to make corrective action possible or to prevent it.

It may well be that there are better points of departure for intellectual endeavors to capture the real form and meaning of Eurocentrism than the life, times, and legacy of Christopher Columbus. Still, since Eurocentrists the world over have so evidently clasped hands in utilizing him as a (perhaps *the*) preeminent signifier of their collective heritage, and are doing so with such an apparent sense of collective jubilation, the point has been rendered effectively moot. Those who seek to devote their scholarship to apprehending the psychopath who sits in our parlor thus have no alternative but to use him as a primary vehicle of articulation. In order to do so, we must employ the analytical tools which allow him to be utilized as a medium of explanation, a way to shed light upon phenomena such as the mass psychologies of fascism and racism, a means to shear Eurocentrism of its camouflage, exposing its true contours, revealing the enduring coherence of the dynamics which forged its evolution.

Perhaps through such efforts we can begin to genuinely comprehend the seemingly incomprehensible fact that so many groups are queueing up to associate themselves with a man from whose very memory wafts the cloying stench of tyranny and genocide. From there, it may be possible to at last crack the real codes of meaning underlying the sentiments of the Nuremberg rallies, those spectacles on the plazas of Rome during which fealty was pledged to Mussolini, and that amazing red-white-and-blue, tie-a-yellow-ribbon frenzy gripping the U.S. public much more lately. If we force ourselves to see things clearly, we can understand. If we can understand, we can apprehend. If we can apprehend, perhaps we can stop the psychopath before he kills again. We are obligated to try, from a sense of sheer self-preservation, if nothing else. Who knows, we may even succeed. But first we must stop lying to ourselves, or allowing others to do the lying for us, about who it is with whom we now share our room.

Notes

1. See, for example, Yehuda Bauer, *The Holocaust in Historical Perspective* (Seattle: University of Washington Press, 1978) and Wiesel, Elie, *Legends of Our Time* (New York: Holt, Rinehart & Winston, 1968). The theme is crystalized in Manvell, Roger, and Heinrich Fraenkel, *Incomparable Crime; Mass Extermination in the 20th Century: The Legacy of Guilt* (London: Heinemannn Publishers, 1967).

2. See, as examples, Richard Falk, "Ethnocide, Genocide, and the Nuremberg Tradition of Moral Responsibility" in Virginia Held, Sidney Morganbesser and Thomas Nagel eds., *Philosophy, Morality, and International Affairs* (New York: Oxford University Press, 1974) pp. 123–37; Beardsley, Monroe C., "Reflections on Genocide and Ethnocide," in Richard Arens, ed., *Genocide in Paraguay* (Philadelphia: Temple University Press, 1976) pp. 85–101; and Robert Jaulin, *L'Ethnocide à travers Les Amériques* (Paris: Gallimard Publishers, 1972) and *La décivilisation, politique et pratique de l'ethnocide* (Brussels: Presses Universitaires de France, 1974).

3. Assaults upon thinking deviating from Eurocentric mythology were published with increasing frequency in U.S. mass circulation publications such as *Time, Newsweek, U.S. News and World Report, Forbes, Commentary, Scientific American* and the *Wall Street Journal* throughout 1990–91. A perfect illustration for our purposes here is Jeffrey Hart, "Discovering Columbus," *National Review,* October 15, 1990, pp. 56–7.

4. See Samuel Eliot Morrison,ed. and trans., *Journals and Other Documents on the Life and Voyages of Christopher Columbus* (New York: Heritage Publishers, 1963).

5. The letter of appointment to these positions, signed by Ferdinand and Isabella, and dated May 28, 1493, is quoted in full in Benjamin Keen, trans., *The Life of the Admiral Christopher Columbus by His Son Ferdinand* (Rutgers University Press, 1959) pp. 105–6.

6. The best sources on Columbus' policies are Troy Floyd, *The Columbus Dynasty in the Caribbean, 1492–1526* (Albuquerque: University of New Mexico Press, 1973) and Stuart B.,Schwartz, *The Iberian Mediterranean and Atlantic Traditions in the Formation of Columbus as a Colonizer* (Minneapolis: University of Minnesota Press, 1986).

7. Regarding the 8 million figure, see Sherburn F. Cook, and Woodrow Borah, *Essays in Population History,* Vol. I (Berkeley: University of California Press, 1971) esp. Chap. VI. The 3 million figure pertaining to the year 1496 derives from a survey conducted by Bartolomé de Las Casas in that year, covered in J.B. Thatcher, *Christopher Columbus,* Vol. 2 (New York: Putnam, 1903–1904) p. 348ff.

8. For summaries of the Spanish census records, see Lewis Hanke, *The Spanish Struggle for Justice in the Conquest of America* (Philadelphia: University of Pennsylvania Press, 1947) p. 200ff. Also see Salvador de Madariaga, *The Rise of the Spanish American Empire* (London: Hollis & Carter, 1947).

9. For aggregate estimates of the precontact indigenous population of the Caribbean Basin, see William Deneven, ed., *The Native Population of the Americas in 1492* (Madison: University of Wisconsin Press, 1976); Henry Dobyns, *Their Numbers Become Thinned: Native American Population Dynamics in Eastern North America* (Knoxville: University of Tennessee Press, 1983); and Russell Thornton, *American Indian Holocaust and Survival: A Population History Since 1492* (University of Oklahoma Press, 1987). For additional information, see Dobyns' bibliographic *Native American Historical Demography* (Bloomington: University of Indiana Press, 1976).

10. These figures are utilized in numerous studies. One of the more immediately accessible is Leo Kuper, *Genocide: Its Political Use in the Twentieth Century* (New Haven, CT: Yale University Press, 1981).

11. See Henry F. Dobyns, "Estimating American Aboriginal Population: An Appraisal of Techniques with a New Hemispheric Estimate," *Current Anthropology,* No. 7, pp. 395–416.

12. An overall pursuit of this theme will be found in P.M. Ashburn, *The Ranks of Death* (New York: Coward Publishers, 1947). Also see John Duffy, *Epidemics in Colonial America* (Baton Rouge: Louisiana State University Press, 1953). Broader and more sophisticated articulations of the same idea are embodied in Alfred W. Crosby, Jr.,*The Columbia Exchange: Biological and Cultural Consequences of 1492* (Westport, CT: Greenwood Press, 1972) and *Ecological Imperialism: The Biological Expansion of Europe, 900–1900* (Melbourne, Australia: Cambridge University Press, 1986).

13. One of the more thoughtful elaborations on this theme may be found in Bradley F. Smith, *Reaching Judgement at Nuremberg* (New York: Basic Books, 1977).

14. See Tzvetan Todorov, *The Conquest of America* (New York: Harper & Row Publishers, 1984).

15. Kirkpatrick Sale, *The Conquest of Paradise: Christopher Columbus and the Columbian Legacy* (New York: Alfred A. Knopf, 1990) p. 155.

16. Bartolomé de Las Casas, *The Spanish Colonie* [*Brevísima relación*], University Microfilms reprint, 1966.

17. Bartolomé de Las Casas, *Historia de las Indias,* Vol. 3, Augustin Millares Carlo and Lewis Hanke, eds. (Mexico City: Fondo de Cultura Económica, 1951) esp. Chap. 29.

18. Las Casas, quoted in Thatcher, *op. cit.,* pp. 348ff.

19. See Lewis Hanke, *Aristotle and the American Indians: A Study in Race Prejudice in the Modern World* (Chicago: Henry Regnery Company, 1959). Also see Rob Williams, *The American Indian in Western Legal Thought* (Oxford University Press, 1989).

20. The most succinctly competent overview of this subject matter is probably Robert Cecil, *The Myth of the Master Race: Alfred Rosenberg and Nazi Ideology* (New York: Dodd & Mead, 1972).

21. The polemics of Columbus' strongest supporters among his contemporaries amplify this point. See, for example, Oviedo, *Historia general y natural de las Indias,* Seville, 1535; Salamanca, 1547, 1549; Valladoid, 1557; Academia Historica, Madrid, 1851–55, esp. Chaps. 29, 30, 37.

22. Sale, *op. cit.,* p. 156.

23. On Columbus' written expression, see V.I. Milani, "The Written Language of Christopher Columbus," *Forum italicum,* 1973. Also see Cecil Jane, "The Question of Literacy of Christopher Columbus," *Hispanic American Historical Review,* Vol. 10, 1930.

24. On Columbus' signature, see Thatcher, *op. cit.,* p. 454.

25. City of Genoa, *Christopher Columbus: Documents and Proofs of His Genoese Origin* (Genoa: Instituto d'Arti Grafiche, 1931) English language edition, 1932.

26. José de la Torre, *Beatriz Enríquez de Harana* (Madrid: Iberoamericana, 1933).

27. Enrique de Gandia, *Historia de Cristóbal Colón: analisis crítico,* Buenos Aires, 1942.

28. Manuel Luciano de Silva, *Columbus Was 100% Portuguese,* Bristol, RI, (self published) 1989.

29. Simon Wiesenthal, *Sails of Hope* (New York: Macmillan, 1973).

30. Henry Vignaud, "Columbus a Spaniard and a Jew?", *American History Review,* Vol. 18, 1913. This initial excursion into the idea was followed in more depth by Francisco Martínez Martínez in his *El descubrimiento de América y las joyas de doña Isabel* (Seville, 1916) and Jacob Wasserman in *Christopher Columbus* (Berlin: S. Fisher, 1929).

31. Salvador de Madariaga, *Christopher Columbus* (London: Oxford University Press, 1939). His lead was followed by Armando Alvarez Pedroso in an essay, "Cristóbal Colón no fue hebero," *Revista de Historica de América,* 1942; and Antonio Ballesteros y Beretta in *Cristóbal Colón y el descubrimiento de América* (Barcelona/Buenos Aires: Savat, 1945).

32. Brother Nectario María, *Juan Colón Was a Spanish Jew* (New York: Cedney, 1971).

33. A much sounder handling of the probabilities of early Jewish migration to the Americas may be found in Meyer Keyserling, *Christopher Columbus and the Participation of the Jews in the Spanish and Portuguese Discoveries* (London: Longmans, Green, 1893 [reprinted, 1963]).

34. For a complete count, see Simonetta Conti, *Un secolo di bibliografia colombiana 1880–1985,* (Genoa: Cassa di Risparmio di Genova e Imperia, 1986).

35. These claims are delineated and debunked in Jacques Heers, *Christophe Columb* (Paris: Hachette, 1981).

GENOCIDE IN THE AMERICAS
Landmarks from "Latin" America, 1492–1992

> I become death, the scatterer of worlds.
>
> —*Bhagavad Gita*

ON October 12, 1492, the day Christopher Columbus first landed in what came to be called the "New World," the western hemisphere was inhabited by a population of well over 100 million people.[1] Two centuries later, it is estimated that the indigenous population of the Americas had been diminished by some 90 percent and was continuing to fall steadily.[2] In the United States, the native population bottomed out during the 1890s at slightly over 237,000—a 98-percent reduction from its original size.[3] Such extreme demographic catastrophe as that evidenced in the United States— indicative of a population "collapse" or "obliteration" rather than of mere "decline" —is not atypical.[4]

To the contrary, the average nadir population for surviving indigenous peoples everywhere in the Americas is about 5 percent (meaning we experienced a reduction of 97–98 percent during the history of invasion, conquest, and colonization which afflicted us all).[5] Moreover, the processes at issue cannot be relegated to some "tragic and regrettable"—but unalterable—past. Instead, they are very much *ongoing* as this is written, imbedded in the policies of the various settler-states of North, South, and Central America, and in the attitudes of the immigrant citizenry of these states.[6]

As I have noted often in my writing and public lectures, the genocide inflicted upon American Indians over the past five centuries is unparalleled in human history, both in terms of its sheer magnitude and in its duration. For the most part, with the exception of occasional forays into describing the real nature of the Columbian endeavor in the Caribbean, I have focused my attention, and that of my readers/listeners, on the genocide perpetrated on my own home ground of North America, mostly by Angloamericans. In this essay, I would like to break with that practice to some extent, laying out what I take to be a few of the landmarks of the post-Columbian record of genocide perpetrated to the south, in what is presumptuously termed "Latin" America, mostly by those of Iberian origin or descent.

Invasion and Conquest

> Into this sheepfold...there came some Spaniards who immediately behaved like ravening beasts... And Spaniards have behaved in no other way during the past forty years down to the present time, for they are still acting like ravening beasts, killing, terrorizing, afflicting, torturing and destroying the native peoples, doing all this with the strangest and most varied new methods of cruelty, never seen or heard of before.
>
> —Bartolomé de Las Casas

In 1519, when the Spanish conquistador, Hernán Cortés, captured the Mexica (Aztec) capital of Tenochtitlán—a huge metropolis constructed in the midst of a volcanic lake—he first laid siege and allowed a smallpox epidemic to run its course, weakening the city's defenses.[7] Then, after a series of assaults which resulted in the Indians being reduced to the point of almost complete defenselessness—"They no longer had nor could find any arrows, javelins or stones" with which to respond, his letters recount—he initiated the wholesale slaughter of those who surrendered, were captured, or who were simply trapped by his troops. Twelve thousand people, many of them noncombatants, were butchered in a single afternoon, another 40,000 the following day, before Cortés withdrew because he and his men "could no longer endure the stench of the dead bodies" that lay in the streets.[8]

When the Spaniards returned the next day, their commander surveyed his "starving, dehydrated, and disease-wracked" opponents, already decimated during the previous assaults, and announced his intent to "attack and slay them all."[9] By the time it was over, perhaps two-thirds of Tenochtitlán's population of about 350,000 was dead.[10]

> The people of the city had to walk upon their dead while others swam or drowned in the waters of that wide lake where they had their canoes; indeed, so great was their suffering that it was beyond our understanding how they came to endure it. Countless numbers of men, women and children came out towards us, and in their eagerness to escape many were pushed into the water where they drowned amidst that multitude of corpses; and it seemed that more than fifty thousand of them had perished from the salt water they had drunk, their hunger and the vile stench... And so in the streets where they were we came across such piles of the dead that we were forced to walk on them.[11]

By 1525, with the conquest of the Mexicas complete, one of Cortés' lieutenants, Pedro de Alvarado, mounted a campaign to the south, against the Mayans and other peoples of what are now the far southern portion of Mexico, as well as Guatemala, Belize, western Honduras and Nicaragua, and Panama. As Las Casas described it at the time, they "advanced killing, ravaging, burning, robbing and destroying all the country" as they went.[12]

> By massacres and murders…they have destroyed and devastated a kingdom more than a hundred leagues square, one of the happiest in the way of fertility and population in the world. This same tyrant [Alvarado] wrote that it was more populous than the kingdom of Mexico; and he told the truth. He and his brothers, together with the others, have killed more than four or five million people in fifteen or sixteen years, from the year 1525 until 1540, and they continue to kill and destroy those who are still left; and so they will kill the remainder.[13]

Northward from the former Mexica empire, things were much the same, or perhaps worse, during the period of conquest.

> Nuño Beltrán de Guzmán was one of those who led armies to the north, torturing or burning at the stake native leaders, such as the Tarascan king, while seizing or destroying enormous native stores of food. Guzmán later was followed by Alvar Nuñez Cabeza de Vaca, by Francisco Vásquez de Coronado, by Francisco de Ibarra, and countless other conquerors and murderers. As elsewhere, disease, depredation, enslavement, and outright massacres combined to extinguish entire Indian cultures in Mexico's northwest.[14]

Meanwhile, Francisco Pizarro's "Conquest of the Incas" in what are now called Peru and Chile, evidenced far less direct killing.[15] In no small part, this was because the conquistadors in this region managed to capture much of the Incan leadership very early on in their campaign, and developed certain methods of "convincing" them to betray their people.

> One ingenious European technique of getting what they wanted involved burying Indian leaders in earth up to their waists… In that helpless position, they were beaten with whips and [given instructions]… When they did not comply…more earth was piled about them and the whippings continued. Then more earth. And more beating. At last, says the Spanish informant on this particular matter, "they covered them to the shoulders and finally to the mouths. He then adds as an afterthought, "I even believe that a great number of natives were burned to death."[16]

By this point, the Portuguese had arrived in March of 1549, with Pedro Alvars Cabral's establishment of his first base of operations at the Bay of Bahía, on the coast of what is now Brazil. For the next decade, Cabral and his colleagues waged a brand of attritional warfare "which destroyed [the

"When the Spaniards had collected a great deal of gold from the Indians, they shut them up in three big houses, crowding in as many as they could, then set fire to the houses, burning alive all that were in them, yet those Indians had given no cause nor made any resistance."
—Bartolomé de Las Casas, *Destruction of the Indies*

natives] little by little," the survivors fleeing into the Amazonian interior.[17] As an unnamed priest explained in a subsequent report to the Church, it was a complete mismatch, the Portuguese, armed with swords and muskets, riding down thousands of unmounted Tupi and Tapuya warriors equipped only with bows and spears. Then "they razed and burned entire villages," the priest said, "which are generally made of dry palm leaves, roasting alive in them those that refused to surrender as slaves."[18] And so it went, area by area, region by region, until the preferred portions of America's southern hemisphere had been "subdued."[19]

Colonization

> Some of the *indias* even as late as the 1580s were being broken physically, their insides literally bursting under the heavy loads they had to carry. Unable to endure more, some of them committed suicide by hanging, starving themselves, or eating poisonous herbs. *Encomenderos* forced them to work in open fields where they tried to care for their children... Mothers occasionally killed their offspring at birth to spare them future agonies... [Others returned] home after weeks or months of separation from their children only to find that they had died or had been taken away.
>
> —William L. Sherman
> *Native Forced Labor*

Horrific as the processes of invasion and conquest must have been to those who suffered them, what came after was far more so, and vastly more consequential in terms of its impact on indigenous populations. In central Mexico, Cortés followed up his "triumph" at Tenochtitlán by establishing a colony dubbed "New Spain" and based on the most brutal use of Indians as slave labor.[20] The methods of pacification and conscription are instructive:

> Numerous reports, from numerous reporters, tell of Indians being led to the mines in columns, chained together at the neck, and decapitated if they faltered. Of children trapped and burned alive in their houses, or stabbed to death because they walked too slowly. Of the routine cutting off of women's breasts, and the tying of heavy gourds to their feet before tossing them to drown in lakes and lagoons. Of babies taken from their mothers' breasts, killed, and left as roadside markers. Of "stray" Indians dismembered and sent back to their villages with their chopped off hands and noses strung around their necks. Of "pregnant and confined women, children, old men, as many as they could capture," thrown into pits in which stakes had been imbedded and "left stuck on the stakes, until the pits were filled." And much, much more.[21]

Within the area of the former Mexica kingdom, the people, who numbered more than 25 million at the time of the conquistadors' arrival, were literally worked to death, mainly in mining and plantation enterprises.[22] According to the Spanish census of that year barely 1.3 million *indios* remained alive in the entire region by 1595.[23] To the north, where Beltrán de Guzmán and his ilk had ventured, it was no better.

> Among the region's Serrano culture groups, in barely more than a century the Tepehuán people were reduced in number by 90 percent; the Irritilla people by 93 percent; the Acaxee people by 95 percent. It took a little longer for the various Yaqui peoples to reach this level of devastation, but they too saw nearly 90 percent of their number perish, while for the varied Mayo peoples the collapse was 94 percent. Scores of other examples from this enormous area followed the same deadly pattern.[24]

To the south, the handiwork of Alvarado and his cohorts was equally evident. Overall, the population of southern Mexico, numbering about 1.7 million at the point of the invasion, dropped to less than a quarter-million over the next century and a half.[25] In Córdoba, on the Gulf of Mexico, the population fell by 97 percent during the century after Tenochtitlán was sacked. Off the coast, on the island of Cozumel, 96 percent of the population was eradicated. Inland, in the province of Jalapa, the die-off was 97 percent.[26] In the Yucatán, "the Spaniards pacified [the Indians of Cochua and Chetumal] in such a way that these provinces which were formerly the thickest settled and most populous, remained the most desolate in the country," recounted Bishop Diego de Landa.[27] Another observer, Alonso de Zorita, added that "certain birds that, when an Indian falls, pick out his eyes and kill and eat him; it is well known that these birds appear whenever the Spaniards make an incursion or discover a mine."[28] The litany goes on in Central America.

> By 1542 Nicaragua alone had seen the export of as many as half a million of its people for slave labor (in effect, a death sentence) in distant areas whose populations had been destroyed. In Panama, it is said, between the years 1514 and 1530 up to 2,000,000 Indians were killed... In the Cuchumatan Highlands of Guatemala the population fell by 82 percent within the first half-century following European contact, and by 94 percent—from 260,000 to 16,000—in less than a century and a half. In western Nicaragua, 99 percent of the people were dead (falling in number from more than 1,000,000 to less than 10,000) before sixty years had passed from the time of the Spaniards' initial appearance. In western and central Honduras, 95 percent of the people were exterminated in little more than a century.[29]

Still further south, in the Andes, where Pizarro's minions wielded the whips and swords, the population dropped from as many as 14 million before the invasion to barely a million by the end of the sixteenth century.[30] The manner of their dying was essentially the same as that of their cousins in Mexico and Central America. As one Spanish observer in Peru put it as early as 1539, "The Indians are being totally destroyed and lost... They [plead] with a cross to be given food for the love of God. [But the soldiers are] killing all the llamas they want for no greater need than to make tallow candles... The Indians are left with nothing to plant, and since they have no cattle and can never obtain any, they cannot fail to die of hunger."[31]

Simultaneously, massive numbers of the sick and starving people were impressed into slave labor on Spanish cocoa plantations, and in silver mines like that at Potosí, in Peru.[32] As Spanish officials estimated, "between a third and a half of the annual quota of cocoa workers died as a result of their five month service."[33] Those who survived were simply subjected to another stint, the cycle repeated again and again, until, as Spain's King Philip remarked in 1551, "an infinite number of Indians perish."[34] Both the scale and rate of death were in some ways as bound up in the attitudes of the colonizers towards native people as it was in the physical conditions they imposed upon them. Consider the following assessment by conquistador Pedro de Cieza de León:

> I would not condemn the employment of Indian [slaves]...but if a [Spaniard] had need of one pig, he killed twenty; if four Indians were wanted, he took a dozen...and there were many who made the poor Indians carry their whores on hammocks borne upon their shoulders. Were one ordered to enumerate the great evils, injuries, robberies, oppression, and ill treatment inflicted upon the natives during these operations...there would be no end of it...for they thought no more of killing Indians than if they were useless beasts.[35]

The silver mines were even worse, the very "mouth of hell," to quote Spanish chronicler Domingo de Santo Tomás.[36] "If twenty healthy Indians enter [a mine] on Monday," wrote Rodrigo de Loaisa in another first-hand account, "half may emerge crippled on Saturday."[37] More often, they did not emerge at all.

> Dropped down a shaft bored as far as 750 feet into the earth, taking with them only "some bags of roasted maize for their sustenance," observed [Loaisa], the miners remained below ground for a week at a time. There, in addition to the dangers of falling rocks, poor ventilation, and the violence of brutal overseers, as the Indian laborers chipped away at the rock faces of the mines they released and inhaled the poisonous vapors of cinnabar, arsenic, anhydride, and mercury... For as long as there appeared to be an unending supply of brute labor it was cheaper to work an Indian to death, and replace him or her with another native, than it was to feed and care for either of them

properly. It is probable, in fact, that the life expectancy of an Indian engaged in forced labor in a mine or on a plantation during these early years of Spanish terror in Peru was not much more than three or four months—about the same as that of someone working at slave labor in the synthetic rubber manufacturing plant at Auschwitz in the 1940s.[38]

The Portuguese, for their part, were proceeding apace in Brazil, primarily through development of the vast plantations which, by 1600, supplied the great bulk of Europe's sugar.[39] Such endeavors entailed equally vast applications of forced labor—over a third of a million Indians were held in bondage at the peak—obtained by slaving expeditions up the Amazon.[40]

> For the Indians brought to the slave markets of the coast, life was frightful. Families were broken up during the raids, and a large proportion of the men were killed. The women and children were taken down river in chains and sold. On the sugar plantations, they were forced to work seven days a week. The work was punishing. It required clearing and irrigating huge tracts of land, building mills, houses and roads, and cutting and pressing cane. Like the Indians who were subjected to the Spanish, the Indians of Brazil, by virtue of enforced labor and the onslaught of disease, suffered greatly. Not many survived.[41]

In fact, less than 10 percent of Brazil's preinvasion indigenous population of approximately 2.5 million lived into the seventeenth century.[42] "In the end," says one account, "things grew so bad that there was no one to make graves and some were buried in dunghills and around huts, but so badly that the pigs routed them."[43] By then, however, the Portuguese had begun the importation of the more than 3.5 million African slaves with which they not only expanded the plantation system, but diversified into timbering and large-scale cattle ranching.[44]

Notes on Genocide as Art and Recreation

> So that their flowers should live, they maimed and destroyed the flowers of others... Marauders by day, offenders by night, murderers of the world.
>
> —*Chilam Balam*

It would be inaccurate and unfair to suggest that life revolved exclusively around matters of commerce and industry for the Iberian colonists. They were, after all, resourceful people, capable of devising forms of entertainment for themselves, even in the midst of the "wilderness" they'd so recently invaded and conquered. One of the favorites, as was the case with Columbus' *hidalgos* on Española a bit earlier, had to do with wagering on the amount of damage which might be inflicted upon an unarmed Indian, often a child, with a single sword stroke.[45] Another commonality of entertainments between the earliest Spanish colonists in the Caribbean and their later mainland counterparts had to do with massacring entire villages, apparently for the sheer "sport" of it.[46]

In Central America, a new innovation, "dogging," shortly made its appearance. This had to do with setting vicious mastiffs and wolfhounds—raised on a diet of human flesh, trained to disembowel upon command, and often equipped with special armor—loose on hapless natives. This was sometimes done to captives in a betting situation, sometimes as a form of "hunting," sometimes in conjunction with pacification efforts, usually in some combination of the three.[47]

> A properly fleshed dog could pursue a "savage" as zealously and effectively as a deer or a boar... To many of the conquerors, the Indian was merely another savage animal, and the dogs were trained to rip apart their human quarry with the same zest as they felt when hunting wild beasts.[48]

In one account, the favorite dog of the noted conquistador Vasco Nuñez de Balboa ripped the head completely off the body of a Cuna leader in Panama, much to the glee of the entourage accompanying the owner of the "pet."[49] At another point, Balboa is recorded as having ordered the bodies of forty of his victims fed to his dogs.[50] In Peru, this practice was so common that Cieza de León found it not particularly remarkable that "a Portuguese named Roque Martin [regularly] had quarters of Indians hanging on his porch to feed his dogs with."[51]

Then there was the matter of sex. For all their supposedly devout Catholicism, the Iberians, Spanish and Portuguese alike, excelled at rape, forced concubinage, and compulsory prostitution. In part, this seems to have been a grotesque psychological stratagem to effect the final degradation and disempowerment of indigenous men as well as women; as a group of Dominican friars reported rather early on, when an enslaved native man emerged from the mines of Mexico at the end of a day, "not only was he beaten or whipped because he had not brought up enough gold, but further, most often, he was bound hand and foot and flung under the bed like a dog, before [a Spanish overseer] lay down, directly over him, with his wife."[52]

> These were just [adjuncts, however,] to the open trade in enslaved women that the Spanish delighted in as the decades wore on. Native women—or *indias*—were gambled away in card games and traded for objects of small value, while stables of them

were rented out to sailors who desired sexual accompaniment during their travels up and down the coast. If an *india* attempted to resist, she was whipped or tortured or burned alive. Even when laws were passed to curb the more extreme of such atrocities, the penalties were a joke. When, for example, an uncooperative Nicaraguan Indian woman was burned to death in her hut by a Spaniard who tried to rape her, he was prosecuted by the governor—and fined five pesos.[53]

Nor was travel neglected, especially of the adventurous and potentially profitable sort. For a long while, expeditions set out with a certain regularity from Peru, in search of a fabled *El Dorado* (City of Gold) believed by the Spanish to lie somewhere along the upper Amazon. "Some two or three hundred Spaniards go on these expeditions," Santo Tomás recorded, "[taking] two or three thousand Indians to serve them and carry their food and fodder… Few or no Indians survive, because of lack of food, the immense hardships of the long journeys through wastelands, and from the loads themselves."[54] Pizzaro himself was more direct in such matters: "When the Indians grew exhausted, they cut off their heads without untying them from their chains, leaving the roads full of bodies, with utmost cruelty."[55]

In sum, Iberian colonization on the American mainland equated to a complete dehumanization and devaluation of indigenous people in the minds of their conquerors. From that sprang the processes in which the native population was consumed, for reasons both systematically calculated and utterly sadistic, in numbers which are truly stupefying. All told, it is plausibly estimated that, from the Río Grande southward into Chile, as many as 80 million human beings were expended in the Spanish/Portuguese drive for wealth and imperial grandeur by the year 1700.[56]

Artistically, the holocaust attending the first two centuries of Iberian rule is still celebrated as a source of tremendous national/cultural pride throughout the "Hispanic" portion of America; paintings, murals, sculpture, and public statuary, much of it officially commissioned, continue to abound in commemoration of the immense "achievement" this "rich Spanish heritage" of rape, pillage, and slaughter invokes. Perhaps exemplary in this regard is the Montejo House in the city of Mérida, on the Yucatán peninsula, near the ancient Mayan centers at Uxmal and Chichén Itzá, locale of some of the worst atrocities of the mid-sixteenth century. There, one may stare in awe and admiration at a façade depicting in lavishly bold relief a pair of noble conquistadors, each of them casually resting a foot atop the severed head of a fallen Indian.[57]

The Maintenance and Expansion of Empire

> This man born in degradation, this stranger brought by slavery into our midst, is hardly recognized as sharing the common features of humanity. His face appears to us hideous, his intelligence limited, and his tastes low; we almost take him to be some intermediary between man and beast.
>
> —Alexis de Tocqueville

As the native populations under Iberian sway eroded like snow beneath an August sun, the intensity of killing necessarily abated. By and large, colonial regimes throughout South and Central America, as well as Mexico and the southwestern portion of the present-day United States, settled in to consolidating the New Order within their domains in accordance with rigid and often elaborate racial codes.

> Every mixture possible, starting from the three pure original racial types [ostensibly Caucasian, Black African and Indian], received its individual name. The terms *mestizo, mulato,* and *zambo* were of long standing, and need no further clarification. *Tercerón, cuarterón* (quadroon), and *quinterón* (quintroon) are self-explanatory. Peruvian Spanish still retains the terms *cholo* and *chino.* But who nowadays remembers the significance of such names as *castizo, morisco, lobo, jíbaro, albarazado, cambujo, barcino, puchel, coyote, chamiso, gálfarro, genizaro, grifo, jarocho,* and *sambago,* or the more picturesque *salta atrás, tente en aire, no te entiendo, ahí estés,* and so forth?[*]

The point is amplified by a portion of one such code, effective in eighteenth-century New Spain, which is illustrative of all such lists compiled in Iberian-occupied America.

1. Spaniard and Indian beget mestizo
2. Mestizo and Spanish woman beget castizo
3. Castizo woman and Spaniard beget Spaniard
4. Spanish woman and Negro beget mulatto
5. Spaniard and mulatto woman beget morisco
6. Morisco woman and Spaniard beget albino
7. Spaniard and albino woman beget torna atrás
8. Indian and torna atrás woman beget lobo
9. Lobo and Indian woman beget zambiago

---

[*] Nicolás Sánchez-Alboronoz, *The Population of Latin America: A History* (Berkeley: University of California Press, 1974) pp. 129–30. I say "ostensibly" in connection with the three "pure" racial classifications because many of the supposed Caucasians from Iberia actually weren't. Of the 200,000-odd "Spaniards" arriving in Mexico by 1570, for example, it has been estimated that about a third were actually of Moorish descent, another third Sephardic Jews who had converted to Catholicism ("*conversos*"); Peter Boyd-Bowman, *Patterns of Spanish Immigration to the New World, 1493–1580* (Buffalo: State University of New York Council on the Humanities, 1973).

10. Zambiago and Indian woman beget cambujo
11. Cambujo and mulatto woman beget albarazado
12. Albarazdo and mulatto woman beget barcino
13. Barcino and mulatto beget coyote
14. Coyote woman and Indian beget chamiso
15. Chamiso woman and mestizo beget coyote mestizo
16. Coyote mestizo and mulatto woman beget ahí te estás[58]

Indians were placed on the very bottom rung of these hierarchies, and were in many cases defined virtually out of existence.[59] Hence, the race codes were coupled directly to an ongoing process of dispossessing native people of their residual landbase, a matter more often accomplished by the eighteenth century through legalistic sleight-of-hand than by armed assault and physical eradication.[60] The two were never mutually exclusive propositions, however.

A prime example is that of the *reduccione* program inaugurated by the Chilean government in 1866, designed to constrict the Mapuche people of that country's southern region to certain specified tracts while opening up the remainder of their holdings to acquisition by members of the ruling Latino oligarchy. This led to the hard-fought Mapuche Revolt of 1880–1882, quelled by Chilean troops with such extreme violence that it has never again been attempted.[61]

> After the final defeat of the Mapuches, the *reducciones indigena*…were further reduced in size, the expropriated land being used to expand the haciendas. The Mapuches…retained less than 500,000 hectares of the 10 million hectares they had held before… Unable to support themselves on their now diminished lands, the Mapuches became a migrant labour force on the haciendas; the reservations became a reservoir of land and labour for the great landowners.[62]

There were, of course, occasional requirements to put down other native insurrections—that of the Mayas in Guatemala during the 1630s and '40s, for instance, the 1680 Pueblo Revolt in New Mexico, the insurgency led by the Manau leader Ajuricaba in Brazil during the mid-1700s, another headed by Túpac Amaru II in Peru in 1780, and several others—but these were mostly transient phenomena, quickly and bloodily suppressed.[63] Mexico also continued right into the twentieth century with its harsh campaigns to subdue the Yaquis and, to a somewhat lesser extent, the Apaches, but the areas concerned were considered to be of such marginal value by ruling elites that, while ferocious in their own right, they were not pursued with the vigor marking the Conquest proper.[64]

Sometimes, however, it was deemed important to expand the reach of empire into localities which had been previously ignored altogether. Then, the genocidal fury that had marked the performances of conquistadors like Cortés and Alvarado would be unleashed full force, albeit on a smaller scale. Such was the case in Argentina when, in 1879, General Julio Roca set out to seize the sprawling pampas south of Buenos Aires, and eventually all of Patagonia below the Río Negro.[65] The idea was to incorporate territory, much of it ideal for ranching, into the country's dominant *estanchieros* system, controlled by a handful of *caudillos* to whom Roca owed his position. The only obstacle was the existence of the Araucaño Indians, perhaps a half-million of them, who occupied the coveted terrain.[66]

> Roca's campaign, he said, was a civilizing mission, intended to bring scientists and engineers to the frontier. Indeed, Roca's army of 6,000 troops was to have the most modern technology available, including four pieces of heavy artillery. In addition, Roca ordered the construction of the first telegraph lines into the countryside, so that his orders could be carried immediately to the front... [Then he directed] lightning raids against unsuspecting villages, killing or imprisoning the inhabitants, seeking to sow terror through the tribes of the pampas. The battles were bloody. Often the Indians realized that their lances were no match for the soldiers' rifles and "they threw their lances to the ground and began to fight with us hand-to-hand, to grab the rifles out of our grasp." Many of the hand-to-hand battles ended with soldiers on horseback trampling fleeing Indians... Roca systematically exterminated the Indians. Vast *estancias* were established on what novelist V.S. Naipaul has called the "stolen, bloody land." Many of the *estancias* were allotted to the victorious generals. Roca himself was rewarded with the presidency.[67]

In the aftermath, surviving Araucaños were interned in concentration camps where many thousands more died of a measles epidemic. What remained were then placed on tiny *colonias* where starvation and disease continued to take a huge toll. In less than a generation these tiny reserves of Indian land were also dissolved, the pitifully small remnants of the Araucanians—fewer than 25,000 by some estimates—dispersed as subsistence labor in urban sweatshops or on the *estancias*.[68] As Naipal has observed, although Argentines tend to be pompous in their pride over an imagined martial prowess, theirs is really only "a simple history of Indian genocide and European takeover."[69] Thus, the Iberian tradition of inflicting the utmost lethal savagery upon the indigenous peoples of America has been maintained up until the present era.

Contemporary Latino Savagery

> I didn't know. But is it only an excuse? I can't think of any other. I didn't know that this evil was going on—was still going on. I didn't know that thirty years after the collapse of the Nazi regime, men and women were still living under its inhuman spell in a so-called free country... I am compelled to make this comparison, even though reluctantly. It is because, until now, I always forbade myself to compare the Holocaust of European Judaism to events which are foreign to it... There are here indications, facts which cannot be denied: it is indeed a matter of a Final Solution.
>
> —Elie Wiesel

These words were written by one of the best-known philosopher/ victims surviving the nazi-induced Holocaust during World War II, a long-time proponent of the "uniqueness of the Jewish experience" of genocide, after he finally consented to review documents concerning the ongoing extermination of the Aché Indians in Paraguay during the 1960s and '70s. After reviewing irrefutable evidence that perhaps 85 percent of the estimated 25,000 Achés still alive in 1959 had already been systematically hunted down and killed by teams of executioners operating under sanction of Paraguayan President Alfredo Stroessner—often dispatched with machetes to "save the expense of bullets"—Wiesel was moved to write that he "read and reread these documents, these testimonies, with a mixed feeling of horror, disgust, and shame."[70]

> These men, hunted, humiliated, murdered for the sake of pleasure; these young girls, raped and sold; these children, killed in front of their parents reduced to silence by pain... [The killers] aim at exterminating this tribe. Morally and physically. So that nothing will remain, not even a cry or a tear. Efficient technique, tested elsewhere. The individual is dragged away from his tribe, from his family, from his past. He is deprived of his strength, his dignity. And of his memory, too. He is diminished. He is forced to look at himself through the eyes of his enemy in order to become his own enemy, and thus wish his own death... Deculturation, ghettos, collective murders, and agonies: that in a country so near ours humans can still be locked with impunity inside stifling camps, can still be tracked down like wild beasts before being reduced to slavery, that husbands can be separated from their wives, children from their mothers, individuals from their language, their religion, their rituals, their songs and litanies, their tales, and their speech, that such torments can be inflicted on a free [people] which thirsts for poetry, torments which, in the past, were inflicted upon another people, this ought to baffle anyone who still believes in Man, in his conscience, and his possibility of survival.[71]

Unfortunately, for all the eloquence of his outrage, Wiesel understated the reality by nearly 100 percent. Not only did he overlook the entire genocidal sweep of history in Iberoamerica—a process of which the Aché slaughter is only the tiniest of recent parts—he managed to miss many contemporaneous examples as well. In 1979, the Fourth International Russell Tribunal was convened in Rotterdam to consider state crimes committed against the indigenous peoples of the western hemisphere. It concluded that in Colombia, for example, genocide was proceeding inexorably as the government, representing the perceived interests of 23 million Spanish-speaking citizens, sought to clear the country's remaining 179,000 Indians from what remained of their territory in the area of the Amazon headwaters.[72]

> The Russell Tribunal found the Colombian government guilty of violating international and [its] own laws in the expropriation of Purace land, and they found the multinational mining company Ceanese and its subsidiary Industrias Purace guilty of violating trade union, pollution, and safety agreements which they had signed in their occupation and exploitation of Purace land. The Tribunal collected evidence of forty-five resistance leaders murdered since 1971 in the Purace area alone. These crimes, however, were only indicative of a much larger government program to "de-Indianize" Colombia.[73]

The residue of Colombia's native population was being "virtually exterminated," a circumstance manifested in actions by both the public and private sectors of the dominant Latino society. The former is indicated by repeated reports of "Colombian navy riverboats [which] cruise the rivers, machine-gunning Indians on the bank."[74] As concerns the private sector, one illustration is that of Anselmo Aguirre and Marcelino Jiménez, a pair of white ranchers, who, in concert with a local policeman named Luis Enrique Morín, invited a group of Cuibas Indians to a "Christmas Feast" in 1967. They then used guns, machetes, clubs, and hatchets to slaughter sixteen of the nineteen Indians present, including an infant and five small children. In this case, there was actually a trial, at which it was admitted that the mass murder had occurred because the perpetrators desired their victims' land. The judge then ordered charges dismissed against the accused because "they did not know it was wrong to kill Indians" in Colombia.[75]

> The systematic extermination of indigenous populations in Colombia has [also] paralleled, predictably, the development plans of energy corporations and other corporate interests in the area. In 1960, a Texaco-Gulf oil consortium began exploration in southern Colombia; by 1968 they operated forty-seven productive wells and a 193-mile pipeline from the region to an oil terminal on the Pacific Coast. In 1970 the World Bank began a loan program to Colombia for development of the remote Amazon region. In March of 1979 the Colombian government under Julio Cesar Tabay signed

111

a $500 million contract with the National Uranium Company of Spain for the exploration of uranium in the southeastern province of Vaupes where the Guahibo Indians had been continuously hunted and slaughtered. In the southern province of Cauca, home of the Purace Indians…51,000 acres of the Indians' subsistence bean crop was reduced to 7,200 acres in the 1960s. During that same time, the multibillion-dollar international farm feeding company, Ralston Purina, had gained control of some 200,000 acres in the province for the production of chicken feed.[76]

In Brazil's Amazon Basin—where a 1972 *U.S. News and World Report* outline of development opportunities listed "soil deficiencies, tropical diseases, insects, and hostile Indian tribes" as being the major barriers to "progress"—the Russell Tribunal found solid evidence of ongoing genocide.[77] Spurred on by the profit incentives embodied in the region's deposits of uranium, bauxite, oil, gold, zinc, copper, nickel, titanium, coal, tin, and other minerals as well as lush timber potentials, the government had entered into "development" relationships with a host of transnational corporations, including Bethlehem Steel, Georgia Pacific, Royal Dutch Shell, Texaco, Gulf Oil, Cominco, Litton Industries, U.S. Steel, Komatsu, Caterpillar, Alcan, Rio Tinto Zinc, Westinghouse, Gulf & Western, and the W.R. Grace Company. The upshot was the beginning of a serious onslaught against the vast Amazon rainforest, vital to planetary ecology, and systematic eradication of the area's 100,000 remaining Indians.[78]

> The most isolated of the Amazon indigenous nations had been the Yanomami Indians until gold, diamonds, and uranium were discovered in their land in 1974. The Yanomami had already been pushed north by early [Portuguese] settlement and the rubber industry, and had established their home in the Branco River Valley, a remote Amazon tributary in the northernmost Brazilian province of Roraima. After the discovery of uranium in the area, the Brazilian government began cutting a road through 225 kilometers of Yanomami land. Fourteen of the southern villages were soon decimated by highway workers, vigilante raids, and disease. Population in the villages was reduced from 400 to 79 by 1975. In 1975 Fernando Ramos Periera, governor of Roraima Province, told the press that the area "is not able to afford the luxury of conserving a half-a-dozen Indian tribes who are holding back development." A 1972 report from the Reuters news service detailed the existence of hunting parties in the Amazon jungles which "murdered and raided the peaceful Indian tribes"… "On other occasions," reported Reuters, "planes bombarded the Indian villages with dynamite or dropped poisoned food into the villages."[79]

Even as the Yanomami, Jivaro, and other Amazonian peoples were being butchered or shunted onto tiny reservations, or "parks" as they are called in Brazil, Chilean military dictator Augusto Pinochet was completing the *reduccione* process imposed upon the Mapuches by his predecessors. On September 12, 1978, he announced "the promulgation in the near future of an act relating to indigenous property. This act…will enable those descendants [of the Mapuche "race"] voluntarily and freely to opt for private land ownership in those cases where they prefer this formula to the present system of community ownership."[80]

> In 1979 Pinochet's government introduced a law designed to divide the Mapuches' communally held lands and turn them into small holdings. The law facilitated the breakup by providing that any one member of an Indian community could require that the land be divided… The draft version of the 1979 law provided that once the land was divided among the Indians, the Indian landholders would no longer be considered to be Indians… Today, only twenty Mapuche reservations remain intact. The new civilian government has agreed to enact a law to stop further division, but given the drastic loss of land already incurred, this is more symbolism than anything else.[81]

In 1977, Antonio Millape, a Mapuche, testified before the United Nations on the methods by which the regime's objectives were already being achieved: "Go to any Mapuche home today, and you will find the dog outside will not bark, because it is too weak. If you go inside you will find one or more children lying sick, dying of starvation. There may be more children outside, and they will tell you their parents are not at home. Do not believe them. If you go inside you will find them, too, dying of starvation and extreme malnutrition. This is the form of extermination today, under Pinochet."[82] Millape also spoke of "torture, murder and the terror of…military death squads. Juan Condori Urichi, a Minka'a Indian from Bolivia spoke of similar atrocities against his people."[83] Delegates representing various indigenous peoples of South America have been testifying to the same effect—and usually providing extensive documentation to substantiate their statements—before the U.N.'s Working Group on Indigenous Populations every year since.[84]

> The stories of other Latin American Indian populations are similar, with local variations. Argentina, like Paraguay, has been ruled by the military, and has systematically exterminated most of the indigenous population; 200,000 survive in a population of 23 million. Uruguay has virtually eliminated all Indians within its borders… In Peru, Quechua-Aymara Andean Indians make up about half of the 11 million population; their land has been continually eroded by forest, oil, and mining industries. Development pressures in Ecuador, Venezuela, Guyana, and Surinam have, likewise, driven the indigenous populations from their traditional lands. The same is true in Central America, from Panama to Mexico.[85]

Actually, in Central America things may be even worse. It has been reliably estimated that, since the overthrow of democratic President Jacobo Arbenz in a CIA-backed coup in 1954, a succession of military governments headed by men like Fernando Lucas García, Efraín Rios Mott, and Mejía Victores have slaughtered somewhere between 100,000 and 150,000 highland Mayans in the country's northern provinces. Another quarter-million have been driven into exile in southern Mexico and Belize.[86] Although the slaughter began in wake of the coup—about 8,000 Indians being killed over a two-year period—and was sustained during much of the 1960s, the process began in earnest in 1976, when "the Guatemalan army occupied El Quiche province; a wave of terror followed. Indians were kidnapped, tortured, assassinated, raped and burned out of their homes and fields."[87]

> In northern Guatemala, a development corridor, the Franja Transversal del Norte was carved out of an isolated territory that is the homeland of the Kekchi and Ixil Indians. Many of the agribusinesses along the corridor are owned by senior members of the armed forces; these estates together are known as the "Zone of the Generals." In May 1978, the Indians who were displaced by the generals staged a march on the city of Panzos... As they reached the town square, government forces and local vigilantes positioned on the roofs of buildings around the square fired into the throng. More than a hundred Indians were killed within minutes, and more died trying to escape the massacre. Their bodies were buried in mass graves that had been prepared by bulldozers the day before.[88]

From there, the military essentially went berserk, butchering Indians with a bestial fury reminiscent of the worst the conquistadors—or the SS— had to offer: "The [soldiers] searched the houses and pulled people out and took us to a churchyard. The Lieutenant walked up and down, pointing at people, saying, 'These will go to hell, these will go to heaven.' The ones he said would go to hell he took...to the cemetery with their hands tied behind their backs. They dug a big ditch and lined them up at the edge. We all had to come and watch... They shot each one with a bullet in the face from about a meter away."[89]

> The people were surrounded and could not leave the church. Then the soldiers called out people's names, including children, and took them to the clinic nearby. All the names were of people who had learned to read and write... The women were raped before the eyes of the men and the children in the clinic. The men and the boys had their testicles cut off. Everybody's tongues were cut out. Their eyes were gouged out with nails. Their arms were twisted off. Their legs were cut off. The little girls were raped and tortured. The women had their breasts cut off.[90]

114

In nearby El Salvador, where dispossession of indigenous people by the ruling Latino elite—the so-called "Fourteen Families" (actually, about 200)—has followed a comparable trajectory, the situation is much the same.[91] In 1961, the number of landless Indians in the country came to 12 percent of the native population. By 1971, the figure had risen to 30 percent; by 1975, 41 percent; in 1980 it was estimated that two–thirds of El Salvador's Indians had been rendered landless as the oligarchy consolidated its *latifundia* system.[92] Those who were evicted were thrown into total destitution while the rest were increasingly constricted upon tiny infertile plots.

Predictably, these expropriations were accomplished through the wholesale application of violence from both the Salvadoran army and "private civic organizations" like ORDEN.* The following account of a November 29, 1974, massacre in the hamlet of La Cayetana in San Vicente Province, carried out jointly by ORDEN and the army, is indicative:

> I saw the plaza covered with people's hair. The National Guard had cut off their hair with machetes, taking part of the skin with it... The National Guard arrived in Cayetana with M-60 machine guns, tear gas, a cannon... When the [Indians] came, they grabbed their machine guns and sprayed them with gunfire... Those they killed, they cut their faces in pieces and chopped up the bodies with machetes. If you like, I will show you where they buried the brains.[93]

Specially trained and equipped "counterinsurgency units" such as the Atlacatl Battalion were also raised during the late 1970s to work in conjunction with the Salvadoran air force in driving Indians from preferred areas. White phosphorous, napalm, and fragmentation ordnance were specifically aimed at native villages during air strikes, driving into the open those who were not killed outright.[94] Concomitantly, the Atlacatl, ORDEN, and cooperation forces would comb targeted areas on foot, often killing whomever they encountered, driving the population before them.

> In the Guazapa area...regular air attacks against civilian targets continued [into the mid-'80s]. The scattered remnants of the population hide from ground sweeps follow-

*"From 1963 to 1970 General 'Chele' Medrano was the closest collaborator of the U.S. military agencies in El Salvador and the main liaison with the CIA. He had a record of extreme brutality and had been responsible for torturing political prisoners and common criminals. In 1967 he became head of the National Guard. It was Medrano, with CIA help, who founded ORDEN in 1968. A U.S. Office of Public Safety (OPS) program was started in El Salvador in 1967 and an OPS adviser was involved in working with Medrano to establish a special intelligence unit in the National Guard and, to work with it, what was described as a 30,000-man informant network—this was to become known as ORDEN"; Pearce, *Under the Eagle, op cit.*, p. 214. On OPS overall, see A.J. Langguth, *Hidden Terrors: The Truth About U.S. Police Operations in Latin America* (New York: Pantheon Books, 1978).

ing the shelling and bombardment by helicopters and jet aircraft, watching their children die of starvation and thirst... "If they find somebody, they kill, they even kill the poor dogs and other animals," [a] refugee testified, reporting night bombing and ambushing of people fleeing in October 1984. The soldiers also destroyed crops and houses "even pans one uses to cook in...in order to leave one without anything." Fleeing women and children were killed by bullets and grenades, or sliced to pieces and decapitated with machetes.[95]

By 1980, at least 30,000 Indians had been exterminated, another 600,000—13 percent of El Salvador's total population—made refugees.[96] Thousands of people, many of them defined as "opposition leaders" were being killed more "surgically" by ORDEN death squads, their bodies dumped at night at locations such as El Playón.[97] Large-scale massacres were also occurring at places like Los Llanitos, the Río Gualsinga, Las Vueltas, and El Mozote.[98]

The first major massacre was at the Río Sampul on May 14 [1980], when thousands of peasants fled to Honduras to escape a military operation. As they were crossing the river, they were attacked by helicopters, members of ORDEN and troops. According to eyewitness testimony reported by Amnesty International and the Honduran clergy, women were tortured, nursing babies were thrown into the air for target practice, children were drowned by soldiers or decapitated or slashed to death with machetes, pieces of their bodies were thrown to dogs... At least 600 unburied corpses were prey for dogs and buzzards while others were lost in the waters of the river, which was contaminated by their dead bodies.[99]

In all of Central America today, only Costa Rica is reputedly free of such treatment of indigenous people. Like Uruguay on the southern continent, however, Costa Rica also claims at this point to have no surviving native population to exterminate.[100] This perhaps is the key to an understanding of the entire phenomenon of genocide in Iberoamerica: left to run its course, the process of liquidating of American Indians, begun the moment the first Spaniard set foot in this hemisphere, will end only when there are no more Indians left to kill. The question thus becomes how to prevent it from running its course.

Denying the Holocaust

> The truth is a weapon more potent than any rifle or bomb.
> —John Trudell
> American Indian Movement

For constructive alteration of any process to occur, it is plainly essential that it be recognized for what it is. As concerns the continuing genocide of the indigenous people of South and Central America, denial rather than recognition have been the norm almost from the moment of inception. As early as the sixteenth century, the Spanish began an endless series of attempts to pass off accounts of their anti-Indian atrocities submitted by their own officials and historians as no more than a "Black Legend," a smear campaign mounted by their Protestant European enemies to discredit them. Despite its patent falsity—comparable to assertions that depictions of the nazi campaign to exterminate Europe's Jews are merely "zionist propaganda"—the Black Legend theme persists through the present day, especially among self-described "Hispanic" polemicists, and is afforded much currency in the mass media.[101]

Closely tied to such outright denial has been the efforts of "minimizers," usually "responsible scholars," who have sought to diminish the magnitude of genocide in America by making it appear that the native population at the outset of the invasion was vastly smaller than it actually was. Preeminent in this regard was the "dean of American anthropology," Alfred L. Kroeber, who in 1939 established as canonical "Truth" the proposition that the hemispheric total of American Indians in 1492—which may have been as high as 125 million—was actually only 8.4 million.[102] Instructively, this technique is identical to that deployed by those who would rehabilitate the reputation of nazism, albeit it would appear they learned the method from "reputable" types like Kroeber rather than the other way around.[103]

In any event, having scaled the American genocide down to more-or-less manageable proportions, deniers have consistently moved to dismiss its significance altogether, conceding that the conquistadors were "perhaps not saints" before arguing that their victims were "as bad or worse," therefore "deserved what they got," and that the "world is a better place" for their demise.[104] A salient theme in this respect, first advanced by Cortés himself in 1522, and established as another modern academic Truth despite a complete absence of tangible evidence by which to support it, is the myth that the Mexicas—described in every standard text as having been a "warlike" and "bloodthirsty" people—were given to ritually sacrificing as many as 20,000 human beings each year.[105] The fact is, as Peter Hassler has explained:

> Bernal Díaz del Castillo is the classic source of information about mass sacrifice by the Aztecs. A literate soldier in Cortés' company, Díaz claimed to have witnessed such a ritual… The observers, however, were watching from their camp…three or four miles away. From that point, Díaz could neither have seen nor heard anything… The only concrete evidence comes to us not from the Aztecs but from the Mayan civilization of the Yucatán. These depictions are found in the records of trials conducted during the Inquisition, between 1561 and 1565. These supposed testimonies about human sacrifice, however, were coerced from the Indians under torture and have been judged worthless as ethnographic evidence… After careful and systematic study of the sources, I find no evidence of institutionalized mass human sacrifice among the Aztecs.[106]

Although one might well be reminded of certain Germanic fables about "Jewish ritual murder," offered as justification of the nazis' treatment of Semitic *Untermenschen* during the 1930s and '40s,[107] such tales of "Aztec sacrifice" are seldom treated with skepticism by the scholarly community, much less classified as being among the rationalizations of mass murderers. To the contrary, such contrived denigration of American Indians—and there are a multitude of variations on the theme[108]—are typically embraced in such a way as to culminate in a note of hearty self-congratulation among the heirs of those who came along to end such savagery once and for all: "[Euroamericans] might as well celebrate the mammoth achievement of the past five centuries… Let's hear it for Columbus."[109]

On balance, eurocentrism and its counterpart, eurosupremacism—the racist fundaments which have always fueled the genocidal process in America—have proven themselves ideologically transcendent among Euroamericans. These mythologies are as rampant in radical dissident circles as they are among conservatives: the Revolutionary Communist Party, U.S.A., has been just as prone to accept Kroeber's low-counting of precolumbian indigenous populations as the Smithsonian Institution ever was;[110] a leftist like Roxanne Dunbar Ortiz has been as quick to repeat the conquistadors' propaganda about human sacrifice in Mesoamerica as any court historian;[111] self-proclaimed "eco-anarchists" such as George Weurthner can hold their own with the most arcane and reactionary anthropologist in decrying imagined "ravages" inflicted by native people upon the environment long before Columbus;[112] Christopher Hitchens has shown himself as apt to applaud the Columbian legacy in the pages of *The Nation* as Jeffrey Hart has been in the pages of *National Review*.[113]

In Peru, the Quechua leader Hugo Blanco, once a hero of the Left, learned such lessons well: "When he turned his support towards Quechua land rights, the Communist Party of Peru dropped him. The rightist government already had a price on his head, so he became a hunted, isolated [indigenist] roaming the hills with three hundred Quechua guerrillas."[114] Today in Peru, a far more extreme leftist formation, the *Sendero Luminoso* ("Shining Path"), conducts a new *requerimiento*, methodically murdering Andean Quechuas in a grotesque effort to compel them to adopt its peculiar "principles of revolutionary Marxism."[115] In the revolutionary Nicaragua of the 1980s, the marxian Sandinista regime employed somewhat gentler methods to the same end, selectively imprisoning and imposing mass relocation upon the Sumu, Miskito, and Rama Indians of the country's Atlantic Coast region to facilitate incorporation of these reluctant people into its Latino-oriented statist structure.[116] In Mexico and other Latin American countries, "indigenista" is a term surpassing even "capitalist" as an expression of revulsion and contempt among marxists.[117]

Even among intellectuals who have devoted themselves explicitly to the task of apprehending the implications of the nazi genocidal campaigns — and of rejoining neonazi attempts to deny, minimize, or negate the meaning of that Holocaust — there has been a thundering silence with regard to the genocide, both historical and contemporary, of American Indians. Indeed, it appears that there is so pervasive a confluence of interest, both real and perceived, underlying denial of the American holocaust that it has assumed the posture of Truth, transcending all ideological boundaries defining Left and Right within the presently dominant society.

On balance, the performance of those American institutions devoted to conditioning public consciousness with regard to American Indians — extending from academia through the mass media to popular literature and the entertainment industry — is about the same as might have been expected of their German counterparts with regard to Jews, Gypsies, Slavs, and others in the aftermath of a nazi victory in World War II. The overall intent is plainly to put a lid on the possibility of any genuine popular consideration of the genocidal dimensions of the post-1492 "American Experience," thus precluding the emergence of any cognitive dissonance which might eventually undermine the smooth functioning of business as usual.

Out of the Maze

> Our sense of history works this way: everything is connected. In order to understand where you're going and how to get there, you must know where you are now; in order to understand that, you must know where it is that you've been.
>
> —Matthew King
> Oglala Lakota elder

Certainly, there have been Euroamerican scholars, intellectuals, and activists who have deviated from the mainstream in these respects. Some, like Woodrow Borah, Sherburn Cook, Henry Dobyns, and Carl O. Sauer, seem to have been motivated by the more or less "pure" academic desire to see the history at last set straight on questions such as the size of precolumbian native populations in America and the manner in which they were reduced.[118] Others, such as David Stannard, Kirkpatrick Sale, and Eduardo Galeano, have evidenced a more consciously political agenda, seeking to use honest depictions of the extermination of American Indians as a lever by which to unravel in its entirety the eurosupremacist hegemony that sustains the ordained order of things in "the modern world."[119]

In this, they have at least figuratively joined hands with a growing number of indigenous scholars like Vine Deloria, Jr., Donald A. Grinde, Jr., and Robert A. Williams, Jr.,[120] who have begun the laborious task of reinterpreting the record of interaction between native and invader in such a way as to conform to reality rather than the ideological prescriptions of domination.[121] In the case of the indigenous scholars, the motivation is one undoubtedly born of an emic knowledge of their people's victimization and marginalization. For the Euroamericans, the process is, to borrow from Edward Said, more one of achieving an hermeneutic understanding of the circumstances experienced by the indigenous, and then acting in ways which at once reveal an unqualified commitment to the pursuit of truth and a bona fide solidarity with the oppressed embodied in that truth.[122] This, in turn, and taken in combination with similar undertakings in related spheres,[123] creates the basis for what may ultimately prove to be a general supplanting of the prevailing hegemony in favor of a new and liberatory one.[124]

This places us at something of a sociopolitical and cultural/intellectual crossroads. As material offering a more accurate and insightful view of the actual history of the Americas becomes increasingly available, those purporting to desire fundamental change confront—many for the first time—the alternative of opting out of eurosupremacist orthodoxy altogether. Therein lie the intellectual tools for creating, not only a whole new vision of our collective past, present, and future, but a practical means of implementing it.

The status quo has been quick to recognize the subversive nature of this project, particularly as regards individuals like Stannard and Sale.[125] Efforts by the champions of orthodoxy to "debunk" their work—mainly by way of personal attacks designed to discredit them as being no more than "academically irresponsible purveyors of political correctitude"—have been widespread.[126] Meanwhile, hack historians like James Axtell, whose self-assigned task appears primarily to be a repackaging of the usual mythology in somewhat more sophisticated wrappers, have been offered up as the new luminaries of "responsible" scholarship.[127]

The choice, ultimately, is ours. If we elect, sheep-like, to accept the definitions of entities like Harvard University, the Smithsonian Institution, and *Newsweek* as to what comprises "proper" or "appropriate" recountings of historical fact and meaning, we will merely have consigned ourselves to more of what has already transpired. If, on the other hand, we move to embrace, absorb and extend the kind of work pioneered by Deloria, Grinde, Williams, Stannard, and Sale, we equip ourselves to change it in a profoundly positive fashion.

Of course, it is true that nothing can undo what has been done. Coming to grips with the significance of the relentless butchery marking the European conquest of America no more changes its nature than does recognition of the horror that was embodied in Auschwitz and the operations of the *Einsatzgruppen* in the western U.S.S.R. serve to alter what transpired during the nazi perpetration of genocide. The point in either case, however, is not to try and make the past go away—that undertaking may be left to the Axtells of the world—but to utilize the insights gained from it in such a way as to intervene constructively in its outcomes, to put an end to the ongoing slaughter of indigenous people in Guatemala, for example, or the obliteration of native environments in Amazonia.

In the end it is a matter of redefining our understanding in such a way as to rearrange our values and priorities. This allows for a thoroughgoing and vitally necessary reconstitution of the relationship between ourselves as individuals, as peoples and, in aggregate, as human beings. In its turn, any such reconstitution sets the stage for the forging of a future which is radically different from our past and present. Together, we have the self-evident capacity to accomplish this. And we have the obligation to do so, not only for ourselves and one another, but for our children, our children's children, and their children on through the coming generations.

Notes

1. Henry F. Dobyns, "Estimating Aboriginal American Population: An Appraisal of Techniques with a New Hemispheric Estimate," *Current Anthropology*, No. 7, 1966; Russell Thornton, *American Indian Holocaust and Survival: A Population History Since 1492* (Norman: University of Oklahoma Press, 1987).

2. Woodrow W. Borah, "Conquest and Population: A Demographic Approach to Mexican History," *Proceedings of the American Philosophical Society*, No. 113, 1968, pp. 177–83; Ann F. Ramenofsky, *Vectors of Death: The Archaeology of European Contact* (Albuquerque: University of New Mexico Press, 1987).

3. U.S. Bureau of the Census, "Indian Population by Divisions and States, 1890–1930," *Fifteenth Census of the United States, 1930: The Indian Population of the United States and Alaska* (Washington, D.C.: U.S. Government Printing Office, 1937) p. 3.

4. I first encountered the useful concept of "population collapse" through historian David E. Stannard, in his fine study of the destruction of Hawai'i's indigenous population, *Before the Horror: The Population of Hawai'i on the Eve of Western Contact* (Honolulu: Social Science Research Institute of Hawai'i Press, 1989). Stannard informs me that he himself adopted the idea from David Nobel Cook's *Demographic Collapse: Indian Peru, 1520–1620* (Cambridge, MA: Cambridge University Press, 1981).

5. Henry F. Dobyns, "More Methodological Perspectives on Historical Demography," *Ethnohistory*, No. 36, 1989.

6. For a survey of such matters, see my *Struggle for the Land: Indigenous Resistance to Genocide, Ecocide and Expropriation in North America* (Monroe, ME: Common Courage Press, 1993).

7. Bernal Díaz Portillo, *The Discovery and Conquest of Mexico, 1517–1521* (London: George Routledge & Sons, 1926); Miguel Leon-Portilla, ed., *The Broken Spears: The Aztec Account of the Conquest of Mexico* (Boston: Beacon Press, 1962).

8. Hernan Cortés, *Letters from Mexico* (New York: Grossman, 1971) pp. 257–62.

9. The first quote is from David E. Stannard, *American Holocaust: Columbus and the Conquest of the New World* (New York: Oxford University Press, 1992) p. 79; for the second, see Cortés, *op. cit.*, p. 263.

10. Tenochtitlán, an architectural marvel, was, with a population of about 350,000, about five times the size of London or Seville. On respective populations, see Rudolph van Zantwijk, *The Aztec Arrangement: The Social History of Pre-Spanish Mexico* (Norman: University of New Mexico) p. 281; Lawrence Stone, *The Family, Sex and Marriage in England, 1500–1800*, p. 147; J.H. Elliot, *Imperial Spain, 1469–1716* (New York: St. Martin's Press, 1964) p. 177.

11. Cortés, *op. cit.*, p. 263.

12. Quoted in Pedro de Alvarado, *An Account of the Conquest of Guatemala in 1524* (Boston: Milford House, 1972) p. 126.

13. Ibid., pp. 131–32.

14. Stannard, *American Holocaust, op. cit.*, p. 81; he is relying primarily on Donald E. Chipman, *Nuño de Guzmán and the Province of Panuco in New Spain, 1518–1610* (Glendale, CA: Arthur C. Clark, 1967).

15. See Nathan Wachtel, *The Vision of the Vanquished: The Spanish Conquest of Peru Through Indian Eyes, 1530–1570* (Sussex: Harvester Press, 1977).

16. Stannard, *American Holocaust, op. cit.*, p. 87; the quotes are taken from John Hemming, *The Conquest of the Incas* (New York: Harcourt Brace Jovanovich, 1970) p. 359.

17. John Hemming, *Red Gold: The Conquest of the Brazilian Indians, 1500–1760* (Cambridge, MA: Harvard University Press, 1978) pp. 139–41.

18. Quoted in Thomas Berger, *The Long and Terrible Shadow: White Values and Native Rights in America, 1492–1992* (Seattle: University of Washington Press, 1991) p. 44.

19. Lyle N. McAlister, *Spain and Portugal in the New World, 1492–1700* (Minneapolis: University of Minnesota Press, 1984).

20. Bernardino de Sahagún, *The Conquest of New Spain* (Salt Lake City: University of Utah Press, 1989 publication of a translation of the original 1585 Spanish-language edition).

21. Stannard, *American Holocaust, op. cit.*, pp. 82–83; he is relying heavily on William L. Sherman, *Native Forced Labor in Sixteenth Century Central America* (Lincoln: University of Nebraska Press, 1979).

22. On demography, see Woodrow Borah and Sherburn F. Cook, *The Aboriginal Population of Central Mexico on the Eve of the Spanish Conquest* (Berkeley: University of California Press, Ibero-Americana No. 45, 1963). On Cortés' colonial enterprises, see France V. Scholes, "The Spanish Conqueror

as Business Man: A Chapter in the History of Fernando Cortés," *New Mexico Quarterly*, No. 28, 1958; Francisco López de Gómara, *Cortés: The Life of the Conqueror by His Secretary* (Berkeley: University of California Press, 1965).

23. Sherburn F. Cook and Woodrow Borah, *The Indian Population of Central Mexico, 1531–1610* (Berkeley: University of California Press, Ibero-Americana 44, 1960).

24. Stannard, *American Holocaust, op. cit.*, pp. 81–83; he is relying on Daniel T. Reff, *Disease, Depopulation, and Culture Change in Northern New Spain, 1518–1764* (Salt Lake City: University of Utah Press, 1991) pp. 194–242. Also see Peter Gerhard, *The Northern Frontier of New Spain* (Princeton: Princeton University Press, 1982) pp. 23–25.

25. Peter Gerhard, *The Southwest Frontier of New Spain* (Princeton: Princeton University Press, 1979) p. 25.

26. Peter Gerhard, *A Guide to the Historical Geography of New Spain* (Princeton: Princeton University Press, 1972) pp. 22–25.

27. Quoted in Grant D. Jones, *Maya Resistance to Spanish Rule: Time and History on a Colonial Frontier* (Albuquerque: University of New Mexico Press) p. 42.

28. Alonzo de Zorita, *Life and Labor in Ancient Mexico: The Brief and Summary Relation of the Lords of New Spain* (New Brunswick, NJ: Rutgers University Press, 1963) p. 210.

29. Stannard, *American Holocaust, op. cit.*, pp. 82, 86; he is relying on W. George Lovell, *Conquest and Survival in Colonial Guatemala: A Historical Geography of the Chuchumatan Highlands, 1500–1821* (Montreal: McGill-Queen's University Press, 1985) p. 145; David R. Randall, "The Indian Slave Trade and Population of Nicaragua During the Sixteenth Century," in William M. Denevan, ed., *The Native Population of the Americas in 1492* (Madison: University of Wisconsin Press, 1976) pp. 67–76; Linda Newson, *The Cost of Conquest: Indian Decline in Honduras Under Spanish Rule* (Boulder, CO: Westview Press, 1986) pp. 107–08.

30. Cook, *The Indian Population of Central Mexico, op. cit.*, p. 114.

31. Quoted in Hemming, *Conquest of the Incas, op. cit.*, p. 351.

32. On Potosí and its significance to funding Europe's "industrial revolution," see Eduardo Galeano, *The Open Veins of Latin America: Three Centuries of the Pillage of a Continent* (New York: Monthly Preview Press, 1975).

33. Quoted in Hemming, *Conquest of the Incas, op. cit.*, p. 368.

34. Ibid.

35. Pedro de Cieza de León, *The Incas* (Norman: University of Oklahoma Press) p. 62.

36. Quoted in Hemming, *Conquest of the Incas, op. cit.*, p. 369

37. Ibid.

38. Stannard, *American Holocaust, op. cit.*, p. 89; on the life expectancy of Buna workers at Auschwitz, he references Raul Hilberg, *The Destruction of the European Jews* (Chicago: Quadrangle Books, 1961) p. 596.

39. Hemming, *Red Gold, op. cit.*, pp. 143–44; *Amazon Frontier: The Defeat of the Brazilian Indians* (Cambridge, MA: Harvard University Press, 1987).

40. Stuart B. Schwartz, "Indian Labor and New World Plantations: European Demands and Indian Responses in Northeast Brazil," *American Historical Review*, No. 83, 1978.

41. Berger, *The Long and Terrible Shadow, op. cit.*, pp. 44–45.

42. Stannard, *American Holocaust, op. cit.*, p. 94.

43. Quoted in Hemming, *Red Gold, op. cit.*, p. 142.

44. Berger, *The Long and Terrible Shadow, op. cit.* pp. 44–45.

45. For descriptions of this "sport" as practiced by Columbus's men and those on the mainland, see, e.g., Tzvetan Todorov, *The Conquest of America: The Question of the Other* (New York: Harper & Row, 1984) pp. 139–141.

46. For accounts of the sort of activity on Española, see, e.g., Bartolomé de Las Casas, *The Devastation of the Indies: A Brief Account* (New York: Seabury Press, 1974); on the mainland, see, e.g., Zorita, *Life and Labor in Ancient Mexico, op. cit.*

47. John Grier Varner and Jeanette Johnson Varner, *Dogs of Conquest* (Norman: University of Oklahoma Press, 1983).

48. Ibid., pp. 192–93.

49. Ibid., pp. 36–37.

50. Ibid., pp. 38–39.

51. Cieza de León, *The Incas, op. cit.*, p. lix.

52. Quoted in Todorov, *Conquest of America, op. cit.*, p. 139.

53. Stannard, *American Holocaust, op. cit.*, p. 85; he draws for his illustration on Sherman, *Native Forced Labor, op. cit.*, p. 311.

54. Quoted in Hemming, *Conquest of the Incas, op. cit.*, p. 363.

55. Diego de Almagro, quoted in ibid., p. 364.

56. The figure derives from Spanish and Portuguese census data showing an aggregate native population of about 10,000,000 for the areas discussed in 1700. This is juxtaposed to Henry Dobyns' figure of approximately 90,000,000 indigenous people in the same regions prior to the invasion; Dobyns, "Estimating Aboriginal American Population," *op. cit.*

57. A photograph of this macabre work is included between pages 158 and 159 in Robert S. Weddle, *Spanish Sea: The Gulf of Mexico in North American Discovery, 1500–1685* (College Station: Texas A&M Press, 1985).

58. Magnus Mörner, *Race Mixture in the History of Latin America* (Boston: Little, Brown, 1967) p. 58.

59. Again, the process is comparable to that later effected in the United States for the same purpose; see "Nobody's Pet Poodle: Jimmie Durham, An Artist for Native America," in my *Indians Are Us? Genocide and Colonization in Native North America* (Monroe, ME: Common Courage Press, 1994).

60. Interestingly, although it was a U.S. jurist, John Marshall, who originally articulated the legal doctrine through which such maneuverings transpired, many South American governments seem to have implemented it in wholesale fashion well before the United States; on Marshall, see, e.g., my "Perversions of Justice: Examining the Doctrine of U.S. Rights to Occupancy in North America," in *Struggle for the Land, op, cit.*, pp. 33–83) on Latino precursors to U.S. implementation in 1887, see Berger, *The Long and Terrible Shadown, op. cit.*, pp. 106–07; on U.S. implementation, see, e.g., Janet A. McDowell, *The Dispossession of the American Indian, 1887–1934* (Bloomington: University Press of Indiana, 1991)

61. Bernardo Berdichewsky, *The Araucanian Indian in Chile* (Copenhagen: IWGIA Doc. No. 20, 1975).

62. Berger, *The Long and Terrible Shadown, op. cit.*, p. 107

63. On the Mayas, see Jones, *Maya Resistance, op. cit.*; on the Pueblo Revolt, see Oakah L. Jones, Jr., *Pueblo Warriors and the Spanish Conquest* (Norman: University of Oklahoma Press, 1966); on the Manaus, see Hemming, *Red Gold, op. cit.*; *Amazon Frontier, op. cit.*; on Peru, see the collected volume *Túpac Amaru II* (Lima: n. p., 1976)

64. On the Yaquis, see Evelyn Hu-DeHart, *Yaqui Resistance and Survival* (Madison: University of Wisconsin Press, 1984); on the Apaches, see Frank C. Lockwood, *The Apache Indians* (Lincoln: University of Nebraska Press, 1938).

65. An earlier campaign to clear the Araucaños from the pampas, undertaken by President Juan Manuel Rosas in 1833, was unsuccessful; David Rock, *Argentina, 1516–1987* (Berkeley: University of California Press, 1987).

66. Juan Carlos Walther, *La Conquista del Desierto* (Buenos Aires: Editorial Universitorio Buenos Aires, 1971).

67. Berger, *The Long and Terrible Shadown, op. cit.*, pp. 96–97; his first quote is of Julio Roca, in Rock, *Argentina, op. cit.*; his second is from V.S. Naipaul, *The Return of Eva Perón* (New York: Alfred A. Knopf, 1980).

68. Rock, *Argentina, op. cit.*

69. Naipaul, *The Return of Eva Perón, op. cit.*, p. 149.

70. On the Aché extermination, see Richard Arens, ed., *Genocide in Paraguay* (Philadelphia: Temple University Press, 1976); Wiesel is quoted from the first page of his epilogue to the volume, "Now We Know," pp. 165–67.

71. Wiesel, "Now We Know," *op. cit.*, pp. 167–68.

72. *Report of the Fourth Russell Tribunal on the Rights of the Indians of the Americas* (Nottingham, UK: Bertrand Russell Foundation, 1980) p. 25.

73. Rex Weyler, *Blood of the Land: The U.S. Government and Corporate War Against the American Indian Movement* (New York: Everest House, 1982) p. 221.

74. *New York Times* News Service, January 6, 1973.

75. Weyler, *Blood of the Land, op. cit.*, p. 221.

76. Ibid., p. 222; the author is relying on Robert L. Ledogar, *Hungry for Profits* (New York: International Documentation, 1975).

77. Reported in *Akwesasne Notes*, Spring 1972, p. 29.

78. *Report of the Fourth Russell Tribunal, op. cit.*, p. 97; on the ecological issues involved, see Susanna Hecht and Alexander Cockburn, *The Fate of the Forest: Developers, Destroyers and Defenders of the Amazon* (London: Verso Books, 1989).

79. Weyler, *Blood of the Land, op. cit.*, p. 224; he is relying on *Brazilian Information Bulletin* (Berkeley: American Friends of Brazil, 1973) and *The Yanomami Indian Park* (Boston: Anthropology Resource Center, 1981).

80. Quoted in Berger, *The Long and Terrible Shadow, op. cit.*, p. 107.

81. Ibid., pp. 107–08.

82. Quoted in Weyler, *Blood of the Land, op. cit.*, p. 229.

83. Ibid., p. 215.

84. For an overview of the Working Group process, see S. James Anaya, "The Rights of Indigenous People and International Law in Historical and Contemporary Perspective," in Robert N. Clinton, Nell Jessup Newton and Monroe E. Price, *American Indian Law: Cases and Material* (Charlottesville, VA: Michie Co., Law Publishers, 1991) pp. 1257–76.

85. Weyler, *Blood of the Land, op. cit.*, p. 229.

86. Noam Chomsky, "Introduction," in Jennifer Harbury, ed., *Bridge of Courage: Life Stories of the Guatemalan Compañeros and Compañeras* (Monroe, ME: Common Courage Press, 1994) p. 17. For background on the 1954 coup, see Bryce Wood, *The Dismantling the Good Neighbor Policy* (Austin: University of Texas Press, 1985); Robert M. Carmack, ed., *Harvest of Violence: The Maya Indians and the Guatemala Crisis* (Norman: University of Oklahoma Press, 1988); Piero Gleijeses, *Shattered Hope: The Guatemalan Revolution and the United States, 1944–1954* (Princeton, NJ: Princeton University Press, 1991).

87. Weyler, *Blood of the Land, op. cit.*, p. 219. For further background, see Julie Hodson, *Witness to Political Violence in Guatemala* (New York: Oxfam America, 1982); Rigoberta Menchú, *I, Rigoberta Menchú* (London: Verso Press, 1983); James Painter, *Guatemala: False Hope, False Freedom* (London: Catholic Institute for International Relations, 1987); Jean-Marie Simon, *Guatemala: Eternal Spring, Eternal Tyranny* (New York: W.W. Norton, 1987); Edward R.F. Sheehan, *Agony in the Garden: A Stranger in Guatemala* (New York: Houghton-Mifflin, 1989).

88. Berger, *The Long and Terrible Shadow, op. cit.*, p. 119.

89. Anonymous Indian, quoted in ibid., p. 114.

90. Anonymous Indian, quoted in Ronald Wright, *Time Among the Maya: Travels in Belize, Guatemala and Mexico* (New York: Viking Press, 1989) p. 220.

91. The families had come to power in 1932, following the "*Matanza*," a series of massacres resulting in the deaths of about 30,000 Indians; Thomas P. Anderson, *Matanza: El Salvador's Communist Revolt of 1932* (Lincoln: University of Nebraska Press, 1971); Philip Russell, *El Salvador in Crisis* (Denver: Colorado River Press, 1984).

92. Jenny Pearce, *Under the Eagle: U.S. Intervention in Central America and the Caribbean* (Boston: South End Press, 1981) p. 209.

93. Anonymous Salvadoran priest, quoted in *El Salvador—A Revolution Brews* (New York: NACLA, 1980).

94. *El Salvador's Other Victims: The War on the Displaced* (New York: Americas Watch/Lawyers Committee for International Human Rights, August 1984).

95. Noam Chomsky, *Turning the Tide: U.S. Intervention in Central America and the Struggle for Peace* (Boston: South End Press, 1985) p. 25; he is relying on two reports by Americas Watch: *Free Fire* (August 1984) and *Draining the Sea…* (March 1985).

96. Cynthia Arnson, *El Salvador: A Revolution Confronts the United States* (Washington, D.C.: Institute for Policy Studies, 1982) pp. 84–85.

97. Ray Bonner, *Weakness and Deceit* (New York: *Times* Books, 1984) pp. 325–26.

98. On the Los Llanitos Massacre, perpetrated by the Atlacatl Battalion in July 1984 (68 dead), as well as the Río Gualsinga Massacre committed by the same unit the same month, see James LeMoyne's article in the *New York Times*, September 9, 1984; on the Las Vueltas Massacre, perpetrated by the Atlacatl Battalion on August 30, 1984 ("several dozen" dead), see *Washington Report on the Hemisphere*, October 30, 1984.

99. Chomsky, *Turning the Tide, op. cit.*, p. 105; he is relying on testimony by U.S. State Department officials before the Senate Select Committee on Foreign Affairs, *Report on Human Rights in El Salvador* (Washington, D.C.: U.S. Government Printing Office, 1983) pp. 57, 168–69.

100. The claim, however, is not entirely true, as it is not in other supposedly "Indian Free Zones" like Cuba and Puerto Rico. In 1986, Colorado AIM leader Glenn Morris and others had occasion to visit a native village in Costa Rica, located in a remote area near the Panamanian border. There are others.

101. See, e.g., Gregory Cerio, "The Black Legend: Were the Spaniards That Cruel?" *Newsweek: Columbus Special Issue*, Fall/Winter 1992; for a good survey of the related brand of "revisionism," see Deborah E. Lipstadt, *Denying the Holocaust: The Growing Assault on Truth and Memory* (New York: Free Press, 1993).

102. For analysis, see Thornton, *American Indian Holocaust, op. cit.*, pp. 20–25; a particularly useful overview of how Kroeber and others "cooked the books" on estimates of precolumbian native population may be found in Francis Jennings, *The Invasion of America: Indians, Colonialism and the Cant of Conquest* (New York: W.W. Norton, 1976) esp. the chapter entitled "The Widowed Land".

103. The classic articulation among nazi apologists is Paul Rassinier's *Debunking the Genocide Myth: A Study of the Nazi Concentration Camps and the Alleged Extermination of European Jewry* (Torrance, CA: Institute for Historical Review, 1978).

104. For recent samples of this sort of argument, see, e.g., Jeffrey Hart, "Discovering Columbus," *National Review*, October 15, 1990; Raymond Sokolov, "Stop Hating Columbus," *Newsweek: Columbus Special Issue*, Fall/Winter 1992.

105. For a good survey, see Elizabeth H. Boone, ed., *Ritual Human Sacrifice in Mesoamerica* (Washington, D.C.: Dumbarton Oaks Research Library, 1984).

106. Peter Hassler, "The Lies of the Conquistadors: Cutting through the Myth of Human Sacrifice," *World Press Review*, December 1992; he is referencing Bernal Díaz del Castillo's *Historia Verdadera de la Conquista de la Nueva España*, published posthumously in 1632, but acknowledges that "Cortés fathered the lie in 1522, when he wrote a shorter version of the tale to Emperor Charles V."

107. R. Po-Chia Hsia, *The Myth of Ritual Murder: Jews and Magic in Reformation Germany* (New Haven: Yale University Press, 1988); Norman Cohn, *Warrant for Genocide: The Myth of the Jewish World-Conspiracy and the Protocols of the Elders of Zion* (New York: Harper & Row, 1967).

108. For instance, the claim that Indians precipitated some sort of never-quite-defined-or-documented environmental devastation of America before the arrival of Europeans; see, e.g., Paul Valentine, "Dancing With Myths," *Washington Post*, April 7, 1991.

109. Sokolov, "Stop Hating Columbus," *op. cit.*

110. "Revolutionary Communist Party, U.S.A., 'Searching for the Second Harvest,' " in Ward Churchill, ed., *Marxism and Native Americans* (Boston: South End Press, 1983) pp. 35–58; the source of the title is the quaint notion—sometimes described as the "Indians Eat Shit Thesis"—that American Indians traditionally ate fecal material as an integral part of their diet.

111. Roxanne Dunbar Ortiz, *Indians of the Americas: Human Rights and Self-Determination* (London: Zed Books, 1984) pp. 5–6: "A religious cult came to dominate which required the daily ritual human sacrifice of thousands of people to the Sun God."

112. George Weurthner, "An Ecological View of the Indian," *Earth First!*, Vol. 7, No. 7, August 1987; for the earlier elaboration of precisely the same view by two of the most inept and reactionary anthropologists in recent memory, see Paul S. Martin and H.E. Wright, *Pleistocene Extinctions: The Search for a Cause* (New Haven: Yale University Press, 1967).

113. *The Nation*, Oct. 19, 1992; Hart, "Discovering Columbus," *op. cit.*

114. Weyler, *Blood of the Land, op. cit.*, p. 230; also see Hugo Blanco, *Land or Death* (New York: Pathfinder Press, 1977).

115. Simon Strong, *Shining Path: Terror and Revolution in Peru* (New York: Times Books, 1992); on the *requerimiento*, the Spanish law requiring Indians to convert to Catholicism on pain of death, see Charles Gibson, *The Spanish Tradition in Mexico* (Columbia: University of South Carolina Press, 1968) pp. 53–60.

116. Glenn T. Morris and Ward Churchill, "Between a Rock and a Hard Place: Left-Wing Revolution, Right-Wing Reaction and the Destruction of Indigenous Peoples," *Cultural Survival Quarterly*, Vol. II, No. 3, Fall 1988.

117. For an especially strong articulation, see Héctor Diaz-Polanco, "Indigenismo, Populism, and Marxism," *Latin American Perspectives*, Vol. 9, No. 2, Spring 1982.

118. Cook and Borah, *The Indian Population of Central Mexico, op. cit.*; Borah and Cook, *The Aboriginal Population of Central Mexico, op. cit.*; Dobyns, "Estimating Aboriginal American Population," *op. cit.*; Carl O. Sauer, *Selected Essays, 1963–1975* (Berkeley: Turtle Island Foundation, 1981).

119. Stannard, *American Holocaust, op. cit.*; Kirkpatrick Sale, *The Conquest of Paradise: Christopher Columbus and the Columbian Legacy* (New York: Alfred A. Knopf, 1990); Eduardo Galeano, *Memory of Fire: Genesis* (New York: Pantheon Books, 1985).

120. See, e.g., Vine Deloria, Jr., *God Is Red* (Golden, CO: Fulcrum Press, [2nd ed.] 1992); Donald A. Grinde, Jr., and Bruce Johansen, *Exemplar of Liberty: Native America and the Evolution of Democracy* (Los Angeles: UCLA American Indian Studies Center, 1991); Robert A. Williams, Jr., *The American Indian in Western Legal Thought: The Discourses of Conquest* (London/New York: Oxford University Press, 1990).

121. Aside from the recent work of various American Indians of both continents, illustrations should include that of indigenous Hawaiians. See, e.g., Lilikala Kame'eleihiwa, *Native Lands and Foreign Desires* (Honolulu: Bishop Museum Press, 1992); Haunani-Kay Trask, *From a Native Daughter: Colonialism and Sovereignty in Hawai'i* (Monroe, ME: Common Courage Press, 1993).

122. Edward Said, *The Pen and the Sword: Conversations with David Barsamian* (Monroe, ME: Common Courage Press, 1994). Also see John D. Caputo, *Radical Hermeneutics: Repetition, Deconstruction, and the Hermeneutic Project* (Bloomington: Indiana University Press, 1987).

123. See, e.g., Edward Said, *Orientalism* (New York: Random House, 1978). Also see Martin Bernal, *Black Athena: The Afroasiatic Roots of Classical Civilization, Vol. 1: The Fabrication of Ancient Greece, 1785–1985* (New Brunswick, NJ: Rutgers University Press, 1987).

124. This is intended in the Gramscian sense. For elaboration, see Walter L. Adamson, *Hegemony and Revolution: A Study of Antonio Gramsci's Political and Cultural Theory* (Berkeley: University of California Press, 1980).

125. The demographers, to be sure, have come in for their fair share of criticism; see, e.g., David Henige, "Their Number Become Thick: Native American Historical Demography as Expiation," in James E. Clifford, ed., *The Invented Indian: Cultural Fictions and Government Policies* (New Brunswick, NJ: Transaction Books, 1990).

126. See, e.g., the review of Stannard by J.H. Elliott in the *New York Review of Books*, June 24, 1993; also see Stannard's reply, published in the *New York Review* on October 21. The nature of the issues in contention is revealed more broadly in Paul Berman, ed., *Debating P.C.: The Controversy Over Political Correctness on College Campuses* (New York: Laurel Books, 1992). The ideological framework employed by Elliot and others of his persuasion is articulated succinctly in an essay by Wilcomb E. Washburn, alleged "dean" of American Indianist historians, entitled "Distinguishing History for Moral Philosophy and Public Advocacy" in Calvin Martin, ed., *The American Indian and the Problem of History* (New York: Oxford University Press, 1987) pp. 91–7.

127. James Axtell, *The European and the Indian: Essays in the Ethnohistory of North America* (New York: Oxford University Press, 1981); *Beyond 1492: Encounters in Colonial North America* (New York: Oxford University Press, 1992).

"NITS MAKE LICE"
The Extermination of North American Indians, 1607–1996

> "Kill and scalp all, little and big... Nits make lice."
>
> —Colonel John M. Chivington
> Instruction to his troops at Sand Creek, Colorado

FROM the time Juan Ponce de León arrived in North America in 1513, searching for gold and a mythical fountain of youth in what the Spanish called *La Florída* (or *Pascua Florída*), until the turn of the twentieth century, up to 99 percent of the continent's indigenous population was eradicated.[*] As of 1900, the U. S. Bureau of the Census reported barely over 237,000 native people surviving within the country's claimed boundaries, and the Smithsonian Institution reported less than a third of a million for all of North America, including Greenland.[1] Although the literature of the day confidently predicted, whether with purported sadness or with open jubilation, that North American Indians would be completely extinct within a generation, two at the most, the true magnitude of the underlying

---

[*] See, e.g., Ann L. Henderson and Gary R. Mormino, eds., *Spanish Pathways in Florida, 1492–1992* (Sarasota, FL: Florida Humanities Council/Pineapple Press, 1991). Ponce de León was by no means the first European to come to North America. While there are various other possibilities, including the Basques, Irish, even the Phoenicians, it is certain that a group of Norse led by Leif Eriksson arrived in present-day Newfoundland—they called it "Vineland"—about 500 years earlier than the initial Columbian voyage. There, they encountered natives, probably Beothuks, possibly Inuits, whom they dubbed "skraelings" ("savages"). Unsure whether these beings were human or some sort of spirit life, the Vikings provided a preview of all that was to follow by killing one (this is interpreted as a kind of "scientific experiment" to determine whether the victim would bleed and die like an ordinary mortal). They then proceeded to kill a group of captives. The skraelings responded by driving most of the Norse away and gradually killing off a hardcore lot who attempted to stay on; see generally, Gwyn Jones, *The Norse Atlantic Saga* (New York: Oxford University Press, 1964); Frederick J. Pohl, *The Viking Settlements of North America* (New York: Clarkson N. Potter, 1972). On the other contenders as "discoverers" of America, see, e.g., Tim Severin, *The Brendan Voyage* (New York: McGraw-Hill, 1978); Barry Fell, *America, B.C.* (New York: Times Books, 1976) and *Saga Americana* (New York: Times Books, 1980); Robert F. Marx with Jennifer G. Marx, *In Quest of the Great White Gods: Contact Between the Old and New World from the Dawn of History* (New York: Crown, 1992).

demographic catastrophe has always been officially denied in both the United States and Canada.[2]

The primary means by which this obfuscation was achieved has been through a systematic and deliberate falsification or suppression of data concerning the size of the pre-invasion aboriginal population.[3] By minimizing estimates as to how many people there were to begin with, the extent of native population reduction was made to seem far less severe than it had actually been. Concomitantly, by making it seem that the continental indigenous population had been extraordinarily sparse, such demographic manipulations fostered the impression that much North American territory consisted of *terra nullius*, vacant land, unoccupied and thus open for the taking by any "hardy pioneer" wishing to invest the time, labor, and privation which came with "settling" it.[4]

In this manner, orthodox historians and their cohorts in cinema and popular literature have been able to present the process of Euroamerican "nation-building" north of the Río Grande as something rather noble, not always entirely fair or devoid of conflict, but basically well intended and ultimately in the best interests of all concerned. In this carefully sanitized version of events, the relatively few indigenous people who were here at the outset did indeed die back to a marked degree, but this "tragedy" was something "unfortunate," "unintended," "inadvertent," and "altogether unavoidable."[5]

Whatever variations of detail may be provided by a particular teller, the story is always the same in its essentials: while it is admitted that some small proportion of the natives were killed outright during the "Indian Wars"—in open and honorable combat, usually provoked at least equally by the Indians—emphasis is placed on the idea that the great bulk of those who disappeared died of diseases "unwittingly" introduced by incoming Europeans, to which America's natives had no immunity.[6] Since there was no intent—neither Europeans nor Euroamericans had a "scientific understanding" of pathogens and epidemiology at the time—there could be no culpability, or so it is said. And without understanding, intent, and consequent culpability among the invaders, any suggestion that the process of native population reduction might have been genocidal are not just "inappropriate" but "wildly irresponsible."[7]

A very tidy rendering, to be sure. The problem is that virtually all of it is untrue. The purpose of this essay is to set the record a bit straighter, first with respect to the real size of North America's indigenous population, circa

1500, and then concerning the true role played by disease in obliterating it, and finally concentrating on what the "disease argument" is designed to divert attention away from: the manner in which those Indians who did *not* die of disease were killed. It will conclude with a survey of the conditions imposed upon the remaining native population of North America in the twentieth-century aftermath of our historic decimation.

Statistical Extermination

Throughout most of the present century, the federally established-and-maintained Smithsonian Institution in Washington, D.C., America's officially ordained repository of Truth in such matters, has categorically asserted the fiction that the size of the indigenous population everywhere north of Mexico added up to "not more than one million" in 1492.[8] Lately, in the face of overwhelming evidence, it has conceded that its estimate was low by a factor of at least 100 percent, that it had "erred." And so, it has now doubled its count, admitting that there "may have been as many as two million" native people on the North American continent before commencement of the European invasion.[9]

As Francis Jennings and others have demonstrated, however, the Smithsonian's supposedly "scientific" estimates have not only been radically low, they have always rested on a combination of blatantly manipulated data and no data at all. The conventional estimate came from "anthropological giant" James M. Mooney, published (posthumously) in 1928.[10]

> A hint of Mooney's method appears in a remark about the estimates for New England. Mooney wrote that "the original Indian population of New England was probably about 25,000 or about one-half what the historian [John Gorham] Palfrey makes it." Apparently Mooney had followed the tradition of Palfrey's own acceptance; that is, he took the estimate of a predecessor and discounted it. The same sort of procedure had been used by every generation of scholars since the original data was recorded in the seventeenth century, and by Mooney's time discount upon discount had reduced the accepted figures to a small fraction of what was mentioned in the sources. It is as if one were to estimate the population of white Americans in 1790 by successive slashes of the census data of that year on the grounds that the census takers were probably exaggerating their numbers for undisclosed reasons. In acknowledging John Gorham Palfrey as an authority superior to the sources, Mooney accepted the implications of Palfrey's own biased interpretation of the source data, and by halving Palfrey's population estimates, he extended Palfrey's spurious logic further than Palfrey himself had gone.[11]

Jennings attributes such biases on the parts of Mooney, Palfrey, and similar "scholars" to an adherence to protonazi doctrines of racist pseudoscience which the American academy had conjured up, beginning in the early nineteenth century.[12] This seems likely, because Mooney's work is littered with terms like "half-negro mongrel" and such phrases as "of fairly healthy blood."[13] In any event, he appears to have "applied the same sort of logic to his estimates for all of North America, [arriving at a] total of 1,100,000."[14] This figure was immediately challenged by more scrupulous researchers—the archaeologist J.H. Spinden, for example, pointed out that construction of the huge burial mound complexes of the Ohio and Mississippi River Valleys required populations vastly larger than those the areas were assigned by Mooney—but to no avail.[15] Mooney's numbers corresponded to the ideological needs of the status quo and were quickly enshrined as dogma.

Actually, they were first subjected to a "rigorous reclassification"—that is, reorganized according to the preferences of Alfred L. Kroeber, reigning dean of American anthropology—and subjected to a further reduction of 10 percent across the board, leaving a "finalized" North American estimate of slightly under a million; his hemispheric estimate came to only 8.4 million.[16] The factual/scientific basis for Kroeber's sweeping diminishment of Mooney's continental estimate is no more apparent than was Mooney's in diminishing Palfrey's, or Palfrey's in diminishing those of his predecessors. As close as Kroeber ever came to stating an actual method was the exercise of what he called "the generic presupposition that the Spaniards counted or estimated excessively."[17] Beyond that, he simply indulged himself in the arbitrary derogation of peoples he himself had never really investigated.

> [Kroeber] emphatically rejected the notion that the nations of North America could be considered capable of so ordering their societies and technologies as to increase their populations beyond a static and sparsely distributed token representation. Kroeber's allotment of one million persons...divides into the total area of Canada and the United States (including Alaska) in the ratio of one person per seven square miles. His explanation for this sparsity virtually blamed the condition of savagery, though he must be credited with avoidance of the term itself. He reasoned that Indian societies were characterized by "insane, unending, continuously attritional" warfare and by "the absence of all effective political organization, of the idea of the state."[18]

Aside from seeming to confuse the history of Native America with that of Europe in terms of "insane" bellicosity, Kroeber appears to have been blissfully unaware that both his findings with respect to indigenous population density, and his assertions concerning their lack of sociopolitical organization, flatly contradict even the possibility of Indians having engaged in the kind of protracted attritional warfare of which he accused them (there being no evidence of it in any case). In the same vein, he disregarded a considerable quantity of hard research running counter to his own gratuitous and degrading characterizations of indigenous agriculture and technology, all of which pointed towards a much larger pre-invasion population than he was willing to admit.[19] Consistency being no more an inherent requirement of propaganda than facts, however, his estimates were published in what he called his "definitive text" in 1939, and immediately accorded the status of Official Truth they were to enjoy for the next fifty years.[20]

Meanwhile, a different sort of work was going on among less establishment-oriented scholars at the University of California at Berkeley, notably Carl O. Sauer, Woodrow W. Borah, Sherburne F. Cook, and Leslie B. Simpson. Working directly from archival records in Mesoamerica, the Caribbean, and New Spain, they began to (re)assemble an overall demographic portrait of the populations the Spanish originally recorded during the early invasion period, a procedure producing estimates several times those sanctioned by Smithsonian orthodoxy.[21] To this, Kroeberians had little to reply other than to insist vacuously that "most anthropologists will consider [Mooney or Kroeber] a safer authority than Cortés or Las Casas, or registers of baptisms and deaths by priests knowing only some missions in one province," and they did what could be done to keep such "dissident" work from being published.[22]

By the early 1950s, the "Berkeley School" had begun increasingly to integrate what, for lack of a better term might be called "agricultural archaeology"—extrapolating from the aggregate acreage in regions known to have been under cultivation at the point of contact, in combination with soil type/richness, types of crops planted, and meteorological records to arrive at carrying capacity for local agricultural systems, and thus population estimates—into their research methods.[23] This allowed them not only a greater degree of precision in computing the numbers of Indians alive in the postinvasion setting, but in the immediate preinvasion context as well.[24] From there, they were able to advance a hemispheric population estimate of up to 100 million—vastly greater than anything sanctioned by the Smithsonian at the time—and to begin probing the real impacts of conquest and colonization in the New World.[25]

The main weakness in the work done by Borah, Cook, and their colleagues concerned North America, a deficiency addressed by others.
Applying the Berkeley group's techniques of archival/agricultural analysis to
an area of northern Florida occupied by the Timucuans before they "became
extinct," Henry F. Dobyns arrived at a maximum pre-invasion population
estimate of over half a million for just that small region.[26] Bruce Trigger similarly compiled and analyzed material on Huron agricultural patterns sufficiently to advance a firm estimate of their pre-invasion population at 32,000,
or forty persons per square mile.[27] In New England, an area where both
Mooney and Kroeber insisted the aboriginal population was not larger than
25,000, Francis Jennings, working primarily from archival materials, arrived
at an estimate for the year 1600 of 72,000 to 90,000 members of the five
great confederacies in the southern portion alone.[28] Even the conservative
National Geographic Society eventually conceded that about 3,000 Indians
still resided on the 109 square miles of Martha's Vineyard during the early
seventeenth century, a population density of 27 persons per square mile; on
the eleven square miles of nearby Block Island, there were approximately
1,200 inhabitants, or 109 persons per square mile.[29]

Dobyns, meanwhile, had begun to compile such data and, by 1966, was
prepared to offer a preliminary estimate of the total aboriginal population
above the Río Grande as having been at least 12.5 million.[30] By his estimation, the Great Lakes region was inhabited by up to 3.8 million people in
1492. Another 1.2 million lived along the Pacific coast; more than 2.7 in the
Sierra, Great Basin, and Plains regions; nearly a million in the upper Sonora
Desert; 5.25 million in "the Great Mississippi River Valley, its major Missouri,
Ohio, Kentucky, Tennessee, and Red River tributaries, and their affluents."[31]

> The southeastern portion of the continent was also thickly populated, with high den-
> sities on or near the coast. The shores of the Gulf of Mexico from the Attakapa peo-
> ple east through the Apalachee may have supported as many as 4.6 persons per square
> kilometer for a total of about 1,100,000 individuals. The Timucuan chiefdoms, the
> Calusa, and smaller groups inhabiting peninsular Florida numbered perhaps 697,000
> persons, with an average density of 5.72 persons per square kilometer. The Atlantic
> coastal plain from Florida to Massachusetts afforded a favorable habitat to about
> 2,211,000 Native Americans. Records of early historic population density rose to as
> many as 13.77 per square kilometer in southern New England. The Virginia-Maryland
> tidewater region was still another area of dense Native American settlement. Population
> densities might appear as high elsewhere in North America were the documentary
> record equally detailed for earlier Colonial years.[32]

After another fifteen years' research, Dobyns concluded there may have been as many as 18.5 million people inhabiting pre-invasion North America, and that the hemispheric population could have reached 112 million.[33] These figures, published in 1983, were immediately subjected to intense scrutiny,[34] most constructively by Cherokee demographer Russell Thornton, whose major concern was to try and establish not so much how many indigenous people *might* have been in North America as how many people there *were*. He therefore reprocessed Dobyns' "maximal" estimates using a set of rather stringent criteria, arriving by 1987 at a "minimal" estimate of 9–12.5 million, some 2 million inhabiting what is now Canada.[35] Lately, a number of scholars have adopted the practice of splitting the difference between Thornton's minimum and Dobyns' maximum estimates, using 15 million as the most likely approximation of the real size of the aboriginal North American population.[36]

Put another way, the demographic reality of aboriginal North America was about *fifteen times* that pretended by Smithsonian convention until well into the 1980s, and about seven-and-a-half times what it is prepared to admit now. While upward revision of estimates to conform with the evidence has elicited all manner of howls from paleoconservatives and allegedly "responsible" academics about the need for exercising "proper scientific caution" in such matters,[37] the fact is that it is orthodoxy itself which threw both science and caution to the winds in deliberately low-counting the pre-invasion population of the continent. Estimates approximating those of Dobyns and Thornton have, after all, been available to anyone who cared to use them since at least as early as 1860.[38] As Jennings observes, they "simply ignored" such inconveniences.[39]

The Smithsonian has never found it necessary to exercise much restraint in embracing all manner of patently idiotic speculations—from Kroeber's absurd contention that the aboriginal population of California hunter-gatherers was somehow larger than that of eastern seaboard agriculturalists,[40] to Vance Haynes' and Paul S. Martin's ridiculous notion that Ice Age Indians were responsible for the extinction of the mastodon and other paleolithic mammals through "jump kills" and the like,[41] to R. Douglas Hurt's nonsensical assertion that crops were grown in the poor and sandy soil of Canyon de Chelly for centuries without native farmers having ever discovered how to fertilize their fields,[42] to the astonishing idea that the Anasazi stored their own excrement, not for use as fertilizer but as a larder of winter nutrients,[*] to perpetual claims of having finally found an American Indian society that actually practiced cannibalism[†]—*whenever* they serve to denigrate indigenous cultures.

In reality, the motives underlying the resistance to revised demography has no more to do with methodological considerations than did Mooney's and Kroeber's original manipulations of the data. The motive in demanding a low count—a sort of retrospective statistical extermination, as it were—is what it has always been: to do otherwise would be, as historian Wilbur Jacobs observed more than twenty years ago, to "change everything" from interpretations of indigenous sociopolitical organization to understandings of aboriginal technologies and economies.[43] Above all, it would destroy the "virgin land" mythology which is key to the prevailing, neatly sanitized version American history, thereby opening the door to a serious and generalized consideration of the question of genocide in North America.[44]

Denial of that genocide is paramount. To observe that the number of native people shrank by three-quarters over four centuries, from a million at the outset to a quarter-million at the end, is to say that something plausibly

---

[*] The so-called "Second Harvest Hypothesis" was advanced by a team of anthropologists from the University of New Mexico in 1980, promptly pronounced "interesting" by the Smithsonian, and, as a consequence, showcased in the *New York Times*. Thereafter, it was picked up by no less than the Revolutionary Communist Party U.S.A. to "prove" that traditional indigenous cultures have nothing of value to offer the world; "The RCP, Searching for the Second Harvest," in Ward Churchill, ed., *Marxism and Native Americans* (Boston: South End Press, 1983).

[†] The idea of indigenous American cannibalism is roughly comparable to the myth of ritual murder used by the nazis against the Jews; see, e.g., John Weiss, *Ideology of Death: Why the Holocaust Happened in Germany* (New York: Ivan R. Dee, 1996) pp. 17–8. It began with Christopher Columbus's attribution of the practice, based upon no direct evidence at all, to the people he called "Caribs," whom he never encountered. Indeed, the very term "cannibal" derives from a mispronunciation of the word "Carib." Although Columbian fable about flesh-eating natives has been long and amply rebutted—most recently by Robert A. Myers in his article, "Island Carib Cannibalism"(see the 1984 edition of Utrecht's *New West Indies Guide*)—it continues to be regurgitated as Truth in standard texts; e.g., Kirby Martin, et al., *America and Its People, op. cit.*, p. 19. Orthodox anthropologists have also proven extraordinarily persistent in attempting to establish its "fundamental validity" with respect to *some* American Indian society, whether it be the Tonkawas, Anasazis, Mohawks, Brazilian forest peoples, or *whoever* (all of these have been disproven). One of the more vicious strains, since it merges with a broader myth of human sacrifice, concerns the Mexicas (Aztecs), perhaps most forcefully presented by Michael Harner in his essays, "The Ecological Basis of Aztec Sacrifice" (*American Ethnologist*, No. 4, 1977) and "The Enigma of Aztec Sacrifice" (*Natural History*, No. 76, 1977); both were rebutted in detail by Marshall Sahlins in the November 23, 1978, issue of the *New York Review of Books*. Despite there never having been a shred of credible evidence to support the cannibalism myth, the Smithsonian establishment has yet to enter anything resembling the categorical skepticism—or outright rejection—of it that it has expressed with respect to the abundantly well-documented case for increased estimates of the size of aboriginal North American population. See additionally, Richard Arens, *The Man-Eating Myth* (New York: Oxford University Press, 1979).

explainable as "benign" occurred. To concede that the population began at two million and fell by seven-eighths during the process of "settlement" is to strain such explanations severely, although they remain at least superficially tenable. But to acknowledge that there were twelve, or fifteen, or eighteen million people in North America in 1492 is to say that somewhere between 96–99 percent of the native inhabitants of the continent were eradicated. Such figures do not lend themselves to facile and blameless explanations, so they must be denied if genocide itself is to be denied.

The practice is no different in principle from that of neonazi "revisionists" who pretend the Jewish population of Europe was much smaller than it actually was in 1939. Their purpose is to minimize impressions of the extent and impact of the nazi Holocaust by comparing these artificially reduced estimates of prewar population to the number of postwar survivors. From there, they move on to deny that the Jews suffered genocide at all.[45] To all appearances, this neonazi assault on truth and memory may well have been informed by the techniques of Smithsonian scholars vis-à-vis American Indians. The only significant distinction to be drawn between the two groups is that the neonazis comprise a sort of pseudointellectual lunatic fringe, while deniers of the American holocaust constitute an elite core of the U.S. and Canadian academic status quo, with all the power to shape public opinion this implies.

Vectors of Death

After minimization, the most common mode of denying that genocide was perpetrated against the indigenous peoples of North America is what is referred to as the "disease factor."[46] The standard histories to which students are exposed belabor the idea that "microbic weapons" to which natives "lacked antibodies" were "unwittingly" introduced, beginning with the conquistadors, and "took a rapid toll." The "native populace… kept dying off from contact with European diseases"—not, apparently, from contact with Europeans themselves—like "smallpox, typhoid, diptheria, the measles, and various plagues and fevers." Consequently, the indigenous population of Mexico, for example, "declined dramatically—by about 90 percent during the 50 years following the invasion of Cortés's army."[47] The army itself, it seems, had nothing to do with it.

Even those scholars who are willing to accept the size of the pre-invasion Native North American population for what it was prove willing to indulge themselves in this manner. Consider Cornell University professor

Steven T. Katz, who cites both Dobyns and Thornton in the relevant sections of his recent study of genocide:

> Very probably the greatest demographic disaster in history, the depopulation of the New World, for all its death and terror, was largely an *unintended* tragedy, a tragedy that occurred despite the sincere and indisputable desire of the Europeans to keep the Indian population alive. The native people died primarily because of pandemics against which there was no protection. Nature, not malice, was the cause of the massive, incomprehensible devastation (emphasis in the original).[48]

There are, of course, elements of truth to this. There can be no question that Christopher Columbus and his crew—and undoubtedly others of the early Spanish invaders as well—were unaware at the outset that they were carrying pathogens to which America's native peoples had never been exposed and therefore possessed no immunity, and of the extent of the lethal effect these microbes would unleash.* Onsets do not, however, last forever. By 1550 at the latest, and probably earlier, it was common knowledge in Europe that there was a firm correlation between the arrival of "explorers, settlers and military expeditions" on the one hand and massive die-offs of native peoples from the above-mentioned diseases on the other. This is frequently remarked upon—piously attributed to the "hand of God" and often *celebrated*—in the literature of the day.[49]

The theme of divine intervention on behalf of Europe's "chosen peoples"—a later regime would describe it as a "master race"—is reiterated endlessly, serving as a near-perfect mystical mask behind which to hide more practical motives and knowledge. A random sampling of contemporaneous quotations might begin with that of a pair of Jesuits explaining in 1570 that the basis for a successful Spanish colonization of San Luis (now Virginia) resided in "Our Lord having chastised it with six years of famine and death,

---

*The very first epidemic, which broke out in Española among the Tainos as a result of Columbus's second voyage, has now been identified as type A influenza, transmitted by hogs acquired in the Canary Islands. It appears to have spread to the mainland independently of the Spanish, decimating the Cakchiquel Maya, beginning in 1523; Francisco Guerra, "La epidemia americana de influenza en 1493," *Revista de Indias*, No. 45, 1985. Juan Ponce de León quite possibly touched off the first North American pandemic, of smallpox upon his arrival in Florida in 1513; Dobyns, *Their Number Become Thinned, op. cit.*, p. 254. The troops of Hernán Cortés then unleashed two epidemics, first of what seems to have been measles (*sarampión*) in 1531 and then of smallpox in 1532, during their conquest of Tenochtitlán. Another apparent smallpox epidemic followed in 1538; Torobio de Motolinía o Benavente, *Memoriales o libro de las cosas Nueva España y de los naturales dello* (Mexico City: UNAM, 1971); Dobyns, *Their Number Become Thinned, op. cit.*, pp. 262–4. These may well have involved a genuinely "unwitting" introduction of pathogens. By the 1540s, however, the connection between European contact and massive native die-off was becoming clear to all concerned.

138

which has brought it about that there is very much less [native] population than usual."[50] Or, as Pedro de Liévano, Dean of the Cathedral of Guatemala, put it 1582, "the secret judgments of God" were responsible for demolishing the Mayan population of his area, thus allowing the easy pacification and colonization of the demoralized survivors by the Spaniards, an inherently superior group selected by heaven itself to perform the task.[51]

Such rationalizations were hardly restricted to the Spanish. The English — Lord Protector Oliver Cromwell himself having proclaimed God an Englishman at about the same time — not only used them, but were far more openly jubilant about it. In describing the consequences of indigenous peoples' "quarrelsome" attitude about being pushed out of their territory around the Massachusetts Bay Colony in 1631, Puritan leader Cotton Mather rejoiced that "God ended the controversy by sending the smallpox amongst the Indians...who were before that time exceedingly numerous."[52] A few years later, the governor of the Carolina Colony solemnly intoned that, "the hand of God was eminently seen in thin[n]ing the Indians, to make room for the English."[53] All of this was a sanctimonious subterfuge, as Jennings has pointed out, rhetoric designed by the European elites — "conquest aristocracies," he calls them — to "overpower their own countrymen's moral scruples" about what was happening to Indians. Consciously "reaching for illegitimate power," he says, they "customarily assume[d] attitudes of great moral rectitude to divert attention from the abandonment" of any recognizable moral standard.[54]

Nowhere does the record reveal anyone, at least nobody in a position of authority, recommending that, in the face of all this "death and terror," contact should be curtailed (at least until some remedy could be found). To the contrary, the rate of expansion was increased as rapidly as possible by every participating European power.[55] Additionally, the evidence is overwhelming that they consistently imposed policy within their areas of acquisition — slave-labor systems, deliberately induced famines, massive dislocations of the populace, etc. — which they *knew* from their own bitter experience with plagues in Europe would greatly exacerbate the effects of whatever diseases were afoot.[*] This is hardly the stuff of "innocence" or "inadvertence."

---

[*]There is abundant evidence that the connection between the physically debilitating effects of these policies and the Indians' catastrophic death rates by disease was well known very early, but that the policies were nonetheless endemic. Consider, for example, an instruction from the utterly ruthless Spanish overlord Pedro de Alvarado to his subordinates in 1533 — a point when he desperately needed an effective native labor force to process his quota of gold for the Crown — that normal practice be temporarily suspended as an expedient to preserving the lives of native workers during an

Absolution from genocidal intent has always been retroactively bestowed upon the early invaders, their own myriad statements to the contrary notwithstanding, by virtue of their lacking any genuine "scientific knowledge" of microbes and epidemiology, understandings unavailable until the late nineteenth century.[56] Such reasoning is obfuscatory at best. I, for one, being virtually illiterate in both ballistics and chemistry, have never acquired a proper scientific understanding of how a .357 magnum handgun actually works. Were I to take such a weapon and fire it pointblank at someone, I doubt very much that the argument of my very real scientific ignorance would stand me in especially good stead at my subsequent murder trial. All that would be required in the minds of the prosecution, judge, jury, and appeals courts would be that I had an average common-sense understanding of the cause and effect involved in what I did. On this basis they would all find me to be criminally culpable, and quite properly so.

No lesser standard is reasonably applicable to the conduct of the Columbian adventurers and those who followed, since the juridical/philosophical concepts involved have been evident in most doctrines of European law, ethics, and morality since well before 1492.[57] In this sense, the apologist routine about not judging the actions and attitudes of historical figures by the allegedly more benevolent mores of today has no bearing at all.[58] With this principle in mind, it would be well to take a close look at a few things which have been passed off under the rubric of "the disease factor" as resulting from "nature, not malice," and, not only unwitting and unintentional, but "despite the sincere and indisputable desire of the Europeans to keep the Indian population alive."

Death by Disease in the Spanish Missions

Some of the worst policy-driven escalations of death from disease north of the Río Grande were the result of slave-labor systems on the Spanish missions in Florida, Texas, California, Arizona, and New Mexico from roughly 1690–1845.[59] Run first by the Jesuits, later by the Franciscans, these institu-

---

epidemic: "Because measles has struck the Indians I order those who hold *encomiendas* and *repartimientos* (categories of slave laborers), on punishment of forfeiting them…to care for and cure their charges without engaging them in any activity, for experience has shown in other similar epidemics that much territory has been depopulated"; quoted in Francisco Antonio de Fuentes y Guzmán, *Recordación Florida* (Guatemala City: Sociedad de Geografía e Historia, 3 Vols., 1932–1933) p. 338. For an overall view of Alvarado's attitude toward Indians, and consequent verification that the directive is not indicative of an overall concern with their well-being, see David E. Stannard, *American Holocaust: Columbus and the Conquest of the New World* (New York: Oxford University Press, 1992) pp. 76, 81, 134.

tions were supposedly devoted to the Indians' physical well-being, as well as their spiritual/moral "enlightenment" through revelation of the "benefits of work."[60] As late as 1865, New Mexico Indian Superintendent Felipe Delgado wrote to U.S. Indian Commissioner William P. Dole, in response to queries concerning traffic in native slaves by the missions in his area (a violation of the 1863 Emancipation Proclamation and pursuant federal legislation), that the object of the priests' efforts "has not been to reduce them to slavery, but rather from a Christian piety…to instruct and educate them in civilization… This has been the practice in this country for the last century and a half, and the result arising from it has been to the captives, favorable, humane and satisfactory."[61]

In actuality, the missions were deathmills in which Indians, often delivered en masse by the military, were allotted an average of seven feet by two feet of living space in what one observer, V.M. Golovin, described as "specially constructed cattle pens."[62] Usually segregated by sex unless married by Catholic ceremony, each gender typically shared an open pit serving as a toilet facility for hundreds of people.[63] Although forced to perform arduous agricultural labor "from morning to night," six days per week, the captives were provided no more than 1,400 calories per day in low-nutrient foods, with missions like San Antonio and San Miguel supplying as little as 715 calories per day.[64] Even Spanish military officials are known to have complained that such rations were grossly insufficient to keep the Indians alive.[65] This was *not* for lack of available foodstuffs:

> [Despite] agricultural crop yields on the Indian-tended mission plantations that Golovin termed "extraordinary" and "unheard of in Europe," along with large herds of cattle and [especially in California] the easily accessible bounty of sea food, the food given the Indians was…"a kind of gruel made from barley meal, boiled in water with maize, beans, and peas; occasionally, they [were] given some beef."[66]

The caloric intake of these Indian mission slaves should be contrasted with that of imported African slaves at about the same time. The best estimates are that Africans were provided on average with slightly over 4,200 calories per day, with field hands often receiving as much as 5,400 calories in relatively high-nutrient foods.[67] The latter, which is not considered excessive, given the strenuous nature of the labor performed, is *eight times* what an Indian received to perform the same tasks. Plainly, the Indians, unlike their black counterparts, were being worked and starved quite literally to death, as the records of their wholesale expiration by "disease" at every mission in California readily attests.

Although there are too many gaps in the archival material to allow a precise estimate as to the number of Indians consumed by the holocaust of the missions, it certainly ran into the hundreds of thousands.[68] From the considerable evidence that *does* exist, it is clear that death rates consistently outstripped birthrates by as much as 800 percent. During the initial three-year period of the mission of San José Cumundi, for instance, 94 Indians were baptized while 241 died. At Nuestra Señora de Loreto, the figures were 76 baptisms and 131 dead. At Nuestra Señora Guadalupe, 53 were baptized and 130 died. Santa Rosalía de Mulegé showed 48 baptisms, 113 deaths; San Ignacio, 115 baptisms and 293 deaths; Purísima de Cadegomó, 39 baptisms and 120 deaths.[69] This comes to over a thousand deaths at just this handful of missions in only three years. There were scores of others, and the process was only beginning. It would continue without interruption—and at a much higher intensity—for another century and a half. It was a rate of death which, "in less than half a century, would completely exterminate a population of any size that was not replenished with new conscripts" brought in ever-increasing numbers by the military.[70]

The reason for this discrepancy in treatment between indigenous slaves and those brought in from Africa had nothing to do with the Spaniards taking a comparatively humane view of Africans.[71] Rather, it was purely economic: importation of Africans was expensive, whereas native people here provided a comparatively cost-free, apparently renewable—and therefore readily *expendable*—source of labor power.[72] As distinguished from blacks (once they were here; millions were sacrificed to precisely the same financial imperatives during their transportation from Africa),* it was simply more profitable to replace native people as they died than to feed them. To that purpose, colonial troops drove the Indians into the yawning maws of the missions until there were none left who could be easily rounded up. By then, the Spanish (later Mexican) dominion over California and the northern Sonora was coming to an end.

Leaving aside differences in scale, technology, and the degree to which sociomilitary organization had evolved among the managers of the mission slave system in North America, it is indistinguishable in its intents and effects

---

*African chattel were readily expendable during the process of transatlantic shipment insofar as their loss simply drove up the "per unit" price of those ultimately delivered to the Americas. Hence, blacks were crammed into the holds of ships under abysmal conditions and fed a diet remarkably similar to that imposed upon the mission Indians. As a result, by what may be considered the most conservative credible estimate, between 1500 and 1900, "of the 12 million [people taken from Africa by] the Atlantic slave trade, around 15 percent, or up to two million...died on the Atlantic Voyage—the dreaded 'Middle Passage' "; Patrick Manning, "The Slave Trade: The Formal Demography of a Global System," in J.I. Inikori and S.L. Engerman, eds., *The Atlantic Slave Trade: Effects on Economies, Societies and Peoples in Africa, the Americas and Europe* (Durham, NC: Duke University Press, 1992) p. 120.

from that administered for the Third Reich by Albert Speer and others during the 1940s.[73] Unlike Speer, who was convicted of crimes against humanity by the Nuremberg Tribunal in 1946 and served twenty years in Spandau prison for the toll taken by his programs—and who openly conceded the criminality of at least part of what he was involved in—his North American Spanish counterparts never recanted their deeds and were never punished.[74] Instead, they went to their graves triumphant, and are now revered and commemorated in books, paintings, place names, and public statuary throughout the area in which they operated.[75]

Probably most remarkable in this regard is Fray Junípero Serra, in charge of the northern California mission complex during its peak period and a man whose personal brutality was noteworthy even by those standards (he appears to have delighted in the direct torture of victims, had to be restrained from hanging Indians in lots, à la Columbus, and is quoted as asserting that "the entire race" of Indians "should be put to the knife").[76] Proposed for canonization as a saint by the Catholic Church, Serra's visage, forty feet tall, today peers serenely down upon motorists driving south from San Francisco along Highway 101 from its vantage point on a prominent bluff.[77]

Another statute of Serra, a much smaller bronze which has stood for decades before San Francisco's city hall, is being moved to a park as part of an expansion/remodeling of the city office facilities. Officials denied requests from local Indians that it be placed in storage, out of public view, offering the compromise of affixing a new plaque to address native concerns about the incipient saint's legacy.[78] Church lobbyists, however, have undermined even that paltry gesture, preventing the inclusion of wording which might have revealed something of the true nature of the mass murder and cultural demolition over which Serra presided. Both the man and the missions, the Vatican insisted, echoing Delgado's 1865 falsehood, were devoted to "mercy and compassion."[79]

Forced Marches and Internments

During the nazi period in Germany, especially from 1942–45, vast numbers of people died in concentration camps, not by direct killing methods such as shooting and gassing, but from disease, starvation, and exposure due to the horrendous conditions imposed upon them.[80] As the Third Reich disintegrated in 1945, many thousands more perished as they were force-marched from camps about to be overrun by the advancing Allies to locations deeper in

German-held territory.[81] In neither of these processes have the deaths which accrued been categorized as inadvertent or accidental. On the contrary, as is entirely appropriate, the victims have been included in the totals of those who fell prey to nazi crimes against humanity,[82] and, in many cases, the perpetrators were tried, convicted, and punished under international law.[83]

Application of the same standard to the supposedly unintentional decimation of the American Indian population by disease produces some illuminating insights. In 1830, for example, the United States Congress passed the Indian Removal Act, a statute authorizing use of military force to compel the relocation of all indigenous people east of the Mississippi River to points west.[84] This precipitated, among numerous other atrocities, the so-called "Trail of Tears" in which the populations of the Cherokee, Choctaw, Chickasaw, Creek, and Seminole nations were rounded up by troops and interned at prearranged points within their own homelands. Once concentrated in this fashion, each people—men, women, children, and elders alike— was marched at bayonet-point for hundreds of miles, without provision of anything approaching adequate food, shelter, or medical support.[85] Needless to say, attrition among those subjected to such treatment was pronounced.

> The Choctaws are said to have lost 15 percent of their population, 6,000 out of 40,000; and the Chickasaw...surely suffered severe losses as well. By contrast, the Creeks and Seminoles are said to have suffered about 50 percent mortality. For the Creeks, this came primarily in the period after removal; for example, of the 10,000 or more who were resettled in 1836–37...an incredible 3,500...died of "bilious fevers."[86]

The toll was perhaps highest of all for the Cherokees. According to the most recent study, which is exceedingly thorough, about 55 percent of all Cherokees alive in 1838, when they were interned, died as a direct result of the extreme privations they suffered along the Trail.[87] Given that the Smithsonian Institution's official estimate of Cherokee losses (advanced by James Mooney in 1900) is still only 25 percent,[88] it seems likely that comparable research with regard to the Choctaws would reveal that they too suffered a much higher proportionate reduction of population than is admitted in conventional histories. A reconstruction of the data with regard to the Chickasaws, which has never been seriously attempted, would undoubtedly lead to much the same conclusion.[89]

Nor was the Trail of Tears "anomalous." Following their military defeat at the hands of Colonel Christopher "Kit" Carson in 1864, the Diné (Navajos) were interned at Fort Defiance, Arizona.[90] From there, they underwent what is called "The Long Walk"; the entire people was force-marched about 300 miles in the dead of winter to a location known as the Bosque Redondo, adjoining old Fort Sumner in eastern New Mexico.[91] Once there, they were reinterned for four years, during which time they were compelled to live in — literally — covered holes in the ground, subsisting on utterly inadequate rations (often a thin gruel made of boiled flour), and with nothing resembling genuine medical care.[92] The most conservative credible estimates place Diné attrition from the ordeal at not less than half the total population.[93]

Very similar conditions of internment were imposed by the United States upon many native peoples throughout the nineteenth century. Prominent examples include the Santee Dakotas in Minnesota, whose keeper, federal Indian agent Andrew Myrick deliberately withheld rations and told the starving people to "eat grass" when they complained. The Santees then revolted — decapitating Myrick and stuffing the mouth of his severed head with grass in the process — only to be put down with great brutality by U.S. troops, who quickly restored the status quo and conducted a mass hanging of Indian leaders in reprisal.[94] Much the same situation prevailed in northern California with respect to the Modoc uprising of 1872–3,[95] and was the precipitating factor attending the so-called "Meeker Massacre" perpetrated by the Utes in 1879.[96]

The list can be continued at length: the Northern Cheyenne lost about half their population while interned at Fort Sill, Oklahoma, from 1876 to 1878;[97] rations, always meager, were suspended altogether for several months in 1876 on the Great Sioux Reservation in present-day South Dakota and were resumed only when the interned Lakotas "consented" to the alienation of most of their land;[98] the conditions under which the Chiricahua and other western Apache groups were incarcerated at San Carlos and other reservations in Arizona during the 1870s and '80s were so grotesque that federal officials referred to them as amounting to an "extermination program."[99] Even peoples who never militarily resisted Euroamerican expropriation of the landbase — the Poncas, for instance — were subjected to such treatment.[*]

---

[*] The unoffending Poncas were forcibly relocated from their Nebraska homeland to the gigantic internment center which was Oklahoma in 1877. Two years later, having meanwhile been reduced to only 530 survivors through "disease attrition," a small group headed by Standing Bear escaped and returned home. Quickly captured by the army, they petitioned for judicial relief, causing a federal judge to enter a decree that Standing Bear should be considered "a person" (i.e., a human being) within the meaning of U.S. law — *United States ex. rel. Standing Bear v. Crook*, 25 Fed. Cas 695 (C.C.D. Ne., 1879) — a matter which had up till then been less than clear. He and his group were therefore allowed to remain on a small parcel of land along Nebraska's Niobrara River. The military and Bureau of Indian affairs openly refused, however, to extend this principle of human rights to the remainder

In each case, spiraling death rates resulted technically from "disease"—always in combination with deliberately induced malnutrition, sustained exposure to the elements, and other physically debilitating circumstances (separating death by disease from death by starvation, etc., in such instances is virtually impossible)—rather than direct killing.* In no case, however, can such fatalities be legitimately described as having accrued from unwitting or unintentional actions on the parts of responsible officials. This is illustrated by the U.S. execution of Captain Henry Wirz, a Confederate officer, after the Civil War. Wirz's offense was that, while serving as commandant of Georgia's Andersonville prison camp, he had caused "needless death and suffering" among Union prisoners by forcing them to endure conditions no worse those experienced by Indian women and children interned by the United States both before and after his trial.† Hence, there can be no question as to whether U.S. officials were fully conscious of the criminal nature of their Indian internment policies, even as they implemented them.

Dislocation, Famine, and Infertility

More pervasive than the effects of the missions, internments, and forced marches discussed above were the effects of the systematic process of dislo-

---

of the Poncas—or any other Indians, for that matter—for another sixty years; see Earl W. Hayter, "The Ponca Removal," *North Dakota Historical Review*, No. 6, 1932; Grant Foreman, *The Last Trek of the Indians* (Chicago: University of Chicago Press, 1946); Thomas Henry Tibbles, *The Ponca Chiefs: An Account of the Trial of Standing Bear* (Lincoln: University of Nebraska Press, 1972).

*The relationship between malnutrition and other forms of physical debilitation (chronic overwork, exposure to the elements, etc.), susceptibility to disease and propensity to succumb to it once it has been contracted are obvious but little studied in this connection. Virtually no effort has been expended in trying to separate victims into groups according to such criteria, which might begin to clarify what was inadvertent—and what was not—in terms of native population decline in America. Rather, all American Indians not killed outright have been conventionally—and all too conveniently—lumped in with the category of unwittingly transmitted disease. Methodologically, the problem might be approached in the manner demonstrated by Andrew B. Appleby, "Disease or Famine? Mortality in Cumberland and Westmoreland," *Economic History Review*, 2nd Ser., No. 26, 1973, and John D. Post in "The Mortality Crisis of the Early 1770s and European Demographic Trends," *Journal of Interdisciplinary History*, No. 21, 1990.

†Shelby Foote, *The Civil War, Vol. III: Red River to Appomattox* (New York: Random House, 1974) pp. 1032–3. Foote describes Wirz's prosecution as "trumped up." Be that as it may, the charges brought against him clearly indicate that the federal government understood imposition of the sort of conditions suffered by Indians interned at many agencies to be criminally actionable, regardless of who committed it. As concerns the U.S. military itself, such treatment of prisoners was explicitly prohibited—under criminal sanction—with its adoption, in April 1863, of a set of field instructions prepared by Dr. Francis Lieber (the so-called "Lieber Code"); Adam Roberts and Richard Guelff, *Documents on the Laws of War* (Oxford: Clarendon Press, 1982) p. 7. Also see Ovid L. Futch, *The History of Andersonville Prison* (Gainesville: University of Florida Press, 1968).

cating indigenous peoples and/or destroying the economic basis of their survival. This began at almost the first moment of the English invasion in the 1580s,[100] escalated steadily for a period of about 200 years, and then increased geometrically during the nineteenth century. Its results were always the consequence of conscious and deliberate policy decisions, constituted the primary causative factor in every "Indian War" fought on the continent, and comprised an essential element of the strategy of all Euroamerican military campaigns conducted against North American Indians.

The pattern was probably set in 1610 by the Jamestown Colony, established in what would become Virginia, with the articulation of an Indian policy based on a presumed "right of Warre" entitling the English, as inherently superior beings, to "invade the Country and destroy them...whereby wee shall enjoy their cultivated places [and] their cleared grounds in all their villages (which are situate in the fruitfullest places of the land) shall be inhabited by us."[101] While there was, as will be seen in the next section, slaughter aplenty attending this obvious prefiguration of what public figures in the United States would later call "Manifest Destiny"—and Adolf Hitler would subsequently term *Lebensraumpolitik*—the main mode of its realization focused on obliteration of the native economy.[102]

In order to accomplish this, it was first necessary to lull the opposition into a false sense of security through a treaty of "peace and friendship" so that the colonists might "have the better Advantage both to surprise them, & cutt down theire Corne."[103] Both the deception and the tactics which followed worked splendidly.

> [The Indians'] canoes and fishing weirs were smashed, their villages and agricultural fields were burned to the ground... In a single raid, the settlers destroyed corn sufficient to feed four thousand people for a year... Starvation [was] becoming the preferred [English] approach to dealing with the natives. By the end of the winter of 1623 the Indians acknowledged that in the past year alone as many of their number [were dead] as had died since the first arrival of the [English] a decade and a half earlier.[104]

Rendered destitute, homeless, harried and harassed relentlessly, the starving and disease-ridden members of the largest mid-Atlantic indigenous confederation—the Pamunkeys, Chickahominies, Naunsemonds, Rappahannocks, Paspaheghs, and several smaller peoples known collectively to Europeans as the "Powhatan Empire"— dwindled to a remnant of no more than 600 by the late 1600s.[105] They had been so thoroughly "rowted, slayne and dispersed" that they were "no longer a nation," as one colonist gloated.[106]

Where there had been perhaps 100,000 or more Indians only a few decades earlier, a burgeoning population upwards of 60,000 English men and women went busily about the business of "civilizing the wilderness" they'd created atop a once-thriving civilization.[107]

Immediately southward, in the Carolinas, things were much the same. Comparable tactics were pursued in the Tuscarora War of 1711–12 and the Yamasee War of 1715–16.[108] Nor were things different to the north, where the Plymouth Colony was established in 1620. There, in a virtual replay of the experience of Sir Walter Raleigh's lost colonists at Roanoak forty years earlier, the "Pilgrim Fathers" had to be saved from starvation during their first winter ashore — an event symbolized to this day in Angloamerica's annual celebration of the "Thanksgiving" holiday — by the local Wampanoags, Pequots, and other Indians, who voluntarily shared their usual bountiful agricultural harvest. The following spring, these pitiful English hunter-gatherers were taught how to plant crops for themselves.[109]

Once they'd achieved self-sufficiency, of course, the Pilgrims set about destroying their native saviors with a vengeance, finishing the first part of the job by 1637.[110] Richard Drinnon, among others, has described the link they forged between total destruction of the indigenous way of life on the one hand and of the very habitat of New England on the other.[111] By 1675, when the colonists of what was by now not only Plymouth, but Massachusetts and Connecticut colonies as well, turned from the now-obliterated Pequots and Western Niantics to tackle the adjacent Wampanoags and Narragansetts, the wholesale and systematic destruction of villages and croplands was standard tactical fare.[112] Ultimately, the application of such techniques of warfare led to what has been called the "Great Dispersal" in which the bedraggled residue of once proud and populous peoples — the Androscoggin, for example, and the Norridgewocks and Pigwackets, Maliseets, Passamequodies and Pocumtucks, Quiripi, Unquahogs, Massachusetts, Mahicans, Abenakis, and many others — fled westward, or north into Canada, in an often futile attempt to escape complete eradication.*

---

*The figures after the period of dislocation and economic warfare are revealing. By 1690, the Norridgewock had been reduced to 100 men, a total which dropped to 25 survivors — a 75-percent decline under *peaceful* conditions — by 1726; the Androscoggin declined from 160 men in 1690 to 10 in 1726; the Pigwackets showed 100 surviving males in 1690, seven in 1726 (all such "warrior counts" should be multiplied by a factor of five to arrive at population totals); Collin G. Calloway, *The Western Abenaki of Vermont, 1600–1800: War, Migration, and the Survival of an Indian People* (Norman: University of Oklahoma Press, 1990) pp. 129–30. The same situation prevails with data reflecting the period

A century later, as the fledgling United States fought its way clear of English colonial dominion, the use of such methods became even more evident. As early as 1776, in an account of the rebel victory in a campaign against England's Cherokee allies, it was reported that the Indians' "towns is all burnt Their Corn cut down and Themselves drove into the Woods to perish."[113] In 1779, Continental Army General John A. Sullivan earned the nickname "Town Destroyer" from the Senecas, another people allied to the English, when he pursued to the letter his orders from overall commander George Washington to "lay waste all the settlements around...that the country not only be overrun but destroyed, [and not to] listen to any overture of peace before the total ruin of their settlements is effected." As Sullivan reported from the field, his troops "destroy[ed] everything that contributes to [the Senecas'] support" turning "that whole beautiful region from the character of a garden to a scene of drear and sickening desolation."[114]

This was followed, in 1780, by a report from General George Rogers Clark, indicative of the type of warfare his ranger unit was conducting deep in what are now the states of Ohio, Indiana, and Illinois, that "it was estimated that at two [Shawnee] towns, Chillicothe and Piqua, more than five hundred acres of corn were destroyed, as well as every species of edible vegetable."[115] Fourteen years later, U.S. General Anthony Wayne, or "Mad Anthony," as he was called by friend and foe alike, reported from an expedition mounted to finish off the Shawnees and their allies that, having won the battle of Fallen Timbers, "we remained for three days and nights on the banks of the Maumee...during which time all the houses and cornfields were consumed and destroyed for a considerable distance." In sum, the troops had burned "immense fields of corn" for a stretch of about fifty miles along the river.[116]

And so it went, from east of the Mississippi to the far west, where, in 1864, Kit Carson's campaigners were finally able to defeat the Diné by laying waste to the Indians' agricultural complex on the floor of Canyon de Chelly, poisoning their wells, and so on.[117] By 1868, units like Custer's

---

1650–1700. The Maliseets and Passamequodies, for instance, were both reduced by 67 percent; the 18,000-strong Pocumticks dropped to 920 (a 95-percent decline); the Quiripi and Unquahogs, who began with a population of around 30,000, were left with fewer than 1,500 (a 95-percent decline); the Massachusetts, numbering at least 44,000 at the onset, could report barely 6,000 survivors (an 81 percent decline); the Mahicans were 92-percent destroyed; the Eastern Abenaki had declined by 78 percent; their cousins, the Western Abenaki, who had numbered about 12,000 had been reduced to some 250 survivors (a destruction rate of 98 percent); Snow and Lamphear, "European Contact and Depopulation in the Northeast," *op. cit.*, p. 24, Table I.

Seventh Cavalry Regiment had adopted the tactic of slaughtering Indian pony herds wherever possible, not only to destroy their opponents' combat mobility, but to deprive them of the ability to subsist by hunting.[*] The capstone to the whole performance was the army's policy, announced by General Phil Sheridan in 1873, of encouraging the deliberate extermination of an entire species of large mammals, the North American bison ("buffalo"), in order to "destroy the commissary" of the Plains Indians.[118]

In every instance, the destruction of indigenous economies was undertaken within the framework of an overarching intent, expressed as a matter of policy by the respective governments involved, to achieve the outright "extermination" of targeted indigenous peoples.[†] In each case, the object was to bring about a massive fatality rate, not just among native combatants but within the target population *as a whole*.[119] Without exception, the desire was, if not to obtain the complete liquidation of given populations during the conduct of "wars" per se, then to take a longer view: extinction might be reasonably expected to claim any survivors, converted as they were into an atomized cloud of refugees, unable to feed, clothe, or house themselves, through a combination of starvation, exposure, and consequent lowered resistance to all manner of diseases.[120]

Another factor concerns the psychological effects on the Indians—

---

[*] Custer's pioneering of the tactic occurred after his bloody attack on a noncombatant Cheyenne winter encampment on the banks of Oklahoma's Washita River on November 28, 1868. After the survivors had fled, an estimated 875 animals were slaughtered. "Additionally, the 7th had captured all the Indians' supply of dried buffalo meat, meal flour, and other provisions, including most of the Cheyennes' clothing. As critical as anything to the Indians was the loss of their lodges, fifty-one of them. A warrior might revere his horse, but it was his lodge that gave him and his family shelter and permitted survival on the open plains." All of it was burned. There can be not doubt that the "Boy General" intended what was left of his vanquished foe to die of starvation, exposure—or disease—as a result of his actions; Stan Hoig, *The Battle of the Washita* (Norman: University of Oklahoma Press, 1976) pp. 137–9.

[†] There was never anything fuzzy about such statements, as is witnessed in those of Thomas Jefferson, reputedly the greatest humanitarian among the "slaveholding philosophers of freedom" who made up America's founding fathers. Writing to his Secretary of War in 1807, Jefferson, at the time President of the United States, instructed that any native resistance to U.S. expansion into their territories should be overcome militarily, with the object that the Indians be "exterminated, or driven beyond the Mississippi." This was sound policy, he argued, based on such examples as the Powhatans and Pequots, because "in war, they will kill some of us; we shall destroy *all* of them." (emphasis added). Five years later, in 1812, he again took up the theme, opining that Euroamericans were "obliged" to drive all Indians they encountered "with the beasts of the forests into the Stony Mountains," concluding in 1813 that this meant pursuing all Indians east of the Mississippi "to extermination, or to drive them to new seats beyond our reach," and that it was probably preferable to "extirpate them from the earth"; quoted in Drinnon, *Facing West, op. cit.*, pp. 96, 98, 116; Ronald T. Takaki, *Iron Cages: Race and Culture in Nineteenth Century America* (New York: Alfred A. Knopf, 1979) pp. 61–5.

acute anxiety, trauma, and depression, generally referred to as "demoralization," which responsible colonial and U.S. officials—and average citizens, for that matter—*knew* resulted from the kind of warfare they were waging. The literature of the entire period from 1607 to 1920 is replete with observations of this or that Indian, or entire people, having "lost the will to live" in the face of the sudden dispossession of both their homeland and their way of life, as well as most of their friends and relatives.[121] The correlation between such psychological devastation and the inability of the average human organism to fend off disease is no mystery today, and it was not *then*. Instead, it was an anticipated by-product of economic warfare, the effects of which were uniformly celebrated.*

Finally, there is another subtext to the psychology of traumatic demoralization, much less remarked upon, although this too was never a great secret: in periods of severe stress and despair the ability of humans to procreate drops off dramatically.[122] Under the conditions imposed upon American Indians, it could have been readily foreseen—and *was*—that their birthrates would plummet in rather direct correlation to their spiraling rates of death.[123] Infertility was as much a part of the calculations of the exterminators as was the inducing of lowered resistance to disease.[124] Altogether, there was nothing at all unwitting, unintentional, accidental, or inadvertent about the way the great bulk of North America's indigenous population was "vanished by microbe."[125] It was *precisely* malice, not nature, which did the deed.

"To Extirpate This Execrable Race"

If there are any lingering doubts as to whether the invaders deliberately spread disease among North American Indians, it is time to lay them to rest once and for all. Contrary to the orthodoxy that the Europeans who came to the New World were ignorant of how disease spread, it had been a practice since at least as early as Tamerlane (Timur), circa 1385, to catapult the corpses of plague victims and the carcasses of diseased animals into besieged

---

*Examples are legion. See, e.g., *Some Meditations Concerning Our Honorable Gentlemen and Fellow Soldiers, in Pursuit of the Barbarous Natives in the Narragansett Country* (Plymouth Colony, 1675), the oldest surviving news broadside printed in North America; reproduced in Drinnon, *Facing West, op. cit.,* p. 54. Or, moving ahead a couple of centuries and more, consider the words of President Theodore Roosevelt: "Of course our whole history has been one of expansion... That the [Indians] recede or are conquered, with the attendant fact that peace follows their retrogression or conquest, is due solely to the power of the mighty civilized races who have not lost their fighting instinct, and which by their expansion are gradually bringing peace into the red wastes where the barbarian peoples of the world hold sway"; Theodore Roosevelt, *The Strenuous Life* (New York: Macmillan, 1901).

cities.[126] While such early experiments in biological warfare were generally unsuccessful, they do demonstrate unequivocally that the Old World, or at least its military leadership, had learned the mechanics of rudimentary epidemiology well before 1492.

In North America, where wave after wave of epidemics, and several pandemics, wracked native populations, often with a timing uncannily convenient to those who had set out to conquer or eradicate them, the first instance in which there is clear reason to suspect these lessons were being applied occurred in 1636.[127] This came with the execution of Captain John Oldham, an officer/diplomat for Massachusetts Colony, by the Narragansetts. The Indians apparently believed—rightly or wrongly—that Oldham had deliberately infected them with smallpox in 1633, probably by dispensing contaminated "gifts," unleashing an epidemic which claimed more than 700 of their people and numerous of their allies.[128] He was therefore brought before the council of Narragansett sachems on Block Island, tried for this and possibly other offenses, and paid the price.[129]

There is considerable duplicity involved in what happened next. While they were certainly aware of who had killed Oldham (and why), both Massachusetts Governor John Winthrop and William Bradford, his counterpart on the Plymouth Plantation, publicly blamed the Pequots for the "murder," thus predicating the almost total annihilation of that people in 1637.[*] Since it was actually the more powerful Narragansetts, not the Pequots, who were convinced the colonists might be seeking to reduce their numbers through intentional contamination, the idea must be considered a contributing factor to the outbreak of "King Philip's War" some forty years later. Such suspicions are known to have been harbored by several of the lesser nations

---

[*] Winthrop in particular had benefit of not less than five eyewitness accounts of Oldham's execution, all of them attributing his death to the Narragansetts; Winthrop, *History of New England, op. cit.*, pp. 191–2. Perhaps realizing that laying the "murder" of Oldham at the feet of the Pequots, whose land was most immediately coveted by the colonists, might not hold up, Winthrop and Bradford quickly added the death of a Plymouth colonist, Captain John Stone, to their list of "grievances." This, too, was pure sophistry. Stone had in fact been killed by the Pequots in 1635, but it was common knowledge that his death resulted from an attempt to kidnap and ransom several Indians. Plymouth had entered no protest at all, both because of the obvious justice of his fate and because he was at the time "banished from the colony on pain of death if he should ever reappear" because of piracy, sexual offenses, and the use of "threatening speech" against officials. He was, moreover, wanted by Dutch authorities in New Amsterdam for a prior kidnapping; Jennings, *The Invasion of America, op. cit.*, pp. 189–90; Winthrop, *History of New England, op. cit.*, pp. 52, 105; William Bradford, *Of Plymouth Plantation, 1620–1647* (New York: Modern Library, 1981 reprint of undated original) pp. 257–60. Also see Alfred A. Cave, "Who Killed John Stone? A Note on the Origins of the Pequot War," *William and Mary Quarterly*, No. 49, 1992.

"Extirpate this execrable race."
In the world's first documented instance of a genocide accomplished by bacteriological means, Lord Jeffrey Amherst — for whom a city in Massachussetts is now named — ordered smallpox-infected blankets to be passed out to Ottawas and Lenni Lenâpés in 1763. How many other occasions in which similar activities occurred is unknown, but Amherst was by no means the only culprit. Photo: Library of Congress

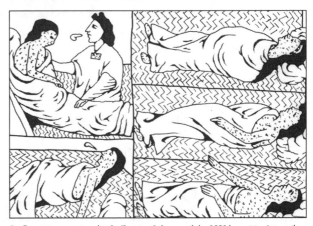

Smallpox victims as portrayed in the Florentine Codex, compiled c. 1550 by surviving Aztec scribes.

—the Eastern Niantics, for example, and the Nipmucks—who, along with the larger Wampanoag confederation under Metacom ("King Philip"), aligned with the Narragansetts against the English in the fighting.*

It is not until another ninety years had passed, however, during the last of the so-called "French and Indian Wars" before positive proof emerges that England was indeed using biological techniques, as such, to eradicate native populations.[130] In 1763, having been fought to a humiliating stalemate in the Ohio River Valley by a French-aligned indigenous military alliance organized by the Ottawa leader Pontiac, Lord Jeffrey Amherst, the English commander-in-chief, wrote a letter to a subordinate, Colonel Henry Bouquet, suggesting that a peace parley be convened and, as was customary at such events, gifts distributed.[131]

> Amherst...wrote in a postscript of the letter to Bouquet that smallpox be sent among the disaffected tribes. Bouquet replied, also in a postscript, "I will try to [contaminate] them with some blankets that may fall into their hands, and take care not to get the disease myself"... To Bouquet's postscript Amherst replied, "You will do well to [infect] the Indians by means of blankets as well as to try every other method that can serve to extirpate this [execrable] race." On June 24, Captain Ecuyer, of the Royal Americans, noted in his journal: "...we gave them two blankets and a handkerchief out of the smallpox hospital. I hope it will have the desired effect."[132]

To say that it did would be to understate the case. The disease spread like wildfire among the Ottawas, Mingos, Miamis, Lenni Lenâpés (Delawares), and several other peoples. By conservative estimate, the toll was over 100,000 dead, a matter which effectively broke the back of native resistance in what the United States would later call the "Northwest Territory," allowing its conquest less than thirty years later.[133] Amherst's maneuver, which displays a considerable familiarity with the notion of disease as a weapon, has been erroneously described as a "milestone of sorts" in military history by Robert O'Connell, in his book *Of Arms and Men*.[134] Actually, since he specified the group targeted for "extirpation" as being not just opposing combatants, but an entire *race*, the "Ohio Valley incident" is not properly understood as an example of biological warfare. Rather, it indisputably an instance of genocide pursued through microbes.[135]

---

*There is no question at all that the Indians felt themselves faced with outright extermination by any and all means, and that this was an exactly accurate interpretation of the desires of colonial officials in Plymouth, Massachusetts, and Connecticut. It is also a certainty that these officials, following the pattern set in the earlier Pequot War, fabricated a pretext to motivate their citizenry to pursue such genocidal ambitions; Jennings, *The Invasion of America, op. cit.*, pp. 298–302; Edward Leach, *Flintlocks and Tomahawks: New England in King Philip's War* (New York: W.W. Norton, 1958).

This was by no means a singular incident, although it is the best documented. Only slightly more ambiguous was the U.S. Army's dispensing of "trade blankets" to Mandans and other Indians gathered at Fort Clark, on the Missouri River in present-day North Dakota, beginning on June 20, 1837. Far from being trade goods, the blankets had been taken from a military infirmary in St. Louis quarantined for smallpox, and brought upriver aboard the steamboat *St. Peter's*. When the first Indians showed symptoms of the disease on July 14, the post surgeon advised those camped near the post to scatter and seek "sanctuary" in the villages of healthy relatives.[136] By then, the disease was already showing up at Fort Union, adjacent to the main Mandan village some forty miles further upriver. The trader there, Jacob Halsey, who was married to an Indian woman, then attempted to administer a vaccine which had been stored by the army rather than used to inoculate the people for whom it was supposedly provided.*

The perfectly predictable result of the "Fort Clark episode"[137] was the igniting of a pandemic which raged for several years, decimating peoples as far north as the Blackfeet, Bloods, and Piegans in southern Alberta and Saskatchewan, to the west as far as the Yuroks and other northern California peoples, and southward to the Kiowas and Comanches on the Staked Plains of Texas.†

---

*Evan S. Connell, *Son of the Morning Star: Custer and the Little Big Horn* (San Francisco: North Point Press, 1984) pp. 15–6. The matter of vaccine is important. Deniers such as Steven Katz are wont to point to a federal policy announced in 1833 "requiring" the inoculation of all Indians against smallpox as "proof" that the U.S. earnestly attempted to prevent the disease from spreading among the indigenous population; Steven T. Katz, "The Uniqueness of the Holocaust: The Historical Dimension," in Alan S. Rosenbaum, ed., *Is the Holocaust Unique? Perspectives on Comparative Genocide* (Boulder, CO: Westview Press, 1996) p. 21. Katz, and those like him, neglect to inquire whether the supposed inoculation requirement was ever acted upon. The answer is a flat no. In post after post, vaccines, when they were provided at all, languished in storerooms rather than being administered. If we've learned anything at all through historical observation of governmental conduct, it should be that ostentatious policy pronouncements lacking anything resembling serious implementation are usually a cover for something else (most often an unstated policy running in the opposite direction). In any event, arguing that the 1833 policy statement proves what Katz says it does is roughly equivalent to arguing that since the nazis maintained medical facilities at Auschwitz they must really have had the Jews' health at heart.

†By the most conservative estimates, the Mandans were virtually exterminated, falling from a population of 2,000 down to perhaps 50 survivors in a matter of weeks; the Blackfeet/Blood/Piegan confederation lost about 8,000 people; the Pawnee, 2,000; one-third of the 9,000 Absarokes (Crows) died; about half the more than 8,000 Assiniboin; as much as three-fifths of several northern California peoples, including the Yurok and Wintu. Peoples suffering substantial but lesser impacts include the Yanktonai Nakota (400), Oklahoma Choctaw (500), and Kansas (100). Although they are known to have been impacted to varying degrees, often heavily, data are unavailable on the Arikara, Hidatsa, Gros Ventre, Lakota, Cheyenne, Arapaho, Kiowa, Kiowa Apache, Jicarilla Apache, Comanche, Winnebago, Oklahoma Chickasaw, Shoshone (both Mountain and Western), Paiute, and several others; Thornton, *American Indian Holocaust and Survival, op. cit.*, pp. 94–5.

There is no conclusive figure as to how many Indians died—it depends a bit on how many one is willing to concede were there in the first place—but estimates run as high as 100,000.[138] However many people perished, their "vanishing" made the subsequent U.S. conquest of the entire Plains region, begun seriously in the 1850s, far easier than it would otherwise have been.

By this point, California, along with its residual population of native people, had been acquired by the United States from Mexico. There is nothing confusing about the meaning of language found in an 1853 San Francisco newspaper, explaining how the incoming Angloamericans were handling their "Indian Question":"people are...ready to knife them, shoot them, or inoculate them with smallpox—*all of which have been done* (emphasis added)."[139] Thus, by the mid-nineteenth century, it appears that the eradication of Indians through *deliberate* infection with plague diseases had become so commonplace that it was no longer a military specialty. Rather, it had been adopted as a method of "pest control" by average civilians. All that is missing are the details as to exactly who did it to which group of northern California natives, how many times and with what overall degree of success. Whatever it was, it fit within a conscious strategy of the citizenry, described in the *San Francisco Bulletin* on July 10, 1860, to effect the "ultimate extermination of the race by disease."[140]

Given these circumstances, as well as those described in this section more generally, it is at best an absurdity to contend that attrition through disease represents anything approximating a "benign" explanation for the complete extinction of numerous North American native peoples—or the near-total disappearance of the "race" as a whole—between 1600 and 1900. To the contrary, based on the evidence the presumption should be—and should have been all along—that the waves of epidemic disease that afflicted indigenous populations during these centuries were deliberately induced, or at least facilitated, by the European invaders.*

---

*The argument that "methodological responsibility" requires conclusive documentary evidence to establish intentionality in each and every instance where it is to be presumed to have played a role holds no water at all. If the historical profession actually adhered to such rarefied standards, it would not even be able to demonstrate that Adolf Hitler played a role in exterminating the Jews and Gypsies; see, e.g., Gerald Fleming, *Hitler and the Final Solution* (Berkeley: University of California Press, 1982). Presumption in historical analysis is based, not on excruciatingly detailed evidence in every instance, but upon assessment of phenomena within the overall context in which they occurred. In view of the overall pattern of their policies, actions, and rhetoric, the nazis are reasonably presumed guilty of a wide range of things by historians, absent compelling evidence to the contrary in any given instance. The same principle holds true for the invaders of America: they should not, and should never have been, automatically presumed innocent *in the face of* their overwhelmingly clear pattern of rhetoric, action, and policy.

To do otherwise is tantamount to arguing, as some "scholars" do, that the approximately 50 percent of the Jews who died as a result of "ghettoization and general privation" at the hands of the nazis shouldn't be tallied into the toll of the Holocaust since, after all, they perished from "natural causes" like starvation and disease.[141] Framed more broadly, it would be the same as saying that of the estimated fifty million fatalities usually attributed to the Second World War, at least two-thirds should not be counted since they died of malnutrition, exposure, disease, and war-related traumas rather than from "direct killing techniques."[142] If such "standards" seem ridiculous when applied in these contexts—and they should—they should seem no less so when applied to the devastation of Native North America.

Profiles in Extermination

Having rebutted the main lines of argument by which the North American holocaust is minimized and denied, it is time to turn to that from which they are designed to divert attention: the matter of direct killing. Here, we again encounter minimization and denial of the first order. Consider a very recent formulation offered by Steven T. Katz to "debunk" the notion that indigenous people suffered literal extermination: "Even Russell Thornton, who has vigorously attempted to highlight the roles of warfare and genocide in the decline of the Indian population, is forced by the unassailable demographic evidence to conclude that, at most, '45,000 American Indians [were] killed in wars with Europeans and Americans between 1775–1890. To this might be added…8,500 American Indians killed in individual conflicts during the period, to arrive at a total of 53,000 killed.'"[143]

> That is to say, in a period of 115 years, during which the indigenous population declined by over 1.5 million, only 53,000 casualties, or 3.7 percent of the total lost, can be counted as having been intentionally murdered. For the pre-1775 period, the percentage of loss due to warfare (and individual murder) is even lower. Thornton, for example, in attempting to configure losses in the prerevolutionary era, suggests doubling the post-1775 figure of 53,000 to arrive at a pre-1775 aggregate. Accordingly, if we follow this suggestion, if only for purposes of argument, we have a projection, however crudely arrived at, of 106,000 casualties due to war and conflict situations in this earlier epoch. However, given the much higher total native population in this native contact period—anywhere up to ten or more times as great as what it was after 1775—the percentage of loss represented by this hypothesized 106,000 casualties shrinks to some fraction of 1 percent.[144]

Leaving aside the transparency of Katz's attempt to constrain the definitional boundaries of "murder" to absurdly narrow limits, there is a more immediate problem: this is not at all what Thornton said. It is worth quoting at length here in order to clearly establish the extent of Katz's manipulation. Thornton himself prefaces the page cited by Katz with a quotation from an 1894 report of the U.S. Bureau of the Census:

> It has been estimated that since 1775, more than [8,500 Indians] have been killed in individual affairs with [whites]... The Indian wars under the government of the United States have been more than forty in number. They have cost the lives of...about 30,000 Indians... The actual number of killed and wounded Indians must be very much greater than the number given, as they conceal, where possible, their actual loss in battle, and carry their killed and wounded off and secrete them. The number above is of those found by whites. Fifty percent additional would be a safe number to add to the numbers given.[145]

He then writes, "Assuming these figures are correct and, for purposes of illustration, adding 50 percent American Indian dead to the 30,000 estimate yields 45,000 American Indians killed in wars with Europeans and Americans between 1775 and 1890. To this might be added the above reported 8,500 American Indians killed in individual conflicts during the period, to arrive at a total of 53,500 killed by the government's own admission. The Indians killed in wars and individual affairs before 1775 might easily double the figure."[146] Far from embracing this governmentally derived estimate as his own, however, Thornton immediately points to one glaring omission in its database — the Indian dead from "intertribal warfare" instigated by the invaders — and then cuts to the heart of his point.[*]

> As these deaths are added, the mortality figures become considerably more substantial: 150,000? 250,000? 500,000? We do not know. Suffice it to say, American Indians suffered substantial population loss due to warfare stemming from the European arrival and colonization... We can only guess at the numbers of American Indians killed by genocide. And it is undoubtedly more problematic to guess the losses from genocide because genocide was neither as well recorded nor as well publicized as warfare.[147]

From there, he provides considerable material to illustrate exactly the sorts and quantities of fatalities he is including within his classification of

---

[*] The argument will no doubt be raised that Indians killed by Indians should not be held against the invaders, regardless of the degree of coercion, etc., employed by the latter to obtain precisely that result. By the same logic, Jews killed by *kapos*, especially those who were themselves Jewish, at Auschwitz, should not be held against the nazis; see Danuta Czech, "The Auschwitz Prisoner Administration," in Yisrael Gutman and Michael Berenbaum, eds., *Anatomy of the Auschwitz Death Camp* (Bloomington/Washington, D.C.: Indiana University Press/U.S. Holocaust Memorial Museum, 1994) esp. pp. 362–5.

genocide,[148] all of which remains as conspicuously unmentioned by Katz as is Thornton's own estimate of up to a half-million dead from warfare alone. Much of what Thornton offers has been covered above. The remainder is included among the matters discussed in the following subsections. Once again, it seems appropriate to begin at the beginning and trace the evolution of the more overt forms of slaughter through to approximately 1900.

Opening Rounds

The "Indian Wars" in North America started at almost the moment the first Europeans set foot upon the continent. Ponce de León's fabled 1513 quest for the Fountain of Youth in Florida—actually, at least in part, a slaving expedition meant to replenish the dwindling supply of fodder for the *encomiendos* on Española and other Caribbean islands—was marked by a series of aggressive acts against, and resultant altercations with, the local Ais and Calusas.[149] In 1521, Ponce returned to set up a permanent colony, only to be mortally wounded by a Calusa arrow while attempting to pacify the indigenous population by cold steel. He died shortly thereafter in Cuba.[150]

By then, Alverde Piñeda had explored the Gulf Coast, come upon the Mississippi River, and set in motion Spanish slaving enterprises on a larger scale.[151] It was slavers who first probed the Atlantic coastline as far north as Maine.[152] One result was the establishment of what was meant to be a permanent slave-trading post dubbed San Miguel de Guadalupe, on Sapelo Sound in present-day Georgia, in 1526. This first European settlement in North America since those of the Vikings had failed five centuries earlier lasted less than a year.[153] Another expedition, this one headed by veteran conquistador Pánfilo de Narváez in 1528, landed on the Florida coast with 400 men and eighty horses and attempted to hack their way through the Apalachees of the panhandle region. Ultimately, there were only five known survivors among the Spanish, four of whom managed to walk all the way to Mexico by 1536.*

---

*The best account of Narváez's expedition comes from one of the four survivors, Alvar Núñez Cabeza de Vaca. See his *Cabeza de Vaca's Adventures in the Unknown Interior of America* (Potomac, MD: Scripta Humanística, 1986 edited translation of the 1542 original); also see Morris Bishop, *The Odyssey of Cabeza de Vaca* (Engelwood Cliffs, NJ: Prentice-Hall, 1933). It should be noted that the group which escaped Florida was much larger, and left on rafts. They were starving and resorted to cannibalism before being wrecked in a storm along the Texas coast, where the few that were left found by local Karankawas. Predictably, the Indians, who were "shocked" to discover evidence that the Spaniards had been devouring one another, were later themselves falsely branded as cannibals by Spanish historians.

The near-total demographic collapse of the indigenous Caribbean population had driven the premium on fresh supplies of slave labor through the roof by the mid-1530s.[154] Simultaneously, the astonishing trove of precious metals garnered by Cortés in his sacking of Tenochtitlán sparked a frenzy to discover further "Cities of Gold." And, of course, Spain was still seeking a water route to India and China.[155] All three factors, combined with an active interest in further territorial expansion, led the Spanish to intensify their activities in North America, mainly through the massive 1539–42 expeditions headed by Francisco Vásquez de Coronado and Fernando de Soto into the southwestern and southeastern portions of the continent, respectively.

Coronado's foray, involving over 300 men-at-arms and about a thousand indigenous mercenaries from northern Mexico, was unabashedly devoted to locating and conquering the fictional "Seven Cities of Cíbola," reputedly somewhere in the area of what are now New Mexico and eastern Arizona.[156] What he found instead were the Tewa and Kerasan pueblos, first Zuni, then Hopi, then the remainder, all the way north and east to Taos.[157] Along the way, his troops emptied native larders, commandeered other property, raped the local women and—to "make an example which would discourage rebellion" at such treatment—laid waste to the village of Arenal, burning its occupants at the stake.[158] This atrocity prompted the very kind of resistance it was meant to deter, and before it was over, thirteen additional pueblos were destroyed along with their inhabitants.[159] By the spring of 1542, having marched as far as central Kansas and killed several thousand Indians in his futile search for golden cities, the would-be Cortés was defeated. He left a small garrison near the present location of Santa Fe and retreated southward into Mexico.*

Meanwhile, to the east in Florida, de Soto's force, 600-strong, had landed near Tampa Bay in May 1539. From there, it moved northward as far as the Carolinas, doubled back into Georgia, then moved erratically westward through what are now Alabama and Mississippi before crossing the great river into Arkansas. Along the way, he encountered a number of indigenous peoples, including the Tocobagans, Timucuans, Apalachees, Tuscaloosas,

---

*Both Coronado and his second-in-command, García López de Cárdenas, suffered the fate of many such failures: they were tried by the Crown for their crimes against Indians. Coronado, still commanding a certain prestige of rank, was exonerated and died in Mexico City, impoverished and eclipsed, in 1544. López, on the other hand, was convicted of the massacre at Arenal and died in prison. This is not proof that Spain was "struggling for justice in the New World" so much as it is evidence that the Spanish were perfectly aware that their treatment of native people was criminal, whether it succeeded or not; Weber, *Spanish Frontier, op. cit.*, p. 49.

Cofitachiquis, Cherokees, Creeks, Choctaws, Chickasaws, Natchez, and perhaps the Caddos.[160]

> De Soto had brought an ambulatory larder in the form of hundreds of pigs whose numbers increased along the march, but he regularly plundered the food supplies of the natives, taking dried corn, squash and beans from storage. He had brought twice the number of Spaniards that Coronado did, but unlike Coronado... de Soto captured slave labor along his route. He had worked out the plan before leaving Spain, for he brought along iron chains and collars to link Indians into human baggage trains. Indian women "who were not old nor the most ugly," de Soto's secretary later explained, the Spaniards "desired both as servants and for foul uses...they had them baptized more on account of carnal intercourse with them than to teach them the faith." Uncooperative Indians might be put to the sword, thrown to the dogs, or burned alive, or might have a hand or nose severed. De Soto killed and mutilated Indians with little provocation, for in the words of one chronicler who knew him, [he] was "much given to the sport of hunting Indians from horseback."[161]

Wherever it went, the expedition "left a trail of shattered lives, broken bodies, ravaged fields, empty storehouses, and charred fields."[162] Resistance mounted as they moved inland and word of their barbarities spread among the native populations ahead of them. Although badly outnumbered, the Spanish, clad in armor and bearing superior weaponry, more than held their own. De Soto buried his dead, had the wounds of his injured treated with the fat of slain Indians, and pressed on.[163] Finally, in late March 1541, a group of Chickasaws made a surprise attack and managed to burn a number of the troops as they slept cooped up in winter shelters.[164] After that, combat was avoided wherever possible and "the invasion of the interior" began to lose steam.[165] It petered out altogether when de Soto himself died in May 1542. What was left of his force —about half of those who had started out—floundered about for some months before making boats and escaping across the Gulf to Mexico.[166]

Although the number of Indians killed in these early expeditions was not great as compared to the scale of butchery that would soon prevail in North America—there were probably around 10,000 native dead, *en toto*—the manner of killing and the attitudes it revealed speak far louder than the bodycount itself.* In this sense, they serve as a preview of things to come, all

---

*This leaves aside the number of Indians taken by Spanish slavers during this period, which is unknown, but must have been considerable. It is certain that Lucas Vasquez de Allyón, for one, took several boatloads, at perhaps 200 per load, to be consumed on the plantations of Española in 1520, and that he operated for another nine years. Esteban Gomez, a Portuguese, not only supplied the Caribbean islands, but delivered a load of fifty Indian slaves, probably from South Carolina, to Spain in 1525. There were a number of others plying their trade along the Atlantic and Gulf coasts between 1515

the more so as they proved to be the fulcrum upon which the weight of the Old World began to swing into the New north of the Río Grande. Only a little more than two decades after Coronado's and de Soto's bedraggled remnants fled back to New Spain, the Spanish had returned to Florida to stay.[167] Before century's end, they would be a permanent presence in New Mexico.[168] Worse, the English, French, and Dutch were coming, too.

A Terrour to the Reste...

The initial effort by the English to establish a colony, led by Martin Frobisher in 1576, was undertaken after a crewman found what was believed to be gold on the shores of Baffin Island during an attempt to discover a northern water route to Asia. When the mineral turned out to be pyrite, Frobisher contented himself with capturing "sundry tokens of people" (Inuits) and taking them back for display before London society.[169] The same sorts of outlooks and practices prevailed during other English voyages of exploration of the era.[170]

In 1585, Sir Walter Raleigh sought to found a permanent colony, Roanoak, near Hatteras, a Croatoan village on the outer banks of North Carolina.[171] Although the local Indians were initially welcoming, feeding the newcomers and teaching them agriculture and other survival skills, the Roanoak colonists proved so belligerently arrogant that a state of virtual low-intensity warfare was quickly established.[172] At some point between 1587, when Raleigh delivered a fresh load of 117 recruits to his enterprise, and 1590, when the next English supply ship arrived, the entire population of the Roanoak Colony simply disappeared. Since this was attributed to defeat at the hands of the Croatoans—literally "eaten by the savages," according to one anthropologist during the 1970s[173]—the venture was thereupon broken off.*

---

and 1560. Additionally, it is known that the de Soto expedition maintained a supply of up to 800 slaves, captured en route, throughout its three years in the field. All told, it is probable that the number of slaves taken was several times the number of Indians killed outright, and the former were just as lost to their people as the latter; see generally, Lauber, *Indian Slavery in Colonial Times, op. cit.*, pp. 48–61.

*The evidence is strong that the fate of the Roanoak colonists was to be adopted ("naturalized") as tribal members ("citizens") by the Croatoans: "Many years later, in 1650, the Croatoan Indians migrated from Hatteras to mainland North Carolina, where they were known as the Lumbees. Some of them were fair-haired and blue-eyed. Among their family names were the names of Roanoak settlers such as Dial, and there was a curious singsong in their speech, reminiscent, it was said, of Elizabethan English"; Ted Morgan, *Wilderness at Dawn: The Settling of the North American Continent* (New York: Simon & Schuster, 1993) p. 82. This, incidentally, was common practice among many, if not most, North American indigenous peoples, who had been adopting/naturalizing one another since time immemorial. Contrary to the rigid insistence upon "blood" evident among many

A bit north, in Virginia, things were moving in a different direction. On May 14, 1607, the English Southern Virginia Company landed a colonizing expedition on a peninsula along what they called the James River, near present-day Williamsburg.[174] Nominally headed by a civilian governor, Sir Thomas West de la Warr, the Jamestown Plantation, as it was quickly dubbed, was actually under command of Captain John Smith, a professional soldier hired to render its planned aggression efficient.* The first violence was on the fourth day, when an Indian was assaulted for "stealing" a hatchet for which he'd apparently traded food (the English, it has been pointed out, seem never to have been able to feed themselves).[175] This led to the first battle, which occurred on May 26.[176]

The colonists had already been busily erecting fortifications against the very Indians who'd been feeding them, a rather obvious indication of their intentions. With his base established and the colonists organized into a coherent military force, and with reinforcements on the way, Smith moved in 1608 to impose the exploitative relationship with the natives he'd been sent to create: "When the Paspaheghs and Chickahominies…refused to trade, he pursued them with such vehemence and did such damage to their houses, boats, and weirs that they quickly sued for peace and loaded his barges with corn. To secure the return of stolen weapons or tools he did not scruple to torture Indian prisoners or, worse yet from their standpoint, shackle them in a dungeon."[177]

contemporary Indians—an attitude clearly internalized from their colonizers—traditional native societies were never plagued with the concepts of "race," exclusivism, and supremacism that mark western European cultures. Native peoples were thus quite uninhibited about incorporating whites, and later blacks, into themselves as full member/citizens. It was English colonialism in particular which sought to abolish the practice on grounds of its presumed racial supremacy, in much the same fashion the Germans would do under the Nuremberg Laws. See, e.g., James Axtell, "The White Indians of North America," in his *The European and the Indian: Essays in the Ethnohistory of North America* (New York: Oxford University Press, 1981); Jack D. Forbes, *Black Africans and Native Americans: Race, Color and Caste in the Making of Red-Black Peoples* (New York: Oxford University Press, 1988); Karen Ordahl Kupperman, *Settling with the Indians: The Meeting of English and American Cultures in America, 1580–1640* (Totowa, NJ: Rowman and Littlefield, 1980); Drinnon, *Facing West, op. cit.*, pp. 3–20. On the nazis' 1935 "Blood Protection Law," see, e.g., Stefan Kühl, *The Nazi Connection: Eugenics, American Racism, and German National Socialism* (New York: Oxford University Press, 1994) pp. 97–9. Overall, see Ashley Montague, *Man's Most Dangerous Myth: The Fallacy of Race* (Cleveland/New York: World, 1964); Joel Kovel, *White Racism: A Psychohistory* (New York: Columbia University Press, 1984 revision of the 1970 Pantheon edition).

*Not only was a subsequent colony, Delaware, named in honor of de la Warr, but the indigenous population there, the Lenni Lenâpé, were called "Delawares" as well. As to aggression, Smith's original instructions were to clear whatever native inhabitants were encountered from the seacoast and then push them further inland at whatever rate seemed practicable; Edward Arber and A.G. Bradley, eds., *Travels and Works of Captain John Smith, President of Virginia and Admiral of New England, 1580–1631*, 2 vols. (Edinburgh: John Grant, 1910) Vol. 1, pp. xxxiii–xxxvii.

His field commanders were equally ruthless. When two English emissaries sent to purchase an island from the Nansemonds were tortured and killed [in retaliation for an earlier English atrocity], troops under Captains John Martin and George Percy "Beate the Salvages outt of the Island, burned their howses, Ransacked their Temples, Tooke downe the Corp[s]es of the dead kings from of[f] their Toambes, and caryed away their pearles, Copper and braceletts, wherewith they doe decor[at]e their king's funeralles." When Captain Francis West and three dozen men were sent to the Potomac to trade for corn, they loaded their pinnace but "used some harshe and Crewell dealinge by cutteinge of[f] towe of the Salvages heads and other extremetyes."[178]

There is solid evidence that Wahunsonacock (whom the English called Powhatan; they called his confederation that, too, although it called itself Tsenacommacah), a Pamunkey and principal leader of the local Indian confederation—which was greatly superior in numbers and could undoubtedly have obliterated the colonists at this point, had they a mind to—made every effort to negotiate some sort of equitable arrangement to end the fighting before it got out of hand.[179] The English, however, were having none of it. Their objective, stripped of all gloss and veneer, was outright extermination: "[It] is infinitely better to have no heathen among us, who at best were but thorns in our sides, then to be at peace and in league with them," as one participant later put it.[180]

Smith was seriously injured by the accidental explosion of a powder cask in 1609, and returned to England (he never came back to Jamestown), but de la Warr launched his war of annihilation the following year.[181] Field command was assigned to Captain George Percy, who pursued the strategy described above, and proved himself every bit as vicious as Smith.

In August, seventy men under command of Percy, led by an Indian prisoner in a handlock, assaulted the Paspahegh town, killing sixteen and capturing the chief's wife and children. After burning the natives' houses and cutting down their corn (which was not unneeded at Jamestown), the soldiers groused that any natives were spared. So a military council met and decided to put the children to death, "which was effected by Throweinge them overboard and shoteinge owt their Braynes in the water." With great difficulty Percy managed to prevent his men from burning the "Queen" at the stake until she could be more humanely put to the sword. On the way home the expedition stopped at Chickahominy to cut down the inhabitants' corn and burn their houses, temples, and religious "idols." Such scenes were repeated up and down the river all fall.*

---

* Axtell, *After Columbus, op. cit.*, p. 207. The exterminationist sensibilities of the colonists, rank-and-file and leadership alike, is readily apparent, not only in the troops' murder of the vanquished Paspahegh leader's children—who might have made good hostages—but in de la Warr's response when Percy arrived at Jamestown with the man's captive wife: "Governor de la Warr was unhappy with him

The following summer saw the arrival of a further 600 troops, well armed and with "a great store of armor." Shortly, a column of a hundred iron-clad men led by Governor Thomas Dale—de la Warr had retired for reasons of health—assaulted the town of the Nansemonds, repeating Percy's performance of the year before, but killing a much larger number of Indians in the process.[182] From then on, the colonists began to build an increasing number of satellite forts, none of which could be approached by an Indian without permission lest he or she suffer, at best, the severing of a hand or, more often, summary execution as "a Terrour to the Reste."[183] The native people, for their part, withdrew further and further, seeking to find to a safe distance.

A war of attrition was pursued until 1614, when a "truce" was arranged after Wahunsonacock's daughter, Pocahantas, was captured by Captain Thomas Argall and held hostage.[184] Although the colonists, now led by George Yeardley, continued to undermine the Tsenacommacahs, encroaching upon their farmlands and killing them at a steady pace—meanwhile tripling their own population—Wahunsonacock appears to have held up his end of the agreement until his death in 1618.* Leadership of the confederation passed to his younger brother, Opechancanough, who began casting about for some means of averting the extinction quite literally staring his people in the face. The Indians had run out of room to retreat, and could afford no more unreturned casualties.†

---

because he had not yet killed the queen. Advised by his chief lieutenant that it would be best to burn her alive, Percy decided instead to end his day of 'so mutche Bloodshedd' with a final act of mercy: instead of burning her, he had the queen killed by stabbing her to death"; Stannard, *American Holocaust, op. cit.*, p. 106. Both authors are quoting from Percy, "'A Trewe Relacyon': Virginia from 1609–1612," *op. cit.*, pp. 271–3.

*The *quid pro quo* seems to have been that, in exchange for his daughter's safety, Wahunsonacock would use his influence to prevent, or at least hold to a minimum, his people's military responses to the colonists. The latter, for their part, promised to cease their physical aggression, but never really did. Rather, they simply throttled back the pace of butchery—with perhaps another 500 Indians killed in the six years from 1615 through 1621—confident that at that rate the "truce" would spare them physical consequences; see generally, Robert Beverley, *The History and Present State of Virginia* (Chapel Hill: University of North Carolina Press, 1947 edited reprint of 1705 original).

†"By 1622 the land-hungry English had claimed most of the excellent waterfront along the James River, interfering with Powhatan access to fields, reed-gathering areas, and the waterway itself; Ian K. Steele, *Warpaths: Invasions of North America* (New York: Oxford University Press, 1994) p. 45. As colonist Edward Waterhouse put it at the time, with considerable accuracy: the Tsenacommacahs experienced "the dayly feare that possest them, that we by our growing continually upon them, would dispossess them of this Country" and their very existence; quoted from Susan Myra Kingsbury, ed., *The Records of the Virginia Company of London*, 4 vols. (Washington, D.C.: Smithsonian Institution, 1906–1935) Vol. 3, pp. 556–7. Another intriguing possibility, unremarked in the literature, is that the Tsenacommacahs were convinced, as the Narragansetts were a bit later, that the colonists had deliberately infected them with an epidemic which took several hundred between 1617 and 1619. It *is* suspicious insofar as the Indians, despite frequent and close proximity to the English for a decade,

Opechancanough's counteroffensive, when it came, was thus born of pure desperation. On March 22, 1622, the Tsenacommacahs rose as a body, killing 347 colonists in a drive to push them back within the boundaries that had prevailed ten years earlier.[185] Sir Francis Wyatt, who had replaced Yeardley as governor, then instructed his military commanders to resume the colony's earlier tactics of total war, "even to...rooting them out from being longer a people uppon the face of the earth...by force, by surprise, by famine in burning their Corne...by pursuing and chasing them with blood-Hounds to draw after them, and Mastives to seaze them...by driving them (when they flye) upon their enemies, who are around them, and by animating and abetting their enemies against them."[*]

The officers complied with a vengeance, laying waste to towns, villages, and fields by the score, stalking the Tsenacommacahs continuously. Perhaps 3,000 Indians were killed in only a few months. When Opechancanough requested a peace parley in May 1623, Wyatt used the occasion to murder "nearly two hundred natives by having them toast the peace with poisoned sack."[186] A second attempt, a few months later, was used as an ambush in which another fifty leaders were shot and hacked to death.[187] In a two-day battle in July 1624, more than 800 Pamunkeys were slaughtered.[188] And so it went until 1632, when it was decided that there were so few remaining Tsenacommacahs that it was no longer worth the time and expense of tracking them down and killing them.[189]

There was one last spasm in 1644, as Opechancanough, by then old and enfeebled, led the starving remains of his once-proud and populous confederacy in a futile attempt to carve out some small niche for themselves in what had been their homeland. Caught by surprise, the colonists lost around 500 killed, but in their thousands they swarmed into action, obliterating the last of the Tsenacommacahs' fighting strength and capturing Opechancanough himself in 1646.[190] The old man was taken in chains to Jamestown and placed on display before being shot to death by a soldier displeased by the fierceness of

showed no signs of illness until the precise moment the latter were sufficiently well established and populous to begin a major territorial expansion. Then, suddenly and mysteriously, the Indians began to die like flies.

[*]Kingsbury, Vol. 3, *The Records of the Virginia Company, op. cit.*, pp. 557–8, 672, 683; Vol. 4, p. 71. This strategy of driving a targeted native population up against other peoples, thus forcing the latter into territorial defense—as was done to the Tsenacommacahs vis-à-vis the far stronger Susquehannocks, as well as the Chesapeak confederation of Patawomecs (Potomacs), Monacans, Accomacs, Accohannocks, and others—would become standard fare in the English inventory of techniques to decimate Indians without appearing to do so.

his pride.[191] This final scourge of the Tsenacommacahs was not so costly in terms of slaughtered native noncombatants because the colony's newest governor, William Berkeley, sensed potential profits and ordered his troops "to spare the women and children," wherever possible, "and sell them" into slavery.[*]

This final liquidation of the "Powhatan Empire" set the stage for equally savage assaults on the other indigenous nations of Virginia and the Maryland Colony, immediately northward.[†] Already, in November 1623, "the Virginia militia had expanded its range and made new enemies by ["mistakenly"] attacking and burning Moyaone, the stockaded Potomac town of the Piscataway."[192] The process was slowed somewhat by political convulsions in England itself, manifested in Virginia as "Bacon's Rebellion" (1675–76)[‡] and some serious sparring with both the Dutch and, briefly, the Swedes over colonial rights.[§] However, the burgeoning numbers of English colonists, their insa-

---

[*] Morgan, *Wilderness at Dawn, op. cit.*, p. 233. About 1,500 native women and children were thus disposed of in the West Indies; Rountree, *The Powhatan Indians, op. cit.*, p. 85–6. The number of Indian dead is, as always, difficult to establish with certainty, but would certainly be at least 500. The result was that the original 100,000 or more Tsenacommacahs had been reduced to about 1,000 by 1675, and continued to decline thereafter.

[†] Actually, the Tsenacommacahs did not go completely out of existence until the early eighteenth century. Until then, a small group, mostly Pamunkeys, was maintained as a Jamestown "tributary." They were led after the murder of Openchancanough, by Necotowance. When he was killed in 1655 while helping defend the colony from a strange group of Indians called "Richahecrians"by the English— they've never been truly identified—who briefly incurred from the west, he was replaced by a woman, Cockacoeske. She seems to have been the last Tsenacommacah leader of any significance; Martha M. McCartney, "Cockacoeske, Queen of the Pamunkey: Diplomat and Suzerain," in Peter H. Wood, Gregory A. Waselkov and M. Thomas Hatley, eds., *Powhatan's Mantle: Indians in the Colonial Southeast* (Lincoln: University of Nebraska Press, 1989).

[‡] The "rebellion" undertaken by colonist Nathaniel Bacon and 200 militia members in 1675 was only marginally connected to the civil war in England of 1642–1649 which resulted in the beheading of Charles I and transformation of the government in the latter year (Bacon claimed he was a "royalist" and that he refused to recognize the legitimacy of the replacement body). More to the point was his desire to assume a dominant position over the Indian slave trade, and, for that purpose, to prosecute wars against the natives more rapidly than the colonial regime desired (all prisoners taken being legally defined as slaves for life). The rebellion petered out when Bacon suddenly died of natural causes in October 1676; Wilcomb E. Washburn, *The Governor and the Rebel: A History of Bacon's Rebellion in Virginia* (Chapel Hill: University of North Carolina Press, 1957) pp. 49–67.

[§] The shortlived colony of New Sweden (1638–1655) had little lasting impact. Over the short run, however, it preoccupied the English, and resulted in the arming of the already powerful Susequehannocks, whom the Swedes were courting as allies against the other European powers, with state-of-the-art weaponry, including cannons. This, in turn, slowed the rate at which England was able to overpower the Susequehannocks themselves; Francis Jennings, "Susequehannocks," in Bruce Trigger, ed., *Handbook of North American Indians, Vol. 15: The Northeast* (Washington, D.C.: Smithsonian Institution, 1978). The Dutch, operating out of their colony of New Amsterdam, later the city of New York, were busily raiding Virginia tobacco shipping during this period as an offshoot of the three rapid-fire Anglo-Dutch wars in Europe (1652–54, 1665–67, and 1672–74); Steele, *Warpaths, op. cit.*, p. 50; more broadly, see Amandua Johnson, *The Swedish Settlements on the Delaware: Their History and Relation to the Indians, 1638–1664* (Philadelphia: University of Pennsylvania Press, 1911).

tiable desire for land on which to expand the increasingly lucrative production of tobacco, and the profitability of the trade in native slaves all combined as incentive for a series of openly exterminatory wars against regional Indians.*

> The spark was ignited in July 1675 by the Doeg, a small tribe on the Maryland side of the Potomac who were now a close neighbor of the [much larger and more powerful] Susquehannock. Angry with Thomas Mathew, a wealthy Virginia planter who reportedly refused to pay for goods received, the Doeg took hogs from one of Mathews' plantations. The English pursued, killing several of the tribe and recovering the hogs; in revenge, a Doeg war party killed one of Mathews' herdsmen. Two Virginia militia captains then led thirty men across the Potomac into Maryland. While one group terrorized a Doeg settlement, killing ten, the other militiamen attacked a nearby cabin, killing fourteen before discovering that they were Susquehannock, erstwhile English allies. Once again, Virginians had displayed surprising, or feigned, difficulty distinguishing between [American Indian] friend and enemy. Maryland protests against both the invasion and the killing of innocent [Indians] were soon forgotten in the midst of a wave of [Indian] attacks on the frontiers of both colonies.[193]

In the fighting which followed, a number of smaller peoples like the Doegs, Occaneechees, and Piscataways were decimated to the point of disappearance.[194] The Susequehannocks proved a much tougher opponent—in 1675, for example, about a hundred of them fortified the remains of the Piscataway town torched in 1623, complete with Swedish cannon, and withstood a siege by 500 Maryland militia for seven weeks—but were eventually worn down.[195] By 1680, harried relentlessly by the militias, the Susequehannocks were effectively dissolved as a people, their survivors absorbed by the five nations of the Haudenosaunee (Iroquois) confederation in what is now Pennsylvania and New York.[196] As of 1700, it is estimated that fewer than 3,000 indigenous people remained within the entire expanse of lush agricultural land extending from the Chesapeake Bay to the Appalachian Mountains, once one of the most densely populated regions in all of Native North America.[197]

---

*By 1672, Virginia was exporting 17 million pounds of tobacco per year to England, aboard more than a hundred ships. Nearly 15,000 indentured servants were among the 38,000 colonists, most of them working in tobacco production. They were augmented by an estimated 2,500 African chattel slaves by that point (native slaves being mainly shipped to Caribbean markets, from whence they could not escape back to their peoples); *Historical Statistics*, series Z, pp. 13–4, 457–9. Also see Robert V. Wells, *The Population of the British Colonies in America before 1776: A Survey of the Census Data* (Princeton: Princeton University Press, 1975).

The record of the English colonists who "settled" the already long- and well-settled area which became "New England" is, if anything, worse than that of their colleagues further south. Things got off to a rocky start in 1602, when an exploratory probe of the area around Cape Cod resulted in hostilities with local Wampanoags (Pokanokets), which caused a hasty departure of the explorers. In 1603 the English returned and attempted to erect a fortification, but were again routed, this time by a group of Nausets. In 1605, George Waymouth, sailing for the Plymouth Company, landed along the Kennebec River, kidnapped five Eastern Abenaki, and returned to England.[198] Two years later, George Popham and Raleigh Gilbert, a pair of former pirates turned Plymouth Company stockholders, returned to the Kennebec with 120 men to establish what they called the Sagadohoc Colony. They built a fort, but shortly ran afoul of the Skidwarre and Tahanedo bands of Abenaki and, by 1608, this beachhead was also abandoned.*

The primary difficulty encountered by all of these ventures was that there were far too many indigenous people in the immediate area—estimates run as high as high as 90,000 in 1600—for them to simply impose themselves.[199] This problem was rectified in 1614 by Captain John Smith, of Jamestown fame, who suddenly materialized on the coastline with a company of Plymouth Company voyagers, shot seven Indians in three quick skirmishes, and abducted 27 Patuxet Wampanaogs and Nausets to sell as slaves in the West Indies on the way home.[200] Mysteriously—the Indians had had close contact with Europeans for years without getting sick—epidemics broke out in the immediate aftermath of Smith's expedition.†

> Between 1616 and 1618, a devastating "virgin soil epidemic"…raged through New England. Fully 90 percent of the Wampanoag died of an unidentified European disease, as did a comparable number of Massachusetts and nearly as many Pawtucket and

---

*The incentive was that the company had been granted the "right" by Charles I to develop a "parcel of 1,000 square miles around anywhere it chose to build a post between 38° and 45° north latitude"; Charles McLean Andrews, *The Colonial Period in American History*, 4 vols. (New Haven: Yale University Press, 1934–1939) Vol. 1, pp. 90–7.

†The earliest known contact in this region occurred when Giovani da Verrazano, sailing for France, landed in 1524. Spanish slavers may well have been there even earlier—certainly, they appeared periodically throughout the sixteenth century—and it is possible the Vikings came this far south five centuries earlier still. Then there are the English ground parties, beginning in 1602, Henry Hudson's 1609 voyage and contacts, and so on. It is indeed "interesting" that none of this often more substantial interaction produced a "virgin soil epidemic," but that one broke out just when it was most convenient—in fact, *necessary*—for the English. Again, God or man?

Eastern Abenaki. Dozens of known coastal villages along Massachusetts Bay were entirely abandoned... [This vastly] improved English chances of establishing a colony successfully in what was now an underpopulated area.[201]

Hence, by the time the "Pilgrims" showed up in 1620, complete with an ample inventory of weapons and a professional soldier, Myles Standish, to oversee their use, there was plenty of "vacant land" for them to select as the site of what was to be England's first durable colony in the north.[202] The Wampanoags, who had been regionally ascendant—and upon whose land the English settled like another plague—were so decimated that the balance of power among the Indians had shifted abruptly to the Narragansetts.[203] They were more or less content, so long as the colonists did not seriously incur upon their territory, a matter which would not become an explosive issue for another half-century.

Under these conditions, there was only minor military scuffling for the next seventeen years as the newcomers consolidated the Plymouth Plantation, as they called it, and imported another thousand constituents.* The Massachusetts Bay Colony, founded in 1629, added another 4,000 English.[204] The Indians, for their part, were preoccupied not only with trying to define their relationship to the invaders but with sorting things out among themselves, given the radical alteration of their respective demographics only a decade before.[205] A very intricate web of diplomacy developed, as all sides maneuvered for an advantageous position,[206] a situation further complicated when a new smallpox epidemic ripped through the native communities in 1633.

There is some indication that the disease was deliberately induced by the English with the aim of reducing the power of the 30,000-strong Narragansetts, who were as inclined to align themselves with the New Amsterdam Dutch as with either Plymouth or Massachusetts Bay.[207] As it turned out, the main effect of the disease was to kill about 10,000 of the estimated 13,000 Pequots by 1635.[208] The English devoted substantial diplomatic energy to isolating what was left of the victims from any possi-

---

* This is not to say the colonists were militarily inactive. For instance, acting on a tip from Massasoit, the principle Wampanoag leader, that the Massachusetts were planning to attack the colonists, Standish took out an eight-man patrol and methodically murdered seven Massachusetts sachems. The tip turned out to be disinformation. Massasoit had in effect used Standish to weaken the Massachusetts to the advantage of his own people. Standish hardly minded, however, given that his major objective was to keep all the Indians as weak as possible, and divided among themselves; Bradford, *Of Plymouth Plantation, op. cit.*, pp. 108–10, 113–9.

bility of defensive alliance other than with their Western Niantic tributaries. With this accomplished by 1637—in fact, the Narragansetts and Mohegans were enlisted as English allies against the Pequots—the leadership of both Plymouth and Massachusetts collaborated with that of the unofficial colony of Connecticut to fabricate a pretext, and then set out on a war of extermination.*

Massachusetts mounted a column of ninety men under Captain John Endicott and dispatched it to heavily populated Block Island. The group's orders were to kill every adult male residing there and capture as many women and children as possible since "they would fetch a tidy sum in the West Indies slave markets."[209] The plan failed when Endicott attempted to engage the Pequots, European-style, in open combat. Instead, the Indians used a meeting on the matter as a delaying tactic while they evacuated their noncombatants. In the end, the Pequots, who seem to have wanted to avoid the war which was being forced upon them, simply melted away into the woods, leaving the frustrated English with no way to vent themselves other than by burning homes and fields.[210]

On the mainland, Captain John Mason was much more crafty. Having augmented his own mixed Massachusetts-Connecticut force of ninety men with about eighty Mohegans under Uncas, their principle leader, and nearly 500 Narragansetts led by Miantonomi, he set out to attack a lesser Pequot "fort" on the Mystic River.[211] Taking a circuitous route which allowed them to bypass the truly fortified Pequot River town of Sassacus, named for the principal Pequot leader, and also the defensive cordon the Indians had thrown up to prevent exactly what it was he meant to do, Mason launched

---

*Jennings, *The Invasion of America, op. cit.* pp. 85–210. As is pointed out at pp. 220–1, the question of prior intent in this respect has always been deliberately obfuscated by American historians, beginning with the Massachusetts Puritans' William Hubbard in 1677. Hubbard, it seems, "edited" the account of Captain John Mason, commander of the militia force which perpetrated the Mystic Massacre. For example, where Mason's text read, "We had formerly concluded to destroy them by the Sword and save the plunder," Hubbard rewrote things to read, "We had resolved a while not to have burned [the village at Mystic], but being we could not come at them, I resolved to set it on fire." Hubbard also altered Mason's 1638 account to make it appear that, rather than being completely defenseless, Mystic was defended by 150 Pequot warriors. Jennings is citing the 1736 reprint of Mason's *A Brief History of the Pequot War* (Ann Arbor: March of America Facsimile Series No. 23, 1966), pp. 7–8; William Hubbard, *The Present State of New England, Being a Narrative of the Troubles with the Indians in New England* (London, printed for Theo. Parkhurst, 1677) p. 126. It should be noted that Plymouth Governor William Bradford (*Of Plymouth Plantation, op. cit.*, p. 296) confirms Mason's rather than Hubbard's version. This information has been equally accessible all along. Consequently, it is obvious that the orthodox interpretation of Puritan objectives during the Pequot War have been quite intentionally distortive of the facts: a calculated pattern of denial lasting three-and-a-half centuries.

his assault in the predawn of May 26.* His men were instructed to take no prisoners at all, and it is apparent that they counted on the "savages" who accompanied them to join in the slaughter with gusto.[212] When they realized what was afoot, however, both the Narragansetts and Mohegans refused to participate.†

Thus left to his own devices, Mason ordered his militiamen to set fire to the entire town, burning alive as many as 900 "women, children and helpless old men."[213] Those who tried to escape the blaze were cut down with swords and axes.‡ As Plymouth Governor William Bradford later described the scene, paraphrasing Mason's own exultant account:

> It was a fearful sight to see them thus frying in the fire and the streams of blood quenching the same, and horrible was the stink and scent thereof; but the victory seemed a sweet sacrifice, and they gave the praise thereof to God, who had wrought so wonderfully for them, thus to enclose their enemies in their hands and give them so speedy a victory over so proud and insulting an enemy.[214]

There were five known survivors, all of whom managed to hide themselves among Uncas' Mohegans, their traditional enemies, who, along with the Narragansetts, were already denouncing the needlessness of the slaughter.§ Arriving too late—the English and their Indian "allies" had already left—the Pequot fighters were "astonished and demoralized."[215] About 200 attempted to surrender themselves to the Narragansetts, but most of these were discovered and killed by colonists.[216] Another fifty or so, led by Sassacus, tried to find refuge among the Mohawks, but, at the

---

*Mason's original orders were to attack Sassacus and destroy the Pequots' fighting capacity. Once in the field, however, he decided "to avoid a direct attack on Sassacus's strongly defended main village in order to attack from the rear"; Jennings, *The Invasion of America, op. cit.*, p. 218. In other words, he was very consciously seeking a "soft target" composed of noncombatants. These, Mason recounted smugly, were caught entirely by surprise, "being in a dead, indeed their last, Sleep"; *Brief History, op. cit.*, p. 7.

†Mason and most subsequent historians have attributed this refusal to "cowardice"; ibid., p. 10. The facts again indicate otherwise. By all appearances, both the Narragansetts and the Mohegans, "primitives" that they were, considered the slaughter of noncombatants dishonorable and declined to have anything to do with it.

‡"Many were burnt in the fort, both men, women, and children. Others, forced out...our soldiers received and entertained with the point of a sword. Down fell men, women, and children." Underhill, who seems to have learned his chaplain's lessons well, justifies this by observing that "sometimes the Scripture declareth women and children must perish with their parents"; Underhill, *Newes from America, op. cit.*, pp. 39–40.

§"Those that escaped us, fell into the hands of the Indians [Mohegans and Narragansetts] that were in the rear of us...not above five of them escaped out of our hands [to be protected by Uncas and Miantonomi]"; Underhill, ibid., p. 296. On Narragansett and Mohegan denunciations of the massacre, see Steele, *Warpaths, op. cit.*, p. 92.

request of the English, were put to death.[217] For more than a year, the militias of the three participating colonies scoured the woods, killing Pequots whenever and wherever they found them.[218] Before it was over, at least two-thirds—probably more—of all Pequots alive at the beginning of the "war" were dead. Those who survived were mostly absorbed by the Mohegans.[219] The Western Niantics were for all practical purposes totally eradicated.[*]

> The Pequots were "rooted out" as a tribe. Winthrop put the body count [for Mystic alone] at between eight and nine hundred. In 1832 one observer counted only "about forty souls, in all, or perhaps a few more or less" living in the township of Groton; in the 1960s the official figure was twenty-one Pequots in all of Connecticut. And there would have been no living members of that tribe had the colonizers had their way. They sought, as Mason said, "to cut off the Remembrance of them from the Earth." After the war, the General Assembly of Connecticut declared the name extinct. No survivors should be called Pequots. The Pequot River became the Thames, and the village known as Pequot became New London.[220]

The message was not lost on the remaining indigenous peoples of the region; "New England" was meant to become exactly that: a vast area utterly depopulated of its native inhabitants, occupied exclusively by the English. Shaken by this realization, and by what he'd witnessed at Mystic, Miantonomi underwent a profound change. No longer devoted to advancing Narragansett interests at the expense of other Indians, he was something of

---

[*]Since the days of William Hubbard, there have been persistent "scholarly" efforts to make the Pequot War appear as something other than an instance of genocide. Samuel G. Drake, Francis Parkman, John Gorham Palfrey, Alden T. Vaughan, and many others have taken their turns at the task. The most recent version is that of Steven T. Katz, who, noting that since "the number killed was probably less than half the tribe," goes on to argue that because *some* Pequots survived, *ipso facto* the Puritan campaign to exterminate them "was not, either in intent or execution, genocidal." Of course, by this "definition," Katz's own Jewish people—whom he claims are unique in having experienced genocide —could not have suffered such a fate, since some of *them* survived as well. He goes on to caution that we should refrain from "misapplying" the term genocide with respect to the extermination of the Pequots and Niantics; "The Pequot War Reconsidered," *New England Quarterly*, No. 64, 1991. As Henry David Thoreau once put it—although he had Francis Parkman in mind—"It frequently happens that the historian, though he professes more humanity than a trapper, mountain man, or gold-digger, who shoots [an Indian] like a wild beast, really exhibits and practices a similar inhumanity to him, wielding a pen instead of a rifle"; quoted in Drinnon, *Facing West, op. cit.* p. 363. Samuel Adams Drake, *The History of the Indian Wars in New England* (Roxbury, MA: C.E. Tuttle, 1965); Francis Parkman, *The Conspiracy of Pontiac and the Indian War After the Conquest of Canada*, 2 vols. (Boston: Little, Brown, 1874); John Gorham Palfrey, *History of New England*, 5 vols. (Boston: Little, Brown, 1858–1890); Alden T. Vaughan, *The New England Frontier: Puritans and Indians, 1620–1675* (Boston: Little, Brown, 1965).

a pioneer, becoming one of the first major figures in North American native history to try and weld together a general alliance of indigenous nations to contain—and possibly expel—the invading Europeans.[221]

The colonists' attentions were subsumed for a while by internal bickering—mainly a squabble over who would gain the territorial spoils of eradicating the Pequots—and with the taking of New Netherlands from the Dutch, but they eventually got around to dealing with the "threat" presented by this precursor of Tecumseh.* Miantonomi, by this point having engineered a compact with the powerful Mohawks to the west, was captured and held in a Connecticut jail for several months.[222] Eventually, he was executed as one by-product of a May 1643 meeting in New Haven at which the New England colonies proclaimed themselves unified against both Dutch and Indians.[223] Thereafter, any attempt by native people to foster a counterbalancing unity among themselves was termed a "conspiracy" and "provocation" to war.[224]

Connecticut was finally chartered as a royal colony in 1662. Rhode Island followed a year later, and, in 1664, the Dutch holding of New Netherlands became the English colony of New York (it was retaken by the Dutch a bit later and had to be "reconquered" in 1674).[225] Working out the relationships presented by these developments—and raiding the French communities of Acadia—again commanded the bulk of English attention for a full decade.[226] By 1675, however, with more than 50,000 colonists in the general area, New England felt itself strong enough to achieve a "final solution" to its "Indian problem."[227] This took the form of an all-out campaign to obliterate the Narragansetts, Wampanoags, and several smaller peoples such as the Nausets and Nipmucks in what was called "King Philip's War."†

---

*There were at the time four competing New England colonies and two more in the making: those of Plymouth Plantation and Massachusetts Bay, the still unofficial Connecticut Colony, and an upstart called New Haven Colony, founded in 1637, more or less specifically to cash in on Pequot land. Uninvolved in the "spoils of war" dispute were the incipient colonies of Rhode Island and New Hampshire. Massachusetts, however, was pressing a claim that Rhode Island was in fact part of itself; Steele, *Warpaths, op. cit.*, pp. 94–6.

†A bit of self-criticism is due. One problem with relying on the sorts of materials I have in this essay is that one's historical reconstruction ends up being decisively—and inaccurately—male-oriented. An instance in which this is plainly true is at hand. Although the war in New England during 1675–76 is associated with the name of Philip (Metacom), because of his position as titular military leader on the Indian side, the likelihood is that he himself took political instruction from Mangus, the preeminent Narragansett sunksquaw (the perfectly honorable Algonkian title—it was, like the male "sachem," bestowed only upon those of stature—from which the derogatory Euroamerican corruption, "squaw,"

Again, there is every indication that the indigenous nations involved did all that was within their power to avert armed conflict.[228] And, again, there is evidence that the Indians had reason to believe they'd been deliberately infected with a disease, possibly influenza.[229] Combined with increasing English encroachments into the very hearts of remaining native territories and an insufferable degree of colonial arrogance, these circumstances had already generated a very high level of volatility among the natives by June of 1675, when three prominent Wampanoags were executed at Plymouth on charges of "plotting" against the English.[230] At that point, Metacom ("King Philip"), successor to Massasoit as principal Wampanoag leader, led a "revolt" intended to reassert some aspect of his people's rights and autonomy.[231]

At first, the Indians did quite well. Metacom, having learned the lesson of Mystic, first moved his noncombatants deep into the swampy Pocasset territory, on the Hoosack River, and placed them under the protection of that people's leader, a woman named Weetamoo.[232] Although he had only about 300 fighters at his disposal, the Wampanoag "king" then conducted a hit-and-run guerrilla campaign that thoroughly demoralized the 10,000 men of the combined Massachusetts, Plymouth, and Connecticut militias.[233] Finally, in dire need of a "victory," and afraid to strike at their real adversary's Hoosack stronghold, the militia did what the Jamestown colonists had done at Piscataway, and what the descendants of both groups would do repeatedly thereafter: they conducted a devastating surprise assault on a completely uninvolved native community, invading the "sister colony" of Rhode Island, where the Narragansetts had been granted sanctuary.[234]

The United Colonies, for reasons that still remain suspicious, chose to attack the winter camp of the still-neutral Narragansett [and] raised nearly a thousand troops for [the purpose]. They were recruited from the militias and supplied and paid in the proportions of Massachusetts, 517; Connecticut, 315; and Plymouth, 158. Josiah Winslow, Plymouth's native-born governor, was given command of the expedition... Attacking [on] December 19, 1675, the impetuous English soldiers...burned food and shelter, which they needed, and killed valuable captives, which they wanted... Of the Narragansett, at least 48 warriors were wounded and 97 were killed, as were [up to]

---

derives). She was one of those executed after the native defeat; Robert Steven Grumet, "Sunksquaws, Shamans, and Tradeswomen: Middle-Atlantic Coastal Algonkian Women During the 17th and 18th Centuries," in Mona Etienne and Eleanor Burke Leacock, eds., *Women and Colonization: Anthropological Perspectives* (New York: Praeger, 1980).

1,000 women and children. The outraged Narragansett survivors fled to join Philip, wintering with the Mahican (not Mohegan).[*]

Thus reinforced—by this point, some Nipmucks had joined them as well—the Wampanoags resumed raiding with even more effectiveness during the spring of 1676, hitting Lancaster, Medfield, Weymouth and Groton, Massachusetts in rapid succession. The Indians still showed no propensity to kill like the English, however, and time was definitely not on their side.[†] Cut off "from the fields which had subsisted them and forced to hunt in unfamiliar territory, the Narragansett and Wampanoag refugee armies and their attending families suffered food shortages" which were grinding them down.[235] It follows that the next great feat of colonial arms came in May, when Captain William Turner of Connecticut—having first ascertained an absence of combatants among them—led 150 of his militia against a large group of Indians gathering food at Peskeompscut on the Connecticut River, about twenty miles north of Hatfield. Attacking at dawn, these brave men managed to slaughter about 300, mostly women, children, and old men.[236]

The colonies finally resorted to a sort of counterguerrilla warfare, fielding small "ranger" units composed of experienced woodsmen. They were motivated to track and kill Indians piecemeal by the placement of a bounty upon any heads they brought in, as well as the promise that they might keep all loot obtained and sell into slavery any prisoners taken.[237] Meanwhile, "Connecticut militia…wantonly slaughtered more people than they captured from two sizable groups of Narragansett who were obviously short of food and gunpowder."[238] In July, a Plymouth soldier wrote his wife that, since May, his unit had "killed and taken upward of one hundred Indians but never an English slain nor wounded."[239] The same month, a Connecticut force invaded

---

[*] Steele, *Warpaths, op. cit.*, p. 102; "Suspicions survive that Plymouth-Massachusetts cooperation already included an agreement that the first would confiscate Wampanoag lands and the second would take those of the Narragansett"; Jennings, *The Invasion of America, op. cit.* p. 304. In any event, the troops, "ran amok, killing the wounded men, women, and children indiscriminately, firing the camp, burning the Indians alive or dead in their huts"; Richard Slotkin and James K. Folsom, eds., *So Dreadful a Judgment: Puritan Responses to King Philip's War, 1676–1677* (Middletown, CT: Wesleyan University Press, 1978) p. 381.

[†] The largest number of fatalities inflicted, about fifty, was at Lancaster, where a woman, Mary Rowlandson was taken captive. She was well treated, especially under the circumstances, and released unharmed a few months later. Her subsequent "journal," however, became a mainstay of anti-Indian propaganda for the next century and more; *The Sovereignty and Goodness of God Together with the Faithfulness of His Promise Displayed: Being the Narrative of the Captivity and Restoration of Mrs. Mary Rowlandson* (Boston, 1682).

Rhode Island again, just long enough to butcher 126 people, 92 of them women, who had taken refuge there.[240] On August 12, Metacom himself was shot in the back and killed while trying to evade an ambush.[241] The severed head of the slain sachem was then paraded as a trophy through the streets of Plymouth, and what was left of his people began to give up the fight.

> For decades, Philip's head was displayed on a pike atop the brick watchtower of Plymouth's Fort Hill. Philip's nine-year-old son escaped execution, but was sold into slavery in Bermuda. Leading Wampanoag warriors who surrendered their entire bands to Benjamin Church, who had promised their lives would be spared, were summarily executed amid public enthusiasm, and their followers sold into slavery. The atmosphere was not unlike that in Marblehead, in neighboring Massachusetts, where a group of women beat and stoned to death two…prisoners being escorted to jail. Of the estimated 3,000 [Indians] killed in the war, at least one-quarter were Wampanoag. All the captured, and many of those who surrendered, were sold into slavery… Wampanoag society was entirely destroyed, and few survivors lived in Plymouth. The aroused citizen armies of New England had once again come to define victory as "extirpation," and this victory seemed their most complete.[*]

The Nausets had ceased to exist altogether, and the Nipmucks were in essentially the same condition.[†] As for the Narragansetts, a number of whom had sought sanctuary in "neutral" Rhode Island, they too were enslaved, albeit mostly within the colony itself rather than being shipped off to the Caribbean.[242] The Indians, wrote a triumphant Puritan leader, Increase Mather, had been "consumed…by Sword & by Famine and by Sickness, it being no unusual thing for those that traverse the woods to find dead Indians up and down… Not above an hundred men [are] left of them who last year were the greatest body of Indians in New England."[243] All in all, the sentiments of the "good Christians" of the colonies is perhaps best summed up in a jingle, very popular at the time, which compared those exterminated to vermin: "A swarm of Flies, they may arise/a Nation to annoy/Yea Rats and

---

[*] Steele, *Warpaths, op. cit.,* p. 107; Other estimates of native casualties run as high as 5–6,000. Enslavement was by no means restricted to "hostiles." Indeed, "early in the war, a group of neutral Wampanoag living near Dartmouth had voluntarily presented themselves to Plymouth authorities for protection, but were promptly sold into slavery [in the West Indies] despite the protests of Benjamin Church, who had negotiated with them." Plainly, the erasure of the Wampanoags was meant to be as complete as that of the Pequots. As for Mr. Church, either he was extraordinarily naïve about his countrymen's intentions (especially the second time around) or he performed an extraordinarily duplicitous function for them.

[†] About a hundred Nipmucks survived, but only by converting to Calvinism and thereby extinguishing themselves as a people; see "John Easton's Relación" in Charles H. Lincoln, ed., *Narratives of the Indian Wars, 1675–1699* (New York: Charles Scribner's Sons, 1913).

Mice or Swarms of Lice/a Nation may destroy."[*] It was an outlook which would prevail among the invaders for the next two centuries.

The Most Savage of Practices...

As Francis Jennings has observed, "So many myths about savage warfare have circulated that the civilized European origin of war against noncombatants needs to be explicitly recognized. The armed conquest in New England [and Virginia]...closely resembled the procedures followed by the English in Ireland in the sixteenth and seventeenth centuries. In these lands, the English...held the simple view that the natives were outside the law of moral obligation. On this assumption, they fought by means that would have been dishonorable, even in that day, in war between civilized peoples."[244]

> Four of their usages, transferred from Ireland and Scotland to America, profoundly affected the whole process of European-Indian acculturation: (1) a deliberate policy of inciting competition in order, by division, to maintain control; (2) a disregard for pledges and promises to natives, no matter how solemnly made; (3) the introduction of total exterminatory war against some communities of natives in order to terrorize others; and (4) a highly developed propaganda of falsification to justify all acts and policies of the conquerors whatsoever.[245]

The answer to the oft-posed question as to why, given their preponder-

---

[*] *Some Meditations, op. cit.* Of course, we have no shortage of "responsible" historians to explain that all this was neither genocidal nor even racist. The classic example is that of Columbia University's Alden T. Vaughan, who not only advances the bald assertion that the colonists' open exterminism was somehow "remarkably humane, considerate and just" but lays responsibility for their annihilation squarely at the feet of the *victims*; "blatant and persistent [Indian] aggression" was the cause of all conflict in New England, he says, as if the slaughtered peoples had traversed the Atlantic and invaded the British Isles. Moreover, he claims, racism is an inapplicable concept in assessing colonial motivations in waging war since the colonies distinguished between Pequots, Narragansetts, Wampanoags, etc., rather than fighting them all at once (as if they had a choice; to have taken them all on in 1637 would plainly have resulted in the English, not the Pequots and Niantics, being exterminated); see Vaughan's "Pequots and Puritans: The Causes of the War of 1637," *William and Mary Quarterly*, 3d Ser. XXI, 1964; and *The New England Frontier: Puritans and Indians, 1620–1675* (Boston: Little, Brown, 1965). The latter was received with great fanfare and fawning reviews in such publications as *Library Journal* ("a model for historians"), *Christian Science Monitor* ("shows Puritans tried to treat Indians with decency and concern"), *Church History* ("will remain the standard work in its field"), *New York Times Book Review* ("throws new light on the nature of Massachusetts Indian society"), *New England Quarterly* ("we can be grateful"), all in 1965. Richard Drinnon, on the other hand, does a fine job of laying bare the implicit teleological racism in Vaughan's denial of the racist content of Puritan views of native people—how *else* are we to understand things like William Bradford's 1637 dictum that the colonists should see "the Pequents, and all other Indeans, as a common enimie"?—and links him solidly to the pattern of systematic historiographic falsification originating with William Hubbard; Drinnon, *Facing West, op. cit.*, pp. 356–64. Also see the critiques of Vaughan offered by Jennings, *The Invasion of America, op. cit.*, pp. 11, 14, 180, 193–5, 217, 221–2, 267, 273; and Stannard, *American Holocaust, op. cit.*, pp. 276–8.

ant military advantage in the early years of Jamestown and Plymouth, the native peoples of each area did not simply annihilate the invaders, is thus rather straightforward: it did not and could not occur to them. Put simply, neither the Tsenacommacahs nor the Pequots, the Narragansetts, the Wampanoags nor any other known preinvasion indigenous people pursued warfare by way of killing their opponents' women, children, and elders.[246] Indeed, the terms of native warfare did not emphasize killing at all.[*] By the standards of what we now call—and, for that matter, what was then called—"civilized behavior," the supposed "savages" were, and in many cases would remain to the end, far more accomplished than their European counterparts.[247]

Reality has, however, been all but entirely inverted over the centuries via the propaganda mechanisms of orthodox historiography and anthropology.[248] A prime signifier is the question of scalping and other forms of bodily mutilation. Invariably ascribed by "responsible scholars" and "objective journalists" to native people as a means of stirring up the requisite popular sentiment for campaigns of extermination, or, *post hoc*, to provide a handy rationalization of what had already occurred, the record of this most "most savage of [the] practices" marking the horrors of Indian-white warfare is actually the reverse.[249]

Although it is likely that at least some Indians practiced scalping in one or another fashion before the European invasion,[†] "there is no doubt that

---

[*] "[As] to pre-Columbian warfare we know almost nothing, and what little we do know suggests that where wars took place, they were infrequent, short, and mild: in fact 'war'… seems a misnomer for the kinds of [fighting that took] place, in which some act of bravery or retribution rather than death, say, or territory, would have been the object, and two 'war parties' might skirmish without [lethal] effect on either one and none at all on home villages. Early European settlers often made a mockery of Indian warfare… John Underhill wrote of the Pequots that their wars were more for pastime than to conquer and subdue their enemies, and Henry Spelman, who lived among the Powhatans, said that 'they might fight seven yeares and not kill seven men'… Organized violence, in short, was not an attribute of traditional Indian societies, certainly not as compared with their European contemporaries, and on the basis of this imperfect record what is most remarkable about them is their apparent lack of conflict and discord"; Sale, *The Conquest of Paradise, op. cit.*, pp. 318–9.

[†] Amid all the vast proliferation of serious misinformation about American Indians screaming to be corrected, James Axtell, in collaboration the Smithsonian's still-reigning "Indian expert," William Sturdevant, determined in the mid-1970s that a top priority for their combined attention should be rebuttal of a "the increasingly popular suggestion in non-Indian literature and the Indian press" that whites might actually have introduced the idea of scalping to Indians. After years of research on this weighty subject—revealing as it is of his own and Sturdevant's powerful racial/cultural biases more than anything else—Axtell offered his proof that the practice preexisted the invasion in an essay entitled "The Unkindest Cut, or Who Invented Scalping? A Case Study," first published in the *William and Mary Quarterly* in 1980. He then went on to pen a second essay, "Scalping: The Ethnohistory of a Moral Question," explaining why he felt the first was so important (in this, Axtell follows directly in the footsteps of his mentor, Smithsonian historian Wilcomb E. Washburn; see, e.g., "A Moral History of Indian-White Relations: Needs and Opportunities for Study," *Ethnohistory*, No. 4, 1957). Both of Axtell's essays are included in his *The European and the Indian, op. cit.*

[generalized] scalp-taking…was due to the barbarity of White men rather than the barbarity of Red men."[250] Or, to put it another way, "contrary to Hollywood's history book, it was the white man who created the tradition of scalping" as we know it today.[251] In truth, the practice probably finds its origins in the same wars of pacification in Scotland and Ireland from whence the English imported the rest of their exterminationist techniques, albeit the entire repertoire mutated into more extreme form when transplanted to North America. Consider the technique employed by Sir Humphrey Gilbert, English commander in Ireland during the late sixteenth century:

> The heddes of all those (of what sort soever thei were) which were killed in the dai, would be cutte off their bodies and brought to the place where he incamped at night, and should there bee laied on the ground by eche side of the waie ledyng into his owne tente so that none could come into his tente for any cause but commonly he muste passe through a lane of heddes which he used *ad terrorum*.[252]

Nearly three centuries later, although such methods had been long abandoned in Europe, U.S. General Alfred Sully would be doing very much the same thing in the Dakota Territory, having the skulls of Lakotas mounted on poles to adorn the entry to his headquarters.[253] As was noted in the preceding section, Massachusetts offered a bounty on Indian heads to rangers during King Philip's War, and the head of Philip himself was displayed at Plymouth for decades.[254] Payment for heads—and possibly a scalp bounty as well—was also offered to the Narragansetts early in the war, an effort to convince them to assist in the slaughter of Wampanoags before the Narragansetts were themselves targeted for extermination.[255] There is no record of the Narragansetts availing themselves much of this opportunity for the obvious reason that the whole concept underlying such atrocities was alien to American Indians.

The English purpose in taking heads was not only to terrorize the populace. It also served to confirm the count of enemy killed, first in Ireland, then in New England. In this, we find the true beginnings of the pervasive scalping and other mutilations which are so much an aspect of "the American way."* The bounty placed on heads was soon transfigured into the

---

*Witness the preoccupation with "bodycount" manifested by American officers in Vietnam, a sensibility reflected in their troops' widespread practice, each time they ventured into "Indian Country," of cutting off ears to confirm their kills, in some units stringing them to wear as necklaces or otherwise displaying them as trophies; Drinnon, *Facing West*, *op. cit.*, p. 451. More generally, see Donald Duncan, *The New Legions* (New York: Random House, 1967); Michael Herr, *Dispatches* (New York: Alfred A. Knopf, 1977).

taking of scalps—other than in the few instances in which authorities were concerned with verifying the death of some particular Indian rather than Indians as a "species"—in order to render the whole increasingly commercialized process less cumbersome.[256]

To be fair, England was hardly alone in facilitating this process, or even necessarily the first to pay for scalps. Willem Kieft, the second governor of New Netherlands offered a reward for the heads of certain Raritans on Staten Island in 1641, and probably introduced the first scalp bounty at the same time.[257] Cornplanter, a Seneca leader, recounted in 1820 his people's recollection that the "French offered to furnish us with instruments of every kind and sharp knives to take the skin off their enemies' heads" at about the same time the Dutch adopted the practice.[258] Susette La Flesche, an Omaha leader of the late nineteenth/early twentieth centuries, also attributed the first such bounty to the French, noting that it was paid for the scalps of Penobscots in what is now Maine at the beginning of the "Beaver Wars" in 1638.[259] By 1688, such bounties were quite regularized, with the governor of Québec offering ten beaver skins to anyone bringing him the scalp of any "enemy of France, Christian or Indian."[260]

The earliest confirmed English bounty for scalps rather than whole heads dates from 1694. On September 12 of that year, the Massachusetts General Court passed an act prohibiting unattended Indians from entering the colony without permission and offering to pay for "every Indian, great or small, which they shall kill, or take and bring in prisoner," the latter to be sold into slavery by the colonial government. Payment listed for native scalps was £50 each, regardless of age or sex, if the killer were an average civilian or professional scalp hunter; £20 each as a supplement to the meager pay of militiamen; and £10 each to regular soldiers.[261] These rates were modified in 1704 so that an incredible £100—*four times* the annual income of a good New England farmer—was paid per man's scalp, £40 per woman's, and £20 per child's. "Men" and "women" were defined as being any Indian over ten years of age.*

Once the English got rolling, moreover, it was like the breaking of a

---

*Steele, *Warpaths, op. cit.*, p. 142. Once it arrived at the idea of a scale graduated by age and sex, the colonial government proved indecisive as to what constituted a "fair rate" for the body parts of murdered women and children. Although the price on adult male scalps remained fixed at £100 until 1722 (it was revised to ensure that "men" would have to be at least twelve years of age), the price on women's went as high as £100, and the price on children's as low as £10; James Axtell, "The Scholastic Philosophy of the Wilderness," in *The European and the Indian, op. cit.*, p. 143.

dam. In 1696, the New York Council, a bit stingy, resolved that, "Six pounds shall be given to each Christian or Indian as a Reward who shall kill a french man or indian Enemy." The proof of death to be submitted for payment was the slain "Enemy's" scalp.[262] By 1717, all the New England colonies had bounties in place,[263] as did New Jersey.* Massachusetts rescinded its Scalp Act in 1722, on the grounds that it had become "ineffectual," but reinstated it by public demand in 1747.[264] Much the same occurred in Pennsylvania, where at the time of the 1763 reinstatement it was noted that "the general cry and wish is for a Scalp Act...Vast numbers of Young Fellows who would not chuse to enlist as Soldiers, would be prompted by Revenge, Duty, Ambition & Prospect of the Reward, to carry Fire & Sword into the Heart of the Indian Country."[265]

This pointed to a real problem, one which had been evident as early as Massachusetts' offering of bounties to prompt the formation of ranger units in 1637: Indian-killing was seen more as a lucrative enterprise than as a civic duty by the average colonist.† Indeed, in many areas it became an outright business.

> The Reverend Thomas Smith of Falmouth [now Portland, Maine]...was one of a group of gentlemen who hired a squad of hardy parishioners to go on a "Scout or Cruse for the killing and capturing of the Indian enemy." In return for supplying the bounty hunters with "Ammunition and Provision," the investors received "one full third Part of fourteen fifteenths of the Province Bounty for Captive or Scalp, and of every Thing else they shall or may recover or obtain." In his journal for June 18, 1757, the minister recorded, along with pious thoughts, "I receive 165 pounds, 3-3...my part of scalp money."[266]

Although the bounties were in principle to be paid only for the deaths of "hostile" Indians, freebooters pursuing the trade realized very early on that

---

* Feeling rather insulated by its neighbors from Indian attack, New Jersey defined an Indian "man" as being over fifteen years of age. Not to be outdone in terms of "humanitarianism," Connecticut, also feeling secure, revised its own code to specify sixteen years as the threshold of male adulthood. Pennsylvania, however, revised its own definition downward, from twelve years to ten, in 1750; *Collections of the New Jersey Historical Society*, No. 4, 1852, pp. 305–6; J. Hammond Trumbull and C.J. Hoadly, eds., *The Public Records of the Colony of Connecticut*, 15 vols. ((Hartford: Connecticut State Historical Society, 1850–90) Vol. 9, p. 229; *Minutes of the Supreme Executive Council of Pennsylvania*, 10 vols. (Philadelphia & Harrisburg: Pennsylvania State Historical Society, 1851–1852) Vol. 9, pp. 191–2.
† Indeed, several colonies found it difficult to mount a militia at all, absent a scalp bounty payable to members; see, e.g., M. Halsey Thomas, ed., *The Diary of Samuel Sewell*, 2 vols. (New York: Farrar, Strauss & Giroux, 1973) Vol. 2, p. 691. As Axtell points out, "the quickest way to mount...an offensive with woodsmen experienced in guerrilla warfare was the scalp bounty," the "Love of Money" being the only thing that would motivate many colonists to "risque [sic] their lives in the service and defense of the country"; Axtell, "Scalping," *op. cit.*, pp. 225, 228.

there was no practical way for paymasters to distinguish the scalp of a "friendly" from that of a foe. It was usually much easier to kill the former than the latter, a circumstance which resulted in Indians—*any* Indians— being killed on sight.[267]

> In 1756 four New Jersey men combined to murder a family of loyal Indians, long-time residents of the area, and to pass their scalps in Philadelphia as having been lifted in Pennsylvania. Armed with "Guns, Cutlasses and an Ax," they attacked the [home] about midnight on April 12. The husband, George, escaped unharmed, but his wife Kate died when one of the men "cut her head all to pieces" with the axe and another fired a "Brace of Balls" into her stomach. An eleven-year-old girl was "much bruised about the Head, stabbed in the Shoulders and her Right hand almost cut off at the Wrist." Her twelve-month-old twin siblings were "cut and gashed in [a] frightful Manner."[268]

So common had such atrocities become by 1723 that in Maine English soldiers had to be assigned to accompany parties of Mohawks—who'd been recruited by the government to help quell raids by Abenakis, Penobscots, and others into the area—as a measure to prevent local scalp hunters and run-of-the-mill colonists from gratuitously killing these allied Indians.[269] In the Ohio/Kentucky region—where scalp bounties never lost their great popularity with the Angloamerican citizenry so long as there were Indians left to kill—it become something of a standing joke that a scalp tendered for payment was as apt to be that of a friendly Chickasaw, Cherokee, or Mingo as it was of a hostile Shawnee.[270]

The situation was made even more complicated by the terms of the so-called "French and Indian Wars," beginning in 1688. As England and France sought to push one other off the continent, indigenous nations were increasingly solicited to act as "allies"—actually surrogates—in the fighting, and were paid premium bounties by both sides for ever-increasing numbers of enemy scalps, white and Indian alike.[271] For many native peoples whose economies were being increasingly undermined by colonial policies of encroachment, participation was already, or would shortly become, a virtual necessity.

> The first change was the transition from a military adventure wholly dominated by the search for personal prestige, tribal honor, and familial revenge to one…subordinated to the commercial constraints and military needs of white foreigners. Once the Indians had been drawn into the English web of trade, the purchasing power to be gained by killing [those] hostile to the economic and political interests of English suppliers could not be rejected lightly. The more dependent on English clothing, food, and guns the

Indians became, the more susceptible their traditional warfare became to commercialization. Indeed, when an Indian leader asked to receive scalp bounties for his military assistance, as did King Hendrick of the Mohawks in 1747 and Teedyuscung of the Delawares ten years later, he effectively certified his dependence on the colonial economy, though not necessarily his political autonomy.[272]

In effect, Europeans were running the show, even when they had Indians doing the killing and scalping for them.[*] There was a catch, however: neither the French nor the English could tell one of their own countrymen's scalps from that of an opponent, a matter which allowed the Indians ample opportunity to avenge relatives killed for bounty by alleged "friends." By 1757, Pennsylvania official Conrad Weiser was calling for an end to bounties, at least on whites, since the colony was ending up "paying for our own Scalps, and those of our Fellow Subjects."[273] In July 1759, English General James Wolfe also tried to constrain things in this regard, issuing instructions to his troops which "strictly forbade the inhuman practice of scalping, except when the enemy are Indians, or Canadians dressed like Indians."[274]

The spiral of violence which had been unleashed was too far gone to be reigned in at this point. By 1758, in response to General Edward Braddock's crushing 1756 defeat at the hands of a mixed force of French and Indians, Pennsylvania, Maryland, Virginia and several other colonies all renewed and increased their scalp bounties.[†] The forests along the Ohio frontier were teeming with quasimilitary groups like Brady's Rangers, who killed and scalped at a professionally steady pace; one sometime member, a certifiable psychopath and a local hero of sorts named Lewis Wetzel, is believed to have taken more than four dozen scalps on his own.[275] At least some in the scalp trade had begun to identify themselves proudly by sport-

---

[*] Axtell concedes that the effect was a "disruption" of native patterns of warfare—to wit, rendering it vastly more lethal—most especially in terms of inducing a "number of adjustments" and "alterations" in scalping practices. In his usual contradictory fashion, he first claims these were "relatively minor," then, four pages later, begins deploying examples to illustrate the "magnitude" of the changes; "Scalping," *op. cit.*, pp. 214–9.

[†] "We must bid up the Scalps and keep the Woods full of our People hunting [Indians]," said Pennsylvania Councilman John Harris, when voting to pay $130 per adult male killed; quoted in Leonard L. Larabee, et al., eds., *The Papers of Benjamin Franklin,* Vol. 6 (New Haven: Yale University Press, 1959) p. 233, n.7. On Braddock, see Charles Hamilton, ed., *Braddock's Defeat* (Norman: University of Oklahoma Press, 1959).

ing breeches made of tanned Indian skin.* Even after the final defeat of France in 1763, when most bounties were terminated, scalp hunts continued almost unabated.[276]

A decade later, during the American War of Independence, with Englishman now scalping Englishman, that and other mutilations escalated even beyond the levels witnessed during the worst of the earlier Ohio fighting. They also turned, if anything, more sadistic and macabre, as when Ranger Colonel George Rogers Clark, during his celebrated siege of Vincennes in 1779, ordered his men to slowly scalp sixteen living captives — both Indian and white—in full view of the English garrison.† The same year, during the Sullivan Campaign against the Seneca, soldiers of the Continental Army weren't content with merely scalping their foes, living or dead. Not uncommonly, they skinned them from the hips down in order to make leggings from the tanned "hides."[277]

Nor did things improve with the rebel victory in 1787. Instead, the newly formed United States Army seems to have institutionalized orgiastic expressions of violence.[278] Consider the performance of troops under future-President William Henry Harrison after their November 6, 1811, defeat of Tecumseh's native alliance at Tippecanoe. While mutilating the dead, they came upon the body of the great Shawnee leader.

> [The] souvenier hunters got to work, and when the warrior had been stripped of his clothing…Kentuckians tore the skin from his back and thigh… The rapacious soldiery

---

*Eckert, *That Dark and Bloody River, op. cit.*, p. 359. A more genteel expression of the same sensibility permeated the upper reaches of colonial society as well. For instance, well into the nineteenth century, scalps taken in the area were displayed on a walls of courthouses in Salem and other Massachusetts communities; Axtell, "Scalping," *op. cit.*, p. 231. The American Museum established in 1782 in Philadelphia by Pierre-Eugène du Simitière included the prominent display of a scalp; Young, "Scalp Bounties," *op. cit.*, p. 217. When Pennsylvania Governor Thomas Penn was presented with the scalp of a Lenni Lenâpé leader after his militia's Mystic-style massacre at Kittanning in 1758, he actively entertained the idea of having a plaque inscribed with an account of the action and sending the grisly trophy to the British Museum; Van Doren and Boyd, *Indian Treaties, op. cit.*, p. lxxiin. English officers like General George Townsend typically took home scalps among the "souvenirs" of service in America with which they later adorned their dens; Hugh Honour, *The New Golden Land: European Images of America from the Discovery to the Present Time* (New York: Pantheon, 1975) p. 128.

†The English commander, Colonel Henry Hamilton, later described the victor, "still reeking with the blood of those unhappy victims," as being "in rapture of his…achievement"; "The Hamilton Papers," *Michigan Pioneer and Historical Collections*, No. 9, 1886, pp. 501–2. Clark, whose nephew later added to the family's fame as the Clark of the Lewis and Clark expedition, became a national hero as a result of his exploits at Vincennes. He still is, being officially cited as the inspiration of elite ranger units in today's "Action Army"; Ian Padden, *The Fighting Elite: U.S. Rangers* (New York: Bantam, 1985), pp. 16–25.

so thoroughly scalped the corpse that some of them came away with fragments the size of a cent piece and endowed with a mere tuft of hair. When [one of them] was interviewed in 1886 he was still able to display a piece of Tecumseh's skin.*

Such behavior was indicative, not exceptional. Witness the performance of troops under another future president after their slaughter of the Muskogee Red Sticks (Baton Rouge) at the Horseshoe Bend of the Tallapoosa River, in Alabama, on March 27, 1814:

> Andrew Jackson…supervised the mutilation of 800 or more Creek Indian corpses—the bodies of men, women and children that they had massacred—cutting off their noses to count and preserve a record of the dead, slicing long strips of flesh from their bodies to tan and turn into bridle reins.[279]

A half-century later, in the aftermath of the Third Colorado Volunteer Cavalry Regiment's November 1864 massacre of Cheyenne and Arapaho noncombatants at Sand Creek, the troops—with the active encouragement of their officers—not only scalped the dead, but performed an altogether astonishing array of other mutilations, including the severing of male genitalia to be turned into tobacco pouches.[280] When the "Bloody Third," returned to parade triumphantly down the streets of Denver a short while later, the citizenry turned out to cheer them as they rode by, waving scalps and with other such "trophies"—female genitals stretched over hats and saddle pommels, for example—plainly in view.† Treated to this display, a local

---

*John Sugden, *Tecumseh's Last Stand* (Norman: University of Oklahoma Press, 1985) p. 180. "One [soldier], more dexterous than the rest, proceeded to *flay* the chief's body; then, cutting the skin in narrow slips, of 10 or 12 inches long, produced, at once, a supply of *razor-straps* for the more 'ferocious' of this brethren" (emphasis in the original); William James, *A Full and Complete Account of the Military Occurrence of the Late War Between Great Britain and the United States of America*, 2 vols. (London: self-published, 1818) Vol. 1, p. 294.

†This is again by no means anomalous. English colonial troops, and their U.S. descendants, seem habitually to have engaged in such jubilant displays of body parts to signify the completeness of their "victories," and the citizenry seems uniformly to have turned out to applaud such representations of the "valor" of their achievements, e.g.: "[Most] memorable for the colonists was the sight of fresh scalps paraded through the streets of colonial towns such as Albany, Dover, Boston, and New York by strutting English woodsmen… Capt. John Lovewell's 'brave company' entering Boston in 1725 'in triumph' with ten hooped trophies on poles ["Indian-style"], could not have failed to stir the blood and admiration of spectators. Only Lovewell's and a Lieutenant Farwell's wearing of wigs made from enemy Indian scalps, which they did to scriptural disapproval—more of the wigs than of the scalps—of a single eccentric minister, may have won more plaudits for patriotic daring"; Axtell, "Scalping," *op. cit.*, pp. 231–2. This raises another point. Much has been made of late with respect to the fact that much of the extermination of European Jewry was carried out, not by the ideologically elite (and thus anomalous) SS, nor even by regular military units, but by average police personnel, often on a purely voluntary basis; Christopher R. Browning, *Ordinary Men: Reserve Police Battalion 101 and the Final Solution in Poland* (New York: HarperCollins, 1992); Daniel Jonah Goldhagen, *Hitler's*

paper, the *Rocky Mountain News*, hailed theirs as being "a brilliant feat of arms" that would "stand in history."[281]

So it would continue until the official close of the U.S. wars against American Indians at the end of the century. Meanwhile, scalp bounties were enacted in every state and territory as the "frontier" advanced across the continent. In the Dakotas, for instance, it stood at $200 for any Lakota male over twelve years of age at the time General Sully decorated his headquarters with native skulls.[282] In Texas, the establishment of a bounty was one of the very first acts of the legislature, initially of the republic, then of the state after Texas was admitted to the Union. It was maintained until the 1880s, by which time the area had been all but entirely cleared of native inhabitants.* In California, even after official bounties were ended, consortia of private businessmen established their own and continued paying until a number of peoples in the northern part of the state—the Yuki, Yahi, Yana, and Tolowa among them—were entirely extinct.†

"The Yuki [were] victims of one of the most organized and intense [private] genocidal campaigns in the state," observes researcher Virginia P. Miller. The most illuminating statement on the number of Yuki murdered comes from Dryden Laycock, one of the settlers in Round Valley. Laycock claimed that beginning in 1856, the first year whites moved into the valley, and continuing through February 1860, parties of Round Valley settlers would...go out "two or three times a week" and kill "on an average, fifty or sixty Indians on a trip." Taking the lower of Laycock's figures, even if only two such trips were made each week and only fifty Indians killed on each trip, then the settlers

---

Willing Executioners: Ordinary Germans and the Holocaust (New York: Alfred A. Knopf, 1996). The authors argue that the willing participation of random Germans in the extermination process demonstrates an "annihilatory" racial consensus across the spectrum of German society as a whole, without which the "Final Solution of the Jewish Problem" could not have occurred (in this, they are building on themes elaborated by Gerald Reitlinger in his *The SS: Alibi of a Nation, 1922–1945* [New York: Viking, 1957]). If such analysis is compelling—as I think it is—it should be considered that at no point were the nazis secure enough in the pervasiveness of German exterminationist sentiments to conduct triumphal marches through the streets of Hamburg in which the body parts of butchered Jews were openly displayed.

*"[The] facts of history are plain: Most Texas Indians were exterminated or brought to the brink of oblivion by Spaniards, Mexicans, Texans, and Americans who often had no more regard for the life of an Indian than they had for that of a dog, sometimes less"; W.W. Newcomb, Jr., *The Indians of Texas* (Austin: University of Texas Press, 1961) p. 334.

†E.g., "A new plan has been adopted by our neighbors opposite this place to chastise the Indians... Some men have been hired to hunt them, who are recompensed by receiving so much for each scalp, or some satisfactory evidence that they have been killed. The money has been made up by subscription"; *Maryville (CA) Weekly Express*, Apr. 16, 1859. Or, "A meeting of citizens was held a day or two ago at Haslerigg's store, and measures taken to raise a fund to be disbursed in payment of Indian scalps for which a bounty is offered... The initial steps have been taken, and it is safe to assert that the extinction of the tribes... will result"; *Maryville Appeal*, May 12, 1861. See generally, Heizer, *The Destruction of California Indians, op. cit.*

would have killed 5,200 Indians in *one* year. And Laycock claimed that settlers' raids went on for five years.[283]

Plainly, the official minimum count of 8,500 Indians killed in "individual conflicts" between 1790 and 1990 was ridiculously low. The northern California tally alone accounts for more than that, and, for its part, Texas paid well over 8,000 scalp bounties between 1858 and 1878.[284] When one adds in all the rest of the country, the real number must exceed 100,000 during the period of U.S. suzerainty. Nor is there evidence of either state or federal prosecution of anyone plying such murderous "private sector" initiatives against even the most unoffending indigenous population in California (or elsewhere, for that matter). On the contrary, the record is replete with examples of official statements whipping up sentiments which could only have led to precisely this result.[285]

Overwhelmed by the sheer viciousness of the European/Euroamerican drive to extermination, and thus confronted with what Tzvetan Todorov has called "facing the extreme," many—but not all—of North America's indigenous peoples internalized much of their exterminators' bloodlust, engaging in largescale killing, scalping, and mutilating in a bitterly desperate effort to forestall their own looming eradication.[286] The dynamic of death imposed upon them left no viable alternative in most cases. Haudenosaunee scholar Ray Fadden thus had it exactly right, in principle if not in literal detail, when he observed that "scalping, skinning alive and burning at the stake were European barbarian inventions, forced on Indian mercenaries," and, eventually, indigenous patriots as well.[287]

War Without Mercy

The entire panorama of colonial warfare in North America, not just that of the English, followed the same exterminatory impulse as was evident at Jamestown and Plymouth, albeit according to the different approaches to colonization exhibited by each colonizing power.[288] If there is an exception, it is the Spanish of *la Florída*, who established permanent installations only to block efforts of French Huguenots to do so in 1564.[289] After effectively exterminating them in 1565, Spanish troops under Pedro Menéndez de Avilés constructed the fort of Castillo de San Marcos (San Augustín) and seven other posts along the Timucuan and Guale coastlines—they called the area, which extended northward through what is now Georgia, "Chicora"— but did not undertake military operations against the natives.[290] Rather, the

Spaniards preferred to missionize, gradually wearing them down through disease and de facto slave labor, and ultimately replacing them with African chattel.[291]

Beginning in the very late seventeenth century, the Apalachees were provided with arms and encouraged to raid northward, into what is now South Carolina—the Spanish regime hoped this might discourage encroaching English colonists—but since Florida was swapped to Britain in 1763 for Caribbean concessions, the effect was minimal.[292] When Spain resumed control of its former colony after the British quitclaimed it at the conclusion of the American War of Independence (1787), it was again with little enthusiasm, and it was wrested away permanently by the more aggressive United States in 1812.[293] With respect to Indians, it had served mainly as a place of refuge for the remnants of peoples devastated by U.S. and English campaigns.

In the upper Sonora, of course, things were different. In 1599, the "last conquistador," Juan de Oñate, pacified the Acoma Pueblo in New Mexico by slaughtering 800 of its residents, capturing another 580, and leveling the town. Oñate then made his captives an example to deter other Pueblo resistance to Spanish rule, placing all between the ages of twelve and twenty-five in slavery and handing everyone under twelve over to Franciscan priests (which, as was discussed above, amounted to the same thing). All Acomas over the age of twenty-five suffered the severing of one foot.[294]

Although their record demonstrates no shortage of such atrocities, usually on a smaller scale, the clearest instance of the Spanish attempting extermination by direct military means north of the Río Grande concerns the various southern Apachean peoples stretching from the Texas Gulf Coast into Arizona and northern Mexico.[295] In 1772, the Marqués de Rubí, Crown Inspector of Presidios, recommended that a state of "continuous offensive war" be declared against the most easterly of these "recalcitrant" groups, the Lipáns, with the goal of extirpating them.[296] A few years later, when Spanish troops had proven themselves inadequate to the task, Interior Minister Toleda de Croix and New Mexico Governor Juan Bautista de Anza, hatched a plan to enlist the Comanches and other native peoples in exchange for horses, weapons, and other manufactured goods, to do the job for them.[297]

This accomplished the objective with respect to the Lipáns—they were virtually wiped out by 1820—but the Spanish had no native takers in their plans to do the same to more westerly Apaches such as the Mescaleros,

Yavapais, and Chiricahuas.[298] This left the Spaniards, and later the Mexicans, to fight a bloody and protracted war of attrition—they initiated scalp bounties on Apaches, and Diné as well, as early as 1790—which they'd still not won by the time the United States seized the northern half of Mexico in 1848.[299] As it turned out, it would take the Americans another thirty years, using a much greater concentration of force, to bring these already badly decimated peoples to heel. By the time it was finished, the Chiricahuas would have joined the Lipáns in near extinction.[300]

The French

More than any other colonizing power in North America, France depended upon the subversion of indigenous societies to act as its surrogates rather than upon great numbers of settlers, troops, and missionaries. At the time of its peak commitment to the New World in the early 1760s, France had fewer than 50,000 of its own people in the colonies—as compared to England's nearly one million.[301] The tremendous human costs of its prolonged effort to assert continental hegemony were thus incurred to a very high degree by its indigenous "allies" and their oft-times native opponents. But, because of the very mode of its manipulations, playing Indians both against one another and against competing European powers, the French have always been able to maintain an air of innocence concerning their genocidal impact and intent.[302]

France's attempt at colonizing the New World began poorly. On his second voyage of reconnaissance up the St. Lawrence in 1536, Jacques Cartier, who had established reasonably cordial relations with both the Micmac (Souriquois) and Laurentian Iroquois during his 1534 expedition, intervened in the internal affairs of the latter in a way he thought would produce a situation favorable to French interests. His approach was to support a leader he thought "friendly," by kidnapping three others who were less so and taking them to France, where they died. Rather than producing the desired effect, the maneuver served to galvanize the powerful Haudenosaunee (Iroquois) confederation—the Mohawks, Senecas, Onondagas, Cayugas, Oneidas, and a number of tributary peoples, often called the "Five Nations"—against the French for the duration of that empire's stay in North America. When Cartier returned for a third time in 1541 and attempted to establish a permanent colony at Cape Diamond, he was repulsed.[303]

The next effort, headed by Pierre du Gua, Sieur de Monts and Samuel de Champlain, commenced in 1604. By this time, seasonal trade in beaver pelts had allowed France to develop a relatively solid web of connections to the Micmac, Algonquin, Montagnais, Huron and, to a somewhat lesser extent, the Maliseets and Abenaki.[304] After a pair of false starts, Champlain was able, in 1608, to set up a permanent base at Stadacona, an abandoned Iroquois town site he renamed Québec.[305] Within a year, he had firmed up France's relations with the Hurons, Algonquins, and Montagnais by promising them arms and other materiel to preempt the trapping territories of their traditional rivals, the Iroquois.[306] On July 29, 1609, he sealed the new arrangement by accompanying a group of sixty of these Indians armed with guns when they overpowered some 200 Mohawks without such weapons.[307] The performance was repeated the following spring.

> Champlain's allies launched their second campaign without waiting for him and his four French companions. Some two hundred Algonquin and Huron warriors discovered a party of about one hundred Mohawks on the lower Richelieu River. The outnumbered Mohawk managed to build a strong, circular barricade, and defended it effectively. When the French finally arrived, delayed by their cumbersome pikesman's armor, they fired into the enclosure, and a passing group of French fur trappers added their arquebuses to the next barrage. After pulling down the barricade with ropes, the allies attacked, killing all but fifteen, who were taken prisoner.[308]

The regional balance of power thus disrupted, the Mohawks withdrew southward for an extended period.[309] During the lull, Champlain busily cultivated new relationships with peoples as far beyond Huronia as the Ottawas, Tionantis (also called "Tobaccos"), and Neutrals of southwestern Ontario. He also began making overtures to the Nipissings. In 1615, he sought to facilitate a further expansion into Haudenosaunee territory by providing advice and firepower to a large group of Hurons who laid siege to a heavily fortified Oneida—or Onondaga, it is unclear which—town. Lacking cannon, and with Champlain unable to convince the Hurons to engage in a European-style assault on their opponents' positions, the attack failed. The Iroquois, however, continued to give ground in order to stay clear of the French musketry which had been placed in the hands of their enemies.[310]

Things might have continued in this vein indefinitely, had it not been for a brief war in Europe between England and France. The major byproduct of this in the New World was that a small English force seized Québec in 1629, evicting Champlain and holding the village until 1631.[311]

By the time it was restored to French control—France had to cede rights to more northerly areas to regain Québec, thereby providing a base for what would become the English Hudson's Bay Company—there had been a number of changes. Paramount was the fact that the Mohawks had forced their way into a trade relationship with the Dutch at Fort Orange (Albany), fighting a sharp little war with the Mahicans to do it, and had begun acquiring firearms of their own.[312] This started to swing the regional pendulum of power back towards its 1615 position, but at a far more lethal level of interaction than had previously prevailed.

> A few Algonquin and Mohawk were prepared to consider intertribal peace in return for exchanging access to European traders, but the Europeans assumed that [American Indian] allies of their European enemies were automatically their enemies [as well], and helped to make it so. Champlain, returning in 1633 as "commander" of New France with a population of only one hundred, nonetheless called for the destruction of the Mohawk by invasion. Failed negotiations in 1635 inaugurated thirty years of intermittent Mohawk war against the French and their allies.[313]

Here is where a truly unintended incidence of disease played into—but hardly accounts for—the obliteration of a people. In their fervor to bolster the French effort in America, and fueled by Cardinal Richelieu's Catholic revitalization movement at home, Jesuit missionaries came flooding into the colony, establishing missions everywhere among their country's native friends, especially the Hurons.[314] In short order, recurrent waves of epidemics had reduced the Huron from about 30,000 in 1630 to fewer than 10,000 a decade later. In the panic of sudden and inexplicable mass death, the Indians cast about for some means of survival.[315] This, the priests gladly offered in the form of wholesale conversions. By 1640, about half of all surviving Hurons were Christians.[318]

This, actually, was the rub. Traditional Hurons would, at this point, have gladly arrived at some accommodation with the Haudenosaunee. The Christian converts, however, were fired with an unconstrained zeal to prove themselves more French than the French, and, provided with a greater number of muskets than ever, they undertook a fresh round of raids against the Mohawks and Senecas in hopes of fulfilling Champlain's languishing objectives.[317] When they violated a painfully negotiated peace agreement in 1645, the Haudenosaunees' patience finally wore out altogether.

> [The] Seneca and Mohawk began recruiting their fellow Iroquois for war… Early in 1648, the Mohawk slaughtered a Huron legation to Onondaga, and a Seneca war party

equipped with firearms destroyed the well-fortified Huron frontier town of Teanaostaiaé. Of its two thousand inhabitants, three hundred were killed, and seven hundred were taken captive, predominately women and children [all of whom were, following Iroquois custom, absorbed into the Haudenosaunee].[318]

This was followed, in March 1649, by an attack by more than a thousand Senecas and Mohawks on Taenhatentaron (St. Ignace), one of the three principal towns of the Huron. After sacking it and taking several hundred prisoners, the Iroquois force assaulted nearby Saint Louis, leveling it, too.[319] By then, the Hurons, who had taken to burning their own villages and food stores in the face of the advancing Iroquois—and who were getting virtually no assistance from their French "friends" now that the chips were down—were starving and beginning to break up. Some of them sought permanent refuge among the nearby Eries, Petuns, and Neutrals. Over the next year, a portion drifted far to the west, eventually becoming Wyandots. Others migrated southward to merge with the Susquehannock, and still others went all the way to the Carolinas, where they joined the Catawbas. The bulk were accepted among the Haudenosaunee themselves.* In any event, "archeologically and anthropologically, the Huron can be regarded as exterminated in 1649."[320]

The abrupt collapse of Huronia created an unprecedented power vacuum among the indigenous nations of the eastern Great Lakes region. For the next fifteen years, the Haudenosaunee were preoccupied with filling it, assuming control over what had been Huron territory and trade networks.

---

*Trigger, "The Destruction of Huronia," *op. cit.* That the Iroquois would absorb so many of a vanquished foe—the Senecas accepted about 500, the Mohawks upwards of 700, the Onondagas about 400, the Oneidas and Cayugas approximately 250–300 apiece—as full citizens of their own polity was simply in keeping with their values and traditions. The same could be said for the other indigenous nations which took in Huron remnants. The whole process stands in stark contrast to that of all the European powers in "disposing" of prisoners; for a broader view of the Iroquoian practice, see Francis Jennings, *The Ambiguous Iroquois Empire: The Covenant Chain Confederation of Indian Tribes with the New England Colonies* (New York: W.W. Norton, 1984). Perhaps ironically, it was their largess in naturalizing the Hurons which sowed the seeds of division among the Haudenosaunee for the first time. Many of the new citizens had been converted to Catholicism and continued their allegiance to both France and the church. Ultimately, the infusion of such views led not only to political confusion within the confederation as a whole but a replication of the factionalism which had beset late Huron society among specific peoples, notably the Mohawks. In 1680 this dynamic would cause a splitting away of Catholic Mohawks from the main body and the establishment of a special mission for them, Caughnawaga (Oka), near the French village of Montréal; Steele, *Warpaths, op. cit.*, pp. 71–2. As was evident in the events at that location in 1990, such things have continuing implications three centuries later; Rick Hornung, *One Nation Under the Gun: Inside the Mohawk Civil War* (New York: Pantheon, 1991).

They extended their reach by fighting a series of short, deadly wars with France's smaller native allies to the west: the Tobaccos in 1649, the Neutrals in 1650, and the Eries in 1656.[321] Southward, in the upper Ohio Valley, they also conducted a campaign against a group they called the Atrakwaeronons during 1651–52.[322] In each case, the outcome was that Iroquois opponents ceased to exist as peoples, since the Haudenosaunee adopted the great majority of their surviving members. By an almost perverse logic, the more they fought, the numerically stronger the Haudenosaunee became.[*]

Another pair of wars, less severe but nonetheless substantial, were waged against the Mahicans of the upper Hudson Valley and the Sokokis of the upper Connecticut in order to secure open access to the Dutch traders of New Netherlands and, increasingly, those of New England as well.[323] By 1655, the Haudenosaunee had emerged from these "Beaver Wars" as the hegemonic power of their region (which kept growing; they were, by this point, already beginning to extend their influence into the Illinois River Valley).[324] The French, whose plan had been to use the now-extinct Hurons and others to eradicate the Five Nations, were becoming desperate. As one consequence, they sued for peace with the Iroquois in 1667 while casting about for new surrogates to equip.[325] As another, they undertook a crash program of bringing in troops and colonists; the European population of New France, which was barely 3,000 in 1660, nearly quadrupled over the next quarter-century.[326]

A problem for France, however, was that rather than simply concentrating its force along the St. Lawrence, it squandered its limited investment of resources in an apparently limitless appetite for territorial/commercial expansion. By 1685, it was pressing claims which followed the Mississippi all the way to New Orleans, and included most of the present United States north of New Spain.[327] It was also attempting to make inroads on a vast territory extending from Hudson's Bay westward to the Pacific, ceded to England in 1631.[328] In every instance, given its paucity of personnel, France relied on an ever-more-complicated web of diplomatic/military/trade

---

[*]It is estimated that the Five Nations took in upwards of 600 Atrakwaeronons alone. The Neutrals, who had been about 10,000 strong in 1600, were reduced to fewer than 800 at the end of 1650, and dissolved altogether thereafter (up to 1,500 joined the Haudenosaunee). Most of the surviving Tobaccos, many of whom were Hurons anyway, went west to become Wyandots. The Eries, who were proportionately most Christianized and thus most heavily motivated by French "ideals," probably suffered the greatest number of fatalities. Still, several hundred of them ended up as Iroquois; Axelrod, *Chronicle of the Indian Wars, op. cit.*, pp. 44–5, Jennings, *Ambiguous Iroquois Empire, op. cit.*

alliances with indigenous nations to accomplish its objectives.* This, in turn, involved it an unending series of brushfire wars on the periphery.

Frustration with this situation led the French to engage in what may be the only two instances in which they directly perpetrated genocide in North America. The first example resulted from a protracted struggle with the Mesquaki, or "Fox," as they were called, beginning in 1712.† Finally, in September 1730, still unable to pacify this small but fiercely independent opponent, French officials determined to exterminate them altogether.[329] Over 1,400 troops were deployed to surround about 1,200 of the 1,600 remaining Mesquakis—about three-quarters of them noncombatants—in Mabichi, a fortified town they'd constructed on the Vermilion River, in Illinois.[330] After an eighteen-day siege, the starving Mesquakis offered to surrender. The French commander, Coulon de Villiers, responded that "no quarter would be given." In the end, there were only 300 survivors, all of whom were parceled out to France's native allies.[331]

The second clear example of French genocide occurred at about the same time, far to the south, in what is now the State of Mississippi, as a subpart of the so-called "Chickasaw Wars."

> The Chickasaw Resistance began in 1720, when the Chickasaws [who were at odds with the French-aligned Choctaws and Muskogees] defied French authority by maintaining trade relations with the English and allowing English traders to "invade" territory claimed by France along the Mississippi River. In an attempt to enforce control, the French incited their Choctaw allies to raid Chickasaw settlements. The Chickasaws retaliated with raids of their own, not only against Choctaw villages, but against French shipping on the river, effectively creating a trade blockade. French authorities redou-

---

* The Indians, of course, usually had their own agendas. In 1685, the French attempted to coopt the Ojibway (Anishinabe, also called "Chippewas") of the western Great Lakes region into the same arrangement as the more northerly Cree. (see note 328) The Ojibway, having perhaps learned something from the Cree experience, demanded more guns and even better trade concessions, which the French provided. The Indians then turned their firepower on their traditional Dakota ("Sioux") rivals, keeping them away from weapons sources altogether. Meanwhile, the Hudson's Bay outposts went largely unscathed; M.L. Brown, *Firearms in Colonial America, op. cit.* Also see William S. Warren, *History of the Ojibway People* (St. Paul: Minnesota Historical Society, 1984 reprint of 1885 original).

† The Mesquaki population, centering originally around Green Bay, Wisconsin, is estimated as having been no more than 4,500 in 1700. They were, however, involved in a conflict with the much more extensive Ojibways, whom France was courting as an ally. Moreover, they were positioned to seriously disrupt broader French operations emanating from Fort Michilimackinac, in the strategic strait at Sault Sainte Marie. The French therefore decided to impress the Ojibways—and preclude a Mesquaki alliance with the English, the Haudenosaunee, or both—by crushing this tiny group. The problem was that the Mesquakis, superb guerrilla fighters, had other ideas; Balesi, *The Time of the French, op. cit.*, Chapter 9, inclusive.

bled their recruitment of [Choctaws] fixing a bounty on Chickasaw scalps and supplying firearms and ammunition.[332]

Unable to defeat the Chickasaws militarily, France formally acknowledged their sovereignty in a 1724 peace accord necessary to end the blockade. Its emissaries then set out to undermine the cohesion of Chickasaw society, flooding it with missionaries and alcohol in roughly equal proportions.[333] Finally, on November 28, 1729, the Natchez and Yazoos, Chicakasaw tributaries from the area near the present-day city of Natchez, had had enough. They attacked Fort Rosalie, a military/missionary post, and put it to the torch.[334] The French response, explicitly intended to make the Natchez an example which would cow the larger body of Chickasaws, was frankly exterminatory. A large force of troops was moved upriver from New Orleans and managed to surprise and butcher about half the Natchez, rather more of the Yazoos.[335] Survivors were mostly taken prisoner and sold into slavery in the Caribbean, a matter which led to the immediate extinction of both peoples.[*]

The reaction of regional natives was exactly the opposite of what the French had hoped. Not only did the Chickasaws rise and impose a veritable stranglehold on French trade, but most Choctaws and Muskogees declined, under the circumstances, to oppose them. The French were forced to import Illinois, Kaskaskias, and other native fighters from far to the north in an ineffectual effort to contain their enraged opponents.[336] In 1736, the Chickasaws defeated the best the French had to offer—a mixed force of 600 regulars and 1,000 Indian mercenaries—in open battle. A second major expedition failed in 1739, and the French gave up. Skirmishing dragged on persistently, a continuous drain on imperial resources, until New France itself was extinguished thirty years later.[337]

The Dutch

Dutch New World colonialism was in some ways more straightforwardly exterminationist than the that of the French, though it, too, typically utilized trade incentives and intricate diplomacy in pursuing its goals. It began in 1609,

---

[*] Steele places the number of those sold into slavery at 500, and says other survivors were incorporated into the Chicakasaw and Cherokee; *Warpaths, op. cit.*, p. 164. Even James Axtell concedes that the French campaigns against the Mesquaki, Natchez, and Yazoo — along with the campaigns of the English against the Powhatans and Pequots, and Amherst's 1763 extirpation of the Ottawas by smallpox—qualify as genocide. He nonetheless contends that, since he himself "knows of only these five instances in which it occurred," genocide is an "inappropriate" descriptor of colonial processes in North America; AHA Q&A, *op. cit.*

when Henry Hudson, an English navigator commissioned by the Netherlands to seek a northerly water route to Asia, sailed up the river that now bears his name.[338] In the vicinity of present-day Albany, he encountered representatives of the 6,400-member Mahican nation and, finding them receptive to the notion of trading beaver pelts and other furs for manufactured goods, initiated transatlantic commerce. By 1614, traders had constructed Fort Nassau, later replaced by Fort Orange, a short distance away, near the location of the first meeting.[339]

Things went along smoothly enough for a few years, with the steadily better-armed Mahicans becoming something of a regional power by virtue of their position as brokers of the Dutch trade to a number of peoples. The first real crisis arose in 1624, when the Mohawks, under heavy pressure from the French and Hurons, determined that their self-interest required direct access to Dutch weaponry. The Mahicans resisted both this erosion of their trade monopoly and the loss of superiority in firepower it would represent.[340] The Dutch backed them, and the resulting "Mohawk-Mahican War"—somehow the Europeans are always left unmentioned in these things—lasted until 1628. The Mahicans were soundly beaten, and the Dutch lost most of the men it had committed to them. The Mohawks got their trade arrangement and their musketry.[341]

Lesson learned, New Netherlands Governor Wouter Van Twiller determined that, as a hedge against the vagaries of the interior, it would be good if the colony were to have an English-style coastal enclave surrounded by cleared lands and settlers. Hence, the port facility of New Amsterdam was established in 1626, and its perimeter was expanded incrementally thereafter. Dutch military capacity was also steadily increased.[342]

> By 1639, when Willem Kieft replaced…Van Twiller as governor of New Netherlands, acquisition of territory became more important to the Dutch than maintaining friendly relations with the Indians. Kieft imposed heavy taxes on the Algonquian tribes of the vicinity of Manhattan and Long Island, claiming that payment of such tribute was necessary to finance the cost of defending them from "hostiles."[343]

This combination of factors led, in 1641, to some minor responses by the Raritans and other small peoples in the area of Staten Island.* Kieft

---

*The catalyst came in the form of a group of Dutch settlers who loosed their livestock in Raritan fields as an expedient for prompting the Indians to abandon lands the settlers coveted for themselves. The Raritans retaliated by slaughtering the animals and burning several farmsteads. Then, in early 1642, a wheelwright named Claes Rademaker, who seems to have murdered a Raritan for scalp bounty (and to steal a batch of beaver pelts the man was bringing in to trade), was in return killed by the victim's nephew; Trelease, *Indian Affairs in Colonial New York, op. cit.*, pp. 60–3.

replied by announcing his intention to "wipe the mouths" of the Indians, placing a bounty on Raritan scalps, enlisting a force of Mohawks in exchange for 400 muskets, and hiring the English mercenary John Underhill to replicate his and his countrymen's feats against the Pequots four years earlier.[344] The first target was the tiny Wappinger Nation, near the mouth of the Hudson River. Attacked by the Mohawks in early February 1643, the Wappingers fled to Pavonia (present-day Jersey City) and asked for the Dutch protection their tributes had supposedly purchased. Kieft not only refused but asked the Mohawks to attack them in their new location. The result was that more than seventy fighting-age males — virtually the entirety of the Wappingers' defensive strength — were killed.[345]

> During the night of February 25–26, Kieft sent in Dutch soldiers to finish off the refugees, mostly women and children, whom the Mohawks had been reluctant to harm. The night of mayhem in Pavonia would become infamous as the Slaughter of the Innocents. The troops returned to New Amsterdam bearing the severed heads of 80 Indians, which soldiers and citizens used as footballs on the streets of New Amsterdam. Thirty prisoners also taken were tortured to death for the public amusement.[346]

The Mohawks absorbed the few Wappingers who remained alive, and that people thereupon went out of existence. Although eleven local peoples, nominally headed by the Raritans, sought to reply to this genocide militarily, they proved no match for the ferocity exhibited by Underhill's troops.[347] For the rest of 1643 and much of 1644, the soldiers engaged in a concerted campaign to completely eradicate all eleven of their opponents.

> The well-armed but cumbersome colonial winter expeditions ransacked and burned deserted...villages, but seldom saw the inhabitants. One important exception occurred in March 1644 [when] Underhill...led 130 men on a night attack against a major Tankiteke or Siwanoy village. Using tactics borrowed from the Pequot War, Underhill's musketeers encircled the village, killed an estimated 180 with initial gunfire, then set fire to the buildings and slaughtered those trying to escape. The [Indians] estimated they'd lost five hundred people in this unequal battle.[348]

All told, at least a thousand native people were killed outright, two or three thousand died of collateral causes, and another thousand captives were shipped off as slaves to the West Indies before the decimated peoples of the New Amsterdam region capitulated in late 1644. The terms of the "peace" imposed upon the Indians were virtually total dispossession and reduction to impoverished servitude.[349] From then on, the Raritans and their allies died off at a very rapid rate; by 1650, they had all joined the Wappingers among the ranks of indigenous nations which had "vanished" under the weight of European conquest and colonization.

In 1655, this extermination was followed by encroachment upon the territory of the much more populous Lenni Lenâpé. In the so-called "Peach War" of that year, Governor Peter Stuyvesant, who had replaced Kieft, called out the militia to lay waste to the Indians' more northerly fields and villages.[350] Native casualties were relatively light only because the Dutch action provoked a significant response from New Sweden, with which the Lenni Lenâpé were aligned, and embroiled New Netherlands in a conflict with the Susquehannocks, an even more powerful Swedish ally.[351] The resulting "Esopus War," which lasted until 1663, saw the Dutch fought to a virtual standstill by an indigenous military alliance which outnumbered, and in some instances outgunned, both the colonists and their Mohawk surrogates.[352] Still, the Hackensacks and Wecquaesgeek peoples of present-day New Jersey, and the Esopus, Minisinks, and Pocumtucks in what is now upstate New York were eradicated in the process.[353]

Although the Swedes were knocked out of North America by the fighting, victory afforded no reprieve for the Dutch, who had seriously overreached themselves. The Susequehannocks and Lenni Lenâpé shifted their alignment to England, Holland's enemy in a costly war being fought in both the Old World and the New.[354] The Mohawks, meanwhile, had been considerably worn down by their effort to simultaneously fight wars with the Susequehannocks and their allies in the south and their French-aligned opponents in the north.[355] By 1664, stripped of both native fodder and the possibility of reinforcement from home, Stuyvesant was reduced to only 150 troops in New Amsterdam; threatened with literal annihilation by English forces, he ceded all of New Netherlands to England.[356]

The English

The most overtly genocidal of the European powers operating in North America was England, a circumstance evinced by that country's ultimate desire not to convert native populations into commercial subordinates or laborers, but to completely replace them on their own land.[357] Along the way, certain indigenous nations might prove to be lucrative (if transitory) trading partners, vital pawns in the empire's military conflicts with its European rivals, and/or a useful pool of expendable slave labor, but there was never really anything very ambiguous about the English goal of creating Indian-free zones of occupation for itself, as rapidly as practicable, in every locality to which it lay claim.[358]

Following hard on the heels of the drives to exterminate first the Pequots, and then the Narragansetts and others in New England, as well as the Tsenacommacahs and Piscataways in Virginia, the colonists of both North and South Carolina set out to eliminate the Tuscaroras, one of the more populous and powerful of the various native peoples within the boundaries of their respective charters.[359] Using the pretext that the Indians had committed "aggression" by repelling a group of would-be Swiss colonists in the vicinity of what is now New Bern, North Carolina, both colonies went to war. From 1711 to 1713, a combined force of colonial volunteers, rangers, and allied Indians (mostly Muskogees, Cherokees, and Catawbas) conducted a series of assaults on Tuscarora villages, perpetrating at least one wholesale massacre after sacking the principle town of Neoheroka in March of 1713.[360]

> In this war, an estimated fourteen hundred [of 6,000] Tuscarora were killed and about one thousand enslaved [probably 2,000 more died "collaterally"]. Most of the tribal territory was confiscated, and survivors "scattered as the wind scatters smoke." Between fifteen hundred and two thousand Tuscarora survivors fled north to join the Five Nations, transforming them into the Six Nations.[361]

Four years later, the Yamasee War erupted in South Carolina. This was in many ways ironic, insofar as the Indians in question, a substantial Chattahoochee River people, had been staunch allies of the English in combatting raids by the Apalachees and other peoples of Spanish Florida. The problem from the native point of view was both the intensifying pressure exerted by South Carolina upon the Yamasees' shrinking territory and the increasing appetite of the Carolinian native slave trade.* On April 15, 1715, the Yamasees seized every English trader within their territory and launched a coordinated series of attacks on encroaching farms and settlements. In short

---

* The colonists were especially interested in impressing Yamasee women and children, an expedient to preventing reproduction. Actually, the problem was endemic. Rather than immediately completing their exterminations of a number of peoples, the Virginians, for example, facilitated the temporary amalgamation of their fragments into new groups like the "Westos," whose sole basis of survival was to conduct slave raids against still-viable neighboring peoples like the Yamasee. Once their utility had passed, of course, the Westos were extinguished altogether; Sanford Winston, "Indian Slavery in the Carolina Region," *Journal of Negro History*, No. 19, 1934; Carol I. Mason, "A Reconsideration of Westo-Yuchi Identification," *American Anthropologist*, No. 65, 1963.

order, they were joined by the Guales, Catawbas, what was left of the old Cofitachiqui chiefdom, a portion of the Muskogees, and strong elements of the Cherokees and Shawnees, all of whom had suffered at the hands of England.[362]

After a brief campaign in which the Indians advanced to within a dozen miles of the South Carolina capital at Charlestown, the bulk of the alliance determined that their point had been made and withdrew from the conflict. A paid force of about 1,500 troops provided by colonies as far north as Virginia then set out to exterminate the Yamasees and the Guales.[363] By 1717, "harried to tribal extinction," the survivors had fled to the very southern reaches of what is now the State of Georgia, finding refuge among the Apalachees.[364] After England took the area from Spain in 1733,[365] the remnants of all three indigenous peoples moved even further south and began to combine themselves in what they called the "Seminole" Nation, strengthening themselves over the next century by admitting the last residue of Cofitachiquis and Timucuans, a portion of the Lower Creeks, and numerous escaped African slaves.[*]

A number of less decisive campaigns were fought by the English during the late seventeenth and most of the eighteenth centuries, always for the purpose of usurping indigenous lands and sovereignty while eroding the physical capacity of native opponents to sustain themselves as peoples. In New England, for example, a war of attrition was fought against the Abenaki of present-day Vermont from 1688–1699, and was abandoned only when other English interests compelled its cessation.[366] It was resumed from 1723–1727 in what was called "Drummer's War" (also known as "Grey Lock's War").[†] During the course of the fighting, the native peoples of Maine—notably the Penobscots, Kennebecs, and Passamaquoddies, all

---

[*] The Yamasees, Guales, Apalachees, Cofitachiquis, and Timucuans were thereafter categorized as extinct by European/Euroamerican ethnographers, a matter which was/is culturally if not literally true. In the late 1980s, a tiny group of Yamasee descendants was finally recognized by the U.S. government as still existing in a genetic sense, a matter which does nothing to mitigate the fact of the genocide perpetrated against them. See Peter H. Wood, "The Changing Population of the Colonial South: An Overview by Race and Region, 1685–1790," in Wood, Waselkov and Hatley, *Powhatan's Mantle, op. cit.*

[†] By this point, the Eastern Abenaki had been "attritted" into a sort of accommodation with the English. The Western Abenaki, however, continued to comport themselves as a completely independent nation. This was contrary to colonial contentions that they were a subject people. The war was fought with the idea of decimating them to the point of utter subjugation and eventual dissolution; Colin G. Calloway, *The Western Abenaki of Vermont, 1600–1800* (Norman: University of Oklahoma Press, 1991) pp. 113–31.

friendly with Abenaki—were also heavily impacted.* The same principle pertained all along the frontier, from Canada to Florida.

The Anglo-French Wars

Several outbreaks of English exterminationism occurred during, or as direct by-products of, the so-called "French and Indian Wars." There were four of these, beginning with King William's War (known as the "War of the League of Augsburg" or "Seven Years' War" in Europe) from 1689 to 1697. This was followed by Queen Anne's War (the "War of the Spanish Succession") from 1702 to 1713, and King George's War (the "War of the Austrian Succession") from 1744–1748. Finally, there was the "Seven Years' War," which actually lasted fourteen years running from 1749 to 1763, and is usually referred to in North America as the "French and Indian War." All were subparts of much larger conflicts, at least one of them global in scope, centering in the power relations of Europe.[367]

Although the configurations of alignment shifted almost continuously during the course of the fighting, the general pattern was that England relied mainly on the relatively high density of its colonizing population, along with the introduction of regiments, to pursue its interests.[368] During all four wars, while the Cherokees, Chickasaws, and others sometimes filled the same role, only the Mohawks sided consistently with the English (after King William's War, the other five nations of the Haudenosaunee attempted, with varying degrees of success, to remain neutral).† The transparently exterminationist nature of England's imperial pretensions in America served to alienate other

---

* In the fall of 1699, for example, as part of their campaign against the Eastern Abenaki, a Massachusetts militia unit swept through Penobscot and Kennebec territory, burning villages, fields, and food stores as they went. Although few Indians were killed outright by the expedition, a number died during the ensuing winter—as was planned by colonial officials—of resultant starvation, exposure, and disease. The Indians of Maine were also subject to the same exterminatory scalp bounties as the Abenakis during this entire period; Steele, *Warpaths, op. cit.*, pp. 146–7; Kenneth M. Morrison, "The Bias of Colonial Law: English Paranoia and the Abenaki Arena of King Philip's War," *New England Quarterly*, No. 53, 1980.

† This was not simply the result of Mohawk Francophobia. From early on, the English began to explore the possibilities of formal diplomatic relations with the Haudenosaunee, the Mohawks in particular. By 1750, they had a permanent diplomatic mission, headed by Sir William Johnson (who broke with English practice by marrying an Indian). England's success in the venture points to the possibilities of what might have happened had they pursued such a strategy more broadly; Francis Jennings, *Empire of Fortune: Crowns, Colonies and Tribes in the Seven Years' War in America* (New York: W.W. Norton, 1988); James Thomas Flexner, *Lord of the Mohawks: A Biography of Sir William Johnson* (Boston: Little, Brown, 1979).

indigenous allies, temporary or potential, almost faster than they could be attracted.*

France, for its part, was able to employ its status as the lesser of evils to considerable advantage, consistently using a preponderance of native surrogates—each of them motivated not by fealty to the French Crown, but by the clear self-interest of eliminating or at least containing the genocidally inclined English—to prosecute its side of the struggle.[369] In the south, France could count on the Choctaws as well as a sizable segment of the Muskogees, and, in the Mississippi Valley, it enjoyed solid relations with the Illinois, Kaskaskias, and others.[370]

> The Delawares and other eastern tribes, having good reason to fear dispossession from their lands at the hands of the English, were fairly reliable French allies... The Delawares were generally supported in the West by the Shawnees. In the Northeast, the Abenakis proved to be extremely reliable allies... Also reliable were the Ojibways, Ottawas, and Potawatomies, Ohio country [nations] known collectively among themselves as the Three Council Fires.[371]

King William's War yielded no decisive results in terms of intercolonial relations. For Indians, however, it was another matter. In 1693, for example, the Haudenosaunee were badly mauled by one of the few largescale French expeditions of the war.[372] Further east, the New England militias managed to batter at least three of the smaller peoples—the Pennacooks, Ossippees, and Pigwackets—to the brink of extinction.[373] By the time the Treaty of Ryswick ended the European conflict in September 1697, the battle lines in North America had been drawn more firmly than ever before. Fighting continued sporadically along the New England frontier until Queen Anne's War commenced exactly five years later.[374]

In this equally inconclusive contest, which involved Spain as well as France and England, the primary victims were the Apalachees, whom the Spaniards sought to deploy in the French manner. In response, former South Carolina governor James Moore mustered a sizable militia force, augmented it with Chickasaws and Yamasees, and marched through Apalachee territory in July 1704. All told, the marauders "killed or captured the inhabitants of

---

*The English blunder in this respect closely prefigures that of the Germans two centuries later, during the invasion of the Soviet Union. In the latter instance, the initial enthusiasm of the Ukrainians and others to fight as German allies was squandered on the shoals of the Germans' unabashed racial arrogance and openly displayed intent to clear the Slavs from their land by all available means; Alexander Dallin, *German Rule in Russia, 1941–1945* (New York: St. Martin's Press 1957).

seven villages and destroyed 13 or 14 Spanish missions in the country, virtually annihilating the Apalachee."[375] To the north, protracted fighting seriously eroded the strength of the Eastern Abenaki and several smaller peoples before the 1713 Treaty of Utrecht brought "peace" in North America.[376]

The interlude between wars was marked by the earlier-mentioned English campaigns of extermination against the Tuscaroras and Yamasees, as well as Drummer's War and the French campaigns to eradicate the Mesquakies and Natchez. It was also during the latter part of this period that the English "pioneers" like Daniel Boone began to make their first serious penetrations into the French-claimed territories of the Shawnees, Mingos, Miamis, and others west of the Appalachians, in what would become Kentucky, West Virginia and Ohio.[377] King George's War brought the era to a close in 1744, sputtering along without much coherence until it flickered out four years later.[378] Basically, it comprised little more than the preliminaries to the real death-struggle, which took place mostly along the heavily contested Ohio River. By 1749, George II was prepared to follow up on this multilayered pattern of aggression by issuing a royal patent to the Ohio Company of Virginia in exchange for its pledge to finance construction of military installations.[379]

For almost a decade, the English suffered badly from almost continuous raiding and a series of defeats at the hands of France's array of indigenous allies.[380] First, an entire army commanded by General Edward Braddock was destroyed in the Battle of the Wilderness by a combined force of Shawnees, Lenni Lenâpés, and Mingos in July 1755.[381] Then, in September of the same year, a second army, commanded by Sir William Johnson and containing a sizable component of Mohawks, was routed.[382] This was followed by the fall of Fort Bull, the furthest outpost along the Ohio, and, in August 1757, a mixed group of French and Indians captured Fort William Henry, at the lower end of Lake George.[383]

Beginning in 1757, the English tried a different tack. William Pitt, the new colonial administrator, offered promisaries to a number of indigenous peoples in exchange for their withdrawal from the conflict, or, in some cases, their active realignment with England.[384] Worn down by sustained combat, several key French allies—notably, the Three Council Fires—accepted the former proposition, while the Lenni Lenâpé switched sides altogether.[385] The Cherokees and Catawbas, who had been neutral, were also coaxed into committing fighting forces to England for the first time.[386] Meanwhile, Pitt landed an army of 2,000 regular troops in Nova Scotia to carry the war into

Canada while a ranger unit led by Colonel Robert Rogers managed to surprise and virtually annihilate the principal Abenaki village at St. François Mission in October 1759.[*]

By 1760, the English had taken the French bastions at Niagara, Québec, Detroit, and Michilimackinac.[387] The following year, a fraudulent treaty was concluded which neutralized the Micmacs, the last major indigenous ally of the French in the northeast, and New France began to disintegrate rapidly.[388] Although the fighting continued fitfully for another year, the end was plainly in sight. With the Treaty of Paris, signed on February 10, 1763, France capitulated, transferring its vast Louisiana Territory, west of the Mississippi River, to Spain. The rights to all remaining French holdings in North American were ceded to England.[†]

This was not the end of the war against the native populations, however. As early as 1759, the English, feeling confident as the French began to crumble, had turned on their Cherokee allies in the south, seeking to drive them from the more easterly portions of their territory. For three consecutive summers, large forces of English regulars and colonial militia ravaged the Cherokees' well-established towns, burning them along with adjoining fields, and clear-cutting the Indians substantial orchards.[389] While native casualties from direct killing were relatively light—not more than 500 in total—the campaign aimed at destroying the basis of the Cherokee economy resulted in about 2,000 collateral fatalities (about a quarter of all Cherokees in the impacted region).[390] The "peace" which was finally declared in December 1761 involved a forced Cherokee cession of huge strip of land along the western frontiers of the Carolinas.[391]

The motives underlying England's pursuit of the "Cherokee War" were also evident in the Ohio River country.[392] Following the advice of a Lenni Lenâpé known as the "Delaware Prophet,"[393] the Ottawa leader Pontiac

---

[*] What was left of the Abenakis were virtually destroyed as a people, and were declared extinct by the English. The United States still declines to recognize the existence of survivor descendants in Vermont; Calloway, *The Western Abenaki of Vermont, op. cit.*, pp. 175–81. Also see Gordon M. Day, "Rogers' Raid in the Indian Tradition," *Historical New Hampshire*, No. 17, 1962; John R. Cuneo, *Robert Rogers of the Rangers* (New York: Oxford University Press, 1959).

[†] It should be noted that such transfers did not convey title to the territories at issue, per se. Rather, what was passed along was the "discovering" power's monopolistic right to acquire land from indigenous owners, free of interference from other European competitors. The international legal construction of "Discovery Doctrine" was thus, more than anything else, a restraint-of-trade mechanism imposed upon native peoples by European colonizers; Williams, *The American Indian in Western Legal Thought, op. cit.*

assembled a strong force of these two peoples, as well as Potawatomies, Wyandots, and Ojibways, in a determined effort to drive the encroaching colonists out of their mutual territories in 1763.[394] Only the resort to bacteriological extermination by the English commander, Lord Jeffrey Amherst, prevented their success. Their decimation by smallpox effectively eliminated the Ottawas, Potawatomies, Wyandots, and Lenni Lenâpés as significant military factors in the events which would shortly follow, placing each of them well along the road to virtual extinction.[395]

The War for Independence

Although Pontiac did not consent to a formal peace until July 1766 — he was then assassinated—George III had already undertaken to assuage native grievances in order to relieve the British Empire from the crushing expense of further Indian fighting.[*] On October 7, 1763, he signed a proclamation repudiating English claims to direct ownership over lands west of the Allegheny and Appalachian mountain chains.[396] In exchange, Crown emissary John Bradstreet was able to negotiate treaties with a number of indigenous nations in which they pledged loyalty to Britian and renounced ties to any other European power.[397]

The colonists, many of whom had considerable speculative interests in the legally proscribed area,[398] reacted with barely restrained hostility, a sentiment compounded by the imposition of substantial tax levies meant to retire debts incurred during England's defeat of France. While these dynamics would eventually spark open revolt against the Crown itself, the initial response was a marked escalation of violence against Indians, especially those who were weakest, most proximate, and friendliest to whites.[399]

In December 1763, for example, a mob of Scotch-Irish immigrants called the "Paxton Boys" vented their rage over the proclamation by slaughtering all remaining members of the tiny and thoroughly Christianized Conestoga people in Lancaster County, Pennsylvania.[†] At about the same time, their neighbors in the Delaware Valley began killing a breakaway group

---

[*]Pontiac entered into an armistice with the English at Detroit on October 3, 1763. His actual agreement to a treaty of peace and friendship, engineered by Sir William Johnson, did not occur until July 24, 1766. He was murdered in March 1769 at Cahokia, Illinois, by a Kaskaskia named Black Dog. Evidence suggests the assassin was hired by the English; Axelrod, *Chronicle of the Indian Wars, op. cit.*, pp. 99–101.

[†]The Conestogas were a dwindling fragment of the once-powerful Susequehannocks. For a reasonably factual—but altogether apologist—account, see Alden T. Vaughan, "Frontier Banditti and the Indians: The Paxton Boys' Legacy, 1763–1775," *Pennsylvania History*, No. 51, 1984.

of Lenni Lenâpés who had converted to the Moravian faith. So extreme was the violence directed against these "Moravian Indians," that the government of Pennsylvania removed them for their own protection to Province Island, in Philadelphia. There, more than fifty of them quickly died of disease, so they were allowed to return to their original settlement, only to find their homes had been burned in their absence.[400] The killing then resumed, and continued sporadically until the survivors were finally exterminated altogether by a militia company commanded by Colonel David Williamson on March 8, 1782.*

By 1773, things were coming to a head. Lord Dunmore, governor of Virginia, defied the Crown by announcing he would begin issuing land patents on both sides of the Ohio River, in areas to which his colony had long laid claim.[401] He then took to the field at the head of 3,000 troops, intent upon clearing the Shawnees from their homeland by "extirpating them, root and branch." When the Shawnee leader Cornstalk attempted to avert war through negotiations, Dunmore used the opportunity to try and murder him. Cornstalk then led a force of his own people, as well as smaller contingents of Mingos, Wyandots, and Lenni Lenâpés, in defeating the Virginians on October 10.[402] A truce was effected two weeks later, but the colonists' exterminationist intentions had once again been made abundantly clear.[403]

"Lord Dunmore's War" served as a warmup for the heavier fighting which occurred three years later, during the American War of Independence. At first, the British were fairly successful in replicating the French strategy of mobilizing indigenous nations along the frontier to join it in fighting the rebellious colonists.[404] The latter, after all, had not only continued swarming into Indian territory after 1763, but were obviously fighting the Crown in large part to enable themselves to take even more. For the Indians, it was as always a choice of the lesser evil, and they availed themselves of the opportunity to try and rid themselves of the more imminent threat to their survival.[405]

In short order, five of the six Haudenosaunee nations and allied Munsees were raiding illegal settlements along the Mohawk River in New York, and in the Wyoming and Cherry Valleys of Pennsylvania.[406] The Shawnees, together with the Mingos, Ojibways, and what was left of the

---

*The Pennsylvania government officially repudiated the massacre, but failed to prosecute Williamson or anyone else. Indeed, the colonel was again commanding troops on behalf of the colony within a month; Eckert, *That Dark and Bloody River, op. cit.*, pp. 314–22.

Lenni Lenâpés, Ottawas, Wyandots, Potawatomies, Miamis, and Tawas were pushing hard throughout the Ohio/Kentucky region.[407] To the south, the Cherokees, Muskogees, and Chickasaws performed much the same function against Georgia and the Carolinas.[408] In addition to inflicting severe damage in outlying areas, thus tying up thousands of militia troops which might otherwise have been deployed against the British, the Indians were decisive in winning two major battles—Oriskiny (New York, 1777) and Sandusky (Ohio, 1782)—against rebel armies.[409]

The response of the colonies was extraordinarily brutal, even by Euroamerican standards. In the south, three columns totaling more than 6,000 men were sent against the Cherokees in 1776, leveling more than two dozen towns, destroying crops, inflicting serious casualties on noncombatants, and sweeping much of the population into Florida.[410] Only the cession of about a third of what remained of Cherokee territory and agreement to the rebel occupation of the Cherokee capitol of Echota brought the annihilatory campaign to a halt.[411] A similar offensive was conducted against the Muskogees and Chickamaugas in 1780, resulting in comparable damage to the former and almost total extermination of the Chickamaugas.[412]

In 1779, rebel commander George Washington ordered 4,000 troops under Major General John Sullivan, assisted by future New York governor James Clinton, to undertake an invasion into the heart of Haudenosaunee territory. Simultaneously, a force of 600 under Colonel Daniel Brodhead was sent against the Mingos, Munsees, and more southerly Seneca towns. Washington's orders were that not only was the Indians' military capacity to be utterly obliterated, but the very basis of their socioeconomic existence.[413] By the time Brodhead was finished with the Munsees, they were virtually extinct.[414] Sullivan also complied enthusiastically with his instructions, implementing what has been called "the most ruthless application of scorched earth policy in American history."[415]

> By October 15, Sullivan considered his work completed and wrote home to John Jay, then President of Congress, that he had destroyed forty towns, 160,000 bushels of corn, and an unknown but vast quantity of vegetables. In all the country of the Six Nations, he reported, one town remained standing. The only part of his assignment he had failed to carry out was the collection of prisoners as hostages. There were [some] he might have taken, but their mutilated bodies lay in the dead villages.[416]

In Ohio, things were more difficult for the exterminators. Although regular troops under Colonel John Bowman were able to burn the Shawnee capital of Chillicothe in 1779, and George Rogers Clark managed the same feat a year later at Piqua, another principal town, the Indians simply rebuilt their communities and, if anything, escalated their own offensive against rebel settlements.[417] Still, the continuous fighting wore the Shawnees and their allies down to the point that, when Britain signed the preliminary articles of peace in November 1782, Clark was in the process of successfully conducting a Sullivan-style campaign against them.[420] Ultimately, it would take the freshly minted United States another generation to finish the Shawnees off altogether.

Nits Make Lice

At the point of its inception, the United States institutionalized the illegitimacy and duplicity which had always marked its leaders' attitudes towards native people. In late 1782, future president George Washington, who "had been feathering his own personal nest with Indian lands ever since his family first became involved with the Ohio Land Company in 1748"—and who had reputedly become the wealthiest man in America in the process—submitted a plan to Congress which he felt might solve certain immediate problems and also serve as a basis for federal policy over the longer term.[419] In many ways, it replicated the prerevolutionary dynamics evident since the Proclamation of 1763: "[Washington's] plan...was in reality no less than a monumental conspiracy, by which the western lands belonging to the Indians could now most easily... and least expensively be wrested from them."[420]

> Since the expense of a major war could not be shouldered by the young and still newly shaping United States government, he recommended that all efforts be made to implant as many new settlers as possible on Indian lands. In order to do this, his plan went on, grants of land should be made to veterans of the Revolutionary War from such parcels in Indian territory as the Virginia Military Lands and the Western Reserve Lands... [He] went on to make mention of the fact that these settlers, being largely veterans of the war and experienced soldiers, might tend to awe the Indians. Even if they did not, his plan continued, and the Indians rose up in arms, these settlers would make excellent militia to protect United States claims in the Ohio country.*

---

* Eckert, *That Dark and Bloody River, op. cit.,* p. 440. Like Dunmore before him, Washington was in some ways building a principle out of an accomplished fact. Unable to pay their troops during the war, the colonies—Virginia, in particular—had taken to issuing warrants for land in Indian territory, redeemable only if victory were achieved; *Revolutionary War Pension and Bounty-and-Warrant Application Files* (Washington, D.C.: National Archives). Once Britain had agreed to U.S. independence, first Virginia, then Connecticut and other states conveyed title to their claims to areas beyond the 1763 Proclamation line (void under Crown law) to the Continental Congress. They then requested—and received—federal grants of the same land. This shell game supposedly vested Virginia with legitimate title to 4,000,200 acres of unceded Indian territory (the "Military Lands"), Connecticut with title to

In order to cut the costs, both human and financial, which might otherwise attend this wholesale takeover of what was unquestionably native territory, Washington borrowed liberally from another English tradition which had been evolving since Jamestown, advising that a series of treaties be negotiated with indigenous nations. The purpose of these was to convince the Indians, people by people, to cede strategic localities to the United States in exchange for solemn guarantees of their remaining landbases.* Thus outpositioned as well as outnumbered and outgunned, they could be eliminated one after another, either by "voluntary" relocation to areas beyond the claimed boundaries of the United States or through liquidation by force.[421]

> Apart from the fact that it was immoral, unethical and actually criminal, this plan placed before Congress by George Washington was so logical and well laid out that it was immediately accepted practically without opposition and immediately put into action. There might be — certainly *would* be — further strife with the Indians, new battles and new wars, but the end result was, with the adoption of Washington's plan, inevitable: Without even realizing it had occurred, the fate of all the Indians in the country was sealed. They had lost virtually everything.[422]

Such a characterization of Washington's stance is neither moralistic nor rhetorical. Rather, given that Article 6 of the U.S. Constitution establishes treaties, "once ratified," as the "Supreme Law of the Land," to describe their deliberate and systematic violation as "criminal" is to be precise within the

---

3,500,000 acres (the "Western Reserve"), and so on. Of course, the entire legal house of cards depended upon the contention made by Washington, John Adams, and others that Great Britain had actually owned the land in question at the time it ceded its non-Canadian territorial rights in North America to the United States. The problem was that Britain never pretended to such ownership (as opposed to the Discovery Right of acquiring it at such point as the native owners decided to sell), a matter of which U.S. officials were well aware. Hence, the entire edifice of U.S. "Indian Law" was from the outset what it is today: an elaborate subterfuge designed to cast an appearance of formal legality to a process of naked and sustained aggression from which even a modicum of adherence to genuine legal principle is conspicuously absent; Reginald Horsman, *Expansion and American Policy, 1783–1812* (Lansing: Michigan State University Press, 1967).

*"In such negotiations, the plan continued, treaty commissioners could promise [Indians] that the United States government 'will endeavor to restrain our people from hunting or settling' on their reserved territories"; Eckert, *That Dark and Bloody River, op. cit.*, p. 440. In other words, since he had just advocated that the government should in reality facilitate the exact opposite, the "Father of His Country" was proposing that U.S. diplomacy with Indians be anchored in deceit—indeed, in boldfaced lies—even before it began. The idea, plainly, was to gain whatever advantage could be gained at the bargaining table, promising whatever was necessary, in full knowledge that such promises would not be kept. In order for this to work out, it was necessary that "commissioners who handled treaties...always deal with tribes on an individual basis and reject any attempt on their part to deal with the government as a unified body." That such a posture serves as a direct precursor to Hitlerian diplomacy, à la Munich, is, or should be, self-evident.

parameters of American legal vernacular.[423] The situation was compounded at the statutory level when, in 1787, Congress passed the Northwest Ordinance, legally binding itself to conduct its relations with Indians on the basis of "utmost good faith" even as it was engaging—and has continued to engage through the present moment—in an exactly contrary course of action.[424]

The legal posture of U.S. Indian policy during the country's formative years was so at odds with itself that it took Chief Supreme Court Justice John Marshall—one of America's brightest legal minds (and recipient of 10,000 acres of Indian land for services rendered during the revolution)—until 1832 to finish contriving the pretense of a reconciling doctrine.[425] Problematically, even this concoction was rejected in practice by the federal executive as being overly restrictive upon the implementation of Indian policy.[426] Hence, the United States has remained, by the standards of its own domestic laws concerning the rights of indigenous peoples, as well as the relevant international legal canons, an outlaw state in the truest sense of the term.*

Clearing and Extirpation

In his 1782 plan, Washington advanced the unequivocal belief that, after all was said and done, the objective of federal policy should be to force the entire indigenous population east of the Mississippi River into the "illimitable regions of the West" to which the United States was not yet pressing claims.[427] Those who physically resisted such a fate in any way would have to be broken by force, or, as Thomas Jefferson bluntly put it, "exterminated."[428] This "removal policy" was in keeping with a sense of "Manifest Destiny"—an outlook founded in precisely the same matrix of virulent Anglo-Saxon supremacism that would later give rise to nazi Aryanist ideology—already pronounced among American leaders and citizens alike.[429]

---

*To be absolutely clear on this point, the only manner in which the United States could ever become a "legitimate" country would be for it to systematically reconstruct its relationships with indigenous peoples in accordance with the requirements of legality, both international and domestic, which it has violated at every step along the way of its expansion and consolidation. Until it does so, it will remain an entirely illegitimate entity, with the power to sustain itself, perhaps, but absent the right. The same principle pertains to Canada, although that country's treaty obligations to Indians were negotiated by—and are therefore inherited from—Great Britain. The fact that Canada accomplished its continental consolidation in a manner relatively free of violence—its only two "Indian Wars" after 1790, were actually fought against Métis insurgents led by Louis Riél, and weren't especially bloody by U.S. standards—does nothing to redeem the situation in a legal sense. On the 1869 and 1885 "Riél Rebellions," see Joseph Howard, *Strange Empire: Louis Riél and the Métis People* (Toronto: James Lewis & Samuel, 1974).

Probably the first to suffer it were the once-powerful Haudenosaunee. Although their rights to about half the present state of New York were recognized in the superficially honorable Treaty of Fort Stanwix in 1784, they were quickly defrauded of the entire area by James Clinton, newly elected governor of the state.* Thoroughly exhausted by nearly two centuries of continuous warfare, and facing what they recognized as the most ruthless foe they'd yet encountered, the Six Nations declined to fight.[430] Instead, they resigned themselves to destitution on postage-stamp-sized reservations within their former homeland, or fled as refugees to Canada, where the British made land available to them.†

The Shawnees were another matter entirely. While the much-battered Wyandots and Lenni Lenâpés agreed to cede the remainder of their territory east of the Ohio in exchange for assurances that tracts to the west would remain free from encroachment, the Shawnees declined even to meet with U.S. negotiators until January 1786.[431] Then, it was only to inform the American commissioner, William Butler, that they had no interest in giving up any land at all. A force of 800 militia under Colonel Benjamin Logan therefore sallied forth in 1787, burning more than a dozen communities and an estimated 15,000 bushels of corn, in an effort to convince them to "reconsider."[432] Instead, the Shawnees, led by Blue Jacket and Tecumseh (Tekamthi), joined briefly with the Cherokees and the remaining handful of Chickamaugas, replying in kind along the Cumberland River in Kentucky during much of 1788.[433]

---

*Henry M. Manley, *The Treaty of Fort Stanwix, 1784* (Rome, NY: Rome Sentinel, 1932). Clinton circumvented constitutional prohibitions on state (rather than federal) acquisition of Indian lands by convincing the Six Nations to lease their territories to New York for 999 years, a matter he said—following Washington's recommended strategy—would "protect" it from white settlement; Georgiana C. Nammack, *Fraud, Politics, and the Dispossession of the Indians: The Iroquois Frontier and the Colonial Period* (Norman: University of Oklahoma Press, 1969); Jack Campisi, "From Stanwix to Canandaigua: National Policy, States' Rights and Indian Land," in Christopher Vescey and William Starna, eds., *Iroquois Land Claims* (Syracuse, NY: Syracuse University Press, 1988). It should be noted that Edward A. Everett, an expert commissioned by the State of New York in 1914 to "dispel the myth" of Haudenosaunee land rights, reached the exact opposite conclusion, confirming the continuing validity of the Indians' title to half the state. His employer promptly suppressed Everett's report, and has proceeded to conduct itself as though it were completely unaware of the document's contents and conclusions; Helen M. Upton, *The Everett Report in Historical Perspective: The Indians of New York* (Albany: New York State Bicentennial Commission, 1980).

†The true nature of U.S. attitudes towards Indians is perhaps best revealed in the fact that the Oneidas —the rebels' staunchest indigenous ally during the War for Independence— were left entirely landless by Clinton's illegal manipulation, and the federal government did absolutely nothing to correct the situation. When the Oneidas were finally granted a parcel on which to try and reconstitute themselves, it was not in New York, but far to the west, near Green Bay, Wisconsin; Arlinda Locklear, "The Oneida Land Claims: A Legal Overview," in Vescey and Starna, *Iroquois Land Claims, op. cit.*

Meanwhile, the Miamis, under Little Turtle (Michikiniqua), were equally adamant in refusing to relinquish their homeland in Ohio. By early 1789, they and the Shawnees had forged a firm alliance to fight a new war of resistance against the Americans, and had attracted small but noticeable contingents of Wyandots, Lenni Lenâpés, Ottawas, Mingos, Ojibways, and Kickapoos to their cause.[434] In 1790, over the protests of Secretary of War Henry Knox (who felt it would be unnecessarily expensive), an army of more than 1,100 militia and 350 regular troops commanded by General Josiah Harmar was dispatched to put down the "insurrection." The column was routed with heavy casualties by Blue Jacket's fighters on October 21 and sent scurrying for safety.[435]

The following spring, General Arthur St. Clair, governor of the Northwest Territory, was sent forth at the head of 2,300 troops by President Washington to "punish" the Indians for the "insolence" of defending their homes. On November 4, 1791, St. Clair was handed a defeat along the banks of the Wabash River which, in "proportion to the number of men fielded that day, stands as the worst loss the United States Army has ever suffered."[436] At that point, the United States effectively sued for peace. At the peace talks, which were held on July 31, 1793, American arrogance was conspicuously lacking.

> The commissioners recanted the previous position of the United States, that the western Indians were a conquered people by virtue of their alliance with the defeated British; they also announced that the government would relinquish all claim to lands north of the Ohio except in the immediate vicinity of Cincinnati and the Scioto and Muskinghum rivers. For these lands, the government would pay the Indians.[437]

The Shawnees rejected the latter proposition, suggesting that the government should take the money it was proposing to pay for their land and divide it among the illegal settlers located there, to compensate them for whatever loss they'd incur by leaving Indian Country altogether.* Thus

---

*The Shawnee response to the American admissions was that, "You agree to do us justice, after having long, and injuriously, withheld it. We mean in the acknowledgment you now have made, that the King of England never did, nor never had a right to, give you our Country by the Treaty of Peace, and you want us to make this act of Common Justice a great part of your concessions, and seem to expect that, because you have at last acknowledged our independence, we should for such favor surrender our country… Money, to us is of no value…and no consideration whatever can induce us to sell the lands on which we get sustenance for our women and children; we hope to point out a mode by which your settlers may be easily removed, and peace thereby obtained… [Divide] this large sum of money, which you have offered us, among these people…and we are persuaded, they would most readily accept of it, in lieu of the lands you sold them… If you add also, the great sums you must expend in raising and paying Armies, with a view to force us to yield to your Country, you will certainly have more than sufficient for the purposes of repaying these settlers for all their labor and improvements"; quoted in Axelrod, *Chronicle of the Indian Wars, op. cit.,* p. 127.

thwarted in his effort to gain even a toehold in Shawnee territory through diplomacy, an enraged George Washington spent the next year putting together still another army, this one composed of nearly 4,000 men and commanded by one of the best American generals, Mad Anthony Wayne. On August 20, 1794, at a place called Fallen Timbers, along the Maumee River in what is now Toledo, Ohio, Wayne was finally able to bring a much-larger force to bear against the Shawnees and Miamis.[438]

In the aftermath of its victory, the United States contented itself with taking "only" the territory lying east of the present Ohio-Indiana line (then called the "Greenville Boundary"). The rest, U.S. representatives claimed, would remain "permanent" Indian territory.[439] The lie imbedded in this promise was already apparent, albeit unknown to the Shawnees at the time, in that William Henry Harrison, governor of the Indiana Territory and another future president, had been assigned as a condition of his appointment to secure American title to the very land in question. Between "1803 and 1806, Harrison acquired 70 million acres west of the 'permanent' Greenville Treaty boundary, trading or negotiating for it with the Sac and Fox and various smaller [peoples], most of which had been broken and impoverished by years of Indian-white warfare."[440]

Predictably, many of these instruments of cession were misrepresented by U.S. negotiators, and were therefore fraudulent. Concerning the largest single purported transfer of property rights, that of fifty million acres in what is now Illinois signed by the Sac leader Black Hawk (Makataimeshekiakiak) in 1804, the Indians had been led by Harrison to believe "that it conveyed nothing more than hunting rights."[441] By 1807, the pattern of expropriation had become so blatant that when the Shawnee leader Tecumseh and his brother Tenskawatawa ("The Prophet") established a resistance center at Tippecanoe ("Prophet's Town"), not only their own people, but Potawatomies, Wyandots, Ottawas, Winnebagos, Lenni Lenâpés, Miamis, Menominees, and Ojibways began to assemble there to plan a joint response.[442] The Sac and Fox also sent delegates, with the result that, from 1808–1811, Black Hawk mounted a sustained effort to contain the settlers moving into the area of Fort Madison, near St. Louis.[443]

In 1808, as the United States and Britain began to drift toward war, Tecumseh, who was attempting to put together an indigenous politicomilitary confederation extending from Canada to Florida, entered into a new alliance with the English.[444] Although there was no raiding outside the reserved Indian territories, the U.S. rejoinder to this "dangerous development" was to send Harrison at the head of 1,000 militia and 350 regulars to invade Shawnee country while Tecumseh was away seeking to bring the Muskogees, Cherokees and Chickasaws into his alliance.[445] Using the pretext of a demand that Tenskawatawa surrender any warriors at Prophet's Town who had participated in raids, "Harrison planned to wipe out the brotherhood's 'capitol' [sic] once and for all."[446] This, he accomplished on November 7, 1811, after a brief battle with about 600 native defenders.[447]

The War of 1812 officially began at this point, with a U.S. invasion of Canada from Detroit.[448] Although the political aspects of the alliance Tecumseh had forged offered the potential of a far more coherent native military strategy than had ever been achieved, the fighting strength of the northern nations had been severely depleted.[449] With the exception of the Red Sticks faction of the Muskogees, the powerful peoples of the south declined to become involved in the fighting, and the British by and large failed to deliver promised weapons, munitions, and other supplies.[450] Hence, despite a few bright spots—as when a combined force of Indians roundly whipped the army of General James Winchester at Frenchtown (Michigan) in 1813—U.S. forces were able engage in miniature Sullivan-style expeditions almost at will. The damages suffered by the Indians, "houses burned, crops destroyed and populations displaced...were terrible."[451]

By the time Tecumseh was killed and his fighters decisively defeated at the Battle of the Thames in 1813, the remaining indigenous societies of the north had suffered their final devastation.[452] Fewer than a thousand of the once-populous Miamis remained alive, while entire subgroups like the Weas had disappeared altogether.[453] The Lenni Lenâpé were equally decimated, as were the Wyandots, Ottawas, Kickapoos, and Potawatomies.[454] Although the Shawnees remained somewhat stronger numerically, their capacity for resistance had finally been broken.[455] By 1820, the remnants of all these peoples had been cleared from their homelands and deported en masse to locales west of the Mississippi.

In the south, the Red Sticks, struggling to repel invaders from their homeland in Georgia, Tennessee, and the Mississippi Territory, had a moment of triumph, destroying Fort Mimms, on the lower Alabama River, on August 30, 1813.[*] It was the last major win by native people east of the

---

[*] The "massacre" of troops and settlers at Fort Mimms is usually considered the first engagement of the "Creek War." The attack on the fort, however, was itself a Red Stick response to the unprovoked (and unsuccessful) ambush of a party of Creeks at Burnt Corn Creek a short time earlier; James Atkins Shackford, *David Crockett: The Man and the Legend* (Lincoln: University of Nebraska Press, 1994

Mississippi. In the aftermath, the Tennessee legislature appropriated the relatively vast sum of $300,000 for purposes of "exterminating the hostiles." General Andrew Jackson then took to the field at the head of an army of 5,000 militiamen and more than a thousand Indian auxiliaries—by far the largest such force mustered before 1850—marching through the heart of Red Stick country, destroying everything in his path.[456] An untold number of noncombatant Muskogees were killed directly,* many more died of collateral causes, and native fighting strength was reduced by about half.†

Then, reinforced by another 800 militia and 600 regular troops, Jackson moved in for the kill. Striking with overwhelming strength against the principal Red Stick bastion at Horseshoe Bend in March 1814, his troops slaughtered all but 150 of the remaining Muskogee combatants, plus a substantial number of women, children, and old men.[457] Virtually obliterated by the offensive, the surviving Red Sticks had no alternative but to surrender (although some escaped to join the Seminoles in Florida). The price of "peace" was their immediate cession of some 23 million acres of land—instructively, this included most of the territory of the White Stick faction of Muskogees, who had fought *with* the Americans[458]—and deportation as a people to points west of the Mississippi after Jackson became president in 1830.[459] By 1840, other U.S. native allies against the Red Sticks—the Cherokees, for instance, had committed nineteen companies of fighters to assist Jackson—had also

---

reprint of 1956 original) p. 18. This is acknowledged in earlier histories, such as H.S. Halbert's and T.H. Ball's *The Creek War* (Chicago: Donohue & Hennebury, 1895). The Mississippi Territory, created by Congress in 1798, was composed of what are now the states of Alabama and Mississippi; Rohrbough, *The Trans-Appalachian Frontier, op. cit.*, p. 115.

* The killing of noncombatants during the November 3, 1813, attack on the Red Stick town at the Tallussahatchee River, for example, is depicted as being "without intention" by Davy Crockett, one of Jackson's best scouts, in his autobiography. A paragraph later, however, Crockett describes a "squaw" being riddled by twenty musket balls, a fate which hardly sounds unintentional. He also acknowledges that the 186 Red Stick fighters who were trapped by more than 900 Americans at the Tallussahatchee attempted to surrender, but were killed "to the last man." The account of this battle concludes with the troops eating potatoes fried in the fat of their fallen foes; Shackford, *op. cit.*, pp. 24–5; also see James A. Shackford and Stanley J. Folmsbee, eds., *A Narrative of the Life of David Crockett of Tennessee* (Knoxville: University of Tennessee Press, 1973 reprint of 1834 original).

† The Red Sticks could put fewer than 3,000 warriors in the field at their peak. In addition to the 186 lost at the Tallussahatchee, another 291 were killed at Talladega later the same month. A further 311 were lost during battles at Emuckfaw and Enotachopo Creek in December (Jackson's men were under orders to cut off noses to confirm bodycounts throughout the campaign). Plainly, losses of this magnitude would quickly result in complete annihilation. The remainder of the "war" consisted of the Indians attempting to find safety deep within their own country, while Jackson and his men pursued them with an unabashed intent to attain their total eradication; Axelrod, *Chronicle of the Indian Wars, op. cit.*, p. 139.

been cleared from their southeastern homelands, force-marched with catastrophic results to the new "Permanent Indian Territory" of Oklahoma.[460]

While most of the eastern Indians were by now too decimated and demoralized to physically resist, the Seminoles were an exception. Consequently, two campaigns were mounted—in 1816–17 and 1835–42—to either compel their "removal" or extinguish them altogether.[461] The second of these proved to be the most proportionately expensive conflict in American history, and it ended inconclusively: while the Seminoles suffered extensive casualties and a number of them eventually submitted to removal, a sizable segment withdrew into the Everglades swamp country, from whence they were never dislodged.[462]

One other "war of removal" was fought in 1832 and '33, this one against the Sac and Fox in Illinois. By 1830, these peoples had in large part followed the almost-extinct Peorias and Kaskaskias, withdrawing, along with the Winnebagos and Kickapoos, into adjoining areas of what are now the states of Iowa and Wisconsin.* The reasons are illuminating:

> As settlers flooded in with the end of the war [against Tecumseh], they pillaged Sac and Fox villages, fenced cornfields, and even plowed up cemeteries. Black Hawk protested to the U.S. Indian agents at Rock Island, who told him to move west, across the Mississippi. In 1829, Black Hawk returned from a hunt to find that a white family had settled in his lodge. Through an interpreter, he told them to leave, explaining that there was plenty of unsettled land available. They ignored his demand. Soon, more whites were settling in Black Hawk's village. Next came an announcement from the General Land Office that the area would be offered for public sale.[463]

In 1832, appalled at their displaced circumstances, Black Hawk attempted to take his people back into a small portion of their home territory, along the Rock River. The response of Illinois Governor John Reynolds was to muster 1,700 militia—future president Zachary Taylor served as an

---

*Most of the remaining Kickapoos—less than a thousand—abandoned Illinois in 1819 when confronted with a war of annihilation by the United States. They drifted southwest, establishing themselves briefly in Texas in 1852, before settling finally in Mexico (where they remain). Two much smaller groups, under the leaders Kennekuk and Mecina, situated themselves in Missouri, from whence they engaged in regular raids into their evacuated Illinois homeland until they merged with Black Hawk's Sacs and Foxes in 1831; Gibson, *The Kickapoos, op. cit.* The much-depleted Winnebagos, who had withdrawn from northern Illinois by 1820, also raided briefly into their former territory in 1827, and promised to ally with Black Hawk in 1832. They reneged on that pledge in the mistaken belief that service to the Americans might assure them a reservation in Iowa or Wisconsin. Instead, their reward was to be pushed all the way into Nebraska; Paul Radin, *The Winnebago Tribe* (Washington, D.C.: Bureau of American Ethnography, Smithsonian Institution, 37th Annual Report, 1923).

officer on this expedition, and Abraham Lincoln, another one-day White House occupant, as a common soldier—to repel the "invasion" by exterminating the 2,000-odd Indians.[464] Confronted by this force, the Sac and Fox retreated, leading the troops on a grueling chase which finally ended on August 3, 1833, when—subsisting on bark and roots, utterly exhausted and reduced by that point to barely 500 survivors—they were trapped by a force of more than 1,300 near the juncture of the Mississippi and Bad Axe Rivers.[465]

> The Indians who had remained on the east bank of the Mississippi attempted to surrender, but the troops, frustrated by weeks of fruitless pursuit...stormed their position in an eight-hour frenzy of clubbing, stabbing, shooting [and] scalping.[466]

Although about 200 of Black Hawk's followers did escape to the west bank, most were later tracked down and killed, completing the Fox extermination initiated by the French a century earlier.[467] The Sac leader was imprisoned for a year, then shipped about as a traveling exhibit illustrating the ability of the government to "humble and humiliate even the most arrogant of savages" (after his death, Black Hawk's bones were disinterred by local whites and displayed as trophies in a "museum" in Iowaville, Iowa).[468] As for the pitifully few remnants of the Sacs and Foxes who survived the "Black Hawk War," they were given a tiny piece of land in central Iowa, but only in exchange for their legitimation by treaty of the seizure of their last six million acres.[469]

Manifest Destiny

By 1840, with the exception of a handful of tiny Iroquois reservations in upstate New York and the remaining Seminoles in the Florida Everglades, the eastern third of what would become the continental United States had been cleared of its indigenous population.[470] The idea that America west of the Mississippi was ever seriously intended to be the exclusive domain of the continent's native peoples was belied—even before their removal was achieved—by the creation of the territories of Missouri (1816), Arkansas (1819) and Iowa (1838).[471] In 1837, Anglo invaders in Texas fought a war of secession from Mexico, creating a temporary republic which became a state in December 1845.[472] Six months later, on June 15, 1846, the United States acquired the Oregon Territory (present-day Oregon, Washington, and Idaho) from Great Britain.[473] Two years after that, in 1848, the northern half of Mexico—California, Arizona, Nevada, Utah, New Mexico, and southern Colorado—was taken by force.[474]

Thomas Jefferson had made the [1803] Louisiana Purchase in large part to acquire seemingly endless space into which white settlement, always moving west, could push the Indian. Andrew Jackson's policy of removal was also a matter of pushing tribes westward. Neither Jefferson, Jackson, nor the other presidents who contemplated or enacted removal considered the possibility that white settlement of the American West might someday proceed from the west as the United States rapidly evolved into a continental nation.[475]

Native North Americans were now caught in a vise from which there was truly no escape. As Maine Senator Lot Morrill would put it to Congress in 1867, "As population has approached the Indian we have removed him beyond population. But population now encounters him from both sides of the continent, and there is no place on the continent to which he can be removed beyond the progress of population."[476] As pronouncements of Angloamerica's "Manifest Destiny" to enjoy limitless expansion intensified, so too did calls for the outright eradication of Indians, or at least large numbers of them, *wherever* they might be encountered.[477]

Aside from the Mandans and other Missouri Valley peoples exterminated by smallpox in 1837,[478] the first victims of this change were the natives—especially Apaches—of western Texas, New Mexico, and Arizona. By the 1880s, not only a number of Apachean bands but other peoples—the Tonkawas, for instance, and the Karankaras—had been totally liquidated, the various Anglo governments involved having depended largely on "free enterprise" rather than troops to accomplish their exterminatory policies.* In this, they drew upon their own heritage as well as the example offered by the Mexican regime they'd displaced.

[They offered] generous bounties for Apache scalps. "Backyard barbering" became a gruesome industry...which became so lucrative that its practicioners did not limit themselves to Apache warrior scalps...Scalp hunters would storm whole villages and kill every man, woman and child. A special examination committee had to be established to certify the authenticity of the scalps, but it soon became evident to the bounty hunters that there was no way to distinguish between the scalps of friendly Indians and those of hostiles. So the harvest of death widened...[T]he examination committee was incapable not only of distinguishing friendly scalps from hostile, but could not tell the difference between Indian hair and Mexican. Remote Mexican villages...now fell victim to bounty hunters.[479]

---

*The once populous Lipán Apaches—the Lipanjenne, Lipanes de Arriba, and Lipanes Abajo—of Texas were reduced to virtually nothing by the 1870s. The last nineteen survivors were absorbed by the more westerly Mescalero Apaches in 1905; Thomas F. Schilz, *The Lipan Apaches in Texas* (El Paso: Texas Western Press, 1987). On the disappearance of the Tonkawas, Karankaras, and others, see Thornton, *American Indian Holocaust and Survival, op. cit.*

A Colorado militia unit mounted a campaign against the Jicarillas in 1854, and the army fought actual wars against the Mescaleros, Chiricahuas, and other western Apache peoples in 1872–73, 1877–80 (the "Victorio Campaign") and 1881–86 (the "Geronimo Campaign"), each of them extraordinarily brutal. But it was the process of "private citizen actions," occurring under state sanction over a sustained period, which ultimately did the job.[480] By 1890, the Apaches had been reduced to less than 10 percent of their original number. More or less the same was true of the other peoples of southern Arizona—the Pimas, Maricopas, and Tohono O'odams (Papagos).[481]

In California and Oregon things got under way a bit later but followed much the same course. Consider a May 1852 "incident," when a peaceful "ranchería of 148 Indians, including women and children, was attacked, and nearly the whole number destroyed," by a mob of whites led by the sheriff of Weaverville, California:[482]

> Of the 150 Indians that constituted the ranchería, only 2 or 3 escaped, and those were supposed to be dangerously wounded; so that probably not one…now remains alive. Men, women and children all shared the same fate—none were spared except one woman and two children, who were brought back as prisoners.[483]

Or, to take another example, there was a "horrible massacre of 200 Indians in Humboldt County," California, in January 1860:

> The attack was made at night, when [the Indians] were in their little settlements or villages at some sort of merrymaking. The men were known to be absent… Under these circumstances, bands of white men, armed with hatchets—small bands, but sufficiently numerous for the purpose—fell on the women and children, and deliberately slaughtered them, one and all. Simultaneous attacks were made on different rancherías or encampments… Regularly organized bodies of armed men attacked the settlements of friendly Indians [and] murdered them in like manner.[484]

That the genocidal implications of these slaughters—just two of several hundred comparable atrocities perpetrated during the period—were well understood is readily evident in editorial commentary: "The perpetrators seem to have acted with a deliberate design to exterminate the Indian race."[485] Such butchery was not "official" policy only in the most technical sense. The massacres were well reported in the local press, and the "vigilantes" who carried them out were paid bounties by the government for the scalps of their victims.[486] Although the military was quite aware of what was being done, as its commanders' own dispatches make clear, no effort was made to intervene or punish the offenders.* Indeed, the process of extermination was often carried out under color of—if not direct participation by—"martial authority."[487]

When the army did take to the field, it was to eliminate whatever capacity the peoples of California had to defend themselves. Thus, in the so-called "Mariposa War" in northern California, troops were used in 1851 to "subdue and disarm" the Miwoks, Tularenos, and Yokuts, who, consequently defenseless, were quickly annihilated by local whites.[488] Much the same pattern prevailed in southern California, where separate campaigns were mounted against the Yumas, Mohaves, Cocopas, and Cahuillas.[489] The final mop-up operation in California was in the north, where in 1872 the army engaged in an especially ugly campaign against the last fifty-or-so Modocs, a peaceful people whose main "offense" was to refuse removal to Oregon.† Small wonder the bulk of all indigenous peoples in California were declared extinct before the end of the nineteenth century—more followed in the twentieth—while the remainder were "pushed into the rocks."[490]

In the Oregon Territory, where "settlers loudly demanded" that the army "annihilate" the region's native peoples, several campaigns for such purposes were undertaken. The first of these, a short 1848 offensive against the Cayuses, set the stage.[491] In 1855, the "Rogue River War" left the the Takelama and Tutuni so decimated that the handful of survivors were lumped together under the heading "Siletz Indians" and confined to a tiny parcel of land near the present-day city of Newport.[492] The same year, an arbitrary declaration by Governor Isaac Stevens that opened the entire territory to white settlement resulted in the so-called "Yakima War," waged not only against the Yakimas, but

---

*E.g., a report from General E.A. Hitchcock, commanding the U.S. Army's Pacific Division, to the adjutant General, dated March 31, 1853: "A party of citizens under the conduct of [militia] Captain Ben Wright last fall massacred over 30 Indians out of a group of 48 who had come into Captain Wright's invitation to make 'peace'… Captain Wright returned to Yreka, which place the papers state he entered in triumph, his men bearing on their rifles the scalps of the Indians, and was received with a general welcome by the citizens of the town"; quoted in Heizer, *Destruction of the California Indians*, *op. cit.*, pp. 247–8.

†As was all too typical of the army's conduct vis-à-vis native opponents, the Modoc leadership— "Captain Jack" and three colleagues—were executed upon surrender; Murray, *The Modocs and Their War, op. cit.* Also see Jeff C. Riddell, *The Indian History of the Modoc War and the Causes That Led to It* (Medford, OR: Pine Cone, 1973). Somewhat less commonly, their heads were severed after their deaths and shipped to Washington, D.C., for "study" by phrenologists. "These relics, symbols of Manifest Destiny's dark side, remained in the nation's capital until 1984, when the Smithsonian Institution returned them to the Modoc people for burial"; Herman J. Viola, *After Columbus: The Smithsonian Chronicle of the North American Indians* (Washington, D.C.: Smithsonian Books, 1990) pp. 178–9.

the Walla Wallas, Umatillas, Palouses, and the remains of the Cayuses as well.[*]

This was followed, in 1857, by the "Coeur d'Alene War," which pitted that people and allied Spokanes, along with a combination of Yakima, Palouse, Umatilla, and Cayuse "recalcitrants," against "a superior force…each man having been issued brand-new long-range rifles."[493] In the aftermath, the leaders of the Indians were executed for the "crime" of having resisted dispossession of their homelands.[494] Thoroughly "dispirited, the tribes of the Columbia Basin waged no more war, but resignedly marched to the reservations prescribed by Governor Stevens' treaties, which the Senate hurriedly ratified on March 8, 1859."[495]

For the next two decades, the army conducted a series of mop-up operations throughout eastern Oregon and most of what is now Idaho, beginning with the "Snake War" of 1866–68, in which the Yahuskin and Walpapi bands of Northern Paiutes were all but obliterated.[496] In 1877, there was the famous and devastating pursuit of the Nez Percé—about a third of whom were killed—driven from their ancestral territory and frantically trying to reach sanctuary in Canada.[497] The Bannocks, as well as remnants of the Cayuses and Northern Paiutes, were mauled in an 1878 campaign.[498] Finally, in 1879, regional warfare died out after troops were dispatched to pacify the "Sheepeaters," a small group of Bannock and Shoshoni holdouts whose name derived from their willingness to subsist almost entirely on mountain sheep rather than surrender their way of life.[499]

The Way West

For a time it appeared that the indigenous population might actually be left with a vast expanse of the continental interior—the "Great American Desert" consisting of the plains region as well as most of the present states of

---

[*]The Indians perhaps fought longer and with more bitterness, and thereby sustained far more damage than might have been the case, because of a specific crime committed by Colonel James Kelley of the Oregon militia early in the war. This occurred during the first week of December, 1855, when the Walla Walla leader Pue Pue Mox Mox led a delegation into Kelley's bivouac to discuss peace terms. Kelley ordered the delegates held hostage against a Walla Walla capitulation. When infuriated Indians attacked the militia instead, Pue Pue Mox Mox was killed, his scalp and ears thereafter displayed as a "trophy of war"; Axelrod, *Chronicle of the Indian Wars, op. cit.*, p. 173; Glassley, *Pacific Northwest Indian Wars, op. cit.*, p. 122. Also see Lucius McWhorter, *Crime Against the Yakimas* (North Yakima, WA: Republic, 1913); Robert H. Ruby, *The Cayuse Indians: Imperial Tribesmen of Old Oregon* (Norman: University of Oklahoma Press, 1972); Clifford E. Trafzer and Richard D. Scheuerman, *Renegade Tribe: The Palouse Indians and the Invasion of the Inland Pacific Northwest* (Pullman: Washington State University Press, 1986).

Utah and Nevada—in which to maintain themselves.[500] Since the land at issue was deemed to be without value to whites, it was considered an ideal dumping ground for peoples displaced from more useful locales. At the outset, all that was required of those native to the region was that they admit such transplants along the fringes of their territories, engage in some limited amount of trade with whites, and allow safe passage to columns of Euroamerican migrants making their way from the East to California and Oregon.[501]

In theory, the overall framework for this was constructed in 1851 through a series of treaties negotiated at Fort Laramie—just west of the Black Hills, in present-day Wyoming—with a number of nations, including the Lakotas, Cheyennes, Arapahos, Crows, Shoshonis, Comanches, Kiowas, and Kiowa Apaches.[502] In the Fort Laramie treaties, the United States formally acknowledged every square inch of the Great Plains as being the sovereign territory of one or another of these counterpart nations and pledged itself to prevent the establishment of permanent communities of its citizens within their domains.[503] Early encounters with these peoples (whom Colonel George Armstrong Custer would later describe as being "the best light cavalry in the world") had convinced the United States that to do otherwise would not be worth the cost of taking a more bellicose stance.[504]

Things more or less worked out for a time, although there were ominous precursors of what would follow.* By the late 1850s, however, gold had been discovered in the Rocky Mountains, leading large numbers of white prospectors and other speculators to establish illegal mining camps in the

---

* One of these, the so-called "Case of the Mormon Cow," is instructive. The terms of the 1851 Fort Laramie treaties with the Lakotas, Cheyennes, and Arapahos allowed for white passage along the Platte River Road in Nebraska. On August 18, 1854, a group of young Lakotas killed and ate a dying cow abandoned by a Mormon wagon train. This "theft" was reported to the army at Fort Kearney. The matter was taken up with Conquering Bear, leader of the band of which the young men were members. Although he offered compensation for the animal, the Mormons demanded that arrests be made. A thirty-man force under Lt. John L. Grattan was dispatched for this purpose. When the Indians refused to turn over the "criminals," Grattan attacked their camp with a cannon, killing Conquering Bear and others. Enraged, the Lakotas promptly wiped out Grattan's entire detachment—there was one survivor, who died of his wounds shortly thereafter—and departed the area. General William S. Harney was then ordered into the field at the head of 600 men to "punish" the "hostiles." On September 3, Harney piled into the peaceful encampment on the Blue Water River of Brûlé Lakota leader Little Thunder—who had had nothing to do with the Grattan fight—and massacred a good portion of it (Harney would thereafter be referred to as "Woman Killer" by the Lakotas). The sequence of events cast the die for U.S./Lakota relations for the rest of the nineteenth century. One of the best accounts is in the early chapters of Mari Sandoz's *Crazy Horse: Strange Man of the Oglalas* (New York: Alfred A. Knopf, 1942). Also see Gerald Baydo, "Overland from Missouri to Washington Territory in 1854," *Nebraska History*, Vol. 52, No. 1, 1971.

western reaches of Cheyenne/Arapaho territory, at places like Denver.[505] Not only did the government not attempt to uphold its treaty commitments to the Cheyennes and Arapahos by preventing this, it engineered a completely fraudulent "supplanting treaty" in 1861, by which the unknowing Indians supposedly ceded more than 90 percent of their central plains homelands.* When the Cheyennes refused to acknowledge the validity of this travesty they were declared to be "aggressors," and military preparations for their outright extermination commenced.[506]

Gold, silver, and other minerals were also discovered in the mountains of western Montana at about the same time. One result was that a new wagon route, the "Bozeman Trail" was cut diagonally through the heart of prime Lakota hunting territory in Wyoming, another direct violation of the 1851 treaty.[507] Since the influx of traffic greatly disrupted the buffalo herds upon which they depended for subsistence, the Indians had little alternative but to respond militarily to this invasion, and the army quickly began building a string of forts along the route in order to secure it.[508] Although eradication was not at that time considered a viable option with regard to the Lakotas, who were much more populous than the Cheyennes, it was believed they might be "chastised" into acquiescence.†

Meanwhile, on the southern plains, Texas cattle interests had begun what was to become a concerted effort to breach the "Comanche Wall," which had prevented all but the most transient white penetration of the Llano

---

*Treaty of Fort Wise, February 18, 1861. The 1851 treaty terms had been ratified by most Cheyennes. Its 1861 "successor" relied upon the ostensible agreement of a handful of "chiefs." Of these, several said they had neither been present during negotiations nor signed the document (suggesting their signatures were forged). The rest maintained the terms of the treaty were radically different than those explained to them during negotiations. This seems due to deliberate misinterpretation of treaty provisions by U.S. representatives during the negotiations, and the fact that the Senate unilaterally altered the terms of the treaty—without consulting the Cheyennes, much less obtaining their consent—before ratifying it. This exceedingly bogus instrument was then pronounced "law" by the United States, and allegedly forms the basis of U.S. title to what is now the eastern two-thirds of the State of Colorado; Hoig, *Battle of the Washita, op. cit.*, pp. 13–7; Thomas F. Dawson, "Colonel Boone's Treaty with the Plains Indians," *The Trail*, Vol. XIV, 1921.

†A preliminary expedition into the Powder River Country of southeastern Montana was mounted in 1865, in an effort to exterminate—or at least intimidate—"every male over twelve years of age" among the Lakotas and allied northern Cheyennes and Arapahos. When the force of nearly 2,000, commanded by General Patrick Connor (fresh from his slaughter of Shoshonis at Bear River) was soundly thrashed and sent scurrying back to Fort Laramie in September of that year, the army temporarily abandoned such ambitious plans; LeRoy R. Hafen and Ann W. Hafen, *The Powder River Campaign and Sawyers' Expedition of 1865* (Glendale, CA: Arthur H. Clark, 1961). Also see James C. Olson, *Red Cloud and the Sioux Problem* (Lincoln: University of Nebraska Press, 1965).

Estacado—the "Staked Plains" or "Texas Panhandle" region—for generations.[509] A special unit, the Texas Rangers, had been assembled to deal with
the "menace" presented by Comanche, Kiowa, and Kiowa Apache defense of
their treaty-guaranteed homelands.[510] However, the Comanches and their
allies proved more than a match for such adversaries. By the late 1850s, Texans
were demanding with increasing shrillness that regular troops be used to clear
these indigenous nations from their homelands, preferably by annihilation.[*]

In all probability the federal government would have accommodated
local exterminationist sentiments on at least one of these three fronts during
the early 1860s, had its ability to do so not been dissolved by the start of the
Civil War in 1861. From then until the war between the states ended in
1865, both the regular army and most militia units, both North and South,
were completely tied up in fighting one another.[511] Indian fighting in the
West was thus consigned mainly to happenstance or to ad hoc units formed
by the territories after official troop levies had been met.[512] This slowed but
by no means halted the process of obliterating the peoples of the plains.[513]
Indeed, it is fair to say that the pattern by which it would proceed was well
established by 1864, catalyzed not by events in the region itself, but by examples set elsewhere, in Minnesota and Utah, by regiments of volunteers.

In 1862, the final "Woodlands" conflict—with the Santee Dakotas in
Minnesota—was provoked by the United States through the simple expedient of cutting off the Indians' food supply while white settlers illegally over-
ran their remaining landbase.[†] When the starving Santees erupted in a

---

[*]Upon its entry into the Union in 1845, "the Texas government made it clear that it would not, then
or later, agree to set aside [any] territory for an Indian reservation. In fact, the state was already busily
granting and selling Indian lands to encourage immigration and development. Meanwhile, both the
state government and a horde of land speculators demanded that the federal government do its duty
and remove [by whatever means] the 'squatting' Indians" whose land it actually was; T.R. Fehrenbach,
The Comanches: The Destruction of a People (New York: Alfred A. Knopf, 1974) p. 379. There is ample
indication that the army would have complied with the wishes of the Texans—and of the manner in
which this compliance would have accrued—had the Civil War not intervened. In late 1858, the so-
called "Wichita Expedition" was mounted out of Fort Belknap, Texas, under command of Captain
(Brevet Major) Earl Van Dorn. Its main "accomplishment" was to attack a small Kotsoteka Comanche
encampment on Crooked Creek, slaughtering 49 Indians, on May 13, 1859. The event understandably
hardened Comanche attitudes against the United States; William Y. Chalfant, *Without Quarter: The
Wichita Expedition and the Fight on Crooked Creek* (Norman: University of Oklahoma Press, 1991).
[†]The Dakotas—composed of the Sisseton, Wahpeton, Santee, and Mdewakanton bands—may have
numbered more than 40,000 at their peak, and originally occupied most of southern Minnesota. Two
deceptive treaties during the 1850s resulted in their loss of about 90 percent of their land, leaving
them constrained to a narrow strip along the Minnesota River, insufficient to provide subsistence for
the 5,000 or so who remained alive at that point. Engulfed by an influx of more than 150,000 whites
who clamored ever more loudly for dissolution of the reservation, the Santees, who were by then

desperate "revolt," they were immediately targeted for total elimination under the premise, voiced by Governor Alexander Ramsey, that "the Sioux Indians must be exterminated or driven from the state."[514] General Henry H. Sibley—called the "Long Trader" by the Santees because of his practice of cheating them in commercial relations—then led several thousand militia troops against the Indians, quickly killing more than a quarter of their fighting men and as many as a thousand noncombatants.[*]

When the bedraggled survivors surrendered—a scalp bounty was proclaimed against all who did not—they were herded into cattle pens at Mankato. The roughly 600 men among the 2,000 captives were chained together, subjected to summary court martial (without benefit of defense counsel), and 303 of them condemned to death. On December 26, thirty-nine of them were hanged in the largest mass execution in U.S. history, and the remainder imprisoned, all for the "crime" of having tried to feed their starving families.[†]

> Sibley [also] decided to keep the remaining 1,700 Santees—mostly women and children—as prisoners, although they were accused of no crime other than having been born Indian. He ordered them transferred overland to Fort Snelling, and along the way they too were assaulted by angry white citizens. Many were stoned and clubbed; a child was snatched from its mother's arms and beaten to death.[515]

---

totally dependent upon the government to feed them, found their rations withheld by officials who wished to compel them to leave. This was the basis of their "revolt"; William W. Folwell, *History of the Santee Sioux* (Lincoln: University of Nebraska Press, 1967); C.M. Oehler, *The Great Sioux Uprising* (New York: Oxford University Press, 1959); Duane Schultz, *Over the Earth I Come: The Great Sioux Uprising of 1862* (New York: St. Martin's Press, 1992).

[*] One reason the Santees were starving was that Sibley had levied a claim of $145,000 for "back debts" they supposedly owed because of his notoriously unscrupulous dealings against a $475,000 federal payment for their lands. Although dubious in the extreme, Sibley's claim was paid as a priority by his business partner, future Minnesota Governor Alexander Ramsey, at the time the federal Indian agent on the Santee Reservation. Another of Sibley's (and Ramsey's) partners, Andrew Myrick, was the trader selected to handle most of the Indians' rations during the early 1860s. Instead of distributing the food to the hungry Santees, he adopted the lucrative practice of selling this windfall inventory at a discount to local whites. When the Indians inquired as to what *they* were supposed to eat, he suggested that grass might be appropriate. This indignity was perhaps the last straw. In any event, one of the Santees' first acts during their revolt was to behead Myrick, leaving the grisly trophy, its mouth stuffed with grass, in front of the storehouse in which he'd kept their food; "Big Eagle's Story of the Sioux Outbreak of 1862," *Collections, Vol. VI* (St. Paul: Minnesota Historical Society, 1894) p. 390; Gerald T. Henig, "A Neglected Cause of the Sioux Uprising," *Minnesota History*, Vol. 45, No. 3, Fall 1976.

[†] The hanging of the 39 Santees at Mankato—including two men executed by mistake—would have been far larger, had the military had its way. Of the 303 men condemned by Sibley's drumhead courts-martial, President Lincoln, who asked to review the records, commuted the sentences of 265 to varying terms of imprisonment; Dee Brown, *Bury My Heart at Wounded Knee: An Indian History of the American West* (New York: Holt, Rinehart & Winston, 1970) p. 58–61. Also see David A. Nichols, *Lincoln and the Indians* (Columbia: University of Missouri Press, 1978).

The killing continued. On July 3, 1863, when Little Crow, the principal Santee leader, attempted to return to his people from asylum in Canada, he was ambushed and shot to death. His murderers were paid a $25 bounty for his scalp, plus a $500 bonus, given the identity of their prize. Little Crow's scalp and skull were then placed on public display for the edification of the gentle souls of St. Paul.[516] Six months later, Minnesota violated Canadian neutrality in order to bring two other Santee leaders, Shakopee and Medicine Bottle, back into U.S. jurisdiction, where they were promptly hanged.[517] Those Santees who escaped the scalping knives were deported en masse, and their remaining lands in Minnesota were impounded as a "reparation" for expenses incurred by the state in annihilating them.[518]

> Crow Creek on the Missouri River was the site chosen for the Santee reservation. The soil was barren, rainfall scanty, wild game scarce, and the alkaline water unfit for drinking. Soon the surrounding hills were covered with graves; of the 1,300 Santees brought there in 1863, less than a thousand survived their first winter.[519]

Meanwhile, far to the west, in Utah, Colonel Patrick E. Connor took to the field at the head of about a thousand California volunteer cavalrymen. His target was the Shoshonis, who had grown increasingly "restive" over Salt Lake City and other Mormon communities recently—and quite illegally—established on their lands.[520] On January 27, 1863, about a third of this force slammed into a sizable village in southern Idaho, along the Bear River. Of the approximately 700 Indians living there as many as 500 were slaughtered with all the savagery customary to such assaults.*

> Soldiers reported…that Indians who were so incapacitated they could not move "were killed by being hit in the head with an axe"… [A] soldier found a dead woman clutching a little infant still alive. The soldier "in mercy to the babe, killed it"… [Numerous women] "were killed because they would not submit quietly to being ravaged, and other squaws were ravaged in the agony of death."[521]

After systematically mutilating the dead, Connor's men loaded their own fourteen casualties of the "battle" aboard sleds and returned to their base camp.[522] Many of them then returned to civilian life in northern California,

---

*The number of Indians killed at Bear River is a matter of some controversy. Connor reported 224 bodies counted on the field, plus another 50 estimated as having washed away after being shot while trying to swim to safety on the far bank. James H. Martineau, an area settler, placed the figure at 368. Another local resident, Richard J.M. Bee, later claimed that the total reached 1,200. Contemporary Park Service personnel have placed the true figure at a little over 500; see generally, Brigham M. Madsen, *The Shoshoni Frontier and the Bear River Massacre* (Salt Lake City: University of Utah Press, 1985) pp. 189–92.

where they immediately resumed the relentless slaughter of the indigenous population in that region.[523] For their part, the Mormons celebrated the colonel's frankly genocidal "victory"—Connor was soon promoted in recognition of his "achievement"—as "an intervention of the Almighty," a sentiment the Puritan Fathers of Plymouth Colony would have expressed neither differently nor better.[524]

Nits Make Lice

In 1864, inspired by the success of Sibley's and Connor's butchery, the government of Colorado Territory, whose two regiments of volunteer troops were fully committed to fighting Confederates further east, mustered in a whole new unit—the Third Colorado Volunteer Cavalry Regiment— exclusively for the purpose of killing Cheyennes, Arapahos and any other native people they might encounter over a 100-day period.* This was done in a climate which was exterminationist in the extreme: "Of twenty-seven stories concerned directly or indirectly with Indians [published in the Denver press during 1863], ten overtly favored 'extermination' of Indians."†️ By mid-1864, the paper's rhetorical advocacy of genocide—mostly written by its publisher, William N. Byers—had, if anything, escalated.

> Eastern humanitarians who believe in the superiority of the Indian race will raise a ter-
> rible howl over this policy [of extermination], but it is no time to split hairs nor stand

---

*As the matter was put in an editorial entitled "Exterminate Them," published in Denver's *Rocky Mountain News* on March 24, 1863, shortly after the Bear River Massacre: "A few such men as Col. Connor could do more to quiet the Indians than a thousand Indian agents with immense trains of annuities to back them." Much was made in the *News* of supposed "depredations" by Cheyennes and Arapahos during this period, although it is clear from the record that noticeably more Indians were being killed by whites than the other way around. Indeed, until "the spring of 1864, more Whites were injured or murdered within the Denver city limits [by other whites] than Whites harmed by Cheyennes or Arapahos during the same period"; Svaldi, *Sand Creek and the Rhetoric of Extermination, op. cit.*, p. 142. Also see George Bird Grinnell, *The Fighting Cheyennes* (Norman: University of Oklahoma Press, 1955 reprint of 1915 original) p. 127; Lilian B. Shields, "Relations with the Cheyennes and Arapahoes in Colorado to 1861," *Colorado Magazine*, Aug. 1927. On the Colorado volunteer regiments, see J.H. Nankivell, *History of the Military Organizations of Colorado, 1860–1935* (Denver: W.H. Kistler, 1935).

†Svaldi, *Sand Creek and the Rhetoric of Extermination, op. cit.*, pp. 149–50; e.g., in the above-cited editorial, "Exterminate Them," *News* publisher William N. Byers sided with the editors of the Santa Fe *New Mexican* in advocating "extermination of the Indians…as the most effective method for life and security." On April 2, 1863, the *News* followed up by declaring emphatically that "we hope [the Cheyennes and Arapahoes] will be exterminated." Two days later, Byers observed that the "feeling" had become "general" among Colorado whites that the "only way" to deal with Indians was to "wage upon them *a war of extermination* (emphasis in the original)." As by far the leading newspaper in the territory, the *Rocky Mountain News* was, of course, also the leading opinion-shaper.

upon delicate compunctions of conscience. Self preservation demands decisive action, and the only way to secure it is [through a] few months of active extermination against the red devils.*

On the day this was written, the publisher was joined by Colorado Governor John Evans who, after announcing—on the basis of no discernible evidence—that the Cheyennes had "declared war on the United States," pronounced his judgment that "Any man who kills a hostile Indian is a patriot!" A day later, the governor clarified his stance, publishing a proclamation in the *News* in which he claimed "the evidence [was] now conclusive" that most Indians on the Plains were "hostile," calling upon area whites to "organize [themselves] to pursue, kill and destroy" Cheyennes and Arapahos wherever they might be found.[525] As the Colorado Third was being formed, Byers chimed in again, inquiring of his readers:"Shall we not go for them, their lodges, squaws and all?"

The answer was shortly announced by Colonel John Milton Chivington, a former Methodist minister with political ambitions, who commanded the unit. "My intention is to kill all Indians I may come across," he explained.[526] The colonel elsewhere elaborated that this included everyone from the most elderly and infirm to newborn infants, the latter for no reason other than that they would one day grow up to become adult Cheyennes. "Nits make lice," Chivington asserted, echoing H.L. Hall, a rather notorious mass-murderer of Indians in northern California.† "I long to be wading in gore," Chivington put

---

*   *Rocky Mountain News*, Aug. 10, 1864. That Byers' formulations constitute a direct prefiguration of Hitlerian rhetoric should be obvious; for comparison, see Hermann Rauschning, *The Voice of Destruction* (New York: G.P. Putnam's Sons, 1940). The Denver publisher also prefigured Goebbels to a noticeable extent; e.g., on April 24, 1864, he whipped up anti-Indian sentiment among Colorado whites by reporting as "news" the "fact" that of 28 persons who had set out for new mine sites that month, "twenty-five have been murdered on the road by the Indians." In actuality, as the *News*'s own stories reveal, this represented a 500-percent inflation of the data; Svaldi, *Sand Creek and the Rhetoric of Extermination, op. cit.*, p. 152. In June, he was still at it, claiming on the 24th that the number of white deaths inflicted by Indians "in recent months" was "daunting," although his own paper's records showed nine dead whites and 69 dead *Indians* as the toll of hostilities by that point in 1864 (this tally included Lean Bear, a prominent Cheyenne peace advocate); for cogent analysis of such techniques, see Jacques Ellul, *Propaganda: The Formation of Men's Attitudes* (New York: Alfred A. Knopf, 1965); Murray Edelman, *Politics as Symbolic Action: Mass Arousal and Quiescence* (Chicago: Markham, 1971); and, most specifically, James Morgan Read, *Atrocity Propaganda, 1914–1919* (New York: Arno Press, 1972).

†   Hall's formulation, which drew on a view articulated in North America at least as early as King Philip's War, was that native babies should be killed without exception because, "a nit would make a louse"; Carranco and Beard, *Genocide and Vendetta, op. cit.*, Chapter 4. It should be noted that, eighty years after Chivington and Hall, SS Reichsführer Heinrich Himmler would also refer to his extermination of Gypsies, Jews, Slavs, and others as being "the same as delousing"; quoted in Robert Jay Lifton, *The Nazi Doctors: Medical Killing and the Psychology of Genocide* (New York: Basic Books, 1986) p. 477.

Poster for the 3rd Colorado Volunteers. Courtesy of Colorado Historical Society

it on another occasion.[527] Such statements quickly became rallying cries for his troops and were enthusiastically embraced by the Colorado citizenry at large.[*]

The problem for Chivington was that his men came across almost no Indians to kill.[†] Aside from an incident on October 10, when forty men led by Captain David Nichols managed to surprise a small Cheyenne hunting camp near Buffalo Springs and slaughter everyone in it—six men, three women, and a fourteen-year-old boy[528]—the only "savages" the colonel and his volunteers had seen by the time the troops' hundred-day enlistments had begun to run out were a group of "peace chiefs"—notably the Cheyennes Black Kettle and White Antelope, and Left Hand (Niwot), an Arapaho—escorted by Major Edward Wynkoop of the First Colorado into Camp Weld, near Denver, in mid-September.[529] Under Wynkoop's watchful eye, these Indians had been allowed to place themselves and their people—about 750 in all-under the protection of the military. In exchange for official recognition of their noncombatant status, they were required to surrender their weapons and accept de facto internment under Wynkoop's supervision at a specified site along Sand Creek, near Fort Lyon in the 1861 reservation area.[‡]

---

[*] Even after Chivington had made his meaning absolutely clear by perpetrating the massacre at Sand Creek, a U.S. Senator who posed the question at a public meeting of Denver citizens as to whether it might not be better to try and "civilize" the Indians than to exterminate them, was confronted with "a shout almost loud enough to raise the roof of the opera house [in which the meeting was held]— 'EXTERMINATE THEM! EXTERMINATE THEM!' "; Letter of Senator Doolittle to Mrs. L.F.S. Foster, March 7, 1881, Notes and Documents," *New Mexico Historical Review*, No. 26, Apr. 1951. Such performances place Colorado's Euroamerican citizenry of 1864 squarely within the ideological/psychological framework attributed to the Germans during the Holocaust.

[†] The reason for this is that there *was* a war going on between the Cheyennes and white settlers. But it was mainly in western Kansas, not Colorado. Hence, the great bulk of the Indians—and *all* of their combatants, the so-called "Dog Soldiers"—were based along the Smoky Hill and Solomon rivers, well east of Chivington's operational area. In effect, despite all the hoopla in the *News*, Colorado was in no danger at all; Hoig, *Battle of the Washita, op. cit.*, Chapter 6, esp. map at p. 93. Also see Grinnell, *The Fighting Cheyennes, op. cit.*; Captain Eugene F. Ware, *The Indian War of 1864* (New York: St. Martin's Press, 1960).

[‡] There is considerable indication that Black Kettle and White Antelope wished to establish residence for their noncombatants in Colorado, not simply because this was the locality of the 1861 reserved area, but because both they and the Cheyenne combatants considered the whole territory to be more or less outside the theater of war. The record is clear that Evans was highly uncomfortable that these representatives of a "race" he and his cohorts had depicted as "bloodthirsty savages" should be so obviously desirous of avoiding war. He officially declined to grant peace, inverting U.S. law—which vests such powers exclusively in civil authority—by arguing that "only the military" could do so. General S.R. Curtis, commander of the entire military district of which Colorado was a part, stated flatly that he wanted "no peace until the Indians suffer more." Both Evans and Chivington did, however, make personal guarantees that, if the peace faction were willing to accept what amounted to prisoner-of-war status at Sand Creek, they would be safe from harm until hostilities ended. Black Kettle and his colleagues agreed, and complied with the military's instructions from then until they were massacred, less than three months later; Hoig, *Sand Creek Massacre, op. cit.*, pp. 112, 116–7, 120.

By early November, Chivington's fearless "Indian fighters" had become a laughingstock, derisively referred to by Coloradans as the "Bloodless Third."[530] At some point mid-month—prompted by a visit by Connor—both the embarrassed officers and their men agreed to serve beyond the expiration of their terms of service in order to make a full-scale assault upon the peace chiefs' immobilized and defenseless village.[531] Moving under cover of a blizzard, the regiment suddenly appeared at Fort Lyon on November 27, and to preserve the secrecy of their arrival—Chivington was determined to preserve the "element of surprise" against his unarmed and woefully outnumbered opponents—"threw a cordon of pickets around the post with orders that no one would be allowed to leave, under penalty of death."[*]

At 8 p.m. that night, the colonel led about 900 soldiers out of the fort and headed for the village, about thirty miles away. He instructed his troops to "use any means under God's heaven to kill [the] Indians" and to be sure to "kill and scalp all, little and big."[532] The volunteers struck at dawn, despite the fact that both American and white flags were flown over the sleeping encampment. When 75-year-old White Antelope, hands open to show he bore no weapons, attempted to halt the attacking cavalrymen, he was unceremoniously shot to death.[†] A soldier who was visiting the village at the time also tried to head off the attackers. Although waving another white flag of surrender, he too was fired upon.[533]

> The Indians fled in all directions, but the main body of them moved up the creek bed, which alone offered some protection from the soldiers' bullets. They fled headlong until they came to a place above the camp where the banks of the river were cut back by

---

[*] Hoig, *Sand Creek Massacre, op. cit.,* p. 140. Wynkoop, to Chivington's knowledge, had left Fort Lyon a day earlier, en route to meet with General Curtis in Kansas. Another officer at the post, Captain Silas S. Soule, tried to intervene with Chivington on the Indians' behalf, explaining that they were not dangerous and considered to be prisoners. Chivington responded that, "They won't be prisoners after we get there." Still another officer, Lt. Joseph A. Cramer, "stated to [Chivington] that I believed [the planned attack] to be 'murder,' and stated the obligations that we of Major Wynkoop's command were under to those Indians… Chivington's reply was…'damn any man that was in sympathy with Indians,' and such men as Major Wynkoop and myself had better get out of the United States service"; quoted in U.S. Dept. of War, "Sand Creek Massacre," *op. cit.,* pp. 11, 47. Soule refused to allow his company to participate in the massacre and later stated a willingness to testify against Chivington and other officers in open court. He was murdered on the streets of Denver prior to taking the stand. No one was ever prosecuted for his death.

[†] Afterwards, his corpse was badly mutilated: "The body of White Antelope, lying solitarily in the creek bed, was a prime target. Besides scalping him, the soldiers cut off his nose, ears and testicles—the last for a tobacco pouch… Some of the men later tried to blame this on Lieutenant Autobee's Company H Mexican troops, but there is much evidence Major [Hal] Sayr and Lieutenant [Harry] Richmond were guilty"; "Sand Creek Massacre," *op. cit.,* p. 153.

breaks. Here, the Indians frantically began digging in the loose sand with their hands to make holes in which to hide. The larger percent of these were women and children...[534]

As the scene was later described by Robert Bent, the mixed-blood son of a local trader and a Cheyenne woman who had guided the attackers from Fort Lyon to the village:

> I saw five squaws under a bank for shelter. When the troops came up to them they ran out and showed their persons, to let the soldiers know they were squaws and begged for mercy, but the soldiers shot them all... There were some thirty or forty squaws collected in a hole for protection; they sent out a little girl about six years old with a white flag on a stick; she had not proceeded but a few steps when she was shot and killed. All the squaws in the hole were afterwards killed... The squaws offered no resistance. Every one I saw dead was scalped. I saw one squaw cut open with an unborn child, as I thought, lying by her side... I saw quite a number of infants in arms killed with their mothers.[535]

Other soldiers were running down Indians who had fled in different directions, killing some as far as five or six miles from the village. By then, mutilation of the dead and dying had begun in earnest, and the few prisoners taken were being summarily executed.* As a lieutenant in the New Mexico Volunteers who'd ridden along "to gain experience," would later testify:

> Of from five to six hundred souls [who were killed], the majority of which were women and children...I did not see a body of man, woman, or child but was scalped, and in many instances their bodies were mutilated in a most horrible manner—men, women, and children's privates cut out, &c; I heard one man say that he had cut out a woman's private parts and had them for exhibition on a stick; I heard another man say he had cut off the fingers of an Indian to get the rings on the hand... I also heard of numerous instances in which men had cut out the private parts of females and stretched them over the saddle bows and wore them over hats while riding in the ranks...I heard one man say that he had cut a squaw's heart out, and he had it stuck up on a stick.†

---

*The best known example is that of Jack Smith, mixed-blood Cheyenne son of army scout John Smith, who was murdered while being held as a prisoner on November 30. Several women prisoners were also shot on the 30th, presumably after suffering gang rape. An infant was kept alive a while longer, but was later discarded as a "nuisance," its throat slit. Chivington's response was simply that he'd ordered that no prisoners be taken in the first place; U.S. Senate, "The Chivington Massacre," *op. cit,* p. 155.

†"The Chivington Massacre," *op. cit.,* p. 53. The number of Indian dead is again controversial. In his after-action report, Chivington claimed a bodycount of "400 to 500," an estimate he later raised to "500 or 600" during congressional testimony. Major Jacob Downing also later testified that there were "five hundred or six hundred Indians killed," that he had personally "counted two hundred and odd [bodies] within a very short distance from where their village stood," and that the dead were strung out as far as "five or six miles" from there. A trooper named Asbury Bird testified that he judged "that between 400 and 500 Indians were killed," that "about half were women and children," and that he'd personally "counted 350 lying up and down the Creek." Sergeant Stephen Decatur place the number of dead at 450; all quoted in Hoig, *Sand Creek Massacre, op. cit.,* pp. 177–92. It seems probable that

Or, to quote from the testimony of John Smith, a frontiersman who served as a scout:

> All manner of depredations were inflicted on their persons. They were scalped, their brains knocked out; the men used their knives, ripped open women, clubbed little children, knocked them in the head with their guns, beat their brains out, mutilated their bodies in every sense of the word…worse mutilated than any I ever saw before… [C]hildren two or three months old; all lying there, from sucking infants up to warriors.[536]

In the aftermath of the massacre the Cheyenne Dog Soldiers, joined by several hundred Lakotas, finally gave Colorado a genuine dose of the "war" its officials had been prattling on about.[537] Denver was virtually sealed off from the east for some months,[538] and it soon became apparent that, however proficient they might be in slaughtering the helpless, outfits like Chivington's "Bloody Third"—as the *News* now proudly dubbed the "bold sojer boys"*—couldn't begin to cope with the response they'd provoked. Infuriated that regular army troops would be required to resolve the situa-

---

these counts were highly inflated. Many other estimates—most importantly, the Cheyennes' own—placed the real toll at less than 200; see, e.g., Simon J. Ortiz, *From Sand Creek* (New York: Thunder's Mouth Press, 1981).

* The verbiage accrues from coverage of the Third's triumphal march through the streets of Denver, displaying Cheyenne body parts before an admiring citizenry: "Headed by the First Regiment band, and by Colonels Chivington and Shoup, Lieut. Col. Bowen and Major Sayr, the rank and file of 'bloody Thirdsters' made an imposing procession, extending, with the transportation trains, from the upper end of Ferry street, through Latimer, G and Blake, almost back to Ferry again. As the 'bold sojer boys' passed along, the sidewalks and corner stands were thronged with citizens saluting their old friends"; *Rocky Mountain News*, Dec. 22, 1864. Pride in what was done to the Cheyennes in 1864 has never abated in Colorado; see, e.g., Lt. Col. William R. Dunn, *"I Stand by Sand Creek": A Defense of Colonel John M. Chivington and the Third Colorado Cavalry* (Ft. Collins, CO: Old Army Press, 1985). Streets all over Denver are named in honor of those responsible, and a town near the massacre site—marked as a "battlefield" by its current owner, Judge William Dawson—is named for Chivington himself. A monument on the grounds of the state capitol commemorates the Third Colorado Volunteers. Until 1988, the University of Colorado at Boulder had a building named after David M. Nichols, perpetrator of the mini-massacre at Buffalo Springs, and a standout performer at Sand Creek; Patricia Nelson Limerick, "What's in a Name? Nichols Hall: A Report" (Boulder: unpublished study commissioned by the Regents of the University of Colorado, 1987). A few years earlier, the same campus was barely prevented from naming a second building after such a figure; Ward Churchill, "A Summary of Arguments Against Naming a University Dormitory After Clinton M. Tyler" (Boulder: unpublished report commissioned by the Vice Chancellor of Academic Affairs, University of Colorado, 1981). It took until late 1995 for the *News*—grudgingly, in limited fashion, and only after years of pressure by the American Indian Movement and other groups—to concede that there might have been anything in the least wrong with Byers' open celebration of genocide; "Siding with the Killers," *Rocky Mountain News*, Dec. 3, 1995. On handling of the subject matter by professional historians, see M.A. Sievers, "The Shifting Sands of Sand Creek Historiography," *Colorado Magazine*, No. 49, 1972; Ward Churchill, "It Did Happen Here: Sand Creek, Scholarship and the American Character," in my *Fantasies of the Master Race: Literature, Cinema and the Colonization of American Indians* (Monroe, ME: Common Courage Press, 1991).

tion, the federal government convened three separate investigations of Sand Creek—one each by the House, Senate, and War Department—all of them concluding that a hideous crime had been committed, and that Chivington, Evans, and other whites were entirely responsible.[*]

Armed with these conclusions, and promising reparations (which were never paid), federal negotiators attempted unsuccessfully to effect an accommodation with the Dog Soldiers through the Treaty of the Little Arkansas during the fall of 1865. Another effort was made via the 1867 Treaty of Medicine Lodge, following a spectacularly unsuccessful military campaign headed up by General Winfield Scott Hancock.[†] This was followed, a year

---

[*] The hype attending these investigations was such that even Colonel Kit Carson, who'd just wrapped up his own campaign against the Diné (see notes 90–93, above)—and whose troops were known to have engaged in recreational activities as playing catch with breasts hacked off living native women—was prepared to denounce the massacre as a "foul deed"; Congress of the United States, *Report of the Joint Special Committee Appointed Under Resolution of March 3, 1865* (Washington, D.C.: 39th Cong., 2d. Sess., 1867) Appendix III, pp. 5–6. Chivington, whose after-action report stated that a single white scalp had been recovered from the Cheyenne lodges at Sand Creek, changed his story during the first hearing, anchoring his defense in the claim that there had been "several scalps of white men and women in Indian lodges." During the second hearing, he revised the facts still further, testifying that "nineteen" scalps were found. By 1883, the fable had evolved to the point that he reminisced about "capturing...an Indian blanket, fringed with white women's scalps"; quoted in Hoig, *Sand Creek Massacre, op. cit.*, pp. 161, 166, 176. In actuality, as Wynkoop and others testified, there had been no scalps found at all (and the massacre would not have been justified, even if such items had been found); Duane Schultz, *Month of the Freezing Moon: The Sand Creek Massacre, November 1864* (New York: St. Martin's Press, 1990) p. 173. A better line of argument was offered by Evans and Byers, who asserted— accurately enough—that "Eastern humanitarians" had no moral standing from which to condemn Coloradoans, since they themselves were comfortably ensconced in Indian-free states made that way by employment of precisely the same methods used at Sand Creek; Svaldi, *Sand Creek and the Rhetoric of Extermination, op. cit.* That the Easterners could make no viable reply to this postulation is probably best evidenced by the fact that, after ostentatiously proving Chivington and numerous others guilty of crimes against humanity, they opted to penalize no one at all. Chivington and the others, it was said, were not subject to prosecution in civilian courts because they'd been in the military at the time their crimes were committed; conversely, the military claimed prosecution could not occur, since the perpetrators' commissions had expired prior to the massacre, meaning they were technically civilians at the time it occurred. On the other hand, while thus finessing such charges as mass murder, federal prosecutors did seriously consider filing charges against several officers they believed to have engaged in the illegal sale of Indian horses taken at Sand Creek (the principle being that such monies were due the government). Hence, while expressing "outrage" at the massacre, the government not only did nothing about it, but sought to profit from it; Hoig, *Sand Creek Massacre, op. cit.*, p. 169. Also see Patrick J. Mendoza, *Song of Sorrow: Massacre at Sand Creek* (Denver: Willow Wind, 1993).

[†] The campaign, conducted mostly in western Kansas by some 4,000 troops was an utter failure. Hancock's crack unit, Custer's elite Seventh Cavalry—much like Chivington's volunteers— floundered around for months on the endless Plains without ever coming to grips with their opponent. Frustrated and exhausted, the army finally gave up the chase and agreed to a treaty preserving much of Cheyenne territory and providing them with much-needed arms and ammunition; Douglas C. Jones, *The Treaty of Medicine Lodge: The Story of the Great Indian Council as Told by Eyewitnesses* (Norman: University of Oklahoma Press, 1966); William E. Connelley, "The Treaty Held at Medicine Lodge," *Collections of the Kansas State Historical Society*, Vol. XVII, 1928.

later, with an offensive commanded by General Phil Sheridan, a leading proponent of "total war."[*] Pursuing a strategy which combined winter campaigning—to catch the Indians in camp, during the period of their least mobility—with wholesale massacre, Sheridan was at last able to drive the Cheyennes virtually out of existence.[539]

> If [a winter campaign] results in the utter annihilation of these Indians...I will say nothing and do nothing to restrain our troops from doing what they may deem proper on the spot, and will allow no vague general charges of cruelty and inhumanity to tie their hands.[540]

The primary instrument of the general's campaign was the newly formed Seventh Cavalry Regiment, commanded by Lt. Colonel George Armstrong Custer.[541] On November 27, 1868, almost four years to the day after Sand Creek, Custer's men attacked an unsuspecting winter encampment on the big bend of the Washita River, in western Oklahoma. The village was again that of Black Kettle, who'd survived Sand Creek and was still vainly seeking to avoid conflict while securing some kind of sanctuary for native noncombatants.[542] Of the 103 people killed in Custer's dawn assault, "93 were women, old men, and children—as well as Black Kettle, who had been cut down with his wife as they were riding double on a pony in a desperate attempt to forestall the attack."[†]

The Washita Massacre took the heart out of most of the remaining Cheyennes in the south. Although a group of Dog Soldiers made their way to the Powder River Country of Montana to merge with their Northern

---

[*] "Sheridan...was convinced that winter would handicap the Indian and benefit the trooper. Indian ponies would be weak and thin and much slower in winter, while the grain-fed army animals would be stronger. Also, he looked to the element of surprise, since the Indians would be around their lodge fires, not expecting the troops to be out. It was obvious that his troops could not catch and defeat the Indians in the field. As he admitted...it would be necessary to hit their home villages even as Chivington had done at Sand Creek"; Stan Hoig, *The Battle of the Washita* (Garden City, NY: Doubleday, 1976) p. 74. Also see DeB. Randolph Keim, *Sheridan's Troopers on the Borders: A Winter Campaign on the Plains* (Philadelphia: David McKay, 1885).

[†] Axelrod, *Chronicle of the Indian Wars, op. cit.*, p. 209. Custer burned the lodges, clothing, and food stores—and had his men slaughter an estimated 900 ponies—intending that any survivors should freeze to death in the bitter cold. He had misjudged the situation, however. Having failed to reconnoiter before he attacked—an habitual failing that would cost him his life at the Little Big Horn eight years later—he was unaware that Black Kettle's was only the most southwesterly of a closely spaced string of winter encampments along the Washita. As substantial numbers of Dog Soldiers and other combatants from these other villages began to appear on the scene, he withdrew in such haste that he abandoned a fifteen-man detail under Major Joel Eliott he'd earlier sent upriver to run down fleeing victims. Eliott's group was consequently annihilated; Don Turner, *Custer's First Massacre: The Battle of the Washita* (Amarillo, TX: Humbolt Gulch Press, 1968).

Cheyenne cousins, the bulk of the survivors surrendered to the army at Fort Sill during the spring and summer of 1869.[543] Thus confined, and with many of their remaining leaders sent to prison at Fort Marion, Florida, a few years later—a policy which led to the Sappa Creek Massacre in 1875[*]—they had declined to near-extinction by the early twentieth century.[544]

The "Conquest of the Southern Plains" was not yet complete, however.[545] Sheridan's campaign in particular had embroiled the Comanches, Kiowas, and Kiowa Apaches. Although these peoples accepted an uneasy "peace" for about three years after the Cheyenne decimation, the army's unofficial policy of fostering the extermination of their traditional "commissary," the buffalo, forced an all-out counteroffensive against white hunters operating in their territory in 1874.[546] Although early victories were won at places like Adobe Walls, none was decisive, and a campaign headed by General Nelson A. Miles was soon mounted to subdue them once and for all.[547]

Miles brought in the Fourth Cavalry, under Colonel Ranald Mackenzie, fresh from a "limited invasion" of Mexico to "punish" a group of long-suffering Kickapoos who had found sanctuary there.[548] Another practitioner of total war, Mackenzie conducted a brutal winter campaign inaugurated by a September 28, 1874, surprise attack on the main body of Comanches and Kiowas, who had withdrawn to what had always been an inaccessible joint refuge in the Palo Duro Canyon, far out on the Llano Estacado. Although few Indians were killed—the various bands quickly scattered when the assault began—the soldiers were able to capture and kill almost all their horses, and to destroy virtually everything else they possessed.[549] Starving, freezing, and harried relentlessly by Mackenzie's patrols during the coldest months, the fragments of each people shortly began to surrender.

By May 25, 1875, the "hard core"—a small group of Kiowas led by Satank, and Quannah Parker's Quahadi Comanches—had laid down their arms. With that, all military resistance by the plains nations south of the Dakota Territory finally ceased.[550] Thereafter, like the Arapahos and

---

[*]The army's policy of more or less arbitrarily sending fighting-age Cheyenne males to the Florida prison caused yet another small group to flee northward in 1875. They were tracked by a group of forty soldiers under Lt. Austin Henely, who managed to locate them in a temporary encampment on the Sappa Creek, in northwestern Kansas, near the Colorado line, on April 20. Making the customary dawn attack, Henely's men were able to trap a group of 27 people—reportedly nineteen men, eight women, and children—and they killed them all. The others, estimated at about thirty, escaped to join the Northern Cheyennes; William D. Street, "Cheyenne Indian Massacre on the Middle Fork of the Sappa," *Transactions of the Kansas State Historical Society*, Vol. X, 1907–1908; G. Derek West, "The Battle of Sappa Creek, 1875," *Kansas Historical Quarterly*, Vol. 34, No. 2, 1968.

Cheyennes (a small number of whom, led by Grey Beard, had joined in the "Buffalo War"), both the Kiowas and Comanches, as well as their Kiowa Apache allies, were stripped of what little land remained to them, rendered absolutely dependent upon their conquerors for subsistence, and rapidly declined to nadir population (by 1900 the Kiowas, for example, who numbered more than 6,000 in 1800, had fewer than 1,300 survivors; there were less than 500 Kiowa Apaches by that point, and the Comanches were reduced by about 90 percent, overall).[551]

Death Song

The northern plains proved a more difficult proposition for the United States. In the summer of 1866, Red Cloud (Mahpiya Luta), a preeminent Oglala political leader, was able to bring all seven bands of his people together, along with the Northern Cheyennes and Arapahos, as well as some refugee Santees, and lay siege to Fort Phil Kearny, most northerly of the posts thus far completed along the Bozeman Trail.[552] With more than 3,000 warriors, the Indians constituted a formidable opponent for the army, especially since the bulk of its available resources were tied up in Kansas and Colorado, trying to contain the indigenous response to Sand Creek.[553]

The situation was greatly exacerbated on December 21, when a unit under Captain William J. Fetterman was annihilated near Fort Kearny.[554] As the months dragged on it became apparent that the Indians were becoming steadily stronger. Unable to muster anything approaching the number of troops needed to defeat Red Cloud's alliance, and in constant danger of suffering even more catastrophic losses in its undermanned Wyoming garrisons, the army began sending out peace feelers during the late summer of 1867.[555] Red Cloud's response was that he would not be interested in negotiating until all U.S. forces had been withdrawn from Lakota territory and the Bozeman Trail posts destroyed. After procrastinating for several months, the army complied with these terms and Red Cloud finally agreed to a treaty, signed at Fort Laramie in November 1868.[556]

This new instrument reaffirmed much of what had been established by its 1851 predecessor with respect to the Lakotas and allied Cheyennes and Arapahos. It defined their territory as extending from the east bank of the Missouri River westward to the Big Horn Mountains, and southward from the upper Missouri to the North Platte River (an area, centering on the Black Hills, totaling about 5 percent of the 48 states). Under the 1868 treaty, the army could not build forts in Indian Country and was required to patrol the borders to prevent U.S. nationals from trespassing therein. No portion of the treaty territory could be sold or otherwise alienated without the express written consent of at least three-quarters of all adult male Lakotas.*

The treaty was actually honored to a large extent for several years while the army concentrated on winning its "Buffalo War" on the southern plains. With the end of that conflict in sight by 1874, however, things began to change in the north. During the summer of that year, Custer's Seventh Cavalry was ordered to make a "reconnaissance in force" into the Black Hills for purposes of assessing potential mineral wealth there.[557] Although it is dubious whether anything was actually found, Custer, writing under a pseudonym, reported in the Eastern press that he'd discovered "gold at the grass-roots."† In short order, whites were pouring into Paha Sapa—as the Lakotas called this, their most sacred area—and the army was doing nothing to fulfill its treaty obligation to prevent their coming.[558]

Indeed, after a follow-up expedition in 1875 (during which gold *was* found), the United States demanded that the Lakotas sell the entire region.[559] When the Indians refused, it was announced in Washington that they'd "declared war on America," and a huge three-pronged invasion of their territory—the so-called "Centennial Campaign"—was set in motion during the spring of 1876.[560] Although the offensive itself fared rather poorly—some 1,200 Lakotas and Cheyennes led by Crazy Horse (Tesunke Witko) defeated a 1,500-man column under General George Crook at the

---

*The Lakota/Cheyenne/Arapaho landbase was divided into three components: everything in present-day South Dakota west of the east bank of the Missouri was designated a "Great Sioux Reservation." All of Nebraska north of the North Platte was designated as a permanent hunting territory, at least "so long as there [was] sufficient game to warrant the chase." All of Wyoming east of the Big Horn Mountains and of Montana and North Dakota south of the upper Missouri were declared "Unceded Indian Territory," for exclusive use and occupancy of the three indigenous nations. This last area included the Bozeman Trail route and the Powder River Country; Kappler, *Indian Treaties, op. cit.*, pp. 998–1007; Roxanne Dunbar Ortiz, *The Great Sioux Nation: Sitting in Judgment on America* (San Francisco/New York: International Indian Treaty Council/Moon Books, 1978).

†The false reports were sent out via Custer's favorite scout, "Lonesome" Charlie Reynolds, who was assigned the dangerous mission of carrying them through hostile territory to Fort Laramie (from whence they were posted by telegraph). Reynolds later admitted that he himself had seen no gold. The expedition's chief geologist, Newton H. Winchell, said the same thing. Custer, however, insisted that he'd found the "New Eldorado" in a letter to the *New York World*, this time using his own name, published Dec. 13, 1874. How frequently the "Boy General" indulged in such deceptions is unclear, but was certainly often. He was, for instance, assigned the code name "Alta" for purposes of submitting whatever stories he chose on "the Black Hills situation," whether "signed or unsigned," to James Gordon Bennett, publisher of the *New York Herald* (letter dated April 1, 1875; Elizabeth Bacon Custer Collection, Little Big Horn National Monument, Package 31).

Rosebud Creek on June 17,[561] and Custer's regiment, overconfident and expecting to perpetrate another Washita-style massacre, was shredded in the valley of the Little Big Horn on the 25th[*]—the writing was on the wall.

As early as 1867, General of the Army William Tecumseh Sherman had opined that, "We must act with vindictive earnestness against the [Lakotas], even to their extermination, men, women and children."[†] During the winter of 1876–77, Ranald Mackenzie was brought to Wyoming to duplicate his success against the Comanches and Kiowas a year earlier. Beginning in mid-October, the colonel's command, as well as forces under Generals Crook and Miles, scoured the Powder River Country, attacking each village they came across.[562] Mackenzie's November 25 assault on the camp of Dull Knife, a noted Cheyenne leader, was indicative:

> It was the month of the Deer Rutting Moon, and very cold, with deep snow in the shaded places and ice-crusted snow in the open places. Mackenzie had brought his troops up to attacking positions during the night, and struck the Cheyennes at first daylight... They caught the Cheyennes in their lodges, killing many of them as they came

---

[*]Custer had definite presidential ambitions by 1876, and felt that one more "great victory" over the Indians would enhance his chances. He therefore disobeyed orders to locate but not to attack the Lakotas on his own. Unaware of the size of the force arrayed against him—nobody knew of Crook's defeat on the Rosebud at this point—and trusting to his fabled "luck," he then repeated his mistake at the Washita by not conducting a proper reconnaissance of his adversary before attacking. Believing he'd encountered merely one more defenseless encampment, he iced the cake by dividing his regiment into three parts in order to trap all who might attempt to escape his intended massacre. The result was that the body of troops under his personal command was completely wiped out, while a second, under Major Marcus Reno, was very nearly so. The Lakotas and Cheyennes, again led by Crazy Horse, then pinned the survivors down for two solid days; Connell, *Son of the Morning Star, op. cit.*; Van de Water, *Glory Hunter, op. cit.*; Edgar I. Stewart, *Custer's Luck* (Norman: University of Oklahoma Press, 1955); Mari Sandoz, *The Battle of the Little Big Horn* (New York: Curtis, 1966); Steven E. Ambrose, *Crazy Horse and Custer: The Parallel Lives of Two American Warriors* (Garden City, NY: Doubleday, 1975).

[†]Quoted in Axelrod, *Chronicle of the Indian Wars, op. cit.*, p. 203. A glimpse of what Sherman had in mind was offered on January 23, 1870, when a cavalry force under Major Eugene M. Baker—who had been instructed by General Sheridan to "strike them hard"—attacked a peaceful Piegan village along the Marias River in northern Montana. Of the 173 Indians killed and mutilated, only fifteen were fighting-age males, while fifty or more were children under twelve. Lt. Gustavus Doan, who had served as a scout on the expedition, later described what had happened as a "complete slaughter." Sheridan—and, by extension, Sherman, who supported him fully—defended Baker's action on the basis that the *Cheyennes* had been raiding settlements in southern Kansas, more than 600 miles away; Athearn, *William Tecumseh Sherman, op. cit.*, pp. 278–9; Wesley C. Wilson, "The Army and the Piegans: The Baker Massacre on the Marias, 1870," *North Dakota History*, No. 32, 1965; Robert J. Ege, *"Tell Baker to Strike Them Hard!": Incident on the Marias, Jan. 23, 1870* (Belleview, NB: Old Army Press, 1970). The impact of the massacre on the Piegans, already much-reduced by the smallpox pandemic unleashed at Fort Clark a generation earlier, is discussed in James Welch, *Killing Custer: The Battle of the Little Big Horn and the Fate of the Plains Indians* (New York: W.W. Norton, 1994). Also see John Canfield Ewers, *The Blackfeet: Raiders of the Northern Plains* (Norman: University of Oklahoma Press, 1958).

Big Foot's band of Miniconjou Sioux, before and after. Above, assembled on the Cheyenne River Sioux Reservation in August 1890; below, after being massacred by the 7th Cavalry at Wounded Knee on December 29, 1890. Top photo: National Archives and Records Administration. Bottom photo: U.S. Army

awake. Others ran out naked into the biting cold, the warriors trying to fight off…the onrushing soldiers long enough for their women and children to escape… Some of the best warriors of the Northern Cheyennes sacrificed their lives in those first furious moments of fighting; one of them was Dull Knife's oldest son. Dull Knife and Little Wolf [another prominent leader] finally managed to form a rear guard along the upper ledges of a canyon, but their scanty supply of ammunition was soon exhausted. Little Wolf was shot seven times before he and Dull Knife broke away to join their women and children in full flight toward the Bighorns. Behind them Mackenzie was burning their lodges, and after that was done he herded their captured ponies against the canyon wall and ordered his men to shoot them down…[563]

More than a hundred Cheyennes, two-thirds of them women, children and elders, had been killed before the survivors managed to get away. Their ordeal, however, was just beginning.

> During the first night of flight, twelve infants and several old people froze to death. The next night, the men killed some of the ponies, disemboweled them, and thrust small children inside to keep them from freezing… For three days they tramped across the frozen snow, their bare feet leaving a trail of blood, [before reaching Crazy Horse's Oglala encampment on the Box Elder Creek].[564]

On January 8, Miles's troops located and attacked this village as well, and so the whole process was repeated.[565] And so it went, month after month. By the end of April 1877, even Crazy Horse's people had surrendered, and the last "Sioux recalcitrants"—a handful of Hunkpapas led by Sitting Bull (Tatanka Yatanka) and Gall (Pizi)—had fled to sanctuary in Canada.* In short order, disarmed, dismounted, and dispirited, the Northern Cheyennes were deported to the reservation of their southern cousins in Oklahoma.[566] In the fall, Crazy Horse was assassinated,[567] and rations to the captive Lakotas were suspended until a scattering of leaders finally agreed to sign a document allegedly transferring ownership of the Black Hills to the United States.†

---

*Crazy Horse was promised a reservation in the Powder River Country—a pledge the United States never had any intention of honoring—in exchange for laying down his arms; Brown, *Bury My Heart at Wounded Knee, op. cit.*, pp. 308–10. On those who went to Canada, see Stanley Vestal, *Sitting Bull: Champion of the Sioux* (Norman: University of Oklahoma Press, 1932).

†Ranald Mackenzie suspended rations to captive Lakotas, pending agreement to a cession of the Black Hills, in September 1876. Ultimately, about 15 percent of all adult male Lakotas signed the transfer instrument—a far cry from the 75 percent required to legitimate such cessions under provision of the still-binding 1868 Fort Laramie Treaty—in order to feed their families. Despite the transparent illegality of the proceedings, Congress passed a law taking formal possession of the Hills in February 1877. At about the same time, contrary to the promises made to Crazy Horse, the Unceded Indian Territory was stripped away, and General Sheridan called for extermination of what remained of the northern buffalo herds, partly to confirm Lakota economic dependency, partly to negate their treaty

In September 1878, about half the remaining Northern Cheyennes, horrified at the attrition they were suffering under the conditions imposed upon them in Oklahoma, broke out of their confinement and attempted to return to their Powder River homeland.[568] Led by Dull Knife and Little Wolf, they were stalked by more than 15,000 troops as they struggled northward, and the initial body of "renegades" was again ground down to about half its size.[569] Finally, in utter exhaustion, Dull Knife's group of some 150 people—composed, as usual, almost exclusively of women, children, and old men—gave themselves up at Camp Robinson, Nebraska. Confined to an unheated guardhouse in the dead of winter, without rations, the prisoners were informed they would be shipped back to the south.[570] At that point, more desperate than ever, they tried to escape again on the night of January 9, 1879.

> [The] soldiers began overtaking scattered bands of women and children, killing many of them before they could surrender… When the morning came, the soldiers herded 65 Cheyenne prisoners, 23 of them wounded, back into [Camp] Robinson… Only 38 of those who had escaped were still alive and free; 32 were together, moving north through the hills and pursued by four companies of cavalry and a battery of mountain artillery… For several days the cavalrymen followed the 32 Cheyennes, until at last they were trapped in a deep buffalo wallow. Charging to the edge of the wallow, the cavalrymen emptied their carbines into it… Only nine Cheyennes survived.[571]

By this point, fewer than 500 Northern Cheyennes—less than 10 percent of their original number—remained alive.[572] Although the Lakotas never came this close to outright extermination, they experienced considerable population losses during the early reservation years. By the late 1880s, nearly 90 percent of their treaty territory had been taken from them, their sociopolitical and spiritual life had been abolished under penalty of law, and they were being deliberately starved.[573] One response to these circumstances was an increasingly widespread adoption of the Ghost Dance—a belief that if certain rituals were performed with sufficient devotion, the whites would disappear, while the buffalo and other dead relatives would be reborn, making life as it had once been.[574]

While it is obvious that this forlorn practice presented absolutely no threat to the United States or its citizens, the army seized upon it as an

---

claim to their Nebraska hunting territory. This history is well-handled in Inouye, "1986 Black Hills Hearing," *op. cit.* Also see Ward Churchill, "The Earth Is Our Mother: Struggles for American Indian Land and Liberation in the Contemporary United States," in my *Since Predator Came, op. cit.*

opportunity to simultaneously break the last traces of native resistance, and to extract another measure of revenge for the humiliations it had experienced at the hands of the Lakotas in 1868 and 1876.[575] More than 3,000 troops were fielded to put down the Ghost Dance "insurrection," Sitting Bull—who had returned from Canada in 1881—was murdered on December 15, 1890,[576] and the reconstituted Seventh Cavalry captured a terrified group of about 350 Minneconjous, led by Big Foot, on the Wounded Knee Creek on December 28.* On the morning of the 29th, the troops proceeded to massacre their unarmed prisoners, using both rifles and Hotchkiss guns carefully placed on surrounding hills for the purpose.

> [All] witnesses agree that from the moment it opened fire, [the Seventh] ceased to be a military unit and became a mass of infuriated men intent on butchery. Women and children attempted to escape by running up a dry ravine, but were pursued and slaughtered—there is no other word—by hundreds of maddened soldiers, while shells from the Hotchkiss guns, which had been moved to allow them to sweep the ravine, continued to burst among them. The line of bodies afterward was found to extend more than two miles from the camp—and they were all women and children. A few survivors eventually found shelter in brushy gullies here and there, and their pursuers had scouts call out that women and children could come out of hiding because they had nothing to fear... Some small boys crept out and were surrounded by soldiers who then butchered them. Nothing Indian that lived was safe.[577]

The dead—more than 300 in all—were buried in a mass grave on New Year's Day 1891,[578] while editorialists like L. Frank Baum of the *Aberdeen Saturday Pioneer* (who would later attain fame as the gentle author of the *Wizard of Oz*) called for the army to "finish the job" by exterminating *all* remaining Indians. "The nobility of the Redskin is extinguished... The Whites, by law of conquest, by justice of civilization, are masters of the American continent, and the best safety of the frontier settlements will be secured by the total annihilation of the few remaining Indians. Why not annihilation? Their glory has fled,

---

*The commander of the Seventh Cavalry at this point was Colonel George A. Forsyth, who, aside from any desire he might have had to "even the score" for the Little Big Horn debacle, had more personal motives for seeking revenge. In September 1868, he had been head of an elite fifty-man ranger unit sent out by Sheridan to track and kill Cheyennes. He had succeeded too well, finding a large group of Dog Soldiers led by Roman Nose on the Beaver Creek, just across the Kansas line in Colorado. The Indians had besieged Forsyth and his erstwhile Indian-killers on a tiny sand spit in the creek for several days, killing or wounding nearly all of them before they suffered the additional indignity of being rescued by a company of Tenth Cavalry troopers (an African American regiment, also called the "Buffalo Soldiers"). Forsyth finally settled accounts for his humiliating ordeal at "Beecher's Island"—so-named in honor of Lt. Frederick Beecher, who died there—on December 29, 1890; Brown, *Bury My Heart at Wounded Knee, op. cit.*, pp. 164–6, 401–2.

their spirit broken, their manhood effaced; better that they should die than live the miserable wretches that they are."[579] Thus ended the "Indian Wars."

Digestion and Domination

It is true that the United States did not follow through on calls such as Baum's to effect the total physical extirpation of indigenous people within its borders. Then again, there was really no need for the country to absorb the expense entailed in doing so. With the native population reduced to not more than 2.5 percent of its original size, the United States had expropriated 97.5 percent of the aboriginal landbase.[580] The fragments of geography left to the Indians by 1900 were considered worthless, unfarmable, arid patches of dust deemed remote enough to allow for the steady die-off of survivors, conveniently out of sight and mind of the dominant society. And there were, of course, federal policies designed to help the process along.[581]

At least as early as the administration of Ulysses S. Grant in the mid-1870s, there was an influential lobby which held that the final eradication of native cultures and population could be achieved more cost-effectively—and with a far greater appearance of "humanitarianism"—through a process of "assimilation" than by force of arms.[582] By the first years of the twentieth century, officials like Indian Commissioner Francis Leupp were explaining that the objective was to "kill the Indian, spare the man," to which end the government's policy of assimilation constituted a "great pulverizing engine for breaking up the tribal mass."[583] A decade later, Leupp's successor, Charles Burke articulated the same principle: "It is not consistent with the general welfare to promote [American Indian national or cultural] characteristics and organization."[584] In effect, it was the express goal of federal policy to bring about the "digestion" of what little remained of Native North America as rapidly and efficiently as possible.

Leupp and Burke were making specific reference to the effects of the 1887 General Allotment Act which voided the customary collectivity of land holdings still prevailing among American Indians during the early reservation period, imposing in its stead the supposedly more "civilized and enlightened" Anglo-Saxon model of individual property ownership.[585] Under provision of the Act, Indians were universally defined on the basis of "blood quantum"—that is, genetic rather than national-political criteria—for the first time under U.S. law.[586] Once each Indian eligible to be considered one under this new definition had been allotted his or her individual 160-acre parcel, the balance of reserved territory was declared "surplus" and opened to corporate use, homesteading by non-Indians, or conversion into national parks, forests, or military reservations. Not only were most indigenous societies thoroughly atomized by the process, which continued until 1934, but about 100 million of the approximately 150 million acres remaining in native hands at the outset were stripped away.[587]

Several other components were attached to this centerpiece of federal assimilationism. By 1894, virtually the entire range of indigenous spiritual practices had been outlawed, a measure expressly intended to eradicate all vestiges of the traditions which afforded cohesion and continuity to native cultures.[588] Meanwhile, the bulk of all American Indian children were forcibly removed from their communities at the earliest possible age and sent to remote boarding schools where they were systematically deculturated. Kept in these institutions for years on end, they were prohibited not only from practicing their religions, but from speaking their languages, dressing or wearing their hair in the customary manner, and often from having even cursory contact with friends and families as well. Meanwhile, they were subjected to sustained indoctrination in Christianity and Western values, in combination with the rudimentary skills which would allow them to serve as laborers and functionaries for the dominant society.[589]

As of 1924, under provision of the Indian Citizenship Act, all indigenous people within U.S. boundaries were unilaterally declared to be citizens of the United States—with all the obligations attending such status—while retaining mere "membership" in their own "tribes."[590] Most likely, this was intended to be the culminating gesture of assimilation in its original form, with all remaining reserved areas to be dissolved and the residual native population dispersed over the next few years.[591] To all appearances, it was only the entirely unforeseen circumstance of certain reservations proving to be extraordinarily mineral-rich which prevented this consummating process of sociocultural digestion from occurring.[592]

By the late 1920s, two belated discoveries had been made. First, it was becoming clear that the "useless" tracts of real estate left to Indians actually contained vast quantities of coal, oil, natural gas, copper, and other minerals (later it was found that about two-thirds of all U.S. "domestic" uranium deposits are also located in reservation areas).[593] Second, as the experience of the Oklahoma oil boom had amply demonstrated, placing these resources in public domain was not the most efficient, or even profitable, manner in which to exploit them.[594]

Only by continuing to hold reserved native lands in trust could the federal government retain its prerogative to engage in centralized planning—which resources would be "developed" at what pace, by whom, and at what royalty rates—with respect to disposition of the minerals within them.[595] It thus became necessary to preserve the reservations and at least some of the peoples resident to them, albeit in a perpetually destitute and subjugated condition.

Almost overnight, the more directly annihilatory aspects of assimilationism were abandoned in favor of a relatively permanent internal colonial model.[596] Under provision of the 1934 Indian Reorganization Act (IRA), the remains of traditional indigenous forms of governance were supplanted by "more democratic" structures designed in Washington and patterned after the sorts of puppet regimes already perfected in Africa and Asia by the European imperial powers (variations of which would shortly be deployed in Europe itself by the nazis).[597] These served—and continue to serve—as the essential apparatus of control by which native resources might be consumed on an almost cost-free basis while providing the illusion of indigenous endorsement of and participation in the process of exploitation.[598]

The most obvious by-product of this arrangement has been that contemporary Native North Americans, given their resource profile and per capita land holdings, should be the wealthiest sector of the continent's populace, but are instead the most impoverished. Indians incur by far the lowest annual and lifetime incomes of any group on the continent, and the highest rates of unemployment. We also experience, by a decisive margin, the highest rates of infant mortality, death by malnutrition, exposure, and plague disease.[599] Such conditions produce the sort of endemic despair that generates chronic alcoholism and other forms of substance abuse among more than half the native population—factors contributing not only to further erosion in physical health but to very high accident rates—as well as rates of teen suicide up to 14.5 times the national average.*

---

*The effects of alcohol, consciously used by Europeans/Euroamericans since colonial times as a sort of "chemical weapon" to dissipate indigenous societies, has received inexcusably short shrift in this essay. The author apologizes for this deficiency and refers readers to Joy Leland's *Firewater Myths: American Indian Drinking and Drug Addiction* (New Brunswick, NJ: Rutgers Center for Alcohol Studies, 1976). For comparable data on Canada, see, e.g., N. Geisbrecht, J. Brown, et al., *Alcohol Problems in Northwestern Ontario: Preliminary Report on Consumption Patterns, and Public Order and Public Health Problems* (Toronto: Addiction Research Foundation, 1977). An excellent case study of the effects of the complex of factors at issue will be found in Anastasia M. Shkilnyk's *A Poison Stronger Than Love: The Destruction of an Ojibwa Community* (New Haven: Yale University Press, 1985).

The upshot is that, during the late twentieth century, reservation-based American Indian men have a life expectancy of only 44.6 years, as compared to a longevity among general-population males of 71.8 years. Reservation-based women can expect to live about three years longer than their male counterparts, as compared to general-population females, who live an average of eight years longer than men. Put another way, every time a reservation Indian dies—or, conversely, every time one is born—approximately one-third of a lifetime is lost.[600] The data among urbanized Indians, at this point about 55 percent of all federally recognized native people, is only marginally better. Hence, the net impact of the modern North American internal colonial order on the indigenous population is something on the order of 30 percent attrition, generation in, generation out.*

"Genocidal" is the only reasonable manner in which to describe the imposition, as a matter of policy, of such physiocultural effects upon any target group.[601] This is all the more true when one factors in specific initiatives undertaken by federal authorities to control the size of the native population, both locally and overall. These include, beginning in the late 1940s—partly to cut the already minimal costs associated with "supporting" them on the reservations, partly to clear portions of the reservation for purposes of mining—the resumption of assimilationism's program of coerced removal of indigenous people from their lands and societies.† During the 1950s and early '60s, this effort was coupled to the outright termination of recognition of the existence of some 108 indigenous nations—none of them possessing substantial mineral wealth—whose reserved landbases were then simply dissolved.[602]

---

* *Chart Series Book, op. cit.* This is not to say that sectors of other population groups—e.g., Latino migrant workers and inner-city blacks—do not share the degree of impoverishment, attendant maladies, and truncated life spans suffered by Native Americans. In these examples, however, it is a portion of the overall population which is at issue. With American Indians, the data derives from the *entire* population aggregate; U.S. Bureau of the Census, *General Social and Economic Characteristics: United States Summary* (Washington, D.C.: U.S. Government Printing Office, 1983). Also see Alan L. Sorkin, *The Urban American Indian* (Lexington, MA: Lexington Books, 1978); M. Belinda Tucker, Waddell M. Herron, Dan Nakasai, Luis Ortiz-Franco, and Lenore Stiffarm, *Ethnic Groups in Los Angeles: Quality of Life Indicators* (Los Angeles: UCLA Ethnic Studies Centers, 1987).

† Donald L. Fixico, *Termination and Relocation: Federal Indian Policy, 1945–1960* (Albuquerque: University of New Mexico Press, 1986). Another aspect concerns the fact that when the Indian landbase was fixed through allotment during the late nineteenth and early twentieth centuries, it was pegged to the approximately 250,000 eligible individuals alive at the time. Given the official anticipation that Indians would shortly die out altogether, no provision was made to accommodate a resurgence in the numbers of native people. Hence, when federal policy shifted to internal colonialism, and the indigenous population consequently began to rebound from its 1890 nadir, the reservation landbase was quickly outstripped; Ethel J. Williams, "Too Little Land, Too Many Heirs: The Indian Heirship Land Problem," *Washington Law Review*, No. 46, 1971.

A decade later, even more draconian methods were employed when the so-called "Indian Health Service" (IHS) of the Bureau of Indian Affairs administered a secret program resulting in the involuntary—and frequently completely uninformed—sterilization of about 42 percent of all American Indian women of childbearing age before it was allegedly halted in 1976.* At about the same time, an ongoing program was initiated to disperse and destroy the largest remaining enclave of traditional Indians in the United States—the approximately 13,000 Diné of the Big Mountain region in Arizona—in order to make way for the draglines of the Peabody Coal Company.[603]

A decade later still, in the mid-to late 1980s, Inuit children on Alaska's oil-rich North Slope were forced to serve as guinea pigs in the "field testing" of hepatitis vaccines which had been banned from international distribution by the World Health Organization (WHO) because of a presumed link to the transmission of HIV microbes. When the WHO report was discovered by Alaska natives, who then refused to allow further inoculation of their offspring, the tests were shifted southward, targeting reservation children in the lower 48 states.[604] Although the WHO's suspicions are as yet unconfirmed, it is undeniable that the federal government demonstrated its willingness to sacrifice an entire generation of several indigenous groups in an effort to challenge the data, primarily to enhance the profitability of at least two major pharmaceutical corporations.†

---

*The government essentially conceded the allegations after hearings on the matter were forced in Oklahoma, and affected an "administrative remedy" by removing the IHS from the BIA and situating it in the Department of Health and Human Services. Needless to say, no one was prosecuted for this perpetration of a genocidal program. Indeed, so far as is known, no one even lost a job; Brint Dillingham, "Indian Women and IHS Sterilization Practices," *American Indian Journal*, Vol. 3, No. 1, Jan. 1977; Janet Larson, "And Then There Were None," *Christian Century*, Jan. 26, 1977; "Women of All Red Nations, Native American Women" (New York: International Indian Treaty Council, 1978); Robin Jarrell, "Women and Children First: The Forced Sterilization of American Indian Women" (undergraduate thesis, Wesley College, 1978). The same sorts of programs were also aimed during this period against other communities of color, e.g.: the forced sterilization of about one-third of the women of child-bearing age in Puerto Rico, 44 percent of the Puertorriqueñas in New Haven, and 51 percent in Hartford, Connecticut; Margarita, *Politica Sexual y Socialización Politica de la Mujer Puertorriqueña la Consolidación del Bloque Histórico Colonial de Puerto Rico* (Río Piedras, P.R.: Ediciones Huracán, 1989); Committee for Abortion rights and Against Sterilization Abuse, *Women Under Attack: Abortion, Sterilization Abuse, and Reproductive Freedom* (New York: CARASA, 1979).

†Such medical experimentation is actually nothing new for the natives of the North Slope. In 1995, it was disclosed on the *60 Minutes* TV news program that, during the early to-mid-1950s, the Department of Defense secretly fed doses of refined uranium to unsuspecting Inuits in order to study the long-term effects of such nuclear contamination on the human organism. It was fully expected that the test subjects would suffer all manner of physical maladies as a result, produce defective offspring (if they were not sterilized by internalized radiation), and mostly suffer miserable deaths from cancer. The mentality which considered this to be acceptable practice is obviously quite consistent

Such priorities correspond perfectly with those evident in federal policymakers' practice, from 1952 onward, of situating U.S. mining and milling of uranium—and with these processes, the highly radioactive waste byproducts which attend them—almost exclusively in reservation areas, despite the fact that substantial ore deposits were known to be available elsewhere.[605] The results of this practice are a maximization of profits for energy corporations with increasingly severe carcinogenic/mutogenic effects on the Diné, Lagunas, and other indigenous peoples.[606] This couples readily to federal plans to locate nuclear-waste storage facilities and accompanying contamination on reservations such as that of the Mescalero Apaches in New Mexico, and in predominately native-occupied environments such as Yucca Mountain, in Newe Segobia, the much-bombed Nevada treaty territory of the Western Shoshoni.[607]

The situation of Native North Americans thus remains much as it has been since the moment the Old World predator landed in the hemisphere. Liquidated to the extent deemed necessary or convenient by the invader—in precisely the fashion, and at exactly the pace the invader's capacity to inflict liquidation has allowed—we are maintained alive at all primarily as a matter of utility by our colonizers, and then only in a form considered acceptable to them. No amount of humanitarian rhetoric, demographic sleights of hand, or deformity and denial of history can alter the substance of these essential realities. The genocide which has been perpetrated against the indigenous peoples of this continent is an experience unparalleled in its scope, magnitude, and duration (other than that of the native peoples of Ibero-America). Moreover, it is a process which is ongoing.[*]

Alternatives

To paraphrase Karl Marx, the purpose of studying history is not so much to understand it—although that is certainly important enough in its own

---

with that analyzed by Robert Jay Lifton in his book, *The Nazi Doctors* (*op. cit.*). Also see Arthur L. Caplan, ed., *When Medicine Went Mad: Bioethics and the Holocaust* (Ottawa, NJ: Humana Press, 1992); George J. Annas, *The Nazi Doctors and the Nuremberg Code: Human Rights in Medical Experimentation* (New York: Oxford University Press, 1992).

[*] This statement is in no way intended to diminish the significance of genocides suffered by other peoples throughout the world, historically or presently, in places like Rwanda and East Timor. One genocide is as horrible as another. Each has its own uniquely awful attributes. The point is that what occurred, and is occurring, in the Americas is indeed as bad as anything that happened to anyone, anywhere, ever, and that there are substantial lessons to be learned from this fact.

right—as it is to acquire the conceptual/intellectual tools with which to change it.[609] This is as true with regard to the perpetration of genocide as it is with anything else. "To identify the relevant parameters is the first step in the prevention of future genocides," observe Frank Chalk and Kurt Jonassohn in an important comparative study of the phenomenon.[609] The identification of these parameters is, however, largely contingent upon the willingness of scholars to call things by their right names, inculcating among people of conscience everywhere an ever-increasing consciousness of what genocide actually is, how and why it has occurred historically, and the ways in which its legacy has shaped our contemporary sociopolitical, cultural, and economic environments.[610]

> This is the only way in which we are ever going to be able to arrive at situation in which genocide is not only "unthinkable" for most people, but impossible or at least much more difficult to perpetrate than it has been for a very long time. It is also the only way in which those who have or do engage in genocidal practices can ever be held accountable for their crimes, both figuratively and literally. We are speaking here not merely of a matter of simple justice, but of the question of sheer survival for millions of human beings.[611]

Of course, the myriad horrors recounted in this essay can never be undone. The outcomes deriving from their cumulative effect can, however. The course of future history *is* alterable. Not only can the continuing genocide of North America's native peoples at last be halted, but the benefits of that genocide—real, potential, and perceived—can ultimately be revoked.[612] Absent the tangible or imaginary attainment of profit, racial/ethnic/national/religious supremacy, and ideological purity which has always motivated genocidal activity, and the incentive to engage in it for the most part disappears. If such lack of likely gain were coupled to the prospect of punishment—whether directly or even indirectly—through the assessments of posterity, we would begin to achieve some degree of genuine disincentive to genocidal behavior.* This last can be made to stand as a barrier against those who would seek to commit genocide against other peoples, in other places, in the years ahead.

---

*The question of "indirect punishment, through the assessments of posterity," may be confusing. This is to say that in heroicizing people like Columbus and Cortés, George Washington and Andrew Jackson, Kit Carson and Custer, society strongly reinforces the notion that their genocidal conduct was/is an appropriate and acceptable manner in which to attain fame and "immortality." Conversely, placing them where they belong in the historical lexicon—alongside the likes of Attila the Hun and Heinrich Himmler—would tend to convey the opposite message. Historical villification is, after all, a form of punishment *not* aspired to by many people.

Creation of such circumstances comprises an agenda truly worthy of pursuit and fulfillment. It can be actualized, however, only through an unflinching willingness to recognize things for what they have been—and, by extension, for what they are—and then to act accordingly. Any such posture entails not only an unstinting and rigorous effort to apprehend the essential meanings of historical processes, but to confront, unmask and thoroughly debunk those who seek, whether individually or institutionally, to obfuscate, degrade, or deny such meanings. If the present essay can be said to have contributed in any way to such an endeavor—and that has been the sole purpose of preparing it—then the effort will have been well warranted.

Notes

1. U.S. Bureau of the Census, *Fifteenth Census of the United States, 1930: The Indian Population of the United States and Alaska* (Washington, D.C.: U.S. Government Printing Office, 1937) esp. Table II, "Indian Population by Divisions and States, 1890–1930," p. 3. The Canadian counts are taken from James M. Mooney, *The Aboriginal Population of America North of Mexico* (Washington, D.C.: Smithsonian Miscellaneous Collections LXXX, No. 7, Smithsonian Institution, 1928) p. 33.

2. See, e.g., B.O. Flower, "An Interesting Representative of a Vanishing Race," *Arena*, July 1896; Simon Pokagon, "The Future of the Red Man," *Forum*, Aug. 1897; William R. Draper, "The Last of the Red Race," *Cosmopolitan*, Jan. 1902; Charles M. Harvey, "The Last Race Rally of Indians," *World's Work*, May 1904; E. S. Curtis, "Vanishing Indian Types: The Tribes of the Northwest Plains," *Scribner's*, June 1906; James Mooney, "The Passing of the Indian," *Proceedings of the Second Pan American Scientific Congress, Sec. 1: Anthropology* (Washington, D.C.: Smithsonian Institution, 1909–1910); Joseph K. Dixon, *The Vanishing Race: The Last Great Indian Council* (Garden City, NY: Doubleday, 1913); Stanton Elliot, "The End of the Trail," *Overland Monthly*, July 1915; Ella Higginson, "The Vanishing Race," *Red Man*, Feb. 1916; Ales Hrdlicka, "The Vanishing Indian," *Science*, No. 46, 1917; J.L. Hill, *The Passing of the Indian and the Buffalo* (Long Beach, CA: n.p., 1917); John Collier, "The Vanishing American," *Nation*, Jan. 11, 1928.

3. This is handled well in Wilber R. Jacobs, "The Tip of the Iceberg: Precolumbian Demography and Some Implications for Revisionism," *William and Mary Quarterly*, 3rd Ser., No. 31, 1974.

4. The concept and its application are well articulated by Boyce Richardson in his *People of Terra Nullius: Betrayal and Rebirth in Canada* (Seattle/Vancouver: University of Washington Press/Douglas McIntire, 1993). More broadly, see L.C. Green and Olive P. Duncan, *The Law of Nations in the New World* (Edmonton: University of Alberta Press, 1989); Robert A. Williams, Jr., *The American Indian in Western Legal Thought: The Discourses of Conquest* (New York: Oxford University Press, 1990).

5. See, e.g., the treatment in James Kirby Martin, Randy Roberts, Steven Mintz, Linda O. McMurry and James H. Jones, *America and Its People, Vol. 1: To 1877* (New York: HarperCollins College, [2nd. ed.] 1993). This is a standard text used in undergraduate American history courses. For analysis of media interface, see my *Fantasies of the Master Race: Literature, Cinema and the Colonization of American Indians* (Monroe, ME: Common Courage Press, 1992).

6. Kirby Martin, et al. (*America and Its People, op. cit.*, pp. 17–19), for example, manage to extol the disease theme three times in three pages.

7. James Axtell, probably the leading U.S. "ethnohistorian"—funny how "history" itself is reserved for matters of specific Euro-derivation while the record of everyone else requires a prefix—of the North American colonial period, made these representative characterizations during a public lecture at the University of Florida, April 1, 1991 (tape on file).

8. See, e.g., Mooney, *Aboriginal Population, op. cit.*; John Reed Swanton, *The Indian Tribes of North America* (Washington, D.C.: Bureau of American Ethnography, Smithsonian Institution, 1952).

9. The new orthodoxy was first enunciated by Douglas H. Ubelaker in his "Prehistoric New World Population Size: Historical Review and Current Appraisal of North American Estimates," *American Journal of Physical Anthropology*, No. 45, 1976. The number he eventually arrives at is precisely 2,171,125 (1,850,011 in the 48 contiguous states area; 73,326 in Alaska; 237,798 in Canada; 10,000 in Greenland). Also see his "The Sources and Methods for Mooney's Estimates of North American Indian Populations" in William H. Deneven, ed., *The Native Population of the Americas in 1492* (Madison: University of Wisconsin Press, 1976), and "North American Indian Population Size: Changing Perspectives," in John W. Verano and Douglas H. Ubelaker, eds., *Disease and Demography in the Americas* (Washington, D.C.: Smithsonian Institution, 1992).

10. Mooney died in 1921. His draft manuscript was then edited by John Reed Swanton, and published in 1928: *The Aboriginal Population of America North of Mexico, op. cit.* As Jennings points out, the "estimates were listed in tabular form, by region and tribe, without specific documentation. Discussion of the figures was general, and authority rested on a rather sketchy bibliography"; Francis Jennings, *The Invasion of America: Indians, Colonialism and the Cant of Conquest* (Chapel Hill: University of North Carolina Press, 1975) pp. 16–7. It should be noted that Colonel Garrick Mallery of the Smithsonian Institution had long argued—and quite vociferously—that the "official" estimate should be far lower still: "Investigation shows that the aboriginal population within the present United States at the beginning of the Columbian

period could not have exceeded much over 500,000"; see his "The Present and Former Number of Our Indians," *Proceedings of the American Association for the Advancement of Science*, No. 26, 1877, p. 365.

11. Ibid., p. 17. The reference is to John Gorham Palfrey, *History of New England* (Boston: Stine, 1858–1890).

12. Jennings, *Invasion of America, op. cit.*, p. 20; at p. 17, he notes that "Palfrey's virulent bias against Indians appears without disguise whenever he mentions them." The emergence of actual "scientific racism" in America—and it was the American prototype which served as a model for the rest of the world, including Germany—can probably be dated from Samuel George Morton's *Crania Americana, or, A Comparative View of the Skulls of Various Aboriginal Nations of North and South America* (Philadelphia: John Pennington, 1839); see generally, William Stanton, *The Leopard's Spots: Scientific Attitudes Towards Race in America, 1815–1859* (Chicago: University of Chicago Press, 1960); Steven Jay Gould, *The Mismeasure of Man* (New York: W.W. Norton, 1981).

13. See, e.g., Mooney, *Aboriginal Population, op. cit.*, p. 3.

14. Jennings, *Invasion of America, op. cit.*, p. 17.

15. J.H. Spinden, "The Population of Ancient America," *Geographical Review*, No. 18, 1928; "Population of Ancient America," in *Anthropological Report* (Washington, D.C.: Smithsonian Institution, 1929).

16. A.L. Kroeber, "Native American Population," *American Anthropologist*, N.S., XXXVI, 1934.

17. A.L. Kroeber, *Cultural and Natural Areas of Native North America* (Berkeley and Los Angeles: University of California Publications in American Archaeology and Ethnology XXXVIII, 1939) p. 177.

18. Jennings, *Invasion of America, op. cit.*, pp. 18–9. He is citing A.L. Kroeber, *Cultural and Natural Areas, op. cit.*, pp. 148, 149.

19. See, e.g., A.L. Kroeber, "Evolution, History and Culture," in Theodora Kroeber, ed., *An Anthropologist Looks at History* (Berkeley: University of California Press, 1966).

20. A.L. Kroeber, *Cultural and Natural Areas, op. cit.*

21. See, e.g., Carl Ortwin Sauer, *The Early Spanish Main* (Berkeley: University of California Press, 1966) and *Sixteenth Century North America* (Berkeley: University of California Press, 1971); Woodrow W. Borah, "New Demographic Research on the Sixteenth Century in Mexico," in Howard F. Cline, ed., *Latin American History, Vol. II: Essays on Its Study and Teaching, 1898–1965* (Berkeley: University of California Press, 1966); Sherburne F. Cook and Woodrow W. Borah, *The Population of Mixteca-Alta, 1520–1960* (Berkeley: University of California Ibero-Americana L, 1968); Sherburne F. Cook and Leslie B. Simpson, *The Population of Mexico in the Sixteenth Century* (Berkeley: University of California Ibero-Americana, No. 31, 1948).

22. A.L. Kroeber, *Cultural and Natural Areas, op. cit.*, pp. 177, 181. As may be seen in the preceding note and those following, the work of the "Berkeley dissidents" didn't really begin to see print until after Kroeber's death, and then only through the press of their home institution.

23. The method is explained most clearly in Henry F. Dobyns, "Estimating Aboriginal American Population: An Appraisal of Techniques and a New Hemispheric Estimate," *Current Anthropology*, No. 7, 1966.

24. Woodrow W. Borah and Sherburne F. Cook, *The Aboriginal Population of Central Mexico on the Eve of the Spanish Conquest* (Berkeley: University of California Ibero-American No. 43, 1963).

25. The estimate was surfaced in Woodrow W. Borah, "America as Model: The Impact of European Expansion on the Non-European World," *Actas y Memorias, XXXV Congreso Internacional de Americanistas, Mexico, 1962: Vol. III* (Mexico City: Editorial Libros de Mexico, 1964). Also see Woodrow W. Borah and Sherburne F. Cook, "Conquest and Population: A Demographic Approach to Mexican History," *Proceedings of the American Philosophical Society*, CXIII, 1969.

26. Dobyns, "Estimating Aboriginal Populations," *op. cit.*

27. Bruce Trigger, "The Destruction of Huronia: A Study in Economic and Cultural Change, 1609–1650," *Transactions of the Royal Canadian Institute*, XXXIII, 1960. Also see Trigger's *The Huron: The Farmers of the North* (New York: Case Studies in Cultural Anthropology, 1969), and John A. Dickinson, "The Pre-Contact Huron Population: A Reappraisal," *Ontario History*, No. 72, 1980.

28. Jennings, *Invasion of America, op. cit.*, p. 29. He relies mainly on the records of Daniel Gookin, dating from 1674, lodged in the Massachusetts State Historical Society Collection (1st Ser., I). Other

references include a 1634 manuscript by William Wood, published under the title *New Englands Prospect* in Boston in 1865.

29. Editors, *The World Almanac, 1973* (New York: National Geographic Society, 1972) p. 470.

30. Dobyns, "Estimating Aboriginal Populations," *op. cit.* The print elements of Dobyns' research base are thorough elaborated and analyzed in his *Native American Historical Demography: A Critical Bibliography* (Bloomington: Indiana University Press, 1976). It was in this period that Jacobs ("The Tip of the Iceberg," *op. cit.*) weighed in with his important essay on the implications of revised demography.

31. Henry F. Dobyns, *Their Number Become Thinned: Native American Population Dynamics in Eastern North America* (Knoxville: University of Tennessee Press, 1983) pp. 34–45.

32. Ibid., p. 41.

33. Ibid., p. 42. In a public lecture delivered at the University of Florida in April 1988, Dobyns indicated his continuing research had led him to conclude that the hemispheric estimate should be revised upward to 145 million. The basis for this determination remains unpublished, however.

34. See, e.g., David Henige, "If Pigs Could Fly: Timucuan Population and Native American Historical Demography," *Journal of Interdisciplinary History*, No. 16, 1985–1986; "On the Current Devaluation on the Notion of Evidence: A Rejoinder to Dobyns," *Ethnohistory*, No. 36, 1989. Also see Russell Thornton, "But How Thick Were They? A Review Essay of *Their Number Become Thinned*," *Contemporary Sociology*, No. No. 13, 1984. Dean R. Snow and Kim M. Lamphear, "European Contact and Depopulation in the Northeast: The Timing of the First Epidemics," *Ethnohistory*, No. 35, 1988.

35. Russell Thornton, *American Indian Holocaust and Survival: A Population History Since 1492* (Norman: University of Oklahoma Press, 1987) pp. xvii, 242. The higher end of the range is expressed in his "American Indian Historical Demography: A Review Essay with Suggestions for the Future," *American Indian Culture and Research Journal*, No. 3, 1979.

36. See, e.g., Kirkpatrick Sale, *The Conquest of Paradise: Christopher Columbus and the Columbian Legacy* (New York: Alfred A. Knopf, 1990) p. 316.

37. For the paleoconservative response, see, e.g., David Henige, "Their Numbers Become Thick: Native American Historical Demography as Expiation," in James A. Clifton ed., *The Invented Indian: Cultural Fictions and Government Policies* (New Brunswick, NJ: Transaction Books, 1990). For analysis of the book itself, which includes not only Henige's masterpiece of reactionary stupidity but another by attorney Allan Van Gestel arguing that Indians never existed at all, see my essay "The New Racism: A Critique of James A. Clifton's *The Invented Indian*" in *Fantasies of the Master Race, op. cit.*

38. A readily accessible estimate of sixteen million for the area north of the Río Grande was published by Emmanuel Henri Dieudonné Domenech in his book *Seven Years Residence in the Great Deserts of North America* (London: Green, Longman & Roberts) in 1860. An even earlier, but perhaps less credible, rendering of exactly the same estimate was given by George Catlin in his 1844 *Letters and Notes on the Manners, Customs and Conditions of the North American Indians* (New York: Dover, 1973 reprint). For analysis, see Russell Thornton, "Implications of Catlin's American Indian Population Estimates for Revision of Mooney's Estimate," *American Journal of Physical Anthropology*, No. 49, 1978.

39. Jennings, *Invasion of America, op. cit.*, p. 24.

40. A.L. Kroeber, *Cultural and Natural Areas, op. cit.*, p. 145. One example: far from challenging it, Smithsonian-aligned luminaries Harold E. Driver and William C. Massey endorsed this antilogical notion, unsupported by any evidence at all, as a "notable" conclusion; *Comparative Studies of North American Indians* (New York: American Philosophical Society, *Transactions*, N.S., XLVII, pt. ii, 1957) p. 214.

41. Vance Haynes, "Elephant-hunting in North America," *Scientific American*, Vol. 214, No. 6, 1966; Paul S. Martin and H.E. Wright, eds., *Pleistocene Extinctions: The Search for a Cause* (New Haven, CT: Yale University Press, 1967); Paul S. Martin and J.E. Moisiman, "Simulating Overkill by Paleo-Indians, *American Scientist*, Vol. 63, No. 3, May–June 1975. Smithsonian dioramas and literature consistently depict such drivel as fact.

42. R. Douglas Hurt, *American Indian Agriculture: Prehistory to the Present* (Lawrence: University Press of Kansas, 1987) pp. 38–9, 55.

43. Jacobs, "The Tip of the Iceberg," *op. cit.*

44. Jennings (*Invasion of America, op. cit.*, p. 30) aptly describes North America as a "widowed" rather than "virgin" land.

45. Paul Rassinier, *Le Drame des Juifs Européens* (Paris: Les Sept Couleurs, 1964), published in English translation as *The Drama of the European Jews* (Silver Springs, MD: Steppingstones, 1975); Richard Harwood *Did Six Million Really Die?* (Richmond, Surrey: Historical Review Press, 1974); Arthur R. Butz, *The Hoax of the Twentieth Century: The Case Against the Presumed Extermination of European Jewry* (Torrance, CA: Institute for Historical Review, 1976) esp. pp. 13–8.

46. See, e.g., Alfred W. Crosby, Jr., "Virgin Soil Epidemics as a Factor in Aboriginal Depopulation in America," *William and Mary Quarterly*, No. 33, 1976.

47. Kirby Martin, et al., *America and Its People, op. cit.*, pp. 17–9.

48. Steven T. Katz, *The Holocaust in Historical Context, Vol. 1: The Holocaust and Mass Death Before the Modern Age* (New York: Oxford University Press, 1992) p. 20.

49. This is quite well documented; see, e.g., Percy M. Ashburn, *The Ranks of Death: A Medical History of the Conquest of America* (New York: Coward-McCann, 1947).

50. Letter of Luís de Quiros and Jean Baptista de Segura to Juan de Hinistrosa, Sept. 12, 1570; quoted in Clifford M. Lewis and Albert J. Loomie, eds., *The Spanish Jesuit Mission in Virginia, 1570–1571* (Chapel Hill: University of North Carolina Press for the Virginia Historical Society, 1953) pp. 89–90.

51. Quoted epigrammatically in Nobel David Cook and W. George Lovell, eds., *"Secret Judgments of God": Old World Disease in Colonial Spanish America* (Norman: University of Oklahoma Press, 1992).

52. Quoted in Ashburn, *The Ranks of Death, op. cit.*, p. 19.

53. Quoted in Alexander S. Salley, Jr., ed., *Narratives of Early Carolina, 1650–1708* (New York: Original Narratives of American History, 1911) pp. 284–5.

54. Jennings, *Invasion of America, op. cit.*, pp. ix–x.

55. Any of a number of works would be adequate to establish this point; see, e.g., J.H. Parry, *The Age of Reconnaissance: Discovery, Exploration and Settlement, 1450–1650* (Berkeley: University of California Press, 1963).

56. The argument is subtly but exceedingly well developed in William McNeill's *Plagues and Peoples* (New York: Doubleday, 1976) and two books by Alfred W. Crosby, Jr., *The Columbian Exchange: Biological and Cultural Consequences of 1492* (Westport, CT: Greenwood Press, 1972) and *Ecological Imperialism: The Biological Expansion of Europe, 900–1900* (Cambridge, MA: Cambridge University Press, 1986).

57. See, e.g., Thomas F.T. Plucknett, *A Concise History of the Common Law* (Rochester, NY: The Lawyers Co-operative, 1936).

58. To the contrary, the relevant legal understandings in the supposedly benighted period of the conquest were in many respects quite sophisticated. As they theoretically applied to Indians, see Lewis Hanke, *The Spanish Struggle for Justice in the Conquest of America* (Philadelphia: University of Pennsylvania Press, 1949); Charles Gibson, ed., *The Spanish Tradition in America* (New York: Harper & Row, 1968); Robert A. Williams, Jr., *The American Indian in Western Legal Thought: The Discourses of Conquest* (New York: Oxford University Press, 1990). Also see the relevant sections of Klaus E. Knorr, *British Colonial Theories, 1570–1850* (London: Frank Cass, 1963).

59. See generally, Michael V. Gannon, *The Cross in the Sand: The Early Catholic Church in Florida, 1513–1870* (Gainesville: University Presses of Florida, [2nd. ed.] 1983); Mardith Keithly Schuetz, *Indians of the San Antonio Missions, 1718–1821* (Austin: University of Texas, Dept. of History, Ph.D. dissertation, 1980); Frances V. Scholes, *Church and State in New Mexico, 1610–1650* (Albuquerque: University of New Mexico Press, 1942).

60. This was always the rationalization for the *encomiendo* system—in which individual Indians were parceled out as laborers to his *hidalgos*—installed by Columbus on Española in 1495, and the later *repartmiento*—doing the same with entire communities, including their land—perfected by Cortés and Alvarado; see Hanke, *Spanish Struggle for Justice, op. cit.*, pp. 182–3, 189. Also see J.H. Elliott, *Imperial Spain, 1469–1716* (New York: Penguin, 1975) pp. 59–63.

61. The missive is dated July 16, 1865; quoted in Frank McNitt, *Navajo Wars: Military Campaigns, Slave Raids, and Reprisals* (Albuquerque: University of New Mexico Press, 1990) p. 441.

62. Sherburne F. Cook, *Indians versus the Spanish Mission* (Berkeley: University of California Ibero-American No. 21, 1943) pp. 89–90; V.M. Golovin, *Around the World on the Kamchatka, 1817–1818* (Honolulu: Hawaiian Historical Society, 1979) pp. 147–8.

63. Golovin (ibid.) noted that, under these circumstances, "cleanliness and tidiness [were] out of the question" and that "a thrifty peasant has a better-kept...barnyard" than the degraded environment in which the mission Indians were forced to live. Such conditions, entirely absent from indigenous tradition —and from the more sanitary facilities enjoyed by priests and troops at the missions—were obvious incubators of all manner of infectious diseases.

64. On caloric intake, see Cook, *The Indian versus the Spanish Mission*, *op. cit.*, p. 37, Table 2. On nutrients-or lack of them; the diet was markedly deficient in highgrade proteins, vitamins A and C, and riboflavin-see Ann Lucy W. Stodder, *Mechanisms and Trends in the Decline of the Costanoan Indian Population of Central California* (Salinas: Coyote Press, 1986).

65. See the quotes in Cook, *The Indian versus the Spanish Mission*, *op. cit.*, p. 54.

66. Stannard, *American Holocaust*, *op. cit.*, p. 138. He is quoting from Golovin, *Around the World*, *op. cit.*, pp. 150, 147.

67. Richard Sutch, "The Care and Feeding of Slaves," in Paul A. David, Herbert G. Gutman, Richard Sutch, Peter Temin and Gavin Wright, *Reckoning with Slavery: A Critical Study in the Quantitative History of American Negro Slavery* (New York: Oxford University Press, 1976).

68. One indication of the impact of the missions may be found in the fact that the California Indian population, conservatively estimated to have been about a third of a million in 1492 had declined to about 85,000 by 1852; Sherburne F. Cook, "Historical Demography," in Robert F. Heizer, ed., *Handbook of the North American Indians, Vol. 3: California* (Washington, D.C.: Smithsonian Institution, 1978). For a more recent, comprehensive and detailed study, see Robert H. Jackson, *Indian Population Decline: The Missions of Northwestern New Spain, 1687–1840* (Albuquerque: University of New Mexico Press, 1995).

69. Fray Francisco Palóu, *Historical Memoirs of New California* (New York: Russell & Russell, 1966) pp. 171–213.

70. Stannard, *American Holocaust*, *op. cit.*, p. 137.

71. To the contrary, even Fray Bartolomé de las Casas, who took the moral high ground in his famous debate in 1550–51 with the nobleman Juan Ginés de Sepúlveda over the intrinsic humanity and consequent rights of Indians, held that blacks were essentially subhuman and thus "natural slaves"; see Lewis Hanke, *Aristotle and the American Indians: A Study in Race Prejudice in the Modern World* (Chicago: Henry Regnery, 1959) p. 9. Also see Robert E. Quirk, "Notes on a Controversial Controversy: Juan Ginés de Sepúlveda and Natural Servitude," *Hispanic American Historical Review*, XXXIV, 1954.

72. Robert W. Fogel and Stanley L. Engerman, *Time on the Cross: The Economics of American Negro Slavery* (Boston: Little, Brown, 1974). Although there is no comparable study of the political economy of the North American mission system per se, it was undoubtedly illuminated by the earlier and more southerly Spanish practices upon which it was based; see William L. Sherman, *Forced Native Labor in Sixteenth Century Central America* (Lincoln: University of Nebraska Press, 1979). Also see Almon Wheeler Lauber's pioneering 1913 study, *Indian Slavery in Colonial Times Within the Present Limits of the United States* (Williamstown, MA: Corner House Social Science Reprints, 1979) and L.R. Bailey's much more recent, but very partial, *Indian Slave Trade in the Southwest* (Los Angeles: Westernlore, 1973).

73. Probably the best overview is provided in Ulrich Herbert, *A History of Foreign Labor in Germany, 1880–1980: Seasonal Workers / Forced Laborers / Guest Workers* (Ann Arbor: University of Michigan Press, 1990). More specifically, see Edward L. Homze, *Foreign Labor in Nazi Germany* (Princeton, NJ: Princeton University Press, 1967) and "Nazi Germany's Forced Labor Program," in Michael Berenbaum, ed., *A Mosaic of Victims: Non-Jews Persecuted and Murdered by the Nazis* (New York: New York University Press, 1990); Peter Black, "Forced Labor in the Concentration Camps, 1942–1944," in Berenbaum, *A Mosaic of Victims, op. cit.* Of additional interest, see generally, Albert Speer, *Inside the Third Reich: Memoirs* (New York: Macmillan, 1970); *The Slave State: Heinrich Himmler's Master Plan for SS Supremacy* (London: Widenfield and Nicholson, 1981).

74. Albert Speer, *Spandau: The Secret Diaries* (New York: Macmillan, 1976). For solid if overly sympathetic analysis of Speer's complicated efforts to redeem himself by assuming responsibility for certain of his own and his countrymen's crimes, even while flatly denying all knowledge of the nazi extermination campaign against the Jews, see Gitta Sereny, *Albert Speer: His Battle with Truth* (New York: Alfred A. Knopf, 1995). A much harsher view is expressed in Matthias Schmidt, *Albert Speer: End of a Myth* (New York: St. Martin's Press, 1984).

75. Wilbur Zelinsky, *Cultural Geography of the United States* (Engelwood Cliffs, NJ: Prentice-Hall, 1973); Charles H. Langham, "From Condemnation to Praise: Shifting Perspectives on Hispanic California," *California Historical Society Quarterly*, No. 61, Winter 1983.

76. Fray Francisco Palóu, *Life and Apistolic Labors of the Venerable Father Junípero Serra* (Pasadena, CA: G.W. James, 1913), pp. 86–7. Also see Omer Englebert, *The Last of the Conquistadors: Junípero Serra (1713–1784)* (New York: Harcourt, Brace and Co., 1956); Daniel Fogel, *Junípero Serra, the Vatican, and Enslavement Ideology* (San Francisco: ism press, 1988).

77. James A. Sandos, "Junípero Serra's Canonization and the Historical Record," *American Historical Review*, No. 93, 1988.

78. See, e.g., California AIM circular, "Junípero Serra: Mass Murderer as Saint" (San Francisco, March 1996); statement of California AIM representative Bobby Castillo on Cable News Network, May 27, 1996.

79. Statement made by the San Francisco Archdiocese on Cable News Network, May 27, 1996.

80. See, e.g., Marcus J. Smith, *Dachau: The Harrowing of Hell* (Albany: State University of New York, 1995); David A. Hackett, *The Buchenwald Report* (Boulder, CO: Westview Press, 1995); Eberhard Kolb, *Bergen-Belsen: From "Detention Camp" to Concentration Camp, 1943–1945* (Göttingen: Vandenhoeck & Ruprecht, [2nd. ed.] 1988).

81. Schmuel Krakowski, "The Death Marches in the Evacuation of the Camps," in *The Nazi Concentration Camps: Structure and Aims, The Image of Prisoners, The Jews in the Camps* (Jerusalem: Yad Vashim, 1984); Yehuda Bauer, "The Death-Marches, January-May, 1945," in Michael R. Marrus, ed., *The Nazi Holocaust: Historical Articles on the Destruction of European Jews, Vol. 9* (Westport, CT: Meckler, 1989).

82. For example: "It is clearly wrong to separate from the essence of the Holocaust those Jews…who starved in the ghettos of eastern Europe, or who were wasted by disease because of malnutrition or neglect"; Robert R. Marrus, *The Holocaust in History* (Hanover, NH: Brandeis University & University Press of New England, 1987) p. 20.

83. For comprehensive information on the prosecutions of these second- and third-tier individuals, see Office of United States Chief Counsel for Prosecution of Axis Criminality, *Trials of War Criminals Before the Nuremberg Military Tribunals under Control Council Law N. 10, Vols. 1–15* (Washington, D.C.: U.S. Government Printing Office, 1951–53).

84. Grant Foreman, *Indian Removal: The Immigration of the Five Civilized Tribes* (Norman: University of Oklahoma Press, 1953); Ronald Satz, *American Indian Policy in the Jacksonian Era* (Lincoln: University of Nebraska Press, 1975); Ernest Downs, "How the East Was Lost," *American Indian Journal*, Vol. 1, No. 2, 1975. For a good dose of the rhetoric attending passage of the Removal Act, see U.S. Congress, *Speeches on the Removal of the Indians, April-May, 1830* (New York: Jonathan Leavitt, 1830; New York: Kraus Reprints, 1973).

85. Gloria Jahoda, *The Trail of Tears: The Story of the Indian Removals* (New York: Holt, Rinehart & Winston, 1975); Thurman Wilkins, *Cherokee Tragedy: The Ridge Family and the Destruction of a People* (New York: Macmillan, 1970); Arthur H. DeRosier, Jr., *The Removal of the Choctaw Indians* (Knoxville: University of Tennessee Press, 1970); Michael D. Green, *The Politics of Indian Removal: Creek Government and Society in Crisis* (Lincoln: University of Nebraska Press, 1982).

86. Russell Thornton, "Cherokee Population Losses During the Trail of Tears: A New Perspective and a New Estimate," *Ethnohistory*, No. 31, 1984, p. 293; included in William L. Anderson, ed., *Cherokee Removal, Before and After* (Athens: University of Georgia Press, 1991).

87. Russell Thornton, *The Cherokees: A Population History* (Lincoln: University of Nebraska Press, 1990) pp. 75–7.

88. James M. Mooney, *Historical Sketch of the Cherokee* (Chicago: Aldine, 1975 reprint of the 1900 edition) p. 127.

89. The best available treatment will be found in Arrel M. Gibson, *The Chickasaws* (Norman: University of Oklahoma Press, 1971).

90. Clifford E. Trafzer, *The Kit Carson Campaign: The Last Great Navajo War* (Norman: University of Oklahoma Press, 1982.).

91. Lynn R. Bailey, *Long Walk* (Los Angeles: Westernlore, 1964); Lawrence C. Kelly, *Navajo Roundup* (Boulder, CO: Pruett, 1970); Ruth Roessel, ed., *Navajo Stories of the Long Walk* (Tsaile, AZ: Navajo Community College Press, 1973).

92. Roberto Mario Salmon, "The Disease Complaint at Bosque Redondo (1864–68)," *The Indian Historian*, No. 9, 1976; Gerald Thompson, *The Army and the Navajo: The Bosque Redondo Reservation Experiment, 1863–1868* (Tucson: University of Arizona Press, 1982).

93. S. Ryan Johansson and S.H. Preston, "Tribal Demography: The Navajo and Hopi Populations as Seen Through Manuscripts from the 1900 Census," *Social Science History*, No. 3, 1978.

94. Kenneth Carley, *The Sioux Uprising of 1862* (St. Paul: Minnesota Historical Society, 1961).

95. Keith A. Murray, *The Modocs and Their War* (Norman: University of Oklahoma Press, 1959).

96. Robert Emmitt, *The Last War Trail: The Utes and the Settlement of Colorado* (Norman: University of Oklahoma Press, 1954); Marshall Sprague, *Massacre: The Tragedy at White River* (Boston: Little, Brown, 1957).

97. Mari Sandoz, *Cheyenne Autumn* (New York: Avon, 1964) pp. 11–30; Donald J. Berthrong, *The Cheyenne and Arapaho Ordeal: Reservation and Agency Life, 1875–1907* (Norman: University of Oklahoma Press, 1976) pp. 17–9, 28–32.

98. Daniel Inouye, "1986 Black Hills Hearings on S. 1453, Introduction," *Wicazo Sa Review*, Vol. IV, No. 1, Spring 1988; Edward Lazarus, *Black Hills, White Justice: The Sioux Nation versus The United States, 1775 to the Present* (New York: HarperCollins, 1991) pp. 72–95.

99. Britton Davis, *The Truth About Geronimo* (Chicago: Lakeside Press, 1951 reprint of 1929 edition) p. 48. Overall, see Richard J. Perry, *Apache Reservation: Indigenous Peoples and the American State* (Austin: University of Texas Press, 1993) pp. 129–36.

100. This was in Roanoak Colony where the first English were welcomed by the local Indians and, as would be the case in Massachusetts forty years later, fed throughout their first winter. The following spring, they were taught to plant and thus to survive. Two years later, when an Indian was accused of having failed to return a borrowed cup, the colonists seized the excuse, sallied forth and burned their benefactors' village and fields, leaving the Indians destitute in the face of oncoming winter; Edmund S. Morgan, *American Slavery-American Freedom: The Ordeal of Colonial Virginia* (New York: W.W. Norton, 1975) pp. 25–43.

101. Edward Waterhouse, *A Declaration of the State of the Colony and Affaires in Virginia* (London, 1622) p. 23; quoted in Stannard, *American Holocaust, op. cit.*, p. 106.

102. An interesting exploration of this connection will be found in an M.A. thesis by Frank Parella entitled *Lebensraum and Manifest Destiny: A Comparative Study in the Justification of Expansion* (Georgetown: Dept. of Political Science, Georgetown University, 1950).

103. Statement of the Council of Virginia, quoted in Morgan, *American Slavery—American Freedom, op. cit.*, p. 99.

104. Stannard, *American Holocaust, op. cit.*, pp. 106–7. On the extent of the indigenous agricultural base that was destroyed—3,000 acres near present-day Hampton, Virginia, alone—see Philip A. Bruce, *Economic History of Virginia* (New York: P. Smith, 1896) pp. 7–13.

105. The smaller peoples included the Kiskiaks, Warraskoyaks, Quiyoughcohannocks, Appamatuks, Orapaks, Youghtanunds, Mattaponis, Payankatanks,. On the size of the residual population, see Robert Beverly, *The History and Present State of Virginia* (Chapel Hill: University of North Carolina Press, 1947 edited reprint of 1705 edition) pp. 232–3.

106. Robert Bennett to Edward Bennett [June 9, 1623], "Bennetes Welcome," *William and Mary Quarterly*, 2nd. Ser., No. 13, 1933, p. 219.

107. On the size of the preinvasion Powhatan population, see J. Leicht Wright, Jr., *The Only Land They Knew: The Tragic Story of the Indians of the Old South* (New York: Free Press, 1981), p. 60. On the settler population, tallied at 62,800 by 1700, see Morgan, *American Slavery—American Freedom, op. cit.*, p. 404.

108. On these and other wars in the region, see Wright, *The Only Land, op. cit.*

109. On Roanoak, see Morgan, *American Slavery—American Freedom, op. cit.* On Plymouth, the "first Thanksgiving," etc., see generally, William Bradford, *Of Plymouth Plantation, 1620–1647* (New York: Random House, 1981 edited reprint of the 1650 original); Francis Dillon, *A Place of Habitation: The Pilgrim Fathers and Their Quest* (London: Hutchinson, 1973).

110. The Puritan campaign against the Pequots and allied peoples relied much more on direct forms of annihilation than on destruction of the native economic base. However, as a prelude, they burned a number of fields of corn and other vegetables both on the mainland and on Block Island, just offshore;

see, e.g., John Mason, *A Brief History of the Pequot War* (Boston: Kneeland & Green, 1736); Jennings, *Invasion of America, op. cit.*, pp. 202–27.

111. Richard Drinnon, *Facing West: The Metaphysics of Indian Hating and Empire Building* (Minneapolis: University of Minnesota Press, 1980).

112. Anonymous, *A True Account of the Most Considerable Occurrences that have Hapned in the Warre Between the English and the Indians in New England* (London, 1676); Douglas Edward Leach, *Flintlock and Tomahawk: New England in King Philip's War* (New York: W.W. Norton, 1958).

113. Quoted in James M. O'Donnell, III, *Southern Indians in the American Revolution* (Knoxville: University of Tennessee Press, 1973) p. 52. Even James Mooney was willing to corroborate the effects. Within months, he wrote, the Cherokees "were on the verge of extinction. Over and over again their towns had been laid in ashes and their fields wasted. Their best warriors had been killed and their women and children had starved and sickened in the mountains"; *Historical Sketch of the Cherokee, op. cit.*, p. 51.

114. Quoted in Drinnon, *Facing West, op. cit.*, pp. 331–2, 65.

115. Quoted in Richard Drinnon, *Keeper of Concentration Camps: Dillon S. Myer and American Racism* (Berkeley: University of California Press, 1987) p. 23.

116. Ibid.

117. Trafzer, *The Kit Carson Campaign, op. cit.*

118. General Philip Sheridan to Commanding General William Tecumseh Sherman, May 2, 1873; quoted in Paul Andrew Hutton, *Phil Sheridan and His Army* (Lincoln: University of Nebraska Press, 1985) p. 246. At one point in the mid-1870s, Congress considered legislation to preserve what was left of the dwindling herds. Sheridan vociferously opposed it, suggesting that the legislators instead "strike a medal, with a dead buffalo pictured on one side and a discouraged Indian on the other," and present it to the buffalo hunters; John R. Cook, *The Border and the Buffalo: An Untold Story of the Southwest Plains* (New York: Citadel Press, 1976) pp. 163–5. Also see William T. Hornaday, *Exterminating the American Bison* (Washington, D.C.: Smithsonian Institution, 1899); Tom McHugh and Victoria Hobson, *The Time of the Buffalo* (New York: Alfred A. Knopf, 1972).

119. General—later U.S. president—Andrew Jackson, for one, was quite explicit about this, making native women and children a *priority* target for American troops. To do otherwise, he explained in his usual "homespun" style, would be like pursuing "a wolf in the hammocks without knowing first where her den and whelps were"; quoted in Takaki, *Iron Cages, op. cit.*, p. 102.

120. As John Mason, captain of the Puritan militia, put it with regard to the Pequots in 1637, the idea was to be so thorough as to "to cut off the Remembrance of them from the Earth"; quoted in Drinnon, *Facing West, op. cit.*, p. 55.

121. For a classic rendering, see H.R. Schoolcraft, *Historical and Statistical Information Respecting the History, Condition, and Prospects of the Indian Tribes of the United States* (Philadelphia: Lippencott, Grambo & Co., 1851).

122. This dynamic is described very well by David E. Stannard in his essay, "The Consequences of Contact: Toward an Interdisciplinary Theory of Native Responses to Biological and Cultural Invasion," in David Hurtz Thomas, ed., *Columbian Consequences, Vol. 3: The Spanish Borderlands in Pan-American Perspective* (Washington, D.C.: Smithsonian Institution, 1991). Also see Henry F. Dobyns, "More Methodological Perspectives on Historical Demography," *Ethnohistory*, No. 36, 1989.

123. See, e.g., J.V. Neel, "Health and Disease in Unacculturated Amerindian Populations," in Ciba Foundation, *Health and Disease in Tribal Societies* (Amsterdam: Elsevier/Excerpta Medica, 1977).

124. See, e.g., David E. Stannard, "Disease and Infertility: A New Look at the Collapse of Native Populations in the Wake of Contact," *Journal of American Studies*, No. 24, 1990.

125. This tidy turn of the phrase may be attributed to James Axtell, during his lecture at the University of Florida, *op. cit.*

126. Robert O'Connell, *Of Arms and Men: A History of War, Weapons, and Aggression* (New York: Oxford University Press, 1989) p. 171.

127. For an overview, see John Duffy, *Epidemics in Colonial America* (Baton Rouge: Louisiana State University Press, 1953); E. Wagner Stearn and Allen E. Stearn, *The Effects of Smallpox on the Destiny of the Amerindian* (Boston: Bruce Humphries, 1945).

128. Jennings, *Invasion of America, op. cit.*, pp. 207–8.

129. The process is described in notations dated July 26 and 30, 1636, in John Winthrop's *The History of New England from 1630 to 1649*, 2 vols. (Boston, 1853 edited reprint of 1690 original) p. 191. It is also covered in a letter from Roger Williams to Governor Winthrop dated Sept. 9, 1637.

130. There were four such conflicts over an eighty-year period.

131. On Pontiac, see generally, Howard Henry Peckham, *Pontiac and the Indian Uprising* (New York: Russell & Russell, 1970).

132. Stearn and Stearn, *The Effects of Smallpox, op. cit.*, pp. 44–5. It should be noted that, according to Yamasee historian Donald A. Grinde, Jr., Howard Peckham, head of the American Historical Association for many years, discovered the Amherst/Bouquet correspondence and related archival materials during the late 1930s. He then proceeded to suppress it "because of the impression it might give" for more than a decade, admitting its existence only when it was independently discovered by Allen Stearn.

133. Stearn and Stearn, *The Effects of Smallpox, op. cit.*, p. 49. Also see John Duffy, "Smallpox and the Indians in the American Colonies," *Bulletin of the History of Medicine*, No. 25, 1951. For a detailed and comprehensive, albeit somewhat biased, overview of the fighting in this region from start to finish, see Allan W. Eckert, *That Dark and Bloody River: Chronicles of the Ohio River Valley* (New York: Bantam, 1995).

134. O'Connell, *Son of the Morning Star, op. cit.*, p. 171.

135. The phrase is again attributable to James Axtell, this time in a talk given during the annual meeting of the American Historical Association (AHA) in Washington, D.C., Dec. 1993 (tape on file).

136. Stearn and Stearn, *The Effects of Smallpox, op. cit.*, pp. 89–94; Francis A. Chardon, *Journal at Fort Clark, 1834–39* (Pierre: State Historical Society of South Dakota, 1932).

137. Attribution of the trivializing phrase is once again to James Axtell, AHA Talk (q & a), *op. cit.*

138. Connell, *Son of the Morning Star, op. cit.*, p. 16.

139. "Exciting News From Tehema-Indian Thefts—Terrible Vengeance of the Whites," *Daily Alta California*, Mar. 6, 1853; excerpted in Robert F. Heizer, ed., *The Destruction of California Indians* (Lincoln: University of Nebraska Press, 1993 reprint of 1974 Peregrine Smith ed.) p. 251.

140. "Indian Butcheries in California," *San Francisco Bulletin*, July 10, 1860; reproduced in Heizer, *Destruction of California Indians, op. cit.*, pp. 253–5.

141. The "ghettoization/privation" phraseology accrues from Raul Hilberg, *The Destruction of European Jews* (New York: Holmes & Meier, 1985). According to Arno J. Meyer, "from 1942 to 1945, certainly at Auschwitz, but probably overall, more Jews were killed by so-called 'natural' causes…sickness, disease, undernourishment, [and] hyperexploitation… than by 'unnatural' ones [like] shooting, hanging, phenol injection, or gassing"; Arno J. Meyer, *Why Did the Heavens Not Darken? The "Final Solution" in History* (New York: Pantheon, 1990) pp. 226–7. David E. Stannard, estimates that a minimum of 2.4 million of 5.1 million Jews who died during the Holocaust perished from these "natural" causes rather than the "unnatural" ones; "The Politics of Holocaust Scholarship: Uniqueness as Denial," in Rosenbaum, *Is the Holocaust Unique?, op. cit.*, p. 178.

142. Peter Calvocoressi, Guy Wint and John Pritchard, *Total War: Causes and Courses of World War II* (New York: Pantheon, [2nd. ed., revised] 1989) pp. 576–8.

143. Katz, "Uniqueness," *op. cit.*, p. 21.

144. Ibid. This is hardly a new game; see, e.g., Don Russell, "How Many Indians Were Killed? White Man Versus Red Man: The Facts and the Legend," *American West*, July 1973.

145. *Report on Indians Taxed and Not Taxed* (1890), *op. cit.*, pp. 637–8; quoted in Thornton, *American Indian Holocaust and Survival, op. cit.*, p.48.

146. Ibid., p. 49.

147. Ibid., p. 49.

148. For example, he quotes no less than James Mooney to the effect that, in California, "the enormous decrease from about a quarter million to less than 20,000 is due chiefly to the cruelties and wholesale massacres perpetrated by the miners and the early settlers"; ibid., quoting Mooney, "Population," *op. cit.*, p. 286.

149. Robert S. Weddle, *Spanish Sea: The Gulf of Mexico in North American Discovery, 1500–1685* (College Station: Texas A&M University Press, 1985) pp. 44–6, 51–3; Randolf J. Widmer, *The Evolution of the Calusa: A Nonagricultural Chiefdom on the Southwest Florida Coast* (Tuscaloosa: University of Alabama Press, 1988).

150. Weddle, *Spanish Sea, op. cit.*, p. 53.

151. John Farmer, "Piñeda's Sketch," *Southwestern Historical Quarterly*, No. 63, 1959; John H. Parry, "The Navigators of the Conquista," *Terra Incognitae*, No. 10, 1978.

152. One of these, Pedro de Salazar, encountered people on the South Carolina coast, probably Yamasees, who treated the Spaniards "graciously" until Salazar's men began to seize them as slave cargo; Paul E. Hoffman, "A New Voyage of North American Discovery: Pedro de Salazar's Visit to the 'Island of Giants'," *Florida Historical Quarterly*, No. 58, April 1980.

153. The intended colony was established by a nobleman, Lucas Vásquez de Ayllón, who invested his family fortune against the potential profits of a thriving trade in native flesh but died of a cold during the first winter; David J. Weber, *The Spanish Frontier in North America* (New Haven: Yale University Press, 1992) p. 35.

154. These economics are well handled in Paul E. Hoffman, "Nature and Sequence of the Spanish Borderlands, 1500–1566," *South Carolina Historical Magazine*, No. 84, 1983.

155. A good overview is provided in Paul E. Hoffman, *A New Andalucia and A Way to the Orient: The American Southeast During the Sixteenth Century* (Baton Rouge: Louisiana State University Press, 1990); also see Ronald Sanders, *Lost Tribes and Promised Lands: The Origins of American Racism* (Boston: Little, Brown, 1978).

156. The Cíbola story—there were supposed to be seven golden cities, of which Cíbola was the most opulent—was promoted by Fray Marcos de Niza, a Franciscan who claimed to have seen it in during a northern reconnaissance in 1538, of which he was the only survivor. The lie was probably designed to draw Spanish presence northward, an idea to which he seems to have been committed, and as a cover for the fact that he had run away and left his comrades in extremis ("If I died, I would not be able to make a report of this country."); Cleve Hallenbeck, ed. and trans., *The Journey of Fray Marcos de Niza* (Dallas: Southern Methodist University Press, 1987); George P. Hammond, "The Search for the Fabulous in the Settlement of the Southwest," in David J. Weber, ed., *New Spain's Far Northern Frontier: Essays on Spain in the American West* (Albuquerque: University of New Mexico Press, 1979).

157. Carl O. Sauer, "The Road to Cíbola," in John Leighy, ed., *Land and Life* (Berkeley: University of California Press, 1963).

158. Herbert Eugene Bolton, *Coronado on the Turquoise Trail: Knight of the Pueblos* (Albuquerque: University of New Mexico Press, 1949) pp. 153–68.

159. George P. Hammond and Agapito Rey, eds. and trans., *Narratives of the Coronado Expedition, 1540–1542* (Albuquerque: University of New Mexico Press, 1940) p. 22, n. 68.

160. Edward Gaylord Bourne, ed., *The Narratives of Hernando de Soto*, 2 vols. (New York: A.S. Barnes, 1904). De Soto, it should be noted, had served as an officer under Pizarro in Peru.

161. Weber, *Spanish Frontier, op. cit.*, p. 51; he is quoting from chronicler Oviedo, who is in turn quoted by Rodrigo Ranjel in his "Narrative of De Soto's Expedition," in Bourne, Vol. 2, *op. cit.*, pp. 117, 60.

162. Weber, *Spanish Frontier, op. cit.*, p. 52.

163. "Relacion of Luys Hernández de Biedma," in Bourne, Vol. 2, *Narratives of Hernando de Soto, op. cit.*, p. 21.

164. Weber, *Spanish Frontier, op. cit.*, p. 54.

165. By this point lacking the strength to militarily confront large bodies of Indians, de Soto attempted a subterfuge which had worked for other conquistadors in Mexico, sending word to the Natchez that he was the "Sun God" in hopes that they might voluntarily submit to his authority. Instead, unimpressed, the Indians sent back word that if he dried up the Mississippi, they'd believe him; Carl O. Sauer, *Sixteenth Century North America: The Land and the Peoples as Seen by Europeans* (Berkeley: University of California Press, 1971) p. 170.

166. John R. Swanton, *Final Report of the United States de Soto Expedition Commission* (Washington, D.C.: Smithsonian Institution, 1939) pp. 83, 88.

167. This was the mission-fort at San Augustín, established on September 8, 1565; Eugene Lyon, *The Enterprise of Florida: Pedro Menéndez de Avilés and the Spanish Conquest, 1565–1568* (Gainesville: University of Florida Press, 1983).

168. Although Santa Fe was not formally established until 1610—it existed as early as 1608 (or earlier, if the small group left behind by Coronado is counted)—the actual Spanish occupation of what

became New Mexico began with the expedition of Juan de Oñate in 1598; Marc Simmons, *The Last Conquistador: Juan de Oñate and the Settling of the Far Southwest* (Norman: University of Oklahoma Press, 1991).

169. Richard Hakluyt, *The Principal Navigations, Voyages, Traffiques & Discoveries of the English Nation, Vol. 5* (London: J.M. Dent & Sons, 1907) pp. 144–5.

170. K.G. Davies, *Europe and the Age of Expansion, Vol. IV: The North Atlantic World in the Seventeenth Century* (Minneapolis: University of Minnesota Press, 1974) p. 17.

171. For the standard interpretation of Roanoak, see Samuel Elliot Morison, *The European Discovery of America, Vol. 2: The Northern Voyages* (New York: Oxford University Press, 1971) pp. 621–84. Also see David Beers Quinn, ed., *The Roanoak Voyages, 1584–1590* (Cambridge: Hakluyt Society, 1955).

172. See note 100, above.

173. John Greenway, *The Inevitable Americans* (New York: Alfred A. Knopf, 1964) p. 34.

174. With typical European arrogance, they immediately named the river after their current ruler, James I, rather than inquiring whether it had already had a name bestowed upon it by the local populace; Philip L. Barbour, ed., *The Jamestown Voyages Under the First Charter, 1606–1609* (Cambridge: Hakluyt Society, 2nd ser., 1969). On the confederation of indigenous peoples who were encountered, and its leaders, see Christian F. Feest, "Powhatan: A Study in Political Organization," *Weiner Völkerkundliche Mitteilungen*, No. 13, 1966; Helen C. Rountree, *The Powhatan Indians of Virginia: Their Traditional Culture* (Norman: University of Oklahoma Press, 1989).

175. Stannard, *American Holocaust, op. cit.*, p. 106.

176. Morgan, *Wilderness at Dawn, op. cit.*, p. 113.

177. James Axtell, *After Columbus: Essays in the Ethnohistory of Colonial North America* (New York: Oxford University Press, 1988) p. 201.

178. Ibid.; Axtell is quoting from George Percy, "'A Trewe Relacyon': Virginia from 1609 to 1612," *Tyler's Quarterly Historical and Genealogical Magazine*, No. 3, 1922, p. 265. Also see J. Frederick Fausz, "An 'Abundance of Blood Shed on Both Sides': England's First Indian War, 1609–1614," *Virginia Magazine of History and Biography*, No. 98, 1990.

179. As Wahunsonacock put it to Smith himself in 1609, after the latter had committed one of his many vile acts, "it is better to eate good meate, lie well, and sleep with my women & children, laugh and be merrie with you, have copper, hatchets, or what I want, being your friend: then bee forced to flie from al[l], to lie cold in the woods, feed upon acorns, roots, and such trash, and be so hunted by you that I can neither rest, eat, nor sleep"; quoted in Barbour, *Jamestown Voyages, op. cit.*, p. 426. Also see Michael J. Puglisi, "Revitalization or Extirpation: Anglo-Powhatan Relations, 1622–1644" (Williamsburg, VA: M.A. thesis, Dept. of History, College of William & Mary, 1982).

180. Governor Francis Wyatt, quoted in H.R. McIlwaine, ed., *Minutes of the Council and General Court of Virginia* (Richmond: Virginia State Historical Society, 1924) p. 484. A good overview of such outlooks is provided in William L. Shea, *The Virginia Militia in the Seventeenth Century* (Baton Rouge: Louisiana State University Press, 1983).

181. Jamestown was actually abandoned altogether just before this. De la Warr left the colony before Smith, dispatching a subordinate, Thomas Gates, to stand in. Gates, however, was shipwrecked off Bermuda while en route. He finally arrived in June 1610, after a winter so bleak the colonists resorted to cannibalism to survive. With his effective strength down to sixty men, Gates immediately gave up and set sail for home, taking the survivors with him. As they sailed down the James for Chesapeak Bay and the Atlantic, however, they were met by de la Warr, who was in the process of returning with 300 men. The war commenced less than sixty days later; Axtell, *After Columbus, op. cit.*, pp. 204–5.

182. It is a safe estimate that upwards of 1,000 Indians were killed by Percy's troops during the late summer and fall of 1610. Dale's men probably killed somewhere between twice and three times that number in the 1611 campaign; see generally, Percy, "A Trewe Relacyon," *op. cit.*, pp. 276–7.

183. Ibid., p. 270.

184. It seems likely that, from 1612–1614, a minimum of 1,000 Indians were killed by English raiders, patrols, sentries, and random acts of violence. The Pocahantas story is too well known to go into here; an interesting twist will be found in J. Frederick Fausz, "George Thorpe, Nemattanew, and the Powhatan Uprising of 1622," *Virginia Cavalcade*, No. 28, 1979.

185. The timing of the attack was wrong for several reasons. March was too early for the trees to have leafed out, providing good cover. Food supplies were also low at the end of a hard winter, and the fighters had not had time to limber up. Opechancanough was forced to move, however, when the Tsenacommacahs' principal military leader, Nemattanow ("Jack-of-Feathers"), was suddenly murdered by a pair of young colonists, taking his place among the growing piles of his gratuitously slain relatives; J. Frederick Fausz, "Opechancanough: Indian Resistance Leader," in David G. Sweet and Gary B. Nash, eds., *Struggle and Survival in Colonial America* (Berkeley: University of California Press, 1981); " 'The Barbarous Massacre' Reconsidered: The Powhatan Uprising of 1622 and the Historians," *Explorations in Ethnic Studies*, No. 1, 1978.

186. Axtell, *After Columbus, op. cit.*, p. 218.

187. Kingsbury, Vol. 4, *Records of the Virginia Company, op. cit.*, pp. 221–2.

188. Kingsbury, Vol. 3, *Records of the Virginia Company, op. cit.*, p. 665; Vol. 4, pp. 10, 507–8.

189. William S. Powell, "Aftermath of the Massacre: The First Indian War, 1622–1632," *Virginia Magazine of History and Biography*, No. 66, 1958.

190. Axtell, *After Columbus, op. cit.*, pp. 219–20.

191. Beverley, *History and Present State of Virginia, op. cit.*, p. 62.

192. Steele, *Warpaths, op. cit.*, p. 47. The Piscataways, a small and unoffending people, never recovered from the disaster, and were very nearly annihilated altogether in the Virginia campaigns conducted a half-century later; James H. Merrell, "Cultural Continuity among the Piscataway Indians of Colonial Maryland," *William and Mary Quarterly*, No. 36, 1979.

193. Steele, *Warpaths, op. cit.*, p. 53; also see Washburn, *The Governor and the Rebel, op. cit.*, pp. 20–1.

194. On the fates of some of these smaller peoples, see Wood, Waselkov and Hatley, *Powhatan's Mantle, op. cit.* Also see Bernard Sheehan, *Savagism and Civility: Indians and Englishmen in Colonial Virginia* (Cambridge: Harvard University Press, 1980).

195. Steele, *Warpaths, op. cit.*, p. 53.

196. See generally, Francis Jennings, *The Ambiguous Iroquois Empire* (New York: W.W. Norton, 1984) pp. 18–22, 127–30; "Glory, Death and Transfiguration: The Susquehannock Indians in the Seventeenth Century," *Proceedings of the American Philosophical Society*, No. 112, 1968.

197. *Historical Statistics, op. cit.*, p. 14; Dobyns computes the preinvasion density of the tidewater area (i.e., Jamestown Colony) at 4.9–6.8 persons per square kilometer. This works out to a beginning population of up to a beginning population for all of Virginia of perhaps 750–800,000; *Their Number Become Thinned, op. cit.*, p. 44.

198. These expeditions are covered in David Beers Quinn, *England and the Discovery of America, 1481–1620* (New York: Alfred A. Knopf, 1974) pp. 419–31; and Neal Salisbury, *Manitou and Providence: Europeans, Indians and the Making of New England, 1500–1643* (New York: Oxford University Press, 1982) pp. 86–93. Also see Colin G. Calloway, *Dawnland Encounters: Indians and Europeans in Northern New England* (Hanover, NH: University Press of New England, 1991).

199. See note 27, above.

200. Philip L. Barbour, ed., *The Complete Works of Captain John Smith, 1580–1631*, 3 vols. (Chapel Hill: University of North Carolina Press, 1986) Vol. 1, pp. 293–4, 433; Vol. 2, pp. 403, 441. Also see Salisbury, *Manitou, op. cit.*, pp. 96–101.

201. Steele, *Warpaths, op. cit.*, p. 84; also see Snow and Lamphear, "European Contact," *op. cit.*

202. The arsenal included twelve cannon; H.L. Peterson, "The Military Equipment of the Plymouth and Bay Colonies, 1620–1690," *New England Quarterly*, No. 20, 1947.

203. Salisbury, *Manitou, op. cit.*, 101–9.

204. For the best overview of colonial demography in this region, see David Cressy, *Coming Over: Migration and Communication between England and New England in the Seventeenth Century* (Cambridge: Harvard University Press, 1987).

205. This process, which continued for more than a century, is addressed in William Cronon, *Changes in the Land: Indians, Colonists and the Ecology of New England* (New York: Hill & Wang, 1983).

206. When you add the intrigues of the French and Dutch to the mix, as well as those of their various indigenous allies, all of them seeking to play the volatile ingredients of New England off in such manner as to end up regionally ascendant, you encounter a confusing welter of alliances, double alliances,

even mutually exclusive triple-alliances, the entirety of which was in almost continuous flux; an excellent snapshot of this complex interplay will be found in Steele, *Warpaths, op. cit.*, pp. 86–90.

207. It should be noted that Narragansett trade with the Dutch predated their trade with the English by more than a decade.

208. William A. Starna, "The Pequots in the Early Seventeenth Century," in Laurence M. Hauptman and James D. Wherry, eds., *The Pequots in Southern New England: The Fall and Rise of an American Indian Nation* (Norman: University of Oklahoma Press, 1990) pp. 45–6.

209. Jennings, *The Invasion of America, op. cit.*, p. 210.

210. There is compelling evidence that the Pequots had no idea a fight was brewing. As John Underhill, a professional mercenary who accompanied the Block Island expedition and then went on to participate in the Mystic Massacre, put it, "they did not think we intended warre"; the Pequots tried to decline warfare with people capable of such savage behavior; *Newes from America; or, A New and Experimental Discovery of New England* (London, 1638) p. 7.

211. On the composition of Mason's forces, see Steele, *Warpaths, op. cit.*, p. 92.

212. It seems there may have been qualms about the nature of the planned slaughter even among some of the militia's officers, notably, Lt. Lion Gardiner and the mercenary Underhill. It was necessary that the proposed course of action be "commended" by a Calvinist chaplain before they consented to go along; Mason, *A Brief History, op cit.*, p. 3.

213. Jennings, *The Invasion of America, op. cit.*, p. 222.

214. Bradford, *Of Plymouth Plantation, op. cit.*, p. 296.

215. Steele, *Warpaths, op. cit.*, p. 93.

216. Jennings, *The Invasion of America, op. cit.*, pp. 215–26; Salisbury, *Manitou, op. cit.*, 218–25.

217. Jennings, *The Invasion of America, op. cit.*, p. 226; Steele, *Warpaths, op. cit.*, p. 93.

218. "For present purposes we need not pursue every last band of Pequots to its final disposition. There were more atrocities; the whole story of the Pequot 'war' is one long atrocity"; Jennings, *The Invasion of America, op. cit.*, p. 226.

219. Ibid.

220. Drinnon, *Facing West*, op. cit., p. 55. It is worth noting that Katz ("Pequot War," *op. cit.*) actually refers to the 21 surviving Pequots of the 1960s as a "proof" that genocide was not committed against their people.

221. In a 1642 meeting with the Montauks, for example, Miantonomi argued that, "we are all Indians as the English are, and say brother to one another; so we must be one as they are, otherwise we shall all be gone shortly"; quoted in Salisbury, *Manitou, op. cit.*, p. 13.

222. On the Mohawk Alliance, see Neal Salisbury, "Towards the Covenant Chain: Iroquois and Southern New England Algonkians, 1637–1685," in Daniel K. Richter and James H. Merrill, eds., *Beyond the Covenant Chain: The Iroquois and Their Neighbors in Indian North America, 1600–1800* (Syracuse, NY: Syracuse University Press, 1987). The Narragansett leader had also seriously proposed that a union between his people and the rival Mohegans be solidified by his marrying of Uncas' daughter. Another union, between the Narragansetts and Wampanoags, would be sealed with the marriage of Miantonomi's brother to the daughter of Massasoit, principal sachem of the latter people; ibid., p. 95.

223. On the meeting and execution, which was actually carried out by Uncas as a gesture of "friendship and good faith," see Salisbury, *Manitou, op. cit.*, pp. 228–35. Overall, see Harry M. Ward, *The United Colonies of New England, 1643–1690* (New York: St. Martin's Press, 1961).

224. War was briefly declared on the Narragansetts by the United Colonies in 1645, just long enough to cow several prominent sachems into repudiating the relationship Miantonomi had established with the Mohawks and consenting to English "protection"; for context, and examples of "conspiracy" rhetoric, see Jennings, *The Invasion of America, op. cit.*, pp. 258–81.

225. Donna Merwick, *Possessing Albany, 1630–1710: The Dutch and English Experiences* (Cambridge: Cambridge University Press, 1990).

226. Concerning the Massachusetts raids on Acadia (Nova Scotia), see George A. Rawlyk, *Nova Scotia's Massachusetts: A Study of Massachusetts-Nova Scotia Relations, 1630 to 1784* (Montréal: McGill-Queens University Press, 1973) pp. 23–7.

227. On colonial population, see *Historical Statistics*, series Z, pp. 5, 6, 8; Wells, *Population, op. cit.*

228. Neal Salisbury, "Indians and Colonists in Southern New England after the Pequot War: An Uneasy Balance," in Hauptman and Wherry, *The Pequots, op. cit.*; Philip Ranlet, "Another Look at the Causes of King Philip's War," *New England Quarterly*, No. 61, 1988.

229. Cook, "The Significance of Disease," *op. cit.*

230. On encroachment, especially in the area of Swansea, see Jennings, *The Invasion of America, op. cit.*, pp. 292–4; on arrogance, see Arthur J. Worrall, "Persecution, Politics and War: Roger Williams, Quaker, and King Philip's War," *Quaker History*, No. 66, 1977; on the executions, see Leach, *Flintlock, op. cit.*, pp. 30–6.

231. "[The] Indians never for a moment aspired to drive out all the English or hoped to gain mastery over them. Their purpose was to salvage some measure of self-government in secure territory"; Jennings, *The Invasion of America, op. cit.*, p. 300. Also see Russell Bourne, *The Red King's Rebellion: Racial Politics in New England, 1675–1678* (New York: Atheneum, 1990).

232. Steele, *Warpaths, op. cit.*, p. 101.

233. On the relative strengths of the two sides at this point, see Adam J. Hirsch, "The Collision of Military Cultures in Seventeenth Century New England," *Journal of American History*, No. 74, 1987–1988.

234. Rhode Island officials protested vehemently that "the Indians had given no cause for warre"; quoted in Jennings, *The Invasion of America, op. cit.*, p. 305.

235. Steele, *Warpaths, op. cit.*, p. 106.

236. Leach, *Flintlock, op. cit.*, pp. 200–4.

237. Steele, *Warpaths, op. cit.*, p. 107.

238. Leach, *Flintlock, op. cit.*, pp. 211–2.

239. Quoted in George D. Langdon, Jr., *Pilgrim Colony: A History of New Plymouth, 1620–1691* (New Haven, CT: Yale University Press, 1966) p. 180.

240. Jennings, *The Invasion of America, op. cit.*, p. 320.

241. Steele, *Warpaths, op. cit.*, p. 107.

242. Leach, *Flintlock, op. cit.*, pp. 226–7.

243. Increase Mather, *A Brief History of the Warr With the Indians in New England* (Boston, 1676), reprinted in Slotkin and Folsom, *So Dreadful a Judgement, op. cit.*, quote at p. 81.

244. Jennings, *The Invasion of America, op. cit.*, p. 212; Nicholas P. Canny, "The Ideology of English Colonization: From Ireland to America," *William and Mary Quarterly*, 3d. Ser., XXX, 1973; James Muldoon, "The Indian as Irishman," *Essex Institute Historical Collections*, No. 111, 1975. More broadly, see David Beers Quinn, *The Elizabethans and the Irish* (Ithaca, NY: Cornell University Press, 1966).

245. Jennings, *The Invasion of America, op. cit.*, pp. 293–4.

246. Ibid., p. 293; Rountree, *The Powhatan Indians, op. cit.*, p. 121; Steele, *Warpaths, op. cit.*, p. 46.

247. This idea has been thoroughly explored elsewhere, notably by Roy Harvey Pierce, *Savagism and Civilization: A Study of the American Indian in the American Mind* (Baltimore: Johns Hopkins University Press, 1953), and *The Savages of America: A Study of the Indian and the Idea of Civilization* (Baltimore: Johns Hopkins University Press, 1965). Also see David R. Wrone and Russell S. Nelson, Jr., *Who's the Savage? A Documentary History of the Mistreatment of the North American Indians* (Greenwich, CT: Fawcett, 1973).

248. There is a strong emergent literature analyzing the overall framework of what is at issue here; for a variety of approaches, see, e.g., Edward Said, *Orientalism* (New York: Pantheon, 1978); Hans Kellner, *Language and Historical Representation: Getting the Story Crooked* (Madison: University of Wisconsin Press, 1989); Robert Young, *White Mythologies: Writing History and the West* (London/New York: Routledge, 1990); Chris Tiffin and Alan Lawson, eds., *De-Scribing Empire: Post-colonialism and Textuality* (London/New York: Routledge, 1994).

249. The phrase quoted comes from Increase Mather, *A Relation Of the Troubles which have hapned in New-England By reason of the Indians there* (1677), later edited and published by Samuel G. Drake under the title *Early History of New England; Being a Relation of Hostile Passages between the Indians and the European Voyagers and Settlers* (Albany: New York State Historical Society, 1864). Cotton Mather, the son of Increase, incorporated the very same language into his *The Life and Death of the Renown'd Mr. John Eliot, Who was the First Preacher of the Gospel to the Indians in America* (London, 2nd ed., 1691), and it was used frequently by historians, including John Palfrey Gorham and Francis Parkman during the nineteenth century. The phrasing itself has been abandoned in the late twentieth century, but the idea remains

entrenched; see, e.g., Duane Schultz, *Month of the Freezing Moon: The Sand Creek Massacre, November 1864* (New York: St. Martin's Press, 1990) p. 16.

250. Peter Farb, *Man's Rise to Civilization as Shown by the Indians of North America from Primeval Times to the Coming of the Industrial State* (New York: Dutton, 1968) pp. 123–4.

251. Edgar S. Cahn, ed., *Our Brother's Keeper: The Indian in White America* (Washington, D.C.: New Community Press, 1969) p. 176.

252. Canny, "Ideology," *op. cit.*, p. 582.

253. Lazarus, *Black Hills, op. cit.*, p. 29. For that matter, as lately as the early 1970s, U.S. troops working with the CIA's notorious Operation Phoenix in Vietnam were busily collecting and displaying heads of suspected Vietcong cadres, as evidenced by photos included in the documentary film *CIA: Phoenix Rising,* shown on The History Channel on July 13, 1996. The matter of "tradition" tends to speak for itself here.

254. This sort of thing was done in Plymouth, almost from the outset, as when Myles Standish killed the Wampanoag leader Wituwamat, took his head, and mounted it atop the Pilgrims' fort; Sidney V. Yates, ed., *Three Visitors to Early Plymouth: Letters about the Pilgrim Settlement in New England during Its First Eleven Years* (Plymouth Plantation, 1963) p. 31.

255. Leach, *Flintlock, op. cit.*, p. 113. Most sources say "heads." However, at least one makes reference to "head-skins"; Lincoln, *Narratives, op. cit.*, p. 37.

256. It was "a convenient way to collect provincial bounties for heads without having to lug the awkward impedimenta attached to the scalps"; Jennings, *The Invasion of America, op. cit.*, p. 160. Bounty hunters "got tired of lugging in the heads so soon they just brought in the scalp to show that they'd killed an Indian… Whites introduced scalping to tribes that had never practiced it themselves"; Alvin M. Josephy, Jr., *The Indian Heritage of America* (New York: Alfred A. Knopf, 1968) p. 305.

257. E. B. O'Callaghan, *Laws and Ordinances of New Netherlands, 1638–1647* (Albany: State Historical Society of New York, 1868) pp. 28–9; Alan Axelrod, *Chronicle of the Indian Wars from Colonial Times to Wounded Knee* (New York: Prentice Hall, 1993) p. 39.

258. "Cornplanter's Talk," Draper Collection, 16 F 277, State Historical Society of Wisconsin, Madison; quoted in Axtell, "The Unkindest Cut," *op. cit.*, p. 18.

259. Quoted in Dorothy Clarke Wilson, *Bright Eyes: The Story of Susette La Flesche* (New York: MaGraw-Hill, 1974) p. 221.

260. E.B. O'Callaghan and Bethold Fernouw, eds., *Documents Relative to the Colonial History of the State of New York,* 15 vols. (Albany: New York State Historical Society, 1856–1857) Vol. 3, p. 562.

261. *The Acts and Resolves of the Province of the Massachusetts Bay,* 21 vols. (Boston: State of Massachusetts Historical Society, 1869–1922) Vol. 1, pp. 175–6, 594.

262. O'Callaghan and Fernouw, *Documents, op. cit.*, Vol. 4, 150*n.*

263. Viola Barnes, *The Dominion of New England* (New Haven: Yale University Press, 1923) pp. 218–9.

264. Axtell, "Scalping," *op. cit.*, pp. 228, 234.

265. The Reverend Thomas Barton, quoted in Carl Van Doren and Julian P. Boyd, eds., *Indian Treaties Printed by Benjamin Franklin* (Philadelphia: University of Pennsylvania Press, 1938) pp. lxxii–lxxiii. Also see Henry J. Young, "A Note on Scalp Bounties in Pennsylvania," *Pennsylvania History*, No. 24, 1957.

266. Clifford K. Shipton, *Sibley's Harvard Graduates: Biographical Sketches of Those Who Attended Harvard College* (Cambridge, MA: Harvard College, 1837) Vol. 6, pp. 407–8; Vol. 7, pp. 176–7.

267. The problem is covered in Richard R. Johnson, "The Search for a Usable Indian: An Aspect of the Defense of New England," *Journal of American History*, No. 64, 1977.

268. Axtell, "Scalping," *op. cit.*, p. 237; he is quoting from William A. Whitehead, ed., *Documents Relating to the Colonial, Revolutionary, and Post-Revolutionary History of the State of New Jersey, Archives of the State of New Jersey* (Trenton: 1st Ser. Vol. 20, 1898) pp. 43–4; *Minutes of the Provincial Council of Pennsylvania, Vol. 7, op. cit.*, p. 89.

269. James Pinney Baxter, ed., *Documentary History of the State of Maine, Collections of the Maine Historical Society* (2nd Ser., No. 23, 1916) pp. 131–2, 139–40.

270. Steele, *Warpaths, op. cit.*, p. 228.

271. The above-mentioned 1688 Québec scalp bounty was the opening round of this, while that of New York in 1696 was the initial English response (notes 260 and 261).

272. Axtell, "Scalping," *op. cit.*, p. 217–8. Analysis of these economic realities will be found in Leroy V. Eid, " 'National' War Among Indians of Northeastern North America," *Canadian Review of American Studies*, No. 16, 1985.

273. Samuel Hazard, et al., eds., *Pennsylvania Archives*, 1st Ser., Vol. 3, 1853, p. 199.

274. Captain John Knox, *An Historical Journal of the Campaigns in North America for the Years 1757, 1758, 1759, and 1760* (London, 1769) pp. 438, 468.

275. The best sources on the group headed by Captain Samuel Brady, and Lewis Wetzel, are the Brady and Wetzel papers, 16 vols., Draper Manuscript Collection, State Historical Society of Wisconsin, Madison.

276. E.g., well after peace was declared, Colonel Henry Bouquet—of smallpox blanket fame—discovered that "one of the Maryland Volunteers, had killed a Shawnee Indian near Fort Pitt & produced a Scalp for the reward; And that Some of the Frontier People were [still] out in the Woods Endeavoring to fall upon some straggling Indians to get their Scalps"; quoted in James Sullivan, et al., eds., *The Papers of Sir William Johnson*, 14 vols. (Albany: State Historical Society of New York, 1921–1965) Vol. 6, p. 102.

277. Peter S. Schmalz, *The Ojibwa of Southern Ontario* (Toronto: University of Toronto Press, 1991) p. 99; Anthony, F.C. Wallace, *The Death and Rebirth of the Seneca* (New York: Alfred A. Knopf, 1970) pp. 141–4.

278. Thomas Harris, *The Silence of the Lambs* (New York: St. Martin's Press, 1988).

279. Stannard, *American Holocaust, op. cit.*, p. 121.

280. There were not less than three official investigations conducted with regard to the Sand Creek Massacre, during which the extent and type of atrocities committed were testified to by participants and other eyewitnesses in excruciating detail; see U.S. House of Representatives, "Massacre of Cheyenne Indians," *Report on the Conduct of the War* (Washington, D.C.: 38th Cong., 2d Sess., U.S. Governing Printing Office, 1865); U.S. Senate, "Sand Creek Massacre," *Report of the Secretary of War* (Washington, D.C.: Sen. Exec. Doc. 26, 39 Cong., 2d Sess., U.S. Government Printing Office, 1867); U.S. Senate, "The Chivington Massacre," *Reports of the Committees* (Washington, D.C.: 39 Cong., 2d Sess., U.S. Government Printing Office, 1867). Verbatim excerpts from testimonies are also included as an appendix to Stan Hoig's *The Sand Creek Massacre* (Norman: University of Oklahoma Press, 1961).

281. The full quote reads, "Among the brilliant feats of arms in Indian warfare, the recent campaign of our Colorado Volunteers will stand in history with few rivals, and none to exceed it in final results... All acquitted themselves well, and Colorado soldiers have again covered themselves with glory"; *Rocky Mountain News*, Dec. 17, 1864. Such sentiments are still widely prevalent; see Reginald S. Craig, *The Fighting Parson: A Biography of Col. John M. Chivington* (Tucson, AZ: Westernlore, 1959); Lt. Colonel William R. Dunn, *"I Stand by Sand Creek": A Defense of Colonel John M. Chivington and the Third Colorado Cavalry* (Ft. Collins, CO: Old Army Press, 1985).

282. Lazarus, *Black Hills, op. cit.*, p. 29.

283. Virginia P. Miller, "Whatever Happened to the Yuki?" *Indian Historian*, No. 8, 1975, pp. 10–1. More extensively, see Lynwood Carranco and Estle Beard, *Genocide and Vendetta: The Round Valley Wars of Northern California* (Norman: University of Oklahoma Press, 1981).

284. Newcomb, *Indians of Texas, op. cit.*

285. See, e.g., the extensive selection of quotations in David Svaldi, *Sand Creek and the Rhetoric of Extermination: A Case Study in Indian-White Relations* (Lanham, MD: University Press of America, 1989).

286. Tzvetan Todorov, *Facing the Extreme: Moral Life in the Concentration Camps* (New York: Henry Holt, 1996). Although scalp bounties were maintained against them in Arizona Territory until well into the 1880s, the "bloodthirsty" Chiricahua and other Apache groups never adopted the practice, considering it beneath their dignity as human beings; E. Leslie Reedstrom, *Apache Wars: An Illustrated Battle History* (New York: Sterling, 1990) p. 51. The same pertained to their cousins, the Diné; Dee Brown, *Bury My Heart at Wounded Knee: An Indian History of the American West* (New York: Holt, Rinehart & Winston, 1970) pp. 24–5.

287. *New Yorker*, Apr. 27, 1971, p. 104; quoted in Axtell, "The Unkindest Cut," *op. cit.*, p. 19.

288. Howard Peckham and Charles Gibson, eds., *The Attitudes of the Colonial Powers Towards the American Indian* (Salt Lake City: University of Utah Press, 1969).

289. Paul Quattlebaum, *The Land Called Chicora: The Carolinas Under Spanish Rule with French Intrusions, 1520–1670* (Gainesville: University of Florida Press, 1956).

290. Lyon, *Enterprise, op. cit.*; Paul E. Hoffman, *The Spanish Crown and the Defense of the Caribbean, 1565–1585: Precedent, Patrimonialism, and Royal Parsimony* (Baton Rouge: Louisiana State University Press, 1980).

291. Kathleen A. Deegan, "Cultures in Transition: Fusion and Assimilation Among the Eastern Timucua"; Lewis H. Larson, Jr., "Historic Guale Indians of the Georgia Coast and the Impact of the Spanish Mission Effort"; both in Jerald T. Milanich and Samuel Proctor, eds., *Tacachale: Essays on the Indians of Florida and Southeastern Georgia During the Historic Period* (Gainesville: University of Florida Press, 1978). Also see John Tate Channing, *The Spanish Missions of Georgia* (Chapel Hill: University of North Carolina Press, 1935).

292. Robert Allen Matter, "Missions in the Defense of Spanish Florida," *Florida Historical Quarterly*, No. 54, 1975; John H. Hann, *Apalachee: The Land Between the Rivers* (Gainesville: University of Florida Press, 1988). On the trade, which was for the Cuban port city of Havana, which the British had recently conquered, see Steele, *Warpaths, op. cit.*, p. 36. It is worth noting that, of the thousands of Indians who had been missionized over the preceding 110 years, only 83 survived at this point.

293. Actually, this happened in stages, with the panhandle region coming under U.S. control in 1812; Joseph Burholder Smith, *The Plot to Steal Florida: James Madison's Phony War* (New York: Arbor House, 1983); Charles Carroll Griffin, *The United States and the Disruption of the Spanish Empire, 1810–1822: A Study of the Relations of the United States with Spain and with the Rebel Spanish Colonies* (New York: Octagon Books, 1968).

294. It would be 1640 before the Acomas began to rebuild their community in its present location; Jack D. Forbes, *Apache, Navajo and Spaniard* (Norman: University of Oklahoma Press, 1960) pp. 89–90. So successful was Oñate's brutality that, in 1680, the Pueblos revolted as a unified people and drove the Spanish out of their territory for a half-century; Robert Silverberg, *The Pueblo Revolt* (New York: Weybright & Talley, 1970). It is worth noting that in 1781, the Yumas managed to accomplish much the same feat in their desert stronghold just north of the Gulf of California; Jack D. Forbes, *Warriors of the Colorado: The Yumas of the Quechan Nation and Their Neighbors* (Norman: University of Oklahoma Press, 1965) pp. 192–200.

295. The plan did not include the two northerly or "Plains" Apache peoples, the Jicarillas and Kiowa Apaches; Delores A. Gunnerson, *The Jicarilla Apaches: A Study in Survival* (DeKalb: Northern Illinois University Press, 1974) pp. 234–92.

296. Rubí also explicitly advocated the killing or capture and enslavement of Apache women so that the "race" would be unable to reproduce itself; Lawrence Kinnard, ed. and trans. *The Frontiers of New Spain: Nicolás de Lafora's Description, 1766–1768* (Berkeley: Quivera Society, 1958) p. 217.

297. Alfred Barnaby Thomas, ed. and trans., *Forgotten Frontiers: A Study of the Spanish Indian Policy of Don Juan Bautista de Anza, Governor of New Mexico, 1777–1787* (Norman: University of Oklahoma Press, 1932) pp. 35–7, 45–6. On the inducements of weapons, etc., an innovation based on contemporaneous French Indian policy in Louisiana, see Elizabeth Howard West, "The Indian Policy of Bernardo de Gálvez," *Proceedings of the Mississippi Valley Historical Association*, No. 8, 1914–1915.

298. José Cortés, *Views from the Apache Frontier: Report on the Northern Provinces of New Spain* (Norman: University of Oklahoma, 1989 edited reprint of 1803[?] original); Max Moorhead, *The Apache Frontier: Jacobo Ugarte and Spanish-Indian Relations in New Mexico, 1769–1791* (Norman: University of Oklahoma Press, 1968). On the demise of the Lipáns, see Henry F. Dobyns, *The Apache People* (Phoenix, Tribal Indian Series, 1971).

299. Forbes, *Apache, Navajo, Spaniard, op. cit.*; McNitt, *Navajo Wars, op. cit.*, pp. 71–2; William B. Griffin, *Utmost Good Faith: Patterns in Apache-Mexican Hostilities in Northern Chihuahua Border Warfare, 1821–1848* (Albuquerque: University of New Mexico Press, 1988).

300. Dan Thrapp, *The Conquest of Apacheria* (Norman: University of Oklahoma Press, 1967). On reduction of Chiricahua population, see Dobyns, *The Apache People, op. cit.*

301. *Historical Statistics*, series Z, pp. 15–6.

302. "The French did…resist the genocidal tendencies exhibited by British colonists who were bent on erasing all Indian presence from the fertile lands the colonists so coveted for their farms"; Charles J. Balesi, *The Time of the French in the Heart of North America, 1673–1818* (Chicago: Alliance Française, 1992) p. 152.

303. Marcel Trudel, *The Beginnings of New France, 1524–1663* (Toronto: University of Toronto Press, 1973) pp. 34–53. The next French attempt to plant a fixed colonial base, the Huguenots in Florida, also failed; see notes 288 and 289, above. Overall, see George M. Wrong, *The Rise and Fall of New France*, 2 vols. (New York: Macmillan, 1928).

304. De Monts had created an entity not unlike the English Virginia Company organized just three years earlier. His and Champlain's initial attempts to establish a base were at the Ile Sainte-Croix, in Passamaquoddy Bay, and at Port Royal; Salisbury, *Manitou, op. cit.*, pp. 56–72.

305. Bruce G. Trigger, *The Children of Aataentsic*, 2 vols. (Montréal: McGill-Queens University Press, 1976) Vol. 1, pp. 214–24; also see Conrad Heidenreich, *Huronia: A History and Geography of the Huron Indians, 1600–1650* (Toronto: McClellan and Stewart, 1971).

306. Trudel, *Beginnings of New France, op. cit.*, pp. 71–81.

307. Trigger, *The Children of Aataentsic, Vol. 1, op. cit.*, pp. 246–56; H.P. Bigger, ed., *The Works of Samuel de Champlain*, 6 vols. (Toronto: University of Toronto Press, 1922–1936) Vol. 2, pp. 82–107.

308. Steele, *Warpaths, op. cit.*, p. 65; Bigger, *Works of Samuel Champlain, op. cit.*, pp. 122–34.

309. The Mohawks, a people of only about 5,000 at the time, were engaged with a long struggle with the Susquehannocks to the south, and could ill-afford a two-front war, even if weaponry had been equal; Trigger, *Children Aataentsic, Vol. 1, op. cit.*, pp. 256–61.

310. Ibid., pp. 308–15; Trudel, *Beginnings of New France, op. cit.*, pp. 119–21.

311. W.J. Eccles, *France in America* (New York: Harper & Row, 1972) pp. 26–9; Trudel, *Beginnings of New France, op. cit.*, pp. 172–8.

312. The Mahicans had sought to be middlemen, positioned to regulate the flow of materiel and brokering whatever goods the Mohawks might receive from the Dutch at a profit to themselves; Bruce G. Trigger, "The Mohawk-Mahican War (1624–28): The Establishment of a Pattern," *Canadian Historical Review*, No. 52, 1971.

313. Steele, *Warpaths, op. cit.*, pp. 69–70; Trigger, *Children of Aataentsic, Vol. 2, op. cit.*, pp. 463–7.

314. Bruce G. Trigger, *Natives and Newcomers: Canada's "Heroic Age" Reconsidered* (Montréal: McGill-Queens University Press, 1985).

315. Susan Johnson, "Epidemics: The Forgotten Factor in Seventeenth Century Native Warfare in the St. Lawrence Region," in Bruce A. Cox, ed., *Native People, Native Lands* (Ottawa: Carlton University Press, 1988) pp. 14–31.

316. Trigger, *Children of Aataentsic, Vol. 2*, pp. 546–51.

317. Ibid.

318. Steele, *Warpaths, op. cit.*, 70–1; Brian J. Givens, "The Iroquois Wars and Native Firearms," in Cox, *Native People, op. cit.*

319. Trigger, *Children of Aataentsic, Vol. 2, op. cit.*, pp. 789–840.

320. Steele, *Warpaths, op. cit.*, p. 71.

321. Axelrod, *Chronicle of the Indian Wars, op. cit.*, pp. 44–5.

322. The evidence suggests this was a northerly branch of the Susquehannock. In any event, their defeat set off renewed fighting between the Haudenosaunee and their powerful southern counterpart which would last for three decades; ibid., p. 45.

323. Axelrod, *Chronicle of the Indian Wars, op. cit.*, p. 45; George T. Hunt, *The Wars of the Iroquois: A Study in Intertribal Relations* (Madison: University of Wisconsin Press, 1960) pp. 151–7. The New England colonists were also interested in developing a commercial relationship with the Mohawks at this time, not only for economic reasons, but to facilitate the emergence of an alliance which might be of use in their intended destruction of the much more proximate Wampanoags and Narragansetts; Bernard Bailyn, *The New England Merchants of the Seventeenth Century* (Cambridge: Harvard University Press, 1955) pp. 125–39.

324. On Haudenosaunee overtures in this area at the time, see Jennings, *Ambiguous Iroquois Empire, op. cit.*; Patricia C. Calloway, ed., *La Salle and His Legacy: Frenchmen and Indians in the Lower Mississippi Valley* (Jackson: Mississippi State University Press, 1982).

325. A campaign to subdue the Mohawks undertaken by 600 freshly imported French regulars and a hundred Algonquins and Huron remnants in 1666 proved, at best, indecisive; Jack Verney, *The Good Regiment: The Carignan-Salières Regiment in Canada, 1665–1668* (Montréal: McGill-Queens University

Press, 1991) pp. 71–84; W.C. Eccles, *Canada Under Louis XIV, 1663–1701* (Toronto: University of Toronto Press, 1964) pp. 41–4. To argue that the fate of the Hurons, Eries and others was "unintended" by the French is irrelevant. Their purpose had been to create a situation in which the Five Nations, or at least the Mohawks, would suffer it. Having quite deliberately set the process in motion for their own purposes, they are responsible for the genocidal nature of the outcome, even though it was, from their perspective, visited upon the "wrong" Indians.

326. Eccles, *France in America, op. cit.*, pp. 63–88.

327. Ibid. Also see Balesi, *Time of the French, op. cit.*; Sauer, *Seventeenth Century North America, op. cit.*, pp. 127–216.

328. The Hudson's Bay Company, following the French example, had long since begun trading guns to the Crees for furs (by 1689, they would have more than 10,000 modern weapons). The French, meanwhile, offered the Indians extraordinary trade inducements—and ample supplies of powder and lead—to turn this newly acquired firepower on the very English who'd provided it. The Cree began attacking Hudson's Bay posts at least as early as 1680; M.L. Brown, *Firearms in Colonial America: The Impact on History and Technology* (Washington, D.C.: Smithsonian Institution, 1980) p. 157.

329. "The most ambitious solution suggested was extermination"; Axelrod, *Chronicle, op. cit.*, p. 64; also see William Eccles, *The Canadian Frontier, 1534–1760* (Albuquerque: University of New Mexico Press, [rev. ed.], 1983), p. 148; R. David Edmunds and Joseph L. Peyser, *The Fox Wars: The Mesquakie Challenge to New France* (Norman: University of Oklahoma Press, 1993).

330. Joseph L. Peyser, "The 1730 Siege of the Foxes," *Illinois Historical Journal*, Vol. LXXX, No. 3, 1967.

331. Joseph L. Peyser, "The Fate of the Fox Survivors: A Dark Chapter in the History of the French in the Upper Country, 1726–1737," *Wisconsin Magazine of History*, Vol. 73, No. 2, 1890–1990.

332. Axelrod, *Chronicle, op. cit.*, p. 67.

333. Patricia D. Woods, "The French and the Natchez Indians in Louisiana, 1700–1731," *Louisiana History*, No. 19, 1978.

334. The Natchez had once been the regional power, having achieved a distinctive Mobilian agricultural civilization well before 1500. A series of epidemics had reduced them by as much as 95 percent by 1700; Charles M. Hudson, *The Southeastern Indians* (Knoxville: University of Kentucky Press, 1976).

335. Axelrod, *Chronicle, op. cit.*, pp. 67–8; Woods, "The French and the Natchez," *op. cit.*

336. Joseph L. Peyser, "The Chickasaw Wars of 1736 and 1740," *Journal of Mississippi History*, February 1982; Balesi, *Time of the French, op. cit.*, Chap. 10, inclusive. Also see Arrell M. Gibson, *The Chickasaws* (Norman: University of Oklahoma Press, 1971).

337. Patricia D. Woods, *French-Indian Relations on the Southern Frontier, 1699–1762* (Ann Arbor: University of Michigan Press, 1980).

338. See generally, the early chapters of C.R. Boxer, *The Dutch Seaborne Empire, 1600–1800* (New York: Alfred A. Knopf, 1965).

339. Allen W. Trelease, *Indian Affairs in Colonial New York: The Seventeenth Century* (Ithaca, NY: Cornell University Press) pp. 25–34.

340. Bruce J. Givens, "The Iroquois Wars and Native Firearms," in Cox, *Native People, op. cit.*

341. Trigger, "The Mohawk-Mohegan War," *op. cit.*; Jennings, *The Ambiguous Iroquois Empire, op. cit.*, 49, 53, 71; Givens, "The Iroquois Wars," *op. cit.*, pp. 3–13; Trelease, *Indian Affairs, op. cit.*, pp. 46–8; Daniel K. Richter, *The Ordeal of the Longhouse: The Peoples of the Iroquois Confederation in the Era of Colonization* (Chapel Hill: University of North Carolina Press, 1992) pp. 1–49.

342. Van Cleaf Bachman, *Peltries or Plantations: The Economic Policies of the Dutch West Indian Company in New Netherland, 1623–1629* (Baltimore: Johns Hopkins University Press, 1969).

343. Axelrod, *Chronicle, op. cit.*, p. 39.

344. On the Dutch provision of muskets to the Mohawks at this time, see Steele, *op. cit.*, p. 115; otherwise, see Trelease, *Indian Affairs, op. cit.*, pp. 64–80.

345. Axelrod, *Chronicle op. cit.*, p. 39.

346. Ibid.

347. Ibid., p. 40.

348. Steele, *Warpaths, op. cit.*, p. 116.

349. Ibid.; Axelrod, *Chronicle, op. cit.*, p. 40.

350. Ibid.

351. Trelease, *Indian Affairs, op. cit.*, pp. 138–68.

352. Jennings, *The Ambiguous Empire, op. cit.*, pp. 108–11.

353. Steele, *Warpaths, op. cit.*, p. 118; Richard I. Melvoin, *New England Outpost: War and Society in Colonial Deerfield* (New York: W.W. Norton, 1989) pp. 35–50.

354. The second Anglo-Dutch War lasted from 1665–67; Steele, *Warpaths, op. cit.*, pp. 118–9.

355. By 1667, the Mohawks had absorbed so many captives in an effort to keep their strength up that they'd become a minority in their own villages. Exhausted, they needed a period of respite to rejuvenate themselves; Gordon G. Day, "The Ouragie War: A Case History in Iroquois-New England Indian Relations," in Michael K. Foster, Jack Campisi and Marianne Mithun, eds., *Extending the Rafters: Interdisciplinary Approaches to Iroquoian Studies* (Albany: State University of New York Press, 1984) pp. 35–50; Richter, *Ordeal, op. cit.*, pp. 50–74; Jennings, *The Ambiguous Iroquois Empire, op. cit.*, pp. 84–112, 128–9.

356. This newest English holding had already been promised as a personal proprietary to the English king's youngest brother, the Duke of York and Albany. Hence the names bestowed upon the colony and its capital; Robert C. Richie, *The Duke's Province: A Study of New York Politics and Society, 1664–1691* (Chapel Hill, NC: University of North Carolina Press, 1977) pp. 9–24.

357. See, overall, Klaus E. Knorr, *British Colonial Theories, 1570–1850* (Toronto: University of Toronto Press, 1944) pp. 68–80.

358. Hugh Edward Egerton, *A Short History of British Colonial Policy* (London: Methuen, 6th ed., 1920). Also see D.K. Fieldhouse, *The Colonial Empires: A Comparative Survey from the Eighteenth Century* (New York: Delacourt, 1967) pp. 55–83.

359. On the Tuscaroras, see Leight Wright, *The Only Land, op. cit.*, pp. 117–20.

360. Douglas W. Boyce, " 'As the Wind Scatters the Smoke': The Tuscarora in the Eighteenth Century," in Richter and Merrill, *op. cit.*

361. Steele, *Warpaths, op. cit.*, p. 160.

362. Steele, *Warpaths, op. cit.*, pp. 165–6.

363. The colonists were so desperate at one point that they armed some 500 African slaves to assist in the defense of Charleston; ibid., p. 166. Also see David H. Corkoran, *The Creek Frontier, 1540–1783* (Norman: University of Oklahoma Press, 1967) pp. 59–81.

364. Axlerod, *Chronicle, op. cit.*, p. 62; Steele, *Warpaths, op. cit.*, p. 166.

365. James Leight Wright, Jr., *The Anglo-Spanish Rivalry in North America* (Athens: University of Georgia Press, 1971) pp. 90–1.

366. Although the Abenaki were aligned with the French as trading partners, they were completely independent and pursued a course of military neutrality which English aggression ultimately denied them; Kenneth M. Morrison, *The Embattled Northeast: The Elusive Ideal of Alliance in Abenaki-Euramerican Relations* (Berkeley: University of California Press, 1984) pp. 117–9.

367. See Edward P. Hamilton, *The French and Indian Wars* (Garden City, NY: Doubleday, 1962); Howard M. Peckham, *The Colonial Wars, 1689–1762* (Chicago: University of Chicago Press, 1964); Albert Marrin, *Struggle for a Continent: The French and Indian Wars, 1690–1760* (New York: Atheneum, 1987).

368. See, e.g., Fred Anderson, *A People's Army: Massachusetts Soldiers and Society in the Seven Years' War* (Chapel Hill, NC: University of North Carolina Press, 1984).

369. "Most [indigenous nations] sided in varying degrees with the French, hoping to eke out some advantage thereby, or hoping merely to survive"; Axelrod, *Chronicle, op. cit.*, p. 76.

370. Balesi, *Time of the French, op. cit.*

371. Axelrod, *Chronicle, op. cit.*, p. 76; also see Randolph C. Downes, *Council Fires on the Upper Ohio* (Pittsburg: University of Pittsburg Press, 1940).

372. Richter, *Ordeal, op. cit.*, pp. 162–213; Dale Miquelon, *New France: "A Supplement to Europe"* (Toronto: McClellan and Stewart, 1987) pp. 18–25.

373. Indeed, by 1730 all three had gone out of existence, their remnants being absorbed mainly by the Penobscots and Abenakis; Calloway, *Western Abenaki, op. cit.*

374. In 1699, for example, France's western allies, particularly the Ojibway, administered a humiliating defeat to the Haudenosaunee on the shores of Lake Erie; Axelrod, *Chronicle, op. cit.*, p. 55.

375. Ibid., p. 56. The captives, of course, were sold into slavery; Hann, *Appalachee, op. cit.*, pp. 264–83.

376. A good overview of the falsity of this "peace" will be found in the early chapters of John Robert McNeill's, *The Atlantic Empires of France and Spain: Louisbourg and Havana, 1700–1763* (Chapel Hill, NC: University of North Carolina Press, 1985). On the impact of the war on the Abenaki and their tributaries, see Calloway, *Western Abenaki, op. cit.*

377. Allan W. Eckert, *The Frontiersmen* (Boston: Little, Brown, 1967).

378. See Charles Morse Stotz, *Outposts of the War for Empire* (Pittsburg: University of Pittsburg Press, 1985); James Titus, *The Old Dominion at War: Society, Politics and Warfare in Late Colonial Virginia* (Columbia, SC: University of South Carolina Press, 1991).

379. See Hamilton, *French and Indian Wars, op. cit.*

380. Probably the best overview of the raiding will be found in Eckert, *That Dark and Bloody River, op. cit.* Also see his *The Wilderness at War* (Boston: Little, Brown, 1978) and Leroy V. Eid, " 'A Kind of Running Fight': Indian Battlefield Tactics in the Late Eighteenth Century," *Western Pennsylvania Historical Magazine*, No. 71, 1988.

381. Lee McCardell, *Ill-Starred General: Braddock of the Coldstream Guards* (Pittsburg: University of Pittsburg Press, 1958); Stanley G. Pargellis, "Braddock's Defeat," *American History Review*, No. 41, 1936.

382. Jennings, *Empire of Fortune, op. cit.*, pp. 162–3; Peter E. Russell, "Redcoats in the Wilderness: British Officers and Irregular Warfare, 1740 to 1760," *William and Mary Quarterly*, No. 35, 1978.

383. Fort William Henry is the installation featured in James Fenimore Cooper's *Last of the Mohicans*. For a much more accurate account of what happened there, see Ian K. Steele, *Betrayals: Fort William Henry and the "Massacre"* (New York: Oxford University Press, rev. ed., 1993).

384. The promisaries devolved upon guarantees of indigenous territoriality. On English diplomacy in this connection, see Wilbur R. Jacobs, *Diplomacy and Indian Gifts: Anglo-French Rivalry Along the Ohio and Northwestern Frontiers, 1748–1763* (Stanford, CA: Stanford University Press, 1950); Richard Middleton, *Bells of Victory: The Pitt-Newcastle Ministry and the Conduct of the Seven Years' War, 1757–1762* (Cambridge: Cambridge University Press, 1985).

385. Downes, *Council Fires, op. cit.* Also see Stephen F. Auth, *The Ten Years' War: Indian-White Relations in Pennsylvania, 1755–1765* (New York: Garland, 1989); Anthony F.C. Wallace, *King of the Delawares: Teedyuscung, 1700–1763* (Philadelphia: University of Pennsylvania Press, 1949).

386. David H. Corkran, *The Cherokee Frontier: Conflict and Survival, 1740–1762* (Norman: University of Oklahoma Press, 1962).

387. Brian Leigh Dunnigan, *Siege 1759: The Campaign Against Niagara* (Youngstown, NY: New York Historical Association, 1986); C.P. Stacy, *Quebec 1759: The Siege and the Battle* (Toronto: Macmillan, 1959).

388. Although English negotiators were officially enjoined by the Crown to assure native land rights through such treaties, the Micmacs were shortly dispossessed through a sleight of hand involving interpretation of the 1713 Treaty of Utrecht; Axelrod, *Chronicle, op. cit.*, pp. 93–4. More generally, see George F. Stanley, *New France: The Last Phase, 1744–1760* (Toronto: McClellan and Stewart, 1968); Francis Gardiner Davenport, ed., *European Treaties Bearing on the History of the United States and Its Dependencies*, 2 vols. (Washington, D.C.: Carnegie Institution, 1917); Dorothy V. Jones, *License for Empire: Colonialism by Treaty in North America* (Chicago: University of Chicago Press, 1982).

389. Corkran, *Cherokee Frontier, op. cit.*, pp. 142–272; Gary C. Goodwin, *Cherokees in Transition: A Study of Changing Culture and Environment prior to 1775* (Chicago: University of Chicago Press, 1977).

390. Thornton, *The Cherokees, op. cit.*, pp. 1–37.

391. Corkran, *Cherokee Frontier, op. cit.*; Goodwin, *Cherokees in Transition, op. cit.*

392. Jack M. Sosin, *Whitehall and the Wilderness: The Middle West in British Colonial Policy, 1760–1775* (Lincoln: University of Nebraska Press, 1961).

393. Duane Champaign, "The Delaware Revitalization Movement of the Early 1760s: A Suggested Reinterpretation," *American Indian Quarterly*, No. 12, 1988; Gregory Evans Dowd, "Thinking and Believing: Nativism and Unity in the Ages of Pontiac and Tecumseh," *American Indian Quarterly*, No. 16, 1992.

394. Peckham, *Colonial Wars, op. cit.*; also see Gregory Evans Dowd, "The French King Wakes Up in Detroit: 'Pontiac's War' in Rumor and History," *Ethnohistory*, No. 37, 1990. On the nature of the alliance Pontiac sought to form, see Gregory Evans Dowd, *A Spirited Resistance: The North American Indian Struggle for Unity, 1745–1815* (Baltimore: Johns Hopkins University Press, 1992). Also see Richard White, *The Middle Ground: Indians, Empires, and Republics in the Great Lakes Region, 1650–1815* (Cambridge: Harvard University Press, 1991).

395. On the demise of these four peoples from the contemporaneous perspective of Amherst's replacement, see Clarence Edwin Carter, ed., *The Correspondence of General Thomas Gage with the Secretaries of State, 1763–1775, Vol. 1* (New Haven: Yale College and University Press, 1931). Also see Thornton, *American Indian Holocaust and Survival, op. cit.*

396. Jack Stagg, *Anglo-Indian Relations in North America to 1763 and an Analysis of the Royal Proclamation of 7 October 1763* (Ottawa: Indian and Northern Affairs Ministry of Canada, 1981).

397. William G. Godfrey, *Pursuit of Profit and Preferment in North America: John Bradstreet's Quest* (Waterloo, Ont.: Wilfred Laurier University Press, 1982).

398. George Washington, to take a prime example, had planned to profit from thousands of acres to which he'd laid claim in Kentucky and Ohio; Eckert, *That Dark and Bloody River, op. cit.*, pp. 13–4. Also see North Callahan, *George Washington: Soldier and Man* (New York: William Morrow, 1972).

399. Bernard Knollenberg, *The Origin of the American Revolution, 1759–1766* (New York: Macmillan, 1960). Also see Peter Marshall, "Colonial Protest and Imperial Retrenchment: Indian Policy, 1764–1768," *Journal of American Studies*, No. 5, 1971; Jack P. Greene, "The Seven Years' War and the American Revolution: The Causal Relationship Reconsidered, *Journal of Imperial and Commonwealth History*, No. 8, 1980.

400. Axelrod, *Chronicle, op. cit.*, p. 99. It is worth noting that no one was ever prosecuted for these crimes.

401. To be fair, Dunmore was doing little more than formalizing an existing situation, since Virginians and others had been literally pouring into the more easterly portions of the proscribed territory despite the Proclamation of 1763; Sosin, *Whitehall, op. cit.*

402. Cornstalk's brother, Silverheels, was killed in the ambush. Thereafter, roughly 700 Indians inflicted 222 fatalities on the governor's 3,000 man column, at which point Dunmore ordered a full retreat; E.O. Randolph, "The Dunmore War," *Ohio Archaeological and Historical Publications*, No. 11, 1931.

403. Axelrod, *Chronicle, op. cit.*, p. 100.

404. Gregory Schaaf, *Wampum Belts and Peace Trees: George Morgan, Native Americans and Revolutionary Diplomacy* (Golden, CO: Fulcrum, 1990).

405. Thomas Perkins Abernathy, *Western Lands and the American Revolution* (New York: Russell & Russell, 1959); Wilbur R. Jacobs, *Dispossessing the American Indian: Indians and Whites on the Colonial Frontier* (New York: Scribner's, 1972); Colin G. Calloway, *The American Revolution in Indian Country: Crisis and Diversity in Native American Communities* (Cambridge: Cambridge University Press, 1995).

406. Although the more populous Senecas probably provided the greater manpower, the sharp end of the Haudenosaunee offensive was as always provided by the Mohawks, this time led by Thayendanegea (Joseph Brant). The Oneidas, alone among the Six Nations, sided with the rebels against the Crown; Barbara Greymount, *The Iroquois in the American Revolution* (Syracuse, NY: Syracuse University Press, 1975).

407. Alan W. Eckert, *The Twilight of Empire* (Boston: Little, Brown, 1988); *That Dark and Bloody River, op. cit.*

408. Corkran, *Cherokee Frontier, op. cit.*, pp. 197–244; R.S. Cotterill, *The Southern Indians: The Story of the Five Civilized Tribes before Removal* (Norman: University of Oklahoma Press, 1954).

409. The implications are analyzed in Eric Robinson's *The American Revolution in Its Political and Military Aspects, 1763–1783* (New York: Oxford University Press, 1955).

410. The commanders were General Andrew Williamson, heading 1,800 troops from Georgia and South Carolina; General Griffith Rutherford, heading 2,500 from North Carolina; and Colonel William Christian, heading another 2,000 from Virginia and North Carolina; Axelrod, *Chronicle, op. cit.*, p. 119.

411. Corkran, *Cherokee Frontier, op. cit.*, pp. 231–5.

412. Axelrod, *Chronicle, op. cit.*, p. 119; also see the final chapters of David H. Corkran, *The Creek Frontier, 1540–1783* (Norman: University of Oklahoma Press, 1967).

413. Quoted in John Tebbel and Keith Jennison, *The American Indian Wars* (New York: Harper & Row, 1960) p. 124.

414. Ibid., p. 125.

415. Page Smith, *A New Age Now Begins: A People's History of the American Revolution*, Vol. 2 (New York: McGraw-Hill, 1976) p. 1172. For details, see Frederick Cook, *Journals of the Military Expedition of Major General John Sullivan against the Six Nations of Indians in 1779* (Auburn, NY: New York Historical Society, 1887).

416. Tebbel and Jennison, *American Indian Wars, op. cit.*, p. 125. Also see the early chapters of Wallace, *The Death and Rebirth of the Senecas, op. cit.*

417. This is well-covered in Frederick Austin Ogg, *The Old Northwest* (New Haven, CT: Yale University Press, 1921). Also see William Albert Galloway, *Old Chillicothe: Shawnees and Pioneer History* (Xenia, OH: Buckeye Press, 1934).

418. Chillicothe had been burned again, and Clark was advancing with little opposition; Axelrod, *Chronicle, op. cit.*, p. 122. The 1782 accords ended the fighting although the actual Treaty of Paris was not finalized and signed until September 3, 1783.

419. Eckert, *That Dark and Bloody River, op. cit.*, p. 440. This and related materials will be found in Alden T. Vaughan, *Early American Indian Documents: Treaties and Laws, 1607–1789* (Washington, D.C.: University Publications of America, 1979).

420. Eckert, *That Dark and Bloody River, op. cit.*, p. 440.

421. As Washington stated it, "There is nothing to be gained by an Indian war but the soil they live on and this can [often] be obtained…at less expense" through the sort of expedients he recommended so long as treaty commissioners did not "grasp at too much" at any given moment. Direct applications of military force should be undertaken only when other means failed; Eckert, *That Dark and Bloody River, op. cit.*, pp. 440–1.

422. Ibid., p. 441.

423. In this, the Constitution merely reflects a longstanding principle of international law, that the legal relations between nations possesses a standing superior to the domestic legal arrangements of any given nation; Emer Vattel, *The Laws of Nations* (Philadelphia: T. & J.W. Johnson, 1855); Alfred Nussbaum, *A Concise History of the Laws of Nations* (New York: Macmillan, 1954). For the perspective of Canada, see George Brown and Ron Mcguire, *Indian Treaties in Historical Perspective* (Ottawa: Indian and Northern Affairs Ministry of Canada, 1979).

424. 1 Stat. 50 (1787). See generally, Francis Paul Prucha, *American Indian Policy in the Formative Years: The Trade and Intercourse Acts, 1790–1834* (Lincoln: University of Nebraska Press, 1970); Vine Deloria, Jr., and Clifford M. Lytle, *American Indians, American Justice* (Austin: University of Texas Press, 1983).

425. On Marshall's holdings, see L. Baker, *John Marshall: A Life in Law* (New York: Macmillan, 1976) p. 80. On his doctrine of Indian law, see my "Perversions of Justice: Examining the Doctrine of U.S. Rights to Occupancy in North America," in David S. Caudill and Steven Jay Gould, *Radical Philosophy of Law: Contemporary Challenges to Mainstream Legal Theory and Practice* (Atlantic Highlands, NJ: Humanities Press, 1995). Also see Donald E. Worcester, ed., *Forked Tongues and Broken Treaties* (Caldwell, ID: Caxton, 1975).

426. Andrew Jackson, who was president at the time Marshall finalized his theory in the so-called "Cherokee Cases" of 1831–32, openly defied the high court's conclusions, announcing that "Justice Marshall has rendered his opinion, now let him enforce it"; Michael P. Rogin, *Fathers and Children: Andrew Jackson and the Subjugation of the American Indian* (New York: Alfred A. Knopf, 1975) pp. 206–48.

427. Quoted in Eckert, *That Dark and Bloody River, op. cit.* p. 440.

428. Quoted in Drinnon, *Facing West, op. cit.*, p. 98.

429. On the common underpinnings of the two pseudophilosophies, see Reginald Horsman, *Race and Manifest Destiny: The Origins of American Racial Anglo-Saxonism* (Cambridge: Harvard University Press, 1981); Parella, *Lebensraum and Manifest Destiny, op. cit.*; Albert K. Weinberg, *Manifest Destiny: A Study of Nationalist Expansion in American History* (Baltimore: Johns Hopkins University Press, 1935); Frederick Merk, *Manifest Destiny and Mission in American History: A Reinterpretation* (New York: Alfred A. Knopf, 1963).

430. As the Seneca leader Red Jacket explained to President Washington in 1792, when his very name was mentioned among the Haudenosaunee, "our women look behind them and turn pale, and our children cling to their mothers' necks"; quoted in Wallace, *The Death and Rebirth of the Seneca, op. cit.*, p. 144. Also see Michael S. Manley, "Red Jacket's Last Campaign," *New York History*, No. 21, April 1950.

431. Axelrod, *Chronicle, op. cit.*, p. 123.

432. The expedition, conducted while the Shawnees were assembled for another round of talks with George Rogers Clark, burned thirteen mostly vacant Shawnee towns. A total of ten men and a dozen women were killed and scalped. "In addition, all the Shawnee crops, ready for the harvesting, had been destroyed." The best rendering of Logan's "campaign" will be found in Allan W. Eckert, *The Frontiersmen* (Boston: Little, Brown, 1967).

433. Axelrod, *Chronicle, op. cit.*, p. 124.

434. Little Turtle served as the principal political strategist of the alliance, while Blue Jacket became its primary military leader; Allan W. Eckert, *A Sorrow in Our Heart: The Life of Tecumseh* (Boston: Little, Brown, 1992).

435. Knox estimated that it would take 2,500 men and $200,000 to defeat the Miami-Shawnee alliance. Plainly not knowing much about Indians, or at least *these* Indians, he calculated that only $15,000 would be needed to "buy their cooperation." Harmar's command, which had lost 31 men to an ambush only two days earlier, suffered losses of 108 dead militiamen and 75 regular army soldiers; Axelrod, *Chronicle, op. cit.*, p. 125.

436. St. Clair had some 1,400 men with him on the day of the battle. Of these, 623 soldiers were killed, as well as 24 civilian teamsters. Another 271 soldiers were wounded. The Indians lost 21 dead and 40 wounded; Axelrod, *Chronicle, op. cit.*, p. 125.

437. Ibid., p. 127.

438. The best overall account of the hostilities is probably Wiley Sword's *President Washington's Indian War* (Norman: University of Oklahoma Press, 1985).

439. Treaty of Greenville, August 1795. For the text of this and 370 other ratified treaties between the U.S. and indigenous peoples, see Charles J. Kappler, ed., *Indian Treaties, 1778–1883* (New York: Interland, 1972). After the treaty, Congress subdivided the old Northwest Territory into three parts: Indiana (est., 1800), Michigan (est., 1805) and Illinois (est., 1809); Malcolm J. Rohrbough, *The Trans-Appalachian Frontier: Peoples, Societies and Institutions, 1775–1850* (New York: Oxford, 1978) p. 115.

440. Axelrod, *Chronicle, op. cit.*, p. 130.

441. Ibid., p. 150; Harrison passed around plenty of liquor before the signing. He then claimed to have "purchased" 50 million acres of prime farmland for $2,234.50 in gifts and a $1,000 annuity in goods. Small wonder Black Hawk considered the whole thing a fraud; Donald Jackson, ed., *Black Hawk: An Autobiography* (Urbana: University of Illinois Press, 1964).

442. Benjamin Drake, *The Life of Tecumseh and His Brother the Prophet* (Cincinnati: Anderson, Gates & Wright, 1841); R. David Edmunds, *The Shawnee Prophet* (Lincoln: University of Nebraska Press, 1983); *Tecumseh and the Quest for Indian Leadership* (Boston: Little, Brown, 1984).

443. Probably the most detailed account is in Armstrong Perry's *The Sauks and the Black Hawk War* (Springfield, IL: H.W. Rokker, 1887).

444. Bradford Perkins, *Prologue to War: England and the United States, 1805–1812* (Berkeley: University of California Press, 1961); Reginald Horsman, *The Causes of the War of 1812* (Philadelphia: University of Pennsylvania Press, 1962).

445. This southern diplomacy is well-handled in Glenn Tucker, *Tecumseh: Vision of Glory* (Indianapolis: Bobbs-Merrill, 1956).

446. Axelrod, *Chronicle, op. cit.*, p. 132. Also see Freeman Cleaves, *Old Tippecanoe: William Henry Harrison and His Times* (Port Washington, NY: Kennikat, 1969 reprint of 1939 ed.); Moses Dawson, *Historical Narrative of the Civil and Military Service of Major-General William Henry Harrison* (Cincinnati: Cincinnati Advertiser, 1824).

447. The implications of this action are analyzed in detail in Philip P. Mason, ed., *After Tippecanoe: Some Aspects of the War of 1812* (East Lansing, MI & Toronto: Michigan State University Press & Ryerson Press, 1963).

448. Pierce Berton, *The Invasion of Canada, 1812–1813* (Boston: Little, Brown, 1980).

449. For analysis, see Carl F. Klinct, ed., *Tecumseh: Fact and Fiction in the Early Records* (Engelwood Cliffs, NJ: Prentice-Hall, 1961).

450. At least one British officer, Major General Henry Proctor, was later prosecuted in this connection; Victor Lauriston, "The Case for General Proctor," in Morris Zaslow and Wesley B. Turner, eds., *The Defended Border: Upper Canada and the War of 1812* (Toronto: Macmillan, 1964).

451. Axelrod, *Chronicle, op. cit.*, p. 135. Winchester lost more than 400 of his 980 men; A.R. Gilpin, *The War of 1812 in the Old Northwest* (East Lansing: Michigan State University Press, 1958) p. 231.

452. See John C. Frederickson, "Kentucky at the Thames, 1813," *Register of Kentucky History*, Spring 1985.

453. Bert Anson, *The Miami Indians* (Norman: University of Oklahoma Press, 1970).

454. The ordeals of these peoples are depicted in Peter D. Clark, *The Origin and Traditional History of the Wyandots* (Toronto: Hunter, Rose, 1870); Arrell M. Gibson, *The Kickapoos: Lords of the Middle Border* (Norman: University of Oklahoma Press, 1963); R. David Edmunds, *The Potawatomies: Keepers of the Fire* (Norman: University of Oklahoma Press, 1978). On the Ottawas, see H. Hickerson, *The Chippewa and Their Neighbors: A Study in Ethnohistory* (New York: Holt, Rinehart & Winston, 1970).

455. Thomas Wildcat Alford, *Civilization and the Story of the Absentee Shawnees* (Norman: University of Oklahoma Press, 1936); James H. Howard, *Shawnee: Ceremonialism of an American Indian Tribe* (Athens, OH: University Press of Ohio, 1981).

456. Jackson's army devastated "every Red Stick town in its path," destroyed winter food stores, and killed whatever Indians it came upon; Axelrod, *Chronicle, op. cit.*, p. 139.

457. For a glowing account of the "heroism "of Jackson's men in shooting hundreds of unarmed Indians who were attempting to swim to safety—but virtually no mention of the wholesale mutilation of their corpses—see William Alexander Caruthers, *The Knights of the Horseshoe* (New York: A.L. Burt, n.d., circa 1835).

458. The Red Stick faction of the (Upper) Creeks, led by William Weatherford (Red Eagle), joined Tecumseh's alliance in an attempt to avert total dispossession of their homeland. They were opposed by the White Sticks (Lower Creek) faction, who erroneously believed some reasonable accommodation might be negotiated with the U.S. The Upper Creeks were virtually exterminated during the war. The Lower Creeks were then almost entirely dispossessed by their American "allies"; Joel W. Martin, *Sacred Revolt: The Muskogees' Struggle for a New World* (Boston: Beacon Press, 1991). Also see Angie Debo, *The Road to Disappearance: A History of the Creek Indians* (Norman: University of Oklahoma Press, 1941); Frank Lawrence Owsley, Jr., *Struggle for the Gulf Borderlands: The Creek War and the Battle of New Orleans, 1812–1815* (Gainesville: University Presses of Florida, 1981).

459. Treaty of Horseshoe Bend, Aug. 9, 1814; Kappler, *Indian Treaties, op. cit.*, pp. 107–10.

460. "Even for admirers of the seventh president of the United States, the name of Andrew Jackson is forever linked to the inequitable, immoral, and inhumane Federal policy of Indian 'removal.' It is true that the Indian Removal Act of 1830 was the work of the Jackson administration and that Jackson, as well as his Indian agents and treaty commissioners, shamelessly manipulated the law and interfered with internal Indian affairs well beyond the point of fraud in order to compel tribal cession of eastern land and the removal of [indigenous nations] to the West." The idea of removal originated with George Washington, however, and was pursued by each of the presidents who followed him; Axelrod, *Chronicle, op. cit.*, p. 137. Also see Louis Filler and Allen Guttmann, eds., *The Removal of the Cherokee Nation: Manifest Destiny or National Dishonor?* (Boston: Heath, 1962).

461. U.S. objectives are spelled out in John K. Mahon, *History of the Second Seminole War, 1835–1842* (Gainesville: University of Florida Press, 1967). The Seminole side of things is reasonably well explained in William Hartley and Ellen Hartley, *Osceola: The Unconquered Indian* (New York: Hawthorn Books, 1973).

462. "For every two Seminoles who were sent West, one soldier died—1,500 in all. The war cost the federal government $20 million, and it ended in 1842 not through any victory on either side, but because the government simply stopped trying to flush out the remaining Seminoles who had hidden themselves deep in the Everglades." A third war was fought with these remnants from 1855 to 1858, with even less-conclusive results; Axelrod, *Chronicle, op. cit.*, pp. 146–7.

463. Ibid., pp. 150–1.

464. Perry, *op. cit.*; Frank E. Stevens, *The Black Hawk War: Including a Review of Black Hawk's Life* (Chicago: Aldine, 1903); Edward J. Nichols, *Zach Taylor's Little Army* (Garden City, NJ: Doubleday, 1963).

465. The best overview of the campaign is in Miriam Gurko's *Indian America: The Black Hawk War* (New York: Crowell, 1970).

466. Axelrod, *Chronicle, op. cit.*, p. 151.

467. Gurko, *Indian America, op. cit.*, p. 238.

468. Jackson, *Black Hawk, op. cit.*

469. William T. Hagan, *The Sac and Fox Indians* (Norman: University of Oklahoma Press, 1958).

470. See my "Like Sand in the Wind: The Making of an American Indian Diaspora," in *Since Predator Came: Notes on the Struggle for American Indian Liberation* (Littleton, CO: Aigis, 1995).

471. By 1821, Missouri had become a state. The last territory east of the Mississippi, Wisconsin, was created in 1836; Rohrbough, *Trans-Appalachian Frontier, op. cit.*, pp. 159, 219, 321.

472. T.R. Fehrenbach, *Lone Star: A History of Texas and Texans* (New York: Macmillan, 1968). Also see Anna Muckleroy, "The Indian Policy of the Republic of Texas" (4 pts.), *Southwestern Historical Quarterly*, Apr., July, Oct. 1922; Jan. 1923.

473. David M. Pelcher, *The Diplomacy of Annexation: Texas, Oregon and the Mexican War* (Columbia: University of Missouri Press, 1973).

474. Gene M. Brack, *Mexico Views Manifest Destiny, 1821–1846: An Essay on the Origins of the Mexican War* (Albuquerque: University of New Mexico Press, 1975); James M. McCaffrey, *Army of Manifest Destiny: The American Soldier in the Mexican War, 1846–1848* (New York: Oxford University Press, 1992).

475. Axelrod, *Chronicle, op. cit.*, p. 155. Also see Merrill D. Peterson, *Thomas Jefferson and the New Nation* (New York: Oxford University Press, 1973); Alexander De Conde, *This Affair of Louisiana* (New York: Scriber's, 1973).

476. Quoted in Axelrod, *Chronicle, op. cit.*, p. 157.

477. Horsman, *Race and Manifest Destiny, op. cit.*; Svaldi, *Sand Creek, op. cit.*

478. See note 138, above.

479. Axelrod, *Chronicle, op. cit.*, p. 162.

480. See, e.g., Gunnerson, *The Jicarilla Apaches, op. cit.*; Thrapp, *op. cit.*; C.L. Sonnichsen, *The Mescalero Apaches* (Norman: University of Oklahoma Press, 1958); Obie B. Falk, *The Geronimo Campaign* (New York: Oxford University Press, 1969); Leigh H. Basso, *The Cibique Apache* (New York: Holt, Rinehart & Winston, 1970); D.C. Cole, *The Chiricahua Apache, 1846–1876: From War to Reservation* (Albuquerque: University of New Mexico Press, 1988).

481. Thornton, *American Indian Holocaust and Survival, op. cit.*

482. *Daily Alta California*, May 4, 1852.

483. Ibid.

484. *San Francisco Bulletin*, June 18, 1860.

485. Ibid.

486. See note 283, above.

487. The reference is to another series of massacres in Mendocino County, California; *San Francisco Bulletin*, June 18, 1860. More broadly, see Carranco and Beard, *Genocide and Vendetta, op. cit.*

488. Cook, *The Conflict Between the California Indians and White Civilization, op. cit.*; William Eccleston, *The Mariposa Indian War, 1850–1851* (Salt Lake City: University of Utah Press, 1957 reprint of 1851 original).

489. Axelrod, *Chronicle, op. cit.*, pp. 171–2. Also see Obie B. Falk, *Destiny Road: The Gila Trail and the Opening of the Southwest* (New York: Oxford University Press, 1973); *Crimson Desert: The Indian Wars of the Southwest* (New York: Oxford University Press, 1974).

490. More than fifty California "mission bands" like the Juaneños were declared extinct by the federal government as part of the "Pit River Land Settlement" during the 1970s; Florence Connolly Shipeck, *Pushed into the Rocks: Southern California Indian Land Tenure, 1769–1986* (Lincoln: University of Nebraska Press, 1988). For selected tribally specific outcomes during the late nineteenth century, see Rose Taylor, *The Last Survivor* (San Francisco: Johnck & Seeger, 1932); Annie Mitchell, *Jim Savage and the Tulareno Indians* (Los Angeles, Westernlore Press, 1957); Frank F. Latta, *Handbook of Yokuts Indians* (Santa Cruz: Bear State Press, 1977); Lowell John Bean, *The Cahuilla* (New York: Chelsea House, 1989). Overall,

see Alberto L. Hurtado, *Indian Survival on the California Frontier* (New Haven, CT: Yale University Press, 1988).

491. Ray Hoard Glassley, *Pacific Northwest Indian Wars* (Portland, OR: Binfords & Mort, 1953) pp. 13–38. This is a horribly racist volume but confirms certain gruesome details of what was done to the indigenous peoples of the region. A much better, but less focused, overview of the same events will be found in David Lavender's *Land of Giants: The Drive to the Pacific Northwest, 1750–1950* (Lincoln: University of Nebraska Press, 1958).

492. Stephen Dow Beckham, *Requiem for a People: The Rogue River Indians and the Frontiersmen* (Norman: University of Oklahoma Press, 1971); Terrance O'Donnell, *An Arrow in the Earth: General Joel Palmer and the Indians of Oregon* (Portland: Oregon Historical Society Press, 1991). Other coastal peoples–such as the Suquamish, Siwash, Nisquallies, Muckleshoots, Puyallups and Lummis–avoided such bloody confrontations only by signing a series of treaties in 1855 in which they relinquished most of their territories in exchange for guarantees of perpetual fishing rights in their "usual and accustomed places." The white citizenry of Washington took the land, then ignored the native right to fish; American Friends Service Committee, *Uncommon Controversy: Fishing Rights of the Muckleshoot, Puyallup, and Nisqually Indians* (Seattle: University of Washington Press, 1970); Faye G. Cohen, *Treaties on Trial: The Continuing Controversy over Northwest Indian Fishing Rights* (Seattle: University of Washington Press, 1986).

493. Axelrod, *Chronicle, op. cit.*, p. 175. Also see B.F. Manring, *The Conquest of the Coeur d'Alenes, Spokanes and Palouses* (Spokane, WA: Inland, 1912); Robert H. Ruby, *The Spokane Indians: Children of the Sun* (Norman: university of Oklahoma Press, 1970).

494. Glassley, *Pacific Northwest Indian Wars, op. cit.*, p. 150.

495. Axelrod, *Chronicle, op. cit.*, p. 175.

496. The two bands—called "Snakes" by local whites—numbered perhaps 1,200 people between them. By mid-1868, they had suffered 329 killed, 20 wounded and 225 captured at the hands of troops commanded by General George Crook. They thereupon surrendered and were dispersed to several reservations; ibid., p. 214. Also see Sarah Winnemuca Hopkins, *Life Among the Piutes: Their Wrongs and Claims* (Bishop, CA: Chalfant Press, 1969 reprint of 1883 original).

497. Harvey Chalmers, *Last Stand of the Nez Percé: Destruction of a People* (New York: Twayne, 1962); Merril D. Beal, *"I Will Fight No More Forever": Chief Joseph and the Nez Percé War* (Seattle: University of Washington Press, 1963); John D. McDermott, *Forlorn Hope: The Battle of Whitebird Canyon and the Beginning of the Nez Percé War* (Boise: Idaho State Historical Society, 1978).

498. Axelrod, *Chronicle, op. cit.*, pp. 236–7.

499. Glassley, *Pacific Northwest Indian Wars, op. cit.*, pp. 239–48.

500. William H. Goetzmann, *Army Exploration and the West, 1803–1863* (New Haven: Yale University Press, 1959); *Exploration and Empire* (New York: Alfred A. Knopf, 1966).

501. On trade, see David Lavender, *Bent's Fort* (Garden City, NY: Doubleday, 1954); *The Great West* (Boston: Houghton-Mifflin, 1987). On passage, see Henry Inman, *The Old Santa Fe Trail: The Story of a Great Highway* (Minneapolis: Ross & Haines, 1966 reprint of the 1897 original); John D. Unruh, *The Plains Across: The Overland Immigrants and the Trans-Mississippi West, 1840–1860* (Urbana: University of Illinois Press, 1979).

502. Burton S. Hill, "The Great Indian Treaty Council of 1851," *Nebraska History*, Vol. 47, No. 1, 1966; also see LeRoy R. Hafen and Francis Marion Young, *Fort Laramie and the Pageant of the West, 1834–1890* (Lincoln: University of Nebraska Press, 1984 reprint of 1938 original).

503. Kappler, *Indian Treaties, op. cit.*, pp. 594–6. Most of Nevada had already been disposed of in similar fashion via the 1863 Treaty of Ruby Valley with the Western Shoshonis; ibid., pp. 851–3.

504. George Armstrong Custer, *My Life on the Plains, or, Personal Experiences with the Indians* (Norman: University of Oklahoma, 1964 reprint of 1873 original) p. 237. Also see Frank Gilbert Roe, *The Indian and His Horse* (Norman: University of Oklahoma Press, 1955).

505. LeRoy R. Hafen, ed., *Colorado Gold Rush* (Glendale, CA: Arthur H. Clark, 1941); *Pike's Peak Gold Rush Guidebooks of 1859* (Glendale, CA: Arthur H. Clark, 1941); Nolie Mumey, *History of the Early Settlements of Denver, 1859–1860* (Glendale, CA: Arthur H. Clark, 1942).

506. At least as early as the beginning of 1863, Major Scott J. Anthony, a ranking army officer in Colorado Territory, noting that the influx of whites had frightened away the buffalo upon which they

subsisted, recommended starving the Cheyennes to death as being "a much easier way of disposing of them" than direct military action; United States Department of War, *The War of Rebellion: A Compilation of the Official Records of the Union and Confederate Armies*, four series, 128 vols. (Washington, D.C.: U.S. Government Printing Office, 1880–1901) Series I, Vol. XXII, Pt. 2, p. 571.

507. Grace Hebard and E.A. Brindenstool, *The Bozeman Trail*, 2 vols. (Glendale, CA: Arthur H. Clark, 1922); Dorothy M. Johnson, *The Bloody Bozeman* (New York: McGraw-Hill, 1971).

508. Dee Brown, *Fort Phil Kearny: An American Saga* (Lincoln: University of Nebraska Press, 1971).

509. Also called the "Comanche Barrier"; see Rupert Norval Richardson, *The Comanche Barrier to Southern Plains Settlement: A Century and a Half of Savage Resistance to Advancing White Settlement* (Glendale, CA: Arthur H. Clark, 1933). Also see Ernest Wallace and E. Adamson Hoebel, *The Comanches: Lords of the Southern Plains* (Norman: University of Oklahoma Press, 1952); Stanley Noyse, *Los Comanches: The Horse People, 1715–1845* (Albuquerque: University of New Mexico Press, 1993).

510. "The Texas Rangers knew best how…to exterminate Indians…and their impatience with [any] humanitarian policy…was colossal"; Walter P. Webb, *The Texas Rangers: A Century of Frontier Defense* (Austin: University of Texas Press, 1989 reprint of 1935 original).

511. Alvin M. Josephy, Jr., *The Civil War in the American West* (New York: Alfred A. Knopf, 1992).

512. Ray C. Colton, *The Civil War in the Western Territories* (Norman: University of Oklahoma Press, 1959).

513. An interesting tangent: factions of the Cherokees, Muskogees, and other southern peoples who had been removed to Oklahoma a generation earlier allied themselves to the Confederate States of America in exchange for promises that, in the event of a secessionist victory, the Indians' fully sovereign national status would be recognized, restored, and respected. The Cherokees in particular, led by Stand Watie, fought well in the Pea Ridge Campaign; Annie Heloise Abel, *The American Indian in the Civil War, 1862–1865* (Lincoln: University of Nebraska Press, 1992); Kenny A. Franks, *Stand Watie and the Agony of the Cherokee Nation* (Memphis: Memphis State University Press, 1979); W. David Baird, ed., *A Creek Warrior for the Confederacy* (Norman: University of Oklahoma Press, 1968); Edwin C. Bearss, "The Battle of Pea Ridge," *Arkansas Historical Quarterly*, Vol. 20, No. 1, 1961.

514. Quoted in Carley, *Sioux Uprising, op. cit.*, p. 54.

515. Brown, *Bury My Heart at Wounded Knee, op. cit.*, p. 60.

516. Gary Clayton Anderson, *Little Crow* (St. Paul: Minnesota Historical Society, 1986); Walter N. Trenerry, "The Shooting of Little Crow: Heroism or Murder?" *Minnesota History*, Vol. 38, 1962.

517. Major Edwin Hatch, a subordinate of Sibley operating out of the village of Pembina, just south of the Canadian border, retained John McKenzie, an American living in Canada, to bribe a pair of Canadian officials into drugging Shakopee and Medicine Bottle during a "friendly meeting." The two unconscious Indians were then handed over to Hatch in Pembina. After the hangings, the Minnesota legislature appropriated the sum of $1,000 to reward McKenzie for his part in the crime; William W. Folwell, *A History of Minnesota* (St. Paul: Minnesota Historical Society, 1924) pp. 443–50. Also see Robin W. Winks, "The British North American West and the Civil War," *North Dakota History*, Vol. 24, 1957.

518. "The uprising had given the white citizens an opportunity to seize the Santees' remaining lands without even a pretense of payment. Previous treaties were abrogated, and the surviving Indians were informed that they would be removed to a reservation in Dakota Territory"; Brown, *Bury My Heart at Wounded Knee, op. cit.*, p. 65. Sibley and Ramsey, as well as their partners, profited mightily from the whole affair, which they had done so much to contrive in the first place.

519. Ibid.

520. Andrew Love Neff, *History of Utah, 1847 to 1869* (Salt Lake City: University of Utah Press, 1940).

521. Madsen, *Shoshoni Frontier, op. cit.*, p. 193.

522. For use of the term "battle" to describe this massacre, see, e.g., Edward Tullidge, "The Battle of Bear River," *Tullidge's Quarterly Magazine*, Jan. 1881; Bill Judge, "The Battle of Bear River," *True West*, Jan.–Feb. 1961.

523. Leo P. Kirby, "Patrick Edward Connor: First Gentile in Utah," *Journal of the West*, Vol. 2, No. 3, 1963; Aurora Hunt, *The Army of the Pacific* (Glendale, CA: Arthur H. Clark, 1951); Irma Watson Hance and Irene Warr, *Johnson, Connor and the Mormons: An Outline of Military History in Northern Utah* (Salt Lake

City: University of Utah Press, 1962); Brigham D. Madsen, *Glory Hunter: A Biography of Patrick Edward Connor* (Salt Lake City: University of Utah Press, 1990).

524. Quoted in Edward Tullidge, "The Cities of Cache Valley and Their Founders," *Tullidge's Quarterly Magazine*, July 1881.

525. This is consistent with a May 1863 statement by Evans that, if there were to be a war against the Cheyennes, "it would be a war of extermination to them"; quoted in U.S. Commissioner of Indian Affairs, *Annual Report* (Washington, D.C.: U.S. Government Printing Office, 1863) pp. 239–46.

526. Quoted in *The War of Rebellion, op. cit.*, Series I, Vol. XLI, Pt. 1, pp. 237–8. It should be noted that all of this was happening during an election year. Both Evans and Chivington, backed by Byers and the *News*, desired to become U.S. senators and were thus key figures in a "Colorado Statehood Party." One organ of the opposition, the *Black Hawk Journal*, opined on August 22 that Byers, Evans, and Chivington "cooked up the Indian war together to prove that only as a state could Colorado get…sufficient troops to control her Indians." On the face of it, the argument is highly plausible. For details on Evans, see Edgar Carlisle McMechen, *Life of Governor John Evans: Second Territorial Governor of Colorado* (Denver: Walgren, 1924); on Chivington, see Reginald S. Craig, *The Fighting Parson: A Biography of Col. John M. Chivington* (Tucson: Westernlore, 1994 reprint of 1959 original).

527. Quoted in Hoig, *Battle of the Washita, op. cit.*, p. 192.

528. The camp was that of Big Wolf, one of the Cheyenne "peace chiefs." Nichols later contended the attack was justified because the scalp and clothing of a white woman was found in Big Wolf's lodge. This evidence of "hostility" was, however, never produced; *The War of Rebellion*, Series I, Vol. XLI, Pt. 3, pp. 789–90.

529. Wynkoop was originally a hardliner, inclined to shooting Indians on sight. After meeting with Black Kettle and White Antelope in September 1864, at their request, he radically altered his view, having been convinced that they and their people bore no ill-intentions towards whites. He therefore engineered the Camp Weld meeting to negotiate terms under which the Cheyenne "peace faction" might be formally recognized as noncombatants by Evans, Chivington, and other territorial authorities. He then accompanied the Indians to the meeting in order to ensure their safety; Stan Hoig, *The Peace Chiefs of the Cheyennes* (Norman: University of Oklahoma Press, 1980).

530. See, e.g., "From Bloodless to Bloody: The Third Colorado Cavalry and the Sand Creek Massacre," *Journal of the American West*, Vol. 6, No. 4, 1967.

531. On Connor's visit and Evans' and Chivington's reaction to it, see *Rocky Mountain News*, Nov. 14, 16, 1864; *Denver Republican*, Nov. 18, 1864. The terms of service of all the roughly 450 enlisted men, and most officers, of the Third Colorado Volunteers who participated in the Sand Creek Massacre—the remainder were drawn primarily from the Colorado First—had expired prior to the event. They were there because they wanted to be, not because they "had" to be; for implications, see Goldhagen, *Hitler's Willing Executioners, op. cit.* On the First Colorado and its participation, see O.J. Hollister, *Boldly They Road: A History of the First Colorado Regiment of Volunteers* (Lakewood, CO: Golden Press, 1965 reprint of 1873 original).

532. Quoted in Hoig, *Sand Creek Massacre, op. cit.*, pp. 142, 147.

533. U.S. Dept. of War, "Sand Creek Massacre," *op. cit.*, p. 138.

534. Hoig, *Sand Creek Massacre, op. cit.*, p. 151.

535. U.S. Senate, "The Chivington Massacre," *op. cit.*, pp. 95–6. Bent places the total number of fighting-age males in the village, all of whom had been disarmed, at 35. There were another 60 "old men" present. The remainder of the several hundred village residents were women and children.

536. "The Chivington Massacre," *op. cit.*, p. 42. Corroborating testimony is too voluminous to review further; see the entire report cited here; "Sand Creek Massacre," *op. cit.*; U.S. House of Representatives, "Massacre of the Cheyenne Indians," *op. cit.*; *The War of Rebellion, op. cit.*; and Hoig, *Sand Creek Massacre, op. cit.*, pp. 177–92.

537. Actually, if it was war he'd wanted, Chivington plainly knew where to find it by the time of the massacre. The Cheyenne combatants, "3,000-strong," were, as he put it in his after action report, camped along the Smoky Hill River, about eighty miles from Sand Creek; *The War of Rebellion, op. cit.*, pp. 950–1. It is instructive that, instead of moving to engage these real "hostiles," the colonel turned tail and ran in the opposite direction; Hoig, *Sand Creek Massacre, op. cit.*, pp. 158–9. Also see Walter S. Campbell,

"The Cheyenne Dog Soldiers," *Chronicles of Oklahoma*, Vol. 1, No. 1, 1923; Grinnell, *Fighting Cheyennes, op. cit.*

538. "In January, 1865, the alliance of Cheyenne, Arapaho, and Sioux launched a series of raids along the South Platte. They attacked wagon trains, stage stations, and small military outposts. They burned the town of Julesburg, scalping the white defenders in revenge for the scalping of Indians at Sand Creek. They ripped out miles of telegraph wire. They raided and plundered up and down the Platte route, halting all communications and supplies. In Denver there was panic as food shortages began to grow"; Brown, *Bury My Heart at Wounded Knee, op. cit.*, pp. 95–6.

539. Stanley Vestal, *Warpath and Council Fire: The Plains Indian Struggle for Survival in War and Diplomacy, 1851–1891* (New York: Random House, 1948); James R. Mead, "The Little Arkansas," *Transactions of the Kansas State Historical Society*, Vol. 10, 1908.

540. General Phil Sheridan to General of the Army William Tecumseh Sherman, Oct. 15, 1868; quoted in Hutton, *Phil Sheridan, op. cit.*, p. 53. Sherman replied that he would back Sheridan with his "whole authority, and stand between you and any effort that may be attempted in your rear to restrain your purpose or check your troops."

541. Custer had been court-martialed by Hancock for deserting his command toward the end of the 1867 campaign, and taken out of active service. He was reinstated in 1868, at the request of Sheridan, for the specific purpose of conducting the sort of operations which occurred on the Washita; Frederick F. Van de Water, *Glory-Hunter: A Life of General Custer* (New York: Bobbs-Merrill, 1934); Jess C. Epple, *Custer's Battle of the Washita and a History of the Plains Indian Tribes* (New York: Exposition Press, 1970).

542. Black Kettle attempted to place his band under the protection of the army at Fort Cobb. This was refused by the post commandant, General William B. Hazen, on November 20, despite the fact that he recognized the group as "friendly"; Hoig, *Battle of the Washita, op. cit.*, p. 91.

543. Col. William Sturtevant Nye, *Carbine and Lance: The Story of Old Fort Sill* (Norman: University of Oklahoma Press, 1937).

544. Berthrong, *Cheyenne and Arapaho Ordeal, op. cit.*; J.H. Moore, *The Cheyenne Nation: A Social and Demographic History* (Lincoln: University of Nebraska Press, 1987); Virginia Cole Trenholm, *The Arapahoes: Our People* (Norman: University of Oklahoma Press, 1970).

545. The expression accrues from Charles J. Brill, *The Conquest of the Southern Plains: Uncensored Narrative of the Battle of the Washita and Custer's Southern Campaign* (Oklahoma City: Golden Saha, 1938). Also see Cyrus T. Brady, *The Conquest of the Southwest: The Story of a Great Spoilation* (New York: Appleton, 1905); William H. Leckie, *The Military Conquest of the Southern Plains* (Norman: University of Oklahoma Press, 1963); Harry A. Stroud, *The Conquest of the Prairies* (Waco, TX: Texian Press, 1968).

546. A total of 4,373,730 buffalo hides were shipped east by rail from Kansas during the years 1872–74 alone; another million are estimated to have been shipped by other means during the same period; James L. Haley, *The Buffalo War: The History of the Red River Indian Uprising of 1874* (Norman: University Oklahoma Press, 1985 reprint of 1976 original) p. 22. On the army's role in promoting this carnage—mainly to destroy the Indians' ability to subsist independently—see note 118, above. Also see John R. Cook, *The Border and the Buffalo* (Topeka, KS: Crane, 1907); Carl Coke Rister, "The Significance of the Destruction of the Buffalo in the Southwest," *Southwestern Historical Quarterly*, Vol. 33, No. 1, 1929; Mari Sandoz, *The Buffalo Hunters: The Story of the Hidemen* (New York: Hasting House, 1954); Wayne Gard, *The Great Buffalo Hunt* (New York: Alfred A. Knopf, 1959).

547. F.A. Hunt, "Adobe Walls Argument: An Indian Attack on a Party of Buffalo Hunters," *Overland Monthly*, May 1909; Rupert N. Richardson, "The Comanche Indians at the Adobe Walls Fight," *Panhandle-Plains Historical Review*, No. 4, 1931; Virginia Wiesel Johnson, *The Unregimented General: A Biography of Nelson A. Miles* (Boston: Houghton-Mifflin, 1962).

548. Edward S. Wallace and Adrian S. Anderson, "R.S. Mackenzie and the Kickapoos: The Raid into Mexico in 1873," *Arizona and the West*, Vol. VII, 1965. On the colonel himself, see Ernest Wallace, *Ranald S. Mackenzie on the Texas Frontier* (Lubbock: West Texas Museum Association, 1964).

549. Haley, *Buffalo War, op. cit.*, pp. 169–94. Also see J. Marvin Hunter, Sr., "The Battle of Palo Duro Canyon," *Frontier Times*, Vol. XXI, No. 4, 1944.

550. Clarence R. Wharton, *Satanta: The Great Chief of the Kiowas and His People* (Dallas: B. Upshaw & Co., 1935); Zoe A. Tilghman, *Quannah: Eagle of the Comanches* (Oklahoma City: Harlow, 1958). The

other Comanche bands—Penatekas, Yapparikas, Kotsotekas, and Nakonis—had already surrendered by the time Quannah and the Quahadis gave up; Colonel W.S. Nye, *Plains Indian Raiders: The Final Phases of Warfare from the Arkansas to the Red River* (Norman: University of Oklahoma Press, 1968).

551. William T. Hagan, *United States-Comanche Relations: The Reservation Years* (Norman: University of Oklahoma Press, 1990 reprint of 1976 original); Mildred P. Mayhall, *The Kiowas* (Norman: University of Oklahoma Press, 1962); John Upton Terrell, *The Plains Apache* (New York: Thomas Y. Crowell, 1975). Also see Rupert N. Richardson, "The Comanche Reservation in Texas," *West Texas Historical Association Yearbook*, Vol. V, 1929; Martha Buntin, "The Removal of the Wichitas, Kiowas, Comanches and Apaches to the Present Agency," *Panhandle-Plains Historical Review*, No. 4, 1931.

552. Brown, *Fort Phil Kearny, op. cit.*; Hebard and Brindenstool, *Bozeman Trail, op. cit.*

553. Olson, *Red Cloud, op. cit.*

554. A good account will be found in the memoirs of the post commander; Colonel Francis C. Carrington, *My Army Life and the Fort Phil Kearny Massacre* (Philadelphia: Lippencott, 1911). Also see John Guthrie, "The Fetterman Massacre," *Annals of Wyoming*, No. 9, 1932; Brown, *Bury My Heart at Wounded Knee, op. cit.*, pp. 135–7.

555. General of the Army William Tecumseh Sherman himself appeared on the scene in an unsuccessful effort to impress the Indians into frittering away by treaty what they had defended on the battlefield; John F. Marszalek, *Sherman: A Soldier's Passion for Order* (New York: Free Press, 1993) pp. 389–91. Also see Robert G. Athearn, *William Tecumseh Sherman and the Settlement of the West* (Norman: University of Oklahoma Press, 1956).

556. "We are on the mountains, looking down on the soldiers and the forts. When we see the soldiers moving away, and the forts abandoned, then I will come down and talk"; quoted in the *Omaha Weekly Herald*, June 10, 1868. The first post abandoned, on July 29, 1868, was an unfinished facility called Fort C.F. Smith. Phil Kearny was next, then the most southerly, Fort Reno. The Lakotas and Cheyennes torched each one before the retreating soldiers were out of sight. On the treaty-signing process, see Remi Nadeau, *Fort Laramie and the Sioux* (Lincoln: University of Nebraska Press, 1967).

557. The expedition was mounted on the basis of 1872 reports by Father Jean de Smet, a Jesuit missionary who had been illegally prospecting in the Hills for some time; Donald Jackson, *Custer's Gold: The United States Cavalry Expedition of 1874* (Lincoln: University of Nebraska Press, 1966); Watson Parker, *Gold in the Black Hills* (Norman: University of Oklahoma Press, 1966).

558. There were at least 800 miners in the Hills within six months; Jackson, *Custer's Gold, op. cit.*, p. 114.

559. This was the "Jenny Expedition," a team of scientists escorted by six companies of cavalry and two of infantry under General George Crook; William Ludlow, *Report of a Reconnaissance of the Black Hills of Dakota* (Washington, D.C.: 43d Cong., 2d Sess., U.S. Government Printing Office, 1875); Walter P. Jenny, *Report on the Mineral Wealth, Climate and Rainfall and Natural Resources of the Black Hills of Dakota* (Washington, D.C.: 44th Cong., 1st Sess., Exec. Doc. No. 51, U.S. Government Printing Office, 1876). The sale was demanded by the Allison Commission during the fall of the same year; U.S. Department of Interior, *Annual Report of the Commissioner of Indian Affairs,* 1875 (Washington, D.C.: 43d Cong., 2d Sess., U.S. Government Printing Office, 1875).

560. An excellent examination of the government's maneuverings to force a war with the Lakotas while making it appear the other way around will be found in Frank Pommershein, "The Black Hills Case: On the Cusp of History," *Wicazo Sa Review*, Vol. 4, No. 1, 1988. Also see Lazarus, *op. cit.* The best account of U.S. military preparations, strategy and the offensive itself is John E. Gray's *The Centennial Campaign: The Sioux War of 1876* (Norman: University of Oklahoma Press, 1988).

561. J.W. Vaughn, *With Crook at the Rosebud* (Harrisburg, PA: Stackpole, 1956).

562. In an opening round of the campaign, one of Crook's unit commanders, Captain Anson Mills, was able to surprise the small Lakota encampment of 37 lodges, led by American Horse at Slim Buttes, north of the Black Hills, on September 9, 1876. The fewer than 40 warriors, short of ammunition, were virtually annihilated by Mills' 150 well-armed soldiers, as were a number of women and children; Jerome A. Greene, *Slim Buttes: An Episode of the Great Sioux War, 1876* (Norman: University of Oklahoma Press, 1982).

563. Brown, *Bury My Heart at Wounded Knee, op. cit.*, p. 306.

564. Ibid. Also see John G. Bourne, *Mackenzie's Last Fight with the Cheyennes* (New York: Argonaut, 1966).

565. The best account is in Sandoz, *Crazy Horse, op. cit.*

566. Berthrong, *Cheyenne and Arapaho Ordeal, op. cit.*

567. The unarmed Oglala leader, his arms pinioned behind his back, was bayoneted in the kidney at Camp Robinson, Nebraska, on September 5, 1877; Robert A. Clark, ed., *The Killing of Chief Crazy Horse* (Lincoln: University of Nebraska Press, 1976).

568. See note 97, above.

569. Sandoz, *Cheyenne Autumn, op. cit.*; Peter M. Wright, "The Pursuit of Dull Knife from Fort Reno, 1878–1879," *Chronicles of Oklahoma*, No. 46, 1968.

570. Dull Knife, 75 years old at the time, responded to this news with the observation that his people would rather "die right here" than return to Oklahoma; quoted in Anonymous, "The Liquidation of Dull Knife," *Nebraska History*, No. 22, 1941.

571. Brown, *Bury My Heart at Wounded Knee, op. cit.*, p. 347. Also see John Edward Weems, *Death Song: The Last of the Indian Wars* (Garden City, NY: Doubleday, 1976).

572. This pitiful handful of survivors, including Little Wolf's group of about 40, was granted a reservation in the Powder River Country later the same year; Berthrong, *Cheyenne and Arapaho Ordeal, op. cit.*

573. On erosion of Lakota territoriality after 1877, mostly under provision of the General Allotment and Homestead Acts, see Lazarus, *Black Hills, op. cit.* On sociopolitical erosion, see Sidney L. Harring, *Crow Dog's Case: American Indian Sovereignty, Tribal Law, and the United States in the Nineteenth Century* (Cambridge: Cambridge University Press, 1994). On the abolition of spiritual practices, see Richard Erdoes, *The Sun Dance People: The Plains Indians, Their Past and Present* (New York: Vintage Books, 1972). As to starvation policies, "The Sioux had been assured they would continue to receive the same rations after giving up so much of their lands, but immediately after[ward], Congress cut the beef ration by 2,000,000 pounds at Rosebud Reservation, by 1,000,000 pounds at Pine Ridge, and by lesser amounts at the other three reservations" left to the Lakotas within what had been one consolidated landbase only a few years before. At Pine Ridge, a further 50-percent reduction was imposed in April 1890; Ralph K. Andrist, *The Long Death: The Last Days of the Plains Indian* (New York: Macmillan, 1964) p. 340.

574. The seven bands are the Oglala, Hunkpapa, Minneconjou, Sicungu (Brûlé), Bohinunpa (Two Kettles), Ituzipco (Sans Arc), Sihasapa (Blackfeet; not to be confused with the indigenous nation of the same name). On the Ghost Dance, as practiced by the Lakotas during this period, see James M. Mooney, *The Ghost Dance Religion and the Sioux Outbreak of 1890* (Washington, D.C.: Bureau of American Ethnology, Smithsonian Institution, 1896); John G. Neihardt, *Black Elk Speaks* (Lincoln: University of Nebraska Press, 1961).

575. See generally, Robert M. Utley, *The Last Days of the Sioux Nation* (New Haven: Yale University Press, 1963).

576. Vestal, *Sitting Bull, op. cit.* Also see Martin F. Schmidt and Dee Brown, *Fighting Indians of the West* (New York: Scribner's, 1948) p. 335.

577. Andrist, *Long Death, op. cit.*, pp. 351–2. Also see James H. McGregor, *The Wounded Knee Massacre from the Viewpoint of the Survivors* (Baltimore: Wirth Brothers, 1940).

578. "No one knows [precisely] how many Indians died on that miserable field, because by the time anyone could count the bodies, some had already been removed"; Andrist, *Long Death, op. cit.*, p. 352. The best firsthand account accrues from the Santee Dakota Charles A. Eastman, who served on the burial detail; see his *From the Deep Woods to Civilization: Chapters in the Autobiography of an American Indian* (Boston: Little, Brown, 1916) pp. 111–2. Also see Raymond Wilson, *Ohiyesa: Charles Eastman, Santee Sioux* (Urbana: University of Illinois Press, 1983).

579. *Aberdeen Saturday Pioneer*, December 20, 1890; quoted in Elliott J. Gorn, Randy Roberts and Terry D. Bilhartz, *Constructing the American Past: A Source Book of a People's History* (New York: HarperCollins, 1972) p. 74.

580. Charles C. Royce, *Indian Land Cessions in the United States: 18th Annual Report, 1896–97*, 2 vols. (Washington, D.C.: Bureau of American Ethnography, Smithsonian Institution, 1899); Jay P. Kinney, *A Continent Lost—A Civilization Won: Indian Land Tenure in America* (Baltimore: Johns Hopkins University

Press, 1937); Imre Sutton, ed., *Irredeemable America: The Indians' Estate and Land Tenure* (Albuquerque: University of New Mexico Press, 1985).

581. For a good overview of policy and sentiment during this period, see Oliver Knight, *Following the Indian Wars* (Norman: University of Oklahoma Press, 1960).

582. Lawrie Tatum, *Our Red Brothers and the Peace Policy of Ulysses S. Grant* (Philadelphia: Winston, 1899); Elsie M. Rushmore, *The Indian Policy During Grant's Administration* (New York: Marion Press, 1914); Henry E. Fritz, *The Movement for Indian Assimilation, 1860–1890* (Philadelphia: University of Pennsylvania Press, 1963); Francis Paul Prucha, *Americanizing the American Indian: Writings of the "Friends of the Indian," 1800–1900* (Lincoln: University of Nebraska Press, 1973).

583. Francis E. Leupp, *The Indian and His Problem* (New York: Scribner's, 1910) p. 93. The attitude expressed is obviously consistent with all of the most authoritarian and paternalistic aspects of U.S. Indian policy; see generally, Francis Paul Prucha, *The Great Father: The United States Government and the American Indian* (Lincoln: University of Nebraska Press, 1984).

584. Letter from Charles Burke to William Williamson, Sept. 12, 1921 (William Williamson Papers, Box 2, File—Indian Matters, Miscellaneous I.D., Weeks Library, University of South Dakota, Vermilion). For further expression of comparable attitudes, see Robert M. Kvasnicka and Herman J. Viola, eds., *The Commissioners of Indian Affairs, 1824–1977* (Lincoln: University of Nebraska Press, 1979).

585. D.S. Otis, *The Dawes Act and the Allotment of American Indian Land* (Norman: University of Oklahoma Press, 1973).

586. According to the Act (ch. 119, 24 Stat. 362, 385, now codified at 18 U.S.C. 331 *et seq.*), to be considered "Indian," and thus eligible to receive a parcel of reservation land, one was required to document being of at least one-half "blood" of a specific and federally recognized "tribal group." One could not be, say, one-quarter by descent of four different indigenous peoples through intermarriage, and still be legally identified as native. Nor could one be adopted or naturalized as a citizen/member of an indigenous nation. Needless to say, such criteria not only negated one of the most important sovereign prerogatives of native peoples—definition of their own polities—it left far fewer eligible Indians than available plots of reserved land. Hence, the massive "surplus" of indigenous property.

587. Kirk Kicking Bird and Karen Ducheneaux, *One Hundred Million Acres* (New York: Macmillan, 1973); Janet A. McDonnell, *The Dispossession of the American Indian, 1887–1934* (Bloomington: Indiana University Press, 1991). Comparable maneuvers were undertaken in Canada, where expropriation occurred with a quantitatively much lesser degree of physical violence; see, e.g., Daniel Raunet, *Without Surrender of Consent: A History of the Nishga Land Claims* (Vancouver, B.C.: Douglas & McIntire, 1984).

588. Similar initiatives were being taken in Canada during this period. See Douglas Cole and Ira Chaikan, *An Iron Hand Upon the People: The Law Against the Potlatch on the Northwest Coast* (Vancouver, B.C.: Douglas & McIntire, Ltd., 1990); Katherine Pettitpas, *Severing the Ties That Bind: Government Repression of Indigenous Religious Ceremonies on the Prairies* (Winnipeg: University of Manitoba Press, 1994).

589. The process had been ongoing in less than systematic fashion since at least as early as John Eliot's establishment of Harvard College; Benjamin Pierce, *A History of Harvard University from Its Founding in the Year 1636 to the Period of the American Revolution* (Cambridge, MA: Brown, Shattuck, 1833). This experiment was rendered somewhat more consistent with Eleazer Wheelock's founding of Moore's Charity School for Indians in 1755 and Dartmouth College in 1769; James D. McCallem, ed., *The Letters of Eleazer Wheelock's Indians* (Hanover, NH: Dartmouth College Pubs, 1932); Leon B. Richardson, *The History of Dartmouth College*, 2 vols. (Hanover, NH: Dartmouth College Pubs., 1932). Wheelock's model was steadily enlarged upon until the point it began to be incorporated into federal policy during the 1870s; Robert F. Berkhofer, Jr., *Salvation and the Savage: An Analysis of Protestant Missions and American Indian Response. 1787–1862* (Knoxville: University of Kentucky Press, 1865); Rushmore, *Indian Policy, op. cit.* By the late 1880s, the structure by which compulsory education might be universally imposed as a means of assimilating native youth was being perfected; Col. Richard H. Pratt, *Battlefield and Classroom: Four Decades with the American Indian* (New Haven, CT: Yale University Press, 1964); Michael C. Coleman, *American Indian Children at School, 1850–1930* (Jackson: University Press of Mississippi, 1993); David Wallace Adams, *Education for Extinction: American Indians and the Boarding School Experience, 1875–1928* (Lawrence: University Press of Kansas, 1995). From roughly 1890 to 1970, an average of more than 70 percent of each succeeding generation of native youngsters was subjected to the boarding school experience;

Thomas Thompson, ed., *The Schooling of Native America* (Washington, D.C.: American Association of Colleges for Teacher Education, 1978). Again, very much the same procedure was followed in Canada; Basil H. Johnson, *Indian School Days* (Norman: University of Oklahoma Press, 1989); J.R. Miller, *Shingwauk's Vision: A History of Native Residential Schools* (Toronto: University of Toronto Press, 1996).

590. Ch. 233, 43 Stat. 25 (1924). For analysis of the effects of the Citizenship Act on indigenous polities, see Hazel W. Hertzberg, *The Search for an American Indian Identity: Modern Pan-Indian Movements* (Syracuse, NY: Syracuse University Press, 1971). For analysis of the implications of the formal redesignation of indigenous nations as "tribes," see my "Naming Our Destiny: Toward a Language of American Indian Liberation" in *Indians Are Us? Culture and Genocide in North America* (Monroe, ME: Common Courage Press, 1994).

591. Such conclusions were reached in a report prepared for the Bureau of Indian Affairs by a committee of 100 individuals selected primarily for their prominence in business and finance; U.S. House of Representatives, *The Indian Problem: Resolution of the Committee of One Hundred by the Secretary of Interior and Review of the Indian Problem* (Washington, D.C.: 68th Cong., 1st Sess., U.S. Government Printing Office, 1925). The same perspective—and practices—prevailed in Canada in somewhat modified form; see the analysis of the handling of Treaty 3 offered by John Kelly in his "We Are All Part of the Ojibway Circle," in Michael Ondaatje, ed., *From Ink Lake* (Toronto: Lester & Orpen Dennys, 1990). Also see J.R. Miller, *Sweet Promises* (Toronto: University of Toronto Press, 1991).

592. The shift in emphasis is evident in a major policy study prepared by the Institute for Government Research; Lewis Meriam, et al., *The Problem of Indian Administration* (Baltimore: Johns Hopkins University Press, 1928). The actual redefinition of policy was engineered by John Collier, Indian Commissioner for the administration of Franklin Delano Roosevelt; Kenneth Philp, *John Collier's Crusade for Indian Reform, 1920–1954* (Tucson: University of Arizona Press, 1977); Lawrence C. Kelly, *Assault on Assimilation: John Collier and the Origins of Indian Policy Reform* (Albuquerque: University of New Mexico Press, 1983). A comparable trajectory is evident in Canada; Indian Affairs of Canada, *Indian Acts and Amendments, 1868–1950* (Ottawa: Indian and Northern Affairs Ministry of Canada, 1981)

593. See, e.g., Ronald L. Trosper, "Appendix I: Indian Minerals," in American Indian Policy Review Commission, *Task Force 7 Final Report: Reservation and Resource Development and Protection* (Washington, D.C.: U.S. Government Printing Office, 1977); U.S. Department of Interior, Bureau of Indian Affairs, *Indian Lands Map: Oil, Gas and Minerals on Indian Reservations* (Washington, D.C.: U.S. Government Printing Office, 1978); Louis R. Moore, *Mineral Development on Indian Lands: Cooperation and Conflict* (Denver: Rocky Mountain Mineral Law Foundation, 1983); Presidential Commission on Indian Reservation Economies, *Report and Recommendation to the President of the United States* (Washington, D.C.: U.S. Government Printing Office, Nov. 1984).

594. C.B. Glasscock, *Then Came Oil: The Story of the Last Frontier* (Indiana: Bobbs-Merrill, 1938); Carl C. Riser, *Oil! Titan of the Southwest* (Norman: University of Oklahoma Press, 1949); H. Craig Miner, *The Corporation and the Indian: Tribal Sovereignty and Industrial Civilization in Indian Territory, 1865–1907* (Columbia: University of Missouri Press, 1976); Terry P. Wilson, *The Underground Reservation: Osage Oil* (Lincoln: University of Nebraska Press, 1985).

595. The legal basis for the presumed right of the U.S. to "manage" indigenous resources in whatever manner it sees fit was articulated in the Supreme Court's ruling in the 1886 *U.S. v. Kagama* case (118 U.S. 375), and again in its 1903 opinion in *Lonewolf v. Hitchcock*. (187 U.S. 553). In both instances, the high court held that the federal government possessed "plenary"—that is, absolute and unchallengeable—power over the affairs of American Indians. In *Lonewolf*, it specifically included disposition of native assets within the scope of such authority.

596. Probably the best examination of the principle involved will be found in Michael Hector, *Internal Colonialism: The Celtic Fringe in British National Development, 1536–1966* (Berkeley: University of California Press, 1975); as applied to American Indians, see Robert K. Thomas, "Colonialism: Classic and Internal," *New University Thought*, Winter 1966–1967.

597. On the IRA, see Graham D. Taylor, *The New Deal and American Indian Tribalism: The Administration of the Indian Reorganization Act, 1934–45* (Lincoln: University of Nebraska Press, 1980); Vine Deloria, Jr., and Clifford M. Lytle, *The Nations Within: The Past and Future of American Indian Sovereignty* (New York: Pantheon Press, 1984). A succinct review of the form of "classic" colonial regimes

will be found in Raymond E. Betts, *Europe Overseas: Phases of Imperialism* (New York: Basic Books, 1968). On the nazi variations, see Dallin, *German Rule, op. cit.*; Pierre Tissier, *The Government of Vichy* (London: Macmillan, 1942). For analysis of the Canadian counterpart to the U.S. internal colonial model, see Bruce Clark, *Native Liberty, Crown Sovereignty: The Existing Aboriginal Right to Self-Government in Canada* (Montréal: McGill-Queens University Press, 1990).

598. See. e.g., Roxanne Dunbar Ortiz, ed., *Economic Development on American Indian Reservations* (Albuquerque: University of New Mexico Native American Development Series, 1979); Michael Garrity, "The U.S. Colonial Empire is as Close as the Nearest Reservation," in Holly Sklar, ed., *Trilateralism: The Trilateral Commission and Elite Planning for Global Management* (Boston: South End Press, 1980); Joseph Jorgenson, ed., *American Indians and Energy Development* (Cambridge, MA: Anthropological Resource Center, 1978) and *American Indians and Energy Development II* (Cambridge, MA: Anthropological Resource Center, 1984); Marjane Ambler, *Breaking the Iron Bonds: Indian Control of Energy Development* (Lawrence: University Press of Kansas, 1990).

599. Reservation unemployment rates have been over 60 percent, nationwide, every year since 1950. On some reservations, like Pine Ridge, the rate has consistently exceeded 85 percent. The poorest locality in the U.S. for 33 of the past 35 years has been Shannon County, on Pine Ridge. During the mid-1970s, per capita annual income on Pine Ridge was $1,200. Adjusted for inflation, the situation there is only marginally better today; U.S. Bureau of the Census, Population Division, Racial Statistics Branch, *A Statistical Profile of the American Indian Population* (Washington, D.C.: U.S. Government Printing Office, Oct. 1984); U.S. Department of Health and Human Services, Public Health Service, *Chart Series Book* (Washington, D.C.: U.S. Government Printing Office, 1988).

600. *A Statistical Portrait of the American Indian Population, op. cit.*, pp. 122–3.

601. The argument to this effect is made exceedingly well in Robert Davis and Mark Zannis, *The Genocide Machine in Canada: The Pacification of the North* (Montréal: Black Rose Books, 1973). Also see my "Genocide: Toward a Functional Definition," in *Since Predator Came, op. cit.*

602. This policy was effected under provision of House Resolution 108 (1953), the complete text of which appears in Edward H. Spicer, *A Short History of the Indians of the United States* (New York: Van Nostrand Rinehold, 1969). For effects, see Gary Orfield, *A Study of Termination Policy* (Denver: National Congress of American Indians, 1965); Oliver LaFarge, "Termination of Federal Supervision: Disintegration and the American Indian," *Annals of the American Academy of Political and Social Science*, No. 311, May 1975; Larry W. Burt, *Tribalism in Crisis: Federal Indian Policy, 1953–1961* (Albuquerque: University of New Mexico Press, 1982). A few of the terminated peoples, such as the Menominee and Siletz, were able to attain reinstatement after protracted struggle; Nicholas Peroff, *Menominee DRUMS: Tribal Termination and Restoration, 1954–1974* (Norman: University of Oklahoma Press, 1982).

603. The program was launched under the "Navajo-Hopi Relocation Act of 1974" (P.L. 93–531); Anita Parlow, *Cry, Sacred Ground: Big Mountain, U.S.A.* (Washington, D.C.: Christic Institute, 1988). It is entirely consistent with a 1972 recommendation of the National Academy of Sciences that the Four Corners region of the Colorado Plateau and the Black Hills Region—the two locales in which reservation concentration is greatest—be declared "National Sacrifice Areas" in the interests of U.S. energy resource development; Thadius Box, et al., *Rehabilitation Potential for Western Coal Lands* (Cambridge, MA: u, 1974). The correlation between sacrificing the landbase of landbased peoples, and sacrificing the peoples themselves, is a well-established principle in applied anthropology; with specific reference to Big Mountain, see, Thayer Scudder, et al., *No Place to Go: Effects of Compulsory Relocation on Navajos* (Philadelphia: Institute for the Study of Human Issues, 1982). The same situation prevails in Canada; see, e.g., John Goddard, *Last Stand of the Lubicon Cree* (Vancouver: Douglas & McIntire, 1991).

604. Andrea Smith, "The HIV-Correlation to Hepatitis-A and B Vaccines," *WARN Newsletter*, Summer 1992.

605. See my "Radioactive Colonization: The Hidden Holocaust in Native American Environments," in *Struggle for the Land, op. cit.*

606. See, e.g., M.J. Samet, et al., "Lung Cancer and Uranium Mining Among Navajo Men," *New England Journal of Medicine*, No. 310, 1984; Christpher McCleod, "Uranium Mines and Mills Have Caused Birth Defects Among Navajo Children," *High Country News*, Feb. 4, 1985.

607. See generally, Charles C. Reith and Bruce M. Thomson, *Deserts as Dumps? The Disposal of*

Hazardous Materials in Arid Ecosystems (Albuquerque: University of New Mexico Press, 1992). On U.S. nuclear testing in the Western Shoshoni treaty territory, see Dagmar Thorpe, *Newe Segobia: The Western Shoshoni People and Land* (Lee, NV: Western Shoshoni Sacred Lands Association, 1982).

608. "The purpose of philosophy is not just to understand history, but to change it," Karl Marx, *The Poverty of Philosophy* (New York: International, 1963); initially penned in "Critique of the Hegelian Dialectic and of Philosophy as a Whole," in *The Economic and Philosophic Manuscripts of 1844* (New York: International, 1964).

609. Frank Chalk and Kurt Jonassohn, *The History and Sociology of Genocide: Analyses and Case Studies* (New Haven: Yale University Press, 1990) p. 4.

610. Chalk and Jonassohn (ibid.) observe that they "take it for granted that we are all against genocide," an assumption unlikely to be valid. Hence, the formulation "people of conscience," used herein.

611. David E. Stannard, response to a question following a lecture at the University of Colorado/Boulder, May 2, 1995 (tape on file).

612. For a prospectus on how this might be accomplished, see my "I Am Indigenist," in *From a Native Son: Selected Essays in Indigenism, 1985–1995* (Boston: South End Press, 1996).

COLD WAR IMPACTS ON NATIVE NORTH AMERICA
The Political Economy of Radioactive Colonization

> When years before they had first come to the people of the Cebolla land grant they had not said what kind of mineral it was. They were driving U.S. government cars, and they paid the land grant association five thousand dollars not to ask questions about the test holes they were drilling... From that time on, human beings were one clan again, united by the fate the destroyers had planned for all of them, for all living things; united by a circle of death that devoured people in cities twelve thousand miles away, victims who had never known these mesas, who had never seen the delicate colors of the rocks which boiled up their slaughter.
>
> —Leslie Marmon Silko
> *Ceremony*

O F all the costs and consequences of the protracted "Cold War" pitting the United States and its "Free World" allies against the "Communist Bloc" after 1945, perhaps the least known—but certainly among the more substantial—have been its impacts upon the indigenous nations of North America. Virtually unremarked in the vast literature on the conflict, these effects extend from the consolidation of what may be history's most-perfected system of internal colonialism to oblique recommendations within at least some sectors of the U.S. government that outright genocide be perpetrated against American Indians.* Along the way, policies which

---

*Internal colonialism differs from the classic variety in that the colonized nation, rather than being maintained as an external source of resources and revenue, is incorporated directly into the claimed "domestic" territory of the colonizing power. For the best, or at least most comprehensive, case study, see Michael Hector, *Internal Colonialism: The Celtic Fringe in British National Development, 1536–1966* (Berkeley: University of California Press, 1975). For application of the concept to the situation of American Indians, see, e.g., Robert K. Thomas, "Colonialism: Classic and Internal," *New University Thought*, Winter 1966–67; Menno Bolt, "Social Correlates of Nationalism: A Study of Native Indian Leaders in a Canadian Internal Colony," *Comparative Political Studies*, Vol. 14, No. 2, Summer 1981; and my own "Indigenous Peoples of the U.S.A.: Struggle Against Internal Colonialism," *Black Scholar*, Vol. 16, No. 1, Feb. 1985.

were—and in many instances continue to be—patently genocidal have been visited upon the peoples native to this continent.[*]

This essay provides an overview of the situation, tracing the evolution, motivations, and effects of such policies, primarily in the United States, with a decidedly secondary emphasis on Canada. It concludes with suggestions as to how the resulting circumstances might be favorably altered, by correcting not only some of the worst material/physical conditions afflicting post–Cold War Native North America, but also the essential structure of relations between indigenous nations and the continent's settler-state governments.

Internal Colonialism

According to the final (1979) report of the federal government's Indian Claims Commission, an entity established by Congress in 1946 to quiet title to the area encompassed by the forty-eight contiguous states, the United States possesses no legal basis for its use and occupancy of approximately one-third of its territory.[†] Leaving aside historical questions con-

---

[*]Although I subscribe to the much more expansive definition of genocide put forth by Raphaël Lemkin when he coined the term to describe nazi policies during the Second World War, I will for purposes of this essay adhere to the narrower criteria advanced in the United Nations 1948 Convention on Prevention and Punishment of the Crime of Genocide (U.S.T._____, T.I.A.S. No._____, 78 U.N.T.S. 277 (Dec. 9, 1948)). Specifically, these include policies implemented "with intent to destroy, in whole or in part, a national, ethnical, racial or religious group, as such" by means of killing members of the group, inflicting systematic physical or mental harm upon group members, and/or creating other conditions leading to group dissolution. Not only the execution of such policies, but their planning or inciting, as well as conspiring and complicity in them, are delineated as crimes of genocide within the convention. See Raphaël Lemkin, *Axis Rule in Occupied Europe: Laws of Occupation, Analysis of Government, Proposals for Redress* (Washington, D.C.: Carnegie Endowment for International Peace, 1944) p. 79; the complete text of the 1948 convention will be found in Ian Brownlie, ed., *Basic Documents on Human Rights* (Oxford: Clarendon Press, [3rd ed.] 1994) pp. 31–4.

[†]U.S. Department of Interior, Indian Claims Commission, *Final Report* (Washington, D.C.: 96th Cong., 1st Sess., U.S. Government Printing Office, 1979); U.S. Department of Interior, Public Land Review Commission, *One-Third of the Nation's Land* (Washington, D.C.: 91st Cong., 2d Sess., U.S. Government Printing Office, 1970). The Claims Commission was an interesting subterfuge. It was created in the aftermath of World War II to manufacture a post-hoc appearance of distinction between the nineteenth-century expansionist policies of the United States and more recent ones pursued by the nazi leaders upon whom the United States was preparing to sit in judgment at Nuremberg; Alice Ehrenfeld and Robert W. Barker, comps. and eds., *Legislative Material on the Indian Claims Commission Act of 1946* (Washington, D.C.: unpublished study, n.d.); Bradley F. Smith, *The Road to Nuremberg* (New York: Basic Books, 1981). The commission's mandate was to examine all claims by indigenous peoples inside U.S. borders with respect to the unlawful taking of land and, where these were found to be valid, to assign payment of compensation in amounts equivalent to the estimated value (without interest accrual) of the property at the time it was taken. No consideration whatsoever was given to whether native peoples wished to alienate their national territories. The commission was *not* authorized to restore stolen property to its rightful owners. In this way, it was intended that a misimpression be fostered that the U.S. acquisition of indigenous territory had been uniformly accomplished through "purchase" rather

cerning fraudulent or coerced transfers of land from indigenous nations to the United States (matters which in themselves would serve to invalidate all pretensions to legitimacy by the acquiring government), the commission admitted that after more than thirty years of exhaustive investigation it was unable to discover "any treaty, any agreement, nor even a unilateral act of Congress" by which the country could legally assert jurisdiction over about 750 million acres of territory it had long since grown accustomed to claiming as its own "domestic" property.[1] By most accounts, the same situation prevails in Canada.[2]

One glaring omission in the Claims Commission's report was that even those areas still recognized by the United States as belonging to indigenous nations—about fifty million acres in 1980—had been directly subordinated to the "plenary power" of the federal government, a juridical concept enunciated by the Supreme Court in its 1903 *Lonewolf* opinion.[3] Under this doctrine, completely antithetical to international legal principles, the United States had unilaterally assigned itself the role of "permanent trustee" over American Indian lands and lives, exercising what the court described as an "absolute and unchallengeable authority" to administer or dispose of native assets in whatever manner it saw fit.*

At the time of *Lonewolf*, the government, having overseen the extermination of the great bulk of all native people within its boundaries, was in the process of formally assimilating (digesting) the residue, both territorially and

---

than aggression; Thomas LaDuc, "The Work of the Indian Claims Commission Under the Act of 1948," *Pacific Historical Review*, No. 26, 1957; John T. Vance, "The Congressional Mandate and the Indian Claims Commission," *North Dakota Law Review*, No. 45, 1969; Richard A. Nielson, "American Indian Land Claims: Land versus Money as a Remedy," *University of Florida Law Review*, Vol. 19, No. 3, 1973.

*Among the other juridical absurdities expressed by the U.S. high court in *Lonewolf* was the idea that the federal government possessed a sort of "line-item veto" over standing treaties with American Indians, allowing it, on its own initiative, to abrogate whatever provisions it found inconvenient—i.e., those obligating it to perform functions such as guaranteeing native borders, paying annuities, and respecting indigenous sovereignty—while still holding the Indians to their sides of the bargains in terms of land cessions and the like. Such a doctrine held—and holds—no validity whatsoever in international law; Samuel Benjamin Crandell, *Treaties: Their Making and Enforcement* (New York: Columbia University Press, [2nd ed.] 1916); Sir Ian Sinclair, *The Vienna Convention on the Law of Treaties* (Manchester: Manchester University Press, [2nd ed., rev.] 1974). Nor does the notion of "permanent trusteeship" hold up to even minimal scrutiny. Since at least as early as the United Nations 1960 Declaration on the Granting of Independence to Colonial Countries and Peoples (U.N.G.A. Res. 1514 (XV), 15 U.N. GAOR, Supp. (No. 16) 66, U.N. Doc. A/4684 (1961)) it has been a requirement of international law that all states exercising trust authority over other entities inscribe them on a list of "Non-Self-Governing Territories" scheduled for timely decolonization under U.N. supervision; Burnard H. Weston, Richard A. Falk, and Anthony D'Amato, *Basic Documents in International Law and World Order* (St. Paul, MN: West, [2nd ed.] 1990) pp. 343–4.

in terms of population.* The high court's articulation was meant to cast a patina of legal rationalization over the results. Only the discovery (during the 1920s) of substantial mineral deposits within the remote and supposedly worthless tracts to which most of the remaining Indians had been consigned to die off, out of sight and mind of the dominant society, averted this planned extinction (which had been scheduled for consummation by the mid-1930s).[4] By the late 1970s, it was estimated that some two-thirds of all "U.S." uranium reserves, as well as about a quarter of the readily accessible low-sulphur coal, one-fifth of the oil and natural gas, and appreciable quantities of other strategic minerals were situated within reservation boundaries.[5]

Insofar as there were always clear advantages for federal economic planners in holding such assets in trust rather than placing them in the public domain—a matter which, given America's alleged "free market" ideology, required the existence of native peoples as justification—governmental policy was quickly retooled to serve the ends of preservation rather than eradication.[6] The instrument by which this vital transformation was accomplished was the Indian Reorganization Act of 1934, a statute that usurped what was left of traditional indigenous governments, replacing them with federally designed-and-maintained "tribal councils" whose function was/is mainly to sign off on federal "development" programs on the reservations, thus fostering the false impression of native consent to massive resource expropriation.[7]

Under this neatly crafted system of internal colonial domination, the federal government determines which resources will be exploited on which

---

*The primary means by which this was to be accomplished was the 1887 General Allotment Act (ch. 119, 24 Stat. 362, 385, now codified at 18 U.S.C. 331 *et seq.*)—which Indian Commissioner Francis Leupp described as a "great engine to grind down the tribal mass"—under provision of which traditional indigenous forms of land tenure were dissolved in favor of the "more civilized" system of individuated land holdings within the reservations. Once each Indian—defined on the basis of a restrictive "blood quantum" formula designed to minimize the number of people eligible—had been allotted his or her individual parcel (averaging 160 acres apiece), the balance of reserved territory was declared "surplus" and opened up to non-Indian usage. Through this mechanism, to which native people never consented, the overall reservation landbase was "legally" reduced by two-thirds, from about 150 million acres at the outset to some 50 million in 1924; Kirk Kicking Bird and Karen Ducheneaux, *One Hundred Million Acres* (New York: Macmillan, 1973); Janet McDowell, *The Dispossession of the American Indian, 1887–1934* (Bloomington: Indiana University Press, 1991). Assimilation policy also worked on a second major track—which was described as an effort to "kill the Indian, spare the man"—through the forced transfer of indigenous children to distant boarding schools, wherein the could be raised in ignorance of their own cultures and indoctrinated in the values and practices of their conquerors; David Wallace Adams, *Education for Extinction: American Indians and the Boarding School Experience, 1875–1928* (Lawrence: University Press of Kansas, 1995). For the quotation from Leupp, see his *The Indian and His Problem* (New York: Scribner's, 1910) p. 93.

reservations, at what pace and for what purpose, by which "vendors," at what royalty rates, under what safety standards, and with what, if any, post-extraction cleanup requirements.[8] The potential superprofits for the government's preferred transnational corporations, many of them defense contractors, are obviously enormous—readily comparable to those accruing through neo-colonialist enterprises conducted in other Third World locales—and they have been consistently realized over the past sixty years.[9] This, in turn, has facilitated America's emergence as the globally dominant economic and military power of the late twentieth century.

For Native North Americans, the costs and consequences have been genuinely catastrophic. Despite the fact that the reservation resource profile is sufficient to make Indians—collectively, and on a per capita basis—the wealthiest people on the continent, we remain by far the poorest, with the lowest annual and lifetime incomes of any group. Reservation unemployment averages 60 percent throughout the United States and, in some places, has hovered in the ninetieth percentile for decades.[10] The effects of such acute impoverishment are more indicative of Third World conditions than of those expected within the world's richest and most advanced postindustrial "democracy." Indians suffer an infant mortality rate up to fifteen times the U.S. national average, and, by a decided margin, the highest rates of death from malnutrition, exposure, and plague disease.[11]

All of this translates into an endemic sense of disempowerment and despair which then generates chronic alcoholism and other kinds of substance abuse, a circumstance contributing heavily to spiraling rates of teen suicide, as well as fatalities from accidents and Fanonesque forms of intragroup violence.[12] As of the mid-1980s, reservation-based American Indian men had a life expectancy of 44.6 years in a country where average male life expectancy was 71.8 years. Reservation-based Indian women could expect to live slightly more than three years longer than their men, but non-Indian females displayed a longevity eight years greater than their male counterparts.[13] Unquestionably, Eduardo Galeano's famous observation that the wealth of the United States is absolutely dependent upon its perpetual and parasitical impoverishment of the South holds equally true for the internal colonies of the native North.[14]

Trinity

In mid-1941, it was discovered for the first time by non-Indians that there were uranium deposits in the northern reaches of the Navajo

293

Reservation called the "Four Corners Region," a high-desert environment where the state boundaries of Arizona, New Mexico, Colorado, and Utah intersect.* Although the mineral was not considered especially valuable at that moment, a limited amount of prospecting began almost immediately, a process which, over the next few years, revealed the contours of what is now called the "Grants Uranium Belt," an almost continuous series of ore pockets stretching roughly two hundred miles across the Colorado Plateau from somewhere west of Tuba City, Arizona, to the area around Albuquerque.[15]

Exploration was intensified in early 1942, after the U.S. entry into World War II, primarily because of the establishment of the Manhattan Project, a highly classified military/scientific effort to develop nuclear weapons for use against Germany and Japan.[16] From that point until July 1945, over 11,000 tons of ore were mined and processed into yellowcake uranium in the Monument Valley and Carrizo Mountain areas of Navajo by a single defense contractor, the Vanadium Corporation of America.[17] The end user of all this material was the Los Alamos National Scientific Laboratory, a huge fortified compound on the Pajarito Plateau, northwest of Santa Fe, created by impounding a tract of land belonging to the San Ildefonso Pueblo.[18] The reasoning bound up in that maneuver is instructive:

> Ironically, the very attributes that protected the Pajarito Plateau from the systematic colonization that engulfed much of New Mexico before the 1940s made it attractive for this secret project. Seeking a remote locale to hide those researching the possibility of creating the single most dangerous human weapon invented up to that time, federal and military officials wanted a place with minimal distraction and little chance of discovery or subversion. The Pajarito Plateau fit such requirements... [It] had never become thoroughly integrated into the economy of modern America, [and] remained as it always had been: remote, peripheral, and marginal to the mainstream.[19]

What was brewed up at Los Alamos was, of course, "Trinity," the first three atomic bombs (uranium fission devices). One of these was test-detonated at the remote Alamagordo Bombing and Gunnery Range—now called the White Sands Missile Range—on July 16, 1945, making the population of the nearby Mescalero Apache Reservation, along with the troops

---

*Although the Bureau of Indian Affairs office at Grants, New Mexico, is usually credited with discovery of the uranium "belt" bearing the town's name, it was actually a Navajo named Martinez who brought in the first samples; see the fine piece on the matter, "It Was That Indian," by the Laguna poet Simon J. Ortiz in his *Woven Stone* (Tucson: University of Arizona Press, 1992) pp. 295–6.

positioned in trenches for experimental purposes, the earliest known victims of nuclear warfare.[20] The test came too late for the remaining pair of devices to be used against the Germans, and barely in time to allow for the strategically unnecessary incineration of the Japanese cities of Hiroshima (August 6, 1945; more than 100,000 dead) and Nagasaki (August 9; at least 50,000 fatalities) in terrifying demonstrations of the newfound American capacity to visit previously unheard-of levels of destruction upon its enemies.[*]

Temporarily sanguine in its monopoly on such weapons—which its experts predicted would last a decade or more, allowing it to achieve a position of unprecedented world dominance—the United States began to build up its nuclear arsenal at a rather leisurely pace.[21] Indeed, while some mining

---

[*] "The [official] justification for these atrocities was that this would end the war quickly, making unnecessary an invasion of Japan. Such an invasion would cost a huge number of lives, the government said—a million, according to Secretary of State [James F.] Byrnes; a half-million, Truman claimed was the figure given him by General George Marshall... These estimates of losses were not realistic, and seemed to be pulled out of the air to justify bombings which, as their effects became known, horrified more and more people... It was known that the Japanese had instructed their ambassador in Moscow to work on peace negotiations with the Allies. Japanese leaders had begun talking of surrender a year before this, and the Emperor himself had begun to suggest, in June 1945, that alternatives to this end be considered. On July 13, Foreign Minister Shigenori Togo had wired his ambassador in Moscow: 'Unconditional surrender is the only obstacle to peace...' If only the Americans had not insisted on unconditional surrender—that is, if they were willing to accept one condition to surrender, that the Emperor, a holy figure to the Japanese, remain in place [a stipulation the United States later decided was in its own interests in any event]—the Japanese would have agreed to stop the war. Why did the United States not take that small step to save American and Japanese lives? Was it because too much money and effort had been invested in the atomic bomb not to drop it?...Or was it, as British scientist P.M.S. Blackett suggested, because the United States was anxious to drop the bomb before the Russians [who had earlier agreed to do so on August 8] entered the war against Japan?... Blackett says, the dropping of the bomb was 'the first major operation of the cold diplomatic war with Russia'... [He] is supported by American historian Gar Alperovitz, who notes a diary entry for July 28, 1945, by Secretary of the Navy James Forrestal, describing Secretary of State James F. Byrnes as 'most anxious to get the Japanese affair over with before the Russians got in'"; Howard Zinn, *A People's History of the United States* (New York: Harper & Row, 1980) pp. 413–5; quoting P.M.S. Blackett, *Fear, War and the Bomb: Military and Political Consequences of Atomic Energy* (New York: McGraw Hill, 1948); Gar Alperovitz, *Atomic Diplomacy: Hiroshima and Potsdam—The Use of the Atomic Bomb and the American Confrontation with Soviet Power* (New York: Vintage, 1967). Zinn also quotes the U.S. War Department's Strategic Bombing Survey: "Based on a detailed investigation of all the facts and supported by the testimony of the surviving Japanese leaders involved, it is the Survey's opinion that certainly prior to 31 December 1945, and probably prior to 1 November 1945, Japan would have surrendered even if atomic bombs had not been dropped, even if Russia had not entered the war, and even if no invasion had been planned or contemplated"; *Japan's Struggle to End the War* (Washington, D.C.: U.S. Government Printing Office, 1946). A superb overview of these factors, as well as the intrinsic racism bound up in U.S. wartime policy, is provided in Ronald Takaki, *Hiroshima: Why America Dropped the Atomic Bomb* (Boston: Little, Brown, 1995). Also see Gar Alperovitz's exhaustive handling of available evidence in *The Decision to Drop the Bomb* (New York: Alfred A. Knopf, 1995). For what may still be the best interpretation, see William Appleman Williams, *The Tragedy of American Diplomacy* (New York: Dell, [2nd. ed.] 1972).

was continued, there is no evidence that a coherent plan was effected by the Pentagon or allied agencies to extract and process further stocks of uranium during the first two years of the postwar period.[22]

A serious ore acquisition program was not inaugurated by the recently formed Atomic Energy Commission (the AEC, established by the Atomic Energy Act of 1946 and now repackaged, innocuously enough, as the "Department of Energy") until late 1947.[23] Even then, the pace did not really begin to pick up until the first, and entirely unpredicted, Soviet test detonation of a nuclear device on September 23, 1949.[24] With U.S. dreams of an uncontested, and therefore relatively inexpensive, planetary military hegemony thus abruptly derailed, the situation was to change radically and with an almost equal degree of suddenness.[25] For the world as a whole, and for Native North America in particular, the results would be disastrous.

Advent of the Cold War
In truth, the Cold War had begun years before, at least as early as 1941, and more likely from the moment of the U.S.S.R.'s inception in 1917.[26] Certainly, the internal security posture of the United States both during and after the Second World War tends to bear out such a view, as does the Truman administration's initial postwar policy of "containment," with its attendant pattern of low-intensity military confrontations with international Soviet "subversion and aggression."[27] However, the Russian acquisition of nuclear weapons in 1949, as well as the "loss" of China to Mao's communist insurgency that same year, upped the ante considerably.[28] On September 30, 1950, just in time for the outbreak of the Korean Conflict, Truman embraced a set of top-secret policy recommendations advanced by the National Security Council (NSC 68), calling for a far more bellicose strategy of "rolling back communist gains" on a worldwide basis.[29]

Among other things, NSC 68 called for the comprehensive restructuring of the U.S. economy to accommodate a massive and perpetual military/technological buildup, with emphasis on nuclear weapons, under what were ostensibly "peacetime" conditions. This open-ended program, which would entail a drastic "reduction of Federal expenditures for purposes other than defense [sic] and foreign assistance…by the deferment of certain desirable [civic] programs," requiring "a large measure of sacrifice and discipline [on the part] of the American people," was expressly designed to force the Soviet Union into a process of martial competition so vastly expensive as to ultimately bankrupt it.*

In order for these objectives to be attained, it was deemed essential by the NSC that an outright "National Security State" posture be adopted by the United States. This involved not just a burgeoning of the military, but also an expansion of its already sprawling counterpart, the Central Intelligence Agency (CIA).† It also entailed placing a permanent mantle of official secrecy over the basis for most governmental decisionmaking, the systematic indoctrination of the public on all sorts of largely fictional external "threats" the military was needed to defend against, and an across-the-board repression of domestic dissent.[30] Shortly, American society, already beset by an escalating series of officially sponsored spy scares and anticommunist witch-hunts in every quarter from the State Department to

---

*Anyone believing that the domestic economic prescription bound up in NSC 68 is in any way anachronistic or unique to the Truman era, should consider Ronald Reagan's February 26, 1982, proposal to cut $41.4 billion (25 percent) from the federal budget for social programs, while on March 8 recommending a 50-percent *increase* in funding for nuclear weapons development and related activities. "Reaganomics," which still holds considerable sway in Washington, was barely more than a recapitualtion of the principles articulated in the 1950 document. In any event, as stated in the original, the idea was to "hasten the decay of the Soviet system [by employing] economic warfare and political and psychological warfare with a view to fomenting and supporting unrest and revolt in selected strategic satellite countries [to] reduce the power and influence of the Kremlin inside the Soviet Union and other areas under its control [and, thereby,] foster the seeds of destruction within" the U.S.S.R.. This was, of course, precisely Reagan's foreign policy recipe. For what may be the best analysis of prereaganite policy implementation in this regard, see Gregg Herken, *The Winning Weapon* (New York: Alfred A. Knopf, 1980). On the early Reagan era, see Chomsky, *Towards a New Cold War, op. cit.* For overviews of effects, see Fred Block, *The Origins of International Economic Disorder* (Berkeley: University of California Press, 1977) and "Economic Instability and Military Strength: The Paradoxes of the 1950 Rearmament Decision," *Politics and Society*, Vol. 10, No. 1, 1980; Noam Chomsky, *World Orders, Old and New* (New York: Columbia University Press, 1995).

†The CIA, which was put together in 1946 and '47, in large part from elements of the wartime Office of Strategic Services (OSS), included not just global intelligence-gathering and -analysis divisions, but an "operations" or "clandestine services" component which was devoted to the active subversion, often through paramilitary means, of ideologically objectionable entities, including governments. This latter dimension of its activities fit well within a second line of attack recommended in NSC 68, that of organizing and supporting anticommunist guerrilla forces within the Soviet sphere—including the U.S.S.R. itself—which would serve over the long run to erode the Kremlin's position politically, economically, and militarily; William Blum, *The CIA: A Forgotten History* (London: Zed Books, 1986). Implementing this strategy entailed a clear nazification of the U.S. defense establishment, at least insofar as it entailed the absorption by the OSS *cum* CIA of Abwehr General Reinhard Gehlen, Hitler's leading anti-Soviet intelligence expert, and the entire apparatus he'd deployed against the U.S.S.R. during World War II. Like Gehlen himself, most of these "operatives" were war criminals or worse—members of the Gestapo and other SS branches, or of openly collaborationist East European fascist movements—but all were shielded from prosecution by the U.S. intelligence "community"; Reinhard Gehlen, *The Service: The Memoirs of General Reinhard Gehlen* (New York: World, 1972); Christopher Simpson, *Blowback: America's Recruitment of Nazis and Its Effects on the Cold War* (New York: Collier Books, 1988).

Hollywood,* was wracked by the full force of McCarthyism (so-called in reference to the "investigative" activities of Wisconsin Senator Joseph R. McCarthy).[31]

The centerpiece of the carefully orchestrated national hysteria which brought McCarthy to the fore was the show trial of a small group of technicians—notably, Julius Rosenberg and Morton Sobell—who had worked on the Manhattan Project, allegedly using their positions to pass nonexistant U.S. nuclear secrets to the Soviets.† The "treason" of these "atom spies" supposedly accounted for the ability of the "Reds" to build a bomb years earlier

---

* The signal investigation of the late 1940s was that involving State Department officials such as Harry Dexter White, accused by a raft of paid witnesses of having acted as real or de facto Soviet agents, selling out American interests to the "international communist conspiracy," especially in Europe and China; David Rees, *Harry Dexter White: A Study in Paradox* (New York: Coward, McCann & Geoghegan, 1973). It was in this context that the FBI was able to manufacture evidence leading to the perjury conviction of Alger Hiss, a former officer at State who had convened the first assembly of the United Nations before going on to work for the Carnegie Endowment for World Peace. Highly sensationalized, this bogus result was peddled to the public as "proof" that the "international communist conspiracy" had penetrated the highest reaches of the American foreign policy establishment, thus accounting for any international posture short of outright U.S. bellicosity in international affairs; Fred J. Cook, *The Unfinished Case of Alger Hiss* (New York: William Morrow, 1958); Alger Hiss, *In the Court of Public Opinion* (New York: Alfred A. Knopf, 1957); Judith Tiger, ed., *In Re Alger Hiss* (New York: Hill & Wang, 1978). Forty years later, after the dissolution of the Soviet Union, its espionage files were searched for any indication that Hiss had been a spy. "Not a single document substantiates the allegation that Mr. A. Hiss collaborated with the Soviet Union," reported General Dimitri Volkogonov; Victor Navasky, "Alger Hiss," *The Nation*, Dec. 9, 1996. On the Hollywood hearings and purges, designed to ensure that American cinema fit into its assigned niche within the official propaganda matrix by restricting its content to only the most "patriotic" fare, see Gordon Kahn, *Hollywood on Trial* (New York: Boni & Gaer, 1948); Robert Vaughn, *Only Victims: A Study of Show Business Blacklisting* (New York: Putnam's, 1972); Dalton Trumbo, *The Time of the Toad: A Study of Inquisition in America* (New York: Harper & Row, 1973). On the quality of the accusatory testimony involved in all this, see Harvey Matusow's autobiographical confession, *False Witness* (New York: Cameron & Kahn, 1955); also see Hyman Lumer, *The Professional Informer* (New York: New Century, 1955) and Herbert L. Packer, *Ex-Communist Witnesses* (Stanford, CA: Stanford University Press, 1962).

† As was admitted as early as 1949 by the Joint Congressional Committee on Atomic Energy, the physics underlying Trinity were no secret at all. From there, it was only a matter of how to manufacture and assemble bomb components, a problem, the solution to which—even if the "atom spies" had provided complete instructions (and no evidence was ever introduced showing that they did)—might have accelerated Soviet bomb production by a few months, not years; Fred J. Cook, *The FBI Nobody Knows* (New York: Macmillan, 1964) pp. 366–7. It is clear that the case presented against Julius Rosenberg, his wife Ethel, and Morton Sobell was largely fabricated. Indeed, it is conclusive that the FBI in particular was aware that Ethel Rosenberg was entirely innocent of the charges brought against her. That she received a death sentence along with her husband—Sobell was sentenced to thirty years' imprisonment—was part of an elaborate ruse designed to coerce Julius into disclosing information about Soviet espionage operations he almost certainly never possessed. The result was that both Rosenbergs were executed at New York's Sing Sing prison on the night of June 19, 1953; Curt Gentry, *J. Edgar Hoover: The Man and His Secrets* (New York: W.W. Norton, 1991) pp. 401–34. Also see Malcolm P. Sharp, *Was Justice Done? The Rosenberg-Sobell Case* (New York: Monthly Review Press, 1956); John Wexley, *The Judgement of Julius and Ethel Rosenberg* (New York: Ballantine, 1977).

than U.S. intelligence analysts had predicted, a matter which placed "the entire citizenry of the Free World in the most extreme peril."* In the trial's aftermath, McCarthy convened well-publicized hearings on what he described as Soviet infiltration of literally the entire "defense" establishment.[†] Even the ranks of the scientists who had overseen Trinity were purged of "communists and communist sympathizers," that is, anyone exhibiting less than full ideological dedication to America's imperial agenda.[‡]

While public consciousness was being thus reshaped, the government began to quietly assemble the infrastructure of its military/industrial/scientific complex. While sharply increasing the funding for existing nuclear research centers at Los Alamos, Oak Ridge and Argonne National Laboratories, and Lawrence Laboratories at Livermore, California, the AEC also broke ground for a new weapons production facility at Rocky Flats, sixteen miles upwind from Denver —augmenting the capacity of the existing

---

*This oft-quoted phrase accrues from U.S. District Judge Irving R. Kaufman, during his sentencing of the Rosenbergs. Their crime, he said, was "worse than murder" in that it put "into the hands of the Russians the A-bomb years before our best scientists predicted Russia would perfect the bomb, [causing] the Communist aggression in Korea, with the resultant casualties exceeding 50,000 and who knows but what…millions more innocent people may the price of your treason"; quoted in Ronald Radosh and Joyce Milton, *The Rosenberg File: A Search for the Truth* (New York: Holt, Rinehart & Winston, 1983) p. 284. It should be noted that the "communist aggression" referred to concerns the effort of Korea to reunify itself after being arbitrarily partitioned by the United States as a part of Truman's postwar containment policy; Clay Blair, *The Forgotten War: America in Korea, 1950–1953* (New York: Times Books, 1987).

†It should be noted that from 1789 until 1947, during which time its role was relatively defensive, the federal executive branch included an entity called the Department of War. In the latter year, at which point the War Department was being retooled for primarily offensive purposes, it was redesignated as being a "Department of Defense." Through such linguistic obfuscations does a good propaganda system function. In any event, by the point McCarthy undertook to purge the defense establishment of ideological impurity, comparable processes were underway in an array of social sectors ranging from public school faculties to the university professorate, from the labor unions to the media, the arts and all areas of government service. For the best overview, see David Caute, *The Great Fear: The Anti-Communist Purge Under Truman and Eisenhower* (New York: Simon & Schuster, 1978). Other fine studies include Robert Griffith, *The Politics of Fear: Joseph R. McCarthy and the Senate* (Lexington: University of Kentucky Press, 1970); Fred J. Cook, *The Nightmare Decade: The Life and Times of Joe McCarthy* (New York: Random House, 1971); David M. Ohshinsky, *A Conspiracy So Immense: The World of Joe McCarthy* (New York: Free Press, 1983).

‡The classic example is that of J. Robert Oppenheimer, who had headed up the Manhattan Project. After Hiroshima and Nagasaki, he became increasingly vocal in his opposition to the development and proliferation of nuclear weapons, especially the new and more powerful fusion (hydrogen) devices. In 1953, he was declared a "potential security risk" on this basis and, a year later, with his clearances revoked, he was forced out of atomic research altogether; Charles P. Curtis, *The Oppenheimer Case: The Trial of a Security System* (New York: Simon & Schuster, 1955); Philip M. Stern, *The Oppenheimer Case: Security on Trial* (New York: Harper & Row, 1969). More broadly, see Morton Grodzins and Eugene Rabinowitch, eds., *The Atomic Age: Scientists in National and World Affairs* (New York: Basic Books, 1962).

plant, situated within the Hanford Military Compound, a large tract abutting the Yakima Indian Reservation in eastern Washington.[32] The extent of corporate interface was soon clear.

> By 1952, thirteen nuclear reactors had been built for weapons production. General Electric built reactors at Hanford, Westinghouse at Argonne, Illinois. Union Carbide ran Oak Ridge [Tennessee]. DuPont was chosen to design, build, and run a giant facility for plutonium waste reprocessing and storage on South Carolina's Savannah River. All government work was contracted out to private firms; the government did not do any direct hiring except for the AEC bureaucracy. From research work to weapons construction, the job was—and is now—done by private firms, think tanks, universities. The new infusion of [taxpayer provided] capital ensured the heavy participation of private industry.[33]

This structural overlap of public finance and private profit was set in concrete through amendment of the Atomic Energy Act in 1954, allowing corporate ownership of reactors and patent rights vis-à-vis the applications discovered for use of fissionable materials, prerogatives formerly reserved for the AEC.[34] The icing on the cake of corporate profit was the passage of the Price-Anderson Indemnity Act in 1957, a statute mandating that public tax revenues would be used to underwrite liability in the event of nuclear accident, even in privately owned facilities.* In order to peddle such an obvious boondoggle to a somewhat skeptical body politic, the government added a carrot to the stick of "national defense."

This took the form of "the friendly atom"—the notion that nuclear power, "properly applied," would ultimately meet the electrical consumption requirements of America, and perhaps the world as a whole, in a clean, efficient, cost-effective, and utterly inexhaustible fashion—a line heavily propagandized by the Eisenhower administration, beginning with the president's "Atoms for Peace" speech in December 1953.† A few months later, the AEC launched a five-year reactor development program.[35]

---

*The act, renewed every decade since it was passed, provided that taxpayers would underwrite $500 million in damages in the event of nuclear accident while requiring responsible corporations to come up with only $60 million—later raised to $125 million—drawn from an industry-wide insurance pool. "In passing the legislation, Congress took the spectre of financial responsibilty in case of accident away from the utilities and nuclear hardware manufacturers"; Gyorgy, et al., *No Nukes, op. cit.,* p. 10; for further details, see Jim Falk, *Global Fission: The Battle Over Nuclear Power* (New York: Oxford University Press, 1982) pp. 78–81.

†Eisenhower also described export of uranium, as applicable to weapons development as to fueling power generation facilities, as a boon to the U.S. trade balance. It is therefore instructive that of 50,000 kilograms earmarked by the AEC for international sale, 90 percent were committed to NATO countries; Robert Rienow and Leona Train Reinow, *Our New Life with the Atom* (New York: Thomas Crowell, 1959) p. 135. By the end of the decade, at least 2.2 million Americans, the majority of them

The first contract was signed in the summer of 1956 with the Yankee Atomic Electric Co., a corporation owned by several New England utilities, for a 185-Mw Westinghouse pressurized water reactor (PWR) in Rowe, Mass. Other permits were issued for Consolidated Edison's PWR at Indian Point, New York, and Commonwealth Edison's G.E. reactor at Dresden, Ill. A construction permit was also [granted] for the first commercial fast breeder, the Enrico Fermi plant in Monroe, Michigan.[*]

Such "civilian" uses of atomic energy had military implications, of course, from lending a benign appearance to whole areas of nuclear research which might otherwise have come to seem menacing much sooner than they did, to stabilizing the basis upon which power generation for key sectors of the politicomilitary command-and-control structure would function during wartime, to providing the raw material from which depleted uranium ammunition would eventually be made.[†] Given the sensitive nature of the materials and technologies

school children, had seen the AEC's traveling multimedia propaganda exhibition, "Atoms for Peace," Cultural Workers Collective, *Workbook on Nuclear Power* (Amherst, MA: Cultural Workers Collective, 1977) p. 102. For a solid dose of Eisenhower-era pro-nuke propaganda, replete with official quotes, see, e.g., Ralph E. Lapp, *The New Force* (New York: Harper & Bros., 1953) and *Atoms and People* (New York: Harper & Bros., 1956); Arnold Kramish and Eugene M. Zuckert, *Atomic Energy For Your Business: Today's Key to Tomorrow's Profits* (New York: David McKay, 1959). Ample indication of the staying power of such tripe will be found in Glenn T. Seaborg and William R. Corliss, *Man and Atom: Building a New World Through Nuclear Technology* (New York: E.P Dutton, 1971).

[*] Gyorgy, et al., *No Nukes, op. cit.*, p. 10. Despite the fact that the AEC's sole attempt to build a functional fast breeder reactor, at its Idaho Falls testing station, had resulted in a near-catastrophic meltdown in November 1955, Detroit Edison was licensed to build the 300-times more powerful Fermi facilty barely a year later, before anything resembling a full assessment of health and safety questions had been attempted (3 million people lived within a thirty-mile radius of the site). Although United Auto Workers President Walter Reuther obtained a court order enjoining Detroit Ed from proceeding, construction continued on AEC authority. The plant opened in February 1966—at a cost of over $130 million to taxpayers—and experienced a near meltdown on October 5 of the same year. Various experiments were undertaken to render the reactor operational before it was finally decommissioned altogether in 1972; John G. Fuller, *We Almost Lost Detroit* (New York: Reader's Digest, 1975).

[†] "The top lobbyist for the nuclear industry, the president of the Atomic Industrial Forum, has confirmed [that] commercial fission began, and was pursued, only because government leaders wanted to justify continuing military expenditures in nuclear-related areas and to obtain weapons-grade plutonium"; K.S. Shrader-Frechette, *Buying Uncertainty* (Berkeley: University of California Press, 1993) p. 15; also see S. Novik, *The Electric War* (San Francisco: Sierra Club Books, 1976) pp. 32–3. As concerns depleted uranium, beginning in the late 1960s, weapons manufacturers like the Olin Corporation and Aerojet Ordnance began to experiment with the use of the substance in both small arms and artillery ammunition. In the former application, the softness of the material—flattening upon impact with the human body, thus creating gaping "explosive type wounds"—lent itself to technical compliance with Geneva Convention prohibitions against military usage of hollowpoint, dum-dum, and soft lead slugs while clearly circumventing the law's intent (the .556 mm. M-16 super-high-velocity "tumbling" ammunition perfected by Colts Arms at about the same time represented a comparable "innovation"). By the mid-'70s, depleted uranium (DU) flechettes had also been developed for use in shotguns and cluster bombs. The great weight of DU uranium also makes it an ideal material for use in artillery-fired armor-piercing projectiles. An added "advantage" in all cases is that

employed, the peddling of "the friendly atom" also facilitated public acceptance of an ever more ubiquitous internal security apparatus.[*] Most of all, it provided a convenient means of funneling vast subsidies into the rapidly growing "defense industry" without including such appropriations in the Pentagon budget.[†]

This, in turn, enabled the Pentagon to lavish its funds, not simply on the development and production of nuclear weaponry, but upon the perfection of more sophisticated "delivery platforms"—the B-52 strategic bomber, for instance, as well as nuclear attack submarines and an array of rockets and ballistic missiles[‡]—and precision electronic paraphernalia allowing better targeting,

anyone or anything hit by the stuff is highly irradiated, thereby increasing "kill rates"; Eric Prokosh, *The Simple Art of Murder: Anti-Personnel Weapons and Their Developers* (Philadelphia: National Action/ Research on the Military-Industrial Complex, 1972); Dr. Malvern Lumsden, *Anti-Personnel Weapons* (Stockholm: International Peace Research Institute, 1975); Philip L. Bolté, "The Tank Killers: Tunsten vs. Depleted Uranium," *National Defense*, May/June 1983; Paul Seideman, "DU: Material with a Future," *National Defense*, Jan. 1984. It should be noted that such ordance, especially Olin's armor-piercing artillery rounds, was used extensively by the U.S. in its 1991 war against Iraq and may therefore account, at least in part, for a mysterious illness—the "Gulf War Syndrome"—which has subsequently appeared among thousands of American troops who fought there; Bill Mesler, "The Pentagon's Radioactive Bullet," *The Nation*, Oct. 21, 1996.

[*] As one French theorist has observed, the very toxicity of the substances inherent to any utilization of atomic energy, whether for military or ostensibly nonmilitary purposes, lead unerringly to a given sociopolitical result: the proliferation of draconian security measures—to prevent contamination—which would be otherwise unacceptable in many societies. "Nuclear society implies the creation of a caste of militarized technicians, who obey like a medieval knighthood its own code and internal heirachy, who are exempt from the common law and are invested with extensive powers of control, surveillance, and regulation... The nuclear knighthood will include tens of thousands of members and will supervise hundreds of thousands of civilians. It will rule as a military apparatus in the name of techical imperatives required by the nuclear megamachine"; André Gorz, "From Nuclear Energy to Electric Fascism," in his *Ecology as Politics* (Boston: South End Press, 1980) pp. 109–10. Also see D. Warnock and K. Bossong, eds., *Nuclear Power and Civil Liberties: Can We Have Both?* (Washington, D.C.: Citizens Energy Project, 1978).

[†] The allocation of tax monies to fund creation of the "civilian" nuclear infrastructure had reached $14 billion annually by 1956 (an amount equal to more than $60 billion at 1996 exchange rates). Correspondingly, the "physical plant and equipment [underwritten] by the federal government [was] greater than the combined value of the [non-federally funded] plant and equipment of the American Telephone and Telegraph Company, General Motors, and United States Steel put together... One plant [Savannah River] built for the AEC by E.I. DuPont de Nemours Corporation cost twice as much as the total value of all plants and facilities owned by DuPont at the time"; Kramish and Zuckert, *Atomic Energy, op. cit.*, p. 11.

[‡] The development of ballistic missiles involved a second major nazification of the U.S. defense establishment. This accrued through its heavy reliance upon the talents of Werner von Braun and his team of some 1,200 scientists and engineers, who had created the V-2 for the Third Reich during World War II. Von Braun, of course, was not only a member of the Nazi Party (as were most of his men), but had made massive use of slave labor in producing the German weapon. He and his associates were in effect immunized for their well-documented crimes against humanity by the United States after the war, and brought to America to head up missile development for the Pentagon. The mentality of those who facilitated this painless "rehabilitation" speaks for itself, being no different in principle from that of any other nazi apologist; Simpson, *Blowback: America's Recruitment of Nazis, op.cit.*, pp. 27–39.

detection and communications.* As these billions of dollars in additional revenues poured into the coffers of corporations like Lockheed, Boeing, McDonnell-Douglas, Grumman, Westinghouse, GE, AT&T, ITT, and Litton Industries, the U.S. economy—indeed, that of the world—underwent an astonishing process of deformation. By 1959, the concentration of wealth among the Pentagon's preferred contractors virtually guaranteed their control over resources and populations, both at home and abroad, in a manner not unlike that evidenced thoughout the internal colonies of Native North America.†

It was in this context, with greater and greater realms of power accumulating in fewer and fewer unelected hands, that even President Dwight David Eisenhower, a former five-star general and avid cold warrior (but apparently a man of at least some degree of democratic sensibility) was to warn before leaving office in January 1960 that the system he himself had done so much to create was threatening, like Frankenstein's monster, to break free of control.[36] Ike's expostulation went unheeded, however, as his "liberal" successor, John F. Kennedy, citing a nonexistent "missile gap" in which he claimed the United States had fallen far behind the U.S.S.R. in its capacity to launch intercontinental nuclear strikes, accelerated rather than reduced America's pursuit of ascendancy in the "strategic arms race."‡

---

* As with missiles, nazification was integral to postwar U.S. electronics development and related military research. "The U.S. share of…scientific and technical booty from all over Germany…included the engineers, technicians, and fifty ME-162 jet turbines—the most advanced in the world—from the Messerschmidt factory at Schönebeck; virtually the entire scientific staff from the Siemens and Zeiss companies; leading chemical and electrical engineers and their equipment from I.G. Farben and Telefunken"; ibid., p. 31.

† It has been reliably estimated that these and about thirty other major defense contractors netted upward of $60 billion—more than $200 billion in 1996 dollars—in research, development, and production allocations during the Eisenhower years alone; William F. Barber and C. Neale Ronning, *Internal Security and Military Power* (Columbus: Ohio State University Press, 1966) p. 13. Also see Nicole Ball and Milton Leitenberg, eds., *The Structure of the Defense Industry* (New York: St. Martin's Press, 1983). By the 1960s, the resulting situation—which involves, not free markets and laissez-faire, but central planning and the systematic governmental transfer of public wealth into corporately private hands—was so pronounced that it had become a mainstay of political-economic analysis from all ideological perspectives; see, e.g., John Kenneth Galbraith, *The New Industrial State* (Boston: Houghton Mifflin, 1967); Ralph Milibrand, *The State in Capitalist Society: An Analysis of the Western System of Power* (New York: Basic Books, 1969); Paul M. Sweezy and Harry Magdoff, *The Dynamics of U.S. Capitalism: Corporate Structure, Inflation, Credit, Gold, and the Dollar* (New York: Monthly Review, 1972). On the impact of this trend abroad, especially in the Third World, see, e.g., Neil Smith, *Uneven Development: Nature, Capital and the Production of Space* (Oxford: Basil Blackwell, 1984); Samir Amin, *Maldevelopment: Anatomy of a Global Failure* (London: Zed Books, 1990).

‡ "[D]eployment of the B-52 jet bomber began in 1955 while the mythical 'bomber gap' was used to muster public support for such spending. The Soviets, being hopelessly outclassed…launched the first intercontinental ballistic missile (ICBM) in 1957. This achievement was soon surpassed by the U.S.…

Radioactive Colonization

Plainly, all the essential ingredients defining the contours of successful American participation in the Cold War were in place by 1951, probably earlier. Their functioning was, however, entirely contingent upon a trio of distinct but closely related needs—a sufficent supply of uranium ore, localities in which the ore could be processed and converted into weapons, and areas in which these weapons and their delivery systems could be tested—none of which had been adequately worked out by that point. Ten years later, a fourth need—locales in which the waste by-products of the whole nuclear cycle might be permanently stored or otherwise disposed of—was to become an increasingly pressing issue.*

The problem was, and remains, that each of these four requirements generates collateral contamination of the environment of varying intensities and durations, but all of it extremely carcinogenic and mutogenic.[37] Both secrecy and propaganda had their limits. There was quite simply no way in which the mainstream American public could be exposed to the brunt of such contamination, thereby suffering the endemic health consequences which could be expected to result, while sustaining the level of popular enthusiasm for nuclear "investment" desired by federal planners.† Insofar as

[However, a 1959 report] probably written by Paul Nitze, created the famous 'missile gap,' which was later shown to be just as fictitious as the earlier 'bomber gap.' It was not until 1964 that the Soviets actually had 100 ICBMs, but by then the U.S. had 400. Meanwhile, the 'missile gap' was used [by Kennedy] to justify the deployment of U.S. Minuteman ICBMs and the Polaris submarine-launched missile system"; Robert C. Aldridge, *Nuclear Empire* (Vancouver, B.C.: New Star Books, 1989) p. 9. For further details on the falsity of Kennedy's posthumous image as a "dove," see Noam Chomsky, *Rethinking Camelot: JFK, the Vietnam War, and U.S. Political Culture* (Boston: South End Press, 1993).

*No thought at all seems to have been given to the ultimate disposition of tailings and other by-products which attend mining and milling in truly massive quantities. In the early days of U.S. nuclear develpment, disposal/storage of spent fuels and similar wastes was also not considered a significant problem since it was estimated that upward of 90 percent of such material could be perpetually reprocessed/reused (thus, among other things, eventually reducing the cost of enriched uranium by as much as one-third). It was only after 1965, when it began to become apparent that reprocessing was not a technically/economically viable option that the disposal issue assumed a critical edge, and not until 1982 that Congress finally passed the Nuclear Waste Policy Act through which taxpayers were, as always, burdened with the expense; "LWR [Light Water Reactor] Spent Fuel Disposition Capabilities," *ERDA [Energy Research and Development Administration] Newsletter*, May 19, 1977; U.S. House of Representatives, Committee on Interior and Insular Affairs, Subcommittee on Energy and the Environment, *Hearings on the Nuclear Waste Policy Act* (Washington, D.C.: 100th Cong., 1st Sess., U.S. Government Printing Office, 1988).

†The bizarre proposition that John Q. Public was somehow "investing" in the creation of a technological infrastructure he did not own, from which he could never gain financially (even hypothetical profits invariably being "reinvested" with neither his knowledge or consent), over which it had no control and about which he in most instances had no accurate information is still being peddled today. To trace the evolution of this bill of goods, see Kramish and Zuckert, *Atomic Energy, op. cit.*; David L. Scott, *Financing the Growth of the Electric Utilities* (New York: Praeger, 1976); U.S.

possible, then, the environmental/health effects of everything from uranium mining and milling to the disposal of radioactive wastes had to be displaced into expendable geographies and onto equally expendable populations.

Although other possibilities were explored over the years, especially with respect to testing, the imagined solutions to such dilemmas were located, by and large, in the "Great American Desert" of the far western regions of the continental United States, conveniently out of sight and mind of the bulk of America's citizens. In these sparsely inhabited areas, taken up mainly by the internal colonial archipelago of American Indian reservations and treaty territories, it was intended that the physiological costs of the country's nuclearization be foisted off more or less exclusively on the indigenous peoples who resided there.[38] To appreciate the extent to which this is true, it is necessary to examine in some detail the evolution of each the four critical elements at issue.

Mining

In 1947, when the AEC began its first, very limited, postwar uranium ore acquisition program, it hit upon an interesting cost-control measure. Since significant uranium deposits along the Grants Belt were known to be concentrated on the Navajo Reservation, and since most Diné (Navajos) had been rendered destitute by federal impoundment of their livestock over the preceeding decade, it was estimated that sufficient ore could be produced by recruiting desperate Indians to undertake individual mining operations.*

Department of Energy, Nuclear Information and Resource Service, *Nuclear Power and National Energy Strategy* (Washington, D.C.: U.S. Government Printing Office, 1991).

*The conventional explanation of the massive stock impoundments on Navajo during the 1930s and '40s—a maneuver which left the reservation's highly self-sufficient population dependent upon the government for survival—has always been that the Diné were heavily overgrazing their land, a circumstance requiring federal intervention to prevent erosion and other environmental degradation; George A. Boyce, *"When the Navajos Had Too Many Sheep":The 1940s* (San Francisco: Indian Historian Press, 1974); Ruth Roessel, ed., *Navajo Livestock Reduction* (Chinle, AZ: Navajo Community College Press, 1975). While this rationalization holds a superficial merit when considered in a policy vacuum, it quickly loses its plausibility when juxtaposed to the eagerness of the very agencies overseeing the impoundments to issue permits for energy corporations to strip-mine the areas they were supposedly protecting thereby. While the effects of overgrazing are largely reversible over a fairly short period, the impact of mineral stripping is permanent in arid locales such as Navajo; Thadias Box, et al., *Rehabilitation Potential for Western Coal Lands* (Cambridge, MA: Ballinger, 1974). The most reasonable policy interpretation is thus one of forcing the Diné into a posture of providing cheap labor to transient mineral extraction interests; Phil Reno, *Navajo Resources and Economic Development* (Albuquerque: University of New Mexico Press, 1981); Donald A. Grinde and Bruce Johansen, *Ecocide of Native America: Environmental Destruction of Indian Lands and Peoples* (Santa Fe: Clear Light, 1995) esp. pp. 113–6.

305

Working through the Department of Labor's Small Business Administration (SBA) and the Interior Department's Bureau of Indian Affairs (BIA), the AEC was even able to promote the proliferation of these tiny "mom and pop" shaft mines—somewhere between one and two hundred of them by 1951—as a "promising new alternative for economic development on American Indian reservations."[39]

Omitted from such glowing projections was the fact that none of the approximately 500 Indians who were provided with SBA loans to establish themselves as "independent suppliers" for the AEC had been warned of the dire health hazards—well known in industrial/governmental circles since the 1930s—involved in working uranium in unventilated mine shafts.

> [R]adon and thoron gases, [which are emitted by uranium,] readily combine with the molecular structure of human cells and decay into radioactive thorium and [polonium]. Radon and thoron gases, if inhaled, irradiate cells in the lining of the respiratory tract, causing cancer.[40]

Even if the miners had been warned, SBA funds were not provided for purposes of installing the equipment necessary to draw off the gases or the equally toxic dust produced in the act of digging. Instead, the miners were left to unwittingly inhale huge doses of such substances day in, day out for years on end.[41] The entirely predictable result was that, by 1980, the first generation of Diné miners had contracted lung cancer in grossly disproportionate numbers.*

> The AEC [later] claimed that it did not possess information about the public health problems for uranium miners. Unions and Public Health Service physicians disagreed. Dr. Victor Archer at NIOSH [National Institute for Occupational Safety and Health] claimed that European physicians had noted a high incidence of lung cancer in ura-

---

*Of the approximately 350 Diné who had worked in the mines before 1955, 25 were dead of lung cancer and at least 45 more had been diagnosed with the disease by 1979; Jack Cox, "Casualties Mounting from U-Rush of '49," *Denver Post*, Sept. 2, 1979; Michael Garrity, "The Pending Energy Wars: America's Final Act of Genocide," *Akwesasne Notes*, Early Spring 1980. In a preview of the far more comprehensive diversion which would afflict the United States by 1990, spokespersons for the uranium industry, tacitly supported by governmental representatives, initially sought to link the epidemic of lung cancer among Diné miners to cigarette smoking; e.g., Bob Beverly, Coordinator of Environmental Control for Union Carbide, quoted in Jack Cox, "Studies Show Radon Guidelines May Be Weak," *Denver Post*, Sept. 4, 1979. The vacuousness of this particular effort to blame personal behaviors rather than systemic causes for mushrooming cancer rates was amply demonstrated when it turned out that most of the victims had never smoked; Dr. Joseph Wagoner, "Uranium Mining and Milling: The Human Costs," unpublished paper quoted in Leslie J. Freeman, *Nuclear Witnesses: Insiders Speak Out* (New York: W.W. Norton, 1982) p. 142. Also see Joseph K. Wagoner, et al., "Radiation as the Cause of Lung Cancer in Uranium Miners," *New England Journal of Medicine*, No. 273, 1965.

nium miners prior to 1940; the National Commission on Radiation Protection and the International Commission on Radiation Protection were aware of potential hazards of radon gas by the early 1940s... As far back as the [early] 1950s, it was widely known that 70 percent of German and Czech pitchblende and uranium miners who worked in the industries in the 1920s and earlier had died of lung cancer.[42]

Things improved little, if at all, after the AEC dramatically stepped up its ore-buying in 1952, contracting with the Kerr-McGee Nuclear Corporation to open the first major uranium mine on Navajo, outside the town of Shiprock, New Mexico. A hundred Diné were hired to perform the underground labor—at about two-thirds the prevailing off-reservation pay scale for comparable work—in what was ostensibly a ventilated mine shaft.[43] When a federal inspector visited the mine a few months after it opened, however, he discovered the ventilator fans were not functioning. When he returned three years later, in 1955, they were still idle.[44] By 1959, radon levels in the mine shaft were routinely testing at 90–100 times the maximum "safe" levels, a circumstance which remained essentially unchanged until the ore played out and Kerr-McGee closed the mine in 1970.[45]

Of the 150-odd Diné miners who worked below ground at Shiprock over the years, eighteen had died of radiation-induced lung cancer by 1975; five years later, another twenty were dead of the same disease, while the bulk of the rest had been diagnosed with serious respiratory ailments.[46] Much the same situation pertained with regard to native employees working in the shaft at Kerr-McGee's second mining operation on Navajo, opened at Red Rock in 1953.[47] The same rates prevail among the men who worked underground for Kerr-McGee at Grants, New Mexico, the largest uranium shaft-mining operation in the world.[48] Of the original six thousand or so miners of all races employed below ground in the Grants Belt as a whole, NIOSH's Victor Archer has estimated that one thousand will eventually die of lung cancer.[49]

Nonetheless, such mines proliferated on the reservation throughout the remainder of the 1950s, as the AEC, with the active complicity of the BIA, entered into a host of additional contracts, not only with Kerr-McGee, but with corporations like Atlantic-Richfield (ARCO), AMEX, Foote Mineral, Utah International, Climax Uranium, United Nuclear, Union Carbide (a chameleon which was formerly known as the Vanadium Corporation of America, and is now called Umetco Minerals Corporation), Gulf, Conoco, Mobil, Exxon, Getty, Sun Oil, Standard Oil of Ohio (Sohio), and Rockwell International.[50] As of 1958, "the Bureau of Indian Affairs reported that over 900,000 acres of tribal land were leased for uranium exploration and development."[51] From 1946 to 1968, over 13 million tons of uranium ore were mined on Navajo—some 2.5 million tons at Shiprock alone—and still the rate of increase grew.[52] By late 1976, at the very peak of the "uranium frenzy" afflicting the Colorado Plateau, the BIA had approved a total of 303 leases encumbering a quarter-million acres of Navajo land for corporate mining and milling purposes.[53]

Aside from its effects upon those working underground, the shaft mining on Navajo had an increasingly negative impact upon the physical well-being of their families and communities. Once real ventilation of the mines began to occur during the mid-'60s, the vents were often situated right in the middle of residential areas, whose inhabitants were then forced to breathe the same potent mixtures of radon, thoron and other toxic substances which were plaguing their husbands, fathers, and neighbors underground.[*] Then there was the matter of pumping out the groundwater which constantly seeped into scores of the deeper shafts—a process called "dewatering"—all of it heavily contaminated. To appreciate the volume of this outpouring, it should be considered that just one site, Kerr-McGee's Church Rock No. 1 Mine, was pumping more than 80,000 gallons of irradiated effluents per day into the local supply of surface water in 1980.[54]

> The millions of gallons of radioactive water [released in this fashion] carry deadly selenium, cadmium, and lead that are easily absorbed into the local food chain, as well as emitting alpha and beta particles and gamma rays. Human ingestion of radioactive water can result in alpha particles recurrently bombarding human tissue and eventually tearing apart the cells comprising that tissue…causing cancer [and/or genetic mutation in offspring].[55]

Small wonder that, by 1981, the Navajo Health Authority (NHA) had documented increasing rates of birth defects—notably cleft palate and Downs Syndrome—among babies born after 1965 in mine-adjacent reservation communities like Shiprock, Red Rock, and Church Rock.[56] At the same time, it was determined that children living in such localities were suffering bone cancer at a rate five times the national average, ovarian cancer at

---

[*] The vents of one mine run by the Gulf Oil Company at San Mateo, New Mexico, for example, were located so close to the town's school that the state's Department of Education ordered closure of the institution—but not the mine—because of the obvious health risk to the children attending it. Meanwhile, the local groundwater was found to be so contaminated by the corporation's activities that the National Guard was forced to truck in drinking water (at taxpayer expense); Clemmer, "Energy Economy," op. cit., p. 98.

a staggering seventeen times the norm.[57] Yet another study concluded that, overall, there was "a twofold excess of miscarriages, infant deaths, congenital or genetic abnormalties, and learning disabilities among uranium-area families (compared with Navajo families in non–uranium areas)."[58] Although funding was requested from the Department of Health, Education and Welfare (DHEW) to conduct more extensive epidemiological studies throughout the Grants Belt, the request was promptly denied.

> In fact, in 1983, one agency, the Indian Health Services [a subpart of DHEW, which was by then redesignated the Department of Health and Human Services] sent a report to Congress…stating that there was "no evidence of adverse health effects on Indians in uranium development areas and there is no need for additional studies or funding for such studies."[59]

Meanwhile, since 1952, an ARCO subsidiary, the Anaconda Copper Corporation, had been operating under AEC/BIA authority on the nearby Laguna Reservation, near Albuquerque. By the early 1970s, the approximately 2,800 acres of Anaconda's Jackpile-Paguate complex at Laguna— from which 22 million tons of ore and more than 44 million tons of other minerals were ultimately removed—was the largest open-pit uranium mine in the world.[60] The excavation went so deep that groundwater seepage became as much an issue as in a shaft mine.

> [Anaconda's] mining techniques require "dewatering," i.e., the pumping of water contaminated by radioactive materials to facilitate ore extraction. Since 1972, the Jackpile Mine has wasted more than 119 gallons per minute through this dewatering procedure. Altogether more than 500 million gallons of radioactive water have been discharged [into] a 260-acre tailings pond [from which it] either sinks back into the acquifer, evaporates, or seeps out into the arroyos and drainage channels of the tiny Río Mequino stream that is fed by a natural spring near the tailings dam.[61]

In 1972, and again in 1977, the Environmental Protection Agency (EPA) notified the Laguna tribal council that both the Río Molino and the nearby Río Paguate, both of which run through the Anaconda leasing area, and which together comprise the pueblo's only source of surface water, were badly contaminated with radium 226 and other heavy metals.[62] This was followed, in 1979, by a General Accounting Office announcement that the acquifer underlying the entire Grants Belt, from which Laguna draws its groundwater, was similarly polluted.[63] The trade-off was, of course, "jobs." But, while most able-bodied Lagunas, and a considerable proportion of neighboring Acomas, were employed by the corporation—a matter touted by the BIA as a "miracle of modernization"—most received poverty-level incomes.* And, although the adverse health effects of open-pit uranium mining seem somewhat less pronounced than those associated with shaft mining, disproportionately high rates of cancer among long-term miners were being noted by the early '80s.[64]

All told, about 3,200 underground and 900 open-pit miners were employed in uranium operations by 1977, and Kerr-McGee was running a multi-million-dollar U.S. Department of Labor-funded job training program in the Navajo community of Church Rock, Arizona, to recruit more.[65] The stated governmental/corporate objective was to create a workforce of 18,400 underground and 4,000 open-pit miners to extract ore from approximately 3.5 million acres along the Grants Belt by 1990.[66] Only the collapse of the market for U.S. "domestic" uranium production after 1980—the AEC met its stockpiling quotas in that year, and it quickly became cheaper to acquire commercially designated supplies abroad, first from Namibia, then from Australia, and finally from the native territories of northern Saskatchewan, in Canada—averted realization of this grand plan.†

As the dust settled around the Four Corners, the real outcomes of uranium mining began to emerge. Although only two-thirds of known uranium resources were located on or near American Indian reservations, some 90 per-

---

*About 450 Lagunas, some three-quarters of the pueblo's labor force, as well as 160 Acomas worked for Anaconda at any given moment. Another 15–20 percent of the Lagunas worked for the BIA or other federal agencies. Yet, even under such "full-employment" conditions, the median income on the reservation was only $2,661 per year (about $50 per week). This was less than half what a non-Indian open-pit miner was earning in an off-reservation locale during the same period; Richard O. Clemmer, "The Energy Economy and Pueblo Peoples," in Jorgenson, *American Indians and Energy Development, op. cit.*, p. 99; Kulentz, *Geographies of Sacrifice, op. cit.*, p. 35.

†The 1972 price of U.S.-produced uranium was $6 per pound. By 1979, the figure had risen to $42, a hugely illegal mark-up which contributed greatly to the accrual of U.S. taxpayer-provided corporate superprofits during the final years of the AEC's ore-buying program (as well as the almost instantaneous bust of the domestic market when the program was phased out); David Burnham, "Gulf Aides Admit Cartel Increased Price of Uranium," *New York Times*, June 17, 1977; John D. Smillie, "Whatever Happened to the Energy Crisis?" *The Plains Truth*, Apr. 1986. Shortly after its closure in 1982, Anaconda's Jackpile-Paguate complex was replaced as the world's largest open-pit uranium mine by Rio Tinto Zinc's Rossing Mine, opened in 1976 in Namibia. Uranium from this de facto South African colony, comprising about one-sixth of the "Free World" supply, was sold not only at a rate of less than $10 per pound to the U.S. and other NATO countries—a factor which drove the highly inflated price of U.S.-mined yellowcake back down to $15, thereby "busting" the profitablity of production— but to Israel, supplying that country's secret production of nuclear weapons. It was also used to underpin South Africa's own illicit nuclear weapons development program; Richard Leonard, *South Africa at War: White Power and Crisis in Southern Africa* (Westport, CT; Lawrence Hill, 1983) pp. 60–9. On Australian uranium mining, and the resistance to it spearheaded by aboriginal peoples, see Falk, *Global Fission, op. cit.*, pp. 256–84. On northern Saskatchewan, see note 178, below. Overall, see A.D. Owen, "The World Uranium Industry," *Raw Materials Report*, Vol. 2, No. 1, Spring 1983.

cent of all mining had occurred on or immediately adjacent to them.[67] The AEC's constellation of corporations had profited mightily as a result, and not just by refusing to meet the expense of providing even the most rudimentary forms of worker safety or their having to pay only the artificially depressed wages prevailing within the reservations' colonial economies. The BIA, exercising the government's self-assigned "trust" prerogatives vis-à-vis Indian uranium, had written contracts requiring the corporations to pay royalties pegged at an average of only 3.4 percent of market price in an environment where 15 percent was the normative standard.[*] Moreover, the contracts often included no clauses requiring post-mining cleanup of any sort, thus sparing Kerr-McGee and its cohorts what would have been automatic and substantial costs of doing business in off-reservation settings. When lucrative mining was completed, the corporations were thus in a position to simply close up shop and walk away.[68]

The impoverished indigenous nations upon which the uranium extraction enterprise had been imposed—who seldom if ever made money from the process and whose prior economies had been demolished in the bargain—were then left holding the bag.[†] On Navajo, this involves the necessity of dealing with hundreds of abandoned mine shafts ranging from fifty to several hundred feet in depth, some subject to caving in and

---

[*] W.D. Armstrong, *A Report on Mineral Revenues and the Tribal Economy* (Window Rock, AZ: Navajo Office of Mineral Development, June 1976); Joseph G. Jorgenson, "The Political Economy of the Native American Energy Business," in his *Native Americans and Energy Development, II, op. cit.*, pp. 9–20. That these rates were approved by "tribal governments" at Navajo, Laguna, and elsewhere means nothing at all insofar as such entities have been created and maintained as instruments of the U.S. colonial administration of Native North America in exactly the same fashion that an "Algerian" government was maintained by colonial France or the Vichy French government by Germany during World War II. Precisely to the point are the observations of Elsie Peshlaskai, an organizer of the Diné resistance to the opening of a mine near the Navajo community of Crown Point, offered in testimony at the National Citizens' Hearings on Radiation Victims in Washington, D.C. (April 12, 1980): In 1979, "I met a lawyer…who showed me a copy of the lease—the United Nuclear Corporation uranium lease negotiating the right to mine and mill and explore the land [where] I was. I was shocked! It had been approved [by the tribal council] in 1971! I couldn't believe it… How come nobody knew about it? The tribal government over in Window Rock wouldn't tell anybody… Thirty-three thousand dollars for 2,500 acres. One dollar for an acre! For rent for one year. And four dollars minimum royalty. I mean, that's nothing… I started to talk to people [and] I found out that the companies had just walked onto the land and started drilling. They hadn't really asked anybody's permission… [The tribal government] must be getting something for it—but the people, no!"; quoted in Freeman, *Nuclear Witnesses, op. cit.*, p. 157.

[†] The federal program to undermine the Diné self-sufficiency economy has already been mentioned. At Laguna, which had enjoyed an agricultural economy since time immemorial, Anaconda's massive strip mining and related activities—which yielded an estimated $600 million in corporate revenues over thirty years—obliterated much of the arable landbase and irradiated most of the rest; Clemmer, "Energy Economy," *op. cit.*, pp. 97–8.

all of them steadily emitting radon and thoron from their gaping maws.[69] At Laguna, conditions are even worse.* As Dr. Joseph Wagoner, Director of Epidemiological Research for NIOSH, would later put it, with conspicuous understatement, the situation presents "serious medical and ethical questions about the responsibility [not just of the corporations, but] of the federal government, which was the sole purchaser of uranium during [much of] the period."[70]

Milling

Milling, the separation of pure uranium from its ore, is the first stage of the production process. Ore pockets across the Grants Belt range from .4–.3 percent uranium content, yielding an average of about four pounds of yellowcake per ton.[71] The remaining 1,996 pounds per ton of waste — reduced to the consistency of coarse sand called "tailings" during milling — invariably accumulates in huge piles alongside the mills which, for reasons of cost efficiency, tend to be situated in close proximity to mines. Tailings retain approximately 85 percent of the radioactivity of the original ore, have a half-life estimated at 10,000 years, and are a source of continuous radon and thoron gas emissions. They are also subject to wind dispersal and constitute an obvious source of groundwater contamination through leaching.[72]

As with uranium mining, about 90 percent of all milling done in the United States during the AEC's ore-buying program occurred on or just outside the boundaries of American Indian reservations.[73] Also as was the case in the mines, "conditions in the mills were deplorable."[74] Even the most elementary precautions to assure worker protection were ignored as an "unnecessary expense." As Laguna poet Simon J. Ortiz, who was employed in a Kerr-McGee mill during the early '60s, would later reflect:

> Right out of high school I worked in the mining and milling region of Ambrosia Lake. I was nineteen years old… At the mill, I worked in crushing, leaching, and yellowcake,

---

* Laguna has been described as the "single most radioactively contaminated area in North America outside of the military reservations in Nevada where nuclear bombs are tested"; Winona LaDuke, interview on radio station KGNU, Boulder, CO., Apr. 15, 1986. Nevertheless, during 1986 "hearings for the environmental impact draft statement for the Jackpile-Paguate mine's reclamation project began with no less than ten Ph.D's and other 'technical' experts in a variety of scientific disciplines, including a mining engineer, a plant ecologist, a radiation ecologist, an expert in biomedicine, and others. All testified in obfuscating language that America's largest uranium mine could be safely unreclaimed. All were under contract to the Anaconda Corporation"; Kulentz, *Geographies of Sacrifice, op. cit.*, p. 42; Marjane Ambler, "Lagunas Face Fifth Delay in Uranium Cleanup," *Navajo Times Today*, Feb. 5, 1986.

Navajos at the Kerr-McGee mine removed uranium ore from the earth much as if it were coal in this photograph taken in 1953. Courtesy of AP/Wide World Photos.

usually at various labor positions... I had a job, and for poor people with low education, no skills and high unemployment, that is the important thing: a job... In 1960, there was no information about the dangers of radiation from yellowcake... In the milling operation at the end of the leaching and settling process, the yellow liquid was drawn into dryers that took the water out. The dryers were screen constructions which revolved slowly in hot air; yellow pellets were extruded and crushed into fine powder. The workers were to keep the machinery operating, which was never smooth, and most of the work was to keep it in free operation; i.e., frequently having to unclog it by hand. There was always a haze of yellow dust flying around, and even though filtered masks were used, the workers breathed in the fine dust. It got in the hair and cuts and scratches and in their eyes. I was nineteen then, and twenty years later I worried about it.[75]

The situation was so acute at Kerr–McGee's first mill on the Navajo Reservation, established at Shiprock in 1953, that after it was abandoned in 1974 inspectors discovered more than $100,000 in uranium dust had settled between two layers of roofing. Former workers recalled having been routinely instructed by their supervisors to stir yellowcake by hand in open, steam-heated floorpans.[76] Needless to say, by 1980, those who had been lured into the mills with the promise of a small but steady paycheck during the 1950s and '60s were suffering rates of lung cancer and other serious respiratory illnesses rivaling those of their counterparts in the mines.[*]

The greater impact of milling, however, has been upon the broader Diné, Laguna, and Acoma communities. The environmental degradation inflicted by a single mill, the Kerr–McGee plant at Grants—once again, the largest such facility in the world—may equal that of all the shaft mines along the uranium belt combined. At its peak, that monstrosity processed 7,000 tons of ore per day, piling up 23 million tons of tailings in a hundred-foot-high mound which covers 265 acres.[77] And this is just one of more than forty mills operating simultaneously on and around Navajo during the late '70s.[78] A similar situation prevailed at plants established by Kerr–McGee, Sohio–Reserve, Bokum Minerals, and several other corporations in the immediate vicinty of Laguna and Acoma.[79]

---

[*] In 1979, several former mill workers with terminal lung cancer joined with eleven similarly afflicted Red Rock miners and the families of fifteen who'd already died in suing the AEC and Kerr–McGee for what had been done to them; "Claims Filed for Red Rock Miners," *Navajo Times*, July 26, 1979; Marjane Ambler, "Uranium Millworkers Seek Compensation," *APF Reporter*, Sept. 1980. In response, "The nuclear industry...commissioned studies which blame [the problem] on smoking, not radiation. 'I'm personally convinced that smoking is helping cause [the cancers] or is the main cause,' [concluded] Dr. Robert W. Buechley, director of the industry-funded study...[He also claimed] researchers had found no excess cancers in New Mexico Navajos"; Freeman, *Nuclear Witnesses, op. cit.*, pp. 141–2; Cox, *Native People, Native Lands, op. cit.* Only one of the plaintiffs had ever smoked.

At the Bluewater Mill, eighteen miles west of the Laguna Reservation [on the western boundary of Acoma, a thirty-mile trip by rail from the Jackpile-Paguate complex, with the raw ore hauled in open gondolas] near the bed of the San Jose River, Anaconda has added a 107–acre pond and a 159–acre pile comprising 13,500,000 tons of "active" tailings and 765,033 tons of "inactive" residues.[80]

In August 1978, it was discovered that Anaconda, as a means of "holding down costs," had made massive use of tailings at Laguna as fill in its "improvement" of the reservation road network. At the same time, it was revealed that tailings had constituted the "sand and gravel mix" of concrete with which the corporation had—with much fanfare about the "civic benefits" it was thereby bestowing upon its indigenous "partners"—poured footings for a new tribal council building, community center, and housing complex.[81] All were seriously irradiated as a result, a matter which may well be playing into increasing rates of cancer and birth defects, even among the nonminer sectors of Laguna's population.[*]

Probably the worst single example of mill-related contamination occurred on July 16, 1979, at the United Nuclear plant in Church Rock, New Mexico, when a tailings dam gave way, releasing more than a hundred million gallons of highly radioactive water into the nearby Río Puerco.[82] About 1,700 Diné living downstream were immediately affected, as were their sheep and other livestock, all of whom depended on the river for drinking water.[†] Shortly thereafter, with spill-area cattle exhibiting unacceptably

---

[*] E.g., in testimony given during 1986 hearings conducted in Denver with regard to the impact of Anaconda's operations around Laguna, Herman Garcia, a resident of the village of Paguate observed that among the nonminers of just that tiny community, in which there is no record of the disease prior to 1965, "last year…we lost five people from cancer… [T]hese people that I'm talking about were nondrinkers and nonsmokers…and I don't know how you'd figure that out"; *Environmental Impact Statement for the Jackpile-Paguate Uranium Mine Reclamation Project, op. cit.*, pp. A-62–3. During the same hearing, a radiation scientist employed by Anaconda testified, contrary to such direct evidence and without offering or being asked to identify the data upon which he based his conclusion, that "individual lifetime risk of cancer in the most exposed individuals at Paguate…is far less than the lifetime risk of dying due to excess cosmic rays received by living in Denver, Colorado." Nor was the good doctor asked to explain why, if this were in any way true, cancer is virtually unknown among populations—the Sherpas of the Himalayas, for instance—residing at elevations much higher than that of Denver; ibid., p. A-10.

[†] In the immediate aftermath, the Río Puerco was testing at over 100,000 picocuries of radioactivity per liter. The maximum "safe" limit is *fifteen* picocuries; Janet Siskind, "A Beautiful River That Turned Sour," *Mine Talk*, Summer/Fall 1982; Steve Hinschman, "Rebottling the Nuclear Genie," *High Country News*, Jan. 19, 1987. Although the July 16 "incident" was the seventh spill from this single dam in five years, United Nuclear had already applied for—and would receive—federal permission to resume use of its tailings pond within two months; Editors, "The Native American Connection," *Up Against the Wall Street Journal*, Oct. 29, 1979.

Cleanup of a nuclear uranium waste spill along the Río Puerco, on the Navajo Nation, 1979. Photo: Dan Budnick.

high levels of lead–210, polonium–210, thorium–230, radium–236, and similar substances in their tissues, all commercial sales of meat from such animals was indefinitely prohibited.[83]

Even as the ban went into effect, Indian Health Services Area Director William Moehler—rather than calling for allocation of federal funds with which to provide emergency rations to those most directly at risk—approved consumption of the very same mutton and beef by local Diné.[84] At about the same time, a request by downstream Diné for United Nuclear to provide them with trucked-in water, at least in quantities sufficient to meet the immediate needs of the afflicted human population, was met with flat refusal.* The corporation stonewalled for another five years—until it was revealed by the Southwest Research and Information Center, an Albuquerque-based environmental organization, that it had known about cracks in the dam at least two months before it broke and had failed to repair it—before agreeing to a minimal, state-facilitated "settlement" of $525,000.[85]

By and large, however, it was not outright disasters such as the Church Rock spill, but the huge and rapidly proliferating accumulation of mill tailings throughout the Four Corners region—more than a half-billion tons in 200 locations by 1979, an amount projected to double by the end of the century—which provoked a team of Los Alamos experts, utterly at a loss as to what to do with such vast quantities of radioactive waste, to recommend the "zon[ing]" of uranium mining and milling districts so as to forbid human habitation."[86] The idea dovetailed perfectly with the conclusions drawn in a contemporaneous study undertaken by the National Academy of Sciences (NAS), that desert lands subjected to stripmining can never be reclaimed.[87]

Since the Peabody Coal Company, among others, was/is engaged in ever more massive coal stripping operations on Navajo,[88] the logical out-

---

*One company spokesperson reportedly informed community representatives that, "This is not a free lunch"; quoted in Dan Liefgree, "Church Rock Chapter Upset at UNC," *Navajo Times*, May 8, 1980. Such behavior is neither unique nor restricted to corporations. When, in 1979, it was discovered that well water in the Red Shirt Table area of the Pine Ridge Reservation in South Dakota was irradiated at a level fourteen times the EPA maximum—apparently as the result of the 3.5 million tons of tailings produced by an isolated AEC mining/milling operation begun in 1954 at Igloo, a nearby army ordnance depot—Tribal President Stanley Looking Elk requested $200,000 in BIA emergency funding to supply potable water to local Oglala Lakota residents. The Bureau approved Looking Elk's request in the amount of $175,000, but stipulated that the water be used *only for cattle*; Madonna Gilbert, "Radioactive Water Contamination on the Redshirt Table, Pine Ridge Reservation, South Dakota" (Porcupine, SD: WARN Reports, Mar. 1980); Women of All Red Nations, "Radiation: Dangerous to Pine Ridge Women" *Akwesasne Notes*, Spring 1980; Patricia J. Winthrop and J. Rothblat, "Radiation Pollution in the Environment," *Bulletin of Atomic Scientists*, Sept. 1981, esp. p. 18.

317

come of the Los Alamos and NAS studies was formulation of a secret federal "policy option" declaring the Four Corners, and also the Black Hills region of the northern plains,[*] "national sacrifice areas in the interests of energy development."[89] Not coincidentally, the pair of locales selected contained the largest and second-largest concentrations of reservation-based Indians in North America: Navajo, with over 120,000 residents in 1980, is by far the biggest reservation both in size and in population in the United States. Also sacrificed in the Four Corners region would be—at a minimum—the Hopi, Zuni, Laguna, Acoma, Isleta, Ramah Navajo, Cañoncito Navajo, Ute Mountain, and Southern Ute reservations. The 50,000 residents of the "Sioux Complex" of reservations in North and South Dakota—Pine Ridge, Rosebud, Crow Creek, Cheyenne River, and Standing Rock in particular—make up the second most substantial concentration. Also sacrificed in the Black Hills region would be the Crow and Northern Cheyenne reservations in Montana, and possibly the Wind River Reservation in Wyoming.[90]

As American Indian Movement leader Russell Means would observe in 1980, shortly after existence of the plan had been disclosed, to sacrifice the landbase of landbased peoples is tantamount to sacrificing the peoples themselves, a prospect he aptly described as genocide while calling for appropriate modes of resistance.[91]

Although a policy of deliberately creating national sacrifice areas out of American Indian reservations was never formally implemented, the indirect effect may well be the same. With windblown tailings spread over wide tracts of Navajo, ground and surface water alike contaminated with all manner of radioactive substances, and Diné children literally using abandoned mounds of tailings as sand piles, it is not unreasonable to suspect that both the land and the people have already been sacrificed on the altar of U.S. Cold War

---

[*] Although little uranium mining or milling had occurred in this region (with the exception of that at Igloo, which ended in 1972, it contains substantial deposits of uranium, low-sulphur coal, and a wealth of other minerals. As was noted by one contemporaneous observer, overall, "the plans for the hills are staggering. They include a giant energy park featuring more than a score of 10,000 megawatt coal-fired plants, a dozen nuclear reactors, huge coal slurry pipelines designed to use millions of gallons of water to move crushed coal thousands of miles, and at least fourteen major uranium mines"; Harvey Wasserman, "The Sioux's Last Fight for the Black Hills," *Rocky Mountain News*, Aug. 24, 1980. Also see Amelia Irvin, "Energy Development and the Effects of Mining on the Lakota Nation," *Journal of Ethnic Studies*, Vol. 10, No. 2, Spring 1982.

arms development.* If so, they and their counterparts at Laguna, Acoma, and elsewhere will have become victims of what may be, to date, history's subtlest form of physical extermination.†

Weapons Research and Production

The Los Alamos lab might well have extended its zoning recommendations to include not just uranium mining and milling districts but localities in which nuclear weapons research and production have been carried out, beginning with itself. Here again, although the sites at which yellowcake is enriched and/or transformed into plutonium have been scattered across the country in localities not typically associated with indigenous people, the great weight of contamination in this connection has been off-loaded by the dominant society onto Indian Country.‡

---

* All told, the official count is "approximately 1,000 significant nuclear waste sites" on Navajo alone; U.S. Department of Interior, Environmental Protection Agency, *Potential Health and Environmental Hazards of Nuclear Mine Wastes* (Washington, D.C.: U.S. Government Printing Office, 1983) pp. 1–23. During the aforementioned April 12, 1980, National Citizens' Hearings on Radiation Victims in Washington, D.C., former uranium miner Kee Begay, dying of lung cancer, testified that he had "lost a son, in 1961. He was one of the many children that used to play in the uranium piles during those years. We had a lot of uranium piles near our homes—just about fifty or a hundred feet away or so—a lot of tailings. Can you imagine? Kids go out and play on those piles!"; quoted in Freeman, *Nuclear Witnesses, op. cit.*, pp. 143–4. Haunting sequences of Diné children playing during the late 1970s in abandoned United Nuclear tailings piles in the reservation community of Tuba City, Arizona, are included in a film by Christopher McCleod, *Four Corners: A National Sacrifice Area?* (San Francisco: Earth Image Films, 1981). Although most of the larger piles have now been fenced off and warning signs posted, there is absolutely no reason to assume kids aren't still playing "king of the mountain" on them from time to time, and suffering the longterm consequences. Besides, radon gas has seldom been known to respect the constraints of a chain-link fence.

† While Grants Belt mining and milling accounted for all but about 10 percent of U.S. uranium production between 1941 and 1982, small amounts were done elsewhere in Indian Country. The AEC facility at Igloo has already been mentioned. Other examples include the Dawn Mining Company's mine and mill which operated at Blue Creek, on the Spokane Reservation in Washington State, from 1964 to 1982, and Western Nuclear's Sherwood facility in the same locale, which operated briefly, from 1978 to 1982. The Blue Creek site in particular has generated contamination of local groundwater at levels forty times the EPA's maximum permissible limit for human consumption (4,000 times the area's natural level); Ambler, *Breaking the Iron Bonds, op. cit.*, p. 176. Another illustration is the Susquehannah-Western Riverton mill site on the Wind River Reservation in Wyoming. Although it ceased operation in 1967, the corporation followed the usual practice of simply walking off and leaving the results for the local Indians, in this case Shoshonis and Arapahos, to deal with; Marjane Ambler, "Wyoming to Study Tailings Issue," *Denver Post*, Feb. 5, 1984; U.S. Department of Energy, *Environmental Assessment on Remedial Action at the Riverton Uranium Mill Tailings Site, Riverton, Wyoming* (Albuquerque: DOE Western Regional Office, June 1987).

‡ The plants in which yellowcake—uranium-238—is enriched to reactor/weapons grade U-235 are the largest and most costly industrial facilities of any kind in the world. Only a handful exist: one each in Britain, France, and China, two in the former Soviet Union, and three in the United States. The U.S. plants are those run by Union Carbide at Oak Ridge, Tennessee and Paduchah, Kentucky, and

319

The extent of radioactive contamination at Los Alamos, which consists, as was noted above, of land "withdrawn" from the San Ildefonso Reservation in 1942, is astonishing. A half-century of nuclear weapons research on the 43-square-mile "campus"—which adjoins not only San Ildefonso, but the Santa Clara, San Juan, Jemez, and Zia reservations—has produced some 2,400 irradiated pollution sites.[92] A single 1950 experiment in which "simulated nuclear devices" were exploded in order to track radioactive fallout patterns was not only kept secret for decades, but left strontium residues in nearby Bayo Canyon which remain clearly detectable more than forty years later.[93] The facility also has a long history of secretly and illegally incinerating irradiated wastes—a practice producing significant atmospheric contamination—as was acknowledged by the EPA in 1991.[94]

The greatest concentration of hazardous materials in the Los Alamos compound is situated in what is called "Area G," which "began taking radioactive waste in 1957. Since 1971, 381,000 cubic feet of [lab]-generated transuranic [plutonium-contaminated] waste has been stored there; no one knows how much went in before 1971, since records are scanty. Wastes were interred without liners or caps, in bulldozed pits" from which they may be presumed to be leaking.[95] This, in combination with the lab's chronic release of radioactive substances into the atmosphere is thought to be correlated to dramatic increases in cancers and birth defects among local native populations over the past twenty years.[96] Plutonium contamination of surface water has been found downstream at least as far as the Cochiti Reservation, thirty miles away.[97]

At present, with a general reorganization/consolidation of U.S. nuclear weapons research and production attending the end of the Cold War—such extraordinarily contaminated sites as Rocky Flats and Hanford have been shut down, and it has been officially suggested that the Lawrence

---

that run by Goodyear Atomic at Portsmouth, Ohio; McKinley C. Olson, *Unacceptable Risk: The Nuclear Power Controversy* (New York: Bantam, 1976) p. 149. Plutonium-239, which requires a breeder reactor for production, was synthesized at the now-closed-off reservation Savannah River facility at Aiken, South Carolina, as well as the also defunct but reservation-abutting Hanford complex in the state of Washington. As concerns the use of plutonium in "civilian" applications like manufacturing reactor fuel rods, "in the early 1970s, there were four companies making [them]: Nuclear Fuel Service, Inc., Nuclear Materials and Engineering Corp. (NUMEC), Gulf United Nuclear Fuels, and the Kerr-McGee Corp. Three of the four plants are now shut down. Gulf United in Long Island quit business after a 1972 fire and explosion killed one worker and contaminated two others.
At Kerr-McGee's Cimarron, Oklahoma plant, 73 workers were contaminated with plutonim during a four-year period… The plant was shut down in December 1975. At present, only the NUMEC plant near Pittsburg is functioning"; Gyorgy, et al., *No Nukes, op. cit.*, p. 49.

Livermore labs follow suit—Los Alamos has been slated to assume an even more prominent role.[98] In the new plan, strongly opposed by area Indians, Area G is also slated for considerable expansion, becoming "a major dumping ground and waste treatment facility for the entire nuclear weapons complex."[99]

About sixty miles as the crow flies south-southwest of Area G, sandwiched between Albuquerque on the north and the Isleta Reservation to its south, is a large fenced-off compound within the Kirtland Air Force Base. This is the home of the Sandia National Scientific Laboratories, a facility second in importance only to Los Alamos in terms of U.S. nuclear weapons research.

> The civilian scientists, engineers, and technicians at Sandia are mostly responsible for the "weaponization" of nuclear bombs which means they "design all the 'peripheral parts and components' that detonate a warhead, and they figure out how to put the guts into delivery packages'—bodies that can be dropped, shot through the water, or whatever the military orders."[100]

Because Kirtland itself has long functioned as the "largest single storage-site for nuclear weapons in the world," maintaining an inventory of over one thousand devices in a vault hollowed out of Manzano Mountain, it is difficult to establish with precision which pollutants accrue from the base and which come from the lab.[101] What *is* known with certainty is that the Río Grande, which flows along the western boundary of the Kirtland/Sandia complex and provides surface water to Isleta, is contaminated with plutonium and a range of other radioactive substances.[102] In 1991, Sandia entered a request—more by way of a notification—to the City of Albuquerque that it wished to increase the "amounts and types" of such materials it was already dumping through municipal sewers into the Río Grande.[103]

A similar though far more extravagant example is that of the Hanford nuclear weapons research and manufacturing facility, a sprawling tract adjoining the town of Richland, about thirty miles upwind/upstream from the Yakima Reservation in western Washington. Opened by the military in 1944, and subsequently operated by the AEC/DOE until its closure in mid-1990, Hanford possessed one of the two U.S. breeder reactors producing plutonium for weapons manufacture.[104] Despite frequent official denials that it presented any sort of public health hazard during the span of its operation, the complex exhibits an unparalleled record of deliberate environmental contamination, beginning with a secret experimental release of radioactive iodides in 1945, the first of a long series, which equaled or surpassed the total quantity of pollutants emitted during the disastrous 1986 Soviet reactor meltdown at Chernobyl.[*]

Also in 1945, Hanford officials secretly instructed staff to begin "disposing" of irradiated effluents by the simple expedient of pouring them into unlined "sumps" from which they leached into the underlying acquifer. All told, before the plant was closed something in excess of 440 *billion* gallons of water laced with everything from plutonium to tritium to ruthenium had been dumped in this "cost efficient" manner.[105] Another 900,000 gallons of even more highly radioactive fluids were stored in a 117–unit underground "tank farm" maintained under contract by ARCO, several components of which were found to be leaking badly. Not only has regional groundwater been severely contaminated, but wastes have been found to have passed into the nearby Columbia River in quantities sufficient to irradiate shellfish at the river's mouth, more than 200 miles distant.[†]

> Not only has the Hanford plant been discharging and leaking radiation into the river for forty-five years, but serious accidents have occurred at the reactors. One could perhaps excuse the accidental release of radiation [if not its cover-up], but on several occasions huge clouds of isotopes were created knowingly and willingly. In December [1952, to provide another example,] about 7,800 curies of radioactive iodine-131 were deliberately [and secretly] released in an experiment designed to detect military reac-

---

[*] Blanche Wiesen Cook, "Cold War Fallout," *The Nation*, Dec. 9, 1996, p. 32. The Chernobyl explosion released, at a minimum, 185 million curies of atmospheric radiation during the first ten days. It has claimed 125,000 dead during the first decade, a rate which is not expected to peak for another ten years. That the 1945 Hanford release—one of seven such—did not claim a similar toll is owing to the fact that the facility is situated in a far less populated area; Alla Yaroshinka, *Chernobyl: The Forbidden Truth* (Lincoln: University of Nebraska Press, 1995). It should also be noted that the faulty helium-cooled graphite block employed at Chernobyl was itself lifted from a reactor constructed at Hanford; Amory B. Lovins and Hunter L. Lovins, *Brittle Power: Energy Strategy for National Security* (Andover, MA: Brickhouse, 1982) p. 197.

[†] There were at least eleven tank failures at Hanford by 1970. Another, reputedly the worst, was discovered on June 8, 1973. Tank 10-6T, a unit installed in 1944, was found to have corroded to the point that it had leaked some 115,000 gallons of high-level waste—containing about 40,000 curies of cesium 137, 14,000 curies of strontium 90, and four curies of plutonium 239—over a 51-day period. Overall, between August 1958 and June 1973 alone, it is estimated that 422,000 gallons of fluids containing more than a half-million curies of radioactivity leaked from the ARCO "farm" at Hanford; Robert Gillette, "Radiation Spill at Hanford: The Anatomy of an Accident," *Science*, No. 181, Aug. 1973. Also see Kenneth B. Noble, "The U.S. for Decades Let Uranium Leak at Weapons Plant," *New York Times*, Oct. 15, 1988; Martha Odom, "Tanks That Leak, Tanks That Explode… Tanks Alot DOE," *Portland Free Press*, May 1989. Concerning shellfish as an indicator of the extent the Columbia River has been contaminated, it should been noted that a Hanford worker who dined on oysters harvested near the river's mouth in 1962 reportedly ingested sufficient radioactivity in the process that he triggered the plant's radiation alarm upon returning to work; Caldicott, *If You Love This Planet, op. cit.*, p. 89.

tors in the Soviet Union (only 15 to 24 curies of iodine-131 escaped at Three Mile Island in 1979).[106]

The true extent of the ecological holocaust perpetrated at and around Hanford is unknown, and is likely to remain so over the foreseeable future, given that most information about the facility is permanently sealed as a matter of "national security," and DOE/Pentagon/corporate officials claim to have "lost" much of what is supposedly accessible.[107] Such information as has come out, however, tends to speak for itself:

> Abnormally high incidence of thyroid tumors and cancers have been observed in populations living downstream from Hanford. People in adjacent neighborhoods [notably, the Yakimas and nearby Spokanes] were kept uninformed about [radioactive] releases—before, during and after—and none were warned that they were at risk for subsequent development of cancer. (Some experts have estimated that downwind farms and families received radiation doses ten times higher than those that reached Soviet people living near Chernobyl in 1986).*

---

*Caldicott, *If You Love This Planet, op. cit.*, p. 90. The cancer correlation at Hanford has not been a mystery in official circles since at least as early as 1972, when an AEC-funded longitudinal study of 3,250 workers employed at the plant from 1944 onward revealed a marked increase in cancers of the lungs, pancreas, and bone marrow. Then, in an independent study conducted under auspices of the Washington State Health Department (WSHD) in 1974, "one of the things that popped out was too much cancer in Hanford workers." The AEC's response to this confirmation of its own findings was to ask the WSHD researcher, Dr. Sam Milham, Jr., *not* to publish his results; David Burnham, "Study of Atom Workers' Deaths Raises Questions About Radiation," *New York Times*, Oct. 25, 1976. When Milham released his data anyway—it was finalized as "Increased Cancer Mortality Among Male Employees of the Atomic Energy Commission Hanford, Washington Facility," in U.S. House of Representatives, Committee on Interstate and Foreign Commerce, Subcommittee on Health and Environment, *Effects of Radiation on Human Health, Vol. 1: Effects of Ionizing Radiation* (Washington, D.C.: 95th Cong., 2d Sess., U.S. Government Printing Office, 1978)— the commission tried to convince its own researcher, Dr. Thomas F. Mancuso, to publish a "strong rebuttal." When Mancuso in turn refused, he was removed from his position and, although he published an overview of his findings anyway—Thomas F. Mancuso, Alice Stewart, and George Kneale, "Radiation Exposures of Hanford Workers Dying of Various Causes," *Health Physics*, No. 33, 1977—his research materials were impounded as "government property"; William Hines, "Cancer Risk at Nuclear Plant? Government Hushes up Alarming Study," *Chicago Sun-Times*, Nov. 13, 1977. As to the spiraling incidence of thyroid cancer among downwinders exposed to massive atmospheric releases of radioactive iodides, the question—given that iodine collects in the thyroid—is the sort of no-brainer which might be adequately addressed by a high school biology student; John W. Gofman, "The Question of Radioactive Causation of Cancer in Hanford Workers," *Health Physics*, No. 37, 1979. Government researchers nonetheless profess to be stymied on the issue of whether there is a "tangible connection" between exposure and cancer; Keith Schneider, "Seeking Victims of Radiation Near Weapons Plant," *New York Times*, Oct. 17, 1988. Meanwhile, we are to believe that researchers can predict within a tenth of a percentage point how many U.S. cancer deaths next year will accrue from the inhalation of "secondhand" cigarette smoke. Indeed.

In sum, the probability is that Los Alamos, Sandia, Hanford, and their surrounding areas should be added to the extensive geographical sacrifices already discussed with respect to uranium mining and milling. To the extent that this is true—and it is almost certainly the case at Hanford—several more colonized indigenous nations must be added to the roster of those peoples whose sacrifice is deemed necessary, useful, or at least acceptable, in the interests of U.S. nuclear development. Nowhere is the intrinsic falsity of the myth that "pure" scientific research is somehow "neutral" or "detached" more conspicuously evident. In this instance at least, without the sacrifices in lands and lives there could be no "science" at all.

Weapons Testing

Nuclear weapons and their "delivery systems," once designed and constructed, must be tested. The first illustration of this principle at work was, of course, Trinity—not only the Alamagordo blast, but perhaps those at Hiroshima and Nagasaki as well—a set of experiences confirming in the minds of U.S. planners and strategists the need for vast tracts of "remote" and "worthless" territory for use in such activities.[108] Probably the most immediate result was an expansion of the original Alamagordo Bombing Range by something over a thousand percent, until by 1950 it had assumed its present 4,000-square-mile incarnation as the White Sands Test Range, a scale making it the largest single military-use parcel in North America and most likely the world.[109]

Although no atomic devices were detonated at White Sands after the original 1945 blast—the limited amount of U.S. postwar nuclear testing was conducted in one of America's newly acquired Pacific colonies, the Marshall Islands, a process which accelerated after 1950 and continued for another eight years*—the compound's expanse of desert terrain has been ravaged over the years by gigantic expenditures of other ordnance, much of it capable of packing a nuclear warhead.

---

*The United States conducted a total of 106 nuclear tests in the Pacific between 1946 and 1958, 101 of them from 1950 onward. Two atolls in the Marshall Islands, Bikini and Enewetak—occupied by the United States in 1943—were subjected to 66 blasts of up to 15 megatons each, beginning in 1946. Among the tests conducted on Enewetak was that of the first hydogen bomb in 1952. The local populations were forcibly relocated to Kili Island, where they were held against their will until 1968. The Bikinians were then told, falsely, that it was safe to return to their homes, which were saturated with the radiation of 23 bombs. A decade later, the Enewetakans were also encouraged to return to their homes, despite the fact that a 1979 General Accounting Office study concluded they would be exposed to dangerously high radiation levels accruing from the 43 tests conducted there

White Sands is used for everything from full-scale battle practice with real jet planes and missiles powered by remote control from the basement of the "Range Control Center" to the development and testing of top secret lasers like Miracl (Mid-Infrared Advanced Chemical Laser), capable of hitting satellites. "White Sands averages more than twenty 'missions' a day"… Electronic warfare is played here, and the Patriot Missile was tested here, as well as "conventional" explosives that can simulate the blast of a nuclear explosion.[110]

The army's Nuclear Effects Directorate also maintains, in the southwest corner of White Sands, a 45x100 ft. "solar furnace" capable of duplicating, in "thermal bursts," the 3000° F. temperatures resulting from a nuclear detonation.[111] For the past quarter-century, a large area within the test range has been devoted more or less exclusively to experimenting with various types of depleted uranium munitions, which has literally saturated its sandy surface with radioactive particles.[112] The Mescalero Apache Reservation, barely a dozen miles downwind at its closest point, has undoubtedly suffered the windblown contamination emanating from White Sands over the years, although the effects are presently unknown.[113]

While it was determined (on the basis of criteria which remain classified) that it would be inappropriate to engage in more extensive nuclear weapons testing at White Sands, the search for a more suitable continental locale began as early as 1948.* Two years later, the AEC/Pentagon combo finally settled on an existing tract in the upper Sonoran desert region of Nevada, an area which it had already decided "really wasn't much good for anything but gunnery practice—you could bomb it into oblivion and never notice the difference."[114]

On October 29, 1940, President Roosevelt established the Las Vegas [Tonopah] Bombing and Gunnery Range. Now called the Nellis Range it is the largest military

prior to 1958; Giff Johnson, "Nuclear Legacy: Islands Laid Waste," *Oceans,* January 1980. The Bikinians were removed from their island again in 1978—at about the same time the people of Enewetak were going home—because cancers, birth defects, and other maladies had become endemic. It is likely that they had been returned in the first place to serve as a test group upon which the effects of plutonium ingestion could be observed; Giff Johnson, "Bikinians Facing Radiation Horrors Once More," *Micronesia Support Committee Bulletin,* May-June 1978. Quite probably, the Enewetakans were slated to serve the same purpose.

*Although various interesting possibilities for a test site were apparently considered—including Cape Hatteras/Cape Fear area of the North Carolina coast—the three real contenders were all in the southwestern desert regions: White Sands-Alamagordo, the Las Vegas-Tonopah Bombing and Gunnery Range, and another portion of Nevada, "about fifty miles wide, extending from Fallon to Eureka"; Robbins, Makhijani, and Yih, *Radioactive Heaven, op. cit.,* p. 55.

range in the Western world [*sic:* standing alone, White Sands is larger]. Executive order 8578 established the range under an obscure legal authority [that] provided for allowing the president to reserve unappropriated public domain lands for aviation fields for testing and experimental work... The original executive order reserved 3.5 million acres on the range.[115]

Of course, nobody bothered to ask the Newe (Western Shoshone) people, within whose treaty-guaranteed territory the entire facility was established, whether they felt this was an acceptable use of their land, or whether they were even willing to have it designated as part of the U.S. "public domain" for *any* purpose.[116] Instead, in 1952, having designated 435,000 acres in the Yucca Flats area of Nellis as a "Nevada Test Site"— another 318,000 acres were added in 1961, bringing the total to 753,000— the AEC and its military partners undertook the first of what by now add up to nearly a thousand atmospheric and underground test detonations.* In the process, it converted the peaceful and pastoral Newes, who had never engaged in an armed conflict with the United States, into "the most bombed nation on earth."[117]

> The deadly atomic sunburst over Hiroshima, in 1945, produced 13 kilotons of murderous heat and radioactive fallout. At least 27 of the 96 above-ground bombs detonated between 1951 and 1958 at the Nevada Test Site produced a total of over 620 kilotons of radioactive debris that fell on downwinders. The radioactive isotopes mixed with the scooped-up rocks and earth of the southwestern desert lands and "lay down a swath of radioactive fallout" over Utah, Arizona, and Nevada. In light of the fact that scientific research has now confirmed that *any* radiation exposure is danger-

---

* On acreage, see Loomis, *Combat Zoning, op. cit.*, p. 31. With respect to the number of test detonations —five of which actually occurred north of the test site, on the Nellis bombing range—the official count was 702 U.S. and 23 British as of early 1992; U.S. Department of Energy, *Announced United States Nuclear Tests July 1945 through December 1991* (Washington, D.C.: U.S. Government Printing Office, 1992). On December 8, 1992, however, the *New York Times* reported that there had been 204 *unannounced* U.S. tests conducted at the Nevada facilty between 1952 and 1990. Adding in the six tests approved by the Clinton administration during 1992, we arrive at an actual total of 953 nuclear bombings of Newe territory by that point (there have been at least a dozen more, since). All told, leaving aside U.S.-British joint tests and detonations carried out as part of "Operation Plowshare" during the 1960s (see notes 126–9, below), but adding in its own testing programs in New Mexico and the Pacific Basin, the United States can be seen to have exploded, at a minimum, 1,018 nuclear devices during the Cold War. By comparison, the U.S.S.R. is known to have triggered 713 detonations—including 115 designated as being for "civilian purposes," comparable to Plowshare— during the same period. Soviet military testing, of course, included a 58–megaton atmospheric blast— about four times larger than "Bravo 1," the largest U.S. counterpart—at Novaya Zemlya in 1961; Robbins, Makhijani, and Yih, *Radioactive Heaven, op. cit.*, p. 91.

ous, the "virtual inhabitants" (more than 100,000 people) residing in the small towns east and south of the test site were placed in...jeopardy by the AEC atomic test program (emphasis added).*

To be sure, those most affected by the estimated 12 billion curies of radioactivity released into the atmosphere over the past forty-five years have been the native communities scattered along the periphery of Nellis.[118] These include not only three Newe reservations—Duckwater, Yomba, and Timbisha—but the Las Vegas Paiute Colony and the Pahrump Paiute, Goshute, and Moapa reservations as well. Their circumstances have been greatly compounded by the approximately 900 underground test detonations which have, in a region where surface water sources are all but nonexistent, resulted in contamination of groundwater with plutonium, tritium, and other radioactive substances at levels up to 3,000 times maximum "safe" limits.[119]

Although the government has been steadfast in its refusal to conduct relevant epidemiology studies in Nevada, especially with respect to indigenous peoples, it has been credibly estimated that several hundred people had already died of radiation-induced cancers by 1981.† The situation concerning birth defects and infant mortality in the area has also been kept deliberately murky, although the hideous aftermath of U.S. testing in the Marshall Islands may give hints as to what can be expected (or may already have occurred in some iso-

---

*Howard Ball, *Justice Downwind: America's Atomic Testing Program in the 1950s* (New York: Oxford University Press) p. 85. A 1956 effort by concerned downwinders to legally enjoin the AEC from testing was defeated by a barrage of testimony and other evidence submitted by government officials and "scientific experts," all of them insisting upon the "truth" that the tests presented "no public health hazard." Although these witnesses were later proven to have lied under oath—that is, they committed perjury in a manner constituting a "reckless disregard for human life," both of which are crimes in the United States—no legal action was ever taken against them; Kulentz, *Geographies of Sacrifice, op. cit.*, p. 99; Randall Smith, "Charge Ike Misled Public on N-Tests," *New York Daily News*, Apr. 20, 1979; Richard D. Lyons, "Public Fears Over Nuclear Hazards Are Increasing," *New York Times*, July 1, 1979. Also see Richard Miller, *Under the Cloud: The Decades of Nuclear Testing* (New York: Free Press, 1986).
†"Report: Feds Snub Tribe's Radiation Exposure," *Reno Gazette-Journal*, June 7, 1994. On estimate of deaths, see James W. Hulse, *Forty Years in the Wilderness* (Reno: University of Nevada Press, 1986) p. 61. Ironically, it appears that one such fatality may have been the hyperpatriotic actor John Wayne—a staunch advocate of U.S. nuclear supremacy—who was heavily irradiated by fallout from a test detonation while filming the movie *The Conqueror* in the Nevada desert during 1956. He, his costars, and most of the film crew later died of cancer; Karen G. Jackovitch and Mark Sennet, "The Children of John Wayne, Susan Hayward and Dick Powell Fear That Fallout Killed Their Parents," *People*, Nov. 10, 1980. Also see Patrick Huyghe and David Konigsberg, "The Grim Legacy of Nuclear Testing," *New York Times Magazine*, Apr. 22, 1979; Anne Fadiman, "The Downwind People: A Thousand Americans Sue for Damage Brought on by Atomic Fallout," *Life*, June 1980.

lated desert communities).* Certainly, none of these effects could have been surprising or mysterious to federal officials, even in the 1950s and '60s, given that the data predicting them had been available to the AEC—and systematically suppressed—since 1947, *years* before massive weapons testing was begun.†

---

*The reference here is to the residents of Rongelap and Utirik atolls. On March 1, 1954, a tremendous cloud of fallout from "Bravo 1," the detonation of a 15-megation hydrogen device on Bikini, 100 miles distant, saturated these unfortunates with fallout. They were left in place for nearly three days before they were evacuated, and were returned to their islands less than three years later despite the fact that radiation levels were known to still be extremely high; Aldridge, *Nuclear Empire, op. cit.*, pp. 23–8. The U.S. military has always contended that the incredible degree of contamination they suffered was an accident, resulting in an unexpected shift in the prevailing winds. In 1981, however, it was revealed by two meteorologists who were "on station" at the time that Bravo 1 had been conducted in full knowledge of wind conditions. It thus seems probable that the residents of Utirik and Rongelap were deliberately exposed in order that the effects of heavy fallout on humans might be studied; Giff Johnson, "Nuclear Clouds Over the Marshalls," *Glimpse*, Vol. 21, No. 4, 1981; "Another Nuclear Cover-Up," *Micronesia Support Committee Bulletin*, Vol. 6, No. 2, Summer 1981. Dr. Merril Eisenbud, who was director of the AEC Health and Safety Laboratory in 1941, and who was also part of the commission's Bravo Test Task Force, has also said as much; quoted in Henry Kohn, *Rongelap Assessment Project Report* (Berkeley: Rongelap Assement Project, University of California, 1989) p. 54. Moreover, in a January 1956 internal document, a member of the AEC's Advisory Committee on Biology and Medicine noted that Rongelap in particular provided a unique opportunity to study the long-term effects of radiation exposure since it "is by far one of the most contaminated areas in the world" and while "it is true that these people do not live…the way Westerners do, civilized people, it is nevertheless true that they are more like us than mice"; Robbins, Makhijani, and Yih, *Radioactive Heaven, op. cit.*, pp. 81–2. Beginning in 1962, thyroid nodules were detected in increasing numbers of Rongelapi and—19 of 22 exposed children required surgery—a total exceeding 50 percent by the 1980s. Thyroid cancer was slower in making its appearance on Utirik, which had been somewhat less exposed, but was spiraling there as well by the late 1970s. Rates of stillbirth and miscarriage also went up on both atolls by a factor of more than 300 percent. Finally, birth defects of the most acute sort—including eyeless, limbless fetuses similar to those evident among Japanese survivors of the Hiroshima and Nagasaki bombings—had made their appearance, especially on Rongelap; J.W. Hollingsworth, "Delayed Effects on Survivors of the Atomic Bombings: A Summary of the Findings of the Atomic Bomb Casualty Commission, 1947–1950," *New England Journal of Medicine*, No. 263, Sept. 1960; Bernard Franke, *Is Rongelap Atoll Safe?* (Takoma Park, MD: Institute for Energy and Environmental Research, 1989). In August 1983, the Congress of the Republic of the Marshall Islands passed a unanimous resolution requesting that the United States relocate the afflicted population. The DOE replied—contrary to all evidence, and its own maps—that the atoll was "safe for human habitation." In the end, it fell to Greenpeace, an international environmental organization, to honor the islanders' pleas by removing some 320 people from Rongelap in 1985; Robbins, Makhijani and Yih, *Radioactive Heaven, op. cit.*, p. 83. Clearly, the attitudes of the U.S. personnel involved in all this—military, bureaucratic, and scientific—exemplified those described by Robert Jay Lifton and Eric Markusen in their penetrating study, *The Genocidal Mentality: Nazi Holocaust and Nuclear Threat* (New York: Basic Books, 1988).

†See generally, Bill Curry, "A-Test Officials Feared Outcry After Health Study," *Washington Post*, Apr. 14, 1979. The mutogenic effects of strontium-90, a major ingredient of fallout, was studied intensively at the Argonne National Laboratory during 1945 and '46. A preliminary report was submitted to the AEC in 1947, a final in 1948. The results were not made "public," until 1969, and then only in an obscure scientific publication; Miriam P. Finkle and Birute O. Briskis, "Pathologic Consequences of Radiostrontium Administered to Fetal and Infant Dogs," in Melvin R. Sikov and D. Dennis Mahlum,

Rather than admit to any aspect of what it was doing, the military simply gobbled up increasingly gigantic chunks of Newe land, pushing everyone off and creating ever-larger "security areas" that rendered its activities less and less susceptible to any sort of genuine public scrutiny. "Military ranges in Nevada alone amount to four million acres. Approximately 40 percent of Nevada's airspace is designated for military use."[120]

Across the state line in California—it is separated from the gargantuan sprawl of military facilities in Nevada only by the width of the interposed

eds., *Radiation Biology of the Fetal and Juvenile Mammal: Proceedings of the Ninth Annual Hanford Biology Symposium at Richland, Washington, 5–8 May 1969* (Springfield, VA: Clearinghouse for Federal Scientific and Technical Information, 1969). Meanwhile, despite its own mounting evidence, the groundbreaking work of Dr. Ernest J. Sternglass—demontrating strong correlations between *any* prenatal radiation exposure and increased rates of miscarriage, stillbirth, childhood leukemia, and other cancers (Sternglass estimated a radiation-induced increase in U.S. infant mortality of 400,000 by 1969)—was publicly assailed as "unproven" and "irresponsible" by the AEC; see, e.g., Ernest J. Sternglass, "Cancer: Relation of Prenatal Radiation to Development of the Disease in Childhood," *Science*, June 7, 1963; "Infant Mortality and Nuclear Tests," *Bulletin of Atomic Scientists*, Apr. 1969; "Can the Infants Survive?" *Bulletin of Atomic Scientists*, June 1969; "The Death of All Children," *Esquire*, Sept. 1969; *Low Level Radiation* (New York: Ballantine, 1972). At about the same time, the AEC set about discrediting the work of Dr. John Gofman, the University of California scientist who discovered both uranium-233 (synthesized from thorium) and the process by which plutonium can be isolated. Gofman's "mistake" was that, as a senior scientist at the Lawrence Livermore Labs during the late 1960s, he had concluded that there is no acceptable level of exposure to radiactive substances, that any exposure results in increased cancer rates, and that the AEC's "safe" limits were therefore invalid; see, e.g., John W. Gofman, "Federal Radiation Council Guidelines for Radiation Exposure of the Population at Large—Protection or Disaster?" in U.S. Congress, Joint Committee on Atomic Energy, *Environmental Effects of Producing Electric Power* (Washington, D.C.: 91st Cong., 1st Sess., U.S. Government Printing Office, 1969); John W. Gofman and Arthur R. Tamplin, "Epidemiologic Studies of Carcinogenesis by Ionizing Radiation," in J. Neyman, ed., *Proceedings of the Sixth Berkeley Symposium on Mathematical Statistics and Probability* (Berkeley: University of California Press, 1971). Gofman's AEC research funding was quickly revoked—this was just before Mancuso's was revoked at Hanford—and the National Cancer Institute (NCI) declined to replace it, a matter which effectively drove him from the field of epidemiology research. Another such casualty was Dr. Rosalie Bertell, an independent medical researcher who conducted studies on the basis of NCI funding until she began in the mid-'70s to publish results showing correlations between radiation exposure, leukemia, and other cancers confirming the findings of Sternglass, Gofman, Mancuso, and others; see, e.g., Rosalie Bertell, "Nuclear Suicide," *America*, No. 131, 1974; "More About Nuclear Suicide," *Nuclear Opponents*, May-June 1975; "Radiation Exposure and Human Species Survival," in Committee on Federal Research into the Biological Effects of Ionizing Radiation, *Issue Papers: Working Documents of 10 March 1980 Public Meeting* (Bethesda, MD: National Institutes of Health, 1980). At that point, NCI suddenly declined to renew her grants, explaining that if she would "like to change [her] line of research" it "would be happy to consider" a new proposal; quoted in Freeman, *Nuclear Witnesses, op. cit.*, p. 43. A common thread running through all of this seems to be Dr. Sidney Marks, a member of the pronuclear Energy Research and Development Association (ERDA) and highly paid "scientist-consultant" to the AEC as well as Union Carbide and other corporations, whose specialization seems to have been to invent pretexts upon which to challenge the validity of the conclusions reached by legitimate researchers like Mancuso and Bertell; *The Effect of Radiation on Human Health, op. cit.*, pp. 72, 714–27, 964–5.

Death Valley National Monument—lies the million-acre China Lake Naval Weapons Center.[121] Butted up against the Army's estate at Fort Irwin (one million acres), and close to both Edwards Air Force Base (500,000 acres) and the Marine Corps Base at Twentynine Palms (800,000 acres), China Lake uses its share of the Mojave Desert in the same manner as White Sands, only more so.[122] Established in November 1943 and expanded steadily thereafter, it was crediting itself by 1968 with being the location in which "over 75% of the airborne weapons of the free world [and] 40% of the world's conventional weapons" had been tested and perfected.[123] As in Nevada, local indigenous communities, both Newe and Paiute, have been pushed out while their lands, including sacred sites, have been bombed, strafed, and shelled relentlessly for more than fifty years.*

Probably the only "concession" made to native peoples in the region during this entire period has been that the three largest nuclear devices ever detonated underground, culminating in a monstrous 5-megaton blast in 1971, were exploded, not at the Nevada Test Site, but on Amchitka Island, off Alaska.† The reason for this change in procedure had nothing to do with concern for the well-being of humans, however. Rather, it was brought on by fears among AEC officials that the shock waves from such large blasts might cause serious damage to casinos and other expensive buildings in downtown Las Vegas, thereby provoking a backlash from segments of the regional "business community."[124] Hence, the brunt of the environmental/biological consequences wrought by the three biggest "bangs" was shifted

---

*One such group of Timbisha Shoshones have more or less established themselves as "squatters" in a Death Valley visitor's center. Others are clustered to the north and west, in the Owens Valley, the Tehachapi Mountains, and the Lake Isabella area. One of their areas of particularly sacred geography, the Coso Range, is now "officially called the Military Target Range, [and] constitutes some 70 square miles of mountainous area…with various targets—bridges, tunnels, vehicles, SAM sites—emplaced in a natural forested environment for tactics development and pilot training under realistic conditions"; R.E. Kistler and R.M. Glen, *Notable Achievements of the Naval Weapons Center* (China Lake Naval Weapons Center: Technical Information Dept. Publishing Division, 1990) p. 17. For further details, see William Thomas, *Scorched Earth: The Military Assault on the Environment* (Philadelphia: New Society, 1995).

†Aside from the 1971 megablast—dubbed "Cannikan," it was about 350 times as powerful as the Hiroshima bomb, but carrying only one-third the force of the Bravo device exploded above ground on Bikini in 1954—the other two Amchitka detonations were Long Shot in 1965 (80 kilotons) and Milrow in 1969 (1 megaton); Robbins, Makhijani and Yih, *Radioactive Heaven, op. cit.*, p. 66; O'Neill, *Firecracker Boys, op. cit.*, pp. 112–5. The United States also engaged in "Operation Dominic," a series of 24 atmospheric tests conducted from April through July 1962, on Johnson Atoll (remotest point in the Hawaiian Archipelago) and British-controlled Christmas Island. The locations were selected to allow the Kennedy administration to avoid undue public outcry over its breach of a supposed moratorium on such tests; Robbins, Makhijani, and Yih, *Radioactive Heaven, op. cit.*, p. 124.

from the Indians of Nevada to the Aleuts, Inuits, and other peoples indigenous to the Aleutian Archipelago.[125]

AEC preoccupation with business sensibilities also led to one of the more bizarre propositions to emerge from the "Atoms for Peace" syndrome. This assumed the form of "Operation Plowshare" a grandiose scheme to detonate thousands of bombs underground, and more than a few in the atmosphere, for "commerial/strategic" purposes.[126] Ideas included a 1966 plan for using 315 megatons of nuclear explosives to cut a wider and deeper canal, either through Panama or the adjoining portion of Colombia — six years and $17 million were spent trying to figure out which was preferable — and the 1967–68 "Project Ketch," in which it was calculated that the use of something over a thousand devices would be sufficient to create a "national storage vault" beneath central Pennsylvania.[127]

Several subsurface blasts, designed to free up natural gas deposits while carving out huge underground vaults in which to store it, actually occurred. The first of a projected 40,000 such detonations, "Project Gasbuggy," was carried out on December 10, 1967, just outside the largely Diné community of Farmington, New Mexico.[128] What gas was released was "radioactive and unusable," and attempts to circumvent the problem resulted in substantial atmospheric contamination.[129] Nonetheless, the AEC followed up in 1969 with "Project Rulison," the simultaneous detonation of three buried devices near the town of Rifle, Colorado. Although the resulting trickle of gas was again too radioactive to use, the AEC went ahead, in 1974, with "Project Rio Blanco," exploding a 50-kiloton bomb about a mile below the nearby Grand River Valley. Failure this time was complete.[130]

The military value of such off-the-books testing must have been great, since during the same period the AEC, while spending some $138 million in tax dollars to produce an estimated $20–30 million in unusable gas for private oil corporations, also carried out similar exercises in the Carslbad Caverns area of New Mexico, just east of the Mescalero Reservation, another outside the town of Fallon, Utah, another in an unpopulated area of central Nevada, and two more near the city of Hattiesburg, Mississippi.[131] It is likely that such operations would have continued indefinitely had not information concerning the accidental 1970 "venting" of "Banebury"—the small (10-kiloton) device was buried 271 meters deep but still ruptured the earth's surface and threw up a cloud of radioactive debris about three kilometers above the Nevada Test Site—produced enough frightened public reaction to force cancelation of the project.[132] Plainly, irradiating the entirety of Newe Segobia was one thing in the minds of American citizens; the prospect of allowing comparable contamination of New York or New Jersey was another.

Exactly how large an area has been sacrificed to nuclear testing and related activities is unclear, but it most certainly includes the bulk of southern Nevada and contiguous portions of California.[133] Indications are that it may encompass northern Nevada as well, given the insistence of Reagan-era Defense Secretary Caspar Weinberger—selected for this position, appropriately enough, on the basis of his credentials as a senior vice president of the Bechtel Corporation, the second-largest U.S. nuclear engineering contractor—that the rail-mounted MX missile system should be sited there, a move which would have effectively precluded human habitation.* Given prevailing wind patterns, the sacrifice area likely encompasses northwestern Arizona as well, including three indigenous nations—Hualapi, Havasupi and the Kaibab Reservation—located there.[134] Also at issue are the more westerly reaches of Utah, a region which includes the small Goshute and Skull Valley reservations in addition to another huge complex of military bases and proving grounds.†

Waste "Disposal"

Plutonium, an inevitable by-product of reactors and the essential ingredient in nearly all nuclear weapons, has been aptly described as being "the

---

*Construction of the MX system—an entirely offensive weapon which was, of course, dubbed the "Peacekeeper"—promised to generate an estimated half-billion in profits for Weinberger's parent corporation; Tristan Coffin, "The MX: America's $100 Billion 'Edsel'," *Washington Spectator*, Oct. 15, 1980. It would also have eliminated the remaining habitable landbase of the Newe; Martha C. Knack, "MX Issues for Native American Communities," in Francis Hartigan, ed., *MX in Nevada: A Humanistic Perspective* (Reno: Nevada Humanities Press, 1980). As it is, the plan, and Newe resistance to it, brought to a head a long-festering conflict between indigenous people in northern Nevada who are continuing to use their land in traditional ways and federal bureaucrats who claim they are an "environmental hazard" which must therefore be removed; Kristine L. Foot, "*U.S. v. Dann*: What It Portends for Millions of Acres in the Western United States," *Public Land Law Review*, No. 5, 1984. Another fine study is to be found in Rececca Solnit's *Savage Dreams: A Journey Into the Hidden Wars of the American West* (San Francisco: Sierra Club, 1994).

†The latter include the 600,000-acre Hill Air Force Training Range, about 30 miles north of the somewhat larger Wendover Range. Adjoining Wendover to the south, is the equally sized Deseret Test Center (containing the Tooele Arms Depot), below which is a much smaller parcel, the Fish Springs Nuclear Weapons Range, where a 20-kiloton Plowshare device was exploded in 1970. Abutting both Wendover and Deseret to the east is another equally sized compound, the Dugway Proving Grounds. No public access is allowed on *any* of these approximately 2,750,000 acres, the combined controlled air space of which exceeds 20,000 square miles; see generally, Ostling and Miller, *Taking Stock, op. cit.*

most toxic substances in the universe."[*] Only ten micrograms, a microscopic quantity, is an amount "almost certain to induce cancer, and several grams...dispersed in a ventilation system, are enough to cause the death of thousands."[135] Indeed, it has been estimated that a single pound of plutonium, if evenly distributed throughout the earth's atmosphere, would be sufficient to kill every human being on the planet.[†] Viewed from this perspective, the quantity of this material created by the United States during the course of its arms race with the Soviet Union—as of 1989, the United States had amassed some 21,000 nuclear weapons—is virtually incomprehensible.[136]

---

[*] Karl Grossman, *Cover Up: What You Are Not Supposed to Know About Nuclear Power* (New York: Permanent Press, 1980) p. 13. The substance does not exist in nature. Plutonium was created on December 2, 1942, when Enrico Fermi's team of Manhattan Project physicists working with an "atomic pile" at the University of Chicago produced the world's first controlled nuclear chain reaction. Subsequently, it was discovered—by future AEC Chairman Glenn T. Seaborg—that the material constituted an entirely new element resulting from the absorption of a fast neutron by a molecule of uranium-238 during the process of nuclear fission. This secondary fusion, it was found, is an inherent aspect of the fission (reaction). Hence, all nuclear reactors produce plutonium as a by-product intermixed with other waste material, although some—fast-breeder reactors such as those at Hanford and Savannah River, the proposed Clinch River facility at Oak Ridge, and the failed Fermi facility near Detroit—are actually designed to produce it in high volume. The reason for this is that plutonium is highly unstable and thus fissionable, making it an ideal material from which to produce both the "business end" of nuclear weapons and the cores of high-output reactors; see generally, David Dietz, *Atomic Science, Bombs and Power* (New York: Collier, 1962); Andrew W. Kramer, *Understanding Nuclear Reactors* (Barrington, IL: Technical, 1970). On commercial breeder reactors, see Creg Darby, "Beware the Fast Flux: Industry Is Readying a New Kind of Nuke," *The Progressive*, Sept. 1980. It should be noted here that "most toxic" status has also been asserted with regard to dioxin, a chemical synthetic commonly found in herbicides—notably Agent Orange and other defoliants used by the military in Vietnam—which is extraordinarily carcinogenic and mutagenic. It is another of those virulent substances in wide official/commercial use which sanctioned epidemiological studies have never been able to "conclusively" tie to the rampant cancers, birth defects, and other maladies incurred by those exposed to them; see, e.g., Fred Wilcox, *Waiting for an Army to Die: The Tragedy of Agent Orange* (New York: Random House, 1983).

[†] As Dr. Helen Caldicott explains, "When exposed to air, plutonium ignites, forming very fine particles—like talcum powder—that are completely invisible. A single one of these particles could give you lung cancer. Hypothetically, if you could take one pound of plutonium and could put a speck of it in the lungs of every human being [she estimates a single microgram is sufficient], you would kill every man, woman, and child on earth—not immediately, but later, from lung cancer"; Freeman, *Nuclear Witnesses, op. cit.*, p. 294. Additionally, "Plutonium is absorbed from the lungs into the blood stream where it can cause liver cancer. It is also taken up in the skeleton, producing bone cancer and leukemia. There is evidence that it collects in the [sex organs] at a concentration twice that of its point of entry into the lung. Infants are especially sensitive to the substance. In pregnant women, it also crosses the placenta into the embryo where it can kill developing cell walls and damage [or kill] the fetus"; Gyorgy, et al., *No Nukes, op. cit.*, p. 79. Also see David Burnham, "Rise in Cancer Death Rate Tied in Study to Plutonium," *New York Times*, June 6, 1976.

By 1995, military weapons-grade plutonium, in the form of active and dismantled bombs, amounted to 270 metric *tons*. The commercial stockpile of plutonium in nuclear-reactor wastes and isoltes from spent fuel amounts to 930 metric tons and will double to 2,130 tons by 2005, only ten years from now. "Every four or five years we're [now] making about as much plutonium in the civil sector as we did during the whole Cold War." And this is only plutonium. Fission reactors create eighty radionuclides that are releasing "ionizing radiation," which causes harm to human beings in the form of genetic mutations, cancer, and birth defects.*

Leaving aside the proliferation of commercial reactors and other such facilities, as well as the mining and milling zones, there are 132 sites in thirty states where one or another facet of nuclear weapons production has left radioactive contamination.[137] The DOE currently estimates that it will cost about $500 billion to return these to habitable condition, an absurdly low figure when it is considered that the department admits elsewhere that neither concepts nor technologies presently exist with which even to begin cleaning up "large contaminated river systems like the Columbia, Clinch, and Savannah rivers, most groundwater [and] nuclear test areas on the Nevada Test Site."[138]

It is also conceded that there is no known method of actually "disposing" of—i.e., decontaminating—plutonium and other radioactive wastes after they've been cleaned from the broader environment.[139] Instead, such materials, once collected, can only be sealed under the dubious premise that they can be somehow safely stored for the next 250,000 years.[140] The sheer volume is staggering: "Hanford [alone] stores 8,200,000 cubic feet of high-level waste and 500,000 cubic feet of transuranic waste. Hanford buried

*Kulentz, *Geographies of Sacrifice, op. cit.*, p. 109; quoting William J. Broad, "The Plutonium Predicament," *New York Times*, May 2, 1995. "There are several types of radiation [given off by these different substances]. *Gamma* radiation is a very high form of electromagnetic energy emitted by many radioactive substances including cesium-137 and iodine-131. It is extremely penetrating; gamma rays can travel hundreds of feet in the air and pass through anything except heavy lead shielding. X-rays are very similar to gamma rays except lower in energy. *Beta* radiation consists of very high energy electrons emitted by radioactive substances such as cesium-137 and iodine-131 as well as substances that emit gamma such as strontium-90. The beta particles are less penetrating than gamma or X-ray but produce more damage in a smaller space. *Alpha* radiation is emitted by radioactive substances such as plutonium-239 and uranium-235. Alpha particles are least penetrating and cannot pass through paper or human skin. It is important to realize, however, that the range of the particle is not the crucial factor once the radioactive substance has been ingested or inhaled since this brings the source of radiation into intimate contact with vulnerable tissue. For example, when substances which release alpha particles are taken into the body they intensely irradiate the cells in their immediate vicinity and are extremely carcinogenic"; Freeman, *Nuclear Witnesses, op. cit.*, p. 229. Also see John W. Gofman, *The Cancer Hazard from Inhaled Plutonium* (San Francisco: Committee for Nuclear Responsibility, May 14, 1975).

18,000,000 cubic feet of 'low-level' waste and 3,900,000 cubic feet of transuranic waste."[141] And, daunting as they are, these numbers—associated exclusively with weapons, weapons production, and commercial reactors—don't begin to include the millions of tons of accumulated mill tailings and similar by-products of "front end" nuclear processing.[142]

Such facilities as now exist to accomodate warhead and reactor wastes—at Hanford, Los Alamos, Rocky Flats, Idaho Falls, Oak Ridge, Savannah River, Paducah, New York's West Valley, and elsewhere—are all temporary installations designed to last a century or less, even under ideal sets of conditions (which seem never to prevail).* The steadily escalating rate of waste proliferation has led to the burning of plutonium and other substances—a practice which certainly reduces the bulk of the offending materials, but also risks sending clouds of radioactivity into the atmosphere†—and an increasingly urgent quest for safer interim facilities, called "monitored retrievable storage" (MRS) sites, and permanent "repositories" into which

---

* All of the facilities have leaked, some for reasons which are simply unbelievable. At Rocky Flats, for example, plutonium-contaminated oil was kept by Dow Chemical in simple 55–gallon drums stacked in a "storage field" during the late 1960s. These corroded away, leaking their contents directly onto the ground. Eight *years* later, 440 cubic yards of dirt were finally dug up, sealed in better containers and transported by truck to the AEC/naval compound at Idaho Falls. There is a lengthy history of such incidents at the facilty; Marcia Klotz, et al., *Citizens' Guide to Rocky Flats: Colorado's Bomb Factory* (Boulder, CO: Rocky Mountain Peace Center, 1992). Small wonder area groundwater is badly contaminated with plutonium, or that breast cancer—not lung cancer, as might be conveniently associated with smoking—has appeared at epidemic rates among west side Denver women over the past two decades; Joan Lowry and Janet Day, "Flats Water Threat Cited," *Rocky Mountain News*, Dec. 7, 1988; Nicholas Lenssen, *Nuclear Waste: The Problem That Won't Go Away* (Washington, D.C.: Worldwatch Institute, 1991) pp. 34–5. It is worth noting that Dow was ultimately fined nothing for the incident in question.

† To use another example from Rocky Flats, on June 6, 1989, a task force of 75 FBI and EPA agents carried out "Operation Desert Glow," the only known "raid" of a military-related nuclear facility. Their purpose was to apprehend Rockwell International employees engaged in the large-scale, systematic, and thoroughly illegal disposal by fire of plutonium-contaminated waste materials. The FBI offered as evidence, among other things, infrared photographs showing nocturnal burnings occurring in a supposedly abandoned building which had been condemned for safety violations. The improperly filtered incinerator which was being used virtually guaranteed the contamination of downwinders on Denver's west side; Bartimus and McCartney, *Trinity's Children, op. cit.*, p. 194. Since Rocky Flats had already been phased out of weapons production, and federal publicists were feeling the need for a show of official"firmness," several corporate officials were actually indicted on this one. Second thoughts soon prevailed, however, since convictions might have an "undesirable chilling effect on the [nuclear] industry." A directed acquittal was entered over the vociferous objections of the grand jury (which then collectively sought to sue both judge and prosecutors). One reason for the government's sandbagging may have been that officials were already aware that they would soon be announcing burning, albeit in a marginally safer manner, as their own preferred "solution" to the plutonium problem; Becky O'Guin, "DOE: Nation to Burn and Vitrify Plutonium Stores," *Colorado Daily*, Dec. 10, 1996.

their contents could eventually be moved.[143] Here, as always, emphasis has been on off-loading the problem onto captive indigenous nations.[144]

The reason, predictably enough, is that despite a chorus of official assurances that neither an MRS nor a repository would present a health hazard, the precise opposite is true.* Dr. John Gofman, a truly pioneering bionuclear scientist, has calculated that if only 0.01 percent of the plutonium now in need of storage were to escape into the environment—a record of efficiency never remotely approximated by the nuclear establishment in either its public or private guise—up to 25 million people could be expected to die of resulting cancers over the following half-century.† Those most proximate to any dump site can of course expect to suffer the worst impact. Consequently,

---

*The refrain, moreover, has been heard before. Consider the case of Edgemont, South Dakota, a community adjoining the Igloo Ordnance Depot, who were given such assurances in 1952 with respect to the uranium mining and milling then being started. Thirty years later, with epidemic cancer rates prevailing in the town for a generation, the DOE suddenly announced that the Edgemont area was so contaminated by mill tailings and other debris that it would be an ideal location for the siting of a high-level waste dump, to be run by the Chemical Nuclear Corporation. Official efforts to sell the plan included both a barrage of promises of significant revenues to "refuel" the depressed local economy and guarantees that the dump would constitute no health hazard for residents of the southern Black Hills region. Once burned, twice wary, the locals voted overwhelmingly to reject the overture; "Nuclear Waste Facility Proposed Near Edgemont," *Rapid City Journal*, Nov. 19, 1982; "Edgemont Waste Facility No Health Hazard Says Chem-Nuclear Corp.," *Rapid City Journal*, Dec. 10, 1982.

†"Plutonium is so hazardous that if you...manage to contain the [amounts projected to exist by the turn of the century] 99.99 percent perfectly, it would still cause somewhere between 140,000 and 500,000 extra lung-cancer fatalities each year... The point is, if you lose a little bit of it—a terribly little bit—you're going to contaminate the earth, and people are going to suffer for thousands of generations"; quoted in Freeman, *Nuclear Witnesses, op. cit.*, pp. 108, 111. With respect to industry efficiency in containing such materials, consider then-governor Nelson Rockefeller's state-of-the-art high-level West Valley Waste Storage Facility, run by the Nuclear Fuels Corporation, a Getty Oil subsidiary, and supposedly offering a perfect "leak-proof environment" for the next three centuries. It failed in just fourteen years, precipitating a 54-percent increase in infant mortality throughout surrounding Cattaraugus County, New York, in the process; Richard Severo, "Too Hot to Handle," *New York Times Magazine*, Apr. 10, 1977. Also consider the fact that, by 1977, the industry as a whole had "lost" some four *tons* of bomb-grade plutonium and uranium-235; David Burnham, "8,000 pounds of Atom Materials Unaccounted for by Plants in U.S.," *New York Times*, Aug. 5, 1977. The fact that part of this missing material may have been "stolen" by Israeli agents as part of that country's drive to develop its own nuclear weapons capacity is no cause for reassurance; Howard Kohn and Barbara Newman, "How Israel Got the Bomb," *Rolling Stone*, No. 253, Jan. 12, 1977; David Burnham, "House Aid Tells of Suspicion U.S. Uranium Was Stolen 10 Years Ago," *New York Times*, Aug. 9, 1977. Interestingly, no "Atom Spy Scare," à la the Rosenberg case, resulted from this bona fide espionage by "agents of a foreign power." Instead, President Lyndon Johnson ordered that the issue be handled as a matter of strictest secrecy, and subsequent chief executives—including that great spy-chaser of the 1940s, Richard M. Nixon—followed suit; David Burnham, "C.I.A. Said in 1974 Israel Had A-bombs," *New York Times*, Jan. 27, 1978; "The Case of the Missing Uranium," *Atlantic Monthly*, Jan. 1979.

only one county in the United States has proven amenable to accepting an MRS within its boundaries, and its willingness to do so was quickly overridden by the state.[145]

Federal pitchmen have therefore concentrated all but exclusively on convincing native governments—which, whenever it's convenient for U.S. authorities, are considered exempt from state and local jurisdiction—to accept the dumps.[146] As longtime indigenous rights activist Grace Thorpe has observed:

> The U.S. government targeted Native Americans for several reasons: their lands are some of the most isolated in North America, they are some of the most impoverished and, consequently, most politically vulnerable citizens and, perhaps most important, tribal sovereignty can be used to bypass state environmental laws... How ironic that, after centuries of attempting to destroy it, the U.S. government is suddenly interested in promoting Native American sovereignty—just to dump its lethal garbage.[147]

There can be little doubt that during the early '90s DOE negotiators played heavily upon the colonially imposed destitution of indigenous peoples in peddling their wares.

> Sixteen tribes initially applied for $100,000 grants from DOE to study the MRS option on Native lands. The lucrative DOE offer included up to $3 million to actually identify a site for an MRS and as much as $5 million per year for any tribe to accept the deal. The government also offered to build roads, hospitals, schools, railroads, airports and recreation facilities [most of which the Indians should have been receiving anyway].[148]

Another $100,000 was passed along in 1992 to the federally oriented National Congress of American Indians (NCAI) to garner its assistance in selling the proposition to its constituents, while a whopping $1.2 million—80 percent of the DOE's budget for such purposes—was lavished on the Council of Energy Resource Tribes (CERT), an entity created for the sole purpose of brokering native mineral rights.[149] Despite the best efforts of both organizations—CERT in particular went beyond the MRS concept to promote acceptance of a repository at Hanford by the Yakimas, Nez Percé, and Umatillas—the campaign was largely a failure.* By 1995, only three reser-

---

* Actually, CERT had been hard at work trying to arrange agreement of these three peoples in the establishment of a repository at Hanford since NWPA was enacted, nearly a decade before. "In 1983 Congress redirected much of DOE's civilian budget toward...waste management. Some of this money went into CERT's coffers when the Confederated Tribes of the Umatilla Reservation and the Nez Percé Tribe [both CERT members] hired CERT to help study the proposed Hanford nuclear waste site... In 1986 DOE still provided $500,000 to CERT through [an] interagency grant [while the] EPA provided half that or $250,000 [per year]... Yakima, Umatilla, and Nez Percé [also] received

vations—Mescalero, Skull Valley, and Ft. McDermitt in northern Nevada—indicated any willingness to accept a dump, regardless of the material incentives offered.

The reasoning which led to this result is instructive. At Skull Valley, the feeling expressed by many residents is that they and their land may already have been sacrificed, in part to radiation blown in over the years from the not-far-distant Nevada Test Site, in part to a host of nuclear, chemical, and bacteriological contaminants emanating from military bases closer to home. Even the specific area committed as an MRS site has long been leased to several corporations as a rocket testing range.[150] As tribal member Leon Bear observes:

> People need to understand that this whole area has already been deemed a waste zone by the federal government, the state of Utah, and the country… Tooele Depot, a military site, stores 40% of the nation's nerve gas and other hazardous gas only 40 miles away from us. Dugway Proving Grounds…is only 14 miles away, and it experiments with viruses like plague and tuberculosis. Within a 40 mile radius there are three hazardous waste dumps and a "low-level" radioactive waste dump. From all directions, north, south, east, and west we're surrounded by the waste of Tooele County, the state of Utah, and U.S. society.[151]

The sentiment at Skull Valley, that it is better to at least charge for one's demise than endure the suffering for free, is shared by an appreciable segment of the Mescalero population. As one reservation resident noted, the feeling of many people is that "since they are getting impacted by nuclear waste [anyway] they should have a chance to benefit economically."[152] Or, as another put it, "The federal government has forced us to choose between being environmentally conscious [and] starving."[153]

More important than subsidies, however, may be the fact that many Mescaleros are now experiencing an overwhelming sense of hopelessness, based in the knowledge that not only are they just downwind from White Sands, but that—over their strong objections—the first U.S. nuclear repository has been sited in the Carlsbad Caverns area, immediately to their east.[154] This is the so-called "Waste Isolation Pilot Plant" (WIPP), a plan to store virtually all military transuranics produced after 1970—57,359 cubic

---

$12.8 million over five years to help them participate in decision making. The money was spent on environmental, social impact, and cultural studies… CERT provided environmental and computer training while the National Congress of American Indians helped…with educational workshops and policy issues"; Ambler, *Breaking the Iron Bonds, op. cit.*, pp. 115, 234.

meters of it—in a subsurface salt bed already scored by one of Operation Plowshare's underground nuclear detonations.*

It now appears that the deep salt beds below Carlsbad are not so dry as was once believed by the National Academy of Sciences, a matter which could lead to the corrosion of the storage cannisters in which the repository's plutonium is to be contained and correspondingly massive contamination of the underlying Rustler Acquifer.[155] Serious questions have also arisen as to whether the mass of materials stored in such close quarters—after accomodating its present allocation of transuranics, the WIPP will still retain some 70 percent of its space availability to meet "future requirements," official shorthand for continuing nuclear weapons production—might not "go critical" and thereby set off an incalculably large atomic explosion.[156] Nevertheless, Secretary of Energy Hazel O'Leary has announced unequivocally that the facility will open in 1998.[157]

Even worse problems are evident at Yucca Mountain, located on the southwestern boundary of the Nevada Test Site, where a $15 billion repository to accommodate 70,000 tons of mostly civilian high-level waste is being imposed on the long-suffering Newes and Western Paiutes.[158] Not only is "spontaneous detonation" just as much a threat as at the WIPP, but Yucca Mountain, located in a volcanically active region, is undercut by no less than 32 geological fault lines.[159] Needless to say, no amount of engineering brilliance can ensure the repository's contents will remain undisturbed through a quarter-million years of earthquakes interspersed with volcanic eruptions. Once again, however, the project is being moved forward as rapidly as possible.[160]

As if this were not enough, it was announced in 1993 by the Southwestern Compact, a consortium of state governments, that it had "decided to keep the option" of siting a huge low-level waste dump in the Mojave Desert's Ward Valley, near the small town of Needles on the California/Arizona boundary.[161] Envisioned as being large enough to accept the contents of all six existing—and failed—low-level facilities in the United States with room to spare for the next thirty years, the proposed site

---

*This, of course, leaves unaddressed the question of transuranic military waste—about 250,000 cubic meters of it—produced *before* 1970. Most of it is buried in shallow trenches at the Nevada Test Site and other locations, and is "difficult to retrieve" since the earth around it is now irradiated to an unknown depth. Present planning has gone no further than to leave it where it is, leaching into the environment at a steady rate; Rosenthal, *At the Heart of the Bomb, op. cit.*, p. 195.

is less than 18 miles from the Colorado River and directly above an acquifer.*
It is also very close to the Fort Mojave, Chemehuavi Valley, and Colorado
River Indian Tribes reservations, and upstream from those of the Cocopahs
and Quechanis around Yuma, Arizona.

Taken as a whole, the pattern of using "deserts as dumps" which has
emerged in nuclear waste disposal practices over the past decade serves to
confirm suspicions, already well founded, that creation of sacrificial geographies within the United States has been an integral aspect of Cold War policies and planning for nearly fifty years.[162] In many ways, the siting of
repositories in particular, since they are explicitly intended to remain in place
"forever," may be seen as a sort of capstone gesture in this regard. And, to be
sure, the collateral genocide of those indigenous peoples whose lands lie
within the boundaries of the sacrifice zones, nations whose ultimate negation has always been implicitly bound up in the very nature and depth of
their colonization, is thus, finally and irrevocably, to be consumated.[163]

Heeding the Miner's Canary

Felix Cohen, widely considered to have been the leading authority on
federal Indian law, once likened the function of indigenous peoples in the
United States to that of a miner's canary. As the bird did for the miner, he
wrote, Indians have been made to serve as an early warning device of impend-
ing danger for the dominant society. By using native people essentially as
guinea pigs for experiments in socioeconomic and political engineering, federal policymakers have been able to assess the relative degrees of efficacy and
consequence attending implementation of their ideas. Based upon these results,
the government can "tune" its programs, enhancing effectiveness and reducing
at least the appearance of likely costs to acceptable levels before exporting them
to the broader U.S. society. In some cases, where the effects of policies have
been found to be unexpectedly unredeeming or counterproductive when
applied to Indians, programmatic export has been avoided altogether, thereby
sparing mainstream America the pain of experiencing such things for itself.[164]

---

*The plan is to "inter" the material—which contains plutonium, strontium, and cesium among a
wide range of hyperactive and longlived substances—in five unlined trenches, each about the
size of a football field. The facility is to be run by U.S. Ecology, formerly Nuclear Engineering, a
corporation whose track record includes oversight of a similar—now closed and badly leaking—
facility at Barnwell, Utah, as well as the disastrous West Valley enterprise in upstate New York;
Kulentz, *Geographies of Sacrifice, op. cit.*, pp. 156–7; John J. Berger, *Nuclear Power: The Unviable Option*
(Palo Alto, CA: Ramparts Press, 1976) p. 104.

At another level, which Cohen does not address, techniques of domination have been consistently field-tested in Native North America, a matter allowing their refinement before they are introduced into other settings both at home and abroad.* At still another, America's internal colonies have been used throughout the second half of the twentieth century, and increasingly so, as laboratories in which the impacts of certain scientific-industrial enterprises could be evaluated and perhaps modified prior to their replication outside reservation boundaries.[165] Beyond that, Indian Country has served as a convenient locale in which to place those sectors of the research, development, and production processes which simply cannot be sufficiently sanitized to be practicable elsewhere.[166]

So it was meant to be with the radioactive colonization of western reservations during the Cold War. They and their occupants were intended to absorb the irremediably dirty parts of the nuclear process—from mining to dumping—while elite sectors of the colonizing society reaped the profits of military/technical ascendancy, with the broader population narcotized by illusions of sharing in this supremacy, as well as the promised benefits of an energy source which was to be cheap, clean, quiet, and endlessly available for their consumption.[167] So long as only the canary died, all was considered to be well; planners and technicians were presumed to learn thereby what not to do, or at least how not to do it, in more "important" locales, among more "significant" concentrations of population. Had it actually worked that way, the unfortunate fact is that most of America would have remained content.[168]

The problem, of course, is that it *didn't* work that way. The marvelously engineered reactors—all 128 of them—invariably leaked radiadion like sieves, as did the research labs and increasingly high-tech production facili-

---

*For example, two operational plans for domestic counterinsurgency, code-named "Garden Plot" and "Cable Splicer," each of them utilizing combinations of federal, state, and local police as well as military personnel and private vigilante organizations to quell "civil insurrections," were field tested against the American Indian Movement on the Pine Ridge Reservation during the mid-'70s. Drafted for then-California Governor Ronald Reagan during the late 1960s by security consultant Louis Giufrida, and revised on the basis of the Pine Ridge exercises, both plans were incorporated into the contingency inventory of the Federal Emergency Management Agency (FEMA) after Giufrida was named its founding director by the Reagan presidential administration in 1981; see Ward Churchill and Jim Vander Wall, *Agents of Repression: The FBI's Secret Wars Against the Black Panther Party and the American Indian Movement* (Boston: South End Press, 1988) pp. 181–98. In the same manner, methods of maintaining a formally democratic veneer over the functioning of what amount to puppet governments were thoroughly worked out on reservations, before they were applied abroad in Third World countries; see Edward S. Herman and Frank Brodhead, *Demonstration Elections: U.S. Staged Elections in the Dominican Republic, Vietnam and El Salvador* (Boston: South End Press, 1984).

ties.[169] Strontium-90–laden fallout from atmospheric bomb testing and the occasional venting of an underground blast failed to confine itself to the remote areas in which most detonations occurred, spreading out rapidly, globally, and with utter unpredictability, to turn faraway places like Albany, New York, into radioactive "hot spots."* It was discovered, moreover, that the lethal filth which was supposed to remain confined to the colonies couldn't be: windblown tailings particles are unaware that they are supposed to quit when they reach a reservation boundary; irradiated surface water does not know it's supposed to stop flowing downstream before reaching a non-Indian community; the radioactive content of groundwater has yet to be informed that it must concentrate itself exclusively beneath the wellheads of indigenous people.

The most obvious result is that, as cancer rates, birth defects, and the like have spiraled out of control at Navajo, Laguna, and other reservations on which the worst impacts of the nuclear process were supposed to have been contained, the same maladies have grown dramatically—albeit to a lesser extent—among the general population. Cancers of all types have increased among American males by 18.6 percent since 1975, 12.4 percent among women.[170]

> The percentage of underweight live births rose by over 40 percent in New York State between 1945 and 1965, as strontium-90 seeped into human bone from atmospheric abuse. [Statistician Jay] Gould charts an epidemic rise in cancer and leukemia during the fifties in children aged 5 to 9. By 1980, they were hit by a wave of immune deficiency diseases never before experienced by this age group [a timing which corresponds well

---

* "There are many so-called hot spots in the United States—that is, areas far from the test location where fallout was much more intense than in surrounding areas. Perhaps the best-known was Albany, New York. The hot spot occurred during the Upshot-Knothole series [of tests in Nevada] due to a severe thunderstorm, which happened just as the fallout cloud passed overhead at an altitude of 40,000 feet... In addition to large gamma doses, it is likely that many people...received large doses of beta radiation to their skin and internal doses due to inhalation or ingestion... In intense hot spot areas, children playing outdoors, and therefore possibly breathing heavily, would have been especially at risk of high inhalation doses... Children who drank milk from cows grazing in these general areas received large iodine-131 doses, increasing their risk of thyroid problems such as hypothyroidism and thyroid cancer... Strontium, whose biological behavior mimics calcium, [also] concentrates in milk and bone"; Robbins, Makhijani, and Yih, *Radioactive Heaven, op. cit.*, pp. 62–3. The issue of hot spots is taken up in more detail in Jacob Shapiro, *Radiation Protection* (Cambridge, MA: Harvard University Press, [3rd ed.] 1990). The citizens of Albany have complained that their arbitrary exposure violated both the "innocence" of their children and the trust they had placed in officials who assurred them they were safe from any possibility of adverse effects from testing. This is true enough. But what led these people to believe their own children were in any way more innocent than those of the Newe and Paiutes around the Nevada Test Site—or those of the Micronesians on Bikini, Enewetak, Utirik, and Rongelap—or that they themselves were more entitled to safety than those peoples, is a bit mysterious. At least in the case of Albany residents, it was their own government doing the testing.

with the epidemic rise of AIDS among adults. He also] documents the impact of radiation on residents of "nuclear counties," the 1,319 counties in proximity to one of the [more than one hundred] civilian and military nuclear reactors in the United States. The results are alarming: Cancer, AIDS, various birth defects and chronic fatigue syndrome occur [much] more frequently in irradiated areas than elsewhere. As compared with every county in the nation, fifty-five of sixty reactor sites had a significantly elevated current breast cancer rate that cannot be explained by chance or genetics.[171]

By 1970, such problems had already become so acute that John Gofman and his colleague Arthur Tamplin were describing what was happening—particularly what they saw as an unstated but very conscious official effort to vector the bulk of the effects into poor communities—"population control through nuclear pollution."[172] It was this understanding, too, which led Gofman a decade later, because of the nature of his earlier work with atomic energy, to publicly pronounce both himself and the institutions in which he had worked guilty of Crimes Against Humanity.

> People like myself and a lot of the atomic energy scientists of the late fifties deserve Nuremberg trials. At Nuremberg we said that those who participate in human experimentation are committing a crime. Scientists like myself who said in 1957, "Maybe Linus Pauling is right about radiation causing cancer, but we really don't know, and therefore we shouldn't stop progress," were saying in essence it's all right to experiment. . . . But once you know that your nuclear power plants are going to release radioactivity, and kill a certain number of people, you are no longer committing the crime of experimentation—you are committing a higher crime. Scientists who support these nuclear plants—knowing the effects of radiation—don't deserve trials for experimentation; they deserve trials for murder.[173]

Theoretically, the impetus leading to all this—the Cold War—ended with the collapse of the Soviet Union in 1989. The goals and objectives outlined in NSC 68 were at that point completely fulfilled. Yet the structural imperatives created by the process—fully a third of the U.S. economy was geared to supporting the military by 1980, and more than half the country's scientific community was harnessed to nuclear research in one form or another—and the mentality it had generated among elites virtually guaranteed a continuation of what one analyst has referred to as "plutonium culture."[174] Indeed, there were strong indications that the nuclear establishment, in both its military and civilian configurations, was preparing to enter a whole new growth phase during the immediate post–Cold War period.

For starters, in 1991 President George Bush advanced a "national energy strategy" of constructing *several hundred* new reactors over twenty years, with an anticipated cost of somewhere between $390 billion and $1.3 *trillion.*[175] Coupled to thus announcement, a mass media advertising blitz was undertaken by the nuclear industry's "big four"—the Westinghouse, Babcock & Wilcox, Bechtel, and Combustion Engineering corporations—featuring a 40ish-looking female yuppie. Purporting to have been an anti-nuclear activist in college who had since "grown up," she warmly endorsed a vast expansion of atomic power generation as "the safe alternative" for her baby daughter.[176] Meanwhile, an ongoing avalanche of extraordinarily dubious, officially endorsed, and massively reported epidemiology studies was initiated, which has diverted the onus of the country's mounting cancer epidemic—and, most recently, responsibility for birth defects as well—further and further away from the systemically crucial nuclear establishment and onto the relatively marginal tobacco industry.*

---

*This is a virtual replay of the scam perpetrated by the nuclear industry—with much official complicity—against Diné miners during the late 1970s and early '80s, only this time writ much larger. That the National Institutes for Health—which have rejected as "inconclusive" literally every study linking the nuclear establishment to cancer, infant mortality, and birth defects, no matter *how* well-substantiated— suddenly showed such enthusiasm for research blaming *any* other substance(s) should have sounded alarms, at least for progressives. This should have been all the more true when well-qualified independent observers like the head of hard sciences at Yale, himself a lifelong non-smoker, publicly categorized the quality of research evident in the Institutes' studies of the effects of secondhand tobacco smoke as being so shoddy that it "would not be accepted as graduate work" at his university. The alarms should have been shrieking by the time the EPA inscribed secondhand smoke as a "Class-A Carcinogen"—dubbing it the "number one preventable environmental health hazard in the country"—despite a finding by the Congressional Research Office that "statistical evidence does not appear to support a conclusion that there are substantial health effects of passive smoking." As Mike Gough, then a senior associate with the congressional Office of Technology Assessment, put it in 1994, "I am adamantly opposed to smoking; I completely agree with the magnitude of the health threat for people who smoke. But I think the EPA played very fast and loose with its own rules in order to come to the conclusion that [secondhand] smoke is a carcinogen"; quoted in David Shaw, *The Pleasure Police* (New York: Doubleday, 1996) p. 143. On December 17, 1996, it was announced on CNN *Headline News* that a team of government-funded researchers in England, another country with a substantial nuclear establishment and escalating consequences, had determined that smoking also causes birth defects at a rate 30 percent higher than among nonsmokers (giving rise to the obvious question of why, if this were true, such a massive disparity wasn't noticed in the aftermaths of either world war, during which the numbers of people smoking skyrocketed). Much ado is made about whether anyone seeking to counter such tripe hasn't been "hired by the cigarette manufacturers"; nobody seems to wonder whether those producing the tripe itself don't owe allegiance to the nuclear industry. Historically, the kind of manipulation we are witnessing on the part of government agencies has *always* served as a means of protecting something officially considered important by jettisoning something else which is deemed less so; see generally, Chomsky, *Necessary Illusions, op. cit.* In this case—since cancer rates, etc., must be blamed on *something*—it appears to have been decided that the incredibly lucrative and strategically central nuclear establishment will be buffered by expending the tobacco industry, either in part, or, if necessary, in its domestic entirety (its profits being largely recoverable in the export trade

The drive to build new reactors was curtailed, at least temporarily, by Bush's electoral defeat at the hands of challenger Bill Clinton in 1992. The latter, however, after a brief moratorium has allowed the resumption of limited weapons testing, especially with regard to neutron devices.* Consideration is also being given to reopening not only the Jackpile Mine at Laguna, but at least some operations on Navajo, Wind River, and Spokane. Additionally, there has been discussion of entirely new extraction and milling facilities being established as "economic stimulants" on the Hualapai, Havasupi, Ute Mountain, Cañoncito Navajo, Zuni, Acoma, Zia, and Jemez reservations in Arizona, Colorado, and New Mexico.[177]

Even if these plans don't bear fruit in the immediate future, their very existence gives ample indication that the genocidal political economy of radioactive colonialism has by no means run its course on American Indian reservations in the United States. Most likely, their delay would indicate only that it remains cheaper for U.S. corporations to acquire yellowcake from Canada, their new NAFTA trading partner to the north, which has itself been engaged in an increasingly intensive plundering of uranium from native lands around Cluff, Key, and Wolleston lakes in northern Saskatchewan.[178] The region has the advantage not only of being more remote from centers of non-Indian population than anything the United States has to offer, but of possessing what is far and away the world's richest known uranium deposit, at Cigar Lake.†

---

anyway). Such a program yields the added advantage of generating a substantial public demand—led, incredibly enough, by self-proclaimed "progressives"—for increased governmental regimentation of individual behavior, thus reinforcing rampant fascistic proclivities on the part of the state; for analysis of this last trend, see Bertram Gross, *Friendly Fascism: The New Face of Power in America* (Boston: South End Press, 1982).

* The plutonium-based neutron bomb, first tested in the early '70s, is designed to employ an ultraintensive spray of radioactivity rather than blast to inflict damage. It will thus kill everything within range upon detonation, but leave buildings and other structures intact; Helen Caldicott, *Nuclear Madness: What You Can Do* (Brookline, MA: Autumn Press, 1978) pp. 159–60.

† The Cigar Lake deposit contains an estimated 100 million kilos of uranium ore averaging over 15-percent purity, with some pockets, perhaps as much as a tenth of the whole, averaging an incredible 60 percent (this is as compared to a worldwide average yield of 3–4 percent). In addition, there are another 50 million kilos of ore averaging 4.7-percent purity. The Cigar Lake deposit, which is at a depth running 410 to 440 meters below ground, will have to be shaft-mined and is therefore simply too hot to be extracted by humans, even a completely expendable native labor force. A special system of robotics is therefore being developed for the purpose; Steven Salaff, "The Cigar Lake Mine: The Real Drilling Begins at Sakatchewan's Prize Uranium Deposit," *Saskatchewan Business*, Mar. 1985. Five new mines have also been opened on the west side of Wolleston Lake and another at Waterbury Lake since 1990. This was to accommodate, as a preliminary to the finalization of NAFTA, increased demand by U.S. corporations; Bud Jorgenson, "Easing of Uranium Export Rules Urged for Canada," *Ottawa Globe and Mail*, May 4, 1986.

In days gone by, when a real miner's canary began to show signs of distress, its owners could immediately abandon it to its fate, themselves scurrying to safety at the mouth of the mine. The cynically analogous use of indigenous nations in the context of nuclear proliferation is unworkable. As should by now be apparent, in this case there is quite simply nowhere safe to run. Rather than serving as an early warning of avoidable danger, then, the fate of radioactively colonized native peoples—whether concentrated in the Grants Uranium Belt or scattered across the upper reaches of Saskatchewan, around the Nevada Test Site or far out in the northern Pacific—should be seen merely as a prefiguration of what will happen—indeed, is *happening*— to everyone else. "The chickens," as Malcolm X once put it with typically eloquent bluntness, have truly "come home to roost."[179]

Reversing the Cold War Legacy

It may be, as Dr. Rosalie Bertell worried more than fifteen years ago, that it is already too late, that Cold War and profit-generated nuclear contamination is already so ubiquitous as to have instigated an irreversible process of human extinction ("species suicide").[180] On the other hand, as Jay M. Gould has more recently suggested, it may be that although it is now very late in the game, there is still hope, the outcome is not yet conclusively determined.[181] Certainly, the marvelously complex organism we call earth possesses recuperative powers unfathomed—and perhaps unfathomable—within the arrogant heritage of Western science. Left to its own devices, it is entirely possible that the planet itself can begin to contain that which America's most accomplished engineers cannot, thus rehabilitating to some extent the global ecosystem upon which they and we are equally dependent for survival.[182]

The buck can be passed to the earth in this regard, however, no more than the impacts of nuclear contamination can be neatly displaced onto the internal colonies of Native North America. People are integral to, not something apart from, the planetary ecology. A certain range of responsibilities thus inhere in us, the shirking of which has led us inerringly to our present circumstance.[183] There is no way out of it: only a conscious and unswerving (re)assumption of these responsibilities by the great mass of humanity can favorably alter the situation in which we now find ourselves. The alternative is a not-so-distant extinction, not just of humans, but more likely of all higher vertebrate species as well.[184]

Within the framework of this discussion, the nature of our responsibilities are not mysterious. It does not devolve upon the cleanup of what has already been done. Rather, it concerns prevention of any further proliferation of radioactive contaminants in the environment. This means that we must, both individually and collectively, devise ways and means of preventing even one of George Bush's hundreds of new reactors from being built.[185] We must find ways to actually stop the testing and production, not only of ever more sophisticated nuclear weapons, but of depleted uranium ammunition and comparable military-scientific innovations. The same holds true for the civil society's technological counterparts, from plutonium-powered pacemakers to neutron-driven spacecraft.[*]

This will be neither easy nor painless. Among the many negative attributes of the U.S.'s Cold War drive to realize itself as a full-fledged "national security state" has been a quintupling of the proportionate level of police power available to the government for purposes of ensuring that the citizenry does not interfere in any meaningful way with the functioning of the military-corporate status quo.[186] More to the point in some ways, the energy corporations themselves have been authorized to form autonomous security forces of their own.[187] In addition to the 110,000 federal and 554,000 state and local police personnel now at large in America, the society is infested with more than 1.5 million "private" cops, all of them armed and provided the power of arrest, tied together by an unprecedentedly sophisticated and continuously evolving web of electronic files and communications, and feeding the world's largest—and steadily burgeoning—prison system.[188]

Plainly, the nuclear establishment has organized itself quite well to prevent any genuine disruption of business as usual. Under such conditions, a dispersal of oppositional energy and resources across a "broad front," combatting the symptomologies of nuclear technology rather than the figuratively physiological cause of the "disease," would prove disastrously self-defeating. A common focus or point of attack is clearly necessary if anything constructive is to be accomplished. In this connection, simple logic dictates—as it always did, if anyone outside the reservations had bothered to look at things honestly—that the crux of of any strategy to halt the nuclear process is at its front end, in the mining and milling zones.

---

[*]The recent atmospheric disentegration of a plutonium-laden Russian satellite should say all that needs saying about why this is so. The "controversy" about whether such a thing might happen has been going on for almost twenty years, since the Soviet Cosmos 954 crashed in Canada on January 24, 1978, without any real alteration in the practice of putting reactors aboard such space vehicles; Richard D. Lyons, "Carter Favors Ban on Atomic Reactors in Earth Satellites," *New York Times*, Jan. 31, 1978.

If the nuclear establishment can't get uranium ore out of the ground, it cannot be milled into yellowcake. Without yellowcake, there can be no production of plutonium or uranium-235.[189] Without these ingredients, both reactors and nuclear weapons are impossible to make. Hence, no future testing or release of a witch's cauldron of radioactive waste by-products from production and reactor sites. It follows, too, that the matter of waste containment becomes self-addressing, at least in the sense that it can be construed as something fixed rather than as a continuously growing phenomenon. The essential question at hand can thus be reduced to how we might most effectively begin choking off the flow of uranium at its source.

Here, another logical sequence presents itself. Since the preponderance of uranium mining in North America has occurred, is occurring, and is projected to *continue* occurring within native territories, and since this has been possible primarily, or even entirely, because of the system of internal colonial domination which has been imposed upon indigenous nations, it is difficult to avoid the conclusion that *de*colonization of these same nations/territories offers the key to resolving the entire nuclear delimma.[190] With native people restored to control over our own lands, lives, and politicoeconomic destinies, the "survivability" of the nuclear establishment is nil, an equation which holds as true in Canada — or in Namibia, Australia, India, China, the former Soviet Union, or anywhere else — as it does in the United States.

To accomplish such a task will require concentration and true clarity of vision. We cannot afford to allow ourselves the distraction of such diversionary silliness as officially sponsored antismoking crusades, or to be deluded into believing that oxymoronic fantasies like Vice President Al Gore's notion of "sustainable development" can do anything but make matters worse than they already are.* If the decolonization of Native North America is to be accomplished — as it must be, if there is to be a sustainable future for anyone,

---

*Albert E. Gore, *Earth in the Balance* (New York: Houghton-Mifflin, 1992). It should be noted that "development" is the standard establishment euphemism for "destruction," e.g., a grassy field has been "developed" when it has been covered under a layer of asphalt for use as a parking lot, a mountain has been "developed" when it has been converted into gravel for use in mixing concrete, a mineral deposit is "developed" when it is dug up and consumed, and so on. Obviously, such processes are fundamentally antithetical to the very possibility of sustainability in a finite system such as the earth. Slowing the rate by which the processes occur, as Gore suggests, does nothing to alter their ultimate effect. The one possible exemption to this rule might be a breeder reactor, an application of technology to which the vice president purports to be strongly opposed. At bottom, his "theory" is little more than another mindless assertion that it is possible to have your cake and eat it, too (which is undoubtedly why it's so popular).

anywhere—it will require every bit of effort, attention, and willingness to absorb punishment that any and all of us can muster, for as long as it takes, until it is done.

Then, and *only* then, can we reasonably expect to be able to ascertain the extent and type of contamination we suffer, chart the boundaries of sacrifice areas with some degree of accuracy, devise methods of neutralizing or encapsulating the toxins which permeate our remaining habitable environments, (re)discover truly sustainable modes of economy and reorganize our longterm relations with one another in a manner which is itself balanced and sustainable. In taking the liberation of the First American as our First Priority we place all of this within our collective grasp, not only because we finally "stop the nukes," but because we will have at long last reversed the polarities of human relations, and the relationship of humanity to the natural order which gave rise to the nukes in the first place. No less total a transformation of consciousness and practice is required if we are to draw back from the abyss which is so rapidly opening beneath our feet.

As the Suquamish leader Sealth (Seattle) reflected in 1854, at a similarly profound juncture in his own people's history, "Tribe follows tribe, and nation follows nation, like the waves of the sea. Your time of decay may be distant, but it must surely come, for even the white man whose god walked with him and talked with him as friend to friend, cannot be exempt from the common destiny. We may be brothers after all. We shall see."[191] If so, it will be possible to say that the Cold War, its antecedent mentalities, and its legacy have been put behind us, once and for all. We can join hands as relatives, heal our mutual wounds, and go forward together as nations of people bound to one another by the reciprocity of our dignity and respect. Are such things possible? In the end, we can only believe that they are and struggle with all our beings to attain them. Our future generations demand no less.

Notes

1. Russel Barsh, "Indian Land Claims Policy in the United States," *North Dakota Law Review*, No. 58, 1982; *One-Third of the Nation's Land, op. cit.*

2. See, e.g., J.R. Miller, *Sweet Promises* (Toronto: University of Toronto Press, 1991).

3. *Lonewolf v. Hitchcock* (187 U.S. 553 (1903)). For analysis, see C. Harvey, "Congressional Plenary Power Over Indian Affairs: A Doctrine Rooted in Prejudice," *American Indian Law Review*, No. 10, 1982; Ann Laquer Estin, "*Lonewolf v. Hitchcock*: The Long Shadow," in Sandra L. Cadwalader and Vine Deloria, Jr., eds., *The Aggressions of Civilization: Federal Indian Policy Since the 1880s* (Philadelphia: Temple University Press, 1984) pp. 215–45.

4. The issue of reservation resources is brought up repeatedly in the major official policy study undertaken during the period, that of the so-called "Committee of One Hundred" prominent civic and business leaders chaired by Lewis Meriam; U.S. House of Representatives, *The Indian Problem: Resolution of the Committee of One-Hundred by the Secretary of Interior and Review of the Indian Problem* (Washington, D.C.: 68th Cong., 1st Sess., U.S. Government Printing Office, 1928); Lewis Meriam, et al., *The Problem of Indian Administration* (Baltimore: Johns Hopkins University Press, 1928).

5. See, e.g., Ronald L. Trosper, "Appendix I: Indian Minerals," in American Indian Policy Review Commission, *Task Force 7 Final Report: Reservation and Resource Development and Protection* (Washington, D.C.: 95th Cong., 1st Sess., U.S. Government Printing Office, 1977); U.S. Department of Interior, Bureau of Indian Affairs, *Indian Lands Map: Oil, Gas and Minerals on Indian Reservations* (Washington, D.C.: U.S. Government Printing Office, 1978).

6. Kenneth Philp, *Assault on Assimilation: John Collier's Crusade for Indian Reform, 1920–1954* (Tucson: University of Arizona Press, 1977).

7. Indian Reorganization Act (ch. 576, 48 Stat. 948, now codified at 25 U.S.C. 461–279 (1934)). The details (but not the conclusions) are provided in Vine Deloria, Jr., and Clifford M. Lytle, *The Nations Within: The Past and Future of American Indian Sovereignty* (New York: Pantheon, 1984). Also see my "American Indian Self-Governance: Fact, Fantasy and Prospects for the Future," in *Struggle for the Land: Indigenous Resistance to Genocide, Ecocide and Expropriation in Contemporary North America* (Monroe, ME: Common Courage Press, 1993) pp. 375–402.

8. Depiction of the structural relationship at issue as "colonialism" is not restricted to "radicals" such as me; see, e.g., U.S. Department of Justice, Commission on Civil Rights, *The Navajo Nation: An American Colony* (Washington, D.C.: U.S. Government Printing Office, 1976). For analysis of the effects of the government's self-assigned "trust" prerogatives vis-à-vis mineral exploitation on reservations, see Joseph Jorgenson, ed., *Native Americans and Energy Development, II* (Cambridge, MA: Anthropological Resource Center/Seventh Generation Fund, 1984).

9. Richard J. Barnet and Ronald E. Müller, *Global Reach: The Power of Multinational Corporations* (New York: Touchstone Books, 1974); Michael Garrity, "The U.S. Colonial Empire is as Close as the Nearest Reservation," in Holly Sklar, ed., *Trilateralism: The Trilateral Commission and Elite Planning for World Management* (Boston: South End Press, 1980) pp. 238–68.

10. U.S. Bureau of the Census, *General Social and Economic Characteristics: United States Summary* (Washington, D.C.: U.S. Government Printing Office, 1983); U.S. Bureau of the Census, Population Division, Racial Statistics Branch, *A Statistical Profile of the American Indian Population* (Washington, D.C.: U.S. Government Printing Office, 1984). An excellent overview of these conditions and their effects is provided in Teresa L. Amott and Julie A. Matthaei, *Race, Gender and Work: A Multicultural History of Women in the United States* (Boston: South End Press, 1991) pp. 31–62.

11. U.S. Department of Health and Human Services, Public Health Service, *Chart Series Book* (Washington, D.C.: U.S. Government Printing Office, 1988).

12. Joy Leland, *Firewater Myths: American Indian Drinking and Alcohol Addiction* (New Brunswick, NJ: Rutgers Center for Alcohol Studies, 1976). On the dynamics of violence involved, see Frantz Fanon, *The Wretched of the Earth* (New York: Grove Press, 1966).

13. *Chart Series Book, op. cit.*; *General Social and Economic Characteristics, op. cit.*

14. Eduardo Galeano, *Open Veins of Latin America: Five Centuries of the Pillage of a Continent* (New York: Monthly Review, 1973) p. 12.

15. Richard Hoppe, "A Stretch of Desert Along Route 66—the Grants Belt—Is Chief Locale for

U.S. Uranium," *Engineering and Mining Journal*, Vol. 79, No. 11, 1978.

16. Leslie R. Groves, *Now It Can Be Told: The Story of the Manhattan Project* (New York: Harper & Bros., 1962); Stephane Groueff, *The Manhattan Project* (Boston: Little, Brown, 1967); Richard Rhodes, *The Making of the Atomic Bomb* (New York: Simon & Schuster, 1986). The official version will be found in Henry DeWolf Smith, *Atomic Energy for Military Purposes: The Official Report on the Development of the Atomic Bomb Under the Auspices of the United States Government, 1940–1945* (Princeton, NJ: Princeton University Press, 1945).

17. Hosteen Kinlicheel, "An Overview of Uranium and Nuclear Development on Indian Lands in the Southwest," *Southwest Indigenous Uranium Forum Newsletter*, Sept. 1993, p. 5.

18. Valerie L. Kulentz, *Geographies of Sacrifice: Nuclear Landscapes and Their Social Consequences, 1940–1996* (forthcoming from Routledge, 1997) mss. pp. 23, 31.

19. Hal Rothman, *On Rims and Ridges: The Los Alamos Area Since 1880* (Lincoln: University of Nebraska Press, 1992) p. 208.

20. Kenneth T. Bainbridge, *Trinity* (Los Alamos, NM: Los Alamos National Scientific Laboratory, 1976 edited release of 1945 original); Kulentz, *Geographies of Sacrifice, op. cit.*, p. 31; Richard Miller, *Under the Cloud: The Decades of Nuclear Testing* (New York: Free Press, 1986) p. 13. On the exposure of U.S. troops for experimental purposes, see Howard I. Rosenberg, *Atomic Soldiers: American Victims of Nuclear Experiments* (Boston: Beacon, 1980); Michael Uhl and Tod Ensign, *G.I. Guinea Pigs: How the Pentagon Exposed Our Troops to Dangers More Deadly Than War* (New York: Playboy Press, 1980).

21. U.S. pretensions in this regard are handled well in Martin Sherwin's *A World Destroyed: The Atomic Bomb and the Grand Alliance* (New York: Alfred A. Knopf, 1975); also see Ronald W. Clark, *The Greatest Power on Earth* (New York: Harper & Row, 1980). A good articulation of the hard Left view will be found in James S. Allen, *Atomic Imperialism: The State, Monopoly and the Bomb* (New York: International, 1952).

22. David Alan Rosenberg, "The U.S. Nuclear Stockpile, 1945 to 1950," *Bulletin of Atomic Scientists*, Mat 1980.

23. Kinlicheel, "An Overview," *op. cit.*; Winona LaDuke, "The History of Uranium Mining: Who Are These Companies and Where Did They Come From?," *Black Hills/Paha Sapa Report*, Vol. 1, No. 1, 1979. On the Atomic Energy Act and establishment of the AEC, see Anna Gyorgy and Friends, *No Nukes: Everyone's Guide to Nuclear Power* (Boston: South End Press, 1979) pp. 7–8.

24. See generally, Debra Rosenthal, *At the Heart of the Bomb: The Dangerous Allure of Weapons Work* (Menlo Park, CA: Addison-Wesley, 1990); Dan O'Neill, *The Firecracker Boys* (New York: St. Martin's Press, 1994).

25. For background to the shift in foreign policy emphasis involved, see Roger Rapaport, *The Great American Bomb Machine* (New York: E.P. Dutton, 1971). Also see the Introduction to Noam Chomsky's *Towards a New Cold War: Essays on the Current Crisis and How We Got There* (New York: Pantheon, 1983) esp. pp. 19–24.

26. For the conservative view, see John Lewis Gaddis, *The United States and the Origins of the Cold War, 1941–1947* (New York: Columbia University Press, 1972); a more reasoned—and better documented—perspective on who did what to whom during the postwar period is offered in Carolyn Eisenberg's recent *Drawing the Line: The American Decision to Partition Germany* (Cambridge, MA: Cambridge University Press, 1996). The bellicosity with which the U.S. received the establishment of the U.S.S.R. from the outset, including participation in a multilateral invasion of Soviet territory in 1918–19 and the relentless hostility with which successive administrations treated the new country during the interwar years, is of course well known. Such facts give rise to the more "radical"—and more accurate—interpretation that a "Cold War" was being waged by the U.S. all along; Denna Frank Fleming, *The Cold War and Its Origins, 1917–1960*, 2 vols. (Garden City, NY: Doubleday, 1961); Desmond Donnelly, *Struggle for the World: The Cold War, 1917–1965* (New York: St. Martin's Press, 1965).

27. On internal security during the period, see, e.g., Alan D. Harper, *The Politics of Loyalty: The White House and the Communist Issue, 1946–1952* (Westport, CT: Greenwood Press, 1969); Walter Goodman, *The Committee: The Extraordinary Career of the House Committee on Un-American Activities* (New York: Farrar, Strauss & Giroux, 1968); Sanford J. Ungar, *FBI: An Uncensored Look Behind the Walls* (Boston: Atlantic-Little, Brown, 1976). For a good range of opinion on Truman's initial postwar strategy, see, e.g.,

Carl Oglesby and Richard Shaull, *Containment and Change: Two Dissenting Views on American Foreign Policy* (New York: Macmillan, 1967); Walter LaFeber, *America, Russia, and the Cold War, 1945–1966* (New York: John Wiley & Sons, 1968); Lloyd Gardner, *Architects of Illusion: Men and Ideas in American Foreign Policy, 1941–49* (Chicago: Quadrangle, 1970).

28. For background, see, e.g., Barbara Tuchman, *Stilwell and the American Experience in China, 1911–45* (New York: Macmillan, 1971); Stanley Karnow, *Mao and China: From Revolution to Revolution* (New York: Viking, 1972); Ranbir Zohra, ed., *The Chinese Revolution, 1900–1950* (Boston: Houghton Mifflin, 1974).

29. NSC 68, which was submitted by the Council to Truman in April 1950, was not declassified until 1975. The complete text is included in Thomas H. Etzold and John Lewis Gaddis, *Containment: Documents on American Foreign Policy and Strategy, 1945–1950* (New York: Columbia University Press, 1978). A fairly candid firsthand account of the context in which the policy was adopted will be found in Dean G. Acheson, *Present at the Creation: My Years in the State Department* (New York: W.W. Norton, 1970).

30. This is not to say that such things did not previously exist in the U.S.—clearly, they did—but that they were greatly amplified, expanded, and systemically perfected after 1950. There is a considerable literature on this score. See, e.g., Morton H. Halperin and Daniel Hoffman, *Freedom vs. National Security* (New York: Chelsea House, 1977) and *Top Secret: National Security and the Right to Know* (Washington, D.C.: New Republic Books, 1977); Richard O. Curry, ed., *Freedom at Risk: Secrecy, Censorship, and Repression in the 1980s* (Philadelphia: Temple University Press, 1988). For more on repression, see Ward Churchill and Jim Vander Wall, *The COINTELPRO Papers: Documents from the FBI's Secret Wars Against Dissent in the United States* (Boston: South End Press, 1990). On the propaganda function, see David Wise, *The Politics of Lying: Government Deception, Secrecy and Power* (New York: Random House, 1973); Edward S. Herman and Noam Chomsky, *Manufacturing Consent: The Political Economy of the Mass Media* (New York: Pantheon, 1988); Noam Chomsky, *Necessary Illusions: Thought Control in Democratic Societies* (Boston: South End Press, 1989); Michael Parenti, *Inventing Reality: The Politics of the News Media* (New York: St. Martin's Press, 1993).

31. For the senator's own definition of his motives and intentions, see Joseph R. McCarthy, *McCarthyism: The Fight for America* (New York: Devon-Adair, 1952). For a contemporary opposing view, see Jack Anderson and Ronald W. May, *McCarthy: The Man, the Senator, the "Ism"* (Boston: Beacon Press, 1952). For several good analyses, see Earl Latham, ed., *The Meaning of McCarthyism* (Boston: D.C. Heath, 1965). On the relationship between McCarthy's especially virulent activities after 1950 and the more "liberal" alternative posed by the Truman administration during the late '40s, see Athan Theoharis, *Seeds of Repression: Harry S. Truman and the Origins of McCarthyism* (Chicago: Quadrangle, 1971); Richard M. Freeland, *The Truman Doctrine and the Origins of McCarthyism* (New York: Alfred A. Knopf, 1972); Cedric Belfrage, *American Inquisition, 1945–1960* (Indianapolis: Bobbs-Merrill, 1973).

32. Gyorgy, et al., *No Nukes, op. cit.*, p. 8; on Rocky Flats, see Rapaport, *Great American Bomb Machine, op. cit.*, pp. 31–49.

33. Gyorgy, et al., *No Nukes, op. cit.*, p. 8.

34. Ralph Nader and John Abbotts, *The Menace of Atomic Energy* (New York: W.W. Norton, 1977) pp. 275–6.

35. In effect, the "AEC's contract system of operation [was used to] build up a powerful industrial alliance that protected it against outside appraisal and political attack"; Cultural Workers Collective, *op. cit.*, p. 6.

36. Quoted in Noam Chomsky, *Deterring Democracy* (New York: Hill & Wang, 1992) p. 21.

37. For a good survey of contemporary understandings of these effects, see Jack Schubert and Ralph E. Lapp, *Radiation: What It Is and How It Affects You* (New York: Viking, 1958).

38. With respect to the official boundaries of reserved lands, see U.S., Department of Interior, Bureau of Indian Affairs, *American Indian Reservations* (Washington, D.C.: U.S. Government Printing Office, 1979). Concerning unceded treaty territories, see the composite map in my *Struggle for the Land, op. cit.*, p. 57.

39. The SBA provided seed money, the BIA, "administrative oversight," the AEC maintained an ore-buying station on the reservation, near Shiprock, New Mexico; Kinlicheel, "An Overview," *op. cit.*; LaDuke, *History, op. cit.*

40. Richard O. Clemmer, "The Energy Economy and Pueblo Peoples," in Jorgenson, *American Indians, op. cit.*, p. 101.

41. Jack Cox, "Effects of Radiation on Early Miners Comes to Light," *Denver Post*, Sept. 3, 1979; Harold Tso and Laura Mangum Shields, "Navajo Mining Operations: Early Hazards and Recent Innovations," *New Mexico Journal of Science*, Vol. 12, No. 1, Spring 1980.

42. Lynn A. Robbins, "Energy Development and the Navajo Nation: An Update," in Jorgenson, *American Indians, op. cit.*, p. 119. The article referenced is V.E. Archer, J.K. Wagoner and F.E. Lundin, "Lung Cancer Among Uranium Miners in the United States," *Health Physics*, No. 25, 1973. Also see Anthony S. Schwagen and Thomas Hollbacher, "Lung Cancer Among Uranium Miners," in *The Nuclear Fuel Cycle* (Cambridge, MA: Union of Concerned Scientists and Friends of the Earth, 1973); James N. Baker, "Keeping a Deadly Secret: The Feds Knew the Mines Were Radioactive," *Newsweek*, June 18, 1990.

43. J.B. Sorenson, *Radiation Issues: Government Decision Making and Uranium Expansion in Northern New Mexico* (Albuquerque: San Juan Regional Uranium Study Working Paper No. 14, 1978) p. 9.

44. Ibid.; also see Tso and Shields, "Navajo Mining," *op. cit.*

45. Jessica S. Pearson, *A Sociological Analysis of the Reduction of Hazardous Radiation in Uranium Mines* (Washington, D.C.: National Institute for Occupational Safety & Health, 1975).

46. V. E. Archer, J.D. Gillan and J.K. Wagoner, "Respiratory Disease Mortality Among Uranium Miners," *Annals of the New York Academcy of Sciences*, No. 271, 1976; M.J. Samet, et al., "Uranium Mining and Lung Cancer Among Navajo Men," *New England Journal of Medicine*, No. 310, 1984, pp. 1481–4.

47. Tom Barry, "Bury My Lungs at Red Rock: Uranium Mining Brings New Peril to the Reservation," *The Progressive*, Oct. 1976; Chris Shuey, "The Widows of Red Rock," *Scottsdale Daily Progress Saturday Magazine*, June 2, 1979; Reed Madsden, "Cancer Deaths Linked to Uranium Mining," *Deseret News*, June 4, 1979; Susan Pearce and Karen Navarro, "The Legacy of Uranium Mining for Nuclear Weapons," *Earth Island Journal*, Summer 1993.

48. Garrity, "The Pending Energy Wars," *op. cit.*, p. 10.

49. Quoted in Shuey, "Widows," *op. cit.*, p. 4; Archer "conservatively" places the lung cancer rate among Diné miners at 1,000 percent of the national average. Also see Robert O. Pohl, "Health Effects of Radon-222 from Uranium Mining," *Science*, Aug. 1979.

50. Norman Medvin, *The Energy Cartel* (New York: Vintage, 1974); Bruce E. Johansen, "The Great Uranium Rush," *Baltimore Sun*, May 13, 1979.

51. Kinlicheel, "An Overview," *op. cit.*, p. 6.

52. Kulentz, *Geographies of Sacrifice, op. cit.*, p. 31; Reno, *Navajo Resources, op. cit.*, p. 138.

53. Marjane Ambler, *Breaking the Iron Bonds: Indian Control Over Energy Development* (Lawrence: University Press of Kansas, 1990) p. 152. For use of the term employed, see Raye C. Ringholz, *Uranium Frenzy: Boom and Bust on the Colorado Plateau* (Albuquerque: University of New Mexico Press, 1989).

54. Although the entire procedure of dewatering was/is in gross violation of both the Clean Water Act of 1972 (P.L. 92–500; 86 Stat. 816) and the Safe Water Drinking Act of 1974 (P.L. 93–523; 88 Stat. 1660), no charges have ever been brought against Kerr-McGee or any other corporation involved in uranium mining; Ambler, *Breaking the Iron Bonds, op. cit.*, p. 175; "Mine Dewatering Operation in New Mexico Seen Violating Arizona water standards," *Nuclear Fuel*, Mar. 1, 1982; Christopher McCleod, "Kerr-McGee's Last Stand," *Mother Jones*, Dec. 1980.

55. Clemmer, "Energy Economy," *op. cit.*, pp. 101–2.

56. Lora Mangum Shields and Alan B. Goodman, "Outcome of 13,300 Navajo Births from 1964–1981 in the Shiprock Uranium Mining Area" (New York: unpublished paper presented at the American Association of Atomic Scientists Symposium, May 25, 1984); Christopher McCleod, "Uranium Mines and Mills May Have Caused Birth Defects among Navajo Indians," *High Country News*, Feb. 4, 1985.

57. "Neoplasms Among Navajo Children" (Window Rock, AZ: Navajo Health Authority, Feb. 24, 1981).

58. Laura Mangum Shields, et al., "Navajo Birth Outcomes in the Shiprock Uranium Mining Area," *Health Physics*, Vol. 63, No. 5, 1992.

59. Kulentz, *Geographies of Sacrifice, op. cit.*, pp. 36, 40; quoting from U.S. Department of Health and Human Services, Indian Health Services, *Health Hazards Related to Nuclear Resources Development on Indian*

Land (Washington, D.C.: 97th Cong. 2d. Sess, U.S. Government Printing Office, 1983).

60. It has been estimated that it would require some 400 million tons of earth—enough to cover the entire District of Columbia 43 feet deep—to fill in the Jackpile-Paguate complex; Dan Jackson, "Mine Development on U.S. Indian Lands," *Engineering and Mining Journal*, Jan. 1980. Overall, see U.S. Department of Interior, Bureau of Land Management, *Final Environmental Impact Statement for the Jackpile-Paguate Uranium Mine Reclamation Project*, 2 vols. (Albuquerque: BLM New Mexico Area Office, 1986) vol. 2, p. A-35.

61. Clemmer, "Energy Economy," *op. cit.*, p. 99.

62. Hope Aldrich, "The Politics of Uranium," *Santa Fe Reporter*, Dec. 7, 1978.

63. U.S. Comptroller General, "EPA Needs to Improve the Navajo Safe Drinking Water Program" (Washington, D.C.: U.S. Government Printing Office, Sept. 10, 1980) p. 5.

64. R. Smith, "Radon Emissions: Open Pit Uranium Mines Said to be Big Contributor," *Nucleonics Week*, May 25, 1978; Linda Taylor, "Uranium Legacy," *The Workbook*, Vol. VIII, No. 6, Nov./Dec. 1983.

65. "Manpower Gap in the Uranium Mines," *Business Week*, Nov. 1, 1977. It should be noted that among the things the Labor Department was spending $2 million per year in tax monies to have Kerr McGee train native workers to believe was that "if they [did] not smoke, they [would] not develop lung cancer from exposure to radiation in the mines"; Dr. Joseph Wagoner, quoted in Denise Tessier, "Uranium Mine Gas Causes Lung Cancer, UNM Group Told," *Albuquerque Journal*, Mar. 11, 1980. There seems to have been no protest from the Surgeon General at the peddling of such quasi-official falsehoods. Instead, the country's "chief doctor" endorsed a battery of studies over the next several years, each of them reinforcing the credibility of such lies by purporting to prove that the "number one cause" of lung cancer even among *non-*smokers was the inhalation of "secondhand" cigarette smoke, even in the most minute quantities, rather than exposure to comparatively massive doses of military-industrial pollutants.

66. "Manpower Gap in the Uranium Mines," *op. cit.*; Ambler, *Breaking the Iron Bonds, op. cit.*, p. 152.

67. Hoppe, "Stretch," *op. cit.*; LaDuke, "History," *op. cit.*

68. For a good summary of such practices, see Richard Nafziger, "Uranium Profits and Perils," in LaDonna Harris, ed., *Red Paper* (Albuquerque: Americans for Indian Opportunity, 1976).

69. Kinlicheel, "An Overview," *op. cit.*, p. 6.

70. Quoted in Tom Barry, "The Deaths Still Go On: New Agencies Ignored Uranium Danger," *Navajo Times*, Aug. 31, 1978.

71. Freeman, *Nuclear Witnesses, op. cit.*, p. 140.

72. "Uranium-bearing tailings are constantly decaying into more stable elements and therefore emit radiation, as do particles of dust that blow in the wind and truck travel on dirt roads"; Clemmer, "Energy Economy," *op. cit.*, p. 102. Also see David Densmore Comey, "The Legacy of Uranium Tailings," *Bulletin of Atomic Scientists*, Sept. 1975.

73. Hoppe, "Stretch," *op. cit.*; LaDuke, "History," *op. cit.* In instances where milling was done in areas populated by "mainstream citizens," it was sometimes disguised as something else. For example, the AEC hid a milling operation, beginning in 1951, in Fernald, Ohio, near Cincinatti, behind the front that it was a "pet food factory." The ruse worked for 37 years; Helen Caldicott, *If You Love This Planet: A Plan to Heal the Earth* (New York: W.W. Norton, 1992) p. 90.

74. Robbins, "Energy Development," *op. cit.*, p. 121.

75. Simon J. Ortiz, "Our Homeland: A National Sacrifice Area," in his *Woven Stone, op. cit.*, pp. 356–8.

76. Robbins, "Energy Development," *op. cit.*, p. 121. It should also be noted that the mill's tailings pile is located only about sixty feet from the San Juan River, Shiprock's only source of surface water, and less than a mile from a daycare center, the public schools and the local business district. The closest residence is less than a hundred yards away; Tso and Shields, "Navajo Mining," *op. cit.*

77. Luther J. Carter, "Uranium Mill Tailings: Congress Addresses a Long Neglected Problem," *Science*, Oct. 13, 1978.

78. See, e.g., the map by Janet Steele entitled "Uranium Development in the San Juan Basin," in Freeman, *Nuclear Witnesses, op. cit.*, p. 139.

79. E.g., the Sohio-Reserve mill at Cebolleta, a mile from the Laguna boundary, processed about 1,500 tons of ore per day during the late 1970s. Its tailings pond covers fifty acres, and the adjoining pile

reached a record 350 feet; Clemmer, "Energy Economy," *op. cit.*, p. 98. Also see Hope Aldrich, "Problems Pile Up at the Uranium Mills," *Santa Fe Reporter*, Nov. 13, 1980.

80. Clemmer, "Energy Economy," *op. cit.*, pp. 97–8.

81. Report by Johnny Sanders (head of Environmental Health Services Branch of the Indian Health Service), T.J. Hardwood (IHS Albuquerque area director) and Mala L. Beard (the district sanitarian) to Laguna Pueblo Governor Floyd Corea, August 11, 1978; copy on file with the Southwest Research and Information Center, Albuquerque. To be "fair" about it, other corporations made similar use of tailings in several backwater non-Indian communities on the Colorado Plateau during this period. These included Moab, Utah, and both Grand Junction and Durango, Colorado.

82. The quantitative release of radioactive substances during the Church Rock spill was several times that of the much more publicized partial meltdown of a reactor at Three Mile Island, near Harrisburg, Pennsylvania, a few months earlier (March 28, 1979); Ambler, *Breaking the Iron Bonds, op. cit.*, pp. 175–6; Mark Alan Pinsky, "New Mexico Spill Ruins a River: The Worst Radiation Accident in History Gets Little Attention," *Critical Mass*, Dec. 1979; Anna Mayo, "The Nuclear State in Ascendancy," *Village Voice*, Oct. 22, 1980.

83. Report of the New Mexico Environmental Improvement Division (EID), dated September 9, 1979, on file with the Southwest Research and Information Center, Albuquerque. The ban lasted a year, virtually destroying the limited cash economy of local Diné sheepherders.

84. J.W. Schomish, "EID Lifts Ban on Eating Church Rock Cattle," *Gallup Independent*, May 22, 1980. Moehler is quoted as cautioning the Diné not to eat organ tissues, where the substances are known to "congregate."

85. On the cracks, see Chris Huey, "The Río Puerco River: Where Did the Water Go?" *The Workbook*, No. 11, 1988. On the settlement, see Frank Pitman, "Navajos-UNC Settle Tailings Spill Lawsuits," *Navajo Times*, Apr. 22, 1985. On state facilitation, which took the form of discounting the extent and degree of damage done, see "EID Finds that Church Rock Dam Break Had Little or No Effect on Residents," *Nuclear Fuel*, Mar. 14, 1983. The questions, of course, are why, if there were "no effect," at least one Diné woman and an untold number of sheep sickened and died in 1979 after wading in the Río Puerco, why several other people died under similar circumstances over the next few years, and why the EID itself prohibited use of the river as a drinking water source until 1990, more than a decade after the spill; Loretta Schwarz, "Uranium Deaths at Crown Point," *Ms. Magazine*, Oct. 1979; Molly Ivins, "100 Navajo Families Sue on Radioactive Waste Spill," *New York Times*, Aug. 15, 1980; Ambler, *Breaking the Iron Bonds, op. cit.*, p. 176.

86. D.R. Dreeson, "Uranium Mill Tailings: Environmental Implications," *Los Alamos Scientific Laboratory Mini-Report*, Feb. 1978.

87. Box, et al., *Rehabilitation Potential, op. cit.*

88. On the extent of Peabody's coal stripping operations on Navajo at the time of the NAS study, see Alvin M. Josephy, Jr., "The Murder of the Southwest," *Audubon Magazine*, July 1971. For a good overview of subsequent expansion and projections, as well as an in-depth assessment of the impact of coal stripping upon the Diné, see my "Genocide in Arizona? The Navajo-Hopi Land Dispute in Perspective," in *Notes From a Native Son: Selected Essays on Indigenism, 1985–1995* (Boston: South End Press, 1996).

89. The Nixon administration reputedly used this vernacular during discussions from 1972 onward. For the first known official print articulation, see U.S. Department of Energy, Federal Energy Administration, Office of Strategic Analysis, *Project Independence: A Summary* (Washington, D.C.: U.S. Government Printing Office, 1974).

90. See generally, Nick Meinhart, "The Four Corners Today, the Black Hills Tomorrow?" *Black Hills/Paha Sapa Report*, Aug. 1979. Also see U.S. Department of the Interior, Bureau of the Census, *1980 Census of Population, Supplementary Reports: Race of the Population of the States by Race, 1980* (Washington, D.C.: U.S. Government Printing Office, 1981) esp. Table 3, "1970"; *1980 Census of the Population, Supplementary Reports: American Indian Areas and Alaska Native Villages* (Washington, D.C.: U.S. Government Printing Office, 1984) esp. Table 4.

91. The statements were made during a speech delivered at the Black Hills International Survival Gathering, near Rapid City, South Dakota, June 12, 1980. The text is included under the title "The Same Old Song," in Ward Churchill, ed., *Marxism and Native Americans* (South End Press, 1983); referenced

material at p. 25. It should be noted that Means' assessment of the severity of the effect of the forced separation of indigenous peoples from their landbase is borne out in the scholarly literature; see, e.g., Thayer Scudder, et al., *No Place to Go: Effects of Compulsory Relocation on Navajos* (Philadelphia: Institute for Study of Human Issues, 1982).

92. Suzanne Ruta, "Fear and Silence at Los Alamos," *The Nation*, Jan. 11, 1993.

93. Concerned Citizens for Nuclear Safety, "LANL [Los Alamos National Laboratory] Deliberately, Secretly Released Radiation on at least Three Separate Occasions in 1950," *The Nuclear Reactor*, Vol. 3, No. 1, Feb.-Mar. 1994.

94. Kulentz, *Geographies of Sacrifice, op. cit.*, pp. 69–70. It appears that legal prohibitions against such "disposal" of nuclear wastes are being circumvented by shipping materials from other DOE facilities to Los Alamos, where they can be secretly burned in the lab's controlled air incinerator. Currently, it is estimated that 1,236 cubic feet of plutonium-contaminated substances are being dispersed in this way each year; Mary Risely, "LANCL Gropes to Find a New Way," *Enchanted Times*, Fall/Winter 1993, p. 6.

95. Ibid.

96. E.g., since 1980, "physicians at the Santa Fe Indian Hospital have noticed an unusual number of thyroid cancer cases [associated with the atmospheric release of radioactive iodides] at the Santa Clara Pueblo, just north of Los Alamos"; Kulentz, *Geographies of Sacrifice, op. cit.*, p. 72. The rate of thyroid cancer at Santa Clara is triple the national average; see the map entitled "New Mexico: A National Sacrifice Area," prepared and distributed by the All People's Coalition, Albuquerque, 1993; reproduced in Kulentz, *Geographies of Sacrifice, op. cit.*, p. 77.

97. Ibid.

98. All research conducted at Lawrence Livermore, for example, would simply be transferred to the "less sensitive environment" of Los Alamos, a move projected as cutting costs while the increasing efficiency of the developmental process; Louis Freedberg, "Livermore: Panel Recommends Ending Nuclear Arms Work," *San Francisco Chronicle*, Feb. 2, 1995.

99. Risely, "LANCL," *op. cit.*

100. Kulentz, *Geographies of Sacrifice, op. cit.*, p. 73; quoting Rosenthal, *At the Heart of the Bomb, op. cit.*, p. 10.

101. Ibid., p. 9.

102. All People's Coalition, "People's Emergency Response Committee," *Enchanted Times*, Summer 1993.

103. "Unlike NRC [Nuclear Regulatory Commission]-regulated industries, DOE [Department of Energy] facilties are not subject to a 7-Curie per year maximum discharge of radioactive wastes into sewers. In fact, DOE's regulations set no limits on the total amount of radioactivity that can be disposed of in a year's time. By simply increasing the amount of water—and thus reducing the [concentration] of radioactive materials—DOE facilities can dump substantial amounts of radioactivity into sewers," which flow directly into the surface water sources for entire regions; All People's Coalition, "Communities Concerned About Potential Radioactive Dumping in Albuquerque Sewers," *Enchanted Times*, Summer 1993.

104. The other, at Savannah River, also closed at this point, has a very bad environmental record as well, but nothing as compared to Hanford; see, e.g., Hartmut Krugman and Frank von Hippel, "Radioactive Wastes: A Comparison of U.S. Military and Civilian Inventories," *Science*, No. 197, Aug. 26, 1977.

105. Elouise Schumacher, "440 Billion Gallons: Hanford wastes could fill 900 King Domes, *Seattle Times*, Apr. 13, 1991.

106. Caldicott, *If You Love This Planet, op. cit.* Also see Susan Wyndham, "Death in the Air," *Australian Magazine*, Sept. 29–30, 1990; Matthew L. Wald, "Wider Peril Seen in Nuclear Waste from Bomb Making," *New York Times*, Mar. 28, 1991.

107. Larry Lang, "Missing Hanford Documents Probed by Energy Department," *Seattle Post-Intelligencer*, Sept. 20, 1991.

108. The upper Chihuahuan Desert area of New Mexico, around Alamagordo, is an environment so harsh that sixteenth-century Spanish explorers dubbed it the "Jornada del Muerto" ("Journey of Death.") It was originally "selected as the best site [for nuclear testing] because it was so remote, the

weather was favorable, and because it was close to the secret laboratory where the weapon was being created"; Tad Bartimus and Scott MacCartney, *Trinity's Children: Living Along America's Nuclear Highway* (Albuquerque: University of New Mexico Press, 1991) pp. 11, 13. On Hiroshima and Nagaski as tests, see Anthony Robbins, Arjun Makhijani and Katherine Yih, *Radioactive Heaven and Earth: The Health and Environmental Effects of Nuclear Weapons Testing In, On, and Above the Earth* (New York/London: Apex Press/Zed Books, 1991) pp. 49–50.

109. Kulentz, *Geographies of Sacrifice, op. cit.,* p. 78. "what became a small drop zone for training bombers grew as planes became larger and faster and squadrons of pilots had to be quickly trained. More land was needed, so ranchers were told to move out. Some were curtly informed at gunpoint that the Army was leasing their land until the end of the war. The army would pay rent, then return their land. They had two weeks to vacate"; Bartimus and MacCartney, *Trinity's Children, op. cit.,* p. 11. The army lied. The ranchers' dispossession was, in fact, permanent, and compensation for lost property was ultimately made at rates the government, not the owners, decided was "fair." The same principle pertained to portions of "remote" American Indian reservations — e.g. Pine Ridge and Spokane — impounded by the military for use as gunnery and bombing practice ranges during World War II, and in which uranium deposits were later discovered; see, e.g., Jacqueline Huber, et al., *The Gunnery Range Report* (Pine Ridge, SD: Office of the President, Oglala Sioux Tribe, 1981).

110. Kulentz, *Geographies of Sacrifice, op. cit.,* pp. 79–80; she is quoting from Bartimus and MacCartney, *Trinity's Children, op. cit.,* p. 32. At p. 40, the latter explain that the "conventional weapon" with which a nuclear blast is simulated is "a bomb that sprays a fine mist of fuel for miles, then erupts in a conflagration that literally sucks molecules out of soldiers."

111. Ibid., p. 40.

112. See "New Mexico: A National Sacrifice Area," *op. cit.*

113. The neglect exhibited by the government in studying the effects of systemically generated radioactive by-products on indigenous populations is, as has already been indicated, notorious. This is as distinguished from instances such as Rongelap and Utirik, where isolated populations seem to have been deliberately exposed for test purposes, and the north slope of Alaska, where a sample group of Inuits were unknowingly fed doses of uranium during the mid-'50s so that the effects might be studied; Valerie Taliman, "Nuclear Guinea Pigs: Native People Were on the Front Lines of Exploitation," *Native American Smoke Signals,* Jan. 1994. One indicator of the situation at Mescalero is that overall childhood leukemia rates among downwinders appear to run at about 2.5 times the national average; *Human and Environmental Effects of Nuclear Testing* (Albuquerque: unattributed activist handout, 1991).

114. David Loomis, *Combat Zoning: Military Land-Use Planning in Nevada* (Las Vegas: University of Nevada Press, 1994) p. 10; citing Michael Skinner, *Red Flag* (Novato, CA: Presidio Press) p. 52. For a more comprehensive overview of how all this evolved, see Gerald D. Nash, *The American West Transformed: The Impact of the Second World War* (Bloomington: University of Indiana Press, 1985).

115. Loomis, *Combat Zoning, op. cit.,* pp. 9–10.

116. Although the United States has long ocupied the area, exhaustive effort by the Indian Claims Commission during the 1960s and '70s could find no evidence that the Indians had ever transferred title; see, e.g., Dagmar Thorpe, *Newe Segobia: The Western Shoshone People and Land* (Lee, NV: Western Shoshone Sacred Lands Association, 1982); Steven J. Crum, *the Road on Which We Came: A History of the Western Shoshone* (Salt Lake City: University of Nevada Press, 1994).

117. Newe Chief Raymond Yowell, quoted in Taliman, "Nine Tribes," *op. cit.* Also see the subsection, "The Most Bombed Nation in the World," in Bernard Neitschmann and William Le Bon, "Nuclear Weapons States and Fourth World Nations," *Cultural Survival Quarterly,* Vol. 11, No. 4, 1987, pp. 5–7.

118. For estimates of atmospheric releases, see Carole Gallegher, *America Ground Zero: The Secret Nuclear War* (New York: Random House, 1993).

119. Kulentz, *Geographies of Sacrifice, op. cit.,* p. 94.

120. Ibid., pp. 93–4; also see Loomis, *Combat Zoning, op. cit.,* p. viii.

121. China Lake, which encompasses 38 percent of the Navy's total land holdings, supports about 1,000 military personnel and over 5,000 civilian scientists, engineers and technicians in more than 1,100 buildings on an annual budget of nearly $1 billion; Kulentz, *Geographies of Sacrifice, op. cit.,* p. 84.

357

122. China Lake commands some 20,000 square miles of air space, as do each of the other three facilities. Quite literally, the sky over the entire Mojave has been appropriated by the military; Loomis, *Combat Zoning, op. cit.*, p. 70.

123. U.S. Navy, *Naval Weapons Center Silver Anniversary* (China Lake Naval Weapons Center: Technical Information Dept. Publishing Division, Oct. 1968).

124. Robbins, Makhijani and Yee, *Radioactive Heaven, op. cit.*, p. 66.

125. Underground detonations of nuclear devices all but invariably cause fissures leading to groundwater contamination of the sort evident in Nevada; Office of Technology Assessment, *The Containment of Underground Nuclear Explosions* (Washington, D.C.: U.S. Government Printing Office, 1989). Also see David Hulen, "After the Bombs: Questions Linger About Amchitka Nuclear Tests," *Anchorage Daily News*, Feb. 7, 1994.

126. As one of Plowshare's leading proponents, AEC Chairman Glenn T. Seaborg , put it at the time: "Large nuclear explosives give us, for the first time, the capability to remedy nature's oversights"; Seaborg and Corliss, *Man and Atom, op. cit.*, p. 188. Another individual who consistently confused himself with God in this manner was Edward Teller, the psychopathic "father of the hydrogen bomb" who replaced Robert Oppenheimer as the preeminent figure in America's "nuclear scientific community"; see, e.g., Edward Teller, et al., *Constructive Uses of Nuclear Explosives* (New York: McGraw-Hill, 1968). Overall, see C.R. Gerber, R. Hamburger and E.W.S. Hull, *Plowshare* (Washington, D.C.: Atomic Energy Commission, 1967). For oppositional views, see Richard Curtis and Elisabeth Hogan, *Perils of the Peaceful Atom* (New York: Ballantine, 1969).

127. On the "New Panama Canal" project, see R. Sanders, *Project Plowshare: The Development of Peaceful Uses of Nuclear Explosives* (Washington, D.C.: Public Affairs Press, 1962). On Project Ketch, see Gyorgy, et al., *No Nukes, op. cit.*, pp. 382, 415; Richard S. Lewis, *The Nuclear Power Rebellion: Citizens vs. the Atomic Industrial Establishment* (New York: Viking, 1972) pp. 207–20.

128. Gyorgy, et al., *No Nukes, op. cit.*, p. 443; Freeman, *Nuclear Witnesses, op. cit.*, p. 66.

129. After the blast itself, the AEC vented "hundreds of millions of cubic feet" of radioactive gas from the resulting subsurface pocket in the vain hope that once the upper levels were thus dispensed with, the remainder might be suitable for commercial sale. All that resulted was a substantial atmospheric dispersal of radioactive substances, especially tritium and krypton 85l across the Navajo Nation; *Nuclear Explosives in Peacetime* (Denver: Scientists Institute for Public Information, 1977) pp. 4–5.

130. Freeman, *Nuclear Witnesses, op. cit.*, p. 68; Gyorgy, et al., *No Nukes, op. cit.*, p. 443.

131. Project Gasbuggy cost some $56 million, returning as much as $18–25 million in useless gas. Project Rulison cost over $11 million and produced about $1.5 million in useless gas. The tab for Project Río Blanco was about $12 million, and the other five detonations a total of just under $60 million. They produced no gas at all; James Robertson and John Lewallen, eds., *The Grass Roots Primer* (San Francisco: Sierra Club Books, 1975) pp. 125–35; Gyorgy, et al., *No Nukes, op. cit.*, pp. 13, 443.

132. On "Banebury," see Robbins, Makhijani and Yih, *Radioactive Heaven, op. cit.*, p. 64. By 1977, it had been revealed that several other underground tests had also vented themselves into the atmosphere, notably the twelve kiloton "Palanquin" device, detonated in April 1965; *Nuclear Explosives in Peacetime, op. cit.*, p. 11. Also see Richard Misrach and Myriam Weisang Misrach, *Bravo Twenty: The Bombing of the American West* (Baltimore: Johns Hopkins University Press, 1990).

133. Kristen Ostling and Joanna Miller, *Taking Stock: The Impact of Militarism on the Environment* (New York: Science for Peace, 1992).

134. Southwestern Arizona also includes another pair of huge military complexes, the half-million-acre Yuma Proving Grounds and adjoining million-acre Luke Air Force Base, both of which engage in activities comparable to those evident at White Sands and China Lake; see generally, Ostling and Miller, *Taking Stock, op. cit.*; Thomas, *op. cit.* The three native peoples in question are thus completely encircled by these facilities to their south, southern California's constellation of bases and test ranges to their west, the Nevada Test Site and related areas to their north, and the Navajo sacrifice zone to their east.

135. P.Z. Grossman and E.S. Cassedy," "Cost Benefit Analysis of Nuclear Waste Disposal," *Science, Technology and Human Values*, Vol. 10, No. 4, 1985.

136. Current planning now entails a "force reduction" in the number of such weapons to 3,500

by the year 2003; Charles Pope, "Nuclear Arms Cleanup Bill: A Tidy $230 Billion," *San Jose Mercury News*, Apr. 4, 1995. The figure advanced here as constituting the "cleanup bill" is low by more than half. The reason for this is that it is based on modes/levels of "site rehabilitation" which leave every location at issue in a highly irradiated condition.

137. Pope, "Nuclear Arms," *op. cit.*

138. U.S. Department of Energy, Office of Environmental Management, *Estimating the Cold War Mortgage: The 1995 Baseline Environmental Management Report* (Washington, D.C.: DOE/EM-0232, Mar. 1995); *Closing the Circle of the Closing of the Atom: The Environmental Legacy of Nuclear Weapons Production in the United States and What the Department of Energy is Doing About It* (Washington, D.C.: DOE/EM-0228, Jan. 1995).

139. John H. Hollocher, "The Storage and Disposal of High Level Wastes," in *The Nuclear Fuel Cycle, op. cit.*; U.S. Department of Energy, Office of Environmental Management, *Environmental Management 1995* (Washington, D.C.: DOE/EM-0228, Feb. 1995).

140. For analysis of the defects in this proposition, see Arjun Makhijana and Scott Saleska, *High-Level Dollars, Low-Level Sense: A Critique of Present Policy for the Management of Long-Lived Radioactive Wastes and Discussion of an Alternative Approach* (Takoma Park, MD: Institute for Energy and Environmental Research, 1992).

141. The Groundwork Collective, "The Illusion of Cleanup: A Case Study at Hanford," *Groundwork*, No. 4, Mar. 1994, p. 14. For the record, the classification scheme involved here, which is incorporated into the 1982 Nuclear Waste Policy Act (P.L. 97–425; 96 Stat. 2201), is problematic. The term "high-level wastes" pertains to spent fuel from nuclear power plants subject to reprocessing for extraction of plutonium and uranium-235. "Transuranic wastes" include substances like plutonium, neptunium, and americium, "bred" from uranium-238. "Low-level wastes" include materials—e.g., worn-out reactor parts—contaminated by exposure to high-level or transuranic substances. The classifications don't necessarily correspond to the degree of threat posed by a given material, only to the nature of the process by which it was produced; Concerned Citizens for Nuclear Safety, *The Nuclear Reactor*, Early Spring 1995.

142. Although tailings cleanup is hypothetically mandated by the Uranium Mill Tailings Radiation Control Act of 1978 (P.L. 95–604; 92 Stat. 3021), the program has been so chronically underfunded that it didn't really get started at all for eight years. When it did, its efforts consisted largely of moving tailings piles from particularly sensitive locations—such as downtown Edgemont, South Dakota, where the AEC had dumped about 3.5 million tons along the banks of the Cottonwood Creek, a quarter-mile upstream from the Cheyenne River—and relocating them to some "preferable" spot a few miles away, where they could be fenced-off for "safety" reasons; Carter, "Uranium Mill Tailings," *op. cit.*; Ambler, *Breaking the Iron Bonds, op. cit.*, pp. 178–90; Peter Matthiessen, *Indian Country* (New York: Viking, 1984) pp. 203–18. Arguably, the dispersal involved in such procedures worsens rather than alleviates the problem. The plain fact is that nobody has a clue what to do this body of carcinogenic material which, by the mid-'70s, was already large enough to "cover a four lane highway one foot deep from coast to coast"; Jeff Cox, "Nuclear Waste Recycling," *Environmental Action Bulletin*, No. 29, May 1976.

143. The need for permanent repositories was formally enunciated for the first time in the Nuclear Waste Policy Act of 1982 (NWPA); the two-part scheme, authorizing establishment of MRS facilities as well as repositories, was included in the 1987 revision of NWPA; U.S. Department of Energy, Monitored Retrievable Storage Commission, "Nuclear Waste: Is There a Need For Federal Interim Storage?" in *Report of the Monitored Retrievable Storage Commission* (Washington, D.C.: U.S. Government Printing Office, 1989); Gerald Jacob, *Site Unseen: The Politics of Siting a Nuclear Repository* (Pittsburg: University of Pittsburg Press, 1990). For insight into the evolution of official thinking on the matter of nuclear waste disposal, see J. Samuel Walker, *Containing the Atom: Nuclear Regulation in a Changing Environment, 1963–1971* (Berkeley: University of California Press, 1992).

144. Valerie Taliman, "Nine Tribes Look at Storage: Signs Point to Nuclear Dump on Native Land, *Smoke Signals*, Aug. 1993.

145. In 1995, the few residents of, Lincoln County, Nevada, attempted to negotiate a hefty fee for themselves in exchange for accepting an MRS. The state government quickly quashed the initiative; Kulentz, *Geographies of Sacrifice, op. cit.*, p. 145.

146. For full exposition of the relevant legal theory, see the references indicated in notes 3 and 7, above.

147. Grace Thorpe, "Radioactive Racism? Native Americans and the Nuclear Waste Legacy," *The Circle*, Apr. 1995. To amplify, in federal doctrine, "Indian reservations…are 'sovereign'—outside the immediate control of the states in which they reside. They are also outside the control of government agencies such as the Environmental Protection Agency… Because they are often extremely impoverished, they are [also] vulnerable to bribes"; ibid., p. 147.

148. Taliman, "Nine Tribes Look at Storage," *op. cit.*

149. On the NCAI grant, see Randel D. Hansen, "Mescalero Apache: Nuclear Waste and the Privatization of Genocide," *The Circle*, Aug. 1994. On the CERT funding, see Winona LaDuke, "Native Environmentalism," *Earth Island Journal*, Summer 1993. CERT, created in the late 1970s by then Navajo Tribal Chairman Peter McDonald and federal lobbyist LaDonna Harris, has long been a major problem for those pursuing indigenous sovereignty and mineral rights; for what is probably the best analysis, see Philip S. Deloria, "CERT: It's Time for an Evaluation," *American Indian Law Newsletter*, Sept./Oct. 1982. Also see Geoffrey O'Gara, "Canny CERT Gets Money, Respect, Problems," *High Country News*, Dec. 14, 1979; Ken Peres and Fran Swan, "The New Indian Elite: Bureaucratic Entrepeneurs," *Akwesasne Notes*, Late spring 1980; Winona LaDuke, "CERT: An Outsider's View In," *Akwesasne Notes*, Summer 1980.

150. The lease, which will soon expire, generates about 90 percent of the reservation's revenues. Without the MRS facility, the Goshutes would not only continue to suffer a high degree of contamination, but be totally without income as well; Kulentz, *Geographies of Sacrifice, op. cit.*, p. 152.

151. Quoted in Randel D. Hanson, "Nuclear Agreement Continues U.S. Policy of Dumping on Goshutes," *The Circle*, Oct. 1995.

152. Unidentified Mescalero, quoted in Winifred E. Frick, "Native Americans Approve Nuclear Waste Dump on Tribal Lands," *Santa Cruz on a Hill Press*, Mar. 16, 1995.

153. Quoted in ibid.

154. Such a sense of emotional/spiritual malaise is hardly unique to Indians, albeit it may manifest itself especially strongly among groups like the Mescaleros, who are placed in extremis; see Joanna Rogers Macy, *Despair and Personal Power in the Nuclear Age* (Baltimore: New Society, 1983).

155. National Academy of Sciences, Division of Earth Science, Committee on Waste Disposal, *The Disposal of Radioactive Waste on Land* (Washington, D.C.: NAS-NRC Pub. 519, 1957); Scientists' Review Panel on the WIPP, *Evaluation of the Waste Isolation Pilot Plant (WIPP) as a Water Saturated Nuclear Waste Repository* (Albuquerque, NM: Concerned Citizens for Nuclear Safety, Jan. 1988).

156. "Scientists Fear Atomic Explosion of Buried Waste," *New York Times*, Mar. 5, 1995.

157. Kulentz, *Geographies of Sacrifice, op. cit.*, p. 133.

158. About 10 percent of Yucca Mountain's capacity is earmarked for military wastes. As to civilian waste, it will have been outstripped by the output of the country's 128 functioning commercial reactors before it is completed. Hence, a third repository is already necessary; ibid., p. 140.

159. Jacob, *Site Unseen, op. cit.*, p. 138.

160. By some estimates, it will be open for business by the turn of the century.

161. The Low-Level Radioactive Waste Policy Act of 1980 makes the states responsible for the disposal of such materials, even if they've been federally/militarily produced (as they almost invariably are, to some extent). California Governor Pete Wilson has apparently opted to "assume the burden" of all 49 of his cohorts—on a fee-for-service basis—by dumping the aggregate contamination on a handful of Indians in a remote and unnoticed corner of his vast domain; Philip M. Klasky, "The Eagle's Eye View of Ward Valley: Environmentalists and Native American Tribes Fight Proposed Waste Dump in the Mojave Desert," *Wild Earth*, Spring 1994.

162. The phrase does not accrue from "radical" rhetoric. See the unabashed advocacy of the trend, both technically and politically, advanced in Charles C. Reith and Bruce M. Thompson, eds., *Deserts as Dumps? The Disposal of Hazardous Materials in Arid Ecosystems* (Albuquerque: University of New Mexico Press, 1992).

163. For a more panoramic view of the phenomenon in its various dimensions, see Donald A. Grinde and Bruce E. Johansen, *Ecocide of Native America: Environmental Destruction of Indian Lands and Peoples* (Santa Fe, NM: Clear Light, 1995).

164. Cohen is mainly known for his definitive *Handbook on Federal Indian Law*, originally published in 1942 and periodically updated by a succession of scholars ever since. For the miner's canary analogy, see Felix S. Cohen, "The Erosion of Indian Rights, 1950–53: A Case-Study in Bureaucracy," *Yale Law Journal*, No. 62, 1953, p. 390.

165. Such experimentation has been by no means restricted to the effects of radioactive substances. Consider, for example, the testing during the late '80s/early '90s of hepatitis vaccines indirectly linked by the World Health Organization to AIDS, on unwitting Inuit and American Indian children; Andrea Smith, "The Correlation of HIV to Hepatitis-A and -B Vaccines," *WARN Newsletter*, Summer 1992.

166. While the great weight of this has fallen on Native North America (Grinde and Johansen, *Ecocide of Native America, op. cit.*), much has also been pushed off on other oppressed population sectors, most especially peoples of color; see, e.g., Robert D. Bullard, ed., *Confronting Environmental Racism: Voices from the Grassroots* (Boston: South End Press, 1993); Andrew Szaz, *Ecopopulism: Toxic Waste and the Movement for Environmental Justice* (Minneapolis: University of Minnesota Press, 1994).

167. It should be noted that early mainstream dissident movements of the late '50s/early '60s, like SANE and Women Strike for Peace, were opposed specifically to proliferation of nuclear weapons, not the development of nuclear power per se. There is no hint in their literature that they were concerned that something akin to genocide might be occurring among indigenous peoples in the mining and milling districts of North America; see, e.g., Arthur J. Laflin and Anne Montgomery, eds., *Swords into Plowshares: Nonviolent Direct Action for Disarmament* (San Francisco: Harper & Row, 1987).

168. One firm indication of this is that in a book like Anna Gyorgy's *No Nukes* (*op. cit.*), a more or less definitive survey put forth by one of the country's premier oppositional publishing houses at the very height of the anti-nuclear movement, only three of 484 pages are devoted to indigenous people. This is true, despite the acknowledgement, at p. 221, that "Native Americans...are affected more than others" by the politicoeconomic and sheer physical structure of nuclear power. In effect, had *only* American Indians been substantially impacted by "the scourge of nuclear energy" (p. 13), opposition would have been minimal to nonexistent, even among the dominant society's self-styled radicals.

169. On the reactors and their safety record, see John W. Gofman and Arthur R. Tamplin, *Poisoned Power: The Case Against Nuclear Plants* (Emmaus, PA: Rodale Press, 1971; rereleased in 1979 with a new subtitle, *The Case Before and After Three Mile Island*); Peter Faulkner, *The Silent Bomb: A Guide to the Nuclear Power Controversy* (New York: Vintage, 1977).

170. Kulentz, *Geographies of Sacrifice, op. cit.*, p. 115.

171. Wiesen Cook, "Cold War Fallout," *op. cit.*, p. 31; her reference is to Jay M. Gould, *The Enemy Within: The High Cost of Living Near Nuclear Reactors* (New York: Four Walls Eight Windows, 1996).

172. John W. Gofman and Arthur R. Tamplin, *Population Control Through Nuclear Pollution* (Chicago: Nelson-Hall, 1970).

173. Quoted in Freeman, *Nuclear Witnesses, op. cit.*, p. 112; the reference is to Linus Pauling, *No More War* (New York: Dodd, Meade, 1958).

174. Gene I. Rochlin, *Plutonium, Power, and Politics* (Berkeley: University of California Press, 1979).

175. U.S. Department of Energy, Nuclear Information and Resource Service, *Nuclear Power and National Energy Strategy* (Washington, D.C.: U.S. Government Printing Office, 1991).

176. It is very interesting that with all the hullabaloo during the past five years over "Joe Camel" and other tobacco advertising campaigns—all of which should probably be banned—there was almost no response from progressives with regard to the far more ominous pronuke ads. Whatever else may be said, simple arithmetic demonstrates that the combined carcinogenic content of all the cigarettes in the world, even if inhaled directly rather than second hand, is relatively benign when compared to a single pound of plutonium.

177. Ambler, *Breaking the Iron Bonds, op. cit.*, p. 173.

178. Uranium mining in northern Saskatchewan began on a fairly small scale in 1952, at an ersatz government-sponsored community called Uranium City. It expanded during the uranium boom of the late 1970s, and really took off after the collapse of U.S. uranium production at the end of the decade. As at Navajo, Laguna, and elsewhere, indigenous habitats and subsistence economies have been devastated as a result; see Miles Goldstick, *Wollaston: People Resisting Genocide* (Montréal: Black Rose Books, 1987). For

an earlier but much broader overview of such processes, see Robert Davis and Mark Zannis, *The Genocide Machine in Canada: The Pacification of the North* (Montréal: Black Rose Books, 1973).

179. Alex Haley, *The Autobiography of Malcolm X* (New York: Ballantine, 1964) p. 329.

180. Rosalie Bertell, "Radiation Exposure and Human Species Survival," in Committee on Federal Research on the Effects of Ionizing Radiation, *Issue Papers: Working Documents of 10 March 1980 Public Meeting, Vol. 1* (Washington, D.C.: National Institutes of Health, 1980); also see her "Nuclear Suicide," *op. cit.*; "More on Nuclear Suicide," *op. cit.*

181. Gould, *The Enemy Within, op. cit.*

182. This is a concept embodied in most, if not all, traditional (indigenous) societies. It has been increasingly incorporated into—more often appropriated by—a fairly broad range of non-native environmentalist theory and activism; see, e.g., Caldicott, *If You Love This Planet, op. cit.*; Vandana Shiva, *Staying Alive: Women, Ecology and Development* (London: Zed Books, 1989); Christopher Manes, *Green Rage: Radical Environmentalism and the Unmaking of Civilization* (Boston: Little Brown, 1990); Paul Virilio, *Popular Defense & Ecological Struggles* (New York: Semiotext[e], 1990); Barry Commoner, *Making Peace with the Planet* (New York: New Press, 1990); Kirkpatrick Sale, *Dwellers in the Land: The Bioregional Vision* (Philadelphia: New Society, 1991); Steve Chase, ed., *Defending the Earth: A Dialogue Between Murray Bookchin and Dave Foreman* (Boston: South End Press, 1991); Jerry Mander, *In the Absense of the Sacred: The Failure of Technology and the Survival of the Indian Nations* (San Francisco: Sierra Club Books, 1991); John Zerzan, *Future Primitive and Other Essays* (Brooklyn, NY: Autonomedia/Anarchy, 1994).

183. This is a theme elaborated very well by Vine Deloria, Jr., in his *God Is Red* (Golden, CO: Fulcrum, [2nd. ed.] 1994).

184. See, e.g., Lewis Regenstein, *The Politics of Extinction* (New York: Macmillan, 1975).

185. The fact that ground has been broken for no new reactor since the late 1980s is, of course, a good sign; Gould, *The Enemy Within, op. cit.*, p. 241.

186. See generally, Frank Donner, *Protectors of Privilege: Red Squads and Police Repression in Urban America* (Berkeley: University of California Press, 1990); Paul Chevigny, *Edge of the Knife: Police Violence in America* (New York: New Press, 1995).

187. In January 1975, the Virginia Electric and Power Company, a utility operating two nuclear reactors and planning four more, became the first such entity to ask for and receive legislative approval to establish a private police force with investigative and arrest prerogatives. On September 9, 1977, it was revealed that a similar unit, created by the George Power Company, was surveilling and compiling files on antinuclear activists. Things have gone steadily downhill from there; Susan Jaffe, "Repression: The New Nuclear Danger," *Village Voice*, Mar. 31, 1980.

188. On sizes and powers of public and private police forces, see Mike Zielinski, "Armed and Dangerous: Private Police Forces on the March," *Covert Action Quarterly*, No. 54, Fall 1995. With respect to files, see, e.g., Fred Hoffman, "Inside the L.A. Secret Police," *Covert Action Quarterly*, No. 42, Fall 1992. Concerning prisons, more citizens are currently behind bars in "the land of the free," proportionately speaking, than in any other country on earth. Official plans include a doubling of lockup capacity by early in the coming century; Marc Bauer, "Americans Behind Bars: A Comparison of International Rates of Incarceration," in Ward Churchill and J.J. Vander Wall, eds., *Cages of Steel: The Politics of Imprisonment in the United States* (Washington, D.C.: Maisonneuve Press, 1992).

189. There is simply no substitute for U-238. Neither plutonium nor U-235 can be synthesized without it, and the thorium-derived U-233 does not fulfill the same requirements; David R. Inglis, *Nuclear Energy: Its Physics and Social Challenge* (Reading, MA: Addison-Wesley, 1973).

190. The term decolonization is employed here in precisely the sense articulated as a fundamental human right under international law, to wit, the United Nations Declaration on the Granting of Independence to Colonial Countries and Peoples, 1960 (U.N.G.A. Res. 1514 (XV), 15 U.N. GAOR, Supp. (No. 16) 66, U.N. Doc. A/4684 (1961)).

191. Quoted in Virginia Irving Armstrong, ed., *I Have Spoken: American History Through the Eyes of American Indians* (Chicago: Swallow Press, 1971) p. 79.

THE UNITED STATES AND THE GENOCIDE CONVENTION
A Half-Century of Obfuscation and Obstruction

> It is clear that the Genocide Convention is a moral document. It is a call for a higher standard of human conduct. It is not a panacea for injustice, [but it is] an important step toward civilizing the affairs of nations.
>
> —Senator William Proxmire

ONE of the earliest matters taken up by the United Nations after its 1945 founding convention in San Francisco was the sponsoring of an international legal instrument to punish and prevent the crime of genocide.[1] In General Assembly Resolution 96(I), passed unanimously and without debate on December 11, 1946, the U.N. made it clear that, although it may have been prompted to act with urgency because of what had been revealed during the recently concluded trials of the major nazi war criminals at Nuremberg, it was more broadly motivated in pursuing the issue: "*Many* instances of such crimes of genocide have occurred when racial, religious, political, and other groups have been destroyed, entirely or in part (emphasis added)."[2] The body's Economic and Social Council (ECOSOC) was mandated by the resolution to produce a draft of the desired convention for consideration at the next annual session of the General Assembly.[3]

ECOSOC immediately turned to the U.N. Secretariat for support in retaining several international legal consultants, including Dr. Raphaël Lemkin, an exiled Polish-Jewish jurist who had coined the term "genocide" in 1944, and who was thus considered a leading expert on the topic.[4] The initial draft, authored primarily by Lemkin, was duly submitted to the Council on the Progressive Development of International Law and Its Codification in June 1947.[5] In July, however, the General Assembly, noting "important philosophical disagreements" among some member states with elements of the draft document, declined to put the matter to a vote. Instead, through Resolution 180(II), the assembly instructed ECOSOC to prepare another draft instrument for consideration the following year.[6]

An ad hoc committee, consisting of representatives of China, France, Lebanon, Poland, the United States, the U.S.S.R., and Venezuela, was then organized by the council to make the necessary revisions.[7] The new document was passed along to ECOSOC's Sixth (Legal) Committee, which made minor alterations, before submitting it to the General Assembly, which unanimously adopted it without further modification on December 9, 1948.[8] By January 12, 1951, a sufficient number of countries had ratified the Convention on Prevention and Punishment of the Crime of Genocide to afford it the status of binding international law (of both "customary" and "black letter" varieties).[9] As of 1990, more than a hundred United Nations member states had tendered valid ratifications.[10] The only significant exception was the United States of America.

The situation remains unchanged today, despite a pretense of ratification made at the behest of the Reagan administration in 1988, *forty years* after the convention first passed muster with the civilized countries of the world.[11] How and why this came to be are questions of no small significance, insofar as they shed a penetrating light on the true character and priorities of this "nation of laws," the self-professed "most humane and enlightened nation in the history of humanity."[12] They are no less important in that the United States, as the planet's only remaining superpower, is now in an unparalleled position to visit its version of "humanitarianism" upon virtually any sector of the species it chooses.[13]

Gutting the Convention

The United States assumed a leading role in formulating the application of international legal principle under which the nazi leadership was tried at Nuremberg, especially with regard to the somewhat nebulous category of "Crimes Against Humanity" under which the regime's most blatantly genocidal policies and practices were prosecuted.[14] Similarly, while engineering establishment of the United Nations in 1945 — ostensibly as a barrier against the sort of "excesses" evidenced by nazism — it did much to promote the idea that each element of customary human rights law, including implicit prohibitions against genocide, should be codified as a "black letter" international legal instrument, formally embraced through a process of treaty ratifications by member states.[15]

When it came time for the drafting of an actual genocide convention, however, the United States conducted itself in what can only be described as a thoroughly subversive fashion. This began with its response to the initial

364

draft instrument, a document which sought to frame the crime in a manner consistent with accepted definition.

> The draft aimed to protect "racial, national, linguistic, religious, or political groups." In sweeping terms it branded as criminal many physical and biological acts aimed at the destruction of such groups in whole or in part, or of "preventing [their] preservation or development." It specified that acts would be punishable, including attempt to commit genocide, participation in genocide, conspiracy to commit genocide, and engaging in a number of "preparatory" acts such as developing techniques of genocide and setting up installations. It called for punishment of "all forms of public propaganda tending by their systematic and hateful character to promote genocide, or tending to make it appear as a necessary, legitimate, or excusable act." It called for the creation of an international court to try offenders in cases when states were unwilling either to try them or extradite them to another country for trial.[16]

As the Saudi Arabian delegation observed at the time, the draft clearly articulated the nature of genocide as consisting not only in the systematic killing of members of a targeted population, but also in policies devoted to bringing about the "planned disintegration of the political, social, or economic structure of a group or nation" and/or the "systematic moral debasement of a group, people, or nation."[17] Things seemed to be moving in the right direction until U.S. representatives, often working through third parties such as Canada and Venezuela, went to work to scuttle what became known as the "Secretariat's Draft" on the grounds that its "net was cast much too wide[ly]" and, if approved as law, might therefore serve to "impair the sovereignty" of signatory states.[18]

The previously mentioned ad hoc committee, chaired by U.S. delegate John Maktos, was then assembled to produce a new draft, with attention focused on "the political as well as the legal dimensions" of the issue.[19] In short order, a *quid pro quo* was effected in which the Soviets were allowed to strike socioeconomic aggregates of the very sort they had been steadily obliterating since the early 1930s from the list of entities to receive protection under the law.[20] In exchange, the United States was able to remove an entire article delineating the criteria of cultural rather than physical or biological genocide, a maneuver serving to exempt a range of its own dirty linen from scrutiny.[*]

---

[*] This is not to say that the United States—or the U.S.S.R., for that matter—were alone in their advocacy of deletion. Most of the countries involved were guilty of one or both categories of violation. Nonetheless, the fact remains that only the Americans and the Soviets possessed sufficient clout to effect the sort of mutual exoneration from culpability through *a priori* alteration of law which ultimately prevailed. In doing so, of course, both parties obviously contravened the most fundamental juridical principle enunciated by Chief U.S. Prosecutor (and Supreme Court Justice) Robert H. Jackson at Nuremberg, that if the legal principles underlying prosecution of the nazis were to serve

The secretariat's draft [had gone] to considerable lengths to detail the specific conditions of the three forms of genocide. In the category of *physical,* it outlined mass extermination and "slow death" measures (i.e., subjection to conditions of life which, owing to lack of proper housing, clothing, food, hygiene and medical care or excessive work or physical exertion are likely to result in the debilitation or death of individuals; mutilations and biological experiments imposed for other than curative purposes; deprivation of all means of livelihood by confiscation of property; looting, curtailment of work, and the denial of housing and supplies otherwise available to the other inhabitants of the territory concerned)... The secretariat's draft took *biological* genocide to mean the restricting of births in the group. It named the methods of sterilization or compulsory abortion, segregation of the sexes and obstacles to marriage... *Cultural* genocide was defined as the destruction of the specific characteristics of the group. Among the acts specified: forced transfer of children to another human group; forced and systematic exile of individuals representing the culture of a group; the prohibition of the use of the national language, or religious works, or the prohibition of new publications; systematic destruction of historical or religious monuments, or their diversion to alien uses; destruction or dispersion of documents and objects of historical, artistic, or religious value and of objects used in religious worship.[*]

---

justice, rather than constituting merely a sophistry masking an exercise in sheer retribution, they would have to be applied equally to all nations, "including those which sit here now in judgment"; Robert H. Jackson, "Opening Statement," in *The Nürnberg Case as Presented by Robert H. Jackson, Chief of Counsel for the United States* (New York: Alfred A. Knopf, 1947) p. 93.

[*]Davis and Zannis, *Genocide Machine, op. cit.,* pp. 19–20. The provision on cultural genocide, as well as Lemkin's original definition of the crime, would have taken in the virtual entirety of U.S. Indian policy from the 1880s onwards. Officially entitled "Assimilation," the goal of the policy was, according to Commissioner of Indian Affairs Francis Leupp, to systematically "kill the Indian, but spare the man" in every native person in the United States, thus creating a "great engine to grind down the tribal mass"; Francis Leupp, *The Indian and His Problem* (New York: Scribner's, 1910) p. 93. The express intent was to bring about the total disappearance of indigenous cultures—as such—as rapidly as possible; Henry E. Fritz, *The Movement for Indian Assimilation, 1860–1890* (Philadelphia: University of Pennsylvania Press, 1963). To this end, the practice of native spiritual traditions were universally forbidden under penalty of law in 1897; Oliver Knight, *Following the Indian Wars* (Norman: University of Oklahoma Press, 1960). A comprehensive and compulsory "educational" system was put in place to "free [American Indian] children from the language and habits of their untutored and often savage parents" while indoctrinating them not only in the language but in the religion and cultural mores of Euroamerican society; U.S. Department of Interior, Bureau of Indian Affairs, *Annual Report of the Commissioner of Indian Affairs to the Secretary of Interior* (Washington, D.C.: U.S. Government Printing Office, 1886) p. xxiv. This was accomplished through a complex of federally run boarding schools which removed native students from any and all contact with their families, communities and cultures for years on end; David Wallace Williams, *Education for Extinction: American Indians and the Boarding School Experience, 1875–1928* (Lawrence: University Press of California, 1995). The structure of indigenous property relations was meanwhile forcibly dissolved under provision of the 1887 General Allotment Act, the populations of all indigenous nations encapsulated by the United States were unilaterally declared to be its subjects via the 1924 Indian Citizenship Act, and traditional forms of native governance were unilaterally dissolved, supplanted by governing council structures designed and implemented by the United States through the 1934 Indian Reorganization Act; Vine Deloria, Jr., and Clifford M. Lytle, *The Nations Within: The Past and Future of American Indian Sovereignty* (New York: Pantheon, 1984). By the 1950s, entire indigenous nations—109 in all—were being declared "extinct"

In the Secretariat's Draft, one crime—genocide—was thus defined as having three distinct but often interactive modes of perpetration. No effort was "made to distinguish the relative seriousness of the modes which are left to stand on par," with the deliberate eradication of cultural existence being treated with as much legal gravity as programs of outright physical annihilation.[21] By the time the United States had completed its overhaul of the text, over the heated objections of the Lebanese delegate, all that remained of the concept of cultural genocide was a provision prohibiting the forced transfer of children.* Even the secretariat's proscription of genocidally oriented propaganda—a concept deployed by the United States in its prosecution of Julius Streicher at Nuremberg—had been scrapped in favor of a much more restrictive clause prohibiting "direct and public incitement."[22] In its final form, the key ingredients of the draft finally presented to the General Assembly had been reduced to the following:

Article II. In the present Convention, genocide means any of the following acts committed to destroy, in whole or in part, a national, ethnical, racial or religious group, as such:

(a) Killing members of the group;
(b) Causing serious bodily or mental harm to members of the group;
(c) Deliberately inflicting on members of the group conditions of life calculated to bring about its physical destruction in whole or in part;
(d) Imposing measures intended to prevent births within the group;
(e) Forcibly transferring children of the group to another group.

---

by unilateral decree of the federal government, through a series of "Termination Acts" passed pursuant to House Resolution 108 (August 1, 1953). Simultaneously, a process was initiated under Public Law 959, the Relocation Act, through which more than half the entire native population was dispersed from its own landbase into urban localities where it was mostly subsumed within "mainstream" society by the 1980s; Donald L. Fixico, *Termination and Relocation: Federal Indian Policy, 1945–1960* (Albuquerque: University of New Mexico Press, 1986). As to the disposition of American Indian religious shrines, one need only consider the creation of the Mt. Rushmore National Monument and a correspondingly vast tourist industry in the Black Hills—the most sacred geography of the Lakotas, Cheyennes, and other peoples—to get the idea.

*If genocide were to be understood as the "actual and intentional destruction of a human group as such," the Lebanese argued, "it would entail giving any group an absolute entity which it would be criminal to attack." Although many states might not yet be prepared to come to grips with the implications of such an understanding, he went on, "certain higher considerations lead world conscience also to revolt at the thought of the destruction of a human group, even though the individual members survived." One purpose of law being to draw adherents into higher standards of consciousness and comportment, he concluded, it was imperative to expand rather than contract the legal definition of genocide; U.N. Doc E/A.C. 25/S.R. (1948), pp. 1–28.

Article III. The following acts shall be punishable:

(a)   Genocide;
(b)   Conspiracy to commit genocide;
(c)   Direct and public incitement to commit genocide;
(d)   Attempt to commit genocide;
(e)   Complicity in genocide.

It was this U.S.-designed and highly truncated instrument, not just diluting but effectively gutting Lemkin's original conception of genocide and the draft convention which arose from it, which was ultimately approved by the General Assembly. From there, it was an easy slide down the slippery slope of definitional erosion into a generalized misunderstanding that genocide occurs *only* within peculiarly focused incidents or processes of mass murder (à la Auschwitz and Babi Yar).* For all practical intents and purposes, then, the United States had attained a diplomatic triumph of sorts, managing to void the very meaning of the crime in question while simultaneously appearing to stand at the forefront of those opposing it.

Nonratification

It appeared for a time that America might be able to have its cake and eat it too, at least on matters of international legality. At home, this liberal accomplishment—not only subversion of the Genocide Convention, but the forging of a position of primacy for the United States within the U.N. itself had been masterminded by Truman-era State Department holdovers from the previous administration of Franklin Delano Roosevelt—foundered on the shoals of extreme right-wing reaction.[23] Beginning in 1945, a strain of radical nativist anticommunism, mixed with overt militarism and white supremacism in a stew every bit as virulent as anything the nazis cooked up, launched an ever more determined campaign to establish an outright fascist order in the United States.[24]

---

*By now, despite the fact that killing is only one of five policy trajectories proscribed under the Convention, even the more insightful literature on the topic is all but exclusively preoccupied with modes of inflicting mass death. There is no major study of genocide which concerns itself equally, or even substantially, with such matters as involuntary sterilization programs and the compulsory transfer of children; see, e.g., Irving Louis Horowitz, *Genocide: State Power and Mass Murder* (New Brunswick, NJ: Transaction Books, 1976); Leo Kuper, *Genocide: Its Political Use in the Twentieth Century* (New Haven, CT: Yale University Press, 1981); Isador Walliman and Michael N. Dobkowski, eds., *Genocide and the Modern Age: Etiology and Case Studies of Mass Death* (Westport, CT: Greenwood Press, 1987); Frank Chalk and Kurt Jonassohn, *The History and Sociology of Genocide: Analyses and Case Studies* (New Haven, CT: Yale University Press, 1990).

Central to this effort—America's "Reichstag Fire," as it were—was a series of dubious but highly sensationalized "spy trials" through which it was purportedly demonstrated that the federal government was literally infested with Soviet agents in all its dimensions and at every level.* Some of these, it was asserted, had worked their way into key positions from which they could pass along to its enemies the country's most closely guarded military secrets—the scientific knowledge underlying the atomic bomb, to take a prominent example—and shape American policy, both foreign and domestic, in such ways as to undermine the national interest.[25] So serious had the threat become, it was proclaimed, that only the exercise of extraordinary powers by the more "patriotic" elements of government could save the United States from being delivered into the totalitarian hands of what was described in perfectly Hitleresque fashion as a "World Communist Conspiracy."† By 1950, a climate of such genuine hysteria had been produced that a nationwide sociopolitical and cultural purge was underway which eventually proved so sweeping that the American polity, never much inclined toward leftism anyway, was shifted significantly and permanently rightward.[26]

The State Department was a particular target of the Right during the entire period. Among those most prominently pilloried were senior diplomat Harry Dexter White and Alger Hiss, a somewhat lesser-ranking official

---

* The first of these was a plainly spurious case brought in 1945 against the editors of *Amerasia*, an obscure academic journal, which had published excerpts from classified documents concerned with the strategic bombing campaign against Japan. The contrived nature of the prosecution shines through even in recent right-wing attempts to make it appear otherwise; see, e.g., Harvey Klehr and Ronald Radosh, *The Amerasia Spy Case: Prelude to McCarthyism* (Chapel Hill: University of North Carolina Press, 1996). Five years later, there was the case of the "atomic spies"—Julius and Ethel Rosenberg, et al.—who supposedly leaked a batch of nonexistent secrets to the KGB, thus "enabling" the Soviets to develop nuclear weapons; William A. Reuben *The Atom Spy Hoax* (New York: Action Books, 1960); Walter and Miriam Schneir, *Invitation to an Inquest* (New York: Pantheon, 3rd ed., 1983). And so it went. Between *Amerasia* and the Rosenbergs, there were about forty other such farces; for a right-wing summary, see Ralph de Toledano and Victor Lasky, *Spies, Dupes and Diplomats* (New Rochelle, NY: Arlington House, 1967). A more balanced contemporaneous view will be found in Vernon Henchley's *The Spies Who Never Were* (New York: Dodd, Meade, 1965).

† This line was put forth from many sources, reinforced by continuous "investigative" hearings conducted by a trio of congressional bodies (the House Committee on Un-American Activities, and the Committee on Internal Security and Joseph McCarthy's Permanent Subcommittee on Investigations in the Senate); Walter Goodman, *The Committee: The Extraordinary Career of the House Committee on Un-American Activities* (New York: Farrar, Strauss & Giroux, 1968); Robert Griffith, *The Politics of Fear: Joseph McCarthy and the Senate* (Lexington: University of Kentucky Press, 1970). The impression was further reinforced by the Truman administration's establishment of "Loyalty Boards" to screen the affiliations, personal associations, and ideological sympathies of everyone in the country employed on the basis of government funding; Ralph Brown, *Loyalty and Security* (New Haven, CT: Yale University Press, 1958).

who had been among the U.S. delegation to the 1945 Yalta Conference (during which America's postwar interests in Europe were supposedly "sold out" to the Soviets) and who then presided over the U.N. founding conference.[*] While White and Hiss were falsely accused of being out-and-out "Russian agents," hundreds of others—notably, the entire roster of State Department China specialists, who were alleged to have deliberately "handed over" that country to Mao Tse Tung's communist insurgents by mid-1949—were branded as "comsymps" (communist sympathizers) or "fellow travelers."[27]

One purpose of the whole charade was to discredit the "communistic" notion of creating a workable system of international problem resolution through nonmilitary means, embodied in the U.N.'s mandate to establish standards of comportment by progressively codifying and gaining universal ratification of the laws of nations.[†] Instead, the American Right sought to impose "world order" through attainment of the very kind of unassailable military ascendancy—and consequent global politicoeconomic dominance—for the United States that Hitler had earlier desired for Germany.[‡] Contrary to most

---

[*] White died before the "case" against him could be brought to fruition; David Rees, *Harry Dexter White: A Study in Paradox* (New York: Coward, McCann & Geoghegan, 1973). Meanwhile, Hiss, who left government service in 1947 for a high position in the Carnegie Endowment for International Peace, was subjected to a lengthy series of highly publicized hearings and trials beginning in 1948. Although never convicted of espionage, he was eventually convicted of having perjured himself when he denied affiliation with members of the Communist Party, largely on the basis of doctored physical evidence and the almost certainly false testimony of former CP member Whittaker Chambers. Such travesties did much to concretize public fears concerning the "Red subversion" of U.S. foreign policy; Fred J. Cook, *The Unfinished Story of Alger Hiss* (New York: William Morrow, 1958); John Chabot Smith, *Alger Hiss, The True Story* (New York: Holt, Rinehart & Winston, 1976); Edith Tiger, ed., *In re Alger Hiss: Petition for a Writ of Error Coram Nobis* (New York: Hill & Wang, 1979); Allen Weinstein, *Perjury: The Hiss-Chambers Case* (New York: Alfred A. Knopf, 1988). Of related interest, see Athan Theoharis, *The Yalta Myths* (Columbia: University of Missouri Press, 1970).

[†] This is not to say that Truman's New Deal holdovers at State were guided by idealism. Rather, they perceived that, given its unrivaled postwar economic position, the United States could achieve global hegemony more cheaply and efficiently via that brand of power projection than through more the traditional approach of military confrontation. Hence, the liberals and their left-wing opposition were agreed on the essential goals of U.S. policy, differing only on the best route by which to attain them; Campbell, *Masquerade Peace, op. cit.*

[‡] Again, the distinction between the Truman administration and its right-wing opposition was one of emphasis, not in kind. The "Truman Doctrine," articulated in NSC 68 (1950), consisted of using military force where necessary to "contain communism" within those countries in which it existed during the late 1940s, then grinding them down economically and politically over the longer term. The Right advocated a more aggressive "roll back" strategy of militarily "liberating" eastern Europe—and perhaps China—thus promoting the internal collapse of the Soviet Union, as the sole remaining socialist state, over the shorter run. Truman's recipe—containment through an unending series of brushfire wars and counterinsurgency campaigns in the periphery, combined with the instigation of a strategic arms race designed to eventually bankrupt the Soviets—eventually won out; Carl Oglesby and Richard Shaull, *Containment and Change: Two Dissenting Views on American Foreign Policy* (New

of what now passes as "responsible" analysis in U.S. scholarship, this bellicosity was not an "outgrowth" of the Cold War. Rather, it was the cause of it.[*]

While such forces never managed to fulfill their original objective of bringing about an actual U.S. withdrawal from the United Nations—after Korea, even the more thoughtful right-wingers could see the utility of remaining within the organization—they were able to neutralize much of what they found most objectionable about it by crafting an American posture of refusing to ratify its promulgation of international legal instruments they perceived as constraining the latitude of U.S. policy options.[†] Among the more important elements of evolving human rights law which the United States still refuses to accept are the International Covenant on Civil and Political Rights (1966); the Covenant on Economic, Social and Cultural Rights (1966); the Convention on the Elimination of All Forms of Racial Discrimination (1966); and the American Convention on Human Rights (1965).[28] The same holds true concerning the Laws of War, specifically the Declaration on the Prohibition of the

York: Macmillan, 1967); Richard M. Freeland, *The Truman Doctrine and the Origins of McCarthyism* (New York: Alfred A. Knopf, 1972); Thomas H. Etzold and John Lewis Gaddis, *Containment: Documents on American Foreign Policy and Strategy, 1945–1950* (New York: Columbia University Press, 1978); Gregg Herkin, *The Winning Weapon* (New York: Alfred A. Knopf, 1980); Noam Chomsky, *Towards a New Cold War: Essays on the Current Crisis and How We Got There* (New York: Pantheon, 1983) esp. pp. 18–25, 195–218.

[*]For a seminal exposition on such analysis, see Noam Chomsky, "Objectivity and Liberal Scholarship," in his *American Power and the New Mandarins* (New York: Pantheon, 1969) pp. 23–158; a more developed perspective will be found in his *Necessary Illusions: Thought Control in Democratic Societies* (Boston: South End Press, 1989). Even the best spin liberalism provides cannot, however, completely obscure the fact that, in 1945, the Soviets were anxious, not for further military confrontation—they were exhausted, having lost as many as 27 million people while fighting the nazis, and their most agriculturally productive/industrially developed regions were devastated—but to reach some accommodation with the West and begin a process of bilateral disarmament which would allow them to rebuild their shattered economy. Only the belligerence of the United States—and, secondarily, Great Britain—forced them into the confrontational mode which became the Cold War; see, e.g., John Lewis Gaddis, *The United States and the Origins of the Cold War* (New York: Columbia University Press, 1972); Thomas G. Patterson, ed., *The Origins of the Cold War* (Lexington, MA: Heath, 1974).

[†]The United States was able to engineer a Security Council Resolution affirming a postwar partition of Korea and condemning efforts by its northern (communist) half to forcibly reunify itself with the southern half (which was occupied by American troops) in 1950. U.N. member states were then required by the organization's charter to provide troops, materiel, and financial support in mounting the massive military campaign by which "order" was restored (the partition was rendered permanent in 1953). During the course of the fighting, the dispute between those supporting Truman's containment doctrine and the Right's rollback advocates was finally resolved in favor of containment when the president sacked General of the Army Douglas MacArthur, American commander of all U.N. forces in Korea, for publicly asserting that the "correct" policy would be to occupy the country as a whole and then proceed with an air and land war against China. All but the most irrational sectors of the Right were properly intimidated by such a prospect; Clay Blair, *The Forgotten War: America in Korea, 1950–1953* (New York: Times Books, 1987).

Use of Thermo-Nuclear Weapons (1961); the Resolution Regarding Weapons of Mass Destruction in Outer Space (1964); the Resolution on the Non-Use of Force in International Relations and Permanent Ban on the Use of Nuclear Weapons (1972); the Resolution on the Definition of Aggression (1974); Protocols Additional to the 1949 Geneva Convention (1977); and the Declaration on the Prohibition of Chemical Weapons (1989).[29]

By and large, the arguments advanced in the Senate against ratification of the treaties accepting each of these legal instruments has been that to do so would "impair U.S. sovereignty" by conceding that there was some body of law "standing at a level higher than that of our own constitution."[30] This follows precisely the logic embodied in a cornerstone of the nazis' Nuremberg defense: insofar as the German government of which the defendants had been a part had never accepted most of the international laws at issue, they had not been required to abide by them.* Rather, the defense contended, they were legally bound only to adhere to the legal code of the sovereign German state, under which authority they asserted legitimation of their various actions.[31] The tribunal rejected this line of reasoning out of hand, countering that the defendants—indeed, the members of *all* governments—were bound under pain of criminal prosecution to conform to "higher laws" than those evidenced in their own domestic constitutions and statutory codes.[32] The U.N. member states, including the United States, went on to affirm this position in December 1946.[33]

Nonetheless, after conducting hearings on the matter in 1950—during which it became clear that many of its members were "profoundly skeptical about, and even hostile to, the notion of assuming an international legal obligation on genocide"[34]—the Senate Committee on Foreign Relations made the Genocide Convention the first casualty of its adoption of nazi legal principles. In this, it was supported not merely by statements from lobbyists of the right-wing lunatic fringe, but by direct testimony offered by men like

---

*The reference was to black letter instruments such as the 1928 Kellogg-Briand Pact (46 Stat. 2343, T.S. No. 796, 2 Bevans 732, L.N.T.S. 57)—to which Germany was not a signatory—outlawing aggressive wars for purposes of seizing territory. As concerned much of what fell under the rubric of "Crimes Against Humanity," it had never been codified in black letter form. The defense therefore argued that no body of law existed prohibiting certain offenses at the time the defendants allegedly committed them, and that—under injunctions against application of *ex post facto* law—they could not thus be legitimately prosecuted; Herbert Wechsler, "The Issues of the Nuremberg Trial," *Political Science Quarterly*, No. 62, Mar. 1947. Some U.S. politicians, of course, agreed with the nazis; see, e.g., Sen. Robert A. Taft, "Equal Justice Under the Law: The Heritage of English-Speaking Peoples and Their Responsibility," *Vital Speeches*, Vol. 13, No. 2, Nov. 1, 1946.

Alfred Schweppe, representing the supposedly more reputable American Bar Association (ABA).[35]

In the aftermath, the committee did not so much as bother to submit the Convention to the full Senate for a vote on ratification.[36] Instead, in 1953, John Bricker, Republican Senator from Ohio, proposed a constitutional amendment barring the federal executive from entering into any treaty obligation which might serve to constrain policy prerogatives, not only on the part of the central government in Washington, but of the individual states of the union.[37] It was in this climate of patent defiance of the international rule of law that the Genocide Convention was left to languish, virtually undiscussed by the U.S. government, for the next twenty years.

Deeper Motives

Beneath the transparently invalid gloss of constitutional argument with which the Senate coated its rejection of the Genocide Convention lay deeper and more important motives.[*] These devolved upon the understanding that certain ongoing U.S. policies and practices abridged the meaning of the Convention, even in its most highly diluted form. In testimony brought before the Foreign Relations Committee, this was expressed in terms of the implications of the treatment accorded racial minorities in light of the Convention's provision that intent to destroy a target group "in part" was sufficient to predicate a charge of genocidal conduct.[38] Witness the following exchange between ABA representative Schweppe and the subcommittee chair, Connecticut Senator Brien McMahon, during the 1950 hearings:

> *Schweppe*: The point is that the intent does not need to exist to destroy the whole group. It needs only to exist to destroy part of the group. Now whether we say part of the group could mean one person or whether we say a substantial part again requires us to inquire into the facts, as you often do in these cases, what is the group and how many were there?

---

[*] Not least of these was entrenched racism/antisemitism and nativism. This was abundantly evident in the treatment accorded Raphaël Lemkin, who, despite the misgivings he must have felt concerning the U.S./Soviet dilution of the Secretariat's Draft, did his best to lobby the 1948 Convention through the Senate. In response, the subcommittee declined to call him as a witness in its hearings on the matter. According to New Jersey's Republican Senator H. Alexander Smith, this was because he and his colleagues were "irritated no end" by the idea that "a Jew…who comes from a foreign country [and] speaks broken English" should be the Convention's "biggest propagandist." Liberals like Brien McMahon (D-Connecticut) and Theodore Francis Green (D-Rhode Island) appear to have substantially agreed, describing Lemkin's conspicuous Jewishness as "the biggest minus quality" of the entire ratification effort; quoted in LaBlanc, *U.S. and the Genocide Convention, op. cit.*, p. 20.

McMahon: Part of the group—but because he is part of the group. Now let's take lynching for example. Let's assume that there is a lynching and a colored man is murdered in this fashion. Is it your contention that that could be construed as being within the confines of the definition; namely, with intent to destroy him as part of a group?

Schweppe: Well, Mr. Chairman, I don't want to answer that categorically... Certainly, it doesn't mean if I want to drive five Chinamen out of town...that I must have the intent to destroy all the 400,000,000 Chinese in the world or the 250,000 within the United States. It is part of a racial group, and if it is a group of 5, a group of 10, a group of 15, and I proceed after them with guns in some community solely because they belong to some racial group that the dictators don't like, I think you have got a serious question. That's what bothers me.[39]

What was bothering both McMahon and Schweppe was not only the gratuitous violence habitually visited upon Chinese immigrants to the United States during the twentieth century, but the history of the lynchings of at least 2,505 black men and women in ten southern states between 1882 and 1930. That comes to an average of one such act of racially explicit lethal mob violence directed against African Americans each week for the entire 48-year period, in an area encompassing only one-fifth of the country.[40] When the remaining 80 percent of the United States is added in, the actual number was probably about double—more than 5,000—a racial murder rate markedly higher than that evidenced in Germany against Jews and Gypsies combined prior to 1939.[41]

As staggering as the lynching toll was, it vastly understates the total volume of violence aimed toward African-American citizens... [The] lynching inventory does not count casualties of the urban race riots that erupted during those years, nor does it embrace victims of a single killer or pairs of assassins. Neither does it include the all-too-frequent beatings, whippings, verbal humiliations, threats, harangues, and other countless indignities suffered by the Black population [in much the same manner as they were undergone by target populations in Germany].[42]

The lynching of African Americans had not ended in 1930, of course. Indeed, with 21 reported fatalities in that year, it represented a high point for the period reported. In 1932, however, there were 22 documented lynchings of blacks in the South, another 18 in 1933.[43] While the level of such violence would abate somewhat after 1935, it could hardly be said to have disappeared by 1950, and it would rise again sharply during the latter part of the decade and on through the mid-'60s.[44] There was, after all, a rather prominent organization, the Ku Klux Klan, which had been openly advocating not only the sort of atrocities at issue, but the sordid racial doctrines underlying them.* Not only had authorities at all levels declined to take decisive action to quell Klan-style activity, they had in many cases encouraged it, and, in more than a few, could be shown to have actively participated in it.[45]

Unquestionably, such a pattern could be argued as falling within the categories of state-sanctioned behavior prohibited by the Genocide Convention. It is therefore instructive that the immediate response of conservatives like Schweppe and McMahon was *not* to embrace the law as a potentially powerful tool which might be useful in an official drive to end the rampant and sustained racist violence plaguing the United States. Instead, it was the opposite: they denounced the Convention on the bizarre premise that such atrocities were somehow or another "constitutionally protected" under the mantle of U.S. sovereignty. Even more revealing in many ways is the fact that liberals agreed, albeit rather than rejecting the Convention outright, they sought to apply finesse by pretending it meant something other than what it said. Consider the following exchange between McMahon and then-Deputy Under Secretary of State Dean Rusk:

> *Rusk*: Genocide, as defined in Article II of the Convention, consists of the commission of certain specified acts, such as killing or causing serious bodily harm to individuals who are members of a national, ethnical, racial or religious group, with the intent to destroy that group. The legislative history of Article II shows that the United Nations negotiators felt that it should not be necessary that an entire human group be destroyed to constitute the crime of genocide, but rather that genocide meant the partial destruction of such a group with the intent to destroy the entire group concerned.
>
> *McMahon*: That is important. They must have the intent to destroy the entire group.
>
> *Rusk*: That is correct.
>
> *McMahon*: In other words, an action leveled against one or two of a race or religion would not be, as I understand it, the crime of genocide. They must have the intent to go through and kill them all.

---

*There is a contemporary misimpression that the Klan is and has always been a "fringe group." To the contrary, during the early part of the twentieth century, it boasted upwards of a million dues-paying members, enjoyed the semiofficial blessing of President Woodrow Wilson, and, during the 1920s, controlled state governments not only in the South (where such power lasted another forty years) but northern states like Indiana, New Jersey, and Colorado as well; William Pierce Randel, *The Ku Klux Klan: A Century of Infamy* (Philadelphia: Chilton, 1965); Wyn Craig Wade, *The Fiery Cross: The Ku Klux Klan in America* (New York: Simon & Schuster, 1987). Nor was the organization exclusively a rural "hick" phenomenon; Kenneth T. Jackson, *The Ku Klux Klan in the City, 1915–1930* (New York: Oxford University Press, 1967).

Rusk: That is correct. The Convention does not aim at the violent expression of prejudice which is directed against individual members of groups.[46]

This, to be sure, was nonsense, as Schweppe later emphatically—and quite correctly—pointed out to the committee.

[Rusk] has undertaken in a gloss to say that basic to any charge of genocide must be the intent to destroy the entire group. Now that is an exact negation of the text which is to be construed not only by [the Senate] but...by the International Court of Justice. Now, the International Court of Justice is not going to say intent to destroy a group in whole or in part means only to destroy a whole group... The Convention says you only need the intent to destroy part of a group; so there is a contradiction, gentlemen...which I suggest you very seriously consider.[47]

If the circumstances attending the lynching of blacks smacked of genocide, their targeting for involuntary sterilization was even worse. Already in 1950 there was considerable discussion in the African American community about this, and in December 1951, a 240-page petition, written by black attorney William L. Patterson for the American Civil Rights Congress (CRC) and entitled "We Charge Genocide," was deposited with the U.N. Secretariat in New York.[48] Although U.S. diplomats were able to prevent the document—which provided copious details on sterilization programs to which the Afroamerican community had been subjected—from being taken up by the U.N.'s Commission on Human Rights, the submission sent lingering shock waves throughout the federal hierarchy.*

By 1970, when an updated version of the CRC petition was deposited with the secretariat, the situation was even more "sensitive."† At that point,

---

*It seems U.S. delegates successfully argued that whatever was being done to poor blacks was being done to them as an economic aggregate rather than as a racial group. Hence, the victims were not subject to protection under the Genocide Convention—thanks to the *quid pro quo* these same delegates had effected with the Soviets during the ad hoc committee process in 1947—and any review of petitions in their behalf claiming otherwise would be "inappropriate." Meanwhile, right-wing senators and expert witnesses like the ABA's Alfred Schweppe were busily rejecting the convention, partly because political and economic aggregates hadn't been retained among the protected groups, thereby "letting the Communists off the hook" for the genocidal aspects of Stalinist and Maoist collectivization policies; *Hearings on the Genocide Convention (1950), op. cit.*; *Hearings on the Genocide Convention (1971), op. cit.*

†Robert Weisbord considered the question at about this time and produced his findings in a book, *Genocide? Birth Control and the Black American* (Westport, CT: Greenwood Press, 1975). Only by resorting to Dean Rusk's bogus contention that it is necessary to demonstrate intent to destroy an *entire* group in order to predicate charges of genocide was Weisbord able to state that from "the evidence available it is fair to conclude that...sterilization [has] never been used to systematically exterminate black Americans," and that there has therefore "never been a genocidal master plan" (p. 178). Had he instead followed the language of the law—and the interpretations of everyone from

the government was not only continuing its "birth control efforts" with regard to poor blacks, it had secretly launched similar programs targeting American Indians and Puerto Ricans which eventually resulted in upwards of 30 percent of the women of childbearing age in each group undergoing involuntary—and in many instances completely unwitting—sterilization.* The only question in this regard which seemed to concern Idaho's liberal Senator Frank Church during testimony provided by Assistant Attorney General (and future Chief Justice of the Supreme Court) William Rehnquist in hearings conducted the same year, was whether responsible officials could be "safeguarded" from meaningful prosecution, perchance charges were ever brought against them under the Genocide Convention.

> *Church*: Another extreme criticism leveled at the Convention is that it would make birth control efforts among the poor blacks an act of genocide. How would you answer this allegation?
>
> *Rehnquist*: I think that any birth control effort that might reasonably be contemplated in this country would certainly be a voluntary one, and would likewise be directed towards all individuals rather than any particular race. I think it inconceivable that any sort of birth control effort that would ever receive public approval in this country would violate the provisions of this treaty.

Raphaël Lemkin to Alfred Schweppe—that intent to destroy any part of a group was sufficient for purposes of predication, Weisbord's conclusions would necessarily have been different. As it was, he was forced to concede that there was plenty in the "historical record and in contemporary societal developments to sustain black fears of such a plan" (ibid.). He also noted that not only had radical groups like the Black Panther Party and Nation of Islam responded to the data on involuntary sterilization of Afroamerican women by labeling it genocidal, but that even such relatively staid organizations as the Urban League had expressed the belief that such practices "opened the way" to genocide (pp. 170, 178).

* As concerns American Indian women, it was determined in 1976 that up to 42 percent were involuntarily sterilized in clinics run by the Indian Health Service, a component of the Interior Department's Bureau of Indian Affairs, between 1970 and 1975. In perhaps a quarter of these cases, the women had not only not consented, they had never been informed that a sterilization had been performed; Brint Dillingham, "Indian Women and IHS Sterilization Practices," *American Indian Journal*, Vol. 3, No. 1, Jan. 1977; Janet Larsen, "And Then There Were None," *Christian Century*, Jan. 26, 1977; Women of All Red Nations, *American Indian Women* (New York: International Indian Treaty Council, 1978); Robin Jarrell, "Women and Children First: The Forced Sterilization of American Indian Women" (undergraduate thesis, Wellesley College, 1978). With respect to Puertorriqueñas, the data were one-third of the women of childbearing age on the island of Puerto Rico, 44 percent of the same target population in New Haven and 51 percent in Hartford, Connecticut; Committee for Abortion Rights and Against Sterilization Abuse, *Women Under Attack: Abortion, Sterilization Abuse, and Reproductive Freedom* (New York: CARASA, 1979); Margarita Ostalaza, *Política Sexual y Socialización Política de la Mujer Puertorriqueña la Consolidación del Bloque Histórico Colonial de Puerto Rico* (Río Piedras, PR: Ediciones Huracán, 1989).

Church: Is it true that if any such effort were to be made, based upon some compulsory method and directed toward some particular group, that the protections of the Constitution would be fully applicable whether or not the United States had ratified and become party to the Genocide Convention?

Rehnquist: Certainly.[49]

Other aspects of U.S. domestic policy were coming into similar focus at about the same time. There were, for instance, potential ramifications to the maintenance of the apartheid structure of Jim Crow segregation throughout much of the nation for more than a hundred years.[50] As ABA representative Eberhard Deutsch put it in his testimony before the subcommittee in 1971, such a systematic pattern of statutory racial discrimination could, at least in part, be seen as a violation of even the most rigorous interpretation of the Convention's injunction against visiting mental harm upon members of a target group.

> In *Brown v. Board of Education,* the leading desegregation case...the Supreme Court of the United States...held expressly that separation of Negro children...from others of similar age and qualifications solely because of their race, generates a feeling of inferiority as to their status in the community that affects their hearts and minds in a way unlikely ever to be undone...and has a tendency to retard their education and mental development... In light of this holding by the Supreme Court, such an understanding as this committee has proposed...that mental harm is to be construed "to mean permanent impairment of mental faculties," would hardly deter any tribunal from determining that any form of local segregation is within the definition of the international crime of genocide under the Convention.[51]

At no point during the subcommission's hearings was there serious discussion of the implications of the Convention's prohibition against the forced transfer of children in light of U.S. policy.[52] The reasons for this are readily apparent. To have done so would have been to expose the entire system of compulsory boarding schools long imposed by the government upon American Indians to the kind of scrutiny it could ill afford.* Any such atten-

---

*There can be no question that the likelihood of such policies falling within the meaning of the Convention was understood, but never raised in the Senate. Consider the following question posed by the Canadian Civil Liberties Union during debates on enabling legislation in that country's parliament—closely monitored by the United States—pursuant to Canada's ratification of the instrument on May 21, 1952: "Could it be argued that...proposals to impose integrated education upon the children of...Indians for example, might fall within this prohibition? The risk contained in this sub-section is that a court might be persuaded that...to transfer children in such a way is intended to 'destroy' a culture, i.e., a group"; quoted in Davis and Zannis, *Genocide Machine, op. cit.*, p. 23. On the native boarding school system in Canada, see J.R. Miller, *Shingwauk's Vision: A History of Native Residential Schools* (Toronto: University of Toronto Press, 1996).

tion to Indian affairs would, moreover, all but inevitably raise the specter of the extermination campaigns waged against America's indigenous peoples in previous centuries.[53] From there, discussion would have led unerringly into the very sphere of consideration the United States had sought to evade when it arranged for deletion of the third article of the Secretariat's Draft: the broad range of culturally genocidal practices through which the Indians' final extinction was still being relentlessly pursued as a matter of policy.* Rather, these genies were left in their bottles altogether, and the subjects of Indians and Indian policy never came up.[54]

Be that as it may, it is unquestionably a matter of record that it was with full knowledge that many of its own undertakings and positions were genocidal by legal definition—and with the stated intention of maintaining its own imagined "sovereign discretion" to continue in exactly the same vein— that the Senate of the United States, cheered on by the country's most representative body of jurists and attorneys, openly rejected the Genocide Convention for fully two generations. By no conceivable definition can it be said that a worse performance on comparable matters was evidenced by Germany's legislators, barristers, and judiciary during the 1930s. Yet the latter were reviled, appropriately enough, as vulgar criminals.[55]

Nonratification, Round Two

During the second half of the 1960s, as the United States mounted an intensifying war of attrition to "contain the spread of communism" in Southeast Asia, a tribunal was convened in Copenhagen to assess America's military and political postures in the region under standards of international legality. Sponsored by British philosopher Bertrand Russell and presided over by the equally eminent French thinker Jean Paul Sartre, the tribunal received

---

*In addition, it might have opened up fresh questions concerning the "Crimes Against the Peace" and "Waging of Aggressive Wars"—to borrow the vernacular employed against the nazis at Nuremberg— by which the United States had expanded from its original narrow band of thirteen states huddled along the Eastern seaboard to its continental proportions. This conceptual/practical linkage between U.S. and nazi postures was hardly unknown—indeed, Adolf Hitler himself had remarked upon it in *Mein Kampf* and elsewhere—and had given birth to the so-called "Indian Claims Commission" on August 13, 1946, a largely cosmetic expedient through which the United States was attempting to distance its image from that of its German counterpart. See Adolf Hitler, *Mein Kampf* (Boston: Houghton-Mifflin, 1962 reprint of 1925 original) pp. 638–44. Also see *Hitler's Secret Book* (New York: Grove Press, 1961) and *Hitler's Secret Conversations* (New York: Signet, 1961). For an overview of the Claims Commission, see Public Land Law Review Commission, *One Third of the Nation's Land* (Washington, D.C.: U.S. Department of the Interior, 1970).

voluminous written evidence, both documentary and scientific, as well as considerable direct testimony over several months.[56] In its findings, advanced in December 1967, the "Russell Tribunal" held that American policies in Indochina violated every element of law enunciated in the Nuremberg Charter, most especially those involving the planning and waging of aggressive war and all manner of crimes against humanity, including genocide.[57] In addition, it was found that numerous U.S. military practices—e.g., the massive use of chemical agents as well as napalm and other incendiary ordnance against civilian targets—violated specific articles of the Geneva Conventions on the Laws of War.[58]

Although the tribunal possessed no enforcement authority, the very prestige of its members, the thoroughness with which they had amassed their evidence, and the eloquent precision with which they delivered their findings did much to undermine the general consensus through which the war was being pursued.[59] In short order, many in the American legal establishment, including even Telford Taylor, Chief U.S. Counsel at Nuremberg, were expressing extraordinary misgivings about the nature and effects of America's martial onslaught.[60] With his capacity to continue the war rapidly eroding, U.S. President Lyndon B. Johnson effectively resigned his office. Beginning in 1969, his replacement, Richard M. Nixon, launched a concerted effort to reverse the appearance—though not necessarily the reality—of illegality in the conduct of America's foreign affairs.* One of the initiatives undertaken to this end was, in 1970, resubmission of the Genocide Convention to the Senate for ratification.[61]

On the face of it, Nixon, whose rightist bona fides were impeccable— he had been a prime mover in the anticommunist purges of the 1940s and '50s, and had once advocated using tactical nuclear weapons to shore up French colonialism in Indochina—should have had all the standing necessary to sell the instrument to those of his ideological stripe.[62] When it came to what amounted to little more than cosmetic acceptance of the most rudi-

---

*Nixon rode into office in no small part on the back of his claim to having a "secret plan to end the war quickly and honorably." His "secret" turned out to be a willingness to greatly intensify aerial bombardment and expand the theater of operations while transferring much of the load of ground fighting onto the backs of South Vietnamese conscripts. American casualty rates thus declined while the numbers of Asian dead rose astronomically; Col. Dewey Waddell and Maj. Norm Wood, *Air War—Vietnam* (New York: Arno Press, 1978); William Shawcross, *Sideshow: Kissinger, Nixon and the Destruction of Cambodia* (New York: Simon & Schuster, 1979); Keith Wilson Nolan, *Into Laos: The Story of Dewey Canyon II/Lam Son 719* (Novato, CA: Presidio Press, 1986).

mentary requirements of international law, however, he proved as unequal to the task as had Harry Truman in 1951. In effect, Nixon's reintroduction of the Genocide Convention simply reopened all the stale arguments which had been raised against it twenty years earlier.[63]

Indeed, Senator John Bricker, long retired, galvanized the opposition with a vociferous letter of protest at Nixon's having "resurrected" the issue at all.* The new champion of Brickerism was Sam Ervin, Jr., a conservative South Carolina Democrat, who picked up his predecessor's "state's rights" theme with a vengeance, arguing that compliance with international legal standards would have the "intolerable" effect of requiring the federal government to constrain the various states—such as his own—from conducting themselves in a manner contrary to international law.

> If the Senate should ratify the Genocide Convention, [Article VI of the U.S. Constitution] would automatically make the Convention the law of the land...and impose upon the United States the obligation to take whatever steps are necessary to make its...provisions effective. This means that the provisions of the Genocide Convention would immediately supersede all State laws and practices inconsistent with them, and would nullify all provisions of all acts of Congress and prior treaties of the United States inconsistent with them.†

The ABA's Eberhard Deutsch also reentered the fray, warning that ratification would imply the precedence of Nuremberg-style international

---

*Bricker contended, probably accurately, that he had been promised by President Dwight D. Eisenhower in 1953 that—in exchange for the senator's not forging ahead with his proposed campaign to pass a constitutional amendment stripping the federal executive of most of its treaty-negotiating authority—the Genocide Convention and comparable international human rights instruments would not be pushed by the White House. He professed considerable outrage that Nixon, who had been Eisenhower's vice president, had violated the agreement after entering the Oval Office; *Hearings on the Genocide Convention (1971), op. cit.*, p. 139. As it turns out, Eisenhower may have had certain rather more personal motives than political science in reaching this accommodation. It appears that, while serving as overall commander of Allied forces in Europe at the end of World War II, he was guilty of precisely the sorts of war crimes for which the nazi defendants were convicted at Nuremberg, albeit on a smaller scale; James Bacque, *Other Losses: The Shocking Truth Behind the Mass Deaths of Disarmed German Soldiers and Civilians Under General Eisenhower's Command* (New York: Prima, 1991). The same pertains to former inmates at Auschwitz and other camps in Poland; John Sack, *An Eye for an Eye: The Untold Story of Jewish Revenge Against Germans in 1945* (New York: Basic Books, [2nd ed.] 1994).

† *Hearings on the Genocide Convention (1970), op. cit.*, p. 196. Ervin professed to be particularly concerned over the implications of a particular case, *Sei Fujii v. California* (217 P.2d 481 (1950)), in which a state court had ruled that the California Alien Land Law was invalid since it conflicted with provisions of the U.N. Charter. This lower court decision was overturned by the California Supreme Court—which invalidated the Alien Land Law on other grounds—but, as has been observed elsewhere, "there was no guarantee that other state or federal courts [wouldn't] strike down other discriminatory state legislation and practices" on the basis of the primacy of international law; Francis A. Boyle, *Defending Civil Resistance Under International Law* (Dobbs Ferry, NY: Transnational, 1987) p. 304.

courts over the U.S. domestic system in the event that the latter failed to impose the rule of law in a meaningful way.[64] This was no abstract threat at a time when the wholesale massacre of Vietnamese civilians at the hamlet of Son My (My Lai 4) by an army unit had been sensationally documented and every official effort was being bent to exonerate the higher-ranking officers responsible.* Equally problematic, Lt. Colonel Anthony Herbert, the most decorated veteran of the Korean War, had come forward with direct evidence of a pervasive pattern of covering up similar atrocities by the military's mid-to-upper echelons.† Worst of all, Daniel Ellsberg, a senior intelligence analyst employed by the Rand Corporation, opted to leak a mass of top-secret government documents verifying many of the conclusions reached by the Russell Tribunal.‡

It was rapidly becoming obvious to anyone paying attention that, by the standards set at Nuremberg, many in the American governmental, corporate, and military leadership belonged in prison cells—or on the gallows—rather than in positions of power.[65] Under such circumstances, there was simply no possibility that these same leaders were going to tie themselves, even symbolically, to any code of legality which led to such

---

* The mass murder of 128 defenseless civilians at Son My occurred on March 16, 1968. It was perpetrated by C Company, 1st Battalion, 11th Brigade, 20th Infantry (Americal) Division. Although solid evidence indicated that the slaughter was approved and covered up at levels at least as high as the brigade commander Colonel Oran B. Henderson—and probably higher—only the company commander, Lt. William Calley, and his immediate superior, Captain Ernest Medina, were tried. Medina was acquitted by a military court after a lackluster prosecution. Calley alone was convicted, but shortly pardoned by President Nixon; Seymour M. Hersh, *My Lai 4: A Report on the Massacre and Its Aftermath* (New York: Random House, 1970); Joseph Goldstein, Burke Marshall, and Jack Schwartz, *The My Lai Massacre and Cover-Up: Beyond the Reach of the Law?* (New York: Free Press, 1976).

† Herbert was reputedly a "super-soldier," an officer whose portrait adorned the cover of the army's Ranger Manual for more than a decade. His credibility with the military should thus have been sterling. Rather than following up on his firsthand accounts of the systematic perpetration of war crimes in Vietnam, however, the army relieved him of his command, isolated him, and forced him into early retirement; Anthony B. Herbert with James T. Wooten, *Soldier* (New York: Holt, Rinehart & Winston, 1973). Herbert was by no means the first or only soldier of conscience to undergo such an experience; see, e.g., Donald Duncan, *The New Legions* (New York: Random House, 1967).

‡ Again the response of the government was to try and suppress the information, and to prosecute Ellsberg for having made it public. No effort whatsoever was made to bring to justice those officials and military leaders who had violated international law (not to mention the U.S. Constitution and an array of domestic statutes); Sanford J. Ungar, *The Papers & The Papers: An Account of the Legal and Political Battle Over the Pentagon Papers* (New York: E.P. Dutton, 1972). For the best selection of the documents released by Ellsberg, see Senator Mike Gavel, *The Pentagon Papers: The Defense Department History of United States Decisionmaking on Vietnam*, 4 vols. (Boston: Beacon Press, 1971). For insight into Ellsberg's motives in going public, see Daniel Ellsberg, *Papers on the War* (New York: Simon & Schuster, 1972).

conclusions.* This became all the more true with the final "communist" victories over U.S. client regimes throughout Indochina in 1975, attended by a marked (if temporary) decline in America's global dominance and a corresponding period of relative insecurity among the country's domestic elites.[66]

For the next decade, the radical Right—spearheaded by the John Birch Society, Phyllis Shlafly's Eagle Forum, and the Liberty Lobby, a neonazi organization headed by Willis Carto—mounted a major campaign to discredit the Convention. In this, such groups were regularly assisted by North Carolina's Jesse Helms—who went so far as to introduce the literature of outright Holocaust denial into Foreign Relations subcommittee records in his efforts to prevent ratification—and other paleoconservatives in the Senate.[67] Throughout the period, with the exception of those advanced by Wisconsin Senator William Proxmire (who spoke in favor of the Convention during every session of Congress from 1967 onward),[68] liberal arguments to counter such propaganda, when they occurred at all, were highly inconsistent and never more than lukewarm.[69]

"Ratification"

It was not until 1985, after the first signs of significant deterioration in the Soviet system signaled the potential for a decisive and potentially permanent shift in global power back to the United States, that a genuine senatorial interest in ratifying the Genocide Convention finally emerged.[70] By then, the Reagan administration had restored a certain "luster and authority" to America's martial image through the conquest of tiny Grenada, endorsement of Israel's invasion and partial occupation of neighboring Lebanon, support for Iraq's bloody attritional contest with Iran, initiation of a pair of substantial low-intensity wars in Nicaragua and El Salvador, and the repeated provocation of lopsided aerial combat over Libya's Gulf of Sidra, among numerous

---

*Indeed, considerable energy was devoted during the period to neutralizing the potential culpability of officials for gross violation of U.S. law. This came mainly through the much-touted congressional "investigative hearings," convened in 1975, after increasingly blatant transgressions by police and intelligence agencies had become too obvious to be concealed. While an incredible panorama of criminal activity was catalogued—everything from assassinations and attempted assassinations of foreign leaders by the CIA, to the overthrow of several governments, to thousands of warrantless wiretaps and burglaries of the homes and offices of U.S. citizens by the FBI, to habitual false arrests and imprisonments of political dissidents, and on and on—the key outcome was that *no one went to jail*. Instead, having engaged in a spectacularly painless ritual *mea culpa*, officialdom was able to peddle the bill of goods that it had thus "fixed itself" and that nothing more than fresh sets of operational guidelines were required as a "penalty" for offending agents and agencies; David Wise, *The American Police State: The Government Against the People* (New York: Random House, 1976).

other things.[71] Moreover, the administration was in the process of repudiating the jurisdiction of the World Court to require U.S. adherence to even those relatively few standards of international legality it had formally embraced.*

Given that these developments dictated an increasing "unenforcability" of the Convention against the United States (to quote Reagan), it was decided that the time was finally ripe for America to reap whatever propaganda benefits might accrue from the "humanitarian gesture" of signing on to what had long since become customary law.[72] It was also discerned by more perceptive officials that, with the United States effectively self-exempted from abiding by provisions of this or any other element of international legality it might find inconvenient, endorsement of the relevant instruments might serve to forge useful new weapons for concrete rather than rhetorical utilization against America's enemies on certain occasions.† A team of leading senatorial conservatives—Indiana's Richard Lugar, Orrin Hatch of Utah, and Jesse Helms—were therefore assembled to sell ratification to the Right.‡

---

*The action—renouncing America's voluntary 1946 acceptance of jurisdiction by the International Court of Justice (ICJ or "World Court")—was taken in response to the ICJ's October 1985 decision in the *Nicaragua v. United States* case, finding the covert U.S. war against the former country to be in violation of international law; "U.S. Terminates Acceptance of ICJ Compulsory Jurisdiction," *Department of State Bulletin,* No. 86, Jan. 1986. As has been observed elsewhere, the case derived from an effort by "Nicaragua to use the peaceful means required by international law in response to U.S. terrorist attack. Nicaragua went to the World Court; the U.S. reacted by withdrawing its acceptance of ICJ jurisdiction. When the Court nonetheless issued a judgment, the U.S. simply dismissed it. Nicaragua then turned to the U.N. Security Council, which passed a resolution calling upon all states to obey international law (11–1, three abstentions; blocked by U.S. veto). Nicaragua tried the General Assembly, where the U.S. again vetoed resolutions in two successive years, once joined by Israel and El Salvador, the second time by Israel alone; a negative U.S. vote amounts to a veto… It would be misleading to say that the World Court was ignored. The Court called upon the U.S. to terminate its 'unlawful use of force' against Nicaragua—[a] war crime—and its illegal economic warfare, and to pay substantial reparations, also explicitly determining that all assistance to the U.S.-run terrorist forces attacking the country is 'military aid,' not 'humanitarian aid'. There was an immediate response. Congress sharply increased military aid to the terrorist forces. The press and intellectual opinion—including well-known advocates of world order and international law—condemned the Court for discrediting itself by issuing its judgment, the essential contents of which were never reported"; Noam Chomsky, *Powers and Prospects: Reflections on Human Nature and the Social Order* (Boston: South End Press, 1996) p. 206; also see LaBlanc, *U.S. and the Genocide Convention, op. cit.* pp. 228–9.

†After the squalid American performance in *Nicaragua v. United States,* enthusiastically endorsed as it was by the *New York Times,* the "newspaper of record" now has the audacity to editorialize (Oct. 28, 1996) on the "urgent need" for "An Effective Global Court" to mete out "justice" to anyone "disorderly" enough to oppose U.S. domination of the planet.

‡The three were apparently selected for this task, not simply on the basis of the their individual credibility with various sectors of the Right, but because each had been prominent in opposing ratification on one or another grounds. Lugar and Hatch also chaired key bodies, the Foreign Affairs Committee and the Subcommittee on the Constitution of the Committee on the Judiciary, respectively; Ben Whitaker, *Revised and Updated Report on the Punishment and Prevention of the Crime of Genocide,* U.N. Doc. E/CN.4/Sub.2/1985/6, pp. 42–4.

Together, the three crafted what they described as a "Sovereignty Package" containing two "reservations" and five "understandings" upon which U.S. "acceptance" of the Genocide Convention would be conditioned. These "clarifications" served to preclude any possibility that its provisions might actually be applied to America by reaffirming U.S. repudiation of the jurisdiction of international courts, asserting the primacy of the United States Constitution over international law (thus assuring American citizens of the "right" to engage in precisely the same activities for which the Nuremberg Tribunal had hanged Julius Streicher), rejecting extradition of U.S. nationals for violation of the Convention (rather than the U.S. "interpretation" of it), and specifically absolving the effects of discriminatory domestic policies and external military actions from being classified as genocidal other than in cases where genocide was a stated intent.* As the package read in its final form:

Resolution of Ratification
(Lugar-Helms-Hatch Sovereignty Package)
Adopted February 19, 1986

Resolved (two-thirds of the Senators present concurring therein), That the Senate advise and consent to the ratification of the International Convention on the Prevention and Punishment of the Crime of Genocide, adopted unanimously by the General Assembly of the United Nations in Paris on December 9, 1948 (Executive O, Eighty-first Congress, first session), *Provided that :*

I.   The Senate's advise and consent is subject to the following reservations:
    (1)   That with reference to Article IX of the Convention, before any dispute to which the United States is a party may be submitted to the International Court of Justice under this article, the specific consent of the United States is required in each case.
    (2)   That nothing in the Convention requires or authorizes legislation or other action by the United States prohibited by the Constitution of the United States as interpreted by the United States.

II.   The Senate's advise and consent is subject to the following understandings, which shall apply to the obligations of the United States under this Convention:
    (1)   That the term "intent to destroy, in whole or in part, a national, ethnical, racial, or religious group as such" appearing in Article II means the

---

*As further indication that the United States waited until the global balance of power shifted emphatically in its favor, thus effectively precluding the possibility that the Genocide Convention might be enforced against it, before ratifying the instrument, it should be noted that all the ingredients that eventually went into the Lugar-Helms-Hatch package had been placed on the table at least as early as 1971; *Hearings on the Genocide Convention (1971), op. cit.*

specific intent to destroy, in whole or in *substantial* part, a national, ethnical, racial, or religious group as such by the acts specified in Article II (emphasis added).

(2) That the term "mental harm" in Article II(b) means the permanent impairment of mental faculties through drugs, torture, or similar measures.

(3) That the pledge to grant extradition in accordance with a state's laws and treaties in force found in Article VII extends only to acts which are criminal under the laws of both the requesting and requested state and nothing in Article VII affects the right of any state to bring trial before its own tribunals any of its nationals for acts committed outside a state.

(4) That acts in the course of armed conflicts committed without the *specific* intent required by Article II are not sufficient to constitute genocide as defined by the Convention (emphasis added).

(5) That with regard to the reference to an international tribunal in Article VI of the Convention, the United States declares that it reserves the right to effect its participation in any such tribunal only by a treaty entered into specifically for that purpose with the advise and consent of the Senate.

III. The Senate's advise and consent is subject to the following declaration: That the President will not deposit the instrument of ratification until after the implementing legislation referred to in Article V has been enacted.[*]

With the force and implications of the instrument thus thoroughly negated, this "ratification" was affirmed by congressional passage of the Genocide Convention Implementation Act—also called the "Proxmire Act," a rather ironic reference to the senator who had been most prominent in advocating adoption of the law in its undiluted form—in October 1988.[73] The resulting documents, including the Lugar-Helms-Hatch package, were deposited by the Reagan administration with the United Nations a month later.[74] The Convention, in its congressionally approved form, became "binding" upon the United States in February 1989.

Long before the process was completed, however, some senators, like

---

[*]U.S. Senate, *Senate Executive Report No. 2* (Washington, D.C.: 99th Cong., 1st Sess., U.S. Government Printing Office, 1985) pp. 26–7. It should be noted that at p. 23, mental harm accruing from the imposition of systematic discrimination against racial groups is specifically exempted from the American definition of genocide: "Psychological harm resulting from living conditions, differential treatment by government authorities and the like is excluded." No other country has ever tried to assert such a qualification. Similarly, no signatory has ever belabored the notion of specific intent in the manner evident in the Lugar-Helms-Hatch package. Nor has any country sought to require the destruction of a "substantial" part of a target group—whatever that means: 10 percent? one-quarter? half? three-quarters? almost all?—as a qualification of genocide (apparently for the explicit purpose of removing the onus from the arbitrary destruction of some smaller portion of the group targeted); LaBlanc, *U.S. and the Genocide Convention, op. cit.*, pp. 52–3.

Connecticut Democrat Christopher Dodd and Charles Mathias, a Maryland Republican, were warning that the U.S. claim to have ratified the Convention in this fashion would likely be rebuffed by the international community on grounds that the U.S. rejection of Article IX "would completely undermine the [law's] effectiveness."[75] Dodd and Mathias were joined by several others when they argued that the *a priori* exoneration entered with respect to military action might have equally adverse effects.

> [A] question arises as to what the United States is really trying to accomplish by attaching this understanding. The language suggests the United States has something to hide. Moreover, the relatively imprecise definition of "armed conflict" in international law is an invitation to problems and will almost certainly draw adverse comments from other nations trying to figure out what the language is intended to do. To call attention to our fears of being brought to account for acts committed in armed conflicts is really an embarrassment to the United States and should have no place in our ratification of the Genocide Convention.[76]

As analyst Lawrence J. LaBlanc has observed, "There is much to commend this viewpoint, though it could be carried further... [Other] provisions—for example, the understandings regarding intent and the meaning of mental harm—seem to carve out exceptions for the United States... [They] could be understood by other parties as being reservations that are incompatible with the object and purpose of the Convention. The considerations that gave rise to these understandings—mainly domestic racial considerations—lend credibility to the viewpoint of those who object."[77]

LaBlanc's assessment is borne out in the fact that, by December 1989, nine European countries—Denmark, Finland, Ireland, Italy, the Netherlands, Norway, Spain, Sweden, and the United Kingdom—had entered formal objections to the "constitutional provision" of the U.S. Sovereignty Package with the U.N. Secretariat, describing it as a violation of international treaty law.[78] The United Kingdom and the Netherlands, joined by Australia, also objected to America's repudiation of World Court jurisdiction.[79] The Netherlands flatly declined to recognize U.S. ratification of the Convention as being valid until such time as these "problems" are corrected.[80] The other objecting governments were not so explicit in this regard, although the legal and diplomatic implications of their filing of objections is the same.[81] Hence, all pretensions to the contrary not withstanding, the United States remains—quite conspicuously—an outlaw state.

Costs and Consequences

The costs and consequences of a half-century of U.S. prevarication, obfuscation, and obstruction concerning the Genocide Convention have been numerous and substantial. For starters, the American initiative in excluding the entire criteria of cultural genocide from the 1948 legal definition has so confused the matter that both academic and popular understandings of the crime itself—never especially well developed or well rooted—have degenerated to the point of synonymity with mass murder.* This has facilitated the continuation—indeed, intensification—of discriminatory policies against America's "domestic minorities" throughout the 1970s and '80s, and on into the '90s.[82] It has also masked the fact that much of what the United States has passed off as "developmental" policy in the Third World, entailing as it does the deliberate underdevelopment of the entire region and emulsification of its "backward social sectors," is not only neocolonialist in its effects but patently genocidal (in Raphaël Lemkin's sense of the term).[83]

Beyond this, the U.S. refusal to ratify even the ludicrously abbreviated conception of genocide it had itself engineered, in effect undermined any attempt to apply the Convention to prevent or punish perpetrators of the global proliferation of systematic mass murder programs which have been documented after 1945.

> [As of 1988,] Ted Gurr and Barbara Harff [had] compiled data on forty-three episodes of mass killings that have occurred since World War II. The data show that many more persons have died since the war as a result of mass killings than from natural disasters, international wars, and colonial and civil wars *combined*. As Gurr and Harff summarize the data, "On average, between 1.6 and 3.9 million unarmed civilians have died at the hands of the state in each decade since the end of World War II, compared with less than a million battle-related deaths in international wars (960,000 per decade) and civil

---

*A survey of the forty leading academic titles purporting to provide political, historical, or sociological analyses of genocide—these range from Irving Louis Horowitz's *Genocide: State Power and Mass Murder* (New Brunswick, NJ: Transaction, 1976; revised edition published under the title *Taking Lives: Genocide and State Power* in 1980) to Leo Kuper's *Genocide: Its Political Use in the Twentieth Century* (New Haven, CT: Yale University Press, 1981), from Isidor Wallimann and Michael N. Dobkowski's edited *Genocide and the Modern Age: Etiology and Case Studies of Mass Death* (Westport, CT: Greenwood, 1987) to Frank Chalk and Kurt Jonassohn's *The History and Sociology of Genocide: Analyses and Case Studies* (New Haven, CT: Yale University Press, 1990)—reveals that *all* are preoccupied with mass killing to the point of excluding consideration and discussion of the other four (nonlethal) criteria of genocidal conduct embodied in the Genocide Convention itself. Needless to say, although every one of these books pays pro forma homage to Raphaël Lemkin—the Wallimann/Dobkowski volume is even dedicated to his memory—none of them accords the least respect to his primary assertion that the essence of genocide resides *precisely* in the "cultural" sphere, i.e., the stamping of the oppressor's "national pattern" upon the oppressed, thus obliterating the national/cultural identity of the oppressed.

wars (890,000 per decade)." Five of the forty-three episodes appear to constitute pure genocides, that is, cases in which the victims appeared to have become victims because of their communal identity. In contrast, Gurr and Harff classified nineteen of the episodes as "politicides," that is, episodes in which the victims "were defined in terms of their hierarchical position or political opposition to the state and dominant group." The remainder of the episodes were classified as mixed, in which the victims were both political and communal groups, seven episodes being more like "genocides" and twelve being more like "politicides." Gurr and Harff argue that the "vast majority of the 6.8 to 16.3 million victims were ordinary people whose only 'offense' was to be on the wrong side of communal, separatist, or revolutionary conflicts."[84]

These totals are hardly complete, since they do not include about half of the more than 3 million Indochinese consumed by the near obliteration of their societies during the the 1960s and '70s in the U.S. drive to convert them into an example of the prohibitive price to be paid for Third World assertions of politicoeconomic independence. Moreover, the compilation was made too early to include the toll of lives attending the Bush administration's brutal invasion of Panama in 1989, or the subsequent and far more massive — not to mention *ongoing*—carnage involved in another American "exemplary action," the war against Iraq.* In addition, the timing of the study precluded

---

*Robert McNamara, U.S. Secretary of Defense under Presidents Kennedy and Johnson (i.e., during the initiation and buildup phases of the war in Southeast Asia), has recently estimated that the total number of Indochinese war dead came to approximately 3.2 million; Robert S. McNamara with Brian VanDeMark, *In Retrospect: The Tragedy and Lessons of Vietnam* (New York: Random House, 1995). The total death toll in Panama is unknown. U.S. officials pronounced the entire 1989 operation (dubbed "Just Cause") as having been "virtually bloodless." They neglected to mention such little details as the bodies of about 5,000 "surgically eliminated" Panamanians having been dumped in a single mass grave, covered with quick lime and bulldozed over; Independent Commission on the U.S. Invasion of Panama, *The U.S. Invasion of Panama: The Truth Behind Operation "Just Cause"* (Boston: South End Press, 1991). Stripped of all rhetoric and rationalization, the war against Iraq was waged to lend force to President Bush's statement that, with the collapse of the Soviet Union, a "New World Order" was emerging within which "what we say, goes." The country's infrastructure—water purification facilities, etc., upon which its *civilian* population depends for survival—was systematically obliterated by airstrikes, resulting in huge losses among Iraq's noncombatant population. Additionally, as many as a quarter-million Iraqi troops were needlessly slaughtered in the course of the war. This total includes thousands who were killed without being afforded an opportunity to surrender—by such expedients as using rome ploughs to bury them alive in their emplacements. As many as 150,000 more were butchered by unopposed air power along the "Highway of Death" as they tried desperately to retreat to safety; Cynthia Peters, ed., *Collateral Damage: The New World Order at Home and Abroad* (Boston: South End Press, 1992); Ramsey Clark, et al., *War Crimes: A Report on U.S. War Crimes Against Iraq* (Washington, D.C.: Maisonneuve Press, 1992). With the capacity of Iraq to militarily defend itself thus effectively neutralized, the United States then declined to consumate its conquest, explaining that it was still needed, relatively intact, to maintain a certain regional balance of power envisioned by America's global planners. In order to ensure the country complied with U.S. dictates in all respects, a limited war—including embargoes of food, medical supplies, and materials needed for infrastructural repair—has been continued through the present. The latter policy has resulted thus far in an estimated 575,000 additional deaths, mostly of children, and the toll is mounting steadily.

inclusion of a pair of recent "pure" genocides in Rwanda and Bosnia-Herzegovina, each of them claiming hundreds of thousands of lives.[85]

In *none* of the "episodes" occurring prior to 1990—encompassing processes of such magnitude as the U.S.-sponsored 1965 Indonesian extermination of perhaps a half-million "communists,"[*] to the holocausts in Burundi and Bangladesh in 1972[86]—was the Genocide Convention invoked by the United Nations.[87] Indeed, with the notable exception of the Khmer Rouge "autogenocide" in Cambodia/Kampuchea—which was showcased in the most propagandistic fashion, as a post hoc justification for U.S. aggression there—none were ever described as being genocidal by mainstream journalists and commentators.[†] It was not until the pretended U.S. ratification of the Convention had gone into effect that it became permissible for the U.N. to employ the term in serious fashion, and then only with respect to *some* perpetrators in *certain* instances.

The most salient illustrations of this concern the recent establishment of international tribunals—the first such since Nuremberg—to prosecute a few of those responsible for bloodbaths in Bosnia-Herzegovina and Rwanda on charges of genocide and other crimes.[88] While this seems at first glance to be a positive development, suggesting that the belated U.S. pretense of ratification, however illegitimate it may have been, is nonetheless serving constructive purposes, closer scrutiny reveals a rather different picture.[‡] Those slated to be hauled into the defendants' dock are composed entirely of those

---

[*]America provided crucial political, economic, and military assistance—including the training of the bulk of the officers corps—to the Indonesian army, which perpetrated the vast slaughter in the interests of the kind of "regional stability" demanded by U.S. policy; Deirdre Griswold, *The Bloodbath That Was* (New York: World View Publishers, 1975).

[†]For a classic example, see William Shawcross, *The Quality of Mercy: Cambodia, Holocaust and the Modern Conscience* (New York: Simon & Schuster, 1984). For analysis of such ideological cant, see Chomsky and Herman, *After the Cataclysm, op. cit.*, pp. 135–294. It should be noted that the genocidal Khmer Rouge, whose butchery was ultimately terminated by Vietnamese military intervention, were shortly adopted by the U.S. as an ally against Vietnam; Chomsky, *Necessary Illusions, op. cit.*, pp. 155–8. Overall, see Michael Haas, *Genocide by Proxy: Cambodian Pawn on a Superpower Chessboard* (New York: Praeger, 1991).

[‡]This is by no means to argue that the tribunals are in themselves inappropriate, or that those suspected of genocide in Africa and the Balkans should not be brought to trial. They should. The principle of equal justice before the law should, however, apply as much to this level of jurisprudence as to any other. Thus, more than a few U.S. friends—Pol Pot, for example, there being no statute of limitations on the crime of genocide—should by rights be seated right alongside the Serbian and Rwandan defendants. For that matter, there is still time to try a number of prominent American officials—from Robert McNamara to Ronald Wilson Reagan, George Herbert Walker Bush and William Jefferson Clinton—for their multitudinous war crimes and implementation of genocidal policies at home and abroad.

who are at most marginal to U.S. policy interests, and whose actions have offered the prospect of disrupting the planetary order that policy is intended to impose.*

To all appearances, the United States, now that it has finally signed on to the Convention, has embarked upon a course of "claiming moral high ground" by instigating show trials on charges of genocide against those it considers essentially irrelevant—as it will undoubtedly do against outright enemies whenever opportunity knocks—the better to immunize itself and governments it deems useful from precisely the same charge. The cynicism inherent to such posturing is nowhere more obvious—although Israel offers a readily comparable example[89]—than with respect to the continued U.S. support to the government of Indonesia, presently in the process of consolidating its blatantly genocidal conquest of East Timor.[90]

The upshot is that after a half-century of blocking implementation of the Genocide Convention, the United States has moved decisively to domesticate it, harnessing international law entirely to the needs and dictates of American policy.† Universal condemnation of the crime of genocide is thus being coopted to a point at which condemnation accrues only to genocides which, whether in form or in function, have failed to receive the sanction of the United States. Those which have not, are to be punished. Those which

---

*No clearer indication of the marginality of the players involved is possible than that offered by U.S. State Department adviser (and former Democratic Senator from Colorado) Tim Wirth when—after State Department official Peter Tarnoff admitted on April 28, 1993, that what was happening in Bosnia–Herzegovina amounted to genocide, and that the U.S. was therefore legally/morally obligated to intervene by all means necessary to stop it—he observed that such a move would be unpopular because America had "no vital interest" in the Balkans. Intervention stood to erode support for the Clinton administration among American citizens, Wirth argued, and "the survival of the fragile liberal [*sic*] coalition represented by this Presidency" was more important than putting a stop to mere genocide; Boyle, *The Bosnian People Charge Genocide, op. cit.*, p. xix. The administration's performance vis-à-vis the slaughter in Rwanda was even more lackluster. It was only after the killing had run its course in both instances, and the perpetrators selected for prosecution were safely out of power, that the administration discovered the "resolve" to "do something"; for further details, see David Rieff, *Slaughterhouse: Bosnia and the Failure of the West* (New York: Touchstone, 1995).

†American demands that the codification of elements of international law be undertaken in conformity with the provisions of the U.S. Constitution (as interpreted by the U.S. Supreme Court)—thereby converting international law into little more than a global adjunct to the federal statutory code—have become endemic. The latest example is the assertion of the U.S. Department of State that it would block a Draft Declaration of the Rights of Indigenous Peoples unless the instrument was written to such specifications. This maneuver, which would have enshrined the denial of the right to self-determination to native peoples as a matter of international as well as U.S. domestic law, precipitated a mass walkout by indigenous delegates from a meeting of the United Nations Working Group on Indigenous Populations on October 22, 1996.

have are to be reinforced, rewarded, defined as anything but what they are, even to the extent of describing them as "democratic."*

This awful parody, which promises to institutionalize genocide as an instrument of state power in ways which even the Hitlerian era did not, is indicative of America's New World Order.[91] The costs and consequences of the U.S. posture vis-à-vis the Convention—indeed, with regard to the whole question of genocide—are already staggering, and are showing signs of becoming steadily worse as we prepare to enter the new millennium. Whether or not we will be able to prevent the unprecedented proliferation of human catastrophe that now looms before us remains to be seen. But we are—every one of us—obligated to try.

---

*Witness the example of Guatemala, which has slaughtered hundreds of thousands of indigenous Mayans since a CIA-sponsored coup in 1954, all the while being described as a "democratizing country" by the U.S. State Department; Robert M. Carmack, ed., *Harvest of Violence: The Mayan Indians and the Guatemala Crisis* (Norman: University of Oklahoma Press, 1988). Another good illustration is Colombia; Javier Giraldo, S.J., *Colombia: The Genocidal Democracy* (Monroe, ME: Common Courage Press, 1996). For a broader overview, see Chomsky, *Deterring Democracy, op. cit.*; Noam Chomsky and Edward S. Herman, *The Political Economy of Human Rights, Vol. 1: The Washington Connection and Third World Fascism* (Boston: South End Press, 1979).

Notes

1. The United Nations Charter (59 Stat. 1031, T.S., No. 993, 3 Bevans 1153, 1976 Y.B.U.N. 1043) was done at San Francisco on June 26, 1945, and entered into force on October 24; Burns H. Weston, Richard A. Falk and Anthony D'Amato, *Basic Documents in International Law and World Order* (St. Paul, MN: West, 2nd. ed., 1990) p. 16.

2. Quoted in Lawrence J. LaBlanc, *The United States and the Genocide Convention* (Durham, NC: Duke University Press, 1991) p. 23. On the fact that there was no operant definition of genocide involved in the Nuremberg proceedings, see Bradley F. Smith, *Reaching Judgment at Nuremberg* (New York: Basic Books, 1977).

3. Ibid. Also see M. Lippman, "The Drafting of the 1948 Convention on the Punishment and Prevention of Genocide," *Boston University International Law Journal*, No. 3, 1984.

4. For Lemkin's original definition of genocide, see his *Axis Rule in Occupied Europe: Laws of Occupation, Analysis of Government, Proposals for Redress* (Washington, D.C.: Carnegie Endowment for International Peace, 1944) pp. 79–94. ECOSOC's request to the Secretariat was made via Resolution 47(IV), March 28, 1947.

5. U.N. Doc. A/362, June 14, 1947.

6. Nehemiah Robinson, *The Genocide Convention: A Commentary* (1960) pp. 18–9.

7. *Report of the Ad Hoc Committee on Genocide,* 3 U.N. ESCOR Supp. 6, U.N. Doc. E/794 (1948).

8. Convention on the Punishment and Prevention of Genocide (U.S.T. _____, T.I.A.S._____, 78 U.N.T.S. 277); done in New York, Dec. 9, 1948; entered into force, Jan. 12, 1951.

9. International Court of Justice, *Reports of Judgments, Advisory Opinions and Orders: Reservations to the Convention on Punishment and Prevention of the Crime of Genocide* (The Hague, 1951) pp. 15–69.

10. *Multilateral Treaties Deposited with the Secretary General: Status as of 31 December 1989,* St/Leg/Ser. E/8 97–98 (1990).

11. LaBlanc, *U.S. and the Genocide Convention, op. cit.,* p. 2.

12. Statement by President Ronald Reagan, as shown on CNN, March 11, 1981.

13. For a good sample of U.S. practice in this regard, see Noam Chomsky, *Deterring Democracy* (New York: Hill & Wang, 1992); Cynthia Peters, ed., *Collateral Damage: The "New World Order" At Home and Abroad* (Boston: South End Press, 1992).

14. Bradley F. Smith, *The Road to Nuremberg* (New York: Basic Books, 1981). The same principles were employed in prosecuting the Japanese leadership a bit later; see Arnold C. Brackman, *The Other Nuremberg: The Untold Story of the Tokyo War Crimes Trials* (New York: William Morrow, 1987).

15. Edwin Tetlow, *The United Nations: The First 25 Years* (New York: Peter Owen, 1970).

16. LaBlanc, *U.S. and the Genocide Convention, op. cit.,* pp. 26–7.

17. Quoted in Robert Davis and Mark Zannis, *The Genocide Machine in Canada: The Pacification of the North* (Montréal: Black Rose Books, 1973) p. 19.

18. 3 U.N. ESCOR, Doc. E/447–623 (1948), esp. pp. 139–47.

19. See, e.g., the Brazilian intervention; ibid., p. 143.

20. On the Soviet policies at issue, see, e.g., Nikolai Dekker and Andrei Lebed, eds., *Genocide in the U.S.S.R.: Studies in Group Destruction* (New York: Scarecrow Press, 1958); Robert Conquest, *The Nation Killers: The Soviet Deportation of Nationalities* (New York: Macmillan, 1970). The compromise was effected by Ernest Gross, U.S. delegate to ECOSOC's Sixth (Legal) Committee; 3 U.N. GAOR C.6 (49th mtg) at 407 (1948).

21. Davis and Zannis, *Genocide Machine, op. cit.,* p. 19.

22. On the Streicher prosecution, see Smith, *Reaching Judgment at Nuremberg, op. cit.,* pp. 200–3.

23. A good analysis, both of the composition of the U.S. diplomatic cadre at the U.N. and the duplicity imbedded in their agenda, is offered in Lloyd Garner's *Architects of Illusion: Men and Ideas in American Foreign Policy, 1941–49* (Chicago: Quadrangle, 1970). Also see Thomas M. Campbell, *Masquerade Peace: America's U.N. Policy, 1944–1945* (Tallahassee: Florida State University Press, 1973).

24. Although the authors usually couch things in somewhat softer terms, substantiation of this view will be found in two books edited by Daniel Bell, *The New American Right* (New York: Criterion, 1955) and *The Radical Right* (New York: Doubleday, 1964). Also see George Nash, *The Conservative Intellectual Movement in America Since 1945* (New York: Basic Books, 1975).

25. For a sample of the relevant propaganda, see Chamber of Commerce of the United States, *Communist Infiltration in the United States* (Washington, D.C.: U.S. Chamber of Commerce, 1946); Rev. John F. Cronin, *Communism: A World Menace* (Washington, D.C.: National Catholic Welfare Conference, 1947); James D. Bales, ed., *J. Edgar Hoover Speaks Concerning Communism* (Nutley, N.J.: Craig Press, 1951); Oliver Pilat, *The Atom Spies* (New York: Putnam, 1952); Joseph R. McCarthy, *McCarthyism: The Fight for America* (New York: Davis-Adair, 1952); James Burnham, *The Web of Subversion: Underground Networks in the U.S. Government* (New York: John Day, 1954); J. Edgar Hoover, *Masters of Deceit: The Story of Communism in America* (New York: Henry Holt, 1958); Albert E. Kahn, *High Treason: The Plot Against the People* (New York: Lear, 1960).

26. See, David Caute, *The Great Fear: The Anti-Communist Purge Under Truman and Eisenhower* (New York: Simon & Schuster, 1978).

27. For a topical sample of such framing, see Frank A. Warren, III, *Liberals and Communism* (Bloomington: Indiana University Press, 1946). For analysis, see E.J. Kahn, Jr., *The China Hands* (New York: Viking, 1975); David Caute, *The Fellow Travelers* (New York: Macmillan, 1973). A good study of the entity most responsible for perpetrating this hoax will be found in Ross Y. Koen, *The China Lobby in American Politics* (New York: Macmillan, 1960).

28. For texts, see Weston, Falk and D'Amato, *Basic Documents in International Law, op. cit.*; also see Ian Brownlie, ed., *Basic Documents on Human Rights* (Oxford: Clarendon Press, 3rd ed. 1992).

29. For texts, see Weston, Falk and D'Amato, *Basic Documents in International Law, op. cit.*; also see Adam Roberts and Richard Guelff, eds., *Documents on the Laws of War* (Oxford: Clarendon Press, 1984).

30. See, e.g., the remarks of Iowa Republican Bourke B. Hickenlooper during the 1950 Senate hearings: "[W]e are in effect, in this Genocide Convention [and other elements of international law] dealing with the question of a certain area of the sovereignty of the United States which amounts to a surrender of that sovereignty"; U.S. Senate, *Hearings on the Genocide Convention Before a Subcommittee of the Senate Committee on Foreign Relations* (Washington, D.C.: 81st Cong., 2d Sess., U.S. Government Printing Office, 1950) p. 36. The Supreme Court sought a way out of this bind in *Reid v. Covert* (354 U.S. 1, 1957) by holding that "any treaty provision that is inconsistent with the United States Constitution would simply be invalid under national law." Article 27 of the Vienna Convention on the Law of Treaties (U.N. Doc. A/CONF.39/27 at 289 (1969)) overrules this opinion, however, by stipulating that no party may "invoke the provisions of its internal law as justification for its failure to perform a treaty" obligation; see generally, Sir Ian Sinclair, *The Vienna Convention on the Law of Treaties* (Manchester: Manchester University Press, 2nd ed., 1984).

31. This position was actually perfectly in keeping with the formulations of German political philosophy, widely admired before the war; see, e.g., Carl Schmidt, *Political Theology: Four Chapters on the Concept of Sovereignty* (Cambridge, MA: MIT Press, 1985 trans. of 1922 original).

32. Quincy Wright, "The Law of the Nuremberg Trial," *American Journal of International Law,* No. 41, Jan. 1947. For interpretation and application, see Richard Falk, *Human Rights and State Sovereignty* (New York: Holmes & Meier, 1981).

33. Affirmation of the Principles of International Law Recognized by the Charter of the Nuremberg Tribunal, adopted by the U.N. General Assembly, Dec. 11, 1946 (U.N.G.A. Res. 95(1), U.N. Doc. A/236 (1946), at 1144); for text, see Weston, Falk and D'Amato, *Basic Documents in International Law, op. cit.*, p. 140. The Charter itself (59 Stat. 1544, 82 U.N.T.S. 279 (Sept. 10, 1945)) appears at pp. 138–9.

34. LaBlanc, *U.S. and the Genocide Convention, op. cit.*, p. 20.

35. *Hearings on the Genocide Convention (1950), op. cit.*, pp. 204–5.

36. LaBlanc, *U.S. and the Genocide Convention, op. cit.*, p. 20.

37. As the senator himself explained it, he did not wish to see "the Constitution and the Bill of Rights become a mere scrap of paper," and he felt that "subordinating" either to international law would have that effect; Natalie Hevener Kaufman and David Whiteman, "Opposition to Human Rights Treaties in the United States Senate: The Legacy of the Bricker amendment," *Human Rights Quarterly,* No. 10, 1988.

38. For a sampling of violence directed against one Asian American target group, see Charles J. McClain, *In Search of Equality: The Chinese Struggle Against Discrimination in the Nineteenth Century* (Berkeley: University of California Press, 1994) pp. 173–90.

39. *Hearings on the Genocide Convention (1950), op. cit.*, p. 205.

40. Stewart E. Tolnay and E.M. Beck, *A Festival of Violence: An Analysis of Southern Lynchings, 1882–1930* (Urbana: University of Illinois Press, 1995). p. 1.

41. For what may be the best survey of comparable prewar violence in Germany, see Raul Hilberg, *The Destruction of the European Jews,* 3 vols. (New York: Holmes & Meier, rev. ed., 1985).

42. Tolnay and Beck, *Festival of Violence, op. cit.* A more detailed examination of lynching in a given subregion will be found in W. Fitzhugh Brundage, *Lynching in the New South, 1880–1930* (Urbana: University of Illinois Press, 1993).

43. Arthur F. Raper, *The Tragedy of Lynching* (Chapel Hill: University of North Carolina Press, 1933) pp. 469–72.

44. For case studies, see James Forman, *Sammy Younge, Jr.* (New York: Grove Press, 1968); Howard Smead, *Blood Justice: The Lynching of Charles Mack Parker* (New York: Oxford University Press, 1986).

45. See, e.g., Leon Friedman, ed., *Southern Justice* (New York: Pantheon, 1965); Robert Sherrill, *Gothic Politics in the Deep South: Stars of the New Confederacy* (New York: Grossman, 1968).

46. *Hearings on the Genocide Convention (1950), op. cit.*, p. 27.

47. U.S. Senate, *Hearings on the Genocide Convention Before a Subcommittee of the Senate Committee on Foreign Relations* (Washington, D.C.: 92d Cong., 1st Sess., U.S. Government printing Office, 1971) p. 189.

48. William L. Patterson, *The Man Who Cried Genocide: An Autobiography* (New York: International, 1971).

49. U.S. Senate, *Hearings on the Genocide Convention Before a Subcommittee of the Committee on Foreign Relations* (Washington, D.C.: 91st Cong., 2d Sess., U.S. Government Printing Office, 1970) pp. 148–9.

50. See generally, C. Vann Woodward, *The Strange Career of Jim Crow* (New York: Oxford University Press, 3rd rev. ed., 1974).

51. *Hearings on the Genocide Convention (1971), op. cit.*, pp. 18–9. Deutsch was undoubtedly correct in his understanding, a matter which could have made the Convention a powerful weapon in any serious effort to abolish institutionalized racial/ethnical discrimination in the U.S. (a goal to which the ABA proclaimed itself "philosophically" committed). As with the earlier-discussed question of lynching however, it was this very potential effectiveness of the Convention in combatting systemic discrimination which seems to have prompted the ABA to oppose its ratification.

52. Indeed, the only reference to the issue devolved upon an absurd query by segregationists as to whether the busing of school children to achieve integration in educational institutions might not qualify as "genocide"; *Hearings on the Genocide Convention (1970), op. cit.*, pp. 138–9, note 11.

53. Although most of it is carefully framed in terms other than genocide, there is a vast literature on these historical processes of extermination. Two excellent works which call things by their right names are David Svaldi's *Sand Creek and the Rhetoric of Extermination: A Case Study in Indian-White Relations* (Washington, D.C.: University Press of America, 1989) and David E. Stannard's *American Holocaust: Columbus and the Conquest of the New World* (New York: Oxford University Press, 1992).

54. There is, for example, not a single reference to "American Indians" or "Native Americans" in the index of LaBlanc's reasonably thorough study.

55. See, e.g., Telford Taylor, "The Nuremberg War Crimes Trials," *International Conciliation,* No. 450, Apr. 1949; Joe Heydecker and Johannes Leeb, *The Nuremberg Trials* (London: Heinemannn, 1962).

56. John Duffett, ed., *Against the Crime of Silence: Proceedings of the International War Crimes Tribunal* (New York: Clarion, 1968).

57. Jean Paul Sartre and Arlette El Kaïm-Sartre, *On Genocide and a Summary of the Evidence and Judgments of the International War Crimes Tribunal* (Boston: Beacon Press, 1968); Ralph Stavins, Richard J. Barnet and Marcus G. Raskin, *Washington Plans an Aggressive War* (New York: Random House, 1971).

58. Bertrand Russell, *War Crimes in Vietnam* (New York: Monthly Review Press, 1967); Barry Weisberg, *Ecocide in Indochina: The Ecology of War* (San Francisco: Canfield Press, 1970); Stockholm International Peace Research Institute, *Incendiary Weapons* (Cambridge, MA: MIT Press, 1975).

59. Paul Joseph, *Cracks in the Empire: State Politics in the Vietnam War* (Boston: South End Press, 1981). It should also be noted that, after 1968, the cohesion of U.S. military units in the field began to disintegrate, a matter which undermined the viability of the war effort in a different but at least equally effective way; Richard Boyle, *Flower of the Dragon: The Breakdown of the U.S. Army in Vietnam* (San

Francisco: Ramparts Press, 1972); Cincinnatus, *Self-Destruction: The Disintegration and Decay of the United States Army During the Vietnam Era* (New York: W.W. Norton, 1981). This was in large part due to the ability of the "enemy" to sustain a very high level of combat effectiveness despite incredibly high casualty rates inflicted by the Americans; Ronald H. Spector, *After Tet: The Bloodiest Year in Vietnam* (New York: Vintage, 1993).

60. See, e.g., Richard A. Falk, ed., *The Vietnam War and International Law* (Princeton, NJ: Princeton University Press, 1970); Telford Taylor, *Nuremberg and Vietnam: An American Tragedy* (Chicago: Quadrangle, 1970); Jay W. Baird, *From Nuremberg to My Lai* (Lexington, MA: D.C. Heath, 1972); Noam Chomsky, *For Reasons of State* (New York: Pantheon, 1973)

61. Nixon's maneuver is covered well in Hevener Kaufman and Whiteman, "Opposition," *op. cit.*

62. See, e.g., William A. Reuben, *The Honorable Mr. Nixon and the Alger Hiss Case* (New York: Action Books, 1956); William Costello, *The Facts About Nixon: An Unauthorized Biography* (New York: Viking, 1960); Jerry Voorhis, *The Strange Case of Richard Milhouse Nixon* (New York: Popular Library, 1973); Anthony J. Lucas, *Nightmare: The Underside of the Nixon Years* (New York: Viking, 1976); Garry Wills, *Nixon Agonistes: The Crisis of a Self-Made Man* (New York: New American Library, 1979).

63. *Hearings on the Genocide Convention (1970), op. cit.; Hearings on the Genocide Convention (1971), op. cit.*

64. *Hearings on the Genocide Convention (1971), op. cit.*, p. 88.

65. This was actually a topic of some discussion in subcommittee proceedings for several years; LaBlanc, *U.S. and the Genocide Convention, op. cit.*, pp. 96−9.

66. Arnold J. Isaacs, *Without Honor: Defeat in Vietnam and Cambodia* (Baltimore: Johns Hopkins University Press, 1983); Noam Chomsky and Edward S. Herman, *The Political Economy of Human Rights, Vol. 2: After the Cataclysm: Postwar Indochina and the Reconstruction of Imperial Ideology* (Boston: South End Press, 1979).

67. E.g., in 1985, Helms, acting on the request of the Liberty Lobby's Trisha Katson, caused the conclusion of one of the organization's publications, a book by Holocaust denier James Martin entitled *The Man Who Invented "Genocide": The Public Career and Consequences of Raphaël Lemkin*, to be printed in the record of subcommittee proceedings; U.S. Senate, *Hearings on the Genocide Convention Before a Subcommittee of the Committee on Foreign Relations* (Washington, D.C.: 99th Cong., 1st Sess., U.S. Government Printing Office, 1985) pp. 132−46.

68. Senator William Proxmire, Senate Floor Debate, Feb. 1986; quoted in LaBlanc, *U.S. and the Genocide Convention, op. cit.*, p. 1.

69. Hearings were conducted on the Convention by the Senate Foreign Relations Committee and/or its subcommittees in 1970, 1971, and 1977, with favorable reports being submitted to the full body in 1970, 1971, 1973, and 1976. Full Senate debate of the matter was attempted only once during this period, however, in 1973–74, and was blocked by a Sam Ervin filibuster; LaBlanc, *U.S. and the Genocide Convention, op. cit.*, p. 6.

70. This followed Reagan's sudden endorsement of the Convention in a speech to the B'nai B'rith during his 1984 reelection campaign. The possibility of ratification was foreclosed that year through a filibuster by Jesse Helms; ibid., pp. 142, 6.

71. As the editors of the *Wall Street Journal* were to put it on January 19, 1989, Reagan "restored the efficiency and morale of the armed forces [and] demonstrated the will to use force in Grenada and Libya." For a thoroughly glorified account of the first of these travesties, see Major Mark Adkin, *Urgent Fury: The Battle for Grenada* (Lexington, MA: D.C. Heath, 1989). On the bloodbath in Lebanon, see Noam Chomsky, *The Fateful Triangle: The U.S., Israel and the Palestinians* (Boston: South End Press, 1983). On U.S. support to Iraq, see Rabab Hadi, "The Gulf Crisis: How We Got There," in Greg Bates, ed., *Mobilizing Democracy: Changing the U.S. Role in the Middle East* (Monroe, ME: Common Courage Press, 1991). On Nicaragua and El Salvador, see Holly Sklar, *Washington's War on Nicaragua* (Boston: South End Press, 1988). On Libya, see Jonathan Bearman, *Qadhafi's Libya* (London: Zed Books, 1986); Noam Chomsky, *Pirates and Emperors: International Terrorism in the Real World* (New York: Claremont, 1986) pp. 138−46. More broadly, see Michael T. Klare, *Beyond the "Vietnam Syndrome": U.S. Interventionism in the 1980s* (Washington, D.C.: Institute for Policy Studies, 1981); Michael T. Klare and Peter Kornbluh, eds., *Low Intensity Warfare: Counterinsurgency, Proinsurgency and Antiterrorism in the Eighties* (New York: Pantheon, 1989); Chomsky,

Deterring Democracy, op. cit.

72. As Reagan described the situation, for the United States, the Convention had been reduced to a "mere symbol of opposition to genocide"; U.S. Senate, *Executive Report No. 2* (Washington, D.C.: 99th Cong., 1st Sess., 1985) p. 4.

73. The act was passed by voice vote—thus preventing a record of how many and which representatives voted for and against it—in the House on April 25, 1988; U.S. Senate, *Senate Report No. 333* (Washington, D.C.: 100th Cong., 2d Sess., U.S. Government Printing Office, 1988) pp. 1–3. The same method was adopted in the Senate on October 14; *Congressional Record,* No. 134, Oct. 14, 1988, S16107–17, S16266–9.

74. *Multilateral Treaties Deposited with the Secretary-General, op. cit.,* p. 101, n. 2.

75. *Hearings on the Genocide Convention (1985), op. cit.,* pp. 24–5.

76. Aside from Dodd and Mathias, the signatories to the statement from which the quoted passage is excerpted were Claiborne Pell (D-Rhode Island), Joseph Biden, Jr. (D-Delaware), Paul Sarbanes (D-Maryland), Alan Cranston (D-California), Thomas Eagleton (D-Missouri) and John Kerry (D-Massachusetts); *Senate Executive Report No. 2, op. cit.,* p. 32.

77. LaBlanc, *U.S. and the Genocide Convention, op. cit.,* pp. 98, 240.

78. *Multilateral Treaties Deposited with the Secretary-General, op. cit.,* pp. 102–4.

79. This result was entirely predictable, given that the same three countries had already entered objections to attempts to avoid ICJ jurisdiction by Bulgaria, Poland and Romania; U.S. Senate, *Hearing on the Genocide Convention Before the Senate Committee on Foreign Relations* (Washington, D.C.: 98th Cong., 2d. Sess., U.S. Government Printing Office, 1984) p. 63.

80. LaBlanc, *U.S. and the Genocide Convention, op. cit.,* p. 12.

81. International Court of Justice, *Reports of Judgments, Advisory Opinions and Orders: Reservations to the Convention on the Prevention and Punishment of the Crime of Genocide* (The Hague: International Court of Justice) pp. 15–69. Also see Sinclair, *Vienna Convention, op. cit.,* pp. 47–69; J. Kohn, "Reservations to Multilateral Treaties: How International Legal Doctrine Reflects World Vision," *Harvard International Law Journal,* No. 71, 1982.

82. As has been demonstrated clearly, the socioeconomic situation of African Americans suffered a marked and policy-driven deterioration from the late 1960s to the early 1980s, with all the adverse physical and psychological effects such a circumstance implies; Manning Marabel, *Race, Rebellion and Reform: The Second Reconstruction in Black America, 1945–1982* (Jackson: University of Mississippi Press, 1984) pp. 168–77. This negative trend was not only continued but accelerated during from 1982–92; Andrew Hacker, *Two Nations: Black and White, Separate and Unequal* (New York: Ballantine, 1992). Much the same data profile pertains to American Indians; see my *Struggle for the Land: Indigenous Resistance to Genocide, Ecocide and Expropriation in Contemporary North America* (Monroe, ME: Common Courage Press, 1992). The same may be said of Latinos and at least some segments of the Asian American population; see, overall, Leslie W. Dunbar, ed., *Minority Report: What Has Happened to Blacks, Hispanics, American Indians and Other Minorities in the Eighties* (New York: Pantheon, 1984); Martin Carnoy, *Faded Dreams: The Politics and Economics of Race in America* (Cambridge, MA: Cambridge University Press, 1994).

83. On the term "neocolonialism," see Kwame Nkrumah, *Neo-Colonialism: The Last Stage of Imperialism* (New York: International, 1965); Jack Woddis, *Introduction to Neo-Colonialism* (New York: International, 1967). On "underdevelopment," see Andre Gunder Frank, *Lumpen-Bourgeoisie/Lumpen-Development: Dependence, Class and Politics in Latin America* (New York: Monthly Review, 1972); Samir Amin, *Imperialism and Unequal Development* (New York: Monthly Review, 1977), and *Maldevelopment: Anatomy of a Global Failure* (London: Zed Books, 1990); Ian Roxborough, *Theories of Underdevelopment* (New York: Macmillan, 1979). On emulsification, see, e.g., Greg Urban and Joel Sherzer, eds., *Nation-States and Indians in Latin America* (Austin: University of Texas Press, 1991).

84. LaBlanc, *U.S. and the Genocide Convention, op. cit.,* p. 84. He is quoting from Ted Gurr and Barbara Harff, "Toward an Empirical Theory of Genocides and Politicides: Identification and Measurement of Cases since 1945," *International Studies Quarterly,* No. 32, 1988.

85. See, e.g., Gérard Prunier, *The Rwanda Crisis: History of a Genocide* (New York: Columbia University Press, 1995), *War Crimes in Bosnia-Herzegovina* (New York: Human Rights Watch, 1992).

86. The respective death tolls were about three million in Bangladesh, some 100,000 in Burundi;

Kalyan Chaudhuri, *Genocide in Bangladesh* (Bombay: Orient Longman, 1972); Réné Lemarchand and David Martin, *Selective Genocide in Burundi* (London: Minority Rights Group Report No. 20, 1974).

87. E.g., the "United Nations [refused] even to discuss the case" of Bangladesh. Similarly, "the United States never publicly rebuked the Burundi government"; Chalk and Jonassohn, *History and Sociology of Genocide, op. cit.*, pp. 397, 391.

88. For examination of the groundwork upon which creation of the first of these tribunals was based, see Francis A. Boyle, *The Bosnian People Charge Genocide: Proceedings at the International Court of Justice Concerning* Bosnia v. Serbia *on the Prevention and Punishment of the Crime of Genocide* (Amherst, MA: Aletheia Press, 1996).

89. On the genocidal aspects of Israeli policies towards Palestinians, see Chomsky, *The Fateful Triangle, op. cit.*; International Organization for the Elimination of All Forms of Racism, *Zionism and Racism: Proceedings of an International Symposium* (New Brunswick, NJ: North American, 1979). For more recent analysis of the U.S. role in supporting Israel, see Edward W. Said, *The Question of Palestine* (New York: Vintage, [2nd ed., rev.] 1992); *The Pen and the Sword: Conversations with David Barsamian* (Monroe, ME: Common Courage Press, 1994).

90. John G. Taylor, *Indonesia's Forgotten War: The Hidden History of East Timor* (London: Zed Press, 1991); Constâncio Pinto, *East Timor's Unfinished Struggle: Inside the Timorese Resistance* (Boston: South End Press, 1996).

91. For further elaboration, see Noam Chomsky, *Year 501: The Conquest Continues* (Boston: South End Press, 1993) and *World Orders, Old and New* (New York: Columbia University Press, 1995).

DEFINING THE UNTHINKABLE
Towards a Viable Understanding of Genocide

> Our review of the history of genocide and its neglect has led us to the con-
> clusion that until recently scholars participated in a process of pervasive and
> self-imposed denial [with the result that no] generally accepted definition of
> genocide is available in the literature... To identify the relevant parameters is
> a first step in the prevention of future genocides.
>
> —Frank Chalk and Kurt Jonassohn
> *The History and Sociology of Genocide*

"GENOCIDE" is perhaps the least properly understood word in the world today. Although it was originally forged from a sense of urgent necessity that a name be finally put to "this most horrible of all crimes,"[1] the term and its underlying concepts have been subject to a bewildering array of misrepresentations and distortions, both unintentional and deliberate, since almost the instant of its coinage during the Second World War. Noteworthy offenders have included most nation-state governments and the international legal bodies they've created, broad nationally/culturally chauvinistic sectors of the academic and scholarly establishments in many societies, the bulk of the literary and artistic communities therein, organized religion, corporations and their lobbyists, advertising and the mass media, political opposition groups, and, as an entirely predictable result of all the rest, the public at large.

For the most part, the very notion of genocide has suffered from the imposition of such arbitrary and inconsistent sets of definitional constraints as to render it inapplicable to "real world" phenomena. Simultaneously, it has been all too frequently employed to rhetorical effect—in official or schol-arly utterances as readily as in vulgar colloquialism—so broadly as to be triv-ialized or voided of meaning altogether.* One result of such confusion has

---

*My personal favorite example of colloquial abuse came in a 1989 letter I received from Bruce Pierce, a member of the neonazi "Brüder Schweigen" and convicted triggerman in the Allen Berg murder in

been a rapid permeation during the late twentieth century of what has been termed a "genocidal mentality," quite often in quarters considering—or at least projecting—themselves as being imbued with the precise opposite.[2] Another has been that, despite a lengthening series of genocides which have occurred since 1948, when a formal convention was effected to codify certain genocidal activities as crimes under international law, no serious effort at enforcement has been undertaken, either by the United Nations or by individual signatory states.[*]

Arguably, under these conditions the physical/cultural eradication of entire human groups, or their systematic reduction to whatever extents are deemed desirable by perpetrator societies, has increasingly become not only a mode by which racial, ethnic and religious conflicts are "resolved," but a fundamental method employed by governments and attendant elites to accomplish everything from the realization of models in social engineering to attainment of political homogeneity, from adjustments at the micro level of their national economies to the tuning at the macro level of the international economy as a whole.[3] A number of analysts have suggested that such trends point towards the (re)emergence of genocide—in fact, if not in name—as a normative aspect of the human condition in the years ahead.[4]

Given the virtual impossibility that a cure can be effected for a malady so widely misunderstood, misnamed and/or misdiagnosed, even (or especially) by the figurative doctors mandated to treat it, it seems that clarification of the nature of the illness itself remains the first order of necessity in combatting it. Labeling a case of AIDS as "the flu," and prescribing aspirin to mask

---

Denver, who claimed that any bestowal of equal rights upon nonwhites in the United States would constitute "the crime of genocide against whites" insofar as it would "deliberately destroy [their] cultural heritage" of racial supremacism; copy on file. On the group in question, see Kevin Flynn and Gary Gerhardt, *The Silent Brotherhood: Inside America's Racist Underground* (New York: Free Press, 1989).

[*]The international tribunals convened to consider charges of genocide against Serbian and Rwandan officials are hopeful signs insofar as they are the first such initiatives since the trials of Axis leaders immediately following World War II. It should be noted, however, that they reveal only an intent to prosecute individuals whose positions have been in governments at or beyond the margins of global power, and, even at that, efforts to apprehend those accused have proven less than awe-inspiring. Only when it is demonstrated that officials of "more important" countries—Indonesia, for example, or India—are subject to the same rules will it be possible to say with a straight face that enforcement has gotten serious. And only when they are applied equally to officials of major states like the United States, England, and China can it be said that the law has been rendered effective. Such an assessment is not especially "radical," deriving as it does from the thought of so conservative a legal theorist as Hugo Grotius; see, e.g., R.J. Vincent, "Grotius, Human Rights and Intervention," in Hedley Bull, Benedict Kingsbury, and Adam Roberts, eds., *Hugo Grotius and International Relations* (Oxford: Clarendon, 1992) esp. 247.

a few of its symptoms, may well be a more pleasant exercise than announcing the truth for physician and patient alike, but it does nothing to facilitate controlling the disease over the long run. On the contrary, temporarily comforting denials can only serve in the end to exacerbate the problem, amplifying its lethal effects. So it is with the epidemic practice of categorizing genocidal attitudes and processes as something (anything) else and otherwise refusing acknowledgment of the pervasiveness of their existence.

For what I hope are obvious reasons then, the purpose of this essay is to make some useful contribution to reaching the degree of definitional clarity which might allow for development of a generalized and popular understanding of what genocide actually is and—by extension, at least—what it is not. It is offered in the sincere belief that only in a genuinely functional and comprehensive explication of the crime can the necessary groundwork be laid for the conceptualization and implementation of methodologies which will lead to its prevention and eventual disappearance from the long list of "odious scourges" afflicting humanity.[5]

Origins of a Concept

"The word is new," as Leo Kuper has observed, "the crime is ancient."[6] He traces the latter back at least as far as the seventh century B.C., when "many cities were razed to the ground and entire populations carried off or brutally exterminated" during the forging of the Empire of Assyria.[7] Subsequent examples which might be drawn from the history of antiquity are legion, and would certainly include the Athenian destruction of Melos [in 416 BC],[*] and Rome's "obliteration [in 150 B.C.] of Carthage, men, women and children, the site of the devastated city sown with salt, symbolic of desolation."[8] A thousand years later, much the same was going on, as is witnessed by accounts of "wolves and ravens [being] the sole living things in once populous lands" through which Mongol leader Genghis Khan had marched with his "Golden Horde."[9] And then there was Tamerlane.

---

* "When the Melians, who were descended from Spartan colonists, rejected Athens's demand for assistance in the Peloponnesian War, the Athenians laid siege, marking their victory by executing all men of the island, enslaving the women and children, and dispatching Athenian citizens (known as cleruchs) to repopulate Melos. By this brutal act of annihilation, the Athenians hoped to terrorize into submission other peoples contemplating resistance or rebellion"; Chalk and Jonassohn, *History and Sociology of Genocide, op. cit.*, p. 65. A comparable genocide, according to Homeric accounts, may have occurred between 1194 and 1184 B.C. when the city of Troy fell to combined Greek forces; Homer, *Iliad* (New York: Penguin, 1981). Overall, see Eli Sagan, *The Lust to Annihilate: A Psychoanalytic Study of Violence in Ancient Greek Culture* (New York: Psychohistory Press, 1979).

[Here was] a monster who razed Isfara'in to the ground in A.D. 1381; built 2,000 prisoners into a living mound and then bricked them over at Sabzawar in 1383; piled 5,000 heads into minarets at Zirih in the same year; cast his Luri prisoners alive over precipices in 1386; massacred 70,000 people and piled the heads into minarets at Isfahan in 1387; massacred 100,000 prisoners at Delhi in 1398; buried alive 4,000 Christian soldiers at Sivas after their capitulation in 1400; and built twenty towers of skulls in Syria in 1400 and 1401.[10]

The religiously cast wars for access to trade routes known as the "Crusades" were also replete with such butchery.[11] When Europe's Christian forces captured Jerusalem in 1099, for example, they first massacred nearly the entire Muslim population, then herded the city's Jewish inhabitants into a synagogue which was promptly torched, killing everyone trapped inside.[12] Such ferocity, indicative of the crusaders' "zeal" from start to finish, was consistently evidenced within Europe itself during the same period.[13] One example concerns the systematic extermination of "witches"—that is, the spiritual/political leadership of the subcontinent's nonchristian cultures—between 1200 and 1600.[14] Another is the so-called "Albigensian Crusades" (1208–1226), the express objective of which was to annihilate the Cathars, adherents to an "heretical" Christian doctrine in southern France, forcing all survivors to assimilate to orthodox Roman Catholicism.

When the [Cathar] city of Bélziers was stormed in A.D. 1209, the crusading army, organized at the instigation of the Pope and the monk Arnold of Cîtreaux, spared "neither dignity, nor sex nor age, nearly 20,000 human beings have perished by the sword... After the massacre the town was plundered and burnt, and the revenge of God seemed to rage upon it in a wonderful manner."[15]

This was the opening round of the Inquisition, a protracted and extraordinarily bloody process of consolidating "European culture" through imposition of Church orthodoxy (and centralized authority).[16] By 1310, it had resulted in the expungement of two more major deviant orders, the Hussites and Knights Templar.[17] Over the following two centuries, a particularly ugly process of religious extermination was also visited upon European Jews, who were confronted with the alternatives of converting to Christianity, forfeiting their property while being expelled from the subcontinent (usually to western Asia or the deserts of northern Africa), or suffering wholesale massacre.[18]

It is startling to find within Christian practice in the period of the Crusades, the Inquisition and the religious wars, all the elements in [a] major genocide of our day, that of the Nazis against the Jews. There were the laws corresponding to the Nuremberg laws, there were the distinguishing badges, the theory of a Jewish conspiracy, appointed centers of annihilation corresponding to Auschwitz, and some systematic organization, with the Dominican friars for example providing the professional expertise and bureaucratic cadres in the Inquisition.[19]

The Inquisition eventually triggered a massive revolt against papal authority known as the "Protestant Reformation" and an extended series of exterminatory campaigns intended to eradicate the insurgents and their doctrines.[20] Kuper notes that many "genocidal massacres marked the course of these conflicts, which culminated in the persecution of the Huguenots in France and the Thirty Years War in Germany. The Massacre of St. Bartholomew in 1572 and the great exodus from France following the revocation of the Edict of Nantes, stand out in the tragic history of the Huguenots. The Thirty Years War in the seventeenth century has always seemed the symbol of extreme devastation wrought by the unbridled passions of religious conflict."[21]

Long before Europe's religious wars had run their course, Portugal's initial forays along Africa's west coast (beginning in 1450) and Spain's into the Americas (from 1492 onward) set in motion an unprecedented and ongoing process of intercontinental mayhem.[22] Although the rape of the "Dark Continent" was largely confined to the burgeoning slave trade until well into the nineteenth century—absence of quinine and other prophylactic drugs to ward off malaria prevented European penetration of the African interior before that point[23]—entire civilizations were eradicated in the Western Hemisphere almost from the outset.[24] By 1800, it has been estimated that upwards of 90 percent of the "New World's" 100 million or more indigenous people had been exterminated, and the killing was continuing.[25]

Shortly thereafter, the conquest and colonization of Africa began in earnest, obtaining in some areas results quite comparable to those prevailing in the Americas by the early twentieth century.[26] Examples abound. During the so-called "Zulu War" of 1878–79, for instance, that proud people—fighting with spears against British rifles and artillery—were so thoroughly decimated that they have never fully recovered.[27] During their 1894 subjugation of the Matabele of what is present-day Zimbabwe, the British relied upon their vastly superior weaponry to inflict casualties at a rate of more than 200 to one.[28] Even worse was the brief 1898 "battle" of Omdurman, in which about 11,000 Sudanese ("Dervishes") were killed outright by British troops equipped with the latest long-range Enfield rifles and dum-dum bullets; in the aftermath, a further 16,000 wounded were slaughtered where they lay.[*]

Nor was Britain the only culprit. The French subjugation of Algeria, beginning in 1830, had been every bit as savage as anything evidenced by Fair Albion,[†] and the near-total extermination of the Hereros and Namas by the Germans in their South-West African colony (Namibia) between 1904 and 1908 surpassed even that.[‡] The English, however, probably remained the

---

[*] As was expected by the British, the Sudanese were never able to get close enough to use their own obsolete weapons. Hence, while they suffered 27,000 dead, the British lost a total of 48 men; Byron Farwell, *Queen Victoria's Little Wars* (New York: Harper & Row, 1972) pp. 335–7. Such butchery—*clearly* genocidal—made a British national hero of the commander, Lord Horatio Herbert Kitchener; E.S. Grew, *Field-Marshall Lord Kitchener, His Life and Work for the Empire*, 3 vols. (London: Gresham, 1916). As has been noted elsewhere, Kitchener's mass execution of prisoners was staunchly defended by the *Saturday Review* on September 3 and again on September 10, 1898; Sven Lindquist, *"Exterminate All the Brutes": One Man's Journey Into the Heart of Darkness and the Origins of European Genocide* (New York: The New Press, 1996) pp. 46, 174–5. Lindquist also observes at p. 52 that dum-dum bullets—so-named because they were first produced by the British Dum Dum Arsenal, near Calcutta—were specially designed to flatten out on impact, creating gaping wounds which would not heal. Prohibited for use against "civilized" combatants under the 1899 Hague Convention, they were thereafter "reserved for big game hunting and colonial wars." Lindquist might have mentioned that the standard-issue U.S. M-16 military rifle, which employs an extremely unstable small-caliber, high-velocity slug which tumbles on impact, was developed during the 1960s with a specific intent to technologically circumvent international legal prohibitions against wartime use of dum-dum ammunition. He might also have added that soft-lead hollow-point ammunition, a variation of the dum-dum, remains in standard usage by police departments throughout the United States against civilians; see my "To Serve and Protect? Police Armaments in the United States," *New Studies on the Left*, Vol. XIV, Nos. 1–2, 1989. For the text of the 1899 Hague Convention 3 Concerning Expanding Bullets, see Adam Roberts and Richard Guelff, eds., *Basic Documents on the Laws of War* (Oxford: Clarendon Press, 1981) pp. 39–42.

[†] Algiers was taken by a force of 30,000 French troops in early 1830, after they used superior firepower to obliterate a larger force of defending Berbers with relatively few losses to themselves. Thereafter, the French commander, the Duc de Rovigo, conducted himself with "unnecessary cruelty" in "true Roman style," sweeping inland across Metidja Plateau like "a destroying angel"; Thomas Campbell, *Letters from the South*, 2 vols. (London: 1837) Vol. I, pp. 316–7. Rovigo's successor in 1840, Marshal T.R. Bugeaud, was an actual "disciple of the Romans" who penned "a classic treatise on colonial warfare for later generations of French soldiers" devolving upon the use of coopted colonial subjects as troops to terrorize their kinsmen into submission by such techniques as random massacres and the impaling of the heads of the slain on bayonets; V.G. Kiernan, *European Empires from Conquest to Collapse, 1815–1960* (Leicester: Leicester University Press, 1982) p. 75. Such aggression unquestionably accounted for at least a quarter-million Algerian casualties during the first generation of French occupation, since the native population—which had been growing—declined from a little over 3 million at the outset to just under 2.8 million according to the 1870 census. Meanwhile, well over 200,000 French settlers had poured into the colony's preferred agricultural areas, thoroughly disrupting the indigenous economy and cultural patterns; Joseph Kraft, *The Struggle for Algeria* (New York: Doubleday, 1961) p. 17.

[‡] When the Hereros and allied Namas revolted against their subjugation in 1904, General Lothar von Trotha, a German officer imported especially for the task, issued an "extermination order" against them on October 2. In it, he announced as official policy his intent to kill as many as possible through employment of overwhelming military force, driving survivors en masse into the waterless Omaheke

global leaders in genocidal activities, both in terms of their overall efficiency—as when they consummated the total extinction of Tasmanians in 1876[*]—and a flair for innovation embodied in their deliberate use of alcohol to effect the dissolution of many of North America's indigenous peoples.[29] Opium was employed in the same fashion against the Chinese.[30] A willingness to rely upon chemistry rather than firepower to accomplish imperialism's more exterminatory objectives was again abundantly manifested in a 1919 recommendation by Winston Churchill to Britain's Colonial Office that order be maintained in "Mesopotamia" (Iraq) by the aerial spraying of poison gas on the Kurds and other "uncivilized tribes."[†]

Naming the Crime

By the early twentieth century, genocidal practices had become so commonplace that they were engendering serious qualms even among some of the worst perpetrator states. Hence, in 1902, "the American Secretary of State addressed to Romania a remonstrance 'in the name of humanity' against Jewish persecutions, stating that his government would not be a tacit party to such international wrongs, and in his message to Congress in 1904, the President of the United States declared, with reference to the Kishniev pogrom in Russia and the 'systematic and long-extended cruel oppression of

---

Desert in order that "the entire nation [will] perish." His instructions had been followed to the letter by the end of 1907. The results of von Trotha's "race war"—this was his term—were shown in a 1911 census revealing only 15,130 Hereros remaining alive out of an initial population exceeding 80,000 (a reduction of 80 percent in only a few years). The Namas had been reduced by more than half, from a starting population of more than 20,000 to 9,781; Chalk and Jonassohn, *History, op. cit.*, pp. 230–48. Also see Helmut Bley, *South West Africa Under German Rule, 1898–1914* (London: Heinemann, 1971); Horst Drechsler, *"Let Us Die Fighting": The Struggle of the Herero and Nama Against German Imperialism, 1884–1915* (London: Zed Press, 1980); Jon Bridgeman, *The Revolt of the Hereros* (Berkeley: University of California Press, 1981).

[*] Much is made of the fact that, after having—through a process of military campaigning and gratuitous murder by settlers—reduced the once-populous Tasmanians to 44 by 1847, the British sought to preserve the residue in a "park." This supposed absolution from allegations of genocide makes about as much sense as to suggest that, had they stopped of their own accord after slaughtering more than 6 million Jews, the World War II nazi extermination program would not have constituted genocide; James Morris, "The Final Solution, Down Under," *Horizon*, Vol. 14, No. 1, Winter 1972.

[†] Arguing that he could "not understand [any sort of] squeamishness about the use of poisoned gas" against the Kurds since it represented just one more of many such "application[s] of Western science to modern warfare [against] tribal insubordination," Churchill contended that "we cannot in any circumstances acquiesce in the non-utilization of any weapons which are available to procure a speedy termination of the disorder which prevails on the frontier" of Mesopotamia; quoted in Noam Chomsky, *Deterring Democracy* (New York: Hill & Wang, 1992) p. 182. Although gas is not known to have been used, the Royal Air Force did conduct what it termed "extensive terror bombing" against Kurdish villages between 1919 and 1924.

the Armenians', that 'there are occasional crimes committed on a vast scale and of such peculiar horror as to make us doubt whether it is not our manifest duty to endeavour at least to show our disapproval of the deed and our sympathy with those who have suffered by it.' "[31]

Such statements contained no small element of hypocrisy, coming as they did from a country which had barely completed a century-long and continent-wide series of unabashedly exterminationist campaigns against American Indian peoples—and which was in the midst of a concerted drive to eradicate their cultural residues through a formal policy of compulsory assimilation. The United States was still wrapping up a similarly annihilatory operation in the Philippines which had resulted in the slaughter of as many as a million native "Moros," and was busily emulsifying the previously vibrant indigenous society of its newly acquired Hawaiian territory.[32] The rhetoric was all the more hypocritical in that the president who enunciated such noble-sounding principles was none other than Theodore Roosevelt, an inveterate racist who openly celebrated such American "accomplishments."[*]

In any event, this U.S. posturing was followed a decade latter with a multilateral declaration issued by France, Great Britain, and Russia on May 24, 1915, condemning as "crimes against humanity and civilization" Turkey's systematic slaughter of more than a million Armenians. An interesting aspect of this document was its inference that "all members of the Turkish government [might] be held responsible together with its agents implicated in the massacres" before some form of international court to be convened for that purpose at an unspecified future date.[33] Although no such body was ever established, a fifteen-member commission to study the possibility was created by the Preliminary Peace Conference of the embryonic League of Nations shortly after the end of World War I. In its final report, submitted on March 29, 1919, the body recommended the chartering of a permanent tribunal to prosecute those thought "guilty of offenses against the laws and customs of war or the laws of humanity."[34]

The idea foundered on strenuous American objections that "laws of humanity" were articulated in no ratified treaties and that, in any event, "stan-

---

[*]Consider the following passage, one of hundreds of comparable examples, written by Roosevelt in his 1901 book, *The Strenuous Life*, published on the very eve of his presidency: "Of course our whole national history has been one of expansion... That the barbarians recede or are conquered, with the attendant fact that peace follows their retrogression or conquest, is due solely to the power of the mighty civilized races which have not lost their fighting instinct, and which by their expansion are bringing peace into the red wastes where the barbarian peoples of the world hold sway."

dards of humanity" could be seen only in situational terms, relative to time, place, and circumstance. In other words, what should be viewed as a crime if committed against "civilized" (white) people might not be considered such if, following U.S. practice, it were committed only against (darker) "savages." Since their own needs were met by such a sliding definition—which precluded the elaboration of black letter law—Europe's imperial powers readily acquiesced in the American obstruction.[35] Interest in the issue remained alive in some quarters, however, as is witnessed by a 1933 proposal submitted to the League of Nations' International Conference for the Unification of Criminal Law by Polish jurist Raphaël Lemkin, arguing that the destruction of any racial, social, or religious collectivity should be declared a "crime of barbarity" under the Laws of Nations.[36]

No action was taken in the matter. Thus, when the nazis' "New Order" was incrementally imposed upon most of Europe itself between 1939 and 1941, no term yet existed which truly encompassed what was occurring. The best that could be managed in the January 1942 Declaration of St. James, issued by the governments-in-exile of nine countries overrun by Germany, was a statement of intent to bring to justice "all those responsible for violence against civilian populations, having nothing in common with acts of war or political crimes, as understood in civilized countries."[37] Little more shape could be found in the December 1942 declaration put forth by the allied powers in which they resolved to punish those responsible for "the bestial policy of cold-blooded extermination" visited upon the Jews and others.[38] The "horror was still nameless" in the October 1943 Moscow Declaration—later used as the basis for the Four-Power Agreement of August 8, 1945, establishing the Nuremberg Tribunal—which reiterated the Allies' intent to prosecute.[39]

Finally, in 1944, Lemkin, who had fled Poland in 1939 and was now working out of Yale and Duke Universities in the United States, stepped into the breach with publication of his *Axis Rule in Occupied Europe*. In it, he offered a new term, "genocide"—derived from the Greek word *genos* (human group) and the Latin *cide* (to "kill" or "put an end to")—to describe any "coordinated and planned annihilation of a national, religious, or racial group by a variety of actions aimed at undermining the foundations essential to the survival of the group as a group."[40] Lemkin conceived of genocide as "a composite of different acts of persecution or destruction." His definition included attacks on political and social institutions, culture, language, national feelings, religion, and the economic existence of the group. Even nonlethal acts that undermined the liberty, dignity, and personal security of members of a group constituted genocide, if they contributed to weakening the viability of the group.[41]

> Lemkin also pioneered the development of a typology of genocide—a set of types clas-
> sifying actual cases of genocide—based on the intent of the perpetrator. In his chap-
> ter [IX] on genocide, he sketched the outline of an evolutionary development
> incorporating three types of genocide. The aim of the first genocides—which he
> related to wars of extermination in antiquity and the middle ages—was the total or
> nearly total destruction of victim groups and nations. A second type of genocide, one
> that had emerged in the modern era, was characterized by the destruction of culture
> without an attempt to destroy its bearers. Nazi-style genocide comprised the third type.
> It combined ancient and modern forms of genocide in a new type in which some
> groups were selected for immediate annihilation while others were selected for [com-
> pulsory] assimilation.*

Lemkin's breakthrough enabled the International Military Tribunal convened at Nuremberg in 1946 to advance an appropriate description of the charges against the major nazi defendants, that is, of having "conducted delib-erate and systematic genocide, *viz.*, the extermination of racial and national groups, against the civilian populations of certain occupied territories in order to destroy certain races and classes of people and national, racial, or religious groups, particularly the Jews, Poles, and Gypsies, and others."[42] Following this lead, the Supreme National Tribunal of Poland, while prosecuting a group of lesser nazis during September and August of the same year, found them guilty on the basis that their "wholesale extermination of Jews and also of Poles had all the characteristics of genocide in the biological meaning of the term, and embraced in addition the destruction of the cultural life of those nations."[43] On December 11, 1946, the newly formed United Nations capped off the institutionalization of Lemkin's definition of the crime with the unanimous passage of General Assembly Resolution 96(I).

---

*Chalk and Jonassohn, *History, op. cit.*, p. 9; referencing Lemkin, *Axis Rule, op. cit.*, pp. 79–82. Actually, things were never so clearcut as it is made to appear here. The nazi mode of genocide was "new" only in terms of scale and efficiency. The total extermination of target populations—or attempts to accomplish it, which is all the nazis managed—were hardly restricted to "antiquity and the middle ages." And deliberate efforts to destroy other cultures dates back as far as physical extermination. Indeed, the "combination of…forms" have *always* gone hand in hand—e.g., Melos and Carthage, each of which contained both elements—albeit the emphasis changes from genocide to genocide. This is what Lemkin was trying to get at in his definitional elaboration. Unfortunately, Chalk and Jonassohn either missed the point, or elected to blur it to a considerable extent. For further detail, see Raphaël Lemkin, "Genocide: A Modern Crime," *Free World*, Apr. 1945.

Genocide is a denial of the right of existence of entire human groups, as homicide is the denial of the right to live of individual human beings; such denial of the right of existence shocks the conscience of mankind, results in great losses to humanity in the form of cultural and other contributions represented by these groups, and is contrary to moral law and the spirit and aim of the United Nations. Many instances of such crimes of genocide have occurred, when racial, religious, political and other groups have been destroyed, entirely or in part. The punishment of the crime of genocide is a matter of international concern.[44]

The General Assembly therefore affirmed "that genocide is a crime under international law which the civilized world condemns, and for the commission of which principals and accomplices—whether private individuals, public officials or statesmen, and whether the crime is committed on religious, racial, political or any other grounds—are punishable."[45] No distinction was drawn in this "norm of international understanding" between genocidal acts or policies implemented abroad and those targeting groups within any state's claimed territoriality, nor between wartime occurrences and those transpiring during times of peace. Similarly, no differentiation in terms of the gravity of the offense was drawn between the accomplishment of genocidal objectives by lethal means and the pursuit of such objectives through processes of deliberate cultural eradication. Thus was the concept of genocide clearly distinguished from the far simpler crime of mass murder.

Definitional Erosion

Resolution 96(I) concluded, in line with the U.N.'s mandate to engage in the formulation of "black letter international law, by assigning its Economic and Social Council (ECOSOC) to draft for adoption by the General Assembly a fullblown Convention delineating the elements of the crime of genocide and appropriate responses by the international community."[46] Through the U.N. Secretariat, Raphaël Lemkin was pressed into service as a consultant, charged with primary responsibility for drafting the instrument.[47] The result, a beautifully crafted and comprehensive document incorporating not only all aspects of genocidal activity but the outlines of an effective means of enforcement, was submitted for review to the Council on the Progressive Development and Codification of International Law in June 1947. There, it immediately stalled because of "concerns" expressed by the representatives of numerous U.N. member states.[48]

With the conclusion of the major Nuremberg Trial, a number of governments had quickly begun to backslide into their prewar postures. Having made grand statements on law and morality against the nazis, they were having second thoughts about the broader implications of such pronouncements and were busily contriving to protect their own "rights" to engage in variations on the same genocidal themes as the leaders of the Third Reich.[*] It was thus necessary for them, collectively, to narrow the Convention's definitional parameters of genocide in such ways as were necessary to exclude many of their own past, present, and anticipated policies/practices from being formally codified as *crimen laesae humanitatis* (crimes against humanity) in international law.[49] Consequently, General Assembly consideration was postponed until 1948, while Lemkin's material—usually referred to as the "Secretariat's Draft"—was handed over to an ad hoc committee of nation-state representatives licensed to rework it in conformity with what were described as the "political realities."[50]

The first task was for the United States to push Lemkin completely out of the process, paving the way for the real bargaining to begin.[†] With this accomplished, the initial modification was proposed by the U.S.S.R., strongly supported by Poland.[51] Lemkin's draft had specified that acts or policies aimed at "preventing the preservation or development" of "racial, national, linguistic, religious or political groups" should be considered genocidal, along with a range of "preparatory" acts, including "all forms of propaganda tending by their systematic and hateful character to provoke genocide, or tending to make it appear as a necessary, legitimate, or excusable act."[52] The Soviet representative, arguing on behalf of a government which had systematically eliminated not only the entirety of its political opposition but whole socioeconomic aggregates during the 1930s and '40s, claimed that inclusion

---

[*]Indeed, there were influential parties in each of the four participating powers—Great Britain, France, the United States and the U.S.S.R.—who had all along opposed the Nuremberg procedure for these very reasons. Winston Churchill and John A. Simon, respectively the English prime minister and lord chancellor, argued strongly for summary execution of the nazi leaders rather than risking the establishment of legal precedents at trial. This view was shared in the United States by Secretary of the Treasury Henry Morgenthau and, in all likelihood, President Franklin Delano Roosevelt; Bradley F. Smith, *The Road to Nuremberg* (New York: Basic Books, 1981) pp. 45–7.

[†]Not only was Lemkin removed from his U.N. role, he was prevented even from testifying before the Senate subcommittees conducting hearings on the possibility of U.S. ratification of the convention itself from 1950 until his death in 1959. Reasons stated included the facts that Lemkin was Jewish, "a man who comes from a foreign country who [spoke] broken English" and thus "irritated [many people] no end" by "running around" while serving as the "biggest propagandist" for the idea that genocide should be outlawed; Republican Senator H. Alexander Smith of New Jersey, quoted in LaBlanc, *U.S. and the Genocide Convention, op. cit.*, p. 20.

of political groups among the entities specifically protected by the Convention would be to cast the net "much too wide."[53]

The United States, which was by then locked into its Cold War confrontation with the U.S.S.R., led the opposition to this change until November 29, 1948, when it suddenly reversed its position.[54] A *quid pro quo* had been effected in which the Soviets would allow the removal of linguistic groups from the roster of protected categories and drop their opposition to deletion of Lemkin's entire second article, devoted to the question of cultural genocide.* In the original draft, Article II had specified as genocidal the "destruction of the specific character of a persecuted 'group' by forced transfer of children, forced exile [i.e., mass expulsion], prohibition of the use of the national language, destruction of books, documents, monuments, and objects of historical, artistic or religious value."[55] It was, as Monroe C. Beardsly later pointed out, meant to get at policies designed "to extinguish, utterly or in substantial part, a culture."[56]

The elimination of such criteria from the legal definition of genocide was strongly desired not only by the United States and other "Western democracies"—most of which were still presiding over "non-self-governing" colonial territories[57]—but by a number of emergent "postcolonial" Third World states even then in the midst of asserting jurisdictional and culturally hegemonic "rights" over divergent national minorities encompassed within their colonially delineated borders.† In the end, Lemkin's list of five protected

---

*The negotiating positions adopted by the two sides hardly presented an accurate reflection of interests. On the "Free World" side, the United States in particular was and would increasingly be involved in types of political repression which might be correlated to genocide, both domestically and, to a far greater extent, in Third World client states; see, e.g., A.J. Langguth, *Hidden Terrors: The Truth About U.S. Police Operations in Latin America* (New York: Pantheon, 1978); Edward S. Herman, *The Real Terror Network: Terrorism in Fact and Propaganda* (Boston: South End Press, 1982). The "Communist Bloc," on the other hand—not only the U.S.S.R., but Yugoslavia, China, Vietnam, and others—has been as committed to the eradication of the "cultural deviations" of ethnic and national minorities as any capitalist power; see generally, Walker Connor, *The National Question in Marxist-Leninist Theory and Strategy* (Princeton, NJ: Princeton University Press, 1984).

†Throughout what is now called the Third World, Europe's imperial powers overrode the traditional boundaries demarcating indigenous nations, creating new colonial entities in which all or parts of several nations were encapsulated; see, e.g., J.M. McKenzie, *The Partition of Africa, 1880–1900* (London: Methuen, 1983). When formal decolonization occurred—that is, when direct European control was terminated—these colonially created geopolitical entities were usually declared to constitute independent nation-states in their own right, without regard to the aspirations for a resumption of self-determining status of the various nations which had been forcibly incorporated into them in the first place. Hence, it is fair to say that most such "countries"—the Congo, for example, or Brazil, or India—went from being externally colonized to being internal colonizers; for a comprehensive examination of the history and conceptual issues involved, see Hugh Seton-Watson, *Nations and States: An Inquiry into the Origins of Nations and the Politics of Nationalism* (Boulder, CO: Westview Press,

411

group classifications was reduced to three—racial, national, and religious—to which a fourth, "ethnical," was then added by way of "compromise." Where he had elaborated three separate articles addressing the distinct but interactive and related categories of what he termed "physical," "biological," and "cultural" genocide, there was now a single abbreviated section.[58]

> *Article II.* In the present Convention, genocide means any of the following acts committed with intent to destroy, in whole or in part, a national, ethnical, racial or religious group, as such:
>
> (a) Killing members of the group;
> (b) Causing serious bodily or mental harm to members of the group;
> (c) Deliberately inflicting on the group conditions of life calculated to bring about its physical destruction in whole or in part;
> (d) Imposing measures intended to prevent births within the group;
> (e) Forcibly transferring children of the group to another group.*

The committee's insertion of the word "intent" was also extremely problematic insofar as it established a predicating requirement for any entity seeking to actually press charges of genocide against another which, on its face, would be virtually impossible to prove.[†] Finally, even in the unlikely event that

---

1977). The elites of such emergent states, thoroughly Europeanized both by their colonial experience and by indoctrination to marxian "alternatives," proved every bit as culturally genocidal in their efforts to forge social homogeneity within their "countries" as had their imperial predecessors; for closer investigations of a specific geographic area, see Greg Urban and Joel Sherzer, eds., *Nation-States and Indians in Latin America* (Austin: University of Texas Press, 1991).

*Brownlie, *Basic Documents, op. cit.*, p. 31. From the background discussions concerning this formulation, it is clear that the ad hoc committee intended the first three criteria to be concerned exclusively with Lemkin's category of "physical" genocide. The fourth criteria is obviously drawn from Lemkin's "biological" category. All that was meant to remain of Lemkin's "cultural" category is the final criterion, concerning the forced transfer of children. The committee's intentions notwithstanding, however, it is plainly possible to argue that the "serious...mental harm" referred to in (b) could derive from criteria—e.g., prohibitions of language and religious practices—included under Lemkin's category of cultural genocide. Similarly, the "deliberate infliction of conditions of life calculated to bring about physical [group] destruction"—although not necessarily the individual group members—contained in (c) can be readily construed as including such culturally genocidal criteria as forced exile and mass expulsions. Try as it might, then, the ad hoc committee could not really get around the fact that Lemkin's physical, biological, and cultural categories of genocide represent inseparable routes to the same end, each of them *equally* deserving of condemnation and punishment.

†The implications were brought out clearly in March 1974, when, in one of the few instances where charges of genocide have ever been filed with the U.N. Secretariat, the International League for the Rights of Man, the Inter-American Association for Democracy and Freedom, and several other organizations did so against the government of Paraguay because of its extermination of Aché Indians. Paraguay's formal response to these allegations was that, "Although there are victims and victimizer, there is not the third element necessary to establish the crime of genocide—that is 'intent.' As there is no 'intent,' one cannot speak of 'genocide' "; Paraguayan Minister of Defense, quoted in Norman Lewis, "The Camp at Cecilio Baez," in Arens, *Genocide in Paraguay, op. cit.*, pp. 62–3.

intent might be demonstrated in a given instance, the ad hoc committee's final draft expunged Lemkin's provision for establishment of a permanent international tribunal to receive and try charges of genocide.* Instead, other than in extraordinary circumstances involving governmental dissolution, it was left to each state to utilize its own juridical apparatus in determining whether it, its officials, or its subjects were to be considered guilty of genocidal conduct.† This was the instrument submitted to and adopted unanimously and without discussion by the General Assembly on December 9, 1948.‡

Conceptual Reinforcement(s)

In the twenty years following passage of the Convention, a remarkable disinterest in the topic of genocide was exhibited by the scholarly community. While there was a burgeoning historical literature chronicling nazism, its leaders, and the war itself—many of these works included material on the exterminations of Jews, Slavs, and others, and several were devoted exclusively to such subject matter—theoretical and social scientific exploration of the concept and its implications languished.[59] Perhaps the only significant

---

*As the Venezuelan representative put it, the question of jurisdiction is "a very delicate matter... The question of the sovereignty of states is involved"; 3 U.N. ESCOR, *op. cit.*, pp. 139–40. For detailed examination of the far more protracted U.S. recalcitrance on this very question, see LaBlanc, *U.S. and the Genocide Convention, op. cit.*, pp. 151–234.

†Suggestions that a "whole new tribunal charter would have been necessary" to have accommodated Lemkin's provision don't hold up to even the most minimal scrutiny. The charter establishing the international tribunal apparatus presiding over the Nuremberg trials has never been rescinded (and the apparatus itself was very much functioning in the period 1946–48, when the Genocide Convention was being drafted and adopted). Indeed, the General Assembly as a whole had affirmed as universal the principles underlying the tribunal charter on December 11, 1946; U.N.G.A. Res. 95(I), U.N. Doc. A/236 (1946), at 1144; see Burns H. Weston, Richard A. Falk, and Anthony D'Amato, eds., *Basic Documents in International Law and World Order* (St. Paul, MN: West, 1960) p. 140. In effect, the U.N. member states were simply unwilling to submit themselves to either the procedures or the principles they insisted—accurately enough—represented justice when imposed upon Germany.

‡It is often argued by apologists that the "compromise wording" forged by the ad hoc committee was necessary to obtain General Assembly acceptance of a Genocide Convention, and that approval of an inadequate or misleading instrument was better than nothing at all; e.g., Chalk and Jonassohn, *History, op. cit.*, p. 11. A more realistic appraisal is offered by Lawrence J. LaBlanc, who observes that, all things considered, "no one could [openly] vote *against* a resolution on genocide (as no one would later vote against the adoption of the Convention itself)"; *U.S. and the Genocide Convention, op. cit.*, p. 26. In other words, had Lemkin's draft been put to the General Assembly, it would have passed, probably unanimously and without discussion. That it was instead gutted is thus solely because certain countries represented in the ad hoc committee—most especially the United States and the U.S.S.R.—found such gutting to be in their own interests, to wit: both fully intended to continue to engage in what they knew to be genocidal activities. Rather than end or otherwise alter these activities in conformity to law, they opted to use their power in the back room to change the law in such manner as to exempt themselves from it before its enactment.

exceptions during the first decade were the final chapter of sociologist Jesse Barnhart's 1948 *American Community Behavior* and Hannah Arendt's ground-breaking *The Origins of Totalitarianism* in 1951.* It was not until 1959 that the first major study, a massive two-volume effort by Dutch law professor Pieter N. Drost, was finally published.[60]

Drost's material set the stage for much of what would come later in two very important ways. First, on the positive side, he entered a scathing critique of the U.N.'s purging of political groups from the Genocide Convention's list of protected classifications, and made a strong case that other entities, especially economic aggregates, should have been included as well.[61] Second, in the negative, he coupled this promising argument to an altogether arbitrary constriction of the criteria of genocidal activities to the realm of the physical, with an emphasis on direct killing. Lemkin's category of cultural genocide disappears altogether, having been rather casually consigned to the classification of "ethnocide," a "more appropriate" term Drost erroneously—or misleadingly—attributes to postwar French scholarship rather than to Lemkin himself.† Moreover, Drost badly blurred Lemkin's distinction

---

*Bernard's *American Community Behavior* (New York: Dryden, 1948) cites Lemkin in the last chapter while arguing that genocide might represent a sort of "ultimate form of conflict resolution" between competing races and ethnicities on the international as well as domestic levels. Although promising in some ways, Bernard's analysis suffered from such a rigid application of criteria drawn from the Genocide Convention that it evinced no further utility for sociological application. The potential impact of Arendt's far better developed *Origins of Totalitarianism* (New York: Harcourt, Brace, Jovanovitch, 1951), which set out the cornerstones for a general theory of genocide as being an inherent characteristic of certain strains of sociopolitical evolution, was greatly undermined by significant sectors of the Jewish intellectual establishment, which had already invested themselves in pseudomystical and deliberately obfuscatory interpretations of Hitler/nazism as representing a "singularity of evil," and the Judaic Holocaust as an "historically unique phenomenon" (views which precluded broader understandings of either totalitarianism or genocide); Dwight Macdonald, "Hannah Arendt and the Jewish Establishment," *Partisan Review*, Spring 1964 (included in Macdonald's *Discriminations: Essays and Afterthoughts, 1938–1974* [New York: Grossman, 1974]).

†Chalk and Jonassohn, for example, replicate this error by describing ethnocide as "a term coined by the French after the war to cover the destruction of a culture without the killing of its bearers," but offer no citation; *History, op. cit.*, p. 9. Elsewhere, they repeat the assertion, pointing to a definition of the term written by Jean Girodet for the *Dictionnaire du Bon Français* (Paris: Bordas, 1981, p. 269) a third of a century "after the war"; Kurt Jonassohn and Frank Chalk, "A Typology of Genocide and Some Implications for the Human Rights Agenda," in Isador Wallimann and Michael Dobkowski, eds., *Genocide and the Modern Age: Etiology and Case Studies of Mass Death* (Westport, CT: Greenwood Press, 1987) pp. 7, 37. In actuality, Lemkin himself coined the term, observing at p. 79 of *Axis Rule* that combining the Greek *ethnos* ("nation") with the Latin *cide* would encompass what he meant by "cultural genocide." He opted to use the latter formulation in an explicit effort to reinforce understandings that ethnocide is a crucial subpart of genocide itself, *not* something distinct from it (pp. 79–82). Those who use Lemkin's name in arguing to the contrary have either never read his work or are intentionally distorting it beyond recognition.

between murder and genocide by emphasizing the fate of individual group members, offering as his own definition of the crime "the deliberate destruction of physical life of individual human beings by reason of their membership of any human collectivity as such."*

Academic silence on the question then resumed and Drost's remained the accepted scholarly definition of genocide until the late 1960s. At that point, the magnitude of carnage inflicted by the United States in Southeast Asia at last compelled serious attention by major intellectuals. The forum through which this occurred was mainly, though by no means exclusively, an international tribunal organized by eminent British philosopher Bertrand Russell to consider the U.S. performance in accordance with the criteria of illegality enunciated in Article 6 of the 1945 Charter for the Nuremberg Tribunal.† These include:

(a) Crimes Against Peace: namely, planning, preparation, initiation or waging of a war of aggression, or war in violation of international treaties, agreements or assurances, or participation in a common plan or conspiracy for the accomplishment of any of the foregoing.

(b) War Crimes: namely, violations of the laws or customs of war. Such violations shall include, but not be limited to, murder, ill-treatment or deportation to slave labor or any other purpose of [the] civilian population of occupied territory, murder or ill-treatment of prisoners of war or persons on the seas, killing of hostages, plunder of public or private property, wanton destruction of cities, towns or villages, or devastation not justified by military necessity.

(c) Crimes Against Humanity: namely, murder, extermination, enslavement, deportation and other inhumane acts committed against any civilian population, before or during the war, or persecutions on political, racial or religious grounds...whether or not in violation of the domestic law of the country where perpetrated.[62]

---

*Drost, *The Crime of State, op. cit.*, p. 125. It is worth noting that Drost was a solid member of the Dutch establishment—he served almost continuously as a legal consultant to the government—with extensive personal experience in that country's colonial possessions in the East Indies. He was therefore not only intimately acquainted with his country's colonial policies, but committed to maintaining them. To all appearances, then, a primary motive in his writing of *The Crime of State* was to create as comprehensive and sophisticated an intellectual barrier as possible against characterizations of Dutch imperialism as being inherently genocidal.

†It is difficult to differentiate between what stems directly from the Russell Tribunal and what does not, since the proceeding was deliberately structured in a diffuse manner designed to continue generating investigations, analyses, and conclusions on an essentially ad hoc basis for the duration of the war. It would be fair to say that its preliminary conclusions, reached as a result of hearings conducted in Stockholm and elsewhere during 1967, were extraordinarily influential, even among critical scholars who were never directly involved; Richard A. Falk, "Genocide, Ecocide and the Nuremberg Tradition," in Virginia Held, Sidney Morgenbesser, and Thomas Nagel, eds., *Philosophy, Morality and International Affairs* (New York: Oxford University Press, 1974) pp. 123–4.

While Russell and numerous others concerned themselves primarily with the issues of war crimes and crimes against peace, French philosopher Jean Paul Sartre focused specifically on the crime of genocide.[63] In his address on the topic to a plenary session of the tribunal—subsequently published in *Ramparts* magazine and, in somewhat expanded form, as a short book—Sartre went very far towards restoring Lemkin's original notion of the nature of the crime.[64]

> He did not assert that there was proof that the United States did in fact envision genocide, but simply that nothing prevented the United States from envisioning it, that genocidal intent was implicit in the facts, and that those who fight the war of the greatest power on earth against a poor peasant people "are *living out* the only possible relationship between an overindustrialized country and an underdeveloped country, that is to say, a genocidal relationship implemented through racism—the only relationship short of picking up and pulling out."[65]

He then proceeded to make a major contribution of his own toward any genuine understanding of genocide, asserting a firm equation between colonialism and genocide:

> Sartre [points to] countless acts of genocide committed by the capitalist powers in the colonial empires where they were established from the year 1830. Since victory, easily achieved by overwhelming fire-power, provokes the hatred of the civilian population, and since civilians are potentially rebels and soldiers, the colonial troops maintain their authority by the terror of perpetual massacre, genocidal in character. This is accompanied by cultural genocide, made necessary by colonialism as an economic system of unequal exchange in which the colony sells its raw materials and agricultural products at a reduced price to the colonizing power, and the latter in return sells its manufactured goods to the colony at world market prices. However, the dependence of the [colonizers] on the subproletariat of the colonized protects the latter, to a certain extent, from physical genocide.[66]

This much-publicized breakthrough was sufficient to finally generate a relatively substantial amount of debate on the question of how genocide should be understood. Probably the most thoughtful rejoinder came from Leo Kuper, an Africanist at UCLA, who, after seemingly visceral responses describing Sartre's perspective as "unbalanced" and "weakened by extravagant overgeneralization," somewhat grudgingly concedes that "the case is [nonetheless] made persuasively by others in more measured...terms," and that the "argument of an affinity between colonialism

and genocide can [therefore] be accepted, with much qualification."*
Moreover:

> The restraints on genocide to which Sartre refers, dependence on the labor of the sub-
> ject peoples and the preservation of the colonial economy, are of a functional nature.
> The corollary will be that the impulse to genocide will be given freer rein where there
> are no material advantages to be derived from restraint, as in the genocides against
> hunting and gathering peoples. This conception of functional restraints on genocide
> seems to have some functional utility.[67]

Ultimately, Kuper expands upon the Sartian position, arguing that:
a) Sartre's timeline for equating colonialism and genocide, which picks up in
1830, should have been rolled back much further, at least as far as the advent
of modern European expansionism in 1450;[68] b) correlating the genocidal
characteristics of many decolonization struggles and postcolonial realities to
the effects of colonialism itself;[69] and c) drawing attention to the question of
internal colonialism, a matter Sartre himself had left entirely unaddressed. In
the latter connection, he observes that "Sartre's discussion of colonialism and

---

*Kuper, Genocide, op. cit., pp. 15, 35; he is following a line of argument advanced by Hugo Adam Bedau
in his "Genocide in Vietnam?" in Held, Morgenbesser and Nagel, op. cit. Kuper's objection to Sartre's
tone of delivery reduces to sheer academic analism. If the substance of an argument is correct—which
Kuper in this case ultimately admits—there is no valid reason to object to it because of its "tenor."
Picking at matters of style where issues so momentous as the then-ongoing genocide in Vietnam are
concerned is intrinsically diversionary, obstructionist, and therefore an objectionable practice in its
own right. The question should never be why, when discussing genocide, Sartre or anyone else might
sound "angry." The real question is why more people, Kuper included, don't demonstrate a more
appropriate degree of passion. Moreover, Kuper's most substantive evidence of Sartre's supposed
"overgeneralization" can be considered such only on the basis of a logical fallacy of his own. At p. 15,
he observes that Sartre describes "colonization as by its very nature an act of cultural genocide:
colonization, he argues, cannot take place without systematically liquidating all the characteristics of
native society." This, Kuper claims, is an "unbalanced perspective" since colonialism clearly did not
have the effect of completely eradicating native cultures in places like Dakar and Calcutta. The
problem is that a genocidal process need not be completely successful in order for it to be genocidal
(if that were the case, the nazis' physical genocide of European Jews could not be considered genocide,
since a third of the Jews survived). For solid evidence that the kind of liquidation of cultural
characteristics Sartre stipulated was in fact the goal of European colonialism in both Africa and Asia,
one need look no further than the "measured terms" of Martin Carnoy's highly detailed study,
Education as Cultural Imperialism (New York: David McKay, 1974). The sort of coerced cultural
indoctrination of colonized populations Carnoy methodically describes represents anything but an
autonomous "borrowing of items of culture [and] transformation of institutions" by the natives which
Kuper suggests. On the contrary, they echo the function if not the form of the openly assimilationist
objectives of comparable "educational" programs imposed upon the indigenous peoples of the
Americas; see, e.g., David Wallace Adams, Education for Extinction: American Indians and the Boarding
School Experience, 1875–1928 (Lawrence: University Press of Kansas, 1995); J.R. Miller, Shingwauk's
Vision: A History of Native Residential Schools (Toronto: University of Toronto Press, 1996). In sum, the
substance of Sartre's argument was correct.

its affinity for genocide is well within the tradition of Marxist-Leninist analysis of capitalism in its imperialist phase. This model of overseas conquest and colonization is now being applied to the internal domestic relations between dominant (or privileged) and subordinate (or underprivileged) racial or ethnic groups in the concept of internal colonialism."[70]

> In the early years of the United Nations the Belgians…attempted to broaden the concept of colonialism to include all ethnically distinct minorities discriminated against in their home countries; and Leo Marquard used the term "internal colonialism" many years ago to describe internal race relations in South Africa. Most recently it has been adopted in Marxist interpretations of black-white relations in the U.S.A. and of Catholic-Protestant relations in Northern Ireland, and it has come into wide currency. Presumably the genocidal conflicts in Burundi and Lebanon [should] be analyzed in these terms. In this use of internal colonialism, there is an identification of ethnic (or racial) group with class. But the concept has also been applied directly to class conflicts.[71]

Like Drost, Kuper assailed the omission of political and economic groups from the Genocide Convention's itemization of protected classes.[*] He was also unequivocal in his opinion that, insofar as it serves no useful purpose and merely "provides an easy means of evading responsibility," the Convention's requirement of demonstrable intent be dropped from the definition of genocide altogether.[72] Unlike Drost, however, he makes no false distinction between "ethnocide" and genocide, treating them as two facets of the same process.[73] Kuper's own exegesis of the crime was thus essentially the same as that originally offered by Lemkin: "genocide [is] quite simply the destruction of a human group," as such, whether wholly or in part, and by whatever means.[74]

This interpretation is one which remained unchanged in a pair of books Kuper published in the mid-1980s, although in the second of these, *The Prevention of Genocide*, he divided the crime into two major classifications, "domestic genocides arising on the basis of internal divisions within a society and genocides arising in the course of international warfare,"

---

[*] In making his point on economic groups at p. 34, Kuper quotes the response of the Brazilian government to allegations during the late 1960s that genocide was being committed against the Yanomami and other native peoples of the Amazon Basin: "The crimes against the Brazilian indigenous population cannot be characterized as genocide, since the criminal parties involved never eliminated the Indians as an ethnic or cultural group. Hence there was lacking the special malice or motivation necessary to characterize the occurrence of genocide. The crimes in question were committed for exclusively economic reasons, the perpetrators having acted solely to take possession of the lands of their victims"; United Nations, Human Rights Communication No. 478, Sept. 29, 1969.

before arranging various illustrations according to a four-part typology:[*]

(1) genocides against indigenous peoples; (2) genocides against hostage groups, a category that includes the Holocaust; (3) genocide following upon decolonization of a two-tier structure of domination; and (4) genocide in the process of struggles by ethnic or racial or religious groups for power or secession, greater autonomy, or more equality.[75]

By then, others had long since weighed in with a range of useful contributions. As early as 1967, Norman Cohn, for example, had advanced a solidly utilitarian interpretation of how certain modes of ideology and propaganda serve to create the psychological context essential to perpetration of genocide, arguing that it is essential for these to be abolished if the genocidal mentality is ever to be rooted out of the sociopolitical environment.[76] In 1974, Armenian scholar Vahakn Dadrian incorporated this construction as well as significant elements of Sartre's functionalism into his own analysis when he observed that "even though in conception, design and execution genocide may be regarded as a phenomenon *sui generis*, in terms of underlying structural contingencies and projected goals, it is functional; it subserves the ultimate end of equilibrium of a system beset by disarray through acute group conflict."[77]

Unfortunately, Dadrian followed up on this insight by extending a somewhat more restrictive overall definition than had either Sartre or Kuper: "Genocide is the successful attempt by a dominant group, vested with formal authority and/or preponderant access to the overall resources of power, to reduce by coercion or lethal violence the number of a minority group whose ultimate extermination is held desirable and useful and whose respective vulnerability is a major factor contributing to the decision for genocide."[78]

Dadrian's definition of genocide, emphasizing the degree and type of disparity between the power of the perpetrator group and the victim group, establishes the matrix for his five-category typology of genocide: (1) cultural genocide, in which assimilation is the perpetrator's aim; (2) latent genocide, in which the perpetrator's activities have unintended consequences, such as civilian deaths during bombing raids or the accidental

---

[*] Leo Kuper, *International Action Against Genocide* (London: Minority Rights Group, [rev. ed.] 1984); *The Prevention of Genocide* (New Haven, CT: Yale University Press, 1985). A problem with Kuper's system of classification is that he seems to accept assertions by internally colonizing states that indigenous and other minority peoples forcibly encompassed within their claimed boundaries are somehow part of the colonizer society itself (a problem which is especially pronounced in systems of "settler state" colonialism. Arguably, the circumstances in which such groups find themselves more nearly resembles that of "international warfare" than of "domestic genocides arising on the basis of internal divisions within a country."

spread of disease during an invasion; (3) retributive genocide, designed to punish a segment of a minority that challenges a dominant group; (4) utilitarian genocide, using mass killing to obtain control of economic resources; and (5) optimal genocide, in which the chief aim of the perpetrator is the total obliteration of the group, as in the Armenian and Jewish holocausts.[*]

A decade later, sociologist Helen Fein produced yet another typology, closely related to those offered by both Kuper and Dadrian, with which she hoped to "replace the U.N. definition with a more analytically rigorous concept."[79] According to Fein, genocide can be of the following types:

> (1) developmental, in which the perpetrator intentionally or unintentionally destroys peoples who stand in the way of the economic exploitation of resources; (2) despotic, which are designed to eliminate a real or potential opposition, as in a new, highly polarized multiethnic state; (3) retributive, in which the perpetrator seeks to destroy a real opponent; and (4) ideological, a category embracing cases of genocide against groups cast as enemies by the state's hegemonic myth or by the need to destroy victims who can be portrayed as the embodiment of absolute evil.[80]

The potential usefulness of Fein's otherwise excellent delineation was seriously undermined by the definition with which she attended it: "Genocide is the calculated murder of a segment or all of a group defined outside the universe of obligation of the perpetrator by a government, elite, staff or crowd representing the perpetrator in response to a crisis or opportunity perceived to be caused by or impeded by the victim."[81] In a 1988 paper, however, she eliminated the worst of what was inadequate in her formulation by recasting it in a manner which includes the full range of non-lethal ingredients, as well direct killing:

> Genocide is a series of purposeful actions by a perpetrator(s) to destroy a collectivity through mass or selective murders of group members and suppressing the biological and social reproduction of the collectivity. This can be accomplished through the imposed proscription or restriction of reproduction of group members, increasing infant mortality, and breaking the linkage between reproduction and socialization of children in the family or group of origin. The perpetrator may be the state of the victim, another state, or another collectivity.[82]

---

[*]Chalk and Jonassohn, *History, op. cit.* pp. 14–5; citing Dadrian, "Typology," *op. cit.* The obvious question here is why "utilitarian genocide" should be in any way confined to mass killing. The answer is that, in Dadrian's handling, it is not (he acknowledges that other methods—such as massive removal or dispersal of population—might well accomplish the same result, both by way of economic benefits to the perpetrators, and in terms the extinguishing of the target group). This is a classic example of those, such as Chalk and Jonassohn, who wish to deny that genocide pertains to processes other than direct killing distorting the conclusions of others to fit their own requirements.

Although he is rather blurry about what he thinks genocide is (and is not), Roger W. Smith offers yet another typology, improving a bit on Fein's:

(1) retributive genocide, which is based on a desire for revenge (for example, the conquests of Genghis Khan); (2) institutional genocide, frequently incidental to military conquest and prevalent in the ancient and medieval worlds; (3) utilitarian genocide, motivated by the desire for material gain and common in the colonial expansions of the sixteenth to nineteenth centuries as well as in the genocides of development devastating small aboriginal groups in the twentieth century [e.g., the Aché in Paraguay and the Amazon Basin peoples of Brazil]; (4) monopolist genocide, originating from the desire to monopolize power, particularly in plural societies (for example, Bangladesh and Burundi); and (5) ideological genocide, motivated by the desire to impose a particular notion of salvation or purification on an entire society and most commonly found in the twentieth century (for example, the Armenians, the Soviet Union, the Holocaust, and Cambodia).[83]

In 1984, University of Washington sociologist Lyman Legters, in an essay marred by its author's preference for the narrowest possible definition of genocide, nonetheless made an important contribution to understandings of the crime by developing the idea that the identity of a target group is to be understood, not by some abstract sociological or anthropological standard, but exclusively in accordance with the perpetrators' operant designation of it (no matter how absurd such a designation may seem).[84]

Legters strongly dissents from the current U.N. definition of genocide in regard to its failure to take into account that "different social orders have diverse ways of classifying their own populations" and that class — a category excluded from the U.N. definition of genocide — "is the primary classificatory device of socialist systems."*

Finally, Robert Melson provides a crucial analytical tool by focusing attention, not just on the dynamics of internal colonialism, but on that more particularized variation known as the "settler state" — a structural innovation evidenced most plainly in the United States, Canada, Australia, New Zealand and Israel (as well as the Hitlerian notion of territorial expansionism known as *Lebensraumpolitik*) — in which an invading group quite literally supplants

---

*Chalk and Jonassohn, *History, op. cit.*, p. 21; quoting Legters, "Soviet Gulag," *op. cit.*, p. 65. Although the focus of his essay induces a certain skew in Legters' handling of the question of how perpetrators define target groups — his examples concentrate entirely on Soviet practice — the underlying principle he elaborates is equally applicable to the racial theories under which nazism functioned, etc. The point is that, at base, it makes no difference whatsoever whether a perpetrator's method of identifying a target group is sound. All that is required is that — in keeping with W.I. Thomas's famous dictum that if people define a situation as real it is real in its consequences — the perpetrator has come up with some criteria of target group identification and then acted upon it.

the indigenous population on its own landbase. Since wholesale displacement, reduction in numbers, and forced assimilation of native peoples is virtually a requirement for the existence of any settler state, Melson suggests they are properly construed as being inherently rather than potentially genocidal in their makeup.[85]

Academic Dilution(s)

By no means were all academic responses to Sartre's postulations so constructive as those sketched above. Indeed, in keeping with academia's traditional role of assembling theoretical support for the status quo, many—if not most—appear to have been designed not only to parry the thrust of his arguments, but to follow the lead of the United Nations member states in diluting the meaning of the term genocide itself.[86] Probably the first major effort in this regard was made by French sociologist Hervé Savon, who, in his 1972 book *Du cannibalism au génocide*, took up Drost's technique of first critiquing the U.N.'s elimination of politicoeconomic groups from its list of protected classes before setting out to narrow the definitional parameters of the crime found in the Genocide Convention.[87]

Here, Savon went Drost one better by restricting his range of genocidal activity exclusively to direct killing ("annihilation"), consigning everything else—including, it seems, such biological criteria as sterilization—to the realm of "ethnocide."[88] He then advanced a three-part typology consisting in genocides of "substitution," "devastation," and "elimination," each of which is determined by the outcomes deriving from the process which engendered it.[89] As has been observed elsewhere, among the many problematic features of this extraordinarily convoluted analytical method is that it precludes even the possibility of an early apprehension of/intervention in the processes themselves—in Savon's "system," one can never be sure a genocide is occurring until after the fact—thus mooting the whole idea of preventing the crime before it occurs.*

In 1976, Rutgers University professor Irving Louis Horowitz not only

---

*Chalk and Jonassohn make the same point with respect to Savon. Later in their book, however, they manifest their own zeal to define genocidal activity as narrowly as possible by arguing that the German genocide of the Hereros occurred exclusively in 1907, "after their warriors had been defeated," rather than beginning in 1904 as an integral part of Germany's war of extermination against them. Hence, Chalk and Jonassohn's methods prove just as subject to obscuring "the events leading up to genocide and the possible methods of halting the process" as did Savon's; Chalk and Jonassohn, *History, op. cit.*, pp. 13, 230.

replicated Savon's circumscription of genocidal criteria—he flatly equates the crime to mass murder—but also attempted to definitionally constrain the range of potential perpetrators to governmental entities.[90] As he puts it in *Taking Lives*, a 1980 rewrite of his earlier book, genocide is merely "a structural and systematic destruction of innocent people by a state bureaucratic apparatus."* In a subsequent essay, however, Horowitz seems to undercut his own argument by contending that while a totalitarian society is a necessary precondition for the genocidal process, it is not in itself a sufficient one. Instead, he casts "national culture" as being of more importance than state ideology in predicating genocide.[91]

> He suggests that totalitarian ideology may make class, race or religion ineradicable sins, thus increasing the potential for genocide, but that the decision to eradicate these sins by committing genocide is largely a function of national culture.†

By the mid-'80s, iterations of the simplistic assertion that "genocide equals mass murder" had accumulated to such an extent that it had come to constitute an orthodoxy of sorts. Perhaps the most crystalline—and certainly among the more reprehensible—enunciations of this definitional truncation is that offered by Frank Chalk and Kurt Jonassohn in their 1990 book, *The History and Sociology of Genocide*:

---

*Irving Louis Horowitz, *Taking Lives: Genocide and State Power* (New Brunswick, NJ: Transaction, 1980). To be fair, Horowitz himself was admitting that his thesis was exceedingly full of holes, focusing as it did exclusively on a handful of twentieth-century genocides, selected, à la Savon, on the basis of outcomes. Moreover, his correlation between totalitarianism and genocide restricted consideration to instances of internal state repression, leaving the question of external projections of genocidal violence entirely unaddressed. Again, it says nothing to the reality that, especially in the Third World, where transnational corporations effectively "own" state governments, the primary instigators of given genocides might well be corporate rather than governmental entities. Finally, it avoids altogether the fact that, especially with respect to recent genocides against the small tribal peoples of the South American interior, perpetrators have often turned out to be aggregations of private citizens rather than governmental or corporate bodies, per se.

†Chalk and Jonassohn, *History, op. cit.*, p. 14. The concept introduced here, at least insofar as the specificities of what is meant by "national culture" are not and probably cannot be defined with any degree of precision, is far more mystifying than clarifying. In resorting to it, Horowitz effectively divorces himself from any pretense of social scientific rigor, entering instead into the inherently obfuscatory "philosophical" discourses on genocide and "human nature" offered by figures such as Elie Wiesel (e.g., *Night* [New York: Hill & Wang, 1972]); Eric Fromm (e.g., *The Anatomy of Human Destructiveness* [Greenwich, CT: Fawcett, 1975]); Conrad Lorenz (e.g., *On Aggression* [New York: Harcourt, Brace & World, 1977]) and Arthur Koestler (e.g., *Janus: A Summing Up* [London: Hutchenson, 1978]). It is noteworthy that Sartre, who was a far more important philosophical figure than anyone listed, refused to philosophize on the matter of genocide precisely because he saw such activity as an all-too-easy means of avoiding more concrete attention to the phenomenon.

> *Genocide* is a form of one-sided mass killing in which a state or other authority intends to destroy a group, as that group and membership in it are defined by the perpetrator.[92]

Here is a definition bound to delight *any* perpetrator, since, on its face, no genocide in history can qualify as such under its terms. Chalk and Jonassohn not only reject out of hand any and all forms of nonlethal activity on the basis that these represent a "phenomenon that is analytically different from the physical extermination of a group,"[*] but they systematically eliminate virtually all forms of mass killing as well. Within their framework, nothing associated with warfare can be considered genocidal, nor can pogroms or massacres, regardless of their scale, duration, or impact upon the victims, absent "intent [by the perpetrator] to destroy all the members of the group."[†] Even nazism's extermination of the Jews cannot be said to qualify as "real" genocide under the authors' "deliberately restrictive" definition, since it does not truly meet their criterion of being "one-sided" (the Jews, after all, sometimes engaged in armed resistance to being slaughtered).[‡]

---

[*] Bauer, et. al., *Remembering, op. cit.* This weighty-sounding distinction is in no sense explained. It is merely posited as a sort of revealed "truth" justifying the authors' express "hope that the term *ethnocide* will come into wider use for those cases in which a group disappears without mass killing." Chalk and Jonassohn also state categorically that bringing about the disappearance of a human group by nonlethal means is less "extreme" than accomplishing the same goal by killing the group members. This, too, is presented as a self-evident fact, with no effort at all to explain why killing should be considered any more extreme in its implications than, say, forcibly sterilizing all group members, or subjecting all women in a group to involuntary abortions whenever they become pregnant. Indeed, there is no attempt to explain why, in terms of bringing about group disappearance—which is, after all, the basic meaning of the term "genocide"—killing should be construed as a more extreme approach than any other method of bringing about the same result.

[†] "We mean to exclude from consideration those cases of mass killing, massacres...and so forth that had a lesser aim, no matter how objectionable such cases are"; ibid. Presumably, the absurd "defenses" offered by the governments of Paraguay and Brazil in countering charges that they were engaged in—or at least allowing—genocide of indigenous peoples within their borders would be perfectly acceptable to Chalk and Jonassohn, since the killings were purportedly conducted without requisite intent. Similarly, so long as the perpetrating "authority" is willing to contend that a "state of war" exists between itself and its target group, it is to be automatically exempted from "legitimate" accusations of genocide. This is because, according to the authors, "When two countries are at war, neither side is defenseless." Leaving aside the obvious question of how, exactly, genocide became a term associated solely with bringing about the disappearance of "defenseless" groups rather than human groups, per se, Chalk and Jonassohn's bland assertion would undoubtedly be treated with considerable astonishment by the thousands of Sudanese slaughtered with such utter impunity by the vastly better-armed British troops at Omdurman or any of several hundred American Indian peoples forced into going up against state-of-the art European firepower with spears, stone clubs, and bows and arrows; see, e.g., Stannard, *American Holocaust, op. cit.*

[‡] "We emphasize *one-sided* to indicate that we are dealing with cases in which there is no reciprocity"; Chalk and Jonassohn, *History, op. cit.*, p. 23. On the following page, the authors attempt to exempt the Jews and several other groups from this stipulation—as usual, without anything approaching adequate

Equally egregious have been the efforts of an uncomfortably large number of Jewish scholars to "prove" that genocide is an historically unique fate suffered by their people alone at the hands of the nazis.[93] Although there have been literally scores of practitioners within this "school," its leading proponent has been, until recently, Yehuda Bauer of Tel Aviv University, whose project has taken the peculiar form of seeking to diminish the relative degree of seriousness implied by the term genocide itself in much the same manner that others have sought to demote genocide's cultural category by retitling it "ethnocide." His method has been to champion the idea that the Holocaust, a term he claims applies exclusively to Jewish victims, represents a category of "unprecedented [and] unparalleled physical destruction" which stand both apart from and above mere genocide.[94]

> [Genocide is] the planned destruction, since the mid-nineteenth century, of a racial, national, or ethnic group as such, by the following means: (a) selective mass murder of elites or parts of the population; (b) elimination of national (racial, ethnic) culture and religious life with the intent of "denationalization"; (c) enslavement, with the same intent; (d) destruction of the national (racial, ethnic) economic life, with the same intent; (e) biological decimation through [sterilization, abortion,] the kidnapping of children, or the prevention of normal family life, with the same intent.[95]

Interestingly, Bauer's definition essentially duplicates Lemkin's up to this point. However, when it comes to "the planned physical annihilation, for ideological or pseudo-religious reasons, of all members of a national, ethnic, or religious group," he parts company, segregating this into a classification of its own, which he labels "holocaust."[96] A hierarchical standing of the respective crimes is assigned via his contention that there is a "kind of continuum of evil that would lead from 'mass murder' in recent times through 'genocide' to 'holocaust' ('shoah')."[97]

---

explanation—but all they manage is to create a deep contradiction within their definition. The matter simply cannot be had both ways. Either the Jews, because at least some of them "reciprocated" nazi violence by way of armed resistance to it, must be excluded from the list of groups suffering genocide, or all groups which have sought to defend themselves against wars of extermination must be included. At that point, virtually all of Chalk and Jonassohn's welter of arbitrary definitional restrictions begin to dissolve into the mist of meaninglessness from which they emerged. On Jewish resistance, see, e.g., Isaiah Trunk, *Jewish Responses to Nazi Persecution: Collective and Individual Behavior in Extremis* (New York: Stein & Day, 1979); Yehuda Bauer, "Jewish Resistance and Passivity in the Face of the Holocaust," in François Furet, ed., *Unanswered Questions: Nazi Germany and the Genocide of the Jews* (New York: Schocken Books, 1989); Hermann Langbein, *Against All Hope: Resistance in the Nazi Concentration Camps, 1938–1945* (New York: Continuum, 1996).

Under genocide, Bauer includes "the Nazi policies towards the Czechs, Poles, or Gypsies...and Soviet policies towards the Chechens, Volga Germans, or Tartars." He also includes "the policies of American settlers toward many native American tribes" and [acknowledges] "it would probably also include the cases of the Hutus, the Biharis and the Ibos." Under holocaust, Bauer lists only the Nazi attempt to destroy the Jews of Europe. Although the term may apply in the future to groups that have not yet become victims, the case of the Jews, in Bauer's view, is "the most thoroughgoing to date, the only case where holocaust would appear fully applicable."[98]

As might be expected, in making his "case" for Jewish exclusivism, Bauer is compelled to engage in the grossest sorts of distortion, not least with respect to the record of the nazi genocide itself. In part, this goes to a consistent and often extravagant overstatement of what was done to the Jews — at one point he actually asserts that all the Jews of Europe were in fact exterminated — as if what really happened were not bad enough.* On the other hand, he has bent himself to the task of falsifying history to make it appear that the Gypsies (Sinti and Romani) — who were subject to exactly the same laws and decrees, and who suffered an equal or even greater proportionate population loss at the hands of the nazis — did not suffer the same horrors as Jews.[99] Nor has he demonstrated the least willingness to admit, as Lemkin did, that nazism had clearly targeted the Poles and several other Slavic peoples for a physical eradication every bit as complete as that intended for the Jews, but were proceeding to accomplish this goal at a different rate and through a somewhat different mode of extermination.[100]

At least it can be said that, regardless of how badly he deforms them for his own purposes, Bauer is knowledgeable with respect to the particulars of the Holocaust and its context. For all his scholarly pretension, however, he has proven not at all squeamish about entering grand historical pronounce-

---

* "Total physical annihilation...was what *happened* to the Jews"; Bauer, "Holocaust and Genocide," *op. cit.*, p. 40 (emphasis added). To be accurate, Bauer is obviously aware that about a third of Europe's Jews survived the Holocaust. His argument, however, seems to be that the nazis' stated intent to effect total annihilation is somehow the same as having achieved it. It is instructive that he applies such "logic" only to the case of his own people, ignoring or dismissing a multitude of comparable statements by ranking nazis with regard to the Gypsies and Slavic peoples (and, for that matter, a host of equally exterminatory utterances by U.S. officials vis-à-vis American Indian peoples). Moreover, it appears Bauer does not even believe his own claim that the nazis intended to accomplish a total annihilation of the Jews themselves. Witness his study of their actual policy, including a 1944 attempt to trade a million Jewish prisoners to the Western Allies in exchange for 10,000 trucks to be used against the Soviet Union; Yehuda Bauer, *Jews for Sale? Nazi-Jewish Negotiations, 1933–1945* (New Haven: Yale University Press, 1994).

ments, whenever these might serve to buttress his argument, on other matters, of which he often displays a truly stunning ignorance. As part of a polemic "refuting" the possibility that certain American Indian peoples were subjected to genocide in a form entirely comparable to that suffered by Holocaust victims, for instance, he discusses the case of what he calls the "Pierce Nez."[101]

> Presumably, he means the Nez Percé people of the American Northwest, whose noses, incidentally, were not pierced, and whose Westernized name apparently is a corruption of the French *nez près*... Clearly, one should avoid declaiming in feigned seriousness on the historical experiences of people whose very name one does not know.[*]

Far worse than Bauer is his apparent successor as dean of the school of Jewish exclusivism, Cornell University professor Steven T. Katz. The latter makes essentially the same claims concerning the uniqueness of the Holocaust as Bauer, and repeats the same catechismic assertions that it was visited upon the Jews alone.[102] Reversing the poles of his predecessor's approach, however, Katz uses the arguments not to separate the Holocaust from genocide, but to make the two terms synonymous. In his rendering, the nazi genocide of the Jews is thus submitted not only as being "phenomonologically unique," and therefore worse than any other, but as the only genocide ever to have occurred.[†] Whatever may have happened to non-Jews, anywhere, during any historical period, is always categorized as having been

---

[*]David E. Stannard, "The Politics of Genocide Scholarship: Uniqueness as Denial," in Rosenbaum, *Is the Holocaust Unique?, op. cit.*, pp. 194–5. Actually, Bauer probably knew at least enough about the Nez Percé to be aware that nobody has ever suggested that they were subjected to a Holocaust-style genocide. If so, then he deliberately set up a straw man with which to lend a false appearance of validity to his sweeping claim that *no* Native North American people ever suffered such a fate. Had he selected as illustration another group—one of the peoples indigenous to northern California, for example—his contention would have been impossible to support.

[†]Steven T. Katz, "Defining the Uniqueness of the Holocaust: Preliminary Clarifications," in Dan Cohn-Sherbok, ed., *A Traditional Quest: Essays in Honor of Louis Jacobs* (London: Routledge, 1991); "Ideology, State Power and Mass Murder/Genocide," in Hayes, *Lessons, op. cit.* Katz attempts to gloss over the intrinsic absurdity of his argument by larding it with obscure terminology, describing the Jewish Holocaust, among other things, as a "*novum.*" By this, he means simply that the Holocaust possesses "singularity as a historical phenomenon." While this is an undoubtedly accurate description, as far as it goes, it by no means yields the connotations Katz would like to assign it. By analogy, his argument reduces to the equivalent of a criminologist who, upon analyzing the details of hideous crime—the 1969 Manson Family murders of Sharon Tate and her friends, for instance—correctly adduces that, as a phenomenon, it was imbued with "a unique historical singularity." The problem enters when our fictive analyst proceeds to extrapolate—à la Katz, and with utter preposterousness—that the Tate murders therefore constitute history's sole "true" murders, and that all other murders must "by definition" be something else.

something else. The Jews, and the Jews *only*, have suffered genocide, according to Katz, and even they experienced it just once: during the Holocaust.[*]

Such a result is not readily apparent in the Katzian definition of the crime—"actualization of the intent, however successfully carried out, to murder in its totality any national, ethnic, racial, religious, political, social, gender or economic group, as these groups are defined by the perpetrator"—although he does restrict the criteria of genocidal activity to modes of direct killing which occur in contexts where there is demonstrable intent to liquidate every member of a target group. One must look to Katz's systematic misrepresentation of the experiences of other peoples—he is presently preparing to publish the second of three massive volumes in which he "contextualizes" his version of the Holocaust by denying the genocides suffered by literally hundreds of groups from ancient times to the present—in order to appreciate how he expects to convince others to share his conclusions.[†]

---

[*] Steven T. Katz, "The Unique Intentionality of the Holocaust," in Steven T. Katz, ed., *Post-Holocaust Dialogues: Critical Studies in Modern Jewish Thought* (New York: New York University Press, 1983). It should be noted that Katz, while he adopts a studied tone of social scientific/philosophical rigor in his much of his own work, seems quite favorably inclined toward more mystical interpretations of the Holocaust; see, e.g., his "Language, Epistemology and Mystical Pluralism," in Steven T. Katz, ed., *Mysticism and Philosophical Analysis* (New York: Oxford University Press, 1978); "The 'Conservative' Character of Mystical Experience," in Steven T. Katz, ed., *Mystical and Religious Traditions* (New York: Oxford University Press, 1983); "Mystical Speech and Mystical Meaning," in Steven T. Katz, ed., *Mysticism and Language* (New York: Oxford University Press, 1992). It thus seems fair to observe that much of what seems otherwise inexplicably wrongheaded in his more "objective" renderings might be understood within a framework of analysis exploring the pseudotheological undercurrent in zionist scholarship which seeks to advance a supposedly unique victimization during the Holocaust as "proof" of Judaism's belief in the status of Jews as a "chosen" people; John Murray Cuddihy, *The Ordeal of Civility: Marx, Freud, Levi-Strauss, and the Jewish Struggle with Modernity* (New York: Basic Books, 1974) pp. 210–2; "The Holocaust: The Latent Issues of the Uniqueness Debate," in Philip F. Gallagher, ed., *Christians, Jews and Other Worlds: Patterns of Conflict and Accommodation* (Lanham, MD: University Press of America, 1988) pp. 62–79.

[†] Steven T. Katz, *The Holocaust in Historical Context, Vol. 1: The Holocaust and Mass Death Before the Modern Age* (New York: Oxford University Press, 1994) p. 131. It is interesting that at p. 137 Katz flatly rejects the appropriateness of the term "ethnocide," insisting that "cultural genocide"—which he defines as "actualization of the intent, however successfully carried out, to destroy the national, ethnic, religious, political, social or class *identity* of a group, as these are defined by the perpetrators (emphasis in original)"—is more precise. This in some ways promising and constructive formulation is then set to the side as constituting a phenomenon entirely apart from physical genocide, which he treats as the only "true" form. Strikingly, in his fervor to validate his emphasis on the latter by segregating the former, he appears to have overlooked the entire category of "biological" genocide, leaving readers to wonder whether he considers compulsory sterilization programs, for example, to be "murder"—his sole criterion for physical genocide—or merely a suppression of cultural identity. In sum, Katz's superficially neat and well-reasoned definitional dichotomizing obscures and confuses far more than it clarifies. It is worth observing at this point that, at p. 129, he declaims that Chalk and Jonassohn's extraordinarily restrictive definition is "surprisingly" like his own. He goes on, however, to argue that their subsequent comparative discussion of historic cases—which, however flawed, is the redeeming

One example should prove sufficient to illuminate the quality of his scholarship as a whole. In "reconsidering" the case of the Pequots, a people indigenous to what is now northern Connecticut who were so thoroughly "extirpated" by English colonists in 1637–38 that even their name was officially expunged, Katz first minimizes their losses, deciding—contrary to conventional estimates that the physical extermination was "almost total"—that "the number killed totaled probably less than half the tribe."[103] On this basis he opines, in what can only be described as a complete nonsequitur by any standard (including his own definition), that the Pequots were subjected, at most, to "cultural genocide."[104] As a final "proof" of his thesis, Katz submits that as "recently as the 1960s, the Pequots were listed as a separate group residing in Connecticut," neglecting to mention that he is referencing a census tally showing that the group included fewer than two-dozen individuals.[105]

Plainly, if one were to advance a similarly squalid line of argument with regard to the Jews of Europe—that they suffered something less than "true" genocide during the Holocaust because, after all, about a third of them survived, and, as recently as 1997, Jews are listed as a separate group residing in Europe (including even Germany!)—one would be branded a neonazi Holocaust denier, and properly so.[106] The same rules apply—or at least should apply—to Steven Katz and his colleagues in the school of Jewish Holocaust exclusivism. Their shameless definitional/analytical manipulations of the concept of genocide amounts to the blanket denial of *many* holocausts.[107]

Unfortunately, such unmitigated cant and duplicity have become normative. The books of Katz, Bauer, and others of the exclusivist persuasion are published, not by obscure and sectarian imprimaturs like the neonazis, but by prestigious academic presses such as Oxford, Temple, and Yale. Chalk and Jonassohn exclude Sartre's work and most other functionalist analysis from the bibliographic survey of "Conceptual and Background Materials" in their "comprehensive" study in comparative genocide.[108] Isador Wallimann and Michael N. Dobkowski, in another currently influential compendium, profess to adhere to a somewhat broader definition of the crime than do Chalk and Jonassohn, but they then ask the latter to produce the typology for their

---

aspect of their book—constitutes "a very real problem" because it admits to instances other than the Jewish portion of the Holocaust in which the requirements of the definition are met. The whole purpose of his own massive exercise in "comparative analysis," is to arrive at the opposite conclusion (a result he announced before he began).

volume, meanwhile refusing to so much as consider essays arguing that "eth-nocide" should be considered equally a part of the phenomenon.[109]

And so it goes. For some time, those anonymous "experts" enlisted by publishers to assess the "merits" of manuscripts dealing with genocide—the fabled "peer review" process which is usually decisive in determining whether a book or journal article sees print, and in what form—have been increasingly of the same general persuasion, a circumstance virtually guaranteeing that contrary views will either be rejected outright or produced only after being "revised" into an acceptable degree of conformity with the requirements of orthodoxy.* The recent establishment of the United States Holocaust Memorial Museum in Washington, D.C., can serve only to exacerbate this already bad situation, creating as it does yet another Smithsonian-like entity through which fact and argument can be filtered, positioned ultimately to lend the luster of its official endorsement to purveyors of convenient "truth."†

---

* It often gets worse than is suggested here. The editor of a recently published forum on the question of Holocaust uniqueness, Alan Rosenbaum, secretly sent copies of all other contributors' submissions to a single participant—Steven Katz—who was then able to tender lists of changes he wished to have made in his adversaries' draft papers (and to modify his own submission in light of their criticisms of his sources, etc.). Rosenbaum was, over his own signature, duly forwarding Katz's individual itemizations of "needed revisions" to each author when he accidentally faxed a memo intended for Katz—updating him on the progress of their covert collaboration—to another contributor (who quickly informed everyone else). With that, the intended orchestration of the outcome of this particular "debate" was brought to a screeching halt. Rosenbaum at least had the good graces to be embarrassed at having been caught engaging in this standard—though institutionally denied—practice among "responsible" academics. Katz, as usual, took a somewhat lower road. Mimicking Newt Gingrich, he responded to exposure of his own dearth of ethics by hurling gratuitous charges of unethical conduct and "incivility" at those who exposed him; see generally, "The Debate Over the Uniqueness of the Holocaust," *Chronicle of Higher Education*, Sept. 13, 1996.

† It is among the most common practices of perpetrator states wishing to divert attention from the realities of their own past or present activities to fetishize genocides occurring elsewhere. A classic example of this sort of subterfuge is the *quid pro quo* between the governments of Turkey and Israel, in which Israel validates the Turkish claim that no genocide was perpetrated against the Armenians in 1915 in exchange for the Turks' formal support for the Israeli contention that the nazi genocide of the Jews was "historically unique." The U.S. Holocaust Memorial Museum has collaborated in this arrangement, at the request of both Israeli and Turkish officials, by omitting all mention of the Armenians, while the federal government has declined to conduct an official Armenian day of remembrance; Roger W. Smith, "Denial of the Armenian Holocaust," in Israel Charny, ed., *Genocide: A Critical Bibliographical Review*, 2 vols. (London: Mansell, 1991) Vol. 2, pp. 63–85. Gypsy scholar Ian Hancock "Uniqueness," (*op. cit.*) details the same sort of posture on the part of the Holocaust Museum with regard to his own people. And, to be sure, indigenous Americans are not included among those enshrined as victims within America's institutional "remembrance" of genocide; see generally, Edward T. Linenthal, *Preserving Memory: The Struggle to Create America's Holocaust Museum* (New York: Viking, 1995).

Towards a Functional Definition

Under such conditions as are described in the preceding section, there is very little possibility that valid apprehensions of the meaning and nature of genocide can be fostered on a widespread enough basis to allow the creation of effective barriers against repetition of the crime.[110] On the contrary, insofar as they deliberately exempt from consideration most genocidal forms and processes, as well as the attitudes and activities underlying them, it seems likely that definitional truncations and analytical manipulations of the sort engaged in by Savon, Horowitz, Chalk, Jonassohn, Bauer and Katz can serve only to facilitate and reinforce rather than retard or halt the steadily accelerating trend towards global proliferation of this most destructive of all human potentials.[111]

As Chalk and Jonassohn themselves acknowledge in the quote used as an epigram at the head of this essay, attainment of some commonly accepted—or at least acceptable—definition of genocide is an absolutely essential prerequisite to changing things for the better.[112] By rights, this might be expected to be achieved, not by advocating yet another arbitrary and exclusionary formulation (as they do), but by incorporating the broadest possible range of contributions offered in consistency with Raphaël Lemkin's original explication since 1944. The purpose is to make the "unthinkable" thinkable,[113] so readily and unavoidably that the occurrence of genocide can be denied the shroud of mystification and denial in which it thrives.

As to the format in which any such inclusive definition can be most effectively advanced, many commentators seem to share the opinion that the motif employed by the framers of the Genocide Convention is best, if for no other reason than that it is by far the most familiar.[114] What follows, then, is an attempt to lay out an adequate and coherent definition of genocide in a manner which lends itself to both popular understanding and functional application to a wide variety of purposes.

Proposed Convention on Prevention and Punishment of the Crime of Genocide (1997)

Although it may or may not involve killing, per se, genocide is a denial of the right of existence of entire human groups, as homicide is the denial of the right to live of individual human beings. Such denial of the right of existence shocks the conscience of mankind, results in great losses to humanity in the form of cultural and other contributions represented by these groups, and is contrary to moral law and the spirit and aim of the United

Nations. Many instances of such crimes of genocide have occurred, when racial, religious, political, and other groups have been destroyed, entirely or in part. The punishment of the crime of genocide is therefore a matter of grave international concern.[115]

The United Nations Member States, *

Having considered the declaration made by the General Assembly of the United Nations in its resolution 96(I) dated 11 December 1946 that genocide is a crime under international law, contrary to the spirit and aims of the United Nations and condemned by the civilized world;

Recognizing that in all periods of history genocide has inflicted great losses on humanity; and

Being convinced that, in order to liberate mankind from such an odious scourge, international cooperation is required,

Hereby agree as hereinafter provided:

Article I

The Member States confirm that genocide, whether committed in time of peace or in time of war, is a crime under international law which they undertake to prevent and punish.[116]

Article II

In the present Convention, genocide means the destruction, entirely or in part, of any racial, ethnic, national, religious, cultural, linguistic, political, economic, gender or other human group, however such groups may be defined by the perpetrator.[117] It is understood that, historically, genocide has taken three (3) primary forms, usually, but not always, functioning in combination with one another.[118]

(a) *Physical Genocide,* by which is meant killing members of the targeted group(s) either directly, by indirect means, or some combination. Indirect means are understood to include, but are not restricted to, the imposition of slave labor conditions upon the target group(s), denial of fundamental medical attention to group members, and forms of systematic economic deprivation leading to starvation and other deteriorations in the physical well-being of group members.[†]

---

* The language here has been changed from "The Contracting Parties" to "The United Nations Member States." My thinking is two-fold. First, insofar as the major elements of international law conform explicitly to the requirements of the U.N. Charter, acceptance of them would seem a concomitant to U.N. membership. Hence, it is arguable that acceptance of instruments such as the Genocide Convention comes with being a member state. Second, insofar as this is true, such instruments constitute customary law, and all states are bound by them, whether or not they have "contracted" to do so.

† The delineation of indirect killing techniques conforms to Lemkin's explication in his chapter on genocide in *Axis Rule, op. cit.,* as well as the realities of nazi policies bearing on the reduction of Slavic populations in Eastern Europe remarked upon in much of the literature. It also encompasses a range of historical phenomena, such as the effects of the Spanish forced labor system upon the native

(b) *Biological Genocide*, by which is meant the prevention of births within the target group(s), either directly, indirectly, or both. Direct means are understood to devolve upon the imposition of involuntary sterilization or abortion measures upon group members. Indirect means include the imposition of degrading physical and/or psychological conditions leading to marked declines in birthrate, heightened rates of infant mortality, and the like.[*]

(c) *Cultural Genocide*, by which is meant the destruction of the specific character of the targeted group(s) through destruction or expropriation of its means of economic perpetuation; prohibition or curtailment of its language; suppression of its religious, social or political practices; destruction or denial of access to its religious or other sites, shrines, or institutions; destruction or denial of use and access to objects of sacred or sociocultural significance; forced dislocation, expulsion or dispersal of its members; forced transfer or removal of its children, or any other means.[†]

It is understood that, insofar as each of these three categories of activity is sufficient in its own right to bring about the complete or partial destruction of human groups, as such, no hierarchy of importance or seriousness can be said to prevail among them. Each will therefore be treated as possessing equal gravity to the other two.[‡]

---

populations of the Americas, the "death by disease" argument in a number of localities, and so on. At present, this is vaguely addressed under Article II(c) of the 1948 Convention, "inflicting on the group conditions of life calculated to bring about its physical destruction in whole or in part."

[*] Although Article II(d) of the 1948 Convention addresses the imposition of "measures intended to prevent births within the group," most literature on genocide fails to mention even sterilization (Katz's massive *Holocaust in Historical Context, Vol. 1*, for example, lacks even an index entry on the subject). (Re)incorporation of Lemkin's category in its full dimension should redress this problem, and clarify its overlap with modes of physical genocide (i.e., creating the conditions enumerated in Article II(c) leads not only to deaths, but declining birth rates, etc., a circumstance also bearing on Article II(b), "causing serious bodily or mental harm to members of the group").

[†] This again follows from Lemkin's chapter on genocide in *Axis Rule*, as well as his 1947 draft Convention. The provision on expropriation of the means of economic perpetuation plainly overlaps with the same criterion under physical genocide, as well as the provision on creation of conditions causing decline in the rate of childbirth under biological genocide, and adheres closely to Sartre's linkage of colonialism and genocide; *On Genocide, op. cit.* The provision on forced relocation, expulsion, and dispersal also bears on biological genocide in particular, and, secondarily, on physical genocide; see, e.g., Thayer Scudder, et al., *No Place to Go: Effects of Compulsory Relocation on Navajos* (Philadelphia: Institute for Study of Human Issues, 1982).

[‡] This is consistent with the way the point is made in a fine but little-acknowledged book by Robert Davis and Mark Zannis, *The Genocide Machine in Canada: The Pacification of the North* (Montréal: Black Rose Books, 1973) p. 20: "A culture's destruction is not a trifling matter… If people suddenly lose their 'prime symbol,' the basis of their culture, their lives lose meaning. They become disoriented, with no hope. As social disorganization often follows such a loss, they are unable to ensure their own survival… The cultural mode of group extermination is genocide, a crime. Nor should 'cultural genocide' be used in the game: 'Which is the more horrible, to kill and torture; or, remove the reason and will to live?' Both are horrible."

Article III

The following acts shall be punishable:

    (a)   Genocide;
    (b)   Conspiracy to commit genocide;
    (c)   Public incitement to commit or advocacy of genocide;[*]
    (d)   Attempt to commit genocide;
    (e)   Complicity in genocide.

Article IV

In keeping with the analogy to murder made in the preamble of this Convention, it is understood that several degrees of culpability pertain to the commission of genocide.[†] These may be taken into consideration for purposes of determining the appropriateness of punishment.

    (a)   *Genocide in the First Degree*, which consists of instances in which evidence of premeditated intent to commit genocide is present.

    (b)   *Genocide in the Second Degree*, which consists of instances in which evidence of premeditation is absent, but in which it can be reasonably argued that the perpetrator(s) acted with reckless disregard for the probability that genocide would result from their actions.

    (c)   *Genocide in the Third Degree*, which consists of instances in which genocide derives, however unintentionally, from other violations of international law engaged in by the perpetrator(s).[‡]

---

[*] The article is identical to its articulation in the 1948 Convention, except that the requirement that incitement be "direct" has been abandoned, and the word "advocacy" has been added for purposes of clarification. These changes follow the precedent set by the Streicher case at Nuremberg in 1946, and conform to the more general theory advanced by Norman Cohn (see note 76, above).

[†] Obviously, it makes little sense to analogize genocide to murder — as most analysts have done — unless all the varying degrees by which murder is customarily defined are also incorporated into the definition of genocide. Such gradation of culpability should go far towards resolving the "intentionalist/functionalist controversy" mentioned in note 67, above. For the original — and to date only — articulation of this concept, see my "Genocide: Toward a Functional Definition," *Alternatives*, Vol. XI, No. 3, 1986; reprinted in *Since Predator Came: Notes from the Struggle for American Indian Liberation* (Littleton, CO: Aigis, 1995).

[‡] The analogous correspondent in U.S. statutory codes would be "felony murder." At issue in connection to genocide, such a charge might devolve upon violations of the laws of war, as suggested by Kuper, among others; e.g., *Genocide, op. cit.*, p. 46. Other likely prospects would include violation of the 1960 Declaration on the Granting of Independence to Colonial Countries and Peoples and/or the 1966 International Covenant on Economic, Social and Political Rights, as suggested by Sartre (*On Genocide, op. cit.*), or violation of the 1979 Convention on Elimination of All Forms of Racial Discrimination, as implied *a priori* by William Patterson and other African Americans; William L. Patterson, *The Man Who Cried Genocide: An Autobiography* (New York: International, 1971).

(d) *Genocide in the Fourth Degree*, which consists of instances in which neither evidence of premeditation nor other criminal behavior is present, but in which the perpetrator(s) acted with depraved indifference to the possibility that genocide would result from their actions and therefore to effect adequate safeguards to prevent it.[*]

Article V

The commission of genocide in any form is not a "right" attending State sovereignty or any other authority. Hence, persons committing genocide or any of the other acts enumerated in Article III shall be punished, whether they are constitutionally responsible rulers, public officials, or private individuals.[†]

Article VI

Insofar as genocide has often been perpetrated as a Crime of State, it may be taken as self-evident that its prosecution lies beyond the competence of the tribunals of individual States. Those charged with genocide in any degree, or with any other act enumerated in Article III of this Convention, shall, therefore, be placed under jurisdiction of an international penal tribunal composed specifically for this purpose. It is this body, not organs of alleged perpetrator states themselves, which shall determine whether sufficient evidence attends given allegations of genocide to warrant their prosecution, and, in instances where this is so, preside over consequent proceedings, pronounce judgments, and affix punishments or other remedies.[‡]

---

[*] The analogous correspondent in U.S. statutory codes would be "negligent homicide."

[†] The second sentence herein is the same as it appears in the 1948 Convention. The first sentence has been added in response to concerns raised during U.N. debates on the matter in 1947 that the Convention contain no provision impairing the "sovereign functioning" of any state. Insofar as no state has a right to perpetrate genocide, however, there can be no infringement of legitimate sovereign prerogative entailed in prohibition of it. To argue otherwise is simply to hold that certain entities are entitled to exercise criminal license under international law. While this may be a practical reality in the world of power politics, it is not a matter deserving of accommodation in the codification of juridical principle.

[‡] This provision, which may in many ways prove to be the most problematic of all, likely represents the only means by which any semblance of "teeth" can ever be put into the Genocide Convention (or any other element of international criminal law). The basis for such a tribunal, which has existed since the 1946 United Nations' Affirmation of the Principles of International Law Recognized by the Charter of the Nuremberg Tribunal (U.N.G.A. Res. 95(I), U.N. Doc. A/235 at 1144), may also be discerned in the September 13, 1993, order of the World Court that tribunal proceedings be instituted in behalf of Bosnia and Herzegovina against Serbia and Montenegro on charges of violating provisions of the 1948 Convention; reproduced in Francis A. Boyle, *The Bosnian People Charge Genocide: Proceedings of the International Court of Justice Concerning* Bosnia v. Serbia *on the Prevention and Punishment of the Crime of Genocide* (Amherst, MA: Altheia Press, 1996) pp. 341–64. A major sticking point will undoubtedly be the formal 1985 U.S. repudiation of World Court authority over its affairs (although not over the affairs of other countries); "U.S. Terminates Acceptance of ICJ Compulsory Jurisdiction," *U.S. Department of State Bulletins*, Jan. 1986.

Article VII

All Member States hereby agree to undertake such policies and other actions as may be necessary to ensure adherence to and enforcement of the provisions of Article VI of this Convention.[119]

Article VIII

It is intended that this instrument shall supersede the United Nations Convention on Prevention and Punishment of Genocide (1948).[*]

While it is by no means anticipated that a U.N. member state will suddenly and voluntarily come to the fore in championing these proposed revisions to the Genocide Convention, especially in view of the provision under Article VI stripping all such entities of their present prerogative of engaging in the charade of self-absolution through resort to their own domestic tribunals, the kind of inclusive, flexible, and typologically nuanced definition of the crime advanced here is not without utility. To the extent that it may be adopted and applied in the discourse of scholarly and activist circles, it can have the positive effect of helping expand and reshape public consciousness of what genocide is, how it functions, and the purposes it serves. This is constructive in the sense that to be able to come to grips with any phenomenon, one must first be able to identify it when it is encountered.[120]

With heightened awareness comes heightened expectations for constructive action. Thus it may be that more than one currently recalcitrant state entity will eventually be compelled by a "creeping enlightenment" among its constituents to lobby for such revisions to the convention, even in contradiction to its own perception of sovereign interest.[121] In the alternative, state authority may be circumvented altogether through the sheer outraged force of popular initiative and determination.[122] In either event—and the reality is likely to play out in some symbiotic intertwining of both dynamics—the result will be a giant step toward achieving the mechanisms necessary to lay history's plague of genocidal actions and outlooks to rest, once and for all.

Posterity, which stands to redeem the richest of rewards from any success obtaining in this regard, will inevitably recall those who met their oblig-

---

[*]This is not so presumptuous a formulation as it may seem at first glance. Even U.S. rapporteur Ben Whitaker has suggested that some form of supersession of the Convention's current terms and provisions is in order; Ben Whitaker, *Revised and Updated Report on the Question of Prevention and Punishment of the Crime of Genocide* (New York: U.N. Economic and Social Council, Commission on Human Rights [E.CN.4.Sub.2.1985.6] July 1985).

ations in the matter with the warmest esteem and affection. To those who now move in the opposite direction, seeking for whatever stupid and misguided reasons to diminish and confuse understandings of genocide to the point that it can never be abolished, will accrue the kind of revulsion and contempt among future generations which are reserved now for the likes of the nazis and their apologists. There can be no forgiveness on this score, no room for further toleration of the squirming sophistries of "responsible" scholarship and statist deceit. The stakes are much too high, and the horror has gone on for far too long to bear further iterations of expedient denial.

Notes

1. David E. Stannard, lecture delivered at the University of Colorado/Boulder, May 2, 1995.

2. Robert Jay Lifton and Eric Markusen, *The Genocidal Mentality: Nazi Holocaust and the Threat of International War* (New York: Basic Books, 1988).

3. For an early and still unequalled elaboration of this argument, albeit one which slights the role of nongovernmental elites in perpetrating many or most genocides, see Pieter N. Drost's two-volume work, *Genocide* (Vol. 1) and *The Crime of State* (Vol. 2) (Leyden: A.W. Sythoff, 1959).

4. Although both works suffer from acute definitional inadequacies, this is the basic prognosis offered by Frank Chalk and Kurt Jonassohn in their *The History and Sociology of Genocide: Analysis and Case Studies* (New Haven: Yale University Press, 1990) and several authors contributing to Isador Wallimann and Michael N. Dobkowski, eds., *Genocide and the Modern Age: Etiology and Case Studies of Mass Death* (Westport, CT: Greenwood Press, 1987). It is also the thesis, better framed, underlying Richard Rubenstein's *The Cunning of History* (New York: Harper & Row, 1975) and, although he refrains from using the term "genocide," Noam Chomsky in his *Year 501: The Conquest Continues* (Boston: South End Press, 1992). A host of other citations might be offered.

5. The terminology accrues from the U.N. General Assembly's characterization of the crime of genocide in 1948; quoted in Leo Kuper, *Genocide: Its Political Use in the Twentieth Century* (New Haven, CT: Yale University Press, 1981) p. 11.

6. Ibid.

7. Ibid. Also see Morris Jastrow, *The Civilization of Babylonia and Assyria* (New York: Benjamin Blom, 1971 reprint of 1915 original).

8. Kuper, *Genocide, op. cit.*, p. 11.

9. Harold Lamb, *Genghis Khan* (New York: Pinnacle Books, 1927) p. 1.

10. Arnold Toynbee, *A Study of History* (New York: Oxford University Press, 1947) p. 347.

11. On the commercial aspects of the Crusades, and their role in consolidating what has come to be known as "European" culture, see Aziz Atiya, *Crusade, Commerce and Culture* (Bloomington: Indiana University Press, 1962). Also see Robert Bartlett, *The Making of Europe: Conquest, Colonization and Cultural Change, 950–1350* (Princeton, NJ: Princeton University Press, 1993).

12. H. Graetz, *History of the Jews*, 3 vols. (Philadelphia: Jewish Publication Society of America, 1894) Vol. III, p. 308. Small wonder that, as was noted by L.C. Lewonton, writing in the June 14, 1990, *New York Review of Books*, the origin of the very word "Europe" may be found in the Semitic term for "darkness."

13. Good overviews of the process, which began in 1095 and lasted until 1270—there were eight Crusades in all—will be found in René Grouset, *The Epic of the Crusades* (New York: Grossman, 1970); Robert Payne, *The Dream and the Tomb: A History of the Crusades* (New York: Stein & Day, 1984).

14. Norman Cohn, *Europe's Inner Demons: An Inquiry Inspired by the Great Witch-hunt* (New York: Basic Books, 1975); Christina Larner, *Witchcraft and Religion: The Politics of Popular Belief* (Oxford: Basil Blackwell, 1984).

15. Kuper, *Genocide, op. cit.*, p. 13, citing an account given to the Pope Innocent III by the monk Arnold, quoted in Graetz, *History of the Jews, op. cit.*, p. 502. Also see generally, Zoé Oldenbourg, *Massacre at Montségur: A History of the Albigensian Crusade* (New York: Pantheon, 1961) and Jacques Madaule, *The Albigensian Crusade* (New York: Fordham University Press, 1967).

16. Hoffman Nickerson, *The Inquisition: A Political and Military History of Its Establishment* (Port Washington, NY: Kennikat Press, 1968 reprint of 1932 original). For longer views, see Wallace K. Ferguson, *Europe in Transition, 1300–1520* (Boston: Houghton Mifflin, 1962) and Mark Greenglass, ed., *Conquest and Coalescence: The Shaping of the State in Early Modern Europe* (London: Edward Arnold, 1991).

17. Jean Guiraud, *The Medieval Inquisition* (New York: AMS Press, 1979); Albert Clement Shannon, *The Popes and Heresy in the Thirteenth Century* (New York: AMS Press, 1979); Malcolm Barber, *The Trial of the Templars* (Cambridge: Cambridge University Press, 1978).

18. To a much lesser extent, the same options were accorded adherents to Islam, mainly remnants of Moorish culture in Iberia; see generally, Cecil Roth, *The Spanish Inquisition* (New York: W.W. Norton, 1964 reprint of 1937 original).

19. Kuper, *Genocide, op. cit.*, pp. 13–4.

20. The fact that the papacy ultimately lacked the strength to accomplish its main objective during

this period—to forcibly eradicate Protestantism—makes its intent no less genocidal in its implications; see, e.g., Geoffrey Parker, *The Thirty Years' War* (New York: Military Heritage Press, 1984).

21. Kuper, *Genocide, op. cit.*, p. 14.

22. For a nice snapshot of how these two avenues of expansion fit together against the backdrop of Europe's religious strife, see Kirkpatrick Sale, *The Conquest of Paradise: Christopher Columbus and the Columbian Legacy* (New York: Alfred A. Knopf, 1990).

23. Daniel R. Headrick, *Tools of Empire: Technology and European Imperialism in the Nineteenth Century* (New York Oxford University Press) pp. 58–79. On the impact of the slave trade, see, e.g., Joseph E. Inikori and Stanley L. Engerman, eds., *The Atlantic Slave Trade: Effects on the Economies, Societies, and Peoples in Africa, the Americas, and Europe* (Durham, NC: Duke University Press, 1992).

24. For a succinct overview, see Thomas R. Berger, *A Long and Terrible Shadow: White Values, Native Rights in the Americas, 1492–1992* (Vancouver, B.C.: Douglas & McIntyre, 1991).

25. David E. Stannard, *American Holocaust: Columbus and the Conquest of the New World* (New York: Oxford University Press, 1992); on precolumbian population, see Appendix 1, pp. 261–8.

26. Probably the best, or at least most comprehensive, account is Thomas Packenham's *The Scramble for Africa: The White Man's Conquest of the Dark Continent from 1876 to 1912* (New York: Random house, 1991).

27. Donald R. Morris, *The Washing of Spears: The Rise and Fall of the Zulu Nation* (New York: Simon & Schuster, 1965).

28. Lord Robert Baden-Powell, the British commander, opined before the fact that fighting the Matabele would be "great sport" since they were clearly "without the capacity to inflict damage on trained soldiers"; Robert S.S. Baden-Powell, *The Matabele Campaign* (London: Bell & Sons, 1897) p. 63.

29. A sketch of what is at issue will be found in William E. Unrah, *White Man's Wicked Water: The Alcohol Trade and Prohibition in Indian Country, 1802–1892* (Lawrence: University Press of Kansas, 1996).

30. See, e.g., Peter Ward Fay, *The Opium War, 1840–1842* (Chapel Hill: University of North Carolina Press, 1975).

31. Kuper, *op. cit.*, p. 20.

32. On U.S. anti-Indian campaigns, see Stannard, *American Holocaust, op. cit.*; David Svaldi, *Sand Creek and the Rhetoric of Extermination: A Case Study in Indian-White Relations* (Washington, D.C.: University Press of America, 1989). On the fate of the Moros, see Stuart Creighton Miller, *"Benevolent Assimilation": The American Conquest of the Philippines, 1898–1903* (New Haven, CT: Yale University Press, 1982). On Hawai'i, see Rich Budnick, *Stolen Kingdom: An American Conspiracy* (Honolulu: Aloha Press, 1992).

33. The text is quoted in Sydney L. Goldenberg, "Crimes Against Humanity, 1945–1970," *Western Ontario Law Review*, No. X, 1971, at pp. 4–5.

34. Egon Schwelb, "Crimes Against Humanity," *The British Yearbook of International Law*, No. 23, 1946.

35. Ibid., pp. 181–3.

36. John Hohenberg, "The Crusade that Changed the U.N.," *Saturday Review*, Nov. 9, 1968.

37. Donnedieu de Vabres, *Le Procès de Nuremberg* (Paris: Éditions Monat Montchrestien, 1947) pp. 81–3.

38. Ibid., pp. 84–5.

39. Kuper, *Genocide, op. cit.*, p. 21; Schwelb, "Crimes," *op. cit.*, pp. 184–6.

40. Raphaël Lemkin, *Axis Rule in Occupied Europe: Laws of Occupation, Analysis of Government, Proposals for Redress* (Washington, D.C.: Carnegie Endowment for International Peace, 1944) p. 79.

41. Chalk and Jonassohn, *History and Sociology of Genocide, op. cit.*, pp. 8–9; quote from Lemkin, *Axis Rule, op. cit.*, p. 92. This definition is reaffirmed in Lemkin's "Genocide," *American Scholar*, Vol. 15, No. 2, 1946.

42. United Nations War Crimes Commission, *Law Reports of Trials of War Criminals*, 24 vols. (London: His Majesty's Stationery Office, 1948) Vol. VII, p. 8.

43. Ibid., pp. 1–10; Kuper, *op. cit.*, pp. 22–3; Analysis of these early trials will be found in the United Nations Sub-Commission on the Prevention of Discrimination and Protection of Minorities, *Study of the Question of the Prevention and Punishment of the Crime of Genocide* (E/CN. 4/Sub. 2/416, 4 July 1978) pp. 6–7.

44. The text of General Assembly Resolution 96(1) is quoted in its entirety in Lawrence J. LaBlanc, *The United States and the Genocide Convention* (Durham, NC: Duke University Press, 1991) pp. 22–3.

45. Ibid., p. 23.

46. Ibid. The resolution also called upon all member states to extend their "cooperation" in the matter.

47. Hohenberg, "Crusade," *op. cit.* Lemkin's schematic for defining genocide in legal terms appears in his "Genocide as a Crime under International Law," *American Journal of International Law*, No. XLI, 1947.

48. M. Lippman, "The Drafting of the 1948 Convention on the Prevention and Punishment of the Crime of Genocide," *Boston University International Law Journal*, No. 3, 1984.

49. As Chalk and Jonassohn put it, "In negotiating the convention the [U.N.] member countries wanted to make sure it applied only to the losers in World War II"; *History, op. cit.*, p. 11.

50. The postponement was provided for by General Assembly Resolution 180(II) in July 1947.

51. Kuper, *Genocide, op. cit.*, p. 24.

52. The full text of the Secretariat's Draft is annexed to Niamiah Robinson, *The Genocide Convention* (New York: Institute of Jewish Affairs, 1960).

53. 3 U.N. ESCOR, Doc. E/447–623 (1948), p. 147. The Polish position was that "the inclusion of provisions relating to political groups, which because of their mutability and lack of distinguishing characteristics do not lend themselves to definition, would weaken and blur the whole Convention"; U.N. ECOSOC, Sess. 7, 26 Aug. 1948, p. 712. On the Soviet record during the 1930s against those defined as political opponents and ideologically objectionable socioeconomic "classes" (often nationalities called by another name), see, e.g., Robert Conquest, *The Great Terror: Stalin's Purge of the Thirties* (New York: Macmillan, 1968) and *The Nation Killers: The Soviet Deportation of Nationalities* (New York: Macmillan, 1970); Nicholai Dekker and Andrei Lebed, eds., *Genocide in the U.S.S.R.: Studies in Group Destruction* (New York: Scarecrow Press, 1958); Aleksandr M. Nekrich, *The Punished Peoples: The Deportation and Fate of Soviet Minorities at the End of the Second World War* (New York: W.W. Norton, 1978) and Lyman J. Letgers, "The Soviet Gulag: Is It Genocidal?" in Israel Charny, ed., *Toward the Understanding and Prevention of Genocide* (Boulder, CO: Westview Press, 1984).

54. Kuper, *Genocide, op. cit.*, p. 29; citing U.N. *Legal Committee*, Sess. 3, Nov. 29, 1948, p. 662.

55. Robinson, *Genocide Convention, op. cit.*

56. Monroe C. Beardsly, "Reflections on Genocide and Ethnocide," in Richard Arens, ed., *Genocide in Paraguay* (Philadelphia: Temple University Press, 1976) p. 86.

57. Under provision of the United Nations Charter (59 Stat. 1031, T.S. No. 993, Bevans 1153, 1976 Y.B.U.N., Oct. 24, 1945), and later the Declaration on the Granting of Independence to Colonial Countries and Peoples (U.N.G.A. Res. 1514 (XV), 15 U.N. GAOR, Supp. (No. 16) 66, U.N. Doc. A/4684, Dec. 14, 1960), all external possessions of the imperial powers were to be inscribed on a list of "non-self-governing territories" scheduled to obtain independent ("self-determining") status within specified time periods; Ian Brownlie, *Basic Documents on Human Rights* (Oxford: Clarendon Press, [3rd ed.] 1992) pp. 9–14, 28–30. There have been a number of attempts to circumvent this requirement, both successful (e.g., the U.S. in Alaska, Hawai'i, Guam, Samoa and Puerto Rico) and unsuccessful (e.g., the French in New Caledonia), but it *is* the law; Lee C. Buchheit, *Secession: The Legitimacy of Self-Determination* (New Haven, CT: Yale University Press, 1978)

58. Robinson, *Genocide Convention, op. cit.*

59. Examples of books focusing on the exterminations drawn from the period include Ernest Kogon, *The Theory and Practice of Hell* (New York: Farrar, Strauss & Giroux, 1984 reprint of 1950 original); Léon Poliakov, *Harvest of Hate: The Nazi Program for the Destruction of the Jews of Europe* (Syracuse, NY: Syracuse University Press, 1954); Primo Levi, *Survival in Auschwitz: The Nazi Assault Upon Humanity* (New York: Collier, 1961); Raul Hilberg, *The Destruction of the European Jews* (Chicago: Quadrangle, 1961); Gerald Reitlinger, *The Final Solution: The Attempt to Exterminate the Jews of Europe, 1939–1945* (New York: Barnes, 1961).

60. Drost, *The Crime of State, op. cit.*

61. Ibid., p. 125.

62. Agreement for the Prosecution and Punishment of the Major War Criminals of the European

Axis Powers and Charter of the International Military Tribunal ("Four Power Agreement," 59 Stat. 1544, 82 U.N.T.S. 279, Sept. 10, 1945); see Weston, Falk and D'Amato, *Basic Documents, op. cit.*, pp. 138–9.

63. See, e.g., Bertrand Russell, *War Crimes in Vietnam* (New York: Monthly Review Press, 1967); John Duffett, ed., *Against the Crime of Silence: Proceedings of the International War Crimes Tribunal* (New York: Clarion, 1970); Richard Stavins, Richard J. Barnet and Marcus G. Raskin, *Washington Plans an Aggressive War* (New York: Random House, 1971); Richard A. Falk, *The Vietnam War and International Law* (Princeton, NJ: Princeton University Press, 1976).

64. Jean Paul Sartre, "On Genocide," *Ramparts*, Feb. 1968; *On Genocide and a summary of the evidence and judgments of the International War Crimes Tribunal* (Boston: Beacon Press, 1968).

65. Kuper, *Genocide, op. cit.*, p. 35, quoting Sartre, "On Genocide," *op. cit.*, p. 41.

66. Kuper, *Genocide, op. cit.*, p. 44.

67. Ibid., p. 46. Arguably, Sartre's approach to understanding genocide set in motion what, by the late 70s, would be known as the "intentionalist/functionalist controversy," a philosophical/methodological dispute between those, like Sartre, who seek to apprehend the meaning and character of the phenomenon in its underlying practical motives, and others, like the framers of the Genocide Convention, who see — or claim to see — the question of ascertaining perpetrator intent as being of decisive importance; see Tim Mason, "Intention and Explanation: A Current Controversy About Interpretation of the Holocaust," in Gerhart Hirschfeld and Lothar Kettenacher, eds., *Der Führerstaat: Mythos und Realität* (Stuttgart: Klett-Gotta, 1981); Adam Schatz, "Browning's Version: A Mild-Mannered Historian's Quest to Understand the Perpetrators of the Holocaust," *Linguafranca*, Vol. 7, No. 2, Feb. 1997.

68. Ibid. Kuper observes that Sartre appears to have selected this year because it corresponds to that of the French invasion of Algeria, the decolonization struggle of which the latter was quite prominently involved. See, e.g., Sartre's preface to Frantz Fanon, *The Wretched of the Earth* (New York: Grove Press, 1966) pp. 7–27.

69. "There is no reference in Sartre's analysis to a frequent source of genocide in decolonization, that is, the struggle between different racial, or ethnic, or religious sections for power. This is one of the consequences flowing from the arbitrary lumping together of different peoples in colonial possessions, and the disruptive impact of the rewards of power with independence"; Kuper, *Genocide, op. cit.*, p. 46. It should be noted that the bulk of Kuper's case-studies — e.g., India/Pakistan/Bangladesh, Biafra, Cambodia — are devoted to illustrating and exploring precisely this phenomenon. In this, he relies heavily on R. Palme Dutt, "India, Pakistan, Bangladesh," *Labour Monthly*, No. 54, Jan. 1972; Victor D. DuBois, *To Die in Burundi* (New York: American University Field Reports, 1972); Charles R. Nixon, "Self-Determination: The Nigeria/Biafra Case," *World Politics*, No. 24, 1972; E.W. Nafzinger and W.L. Richter, "Biafra and Bangladesh: The Political Economy of Secessionist Conflict," *Peace Research Journal*, Vol. 13, No. 2, 1976; François Ponchaud, *Cambodia Year Zero* (New York: Penguin, 1978).

70. Ibid. The primary reference here is to V.I. Lenin, *Imperialism: The Highest Stage of Capitalism* (Moscow: Foreign Languages Publishing House, 1952 translation of 1917 original). For doctrinaire efforts to conform the leninist model to the requirements of internal colonial analysis, see the compilation of essays offered by the Soviet government under the title *Genocide* (Moscow: Progress Publishers, 1985).

71. Kuper, *Genocide, op. cit.*, pp. 47–8. On the so-called "Belgian Thesis," see Buchheit, *Secession, op. cit.*; Foreign Office of Belgium, *The Belgian Thesis: Sacred Mission of Civilization, To Which Peoples Should the Benefit Be Extended?* (New York: Belgian Government Information Center, 1953); Gordon Bennett, *Aboriginal Rights in International Law* (London: Royal Anthropological Society, 1978). Other references made in this passage are to John Darby, *Conflict in Northern Ireland* (New York: Barnes & Noble, 1976); Michael Hector, *Internal Colonialism: The Celtic Fringe in British National Development, 1536–1966* (Berkeley: University of California Press, 1975); M. Bowen, G. Freeman and Kay Miller, *Passing By: The United States and Genocide in Burundi* (Washington, D.C.: Carnegie Endowment for International Peace, 1973); René Lemarchand and David Martin, *Selective Genocide in Burundi* (London: Minority Rights Group Report No. 20, 1974); John Bullock, *Death of a Country: The Civil War in Lebanon* (London: Weidenfeld & Nicolson, 1977). The groundwork for treating black-white relations in the U.S. as an intersection between colonial and class analysis was laid by W.E.B. DuBois during the 1920s; see, e.g., the cluster of short essays included in Meyer Weinberg, ed., *W.E.B. DuBois: A Reader* (New York: Harper Torchbooks, 1970) pp. 335–54. Kuper points to Alvin Gouldner as having developed a comparable sort

of analytical approach regarding the U.S.S.R.; Alvin W. Gouldner, "Stalinism: A Study in Internal Colonialism," *Telos*, No. 34, Winter 1977–78.

72. Kuper, *Genocide, op. cit.*, p. 35.

73. Indeed, Kuper uses the term "ethnocide" just once in his entire book, and then only to show that it is intended to encompass what he himself continues to describe as "cultural genocide"; ibid., p. 31.

74. Ibid., pp. 35–6.

75. Chalk and Jonassohn, *History, op. cit.*, p. 17.

76. Norman Cohn, *Warrant for Genocide: The Myth of the Jewish World Conspiracy and the Protocols of the Elders of Zion* (New York: Harper & Row, 1967); Robert Jay Lifton and Eric Markusen, *The Genocidal Mentality: Nazi Holocaust and Nuclear Threat* (New York: Basic Books, 1990). Cohn's argument should be legally interpreted in terms of the provision under Article III of the Genocide Convention prohibiting "incitement" of the crime. This, in turn, can be best interpreted on the basis of the precedent established by the case brought against nazi party racial propagandist Julius Streicher at Nuremberg; Eugene Davidson, *The Trial of the Germans, 1945–1946* (New York: Macmillan, 1966) pp. 39–58. For further details on the defendant, see Randall L. Bytwerk, *Julius Streicher: The Man Who Persuaded a Nation to Hate Jews* (New York: Dorset, 1983).

77. Vahakn N. Dadrian, "The Structural-Functional Components of Genocide," in Israel Drapkin and Emilio Viano, eds., *Victimology: A New Focus* (Lexington, MA: C.C. Heath, 1974) p. 123. A fairly close approximation will be found in Henry Huttenbach, "Locating the Holocaust on the Genocide Spectrum: Towards and Methodology of Definition and Categorization," *Holocaust and Genocide Studies*, Vol. 3, No. 3, 1988.

78. Vahakn N. Dadrian, "A Typology of Genocide," *International Review of Modern Sociology*, No. 5, Fall 1975. The most problematic aspect of the author's definition is plainly his inclusion of the word "successful." How this might be construed in any instance short of total physical extermination of a target group is anything but clear. Another subjective consideration—at least as slippery as the Genocide Convention's requirement that "intent" be demonstrated—is thus unnecessarily introduced. In effect, *any* attempt by a dominant group to actually do what Dadrian describes amounts to genocide.

79. Helen Fein, "Scenarios of Genocide: Models of Genocide and Critical Responses," in Charny, *Toward the Understanding, op. cit.*, p. 4.

80. Chalk and Jonassohn, *History, op. cit.*, p. 17; following Fein, *Accounting for Genocide, op. cit.*

81. Fein, *Accounting for Genocide, op cit.*, p. 4.

82. Helen Fein, "Towards a Sociological Definition of Genocide," unpublished paper presented at the International Studies Association annual conference, St. Louis, April 2, 1988, p. 9.

83. Chalk and Jonassohn, *History, op. cit.*, p. 22; following from Roger W. Smith, "Human Destructiveness and Politics: The Twentieth Century as an Age of Genocide," in Wallimann and Dobkowski, *Genocide, op. cit.* The use of Genghis Khan to illustrate "retributive genocide" seems a bit problematic since his resort to genocidal methods was clearly to instill terror as a means of curbing resistance to conquest. His name should therefore be placed under the heading "institutional genocide."

84. Lyman H. Legters, "The Soviet Gulag: Is It Genocidal?" in Charny, *Toward the Understanding, op. cit.* Legters confines his criteria of genocide to mass murder. Overall, his views coincide closely with those elaborated by Barbara Harff and Ted Gurr in their "Toward an Empirical Theory of Genocide and Politicide: Identification and Measurement of Cases Since 1945," *International Studies Quarterly*, Vol. 32, No. 3, Sept. 1988.

85. Robert Melson, "Provocation or Nationalism: A Critical Inquiry into the Armenian Genocide of 1915," in Richard G. Hovannisian, ed., *The Armenian Genocide in Perspective* (New Brunswick, NJ: Transaction, 1986). For detailed examination of Hitlerian and U.S. doctrines in this connection, see Frank Parella, *Lebensraum and Manifest Destiny: A Comparative Study in the Justification of Expansionism* (Washington, D.C.: MA Thesis, George Washington University Graduate School of International Relations, 1950). An excellent analysis of the theological underpinnings of at least some variants of the settler state will be found in Donald Harmon Atkinson's *God's Peoples: Covenant and Land in South Africa, Israel, and Ulster* (Ithaca, NY: Cornell University Press, 1992). Still another useful perspective is offered in J. Sakai's *Settlers: The Myth of the White Proletariat* (Chicago: Morningstar Press, 1983).

86. Noam Chomsky has contributed major insights into the functioning of the academic

community as a bolster to the status quo. For a seminal essays on this topic, see his "Objectivity and Liberal Scholarship," "Some Thoughts on Intellectuals and the Schools," and "The Responsibility of Intellectuals" in *American Power and the New Mandarins* (New York: Pantheon, 1967).

87. Hervé Savon, *Du cannibalisme au génocide* (Paris: Hachette, 1972); the author is also highly critical of the U.N.'s apparent abandonment of historical context in its formulation of the Convention.

88. Ibid. Other French writers were more fully articulating the handy catch-all notion of "ethnocide" at about the same time; see, e.g., Robert Jaulin, *L'Ethnocide à travers Les Ameriques* (Paris: Fayard, 1972); *La décivilization, politique et pratique de l'ethnocide* (Brussels: Presses Universitaires de France, 1974); Pierre Clastres, "De l'ethnocide," *L'Homme*, July-Dec. 1974.

89. Savon, *Du Cannibalisme, op. cit.*, pp. 119–24; the categories are ambiguous and overlapping, and, despite his disavowals, require considerable measures of nonlethal ingredients in order to enjoy any sort of functional reality.

90. Irving Louis Horowitz, *Genocide: State Power and Mass Murder* (New Brunswick, NJ: Transaction, 1976). Horowitz appears to have been heavily influenced by Hannah Arendt's earlier investigations of the bureaucratic aspects of nazi genocide, both in *The Origins of Totalitarianism, op. cit.*, and her subsequent *Eichmann in Jerusalem: A Report on the Banality of Evil* (New York: Penguin, 1964). However, he frames her arguments in terms of a kind of universalization and finality that she herself not only avoided, but would likely have rejected had she encountered it.

91. Irving Louis Horowitz, "Genocide and the Reconstruction of Social Theory: Observations on the Exclusivity of Collective Death," *Armenian Review*, No. 37, 1984.

92. Chalk and Jonassohn, *History, op. cit.*, p. 23. This is essentially the definition arrived at independently by Chalk in his "Definitions of Genocide and Their Implications for Prediction and Prevention," in Yehuda Bauer, et al., eds., *Remembering for the Future: Working Papers and Addenda*, 2 vols. (Oxford: Pergamon Press, 1989) Vol. 2, pp. 76–7.

93. Aside from materials otherwise cited herein, a light sampling of the work at issue includes Lucy S. Dawidowicz, "The Holocaust Was Unique in Intent, Scope and Effect," *Center Magazine*, July-Aug. 1981; Arthur A. Cohen, *The Tremendium: A Theological Interpretation of the Holocaust* (New York: Holmes & Meier, 1981); Martin Gilbert, *The Holocaust: A History of the Jews During the Second World War* (New York: Henry Holt, 1985); Michael R. Marrus, *The Holocaust in History* (Hanover, NH: Brandeis University/University Press of New England, 1987); Leni Yahil, *The Holocaust: The Fate of European Jewry, 1932–1945* (New York: Oxford University Press, 1990); Michael Berenbaum, *The World Must Know: The History of the Holocaust as Told by the American Holocaust Museum* (Boston: Little, Brown, 1993); Edward Alexander, *The Holocaust and the War of Ideas* (New Brunswick, NJ: Transaction, 1994). For a succinct overview of argumentation, see Liz McMullen, "The Uniqueness of the Holocaust," *Chronicle of Higher Education*, June 22, 1994.

94. Yehuda Bauer, "Holocaust and Genocide: Some Comparisons," in Peter Hayes, ed., *Lessons and Legacies: The Meaning of the Holocaust in a Changing World* (Evanston, IL: Northwestern University Press, 1991).

95. Yehuda Bauer, "The Place of the Holocaust in Contemporary History," in Jonathan Frankel, ed., *Studies in Contemporary Jewry, Vol. 1* (Bloomington: Indiana University Press, 1984) p. 213.

96. Ibid.

97. Ibid., p. 216.

98. Chalk and Jonassohn, *History, op. cit.*, p. 20; quoting Bauer, "The Place of the Holocaust," *op. cit.*, pp. 213–4. It should be noted that much of the spadework for this assessment was done in Bauer's *The Holocaust in Historical Perspective* (Seattle: University of Washington Press, 1978) pp. 31–6.

99. Yehuda Bauer, "Whose Holocaust?" *Mainstream*, Vol. 26, No. 9, Nov. 1980; "Gypsies," in Yisrael Gutman, ed., *Encyclopedia of the Holocaust* (New York: Macmillan, 1990). For countering information, see Ian Hancock, " 'Uniqueness' of the Victims: Gypsies, Jews and the Holocaust," *Without Prejudice*, Vol. 1, No. 2, 1988; "Responses to the *Porrajmos*: The Romani Holocaust," in Alan S. Rosenbaum, ed., *Is the Holocaust Unique? Perspectives on Comparative Genocide* (Boulder, CO: Westview Press, 1996); Benno Müller-Hill, *Murderous Science: Elimination by Scientific Selection of Jews, Gypsies and Others, 1933–1945* (Oxford: Oxford University Press, 1988). On genocide against the Poles, see Richard C. Lukas, *Forgotten Holocaust: The Poles Under German Occupation, 1939–1944* (Lexington: University Press of Kentucky,

1986). More broadly still, see Michael Berenbaum, ed., *A Mosaic of Victims: Non-Jews Persecuted and Murdered by the Nazis* (New York: New York University Press, 1990).

100. E.g., Lemkin quotes Hitler's *Mein Kampf*, at pp. 588 and 590, on the intended fates of the Poles and Slovenes; *Axis Rule, op. cit.*, pp. 81–2.

101. Yehuda Bauer, "Is the Holocaust Explicable?" in *Remembering for the Future, op. cit.*, p. 1969.

102. Steven T. Katz, "Organizing Genocide: Reflections on the Role of Technology and Bureaucracy in the Holocaust," in Alan Rosenberg and Gerald E. Meyers, eds., *Echoes from the Holocaust: Philosophical Reflections on a Dark Time* (Philadelphia: Temple University Press, 1988).

103. Steven T. Katz, "The Pequot War Reconsidered," *New England Quarterly*, No. 64, 1991, p. 223. On the actualities of the Pequot extermination, see Stannard, *American Holocaust, op. cit.*, pp. 111–5.

104. Katz, "Pequot War," *op. cit.*

105. Ibid.

106. A comprehensive survey of the neonazi literature in question will be found in Deborah Lipstadt, *Denying the Holocaust: The Growing Assault on Truth and Memory* (New York: Free Press, 1993). Also see Pierre Vidal-Naquet, *Assassins of Memory: Essays on Denial of the Holocaust* (New York: Columbia University Press, 1992).

107. The best articulation of this argument is made in Stannard, "The Politics of Genocide Scholarship," *op. cit.*

108. Chalk and Jonassohn, *History, op. cit.*, pp. 430–2.

109. Jonassohn and Chalk, *History, op. cit.* Wallimann and Dobkowski's dismissive attitude concerning potential submissions arguing that "ethnocide" constitutes an integral subpart of genocide was experienced by the author on a firsthand basis in 1986 and again during the summer of 1996.

110. The importance of the cognitive dimension is emphasized by virtually all serious commentators on the question of prevention; see, e.g., Kuper, *The Prevention of Genocide, op. cit.*; Israel W. Charny, ed., *Toward the Understanding and Prevention of Genocide: Proceedings of the International Conference on the Holocaust and Genocide* (Boulder, CO: Westview Press, 1984).

111. Although she takes a some different tack—and doesn't focus upon the named individuals— this is an important point raised by Barbara Harff in her *Genocide and Human Rights: International Legal and Political Issues* (Denver: University of Denver Graduate School of International Studies, Monograph Series in World Affairs, 1984). Also see Kuper, *International Action Against Genocide, op. cit.*

112. Chalk and Jonassohn, *History, op. cit.*, pp. 7, 4.

113. The phrasing used here is borrowed from Israel Charny, *How Can We Commit the Unthinkable? Genocide, the Human Cancer* (Boulder, CO: Westview Press, 1982).

114. E.g., Kuper, *Genocide, op. cit.*, p. 39; Chalk and Jonassohn, *History, op. cit.*, p. 11;

115. With the exception of the first phrase, added for purposes of clarification, this is virtually a recapitulation of the relevant passage contained in U.N. Resolution 96(I).

116. Aside from duplicating the modification of "The Contracting Parties" to "The Member States" this is a verbatim recapitulation of the Convention's present language.

117. The itemization of groups used here includes all those put forward since 1946, adhering most closely to that offered by Katz, *Holocaust in Historical Context, Vol. 1, op. cit.*, p. 131.

118. This imbricated triadic formulation conforms to that put forward by Raphaël Lemkin in his 1947 draft Convention.

119. Again, this is a close paraphrase of existing language.

120. The necessity of such a first step is agreed to by virtually all analysts and commentators; e.g., Chalk and Jonassohn, *History, op. cit.*; Kuper, *The Prevention of Genocide, op. cit.*; Harff, *Genocide and Human Rights, op. cit.*; Fein, "Scenarios of Genocide," *op. cit.*; Israel W. Charny, "Intervention and Prevention of Genocide," in Israel W. Charny, ed., *Genocide: A Critical Bibliography* (New York/London: Facts on File/Mansell, 1988).

121. This is a prospect suggested by international legal scholar Richard A. Falk, in his *The End of World Order: Essays on Normative International Relations* (New York: Holmes & Meier, 1983).

122. Such an implication might be drawn from the discussion of the International Peoples' Tribunal formed by Lelio Basso pursuant to the 1976 Algiers Declaration found in Richard A. Falk, *Human Rights and State Sovereignty* (New York: Holmes & Meier, 1981) pp. 200–1.

Bibliography

Publications Originating Before 1900

Anonymous, *A True Account of the Most Considerable Occurences that have Hapned in the Warre Between the English and the Indians in New England* (London, 1676).

Alvarado, Pedro de, *An Account of the Conquest of Guatemala in 1524* (Boston: Milford House, 1972 translation of Spanish language original).

Arber, Edward, and A.G. Bradley, eds., *Travel and Works of Captain John Smith, President of Virginia and Admiral of New England, 1580–1631,* 2 vols. (Edinburgh: John Grant, 1910).

Baden Powell, Robert S.S., *The Matebele Campaign* (London: Bell & Sons, 1897).

Barbour, Philip L., ed., *The Jamestown Voyages Under the First Charter, 1606–1609* (Cambridge: Hakluyt Society, 2nd ser., 1969).

————, ed., *The Complete Works of Captain John Smith, 1580–1631,* 3 vols. (Chapel Hill: University of North Carolina Press, 1986).

Baxter, James Pinney, ed., *Documentary History of the State of Maine* (Collections of the Maine Historical Society, 2nd ser., No. 23, 1916).

Bennett, Robert, and Edward Bennett [June 9, 1623], "Bennetes Welcome," *William and Mary Quarterly,* 2nd. Ser., No. 13, 1933.

Beverly, Robert, *The History and Present State of Virginia* (Chapel Hill: University of North Carolina Press, 1947 edited reprint of 1705 edition).

Bigger, H.P., ed., *The Works of Samuel de Champlain,* 6 vols. (Toronto: University of Toronto Press, 1922–1936).

Bourne, Edward Gaylord, ed., *The Narratives of Hernando de Soto,* 2 vols. (New York: A.S. Barnes, 1904).

Bradford, William, *Of Plymouth Plantation, 1620–1647* (New York: Random House, 1981 edited reprint of the 1650 original).

Bruce, Philip A., *Economic History of Virginia* (New York: P. Smith, 1896).

Caruthers, William Alexander, *The Knights of the Horsehoe* (New York: A.L. Burt, n.d., circa 1835).

Cabeza de Vaca, Alvar Nunez, *Cabeza de Vaca's Adventures in the Unknown Interior of America* (Potomoc, MD: Scripta Humanística, 1986 edited translation of the 1542 original).

Carlo, Augustin Millares, and Lewis Hanke, eds., *Historia de Las Indias,* 3 vols. (Mexico City: Fondo de Cultura Economica, 1951).

Catlin, George, *Letters and Notes on the Manners, Customs and Conditions of the North American Indians* (New York: Dover, 1973 reprint of 1844 original).

Carter, Clarence Edwin, ed., *The Correspondence of General Thomas Cage with the Secretaries of State, 1763–1775, Vol. 1* (New Haven: Yale College and University Press, 1931).

Chardon, Francis A., *Journal at Fort Clark, 1834–39* (Pierre: State Historical Society of South Dakota, 1932).

Clark, Peter D., *The Origin and Traditional History of the Wyandots* (Toronto: Hunter, Rose, 1870).

Cook, Frederick, *Journals of the Military Expedition of Major General John Sullivan Against the Six Nations in 1779* (Auburn, New York, 1887).

Cortés, Hernán, *Letters from Mexico* (New York: Grossman, 1971).

Cortes, Jose, *Views from the Apache Frontier: Report on the Northern Provinces of New Spain* (Norman: University of Oklahoma, 1989 edited reprint of 1803 original).

Custer, George Armstrong, *My Life On the Plains, or Personal Experiences with the Indians* (Norman: University of Oklahoma, 1964 reprint of 1873 original).

Davenport, Francis Gardiner, ed., *European Treaties Bearing on the History of the United States and Its Dependencies,* 2 vols. (Washington, D.C.: Carnegie Institution for International Peace, 1917).

Dawson, Moses, *Historical Narrative of the Civil and Military Service of Major-General William Henry Harrison* (Cincinnati: Cincinnati Advertiser, 1824).

Díaz del Castillo, Bernal, *The Discovery and Conquest of Mexico, 1517–1521* (London: George Routledge & Sons, 1926 translation of Spanish language original).

————, *The Conquest of New Spain* (New York: Penguin, 1963 of the posthumously published 1623 Spanish language original, *Historia Verdadera de la Conquista de la Nueva*).

Domenech, Emmanuel Henri Dieudonne, *Seven Years Residence in the Great Deserts of North America* (London: Green, Longman & Roberts, 1860).

Drake, Benjamin, *The Life of Tecumseh and His Brother the Prophet* (Cincinnati: Anderson, Gates & Wright, 1841).

Eccleston, William, *The Mariposa Indian War, 1850–1851* (Salt Lake City: University of Utah Press, 1957 reprint of 1851 original).

Golovin, V.M., *Around the World on the Kamchatka, 1817–1818* (Honolulu: Hawaiian Historical Society, 1979 reprint of 1819 original).

Graetz, H., *History of the Jews*, 3 vols. (Philadelphia: Jewish Publication Society of America, 1894).

Halbert, H.S., and T.H. Ball, *The Creek War* (Chicago: Donohue and Hennebury, 1895).

Hammond, George P., and Agapito Rey, eds. and trans., *Narratives of the Coronado Expedition, 1540–1542* (Albuquerque: University of New Mexico Press, 1940).

Hollister, O.J., *Boldly They Road: A History of the First Colorado Regiment of Volunteers* (Lakewood, CO: Golden Press, 1965 reprint of 1873 original).

Hopkins, Sarah Winnemuca, *Life Among the Paiutes: Their Wrongs and Claims* (Bishop, CA: Chalfont Press, 1969 reprint of 1883 original).

Hornaday, William T., *Exterminating the American Bison* (Washington, D.C.: Smithsonian Institution, 1899).

Hubbard, William, *The Present State of New England, Being a Narrative of the Troubles with the Indians in New England* (London: Theo. Parkhurst, 1677).

Inman, Henry, *The Old Santa Fe Trail: The Story of a Great Highway* (Minneapolis: Ross & Haines, 1966 reprint of the 1897 original).

James, William, *A Full and Complete Account of the Military Occurence of the Late War Between Great Britain and the United States of America*, 2 vols. (London: self-published, 1818).

Jenny, Walter P., *Report on the Mineral Wealth, Climate and Rainfall and Natural Resources of the Black Hills of Dakota* (Washington, D.C: 44th Cong., 1st Sess., Exec. Doc. No. 51, U.S. Government Printing Office, 1876).

Kappler, Charles J., ed., *Indian Treaties, 1778–1883* (New York: Interland, 1972).

Keen, Benjamin, trans., *The Life of the Admiral Christopher Columbus by His Son Ferdinand* (New Brunswick, NJ: Rutgers University Press, 1959 reprint of circa 1540 original).

Keim, DeB. Randolph, *Sheridan's Troopers on the Borders: A Winter Campaign on the Plains* (Philadelphia: Davis McKay, 1885).

Keyserling, Meyer, *Christopher Columbus and the Participation of the Jews in the Spanish and Portuguese Discoveries* (London: Longman, Green, 1963 reprint of 1893 original).

Kingsbury, Susan Myra, ed., *The Records of the Virginia Company of London*, 4 vols. (Washington, D.C.: Smithsonian Institution, 1906–1935).

Kinnard, Lawrence, ed. and trans., *The Frontiers of New Spain: Nicolas de Lafora's Description, 1766–1768* (Berkeley: Quivera Society, 1958).

Knox, Captain John, *An Historical Journal of the Campaigns in North America for the Years 1757, 1758, 1759, and 1760* (London, 1769).

Larabee, Leonard L., et al., eds., *The Papers of Benjamin Franklin, Vol. 6* (New Haven: Yale University Press, 1959).

Las Casas, Bartolomé de, *The Spanish Colonie (Brevísima relacíon)* (University Microfilms Reprint, 1966).

————, *Historia de las Indias*, 3 vols. (Mexico City: Fondo de Cultura Económica, 1951 reprint of 1541 edition).

Lincoln, Charles H., ed., *Narratives of the Indian Wars, 1675–1699* (New York: Charles Scribner's Sons, 1913).

López de Gómara, Francisco, *Cortés: The Life of the Conqueror by His Secretary* (Berkeley: University of California Press, 1965 translation of the 1539 Spanish language original).

Ludlow, William, *Report of a Reconnaissance of the Black Hills of Dakota* (Washington, D.C.: 43d Cong., 2d Sess., U.S., Government Printing Office, 1875).

McCallem, James D., ed., *The Letters of Eleazer Wheelock's Indians* (Hanover, NH: Dartmouth College Pubs, 1932).

McIlwaine, H.R., ed., *Minutes of the Council and General Court of Virginia* (Richmond: Virginia State Historical Society, 1924).

Mallery, Colonel Garrick, "The Present and Former Number of Our Indians," *Proceedings of the American Association for the Advancement of Science*, No. 26, 1877.

Mason, John, *A Brief History of the Pequot War* (Ann Arbor: March of America Facimile Series No.23, 1966 reprint of the 1763 reprint of the 1677 original).

Mather, Cotton, *The Life and Death of the Renown'd Mr. John Eliot, Who Was the First Preacher of the Gospel to the Indians in America* (London, 2nd ed., 1691).

Mather, Increase, *A Brief History of the Warr With the Indians in New England* (Boston, 1676).

————, *Early History of New England; Being a Relation of Hostile Passages Between the Indians and the European Voyagers and Settlers* (Albany: State University Press of New York, 1864 reprint of the 1677 original).

Mooney, James M., *The Ghost Dance Religion and the Sioux Outbreak of 1890* (Washington, D.C.: Bureau of American Ethnology, Smithsonian Institution, 1896).

Morison, Samuel Elliot, ed. and trans., *Journals and Other Documents on the Life and Voyages of Christopher Columbus* (New York: Heritage Publishers, 1963).

Morton, Samuel George, *Crania Americana; or, A Comparitive View of the Skulls of Various Aboriginal Nations of North and South America* (Philadelphia: John Pennington, 1839).

O'Callaghan, E. B., *Laws and Ordinances of New Netherlands, 1638–1647* (Albany: State Historical Society of New York, 1868).

O'Callaghan, E.B., and Bethold Fernouw, eds., *Documents Relative to the Colonial History of the State of New York,*, 15 vols. (Albany: State University Press of New York, 1856–1857).

Oviedo, *Historia general y natural de las Indias*, 4 vols. (Madrid: Academia Historica, 1851–1855).

Palfrey, John Gorham, *History of New England*, 5 vols. (Boston: Little, Brown, 1858–1890).

Parkman, Francis, *The Conspiracy of Pontiac and the Indian War After the Conquest of Canada*, 2 vols. (Boston: Little, Brown, 1874).

Perry, Armstrong, *The Sauks and the Black Hawk War* (Springfield, IL: H. W. Rokker, 1887).

Pierce, Benjamin, *A History of Harvard University from Its Founding in the Year 1636 to the Period of the American Revolution* (Cambridge, MA: Brown, Shattuck, 1833).

Rowlandson, Mary, *The Sovereignty and Goodness of God Together with the Faithfulness of His Promise Displayed: Being the Narrative of the Captivity and Restoration of Mrs. Mary Rowlandson* (Boston, 1682).

Royce, Charles C., *Indian Land Cessions in the United States: 18th Annual Report, 1896–97*, 2 vols. (Washington, D.C.: Bureau of American Ethnography, Smithsonian Institution, 1899).

Salley, Alexander S. Jr., ed., *Narratives of Early Carolina, 1650–1708* (New York: Original Narratives of American History, 1911).

Sahagún, Bernardino de, *The Conquest of New Spain* (Salt Lake City: University of Utah Press, 1989 translation 1585 Spanish language original).

Schoolcraft, H.R., *Historical and Statistical Information Respecting the History, Condition, and Prospects of the Indian Tribes of the United States* (Philadelphia: Lippencott, Grambo & Co., 1851).

Shackford, James A., *David Crockett: The Man and the Legend* (Lincoln: Uinversity of Nebraska Press, 1994 reprint of 1856 original).

Shackford, James A., and Stanley J. Folmsbee, ed., *A Narrative of the Life of David Crockett of Tennessee* (Knoxville: University of Tennessee Press, 1973 reprint of 1834 original).

Shipton, Clifford K., *Sibley's Harvard Graduates: Biographical Sketches of Those Who Attended Harvard College* (Cambridge, MA: Harvard College, 1837).

Sullivan, James, et al., eds., *The Papers of Sir William Johnson*, 14 vols. (Albany: State Historical Society of New York, 1921–1965).

Tatum, Lawrie, *Our Red Brothers and the Peace Policy of Ulysses S. Grant* (Philadelphia: Winston, 1899).

Thomas, Alfred Burnaby, ed. and trans., *Forgotten Frontiers: A Study of the Spanish Indian Policy of Don Juan Bautista de Anza, Governor of New Mexico, 1777–1787* (Norman: University of Oklahoma Press, 1932).

Thomas, M. Halsey, ed., *The Diary of Samuel Sewell*, 2 vols. (New York: Farrar, Strauss & Giroux, 1973).

Trumbull, J. Hammond and C. J. Hoadly, eds., *The Public Records of the Colony of Connecticut*, 15 vols. (Hartford: Connecticut State Historical Society, 1850–90).

Tullidge, Edward, "The Battle of Bear River," *Tullidge's Quarterly Magazine*, Jan. 1881.

———, "The Cities of Cache Valley and Their Founders," *Tullidge's Quarterly Magazine*, July 1881.

Underhill, John, *Newes from America; or, A New and Experimental Discovery of New England* (London, 1638).

U.S. Congress, *Speeches on the Removal of the Indians, April-May, 1830* (New York: Kraus, 1973 reprint of 1830 original).

———, *Report of the Joint Committee Appointed Under Resolution of March 3, 1865* (Washington, D.C.: 39th Cong., 2nd. Sess., 1867).

U.S. Department of Interior, Bureau of Indian Affairs, *American Indian Reservations* (Washington, D.C.: U.S. Government Printing Office, 1979).

———, Bureau of the Census, *Annual Report of the Commissioner of Indian Affairs, 1863* (Washington, D.C.: Government Printing Office. 1863).

———, Bureau of Indian Affairs, *Annual Report of the Commissioner of Indian Affairs, 1875* (Washington, D.C.: 43d Cong., 2d Sess., U.S., U.S., Government Printing Office, 1875).

———, Bureau of Indian Affairs, *Annual Report of the Commissioner of Indians Affairs to the Secretary of the Interior* (Washington, D.C.: U.S. Government Printing Office, 1886).

U.S. Department of War, "Sand Creek Massacre," *Report of the Secretary of War* (Washington, D.C.: Sen. Exec. Doc. 26, 39 Cong., 2d Sess., U.S. Government Printing Office, 1867).

U.S. House of Representatives, "Massacre of Cheyenne Indians," *Report on the Conduct of the War* (Washington, D.C.: 38th Cong., 2d Sess., U.S. Governing Printing Office, 1865).

U.S. Senate, "The Chivington Massacre," *Reports of the Committees* (Washington, D.C.: 39 Cong., 2d Sess., U.S. Government Printing Office, 1867).

Vattel, Emer, *The Laws of Nations* (Philidelphia: T. & J.W. Johnson, 1855).

Vaughan, Alden T., ed., *Early American Indian Documents: Treaties and Laws, 1607–1789* (Washington, D.C.: University Publications of America, 1979).

Waterhouse, Edward, *A Declaration of the State of the Colony and Affaires in Virginia* (London, 1622).

Whitehead, William A., ed., *Documents Relating to the Colonial, Revolutionary, and Post-Revolutionary History of the State of New Jersey, Archives of the State of New Jersey* (Trenton: 1st ser., Vol. 20, 1898).

Winthrop, John, *The History of New England from 1630 to 1649*, 2 vols. (Boston, 1853 edited reprint of 1690 original).

Yates, Sidney V., ed., *Three Visitors to Early Plymouth: Letters About the Pilgrim Settlement in New England during Its First Eleven Years* (Plymouth, MA: Plymouth Plantation, 1963).

Publications Originating After 1900

Books

Abel, Annie Heloise, *The American Indian in the Civil War, 1862–1865* (Lincoln: University of Nebraska Press, 1992).

Abernathy, Thomas Perkins, *Western Lands and the American Revolution* (New York: Russell & Russell, 1959).

Abrahamson, Irving, ed., *Against Silence: The Voice and Vision of Elie Wiesel* (New York: Holocaust Society, 1985).

Acheson, Dean G., *Present at the Creation: My Years in the State Department* (New York: W.W. Norton, 1970).

Adamic, Louis, *My Native Land* (New York: Harper & Brothers, 1943).

Adams, David Wallace, *Education for Extinction: American Indians and the Boarding School Experience, 1875–1928* (Lawrence: University Press of Kansas, 1995).

Adamson, Walter, *Hegemony and Revolution: A Study of Antonio Gramsci's Political and Cultural Theory* (Berkeley: University of California Press, 1980).

Adkin, Major Mark, *Urgent Fury: The Battle for Grenada* (Lexington, MA: D.C. Heath, 1989).

Ainstein, Reubin, *Jewish Resistance in Nazi-Occupied Eastern Europe* (New York: Barnes & Noble, 1974).

Alan, Alexrod, *Chronicle of the Indian Wars from Colonial Times to Wounded Knee* (New York: Prentice Hall, 1993).

Aldridge, Robert C., *Nuclear Empire* (Vancouver, B.C.: New Star Books, 1989).

Alexander, Edward, *The Holocaust and the War of Ideas* (New Brunswick, NJ: Transaction, 1994).

Alford, Thomas Wildcat, *Civilization and the Story of the Absentee Shawnees* (Norman: University of Oklahoma Press, 1936).

Allen, James S., *Atomic Imperialism: The State, Monopoly and the Bomb* (New York: International, 1952).

Alperovitz, Gar, *Atomic Diplomacy: Hiroshima and Potsdam—The Use of the Atomic Bomb and the American Confrontation with Soviet Power* (New York: Vintage, 1967).

———, *The Decision to Drop the Bomb* (New York: Alfred A. Knopf, 1995).

Ambler, Marjane, *Breaking the Iron Bonds: Indian Control of Energy Development* (Lawrence: University Press of Kansas, 1990).

Ambrose, Steven E., *Crazy Horse and Custer: The Parallel Lives of Two American Warriors* (Garden City, NY: Doubleday, 1975).

American Friends Service Committee, *Uncommon Controversy: Fishing Rights of the Muckleshoot, Puyallup, and Nisqually Indians* (Seattle: University of Washington Press, 1970).

Amin, Samir, *Maldevelopment: Anatomy of a Global Failure* (London: Zed Books, 1990).

Amott, Teresa L., and Julie A. Matthaei, *Race, Gender and Work: A Multicultural History of Women in the United States* (Boston: South End Press, 1991).

Anderson, Fred, *A People's Army: Massachusetts Soldiers and Society in the Seven Years' War* (Chapel Hill; University of North Carolina Press, 1984).

Anderson, Gary Clayton, *Little Crow* (St. Paul: Minnesota Historical Society, 1986).

Anderson, Jack, and Ronald W. May, *McCarthy: The Man, the Senator, the "Ism"* (Boston: Beacon Press, 1952).

Anderson, Thomas P., *Matanza: El Salvador's Communist Revolt of 1932* (Lincoln: University of Nebraska Press, 1971).

Anderson, William L., ed., *Cherokee Removal, Before and After* (Athens: University of Georgia Press, 1991).

Andreopoulos, George J., ed., *Genocide: Conceptual and Historical Dimensions* (Philadelphia: University of Pennsylvania Press, 1994).

Andrews, Charles McLean, *The Colonial Period in American History,* 4 vols. (New Haven: Yale University Press, 1934–1939).

Andrist, Ralph K., *The Long Death: The Last Days of the Plains Indian* (New York: Macmillan, 1964).

Ann, Isador Walliamn, and Mchael N. Dobkowski, eds., *Genocide and the Modern Age: Etiology and Case Studies of Mass Death* (Westport, CT: Greenwood Press, 1987).

Annas, George J., *The Nazi Doctors and the Nuremberg Code: Human Rights in Medical Experimentation* (New York: Oxford University Press, 1992).

Anson, Bert, *The Miami Indians* (Norman: University of Oklahoma Press, 1970).

Anti-Defamation League of B'nai Brith, *Hitler's Apologists: The Anti-Semitic Propaganda of Holocaust "Revisionism"* (New York: ADL, 1993).

App, Austin J., *The Six Million Swindle: Blackmailing the German People for Hard Marks with Fabricated Corpses* (Tacoma Park, MD: St. Boniface Press, 1973).

———, *A Straight Look at the Third Reich: Hitler and National Socialism, How Right? How Wrong?* (Tacoma Park, MD: St. Boniface Press, 1974).

Arad, Yitzak, Shmuel Krakowski and Schmuel Spector, eds., *The Einsatzgruppen Reports: Selections from the Nazi Death Squads' Campaign Against the Jews in Occupied Territories of the Soviet Union, July 1941–January 1943* (New York: Holocaust Library, 1989).

Arendt, Hannah, *The Origins of Totalitarianism* (Cleveland: World, [2nd ed.] 1958).

————, *Eichmann in Jerusalem: A Report on the Banality of Evil* (New York: Penguin, 1964).

Arens, Richard, ed., *Genocide in Paraguay* (Philadelphia: Temple University Press, 1976).

Arens, W., *The Man-Eating Myth* (New York: Oxford University Press, 1979).

Armstrong, Virginia Irving, ed., *I Have Spoken: American History Through the Eyes of American Indians* (Chicago: Swallow Press, 1971).

Armstrong, W.D., *A Report on Mineral Revenues and the Tribal Economy* (Window Rock, AZ: Navajo Office of Mineral Development, June, 1976).

Arnson, *El Salvador: A Revolution Confronts the United States* (Washington, D.C.: Institute for Policy Studies, 1982).

Aronsfeld, C.C., *The Text of the Holocaust: A Study of the Nazis' Extermination Propaganda, 1919–1945* (Marblehead, MA: Micah, 1985).

Ashburn, P.M., *The Ranks of Death* (New York: Coward Publishers, 1947).

Athearn, Robert G., *William Tecumseh Sherman and the Settlement of the West* (Norman: University of Oklahoma Press, 1956).

Auth, Stephen F., *The Ten Years' War: Indian-White Relations in Pennsylvania, 1755–1765* (New York: Oxford University Press, 1989).

Atkinson, Donald Harmon, *God's Peoples: Covenant and Land in South Africa, Israel, and Ulster* (Ithaca, NY: Cornell University Press, 1992).

Axelrod, Alan, *Chronicle of the Indian Wars from Colonial Times to Wounded Knee* (New York: Prentice Hall, 1993).

Axtell, James, *The European and the Indian: Essays in the Ethnohistory of North America* (New York: Oxford University Press, 1981).

————, *After Columbus: Essays in the Ethnohistory of North America* (New York: Oxford University Press, 1988).

————, *Beyond 1492: Encounters in Colonial North America* (New York: Oxford University Press, 1992).

Azis, Atiya, *Crusade, Commerce and Culture* (Bloomington: Indiana University Press, 1962).

Bachman, Van Cleaf, *Peltries or Plantations: The Economic Policies of the Dutch West Indian Company in New Netherland, 1623–1629* (Baltimore: John Hopkins University Press, 1969).

Bacque, James, *Other Losses: The Shocking Truth Behind the Mass Deaths of Disarmed German Soldiers and Civilians Under General Eisenhower's Command* (New York: Prima, 1991).

Bailey, L.R., *Long Walk* (Los Angeles: Westernlore, 1964).

————, *Indian Slave Trade in the Southwest* (Los Angeles: Westernlore, 1973).

Bailyn, Bernard, *The New England Merchants of the Seventeenth Century* (Cambridge: Harvard University Press, 1955).

Baird, W. David, ed., *A Creek Warrior for the Confederacy* (Norman: University of Oklahoma Press, 1968).

Baird, Jay W., *From Nuremberg to My Lai* (Lexington, MA: D.C.: Heath, 1972).

Baker, L., *John Marshall: A Life in Law* (New York: Macmillan, 1976).

Balabkins, Nicholas, *West German Reparations to Israel* (New Brunswick, NJ: Princeton University Press, 1971).

Bales, James D., ed., *J. Edgar Hoover Speaks Concerning Communism* (Nutley, N.J.: Craig Press, 1951).

Balesi, Charles J., *The Time of the French in the Heart of North America, 1673–1818* (Chicago: Alliance Française, 1992).

Ball, Howard, *Justice Downwind: America's Atomic Testing Program in the 1950s* (New York: Oxford University Press).

Ball, Nicole, and Milton Leitenberg, ed., *The Structure of the Defense Industry* (New York: St. Martin's Press, 1983).

Barber, Malcolm, *The Trial of the Templars* (Cambridge: Cambridge University Press, 1978).

Barber, William F., and C. Neale Ronning, *Internal Security and Military Power* (Columbus: Ohio State University Press, 1966).

Barnes, Harry Elmer, *The Barnes Trilogy: Three Revisionist Booklets by Henry Elmer Barnes, Historian, Sociologist, Criminologist, Economist* (Torrance, CA: Institute for Historical Review, 1979).

————, *Who Started World War I?* (Torrance, CA: Institute for Historical Review, 1983 reprint of 1929 original).

Barnes, Viola, *The Dominion of New England* (New Haven: Yale University Press, 1923).

Barnet, Richard J., and Ronald Müller, *Global Reach: The Power of Multinational Corporations* (New York: Touchstone Books, 1974).

Barrett, Stanley R., *Is God a Racist? The Right Wing in Canada* (Toronto: University of Toronto Press, 1987).

Bartimus, Tad, and Scott MacCartney, *Trinity's Children: Living Along America's Nuclear Highway* (Albuquerque: University of New Mexico Press, 1991).

Bartlett, Robert, *The Making of Europe: Conquest, Colonization and Cultural Change, 950–1350* (Princeton, NJ: Princeton University Press, 1993).

Basso, Leigh H., *The Cibique Apache* (New York: Holt, Rinehart & Winston, 1970).

Bates, Gregg, ed., *Mobilizing Democracy: Changing the U.S. Role in the Middle East* (Monroe, ME: Common Courage Press, 1991).

Bauer, Yehuda, *The Holocaust in Historical Perspective* (Seattle: University of Washington Press, 1978).

————, *The Jewish Emergence from Powerlessness* (London: Macmillan, 1979).

————, *A History of the Holocaust* (New York: Franklin Watts, 1982).

Bauer, Yehuda, and Nathan Rosenstreich, eds., *The Holocaust as Historical Experience* (Chicago: Quadrangle, 1981).

Bauer, Yehuda, et al., *Remembering for the Future: Working Papers and Addenda*, 2 vols. (Oxford: Pergamon Press, 1989).

Bauman, Zygmunt, *Modernity and the Holocaust* (Cambridge: Polity Press, 1989).

Beal, Merrill D., *"I Will Fight No More Forever": Chief Joseph and the Nez Percé War* (Seattle: University of Washington Press, 1963).

Bean, Lowell John, *The Cahuilla* (New York: Chelsea House, 1989).

Bearman, Jonathan, *Qadhafi's Libya* (London: Zed Books, 1986).

Beckham, Stephen Dow, *Requiem for a People: The Rogue River Indians and the Frontiersmen* (Norman: University of Oklahoma Press, 1971).

Belfrage, Cedric, *American Inquisition, 1945–1960* (Indianapolis: Bobbs-Merrill, 1973).

Bell, Daniel, *The New American Right* (New York: Criterion, 1955).

————, *The Radical Right* (New York: Double, Day 1964).

Bennett, Gordon, *Aboriginal Rights in International Law* (London: Royal Anthropological Society, 1978).

Berdechewsky, Bernardo, *The Aracuanian Indian in Chile* (Copenhagen: IWGIA Doc. No. 20, 1975).

Berenbaum, Michael, ed., *A Mosaic of Victims: Non-Jews Persecuted and Murdered by the Nazis* (New York: New York University Press, 1990).

————, *The World Must Know: The History of the Holocaust as Told by the American Holocaust Memorial Museum* (Boston: Little, Brown, 1993).

Berger, John J., *Nuclear Power: The Unviable Option* (Palo Alto, CA: Ramparts Press, 1976).

Berger, Thomas R., *The Long and Terrible Shadow: White Values, Native Rights in the Americas, 1492–1992* (Vancouver, B.C.: Douglas & McIntyre, 1991).

Berkhofer, Robert F., Jr., *Salvation and the Savage: An Analysis of Protestant Missions and American Indian Response, 1787–1862* (Knoxville: University of Kentucky Press, 1965).

Berman, Paul, ed., *Debating P.C.: The Controversy Over Political Correctness on College Campuses* (New York: Laurel Books, 1992).

Bernal, Martin, *Black Athena: The Afroasiatic Roots of Classical Civilization, Vol. 1: The Fabrication of Ancient Greece, 1785–1985* (New Brunswick, NJ: Rutgers University Press, 1987).

Berthrong, Donald, *The Cheyenne and Arapaho Ordeal: Reservation and Agency Life, 1875–1907* (Norman: University of Oklahoma Press, 1976).

Betts, Raymond E., *Europe Overseas: Phases of Imperialism* (New York: Basic Books, 1968).

Binding, Karl, and Alfred Hoche, *Die Freigabe der Vernichtung Lebensunwerten Lebens* (Leipzig: Felix Meiner, 1920).

Bird, Kirk Kicking, and Karen Ducheneaux, *One Hundred Million Acres* (New York: Macmillan, 1973).

Bishop, Morris, *The Odyssey of Cabeza de Vaca* (Englewood Cliffs, NJ: Prentice-Hall, 1933).

Black, Edwin, *The Transfer Agreement* (New York: Macmillan, 1984).

Blackett, P.M.S., *Fear, War and the Bomb: Military and Political Consequences of Atomic Energy* (New York: McGraw Hill, 1948).

Blair, Clay, *The Forgotten War: America in Korea, 1950–1953* (New York: Times Books, 1987).

Blanco, Hugo, *Land or Death* (New York: Pathfinder, 1977).

Bley, Helmut, *South West Africa Under German Rule, 1898–1914* (London: Heinemann, 1971).

Block, Fred, *The Origins of International Economic Disorder* (Berkeley: University of California Press, 1977).

Blum, William, *The CIA: A Forgotten History* (London: Zed Books, 1986).

————, *Killing Hope: U.S. Military and CIA Interventions Since World War II* (Monroe, ME: Common Courage Press, 1995).

Bolger, Daniel P., *Savage Peace: Americans at War in the 1990s* (San Francisco: Presidio Press, 1995).

Bolton, Herbert Eugene, *Coronado on the Turquois Trail: Knight of the Pueblos* (Albuqueque: University of New Mexico Press, 1949).

Bonner, Ray, *Weakness and Deceit* (New York: *Times* Books, 1984).

Boone, Elizabeth, ed., *Ritual Human Sacrifice in Mesoamerica* (Washington, D.C.: Dumbarton Oaks Research Library, 1984).

Bourne, John G., *Mackenzie's Last Fight with the Cheyennes* (New York: Argonaut, 1966).

Bourne, Russell, *The Red King's Rebellion: Racial Politics in New England, 1675–1678* (New York: Atheneum, 1990).

Borah, Woodrow W. and Sherburne F. Cook, *The Aboriginal Population of Central Mexico on the Eve of the Spanish Conquest* (Berkeley: University of California Ibero-American No. 43, 1963).

Boshyk, Y., ed., *Ukraine During World War II: History and Aftermath* (Edmunton: Canadian Institute for Ukrainian Studies, University of Alberta, 1986).

Bowen, M., G. Freeman and Kay Miller, *Passing By: The United States and Genocide in Burundi* (Washington, D.C.: Carnegie Endowment for International Peace, 1973).

Box, Thadius, et al., *Rehabilitation Potential for Western Coal Lands* (Cambridge, MA: u, 1974).

Boxer, C. R., *The Dutch Seaborne Empire, 1600–1800* (New York: Alfred A. Knopf, 1965).

Boyce, George A., *When the Navajos Had Too Many Sheep: The 1940s* (San Francisco: Indian Historian Press, 1974).

Boyd-Bowman, Peter, *Patterns of Spanish Immigration to the New World, 1493–1580* (Buffalo: State University of New York Council on the Humanities, 1973).

Boyle, Francis A., *Defending Civil Resistence Under International Law* (Dobbs Ferry, NY: Transnational, 1987).

————, *The Bosnian People Charge Genocide: Proceedings of the International Court of Justice Concerning Bosnia v. Serbia on the Prevention and Punishment of the Crime of Genocide* (Amherst, MA: Alethia Press, 1996).

Boyle, Richard, *Flowers of the Dragon: The Breakdown of the U.S. Army in Vietnam* (San Francisco: Ramparts Press, 1972).

Brack, Gene M., *Mexico Views Manifest Destiny, 1821–1846: An Essay on the Origins of the Mexico War* (Albuquerque: University of New Mexico Press, 1975).

Brackman, Arnold C., *The Other Nuremberg: The Untold Story of the Tokyo War Crimes Trials* (New York: William Morrow, 1987).

Bridgeman, Jon, *The Revolt of the Hereros* (Berkeley: University of California Press, 1981).

Brady, Cyrus T., *The Conquest of the Southwest: The Story of a Great Spoilation* (New York: Appleton, 1905).

Braham, Randolph, *The Politics of Genocide: The Holocaust in Hungary*, 2 vols. (New York: Columbia University Press, 1981).

Brainbridge, Kennth T., *Trinity* (Los Alamos, NM: Los Alamos National Scietific Laboratory, 1976 edited release of 1945 original).

Breitman, Richard, *Architect of Genocide: Himmler and the Final Solution* (Hanover, NH: University Press of New England, 1991).

Brill, Charles J., *The Conquest of the Southern Plains: Uncensored Narrative of the Battle of the Washita and Custer's Southern Campaign* (Oklahoma City: Golden Saha, 1938).

Brown, Dee, *Bury My Heart at Wounded Knee: An Indian History of the American West* (New York: Holt, Rinehart & Winston, 1970).

———, *Fort Phil Kearny: An American Saga* (Lincoln: University of Nebraska Press, 1971).

Brown, M.L., *Firearms in Colonial America: The Impact on History and Technology* (Washington, D.C.: Smithsonian Institution, 1980).

Brown, Ralph, *Loyalty and Security* (New Haven, CT: Yale University Press, 1958).

Browning, Christopher R., *The Fateful Months: Essays on the Emergence of the Final Solution* (New York: Holmes & Meier, 1985).

———, *Ordinary Men: Reserve Police Battalion 101 and the Final Solution in Poland* (New York: HarperCollins, 1992).

Brownlie, Ian, ed., *Basic Documents on Human Rights* (Oxford: Clarendon Press, [3rd ed.] 1988).

Brundage, W. Fitzhugh, *Lynching in the New South, 1880–1930* (Urbana: University of Illinois Press, 1993).

Buchheit, Lee C., *Secession: The Legitimacy of Self-Determination* (New Haven: Yale University Press, 1978).

Budnick, Rich, *Stolen Kingdom: An American Conspiracy* (Honolulu: Aloha Press, 1992).

Bull, Hedley, Benedict Kingsbury and Adam Roberts, eds., *Hugo Grotius and International Relations* (Oxford: Clarendon Press, 1992).

Bullard, Robert D., ed., *Confronting Environmental Racism: Voices from the Grassroots* (Boston: South End Press, 1993).

Burleigh, Michael, and Wolfgang Wipperman, *The Racial State: Germany, 1933–45* (Cambridge: Cambridge University Press, 1991).

Burnam, James, *The Web of Subversion: Underground Networks in the U.S. Government* (New York: John Day, 1954).

Burt, Larry W., *Tribalism in Crisis: Federal Indian Policy, 1953–1961* (Albuquerque: University of New Mexico Press, 1982).

Butz, Arthur R., *The Hoax of the Twentieth Century: The Case Against the Presumed Extermination of European Jewry* (Torrance CA: Institute for Historical Review, 1976).

Bytwerk, Randall B., *Julius Streicher: The Man Who Persuaded a Nation to Hate Jews* (New York: Dorset, 1983).

Cadwalader, Sandra L., and Vine Deloria, Jr., eds., *The Aggressions of Civilization: Federal Indian Policy Since the 1880's* (Philadelphia: Temple University Press, 1984).

Cahn, Edgar S., ed., *Our Brother's Keeper: The Indian in White America* (Washington, D.C.: New Community Press, 1969).

Caldicott, Helen, *Nuclear Madness: What You Can Do* (Brookline, MA: Autumn Press, 1978).

———, *If You Love This Planet: A Plan to Heal the Earth* (New York: W.W. Norton, 1992).

Callahan, North, *George Washington: Soldier and Man* (New York: William Morrow, 1972).

Calloway, Collin G., *The Western Abenaki of Vermount, 1600–1800: War, Migration, and the Survival of an Indian People* (Norman: University of Oklahoma Press, 1991).

———, *The American Revolution in Indian Country: Crisis and Diversity in Native American Communties* (Cambridge: Cambridge University Press, 1995).

Calloway, Patricia C., ed., *La Salle and His Legacy: Frenchmen and Indians in the Lower Mississippi Valley* (Jackson: Mississippi State University Press, 1982).

Calvocoressi, Peter, Guy Wint and John Pritchard, *Total War: Causes and Courses of World War II* (New York: Pantheon, [2nd. ed. revised] 1989).

Campbell, Thomas M., *Masquerade Peace: America's U.N. Policy, 1944–45* (Tallahasee: Florida State University Press, 1973).

Caplan, Arthur L., ed., *When Medicine Went Mad: Bioethics and the Holocaust* (Ottawa, NJ: Humana Press, 1992).

453

Caputo, John D., *Radical Hermeneutics: Repetition, Deconstruction, and the Hermeneutic Project* (Bloomington: Indiana University Press, 1987).

Carmack, Robert M., *Harvest of Violence: The Mayan Indians and the Guatemala Crisis* (Norman: University of Oklahoma Press, 1988).

Carnoy, Martin, *Education as Cultural Imperialism* (New York: David McKay, 1974).

Carranco, Lynwood, and Estle Beard, *Genocide and Vendetta: The Round Valley Wars of Northern California* (Norman: University of Oklahoma Press, 1981).

Carrington, Colonel Francis C., *My Army Life and the Fort Phil Kearny Massacre* (Philadelphia: Lippencott, 1911).

Caudill, David S., and Stephen Jay Gould, eds., *Radical Philosophy of Law: Contemporary Challenges to Mainstream Legal Theory and Practice* (Atlantic Highlands, NJ: Humanities Press, 1995).

Caute, David, *The Fellow Travelers* (New York: Macmillan, 1973).

———, *The Great Fear: The Anti-Communist Purge Under Truman and Eisenhower* (New York: Simon & Schuster, 1978).

Cecil, Robert, *The Myth of the Master Race: Alfred Rosenburg and Nazi Ideology* (New York: Dodd, Mead, 1972).

Central Commission for the Investigation of German Crimes in Poland, *German Crimes in Poland* (Warsaw: State Publishing House, 1947).

Chalfant, William Y., *Without Quarter: The Witchita Expedition and the Fight on Crooked Creek* (Norman: University of Oklahoma Press, 1991).

Chalk, Frank, and Kurt Jonassohn, *The History and Sociology of Genocide: Analyses and Case Studies* (New Haven, CT: Yale University Press, 1990).

Chalmers, Harvey, *Last Stand of the Nez Percé: Destruction of a People* (New York: Twayne, 1962).

Chamber of Commerce of the United States, *Communist Infiltration in the United States* (Washington, D.C.: U.S. Chamber of Commerce, 1946).

Channing, John Tate, *The Spanish Missions of Georgia* (Chapel Hill: University of North Carolina Press, 1935).

Charny, Israel, *How Can We Commit the Unthinkable? Genocide, the Human Cancer* (Boulder, CO, Westview Press, 1982).

———, ed., *Toward the Understanding and Prevention of Genocide: Proceedings of the International Conference on the Holocaust and Genocide* (Boulder, CO: Westview Press, 1984).

———, *Genocide: A Critical Biography* (New York and London: Facts on File/Mansell, 1988).

Chase, Steve, ed., *Defending the Earth: A Dialogue Between Murray Bookchin and Dave Foreman* (Boston: South End Press, 1991).

Chevigny, Paul, *Edge of the Knife: Police Violence in America* (New York: New Press, 1995).

Chipman, Donald E., *Nuño de Guzmán and the Province of Panuco in New Spain, 1518–1610* (Glendale, CA: Arthur C. Clark, 1967).

Chomsky, Noam, *American Power and the New Mandarins* (New York: Pantheon, 1969).

———, *For Reasons of State* (New York: Pantheon, 1973).

———, *Towards a New Cold War: Essays on the Current Crisis and How We Got There* (New York: Pantheon, 1983).

———, *The Fateful Triangle: The United States, Israel and The Palestinians* (Boston: South End Press, 1983).

———, *Turning the Tide: U.S. Intervention in Central America and the Struggle for Peace* (Boston: South End Press, 1985).

———, *Pirates and Emperors: International Terrorism in the Real World* (New York: Claremont, 1986).

———, *Necessary Illusions: Thought Control in Democratic Societies* (Boston: South End Press, 1989).

———, *Deterring Democracy* (New York: Hill & Wang, 1992).

———, *Rethinking Camelot: JFK, the Vietnam War, and U.S. Political Culture* (Boston: South End Press, 1993).

———, *World Orders, Old and New* (New York: Columbia University Press, 1995).

———, *Powers and Prospects: Reflections on Human Nature and the Social Order* (Boston: South End Press, 1996).

Chomsky, Noam, and Edward S. Herman, *After the Cataclysm: Postwar Indochina and the Reconstruction of Imperial Ideology* (Boston: South End Press, 1979).

Churchill, Ward, ed., *Marxism and Native Americans* (Boston: South End Press, 1983).

———, *Fantasies of the Master Race: Literature, Cinema and the Colonization of American Indians* (Monroe, ME: Common Courage Press, 1992).

———, *Struggle for the Land: Indigenous Resistance to Genocide, Ecocide and Expropriation in Contemporary North America* (Monroe, ME: Common Courage Press, 1993).

———, *Since Predator Came: Notes on the Struggle for American Indian Liberation* (Littleton, CO: Aigis, 1995).

———, *Notes From a Native Son: Selected Essays on Indigenism, 1985–1995* (Boston: South End Press, 1996).

Churchill, Ward, and Jim Vander Wall, *Agents of Repression: The FBI's Secret Wars Against the Black Panther Party and the American Indian Movement* (Boston: South End Press, 1988).

———, *The COINTELPRO Papers: Documents from the FBI's Secret Wars Against Dissent in the United States* (Boston: South End Press, 1990).

———, eds., *Cages of Steel: The Politics of Imprisonment in the Uinited States* (Washington, D.C.: Maisonneuve Press, 1992).

Ciba Foundation, *Health and Disease in Tribal Societies* (Amsterdam: Elsevier/Excerpta Medica, 1977).

Cieza de Léon, Pedro de, *The Incas* (Norman: University of Oklahoma Press, 1959).

Cincinnatus, *Self-Destruction: The Disintegration and Decay of the United States Army During the Vietnam War Era* (New York: W.W. Norton, 1981).

City of Genoa, *Christopher Columbus: Documents and Proofs of His Genoese Origin* (Genoa: Instituto d'Arti Grafiche, 1931).

Clark, Bruce, *Native Liberty, Crown Sovereignty: The Existing Aboriginal Right of Self-Government in Canada* (Montréal: McGill-Queens University Press, 1990).

Clark, Robert A., ed., *The Killing of Chief Crazy Horse* (Lincoln: Uinversity of Nebraska Press, 1976).

Clark, Ronald W., *The Greatest Power on Earth* (New York: Harper & Row, 1980).

Cleaves, Freeman, *Old Tippecanoe: William Henry Harrison and His Times* (Port Washington, NY: Kennikat, 1969 reprint of 1939 ed.).

Clifford, James A., *The Invented Indian: Cultural Fictions and Government Policies* (New Brunswick, NJ: Transaction Books, 1990).

Cline, Howard F., *Latin American History, Vol. II: Essays on Its Study and Teaching, 1898–1965* (Berkeley: University of California Press, 1966).

Clinton, Robert N., Nell Jessup Newton and Monroe E. Price, eds., *American Indian Law: Cases and Materials* (Charlottesville, VA: Michie, 1991).

Cohen, Arthur A., *The Tremendium: A Theological Interpretation of the Holocaust* (New York: Holmes & Meier, 1981).

Cohen, Faye G., *Treaties on Trial: The Continuing Controversy over Northwest Indian Rights* (Seattle: Unioversity of Washington Press, 1986).

Cohn, Norman, *Warrant for Genocide: The Myth of the Jewish World Conspiracy and the Protocols of the Elders of Zion* (New York: Harper & Row, 1967).

———, *Europe's Inner Demons: An Inquiry Inspired by the Great Witch-hunt* (New York: Basic Books, 1975).

Cohn-Sherbok, Dan, ed., *A Traditional Quest: Essays in Honor of Louis Jacobs* (London: Routledge, 1991).

Cole, D.C., *The Chiricahua Apache, 1846–1876: From War to Reservation* (Albuquerque: University of New Mexico Press, 1988).

Cole, Dougals, and Ira Chaikan, *An Iron Hand Upon the People: The Law Against the Potlatch on the Northwest Coast* (Vancouver, B.C.: Douglas & McIntire, Ltd., 1990).

Cole, Wayne S., *Charles A. Lindbergh and the Battle Against American Intervention in World War II* (Garden City, NY: Doubleday, 1974).

————, *Roosevelt and the Isolationists, 1932–1945* (Lincoln: University of Nebraska Press, 1983).

Coleman, Michael C., *American Indian Children at School, 1850–1930* (Jackson: University Press of Mississippi, 1993).

Collier, Ellen C., *Instances of Use of United States Armed Forces Abroad, 1798–1989* (Washington D.C.: Congressional Research Service, 1989).

Collins, John M., *America's Small Wars* (McLean, VA: Brassey's, 1991).

Colton, Ray C., *The Civil War in the Western Territories* (Norman: University of Oklahoma Press, 1959).

Committee for Abortion Rights and Against Sterilization Abuse, *Women Under Attack: Abortion: Sterilization Abuse, and Reproductive Freedom* (New York: CARASA, 1979).

Commoner, Barry, *Making Peace with the Planet* (New York: New Press, 1990).

Connell, Evan S., *Son of the Morning Star: Custer and the Little Big Horn* (San Francisco: North Point Press, 1984).

Connor, Walker, *The National Question in Marxist-Leninist Theory and Strategy* (Princeton, NJ: Princeton University Press, 1984).

Conquest, Robert, *The Great Terror: Stalin's Purge of the Thirties* (New York: Macmillan, 1968).

————, *The Nation Killers: The Soviet Deportation of Nationalities* (New York: Macmillan, 1970).

————, *Harvest of Sorrow: Soviet Collectivization and the Terror Famine* (New York: Oxford University Press, 1986).

Cook, Fred J., *The Unfinished Story of Alger Hiss* (New York: William Morrow, 1958).

————, *The FBI Nobody Knows* (New York: Macmillan, 1964).

————, *The Nightmare Decade: The Life and Times of Joe McCarthy* (New York: Random House, 1971).

Cook, John R., *The Border and the Buffalo: An Untold Story of the Southwest Plains* (New York: Citadel Press, 1976).

Cook, Nobel David, *Demographic Collapse: Indian Peru, 1520–1620* (Cambridge: Cambridge University Press, 1981).

Cook, Nobel David, and W. George Lovell, eds., *"Secret Judgements of God": Old World Disease in Colonial Spanish America* (Norman: University of Oklahoma Press, 1992).

Cook, Sherburne F., *Indians Versus the Spanish Missions* (Berkeley: University of California Ibero-Americana No. 21, 1943).

Cook, Sherburne F., and Leslie B. Simpson, *The Population of Mexico in the Sixteenth Century* (Berkeley: University of California Ibero-Americana, No. 31, 1948).

Cook, Sherburne F., and Woodrow W. Borah, *The Indian Population of Central Mexico, 1531–1610* (Berkeley: University of California Press, Ibero-Americana No. 44, 1960).

————, *The Population of Mixteca-Alta, 1520–1960* (Berkeley: University of California Ibero-Americana L, 1968).

————, *Essays in Population History, Vol. I* (Berkeley: University of California Press, 1971).

Cooper, Milton William, *Behold a Pale Horse* (Sedona, AZ: Light Technology, 1991).

Corkran, David H., *The Cherokee Frontier: Conflict and Survival, 1740–1762* (Norman: University of Oklahoma Press, 1962).

————, *The Creek Frontier, 1540–1783* (Norman: University of Oklahoma Press, 1967).

Costello, William, *The Facts About Nixon: An Unauthorized Biography* (New York: Viking, 1960).

Cotterill, R.S., *The Southern Indians: The Story of the Five Civilized Tribes Before Removal* (Norman: University of Oklahoma Press, 1954).

Cox, Bruce A., ed., *Native People, Native Lands* (Ottawa: Carlton University Press, 1988).

Craig, Reginald S., *The Fighting Parson: A Biography of Col. John M. Chivington* (Tucson, AZ: Westernlore, 1994 reprint of 1959 original).

Crandell, Samuel Benjamin, *Treaties: Their Making and Enforcement* (New York: Columbia University Press, [2nd ed.] 1916).

Creighton Miller, Stuart, *"Benevolent Assimilation": The American Conquest of the Philippines, 1898–1903* (New Haven, CT: Yale University Press, 1982).

Cressy, David, *Coming Over: Migration and Communication Between England and New England in the*

Seventeenth Century (Cambridge: Harvard University Press, 1987).

Cronin, Rev. John F., *Communism: A World Menace* (Washington, D.C.: National Welfare Conference, 1947).

Cronon, William, *Changes in the Land: Indians, Colonists and the Ecology of New England* (New York: Hill & Wang, 1983).

Crosby, Alfred W., Jr., *The Columbian Exchange: Biological and Cultural Consequences of 1492* (Westport, CT: Greenwood Press, 1972).

————, *Ecological Imperialism: The Biological Expansion of Europe, 900–1900* (Cambridge: Cambridge University Press, 1986).

Crum, Steven J., *The Road on Which We Came: A History of the Western Shoshone* (Salt Lake City: University of Nevada Press, 1994).

Cuddihy, John Murray, *The Ordeal of Civility: Marx, Freud, Levi-Strauss, and the Jewish Struggle with Modernity* (New York: Basic Books, 1974).

Cuneo, John R., *Robert Rogers of the Rangers* (New York: Oxford University Press, 1959).

Curry, Richard O., ed., *Freedom at Risk: Secrecy, Censorship, and Repression in the 1980s* (Philadelphia: Temple University Press, 1988).

Curtis, Charles P., *The Oppenheimer Case: The Trial of a Security System* (New York: Simon & Schuster, 1955).

Curtis, Richard, and Elizabeth Hogan, *Perils of the Peaceful Atom* (New York: Ballentine, 1969).

Dadrian, Vahakn N., *History of the Armenian Genocide: Ethnic Conflict from the Balkans to Anatolia to the Caucasus* (Providence, RI: Berghahn, 1995).

Dallin, Alexander, *German Rule in Russia, 1941–1945: A Study of Occupation Policies* (New York: St. Martin's Press, 1957).

Daly, Mary, *Gyn/Ecology: The Metaethics of Radical Feminism* (Boston: Beacon Press, 1978).

Datner, Szymon, *Crimes Against POWs: Responsibility of the Wehrmacht* (Warsaw: Zachodnia Agencja Prasowa, 1964).

David, Paul A., Herbert G. Gutman, Peter Temin and Gavin Wright, *Reckoning with Slavery: A Critical Study in the Quantitive History of American Negro Slavery* (New York: Oxford University Press, 1976).

Davidson, Basil, *The African Slave Trade* (Boston: Little, Brown, [rev. ed.] 1980).

Davies, K.G., *Europe and the Age of Expansion, Vol. IV: The North Atlantic World in the Seventeenth Century* (Minneapolis: University of Minnesota Press, 1974).

Davidson, Eugene, *The Trial of the Germans, 1945–1946* (New York: Macmillan, 1966).

Davies, Alan, ed., *Antisemitism in Canada* (Rexdale, Ont.: John Wiley & Sons, 1992).

Davis, Britton, *The Truth About Geronimo* (Chicago: Lakeside Press, 1951 reprint of 1929 edition).

Davis, Robert, and Mark Zannis, *The Genocide Machine in Canada: The Pacification of the North* (Montréal: Black Rose Books, 1973).

Dawidowicz, Lucy S., *The War Against the Jews, 1933–1945* (New York: Holt, Rinehart & Winston, 1975).

————, *The Holocaust and the Historians* (Cambridge: Harvard University Press, 1981).

De Conde, Alexander, *This Affair of Louisiana* (New York: Scribner's, 1973).

Dekker, Nikolai and Andrei Lebed, eds., *Genocide in the U.S.S.R.: Studies in Group Destruction* (New York: Scarecrow Press, 1958).

Deloria, Vine Jr., and Clifford M. Lytle, *American Indians, American Justice* (Austin: University of Texas Press, 1983).

————, *The Nations Within: The Past and Future of American Indian Sovereignty* (New York: Pantheon Press, 1984).

————, *God Is Red* (Golden, CO: Fulcrum, [2nd. ed.] 1994).

Denevan, William, ed., *The Native Population of the Americas in 1492* (Madison: University of Wisconsin Press, 1976).

DeRosier Jr., Arthur H., *The Removal of the Choctaw Indians* (Knoxville: University of Tennessee Press, 1970).

Dietz, David, *Atomic Science, Bombs and Power* (New York: Collier, 1962).

Dillon, Francis, *A Place of Habitation: The Pilgrim Fathers and Their Quest* (London: Hutchinson, 1973).

Dishnyck, Walter, *Fifty Years Ago: The Famine Holocaust in the Ukraine* (New York & Toronto: World Congress of Free Ukrainians, 1980).

Diwald, Hellmut, *Geshichte der Deutschen* (Frankfurt a.M.: Suhrkamp, 1978).

Dixon, Joseph K., *The Vanishing Race: The Last Great Indian Council* (Garden City, NY: Doubleday, 1913).

Dobyns, Henry, *The Apache People* (Phoenix, Tribal Indian Series, 1971).

———, *Native American Historical Demography: A Critical Bibliography* (Bloominton, IN: University of Indiana Press, 1976).

———, *Their Numbers Become Thinned: Native American Population Dynamics in Eastern North America* (Knoxville, TN: University of Tennessee Press, 1983).

Donnelly, Desmond, *Struggle for the World: The Cold War, 1917–1965* (New York: St. Martin's Press, 1965).

Donner, Frank, *Protectors of Privilege: Red Squads and Police Repression in Urban America* (Berkeley: University of California, 1990).

Doren, Carl Van, and Julian P. Boyd, eds., *Indian Treaties Printed by Benjamin Franklin* (Philadelphia: University of Pennsylvnia Press, 1938).

Dowd, Gregory Evans, *A Spirited Resistance: The North American Indian Struggle for Unity, 1745–1815* (Baltimore: John Hopkins University Press, 1992).

Downes, Randolph C., *Council Fires on the Upper Ohio* (Pittsburg: University of Pittsburg Press, 1940).

Drake, Samuel G., *The History of the Indian Wars in New England* (Roxbury, MA: C. E. Tuttle, 1965).

Drapkin, Israel, and Emilio Viano, eds., *Victimology: A New Focus* (Lexington, MA: C.C. Heath, 1974).

Drechsler, Horst, *"Let Us Die Fighting": The Struggle of the Herero and Nama Against German Imperialism, 1884–1915* (London: Zed Books, 1980).

Drinnon, Richard, *Facing West: The Metaphysics of Indian Hating and Empire Building* (Minneapolis: University of Minnesota Press, 1980).

———, *Keeper of Concentration Camps: Dillon S. Myer and American Racism* (Berkeley: University of California Press, 1987).

Driver, Harold E., and William C. Massey, *Comparative Studies of North American Indians* (New York: American Philosophical Society, Transactions, N.S., XLVII, pt. ii, 1957).

Drost, Pieter N., *Genocide* (Leyden: A.W. Sythoff, 1959).

———, *The Crime of State* (Leyden: A.W. Sythoff, 1959).

DuBois, Victor, *To Die in Burundi* (New York: American University Field Reports, 1972).

Duffet, John, ed., *Against the Crime of Silence: Proceedings of the International War Crimes Tribunal* (New York: Clarion, 1968).

Duffy, John, *Epidemics in Colonial America* (Baton Rouge: Louisiana State University Press, 1953).

Dunbar Ortiz, Roxanne, *The Great Sioux Nation: Sitting in Judgment on America* (San Francisco/New York: International Indian Treaty Council/ Moon Books, 1978).

———, ed., *Economic Development on American Indian Reservations* (Albuquerque: University of New Mexico Native American Development Series, 1979).

———, *Indians of the Americas: Human Rights and Self-Determination* (London: Zed Books, 1984).

Duncan, Donald, *The New Legions* (New York: Random House, 1967).

Dunn, Lt. Colonel William R., *"I Stand by Sand Creek": A Defense of Colonel John M. Chivington and the Third Colorado Cavalry* (Ft. Collins, CO: Old Army Press, 1985).

Dunnigan, Brian Leigh, *Siege 1759: The Campaign Against Niagara* (Youngstown, NY: 1986).

Dworkin, Andrea, *Woman Hating* (New York: Dutton, 1974).

Eastman, Charles A., *From the Deep Woods to Civilization: Chapters in the Autobiography of an American Indian* (Boston: Little, Brown, 1916).

Eccles, W.C., *Canada Under Louis XIV, 1663–1701* (Toronto: University of Toronto Press, 1964).

———, *France in America* (New York: Harper & Row, 1972).

————, *The Canadian Frontier, 1534–1760* (Albuquerque: University of New Mexico Press, rev. ed., 1983).

Eckert, Allan W., *The Frontiersmen* (Boston: Little, Brown, 1967).

————, *The Wilderness at War* (Boston: Little, Brown, 1978).

————, *The Twilight of Empire* (Boston: Little, Brown, 1988).

————, *A Sorrow in Our Heart: The Life of Tecumseh* (Boston: Little, Brown, 1992).

————, *That Dark and Bloody River: Chronicles of the Ohio River Valley* (New York: Bantam, 1995).

Edelman, Murray, *Politics as Symbolic Action: Mass Arousal and Quiescence* (Chicago: Markham, 1971).

Editors, *The World Almanac, 1973* (New York: National Geographic Society, 1972).

Edmunds, R. David, *The Powawatomies: Keepers of the Fire* (Norman: University of Oklahoma Press, 1978).

————, *The Shawnee Prophet* (Lincoln: University of Nebraska Press, 1983).

————, *Tecumseh and the Quest for Indian Leadership* (Boston: Little, Brown, 1984).

Eisenberg, Carolyn, *Drawing the line: The American Decision to Partition Germany* (Cambridge, MA: Cambridge University Press, 1996).

Ege, Robert J., *"Tell Baker to Strike Them Hard!": Incident on the Marias, Jan. 23, 1870* (Belleview, NB: Old Army Press, 1970).

Egerton, Hugh Edward, *A Short History of British Colonial Policy* (London: Metheun, [6th ed.] 1920).

Ehrenfeld, Alice, and Robert W. Barker. comps. and eds., *Legislative Material on the Indian Claims Commission Act of 1946* (Washington, D.C.: unpublished study, n.d.).

Elliott, J.H., *Imperial Spain, 1469–1716* (New York: St. Martin's Press, 1964).

Ellis, Marc H., *Beyond Innocence and Redemption: Confronting the Holocaust and Israeli Power* (New York: Harper & Row, 1990).

Ellsberg, Daniel, *Papers on the War* (New York: Simon & Schuster, 1972).

Ellul, Jacques, *Propaganda: The Formation of Men's Attitudes* (New York: Vintage, 1965).

Emmitt, Robert, *The Last War Trail: The Utes and the Settlement of Colorado* (Norman: University of Oklahoma Press, 1954).

Engelhardt, Zephyrin, *The Missions and Missionaries of California, 15 vols.* (San Francisco: 1908–1916).

Engelbert, Omer, *The Last of the Conquistadors: Juniper Serra (1713–1784)* (New York: Harcourt, Brace and Co., 1956).

Epple, Jess C., *Custer's Battle of the Washita and a History of the Plains Indian Tribes* (New York: Exposition Press, 1970).

Erdoes, Richard, *The Sun Dance People: The Plains Indians, Their Past and Present* (New York: Vintage Books, 1972).

Etienne, Mona, and Eleanor Burke Leacock, eds., *Women and Colonization: Anthropological Perspectives* (New York: Praeger, 1980).

Etzold, Thomas H., and John Lewis Gaddis, *Containment: Documents on American Foreign Policy and Strategy, 1945–1950* (New York: Columbia University Press, 1978).

Evans, Richard, *In Hitler's Shadow: West German Historians and the Attempt to Escape from the Nazi Past* (New York: Alfred A. Knopf, 1989).

Ewell, John, and Chris Dodge, *Confronting Columbus: An Anthology* (Charlotte, NC: McFarland, 1992).

Ewers, John Canfield, *The Blackfeet: Raiders of the Northern Plains* (Norman: University of Oklahoma Press, 1958).

Fackenheim, Emil, *To Mend the World: Foundations of Future Jewish Thought* (New York: Holmes & Meier, 1982).

Falk, Jim, *Global Fission: The Battle Over Nuclear Power* (New York: Oxford University Press, 1982).

Falk, Obie B., *The Geronimo Campaign* (New York: Oxford University Press, 1969).

————, *Destiny Road: The Gila Trail and the Opening of the Southwest* (New York: Oxford University Press, 1973).

————, *Crimson Desert: The Indian Wars of the Southwest* (New York: Oxford University Press, 1974).

Falk, Richard A., ed., *The Vietnam War and International Law* (Princeton, NI: Princeton University Press, 1970).

———, *Human Rights and State Sovereignty* (New York: Holmes & Meier, 1981).

———, *The End of World Order: Essays on Normative International Relations* (New York: Holmes & Meier, 1983).

Farwell, Byron, *Queen Victoria's Little Wars* (New York: Harper & Row, 1972).

Fanon, Frantz, *The Wretched of the Earth* (New York: Grove, 1966).

Farb, Peter, *Man's Rise to Civilization as Shown by the Indians of North America from Primeval Times to the Coming of the Industrial State* (New York: Dutton, 1968).

Faulkner, Peter, *The Silent Bomb: A Guide to the Nuclear Power Controversy* (New York: Vintage, 1977).

Fay, Peter Ward, *The Opium War, 1840–1842* (Chapel Hill: University of North Carolina Press, 1975).

Fehrenbach, T.R., *Lone Star: A History of Texas and Texans* (New York: Macmillan, 1968).

———, *The Commanches: The Destruction of a People* (New York: Alfred A. Knopf, 1974).

Fein, Helen, *Accounting for Genocide: National Responses and Jewish Victimization During the Holocaust* (New York: Free Press, 1979).

Feingold, Henry L., *The Politics of Rescue* (New Brunswick, NJ: Rutgers University Press, 1970).

Fell, Barry, *America, B.C.* (New York: Times Books, 1976).

———, *Saga Americana* (New York: Times Books, 1980).

Ferguson, Wallace K., *Europe in Transition, 1300–1520* (Boston: Houghton Mifflin, 1962).

Fest, Joachim, *The Face of the Third Reich* (New York: Pantheon, 1970).

Fickowski, Jerzy, *The Gypsies in Poland* (Warsaw: Interpress, 1989).

Fieldhouse, D.K., *The Colonial Empires: A Comparative Survey from the Eighteenth Century* (New York: Delacourt, 1967).

Filler, Louis, and Allen Guttmann, eds., *The Removal of the Cherokee Nation: Manifest Destiny or National Dishonor?* (Boston: Heath, 1962).

Fixico, Donald L., *Termination and Relocation: Federal Indian Policy, 1945–1960* (Albuquerque: University of New Mexico Press, 1986).

Fleming, Denna Frank, *The Cold War and Its Origins, 1917–1960* (Garden City, NY; Doubleday, 1961).

Fleming, Gerald, *Hitler and the Final Solution* (Berkeley: University of California Press, 1982).

Flexner, James Thomas, *Lord of the Mohawks: A Biography of Sir William Johnson* (Boston: Little, Brown, 1979).

Floyd, Troy, *The Columbus Dynasty in the Caribbean, 1492–1526* (Albuerque: University of New Mexico Press, 1793).

Flynn, Kevin, and Gary Gerhart, *The Silent Brotherhood: Inside America's Racist Underground* (New York: Free Press, 1989).

Fogel, Daniel, *Junípero Serra, the Vatican, and Enslavement Theology* (San Francisco: ism press, 1988).

Fogel, Robert W., and Stanley L. Engerman, *Time on the Cross: The Economics of American Negro Slavery* (Boston: Little, Brown, 1974).

Folwell, William W., *A History of Minnesota* (St. Paul: Minnesota Historical Society, 1924).

———, *History of the Santee Sioux* (Lincoln: University of Nebraska Press, 1967).

Foote, Shelby, *The Civil War, Vol. III: Red River to Appomattox* (New York: Random House, 1974).

Forbes, Jack D., *Apache, Navajo and Spaniard* (Norman: University of Oklahoma Press, 1960).

———, *Warriors of the Colorado: The Yumas of the Quechan Nation and Their Neighbors* (Norman: University of Oklahoma Press, 1965).

———, *Black Africans and Native Americans: Race, Color and Caste in the Making of Red-Black Peoples* (New York: Oxford University Press, 1988).

Foreign Office of Belgium, *The Belgian Thesis: Sacred Mission of Civilization, To Which Peoples Should the Benefit Be Extended?* (New York: Belgian Government Information Center, 1953).

Foreman, Grant, *The Last Trek of the Indians* (Chicago: University of Chicago Press, 1946).

———, *Indian Removal: The Immigration of the Five Civilized Tribes* (Norman: University of Oklahoma Press, 1953).

Forman, James, *Sammy Younge, Jr.* (New York: Grove Press, 1968).

Foster, Micheal K., Jack Campisi and Marianne Mithun, eds., *Extending the Rafters: Interdisciplinary Approaches to Iroquoian Studies* (Albany: State University Press of New York, 1984).

Fox, Robin Lane, *Pagans and Christians* (San Francisco: HarperCollins, 1986).

Fraenkel, Manvell, Roger and Heinrich, *Incomparable Crime; Mass Extermination in the 20th Century: The Legacy of Guilt* (London: Heinemann, 1967).

Franke, Bernard, *Is Rongelap Atoll Safe?* (Takoma Park, MD: Institute for Energy & Environmental Research, 1989).

Frankel, Jonathan, ed., *Studies in Contemporary Jewry, Vol. 1* (Bloomington: Indiana University Press, 1984).

Franks, Kenny A., *Stand Watie and the Agony of the Cherokee Nation* (Memphis: Memphis State University Press, 1979).

Fraser, Angus, *The Gypsies* (Oxford: Blackwell, 1992).

Freeland, Richard M., *The Truman Doctrine and the Origins of McCarthyism* (New York: Alfred A. Knopf, 1972).

Freeman, Leslie J., *Nuclear Witnesses: Insiders Speak Out* (New York: W.W. Norton, 1982).

Friedman, Leon, ed., *Southern Justice* (New York: Pantheon, 1965).

Friedman, Philip, *Roads to Extinction: Essays on the Holocaust* (New York & Philadelphia: Jewish Publication Society of America, 1980).

Friedrich, Christof, and Eric Thompson, *The Hitler We Loved and Why* (Reedy, WV: White Power, 1978).

Fritz, Henry E., *The Movement for Indian Assimilation, 1860–1890* (Philadelphia: University of Pennsylvania Press, 1963).

Fromm, Eric, *The Anatomy of Human Destructiveness* (Greenwich, CT: Faucett, 1975).

Fuentes y Guzmán, Francisco Antonio de, *Recordacion Florida, 3 vols.* (Guatemala City: Sociedad de Geografía e Historia, 1932–1933).

Fuller, John G., *We Almost Lost Detroit* (New York: Reader's Digest, 1975).

Furet, François, ed., *Unanswered Questions: Nazi Germany and the Genocide of the Jews* (New York: Schocken Books, 1989).

Futch, Ovid L., *The History of Andersonville Prison* (Gainesville: University of Florida Press, 1968).

Gaddis, John Lewis, *The United States and the Origins of the Cold War* (New York: Columbia University Press, 1972).

Galbraith, John Kenneth, *The New Industrial State* (Boston: Houghton Mifflin, 1967).

Galeano, Eduardo, *Open Veins of Latitn America: Five Centuries of the Pillage of a Continent* (New York: Monthly Review, 1973).

——, *Memory of Fire: Genesis* (New York: Pantheon, 1985).

Gallagher, Philip F., ed., *Christians, Jews, and Other Worlds: Patterns of Conflict and Accommodation* (Lanham, MD: University Press of America, 1988).

Gallegher, Carole, *America Ground Zero: The Secret Nuclear War* (New York: Random House, 1993).

Galloway, William Albert, *Old Chillocothe: Shawnees and Pioneer History* (Xenia, OH: Buckeye Press, 1934).

Gannon, Michael V., *The Cross in the Sand: The Early Catholic Church in Florida, 1513–1870* (Gainesville: University Presses of Florida, [2nd. ed.] 1983).

Gard, Wayne, *The Great Buffalo Hunt* (New York: Alfred A. Knopf, 1959).

Gardner, Lloyd, *Architects of Illusion: Men and Ideas in American Foreign Policy, 1941–49* (Chicago: Quadrangle, 1970).

Gavel, Mike, *The Pentagon Papers: The Defense Department History of United States Decisionmaking on Vietnam, 4 vols.* (Boston: Beacon Press, 1971).

Gehlen, Rehnhard, *The Service: The Memoirs of General Reinhard Gehlen* (New York: World, 1972).

Geisbrecht, N., J. Brown, et al., *Alcoholic Problems in Northwestern Ontario: Preliminary Report on Consumption Patterns, and Public Order and Public Health Problems* (Toronto: Addiction Research Foundation, 1977).

Gentry, Curt, *J. Edgar Hoover: The Man and His Secrets* (New York: W.W. Norton, 1991).

461

Gerard-Libois, Jules, *Katanga Secession* (Madison: University of Wisconsin Press, 1966).

Gerber, C.R., R. Hamburger, and E.W.S. Hull, *Plowshare* (Washington D.C.: Atomic Energy Commission, 1967).

Gerber, David, *Antisemitism in American History* (Urbana: University of Illinois Press, 1986).

Gerhart, Peter, *A Guide to the Historical Geography of New Spain* (Princeton, NJ: Princeton University Press, 1972).

————, *The Southwest Frontier of New Spain* (Princeton, NJ: Princeton University Press, 1979).

————, *The Northern Frontier of New Spain* (Princeton, NJ: Princeton University Press, 1982).

Gibson, Arrel M., *The Kickapoos: Lords of the Middle Border* (Norman: University of Oklahoma Press, 1963).

————, *The Chicksaws* (Norman: University of Oklahoma Press, 1971).

Gibson, Charles, *The Spanish Tradition in Mexico* (Columbia: University of South Carolina Press, 1968).

————, ed., *The Spanish Tradition in America* (New York: Harper & Row, 1968).

Gilbert, Martin, *The Holocaust: A History of the Jews of Europe During the Second World War* (New York: Henry Holt, 1985).

Gilpin, A.R., *The War of 1812 in the Old Northwest* (East Lansing: Michigan State University Press, 1958).

Giroux, Henry A., *Ideology, Culture and the Process of Schooling* (Philadelphia: Temple University Press, 1981).

Glasscock, C.B., *Then Came Oil: The Story of the Last Frontier* (Indiana: Bobbs-Merrill, 1938).

Glassley, Ray Hoard, *Pacific Northwest Indian Wars* (Portland, OR: Binfords & Mort, 1953).

Gleijeses, Piero, *Shattered Hope: The Guatemalan Revolution and the United States, 1944–1954* (Princeton, NJ: Princeton University Press, 1991).

Goddard, John, *Last Stand of the Lubicon Cree* (Vancouver: Douglas and McIntire, 1991).

Godfrey, William C., *Pursuit of Profit and Preferment in North America: John Bradsteet's Quest* (Waterloo, Ont.: 1982).

Goetzmann, William H., *Army Exploration and the West, 1803–1863* (New Haven: Yale University Press, 1959).

————, *Exploration and Empire* (New York: Alfred A. Knopf, 1966).

Gofman, John W., *The Cancer Hazard from Inhaled Plutonium* (San Francisco: Committee for Nuclear Responsibility, May 14, 1975).

Gofman, John W., and Arthur R. Tamplin, *Population Control Through Nuclear Pollution* (Chicago: Nelson-Hall, 1970).

————, *Poisoned Power: The Case Against Nuclear Plants* (Emmaus, PA: Rodale Press, 1971; rereleased in 1979 with a new subtitle, *The Case Before and After Three Mile Island*).

Goldhagen, Daniel Jonah, *Hitler's Willing Executioners: Ordinary Germans and the Holocaust* (New York: Alfred A. Knopf, 1996).

Goldstein, Joseph, Burke Marshall and Jack Schwartz, *The My Lai Massacre and Cover-Up: Beyond the Reach of the Law?* (New York: Free Press, 1976).

Goldstein, Robert Justin, *Political Repression in Modern America, 1870 to the Present* (Cambridge/New York: Schenkman/Two Continents, 1978).

Goldstick, Miles, *Wollaston: People Resisting Genocide* (Montréal: Black Rose Books, 1987).

Goodman, Walter, *The Committee: The Extraordinary Career of the House on Un-American Activities* (New York: Farrar, Straus & Giroux, 1968).

Goodwin, Gary C., *Cherokees in Transition: A Study of Changing Culture and Environment Prior to 1775* (Chicago: University of Chicago Press, 1977).

Gore, Albert E., *Earth in the Balance* (New York: Houghton-Mifflin, 1992).

Gorn, Elliot J., Randy Roberts and Terry D. Bilhartz, *Constructing the American Past: A Source Book of a People's History* (New York: HarperCollins, 1972).

Gorz, André, *Ecology as Politics* (Boston: South End Press, 1980).

Gould, Steven Jay, *The High Cost of Living Near Nuclear Reactors* (New York: Four Walls Eight Windows, 1996).

Gould, Steven Jay, *The Mismeasure of Man* (New York: W.W. Norton, 1981).

Gray, John E., *The Centennial Campaign: The Sioux War of 1876* (Norman: University of Oklahoma Press, 1988).

Green, L.C., and Olive P. Duncan, *The Law of Nations in the New World* (Edmonton: University of Alberta Press, 1989).

Green, Michael D., *The Politics of Indian Removal: Creek Government and Society in Crisis* (Lincoln: University of Nebraska Press, 1982).

Greene, Jerome A., *Slim Buttes: An Episode of the Great Sioux War, 1876* (Norman: University of Oklahoma Press, 1982).

Greenglass, Mark, ed., *Conquest and Coalescence: The Shaping of Early Modern Europe* (London: Edward Arnold, 1991).

Grew, E.S., *Field Marshall Lord Kitchener, His Life and Work for the Empire, 3 vols.* (London: Gresham, 1916).

Greymount, Barbara, *The Iroquois in the American Revolution* (Syracuse, NY: Syracuse University Press, 1975).

Griffin, Charles Carroll, *The United States and the Disruption of the Spanish Empire, 1810–1822: A Study of the Relations of the United States with Spain and with the Rebel Spanish Colonies* (New York: Octagon Books, 1968).

Griffin, William B., *Utmost Good Faith: Patterns in Apache-Mexican Hostilities in Northern Chihuhua Border Warfare, 1821–1848* (Albuqueque: University of New Mexico Press, 1988).

Griffith, Robert, *The Politics of Fear: Joseph McCarthy and the Senate* (Lexington: University of Kentucky Press, 1970).

Grinde, Donald A., and Bruce Johansen, *Exemplar of Liberty: Native America and the Evolution of Democracy* (Los Angeles).

————, *Ecocide of Native America: Environmental Destruction of Indian Lands and Peoples* (Santa Fe: Clear Light, 1995).

Grinnell, Bird, *The Fighting Cheyennes* (Norman: University of Oklahoma Press, 1955 reprint of 1915 original).

Griswold, Deirdre, *Indonesia: The Bloodbath That Was* (New York: World View, 1975).

Grobman, Alex, and Daniel Landes, eds., *Genocide: Critical Issues of the Holocaust* (Los Angeles: Rossell, 1983).

Grodzins, Morton, and Eugene Rabinowitch, eds., *The Atomic Age: Scientists in National and World Affairs* (New York: Basic Books, 1962).

Gross, Bertram, *Friendly Fascism: The New Face of Power in America* (Boston: South End Press, 1982).

Grossman, Karl, *Cover Up: What You Are Not Supposed to Know About Nuclear Power* (New York: Permanent Press, 1980.

Groueff, Stephane, *The Manhattan Project* (Boston: Little, Brown, 1967).

Grousett, René, *The Epic of the Crusades* (New York: Grossman, 1970).

Groves, Leslie R., *Now It Can Be Told: The Story of the Manhattan Project* (New York: Harper & Bros., 1962).

Guiraud, Jean, *The Medieval Inquisition* (New York: AMS Press, 1979).

Gunnerson, Dolores A., *The Jicarilla Apaches: A Study in Survival* (DeKalb: Northern Illinois Uniersity Press, 1974).

Gurko, Miriam, *Indian America: The Black Hawk War* (New York: Crowell, 1970).

Gutman, Yisrael, ed., *Encyclopedia of the Holocaust* (New York: Macmillan, 1990).

Gutman, Yisrael, and Gideon Grief, eds., *The Historiography of the Holocaust Period* (Jerusalem: Hebrew University Monographs, 1988).

Gutman, Yisreal, and Michael Berenbaum, eds., *Anatomy of the Auschwitz Death Camp* (Bloomington/Washington, D.C.: Indiana University Press/U.S. Holocaust Memorial Museum, 1994).

Gyorgy, Anna, and Friends, *No Nukes: Everyone's Guide to Nuclear Power* (Boston: South End Press, 1979.

Hackett, David A., *The Buchenwald Report* (Boulder, CO: Westview Press, 1995).

Hafen, Leroy R., ed., *Colorado Gold Rush* (Glendale, CA: Arthur H. Clark, 1941).

Hafen, Leroy R., *Pike's Peak Gold Rush Guidebooks of 1859* (Glendale, CA: Arthur H. Clark, 1941).

Hafen, Leroy R., and Ann W. Hafen, *The Powder River Campaign and Sawyers' Expedition of 1865* (Glendale, CA: Athur H. Clark, 1961).

Hafen, Leroy R., and Francis Marion Young, *Fort Laramie and the Pageant of the West, 1834–1890* (Lincoln: University of Nebraska Press, 1984 reprint of 1938 original).

Haffner, Sebastian, *The Meaning of Hitler* (New York: Macmillan, 1979).

Hagan, William T., *The Sac and Fox Indians* (Norman: University of Oklahoma Press, 1958).

———, *United States–Comanche Relations: The Reservation Years* (Norman: University of Oklahoma Press, 1990 reprint of 1976 original).

Hakluyt, Richard, *The Principal Navigations, Voyages, Traffiques & Discoveries of the English Nation, Vol. 5* (London: J.M. Dent & Sons, 1907).

Haley, Alex, *The Autobiography of Malcolm X* (New York: Ballantine, 1964).

Haley, James L., *The Buffalo War: The History of the Red River Indian Uprising of 1874* (Norman: University of Oklahoma Press, 1985 reprint of 1976 original).

Hallenbeck, Cleve, ed. and trans., *The Journey of Fray Marcos de Niza* (Dallas: Southern Methodist University Press, 1987).

Halperin, Morton H., and Daniel Hoffman, *Freedom vs. National Security* (New York: Chelsea House, 1977).

———, *Top Secret: National Security and the Right to Know* (Washington, D.C.: New Republic Books, 1977).

Hamilton, Charles, ed., *Braddock's Defeat* (Norman: University of Oklahoma Press, 1959).

Hamilton, Edward P., *The French and Indian Wars* (Garden City, NY: Doubleday, 1962).

Hance, Irma Watson, and Irene Warr, *Johnson, Connor and the Mormans: An Outline of Military History in Northern Utah* (Salt Lake City: University of Utah Press, 1962).

Hanke, Lewis, *The Spanish Struggle for Justice in the Conquest of America* (Philadelphia: University of Pennslyvanis Press, 1947).

Hann, John H., *Apalachee: The Land Between the Rivers* (Gainesville: University of Florida Press, 1988).

———, *Aristotle and the American Indians: A Study in Race Prejudice in the Modern World* (Chicago: Henry Regnery Company, 1959).

Harbury, Jennifer, ed., *Bridge of Courage: Life Stories of the Guatemala Compañeros and Compañeras* (Monroe, ME: Common Courage Press, 1994).

Harff, Barbara, *Genocide and Human Rights: International Legal and Political Issues* (Denver: University of Denver Graduate School in International Studies, Monograph Series in World Affairs, 1984).

Harper, Alan D., *The Politics of Loyalty: The White House and the Communist Issue, 1946–1952* (Westport, CT: Greenwood Press, 1969).

Harring, Sidney L., *Crow Dog's Case: American Indian Sovereignty, Tribal Law, and the United States in the Nineteenth Century* (Cambridge: Cambridge University Press, 1994).

Harris, LaDonna, ed., *Red Paper* (Albuqueque: Americans for Indian Opportunity, 1976).

Hart, Newell, *The Bear River Massacre* (Preston, ID: 1982).

Hartigan, Francis, ed., *MX in Nevada: A Humanistic Perspective* (Reno: Nevada Humanities Press, 1980).

Hartley, William and Ellen Hartley, Osceola: *The Unconquered Indian* (New York: Hawthorn Books, 1973).

Hartman, Geoffrey, ed., *Bitburg in Moral and Political Perspective* (Bloomington: University Press of Indiana, 1986).

Harvey Pierce, Roy, *Savagism and Civilization: A Study of the American Indian in the American Mind* (Baltimore: John Hopkins University Press, 1953).

———, *The Savages of America: A Study of the Indian and the Idea of Civilization* (Baltimore: John Hopkins University Press, 1965).

Harwood, Richard, *Did Six Million Really Die? The Truth at Last* (Richmond, Surrey: Historical Review Press, 1974).

Hauptman, Laurence M., and James D. Wherry, eds., *The Pequots in Southern New England: The Fall and Rise of an American Indian Nation* (Norman: University of Oklahoma Press, 1990).

Hayes, Peter, ed., *Lessons and Legacies: The Meaning of the Holocaust in a Changing World* (Evanston, IL: Northwestern University Press, 1991).

Headrick, Daniel R., *Tools of Empire: Technology and European Imperialism in the Nineteenth Century* (New York: Oxford University Press, 1981).

Hebard, Grace, and E.A. Brindenstool, *The Bozeman Trail, 2 vols.* (Glendale, CA: Arthur H. Clark, 1992).

Hect, Susanna, and Alexander Cockburn, *The Fate of the Forest: Developers, Destroyers and Defenders of the Amazon* (London: Verso, 1989).

Hector, Michael, *Internal Colonialism: The Celtic Fringe in British National Develoment, 1536–1966* (Berkeley: University of California Press, 1975).

Heers, Jacques, *Christophe Columb* (Paris: Hachette, 1981).

Heidenreich, Conrad, *Huronia: A History and Geography of the Huron Indians, 1600–1650* (Toronto: McClellan & Stewart, 1971).

Heizer, Robert F., ed., *The Destruction of California Indians* (Lincoln: University of Nebraska Press, 1993 reprint of 1974 Peregrine Smith ed.).

———, *Handbook of the North American Indians, Vol. 3:* California (Washington, D.C.: Smithsonian Institution, 1978).

Held, Virginia, Sidney Morganbesser and Thomas Nagel, eds., *Philosophy, Morality, and International Affairs* (New York: Oxford University Press, 1974).

Hemming, John, *The Conquest of the Incas* (New York: Harcourt Brace Jovanovich, 1970).

———, *Red Gold: The Conquest of the Brazilian Indians, 1500–1760* (Cambridge: Harvard University Press, 1978).

———, *The Amazon Frontier: The Defeat of the Brazilian Indians* (Cambridge: Harvard University Press, 1987).

Henchley, Vernon, *The Spies Who Never Were* (New York: Dodd, Meade, 1965).

Henderson, Ann L., and Gary R. Momino, eds., *Spanish Pathways in Florida, 1492–1992* (Sarasota, FL: Florida Humanities Council/Pineapple Press, 1991).

Herbert, Anthony B., and James T. Wooten, *Soldier* (New York: Holt, Rinehart & Winston, 1973).

Herbert, Ulrich, *A History of Foreign Labor in Germany, 1880–1980: Seasonal Workers/Guest Workers* (Ann Arbor: University of Michigan Press, 1990).

Herken, Gregg, *The Winning Weapon* (New York: Alfred A. Knopf, 1980).

Herman, Edward S., and Frank Brodhead, *Demonstration Elections: U.S. Staged Elections in the Dominican Republic, Vietnam and El Salvador* (Boston: South End Press, 1984).

Herman, Edward S., and Noam Chomsky, *Manufacturing Consent: The Political Economy of the Mass Media* (New York: Pantheon, 1988).

Herman, Edward S., *The Real Terror Network: Terrorism in Fact and Propaganda* (Boston: South End Press, 1982).

Herr, Michael, *Dispatches* (New York: Alfred A. Knopf, 1977).

Hersh, Seymour M., *My Lai 4: A Report on the Massacre and Its Aftermath* (New York: Random House, 1970).

Hertzberg, Hazel W., *The Search for an American Indian Identity: Modern Pan-Indian Movements* (Syracuse, NY: Syracuse University Press, 1971).

Heydecker, Joe, and Johannes Leeb, *The Nuremberg Trials* (London: Heinemannn, 1962).

Hickerson, H., *The Chippewa and Their Neighbors* (New York: Holt, Rinehart & Winston, 1970).

Hilberg, Raul, *The Destruction of the European Jews* (Chicago: Quadrangle, 1961).

———, *The Destruction of the European Jews, 3 vols.* (New York: Holmes & Meier, [3rd ed., definitive] 1985).

Hill, J.L., *The Passing of the Indian and the Buffalo* (Long Beach, CA: n.p., 1917).

Hillgruber, Andreas, *Zweierlei Untergang: Die Zerschlagung des Deutschen Reiches und das Ende des Europäischen Judentums* (Berlin: Corso bei Siedler, 1986).

Hirabayashi, Lane Ryo, *Inside an American Concentration Camp: Japanese American Resistance at Poston, Arizona* (Tucson: University of Arizona Press, 1995).

Hirschfeld, Gerhart, and Lothar Kettenacher, eds., *Der Führerstaat: Mythos und Realität* (Stuttgart: Klett-Gotta, 1981).

Hiss, Alger, *In the Court of Public Opinion* (New York: Alfred A. Knopf, 1957).

Hitler, Adolph, *Mein Kampf* (Boston: Houghton-Mifflin, 1962 reprint of 1925 original).

———, *Hitler's Secret Book* (New York: Grove Press, 1961).

———, *Hitler's Secret Conversations* (New York: Signet, 1961).

Hodson, Julie, *Witness to Political Violence in Guatemala* (New York: Oxfam America, 1982).

Hoffman, Paul E., *The Spanish Crown and the Defense of the Caribbean, 1565–1585: Precedent, Patrimonialism, and Royal Parsimony* (Baton Rouge: Louisiana State University Press, 1980).

———, *A New Andalucia and a Way to the Orient: The American Southeast During the Sixteenth Century* (Baton Rouge: Louisiana State University Press, 1990).

Hoggan, David Leslie, *The Myth of the Six Million* (Tacoma Park, MD: Noontide Press, 1969).

———, *The Forced War: When Peaceful Revision Failed* (Tacoma Park, MD: Noontide Press, 1983 translation of 1961 German original).

Hoig, Stan, *The Sand Creek Massacre* (Norman: University of Oklahoma Press, 1961).

———, *The Battle of the Washita* (Garden City, NY: Doubleday, 1976).

Hoig, Stan, *The Peace Chiefs of the Cheyennes* (Norman: University of Oklahoma Press, 1980).

Homer, *Iliad* (New York: Penguin, 1981).

Homze, Edward L., *Foreign Labor in Nazi Germany* (Princeton, NJ: Princeton University Press, 1967).

Honour, Hugh, *The New Golden Land: European Images of America from the Discoveries to the Present Time* (New York: Pantheon, 1975).

Hoover, J. Edgar, *Masters of Deceit: The Story of Communism in America* (New York: Henry Holt, 1958).

Hornung, Rick, *One Nation Under the Gun: Inside the Mohawk Civil War* (New York: Pantheon, 1991).

Horowitz, Irving Louis, *Taking Lives: Genocide and State Power* (New Brunswick, NJ: Transaction, [3rd ed.] 1982).

———, *Genocide: State Power and Mass Murder* (New Brunswick, NJ: Transaction Books, 1976).

Horsman, Reginald, *The Causes of the War of 1812* (Philadelphia: University of Pennsylvania Press, 1962).

———, *Expansion and American Policy, 1783–1812* (Lansing: Michigan State University Press, 1967).

———, *Race and Manifest Destiny: The Origins of American Racial Anglo-Saxonism* (Cambridge: Harvard University Press, 1981).

Hovannisian, Richard G., ed., *The Armenian Genocide in Perspective* (New Brunswick, NJ: Transaction, 1986).

———, *The Armenian Genocide: History, Politics, Ethics* (New York: St. Martin's Press, 1992).

Howard, James H., *Shawnee: Ceremonialism of an American Indian Tribe* (Athens: University Press of Ohio, 1981).

Hoxie, Frederick E., *A Final Promise: The Campaign to Assimilate the Indians, 1880–1920* (Lincoln: University of Nebraska Press, 1985).

Hoyt, Edwin P., *America's Wars and Military Incursions* (New York: McGraw-Hill, 1987).

Hu-DeHart, Evelyn, *Yaqui Resistance and Survival* (Madison: University of Wisconsin Press, 1984).

Huber, Jacqueline, et al., *The Gunnery Range Report* (Pine Ridge, SD: Office of the President, Oglala Sioux Tribe, 1981).

Hudson, Charles M., *The Southeastern Indians* (Knoxville: University of Kentucky Press, 1976).

Hulse, James W., *Forty Years in the Wilderness* (Reno: University of Nevada Press, 1986).

Hunt, Aurora, *The Army of the Pacific* (Glendale, CA: Arthur H. Clark, 1951).

Hunt, George T., *The Wars of the Iroquois: A Study in Intertribal Relations* (Madison: University of Wisconsin Press, 1960).

Hurt, R. Douglas, *American Indian Agriculture: Prehistory to the Present* (Lawrence: University Press of Kansas, 1987).

Hurtado, Albert L., *Indian Survival on the California Frontier* (New Haven, CT: Yale Universsity Press, 1988).

Hutton, Paul Andrew, *Phil Sheridan and His Army* (Lincoln: University of Nebraska Press, 1985).

Indian Affairs of Canada, *Indian Acts and Amendments, 1868–1950* (Ottawa: Indian & Northern Affairs Ministry of Canada, 1981).

Inglis, David, R., *Nuclear Energy: Its Physics and Social Challenge* (Reading, MA: Addison-Wesley, 1973).

Inikori, Joseph E., and Stanley L. Engerman, eds., *The Atlantic Slave Trade: Effects on Economies, Societies, and Peoples, in Africa, the Americas, and Europe* (Durham: Duke University Press, 1992).

International Court of Justice, *Reports of Judgments, Advisory Opinions and Orders: Reservations to the Convention on Punishment and Prevention of the Crime of Genocide* (The Hague, 1951).

International Organization for the Elimination of All Forms of Racism, *Zionism and Racism: Proceedings of an International Symposium* (New Brunswick, NJ: North American, 1979).

Irving, David, *Hitler's War* (London & New York: Macmillan, 1977).

Isaacs, Arnold J., *Without Honor: Defeat in Vietnam and Cambodia* (Baltimore: John Hopkins University Press, 1983).

Jackson, Donald, ed., *Black Hawk: An Autobiography* (Urbana: University of Illinois Press, 1964).

———, *Custer's Gold: The United States Cavalry Expedition of 1874* (Lincoln: University of Nebraska Press, 1966).

Jackson, Kenneth T., *The Ku Klu Klan in the City, 1915–1930* (New York: Oxford University Press, 1967).

Jackson, Robert H., *The Nürnberg Case as Presented by Robert H. Jackson, Chief Counsel for the United States* (New York: Alfred A. Knopf, 1947).

Jackson, Robert H., *Indian Population Decline: The Missions of Northwestern New Spain, 1687–1840* (Albuquerque: University of New Mexico Press, 1995).

Jacob, Gerald, *Site Unseen: The Politics of Siting a Nuclear Repository* (Pittsburg: University of Pittsburg Press, 1990).

Jacobs, Wilbur R., *Dispossessing the American Indian: Indians and Whites on the Colonial Frontier* (New York: Scribner, 1972).

Jacobs, William R., *Diplomacy and Indian Gifts: Anglo-French Rivalry Along the Ohio and Northwestern Frontiers, 1748–1763* (Standford, CA: Standford University Press, 1950).

Jahoda, Gloria, *The Trail of Tears: The Story of the Indian Removals* (New York: Holt, Rinehart & Winston, 1975).

Jastrow, Morris, *The Civilization of Babylonia and Assyria* (New York: Benjamin Blom, 1971 reprint of 1915 original).

Jaulin, Robert, *L'Ethnocide à travers les Amériques* (Paris: Gallimard Publishers, 1972).

———, *La décivilisation, politique et pratique de l'ethnocide* (Brussels: Presses Universitaires de France, 1974).

Javier Giraldo, S.J., *Columbia: The Genocidal Democracy* (Monroe, ME: Common Courage Press, 1996).

Jennings, Francis, *The Invasion of America: Indians, Colonialism and the Cant of Conquest* (Chapel Hill: University of North Carolina Press, 1975).

———, *The Ambiguous Iroquois Empire: The Covenant Chain Confederation of Indian Tribes with the New England Colonies* (New York: W.W. Norton, 1984).

———, *Empire of Fortune: Crowns, Colonies and Tribes in the Seven Years' War in America* (New York: W.W. Norton, 1988).

Johnson, Amandua, *The Swedish Settlements on the Delaware: Their History and Relation to the Indians, 1638–1664* (Philadelphia: University of Pennsylvania Press, 1911).

Johnson, Basil H., *Indian School Days* (Norman: University of Oklahoma Press, 1989).

Johnson, Dorothy M., *The Bloody Bozeman* (New York: McGraw-Hill, 1971).

Johnson, George, *Architects of Fear: Conspiracy Theories and Paranoia in American Politics* (Boston: Beacon Press, 1983).

Johnson, Virginia Wiesel, *The Unregimented General: A Biography of Nelson A. Miles* (Boston: Houghtn-Mifflin, 1962).

Jones, Dorothy V., *License for Empire: Colonialism by Treaty in North America* (Chicago: University of Chicago Press, 1982).

Jones, Douglas C., *The Treaty of Medicine Lodge: The Story of the Great Indian Council as Told by Eyewitnesses* (Norman: University of Oklahoma Press, 1966).

Jones, Grant D., *Maya Resistance to Spanish Rule: Time and History on a Colonial Frontier* (Albuquerque: University of New Mexico Press, 1989).

Jones, Gwyn, *The Norse Atlantic Saga* (New York: Oxford University Press, 1964).

Jones, Oakah L. Jr., *Pueblo Warriors and the Spanish Conquest* (Norman: University of Oklahoma Press, 1966).

Jorgenson, Joseph, ed., *American Indians and Energy Development* (Cambridge, MA: Anthropological Resource Center, 1978).

———, *American Indians and Energy Development II* (Cambridge, MA: Anthropological Resource Center, 1984).

Joseph, Paul, *Cracks in the Empire: State Politics in the Vietnam War* (Boston: South End Press, 1981).

Josephy, Jr., Alvin M., *The Indian Heritage of America* (New York: Alfred A. Knopf, 1968).

———, *The Civil War in the American West* (New York: Alfred A. Knopf, 1992).

Kahn, Albert E., *High Treason: The Plot Against the People* (New York: Lear, 1960).

Kahn, E.J., Jr., *The China Hands* (New York: Viking, 1975).

Kahn, Gordon, *Hollywood on Trial* (New York: Boni & Gaer, 1948).

Kame'eleihiwa, Lilikala, *Native Lands and Foreign Desires* (Honolulu: Bishop Museum Press, 1992).

Kamenesky, Ihor, *Secret Nazi Plans for Eastern Europe: A Study of Lebensraum Policies* (New York: Bookman, 1961).

Karmasian, Fritz, *Austrian Attitudes Towards Jews, Israel and the Holocaust* (New York: American Jewish Committee, 1992).

Karnow, Stanley, *Mao and China: From Revolution* (New York: Viking, 1972).

Katz, Steven T., ed., *Post-Holocaust Dialogues: Critical Studies in Modern Jewish Thought* (New York: New York University Press, 1983).

———, ed., *Mystical and Religious Traditions* (New York: Oxford University Press, 1983).

———, ed., *Mysticism and Language* (New York: Oxford University Press, 1992).

———, *The Holocaust in Historical Context, Vol. 1: The Holocaust and Mass Death Before the Modern Age* (New York: Oxford University Press, 1992).

Katz, Steven T., *Post-Holocaust Dialogues: Critical Studies in Modern Jewish Thought* (New York: New York University Press, 1983).

Kellner, Hans, *Language and Historical Representation: Getting the Story Crooked* (Madison: University of Wisconsin Press, 1989).

Kelly, Lawrence C., *Navajo Roundup* (Boulder, CO: Pruett, 1970).

———, *Assault on Assimilation: John Collier and the Origins of Indian Policy Reform* (Albuquerque: University of New Mexico Press, 1983).

Kendrick, Donald, *Gypsies Under the Swastika* (Hartfield: Hertfordshire University Press, 1995).

Kendrick, Donald, and Grattan Paxton, *The Destiny of Europe's Gypsies* (London: Sussex University Press, Chatto & Heinemann, 1972).

Kenneth, Carley, *The Sioux Uprising of 1862* (St. Paul: Minnesota Historical Society, 1961).

Kicking Bird, Kirk, and Karen Ducheneaux, *One Hundred Million Acres* (New York: Macmillan, 1973).

Kiernan, V.G., *European Empires from Conquest to Collapse, 1815–1960* (Leicester: Leicester University Press, 1982).

King, Dennis, *Lyndon LaRouche and the New American Fascism* (Garden City, NY: Doubleday, 1989).

Kinney, Jay P., *A Continent Lost—A Civilization Won: Indian Land Tenure in America* (Baltimore: John Hopkins University Press, 1937).

Kistler, R.E., and R.M. Glen, *Notable Achievements of the Naval Weapons Center* (China Lake Weapons Center: Technical Information Dept. Publishing Division, 1990).

Klare, Michael T., *Beyond the "Vietnam Syndrome": U.S. Interventionism in the 1980s* (Washington, D.C.: Institute for Policy Studies, 1981).

Klare, Michael T., and Peter Kornbluh, eds., *Low Intensity Warfare: Counterinsurgency, Proinsurgency and Antiterrorism in the Eighties* (New York: Pantheon, 1989).

Klehr, Harvey, and Ronald Radosh, *The Amerasia Spy Case: Prelude to McCarthyism* (Chapil Hill: University of North Carolina Press, 1996).

Kleist, Peter, *Auch Du Warst Dabei!* (Heidelberg: Wehr & Wissen, 1952).

Klinct, Carl F., ed., *Tecumseh: Fact and Fiction in the Early Records* (Englewood Cliffs, NJ: Prentice-Hall, 1961).

Klotz, Marcia, et al., *Citizens' Guide to Rocky Flats: Colorado's Bomb Factory* (Boulder, CO: Rocky Mountain Peace Center, 1992).

Knight, Oliver, *Following the Indian Wars* (Norman: University of Oklahoma Press, 1960).

Knollenberg, Bernard, *The Origin of the American Revolution, 1759–1766* (New York: Macmillan, 1960).

Knorr, Klaus E., *British Colonial Theories, 1570–1850* (London: Frank Cass, 1963 reprint of 1944 original).

Koch, H.W., ed., *Aspects of the Third Reich* (London: Allen & Unwin, 1985).

Koehl, Robert, *RKFDV: German Resettlement and Population Policy, 1939–1945* (Cambridge: Cambridge University Press, 1957).

Koen, Ross Y., *The China Lobby in American Politics* (New York: Macmillan, 1960).

Koestler, Arthur, *Janus: A Summing Up* (London: Hutchenson, 1978).

Kogon, Ernest, *The Theory and Practice of Hell* (New York: Farrar, Strauss & Giroux, 1984 reprint of 1950 original).

Kohn, Henry, *Rongelap Assessment Project Report* (Berkeley: Rongelap Assessment Project, University of California, 1989).

Kolb, Eberhard, *Bergen-Belsen: From "Detention Camp" to Concentration Camp, 1943–1945* (Gottingen: Vandenhoeck & Ruprecht, [2nd. ed.] 1988).

König, Ulrich, *Sinti und Roma unter dem Nationalsocialismus* (Bochum: Brockmeyer Verlah, 1989).

Kovel, Joel, *White Racism: A Psychohistory* (New York: Columbia University Press, 1984 revision of the 1970 Pantheon edition).

Kraft, Joseph, *The Struggle for Algeria* (Garden City, NY: Doubleday, 1961).

Kramer, Andrew W., *Understanding Nuclear Reactors* (Barrington, IL: Technical, 1970).

Kramish, Arnold, and Eugene M. Zuckert, *Atomic Energy For Your Business: Today's Key to Tomorrow's Profits* (New York: David McKay, 1959).

Kren, George M. and Leon Rappoport, *The Holocaust and the Crisis of Human Behavior* (New York: Holmes & Meier, 1980).

Kroeber, A.L., *Cultural and Natural Areas of Native North America* (Berkeley & Los Angeles: University of California Publications in American Archaeology and Ethnology XXXVIII, 1939).

Kroeber, Theodora, *An Anthropologist Looks at History* (Berkeley: University of California Press, 1966).

Kühl, Stefan, *The Nazi Connection: Eugenics, American Racism, and German National Socialism* (New York: Oxford University Press, 1994).

Kulentz, Valerie L., *Geographies of Sacrifice: Nuclear Landscapes and Their Social Consequences, 1940–1996* (forthcoming from Routledge, 1997).

Kuper, Leo, *Genocide: Its Political Uses in the Twentieth Century* (New Haven, CT, Yale University Press, 1981).

———, *International Action Against Genocide* (London: Minority Rights Group, [rev. ed.] 1984).

———, *The Prevention of Genocide* (New Haven, CT: Yale University Press, 1985).

Kupperman, Karen Ordahl, *Settling With the Indians: The Meeting of English and American Cultures in America, 1580–1640* (Totowa, NJ: Rowman & Littlefield, 1980).

Kvasnicka, Robert M., and Herman J. Viola, eds., *The Commissioners of Indian Affairs, 1824–1977* (Lincoln: University of Nebraska Press, 1979).

LaBlanc, Lawrence J., *The United States and the Genocide Convention* (Durham, NC: Duke University Press, 1991).

Laflin, Arthur J., and Anne Montgomery, eds., *Swords into Plowshares: Nonviolent Direct Action for Disarmament* (San Francisco: Harper & Row, 1987).

Lamb, Harold, *Genghis Khan* (New York: Pinnacle Books, 1927).

Langbein, Hermann, *Against All Hope: Resistance in the Nazi Concentration Camps, 1938–1945* (New York: Continuum, 1996).

Langdon, Jr., George D., *Pilgrim Colony: A History of New Plymouth, 1620–1691* (New Haven, CT: Yale University Press, 1966).

Langguth, A.J., *Hidden Terrors: The Truth About U.S. Police Operations in Latin America* (New York: Pantheon, 1978).

Lapp, Ralph E., *The New Force* (New York: Harper & Bros., 1953).

———, *Atoms and People* (New York: Harper & Bros., 1956).

Laqueur, Walter, *The Terrible Secret: Suppression of the Truth About Hitler's "Final Solution"* (Boston: Little, Brown, 1981).

Larner, Christina, *Witchcraft and Religion: The Politics of Popular Belief* (Oxford: Basil Blackwell, 1984).

Lasky, Toledano and Victor, *Spies, Dupes and Diplomats* (New Rochelle, NY: Arlington House, 1967).

Latham, Earl, ed., *The Meaning of McCarthyism* (Boston: D.C. Heath, 1965).

Latta, Frank F., *Handbook of Yokuts Indians* (Santa Cruz: Bear State Press, 1977).

Lauber, Almon Wheeler, *Indian Slavery in Colonial Times Within the Present Limits of the United States* (Williamstown, MA: Corner House Social Science Reprints, 1979).

Lavender, David, *Bent's Fort* (Garden City, NY: Doubleday, 1954).

———, *Land of Giants: The Drive to the Pacific Northwest, 1750–1950* (Lincoln: University of Nebraska Press, 1958).

———, *The Great West* (Boston: Houghton-Mifflin, 1987).

Lazarus, Edward, *Black Hills, White Justice: The Sioux Nation versus The United States, 1775 to the Present* (New York: HarperCollins, 1991).

Leach, Douglas Edward, *Flintlock and Tomahawk: New England in King Philip's War* (New York: W.W. Norton, 1958).

Leckie, William H., *The Military Conquest of the Southern Plains* (Norman: University of Oklahoma Press, 1963).

Ledogar, Robert L. *Hungry for Profits* (New York: International Documentation, 1975).

LeFeber, John, *America, Russia, and the Cold War, 1945–1966* (New York: John Wiley & Sons, 1968).

Leighy, John, ed., *Land and Life* (Brekeley: University of California Press, 1963).

Leland, Joy, *Firewater Myths: American Indian Drinking and Drug Addiction* (New Brunswick, NJ: Rutgers Center for Alcoholic Studies, 1976).

Lemarchand, Réné, and David Martin, *Selective Genocide in Burundi* (London: Minority Rights Group Report No. 20, 1974).

Lemkin, Raphaël, *Axis Rule in Occupied Europe: Laws of Occupation, Analysis of Government, Proposals for Redress* (Washington, D.C.: Carnegie Endowment for International Peace, 1944).

Lenin, V.I., *Imperialism: The Highest Stage of Capitalism* (Moscow: Foreign Languages Publishing House, 1952 translation of 1917 original).

Lens, Sidney, *The Forging of the American Empire* (New York: Thomas Y. Crowell, 1971).

Lenssen, Nicholas, *Nuclear Waste: The Problem That Won't Go Away* (Washington, D.C.: Worldwatch Institute, 1991).

Leonard, Richard, *South Africa at War: White Power and Crisis in Southern Africa* (Westport, CT: Lawrence Hill, 1983).

Leon-Portilla, Miguel, ed., *The Broken Spears: The Aztec Account of the Discovery of Mexico* (Boston: Beacon Press, 1962).

Leuchter, Frederick A., *The End of the Line: The Leuchter Report-The First Forensic Examination of Auschwitz* (London: Focal Point, 1989).

Leupp, Francis E., *The Indian and His Problem* (New York: Scribner's, 1910).

Levi, Primo, *Survival in Auschwitz: The Nazi Assault on Humanity* (New York: Collier, 1961).

Levkov, Ilya, ed., *Bitburg and Beyond: Encounters in American, German, and Jewish History* (New York: Shapolsky, 1987).

Lewis, Clifford M., and Albert J. Loomie, eds., *The Spanish Jesuit Mission in Virginia, 1570–1571* (Chapel Hill: University of North Carolina Press for the Virginia Historical Society, 1953).

Lewis, Richard S., *The Nuclear Power Rebellion: Citizens vs. the Atomic Industrial Establishment* (New York: Viking, 1972).

Lifton, Robert Jay, *The Nazi Doctors: Medical Killing and the Psychology of Genocide* (New York: Basic Books, 1986).

Lifton, Robert Jay, and Eric Markusen, *The Genocidal Mentality: Nazi Holocaust and Nuclear Threat* (New York: Basic Books, 1988).

Lindquist, Sven, *"Exterminate All the Brutes": One Man's Journey Into the Heart of Darkness and the Origins of Modern Genocide* (New York: New Press, 1996).

Linenthal, Edward T., *Preserving Memory: The Struggle to Create America's Holocaust Museum* (New York: Viking, 1995).

Lipstadt, Deborah, *Denying the Holocaust: The Growing Assault on Truth and Memory* (New York: Free Press, 1993).

Lockwood, Frank C., *The Apache Indians* (Lincoln: University of Nebraska Press, 1938).

Loomis, David, *Combat Zoning: Military Land-Use Planning in Nevada* (Las Vegas: University of Nevada Press, 1994).

Lorenz, Konrad, *On Aggression* (New York: Harcourt, Brace & World, 1977).

Lovell, W. George, *Conquest and Survival in Colonial Guatemala: A Historical Geography of the Chuchumatan Highlands, 1500–1821* (Montréal: McGill-Queens University Press, 1985).

Lovins, Armory B., and Hunter L. Lovins, *Brittle Power: Energy for National Security* (Andover, MA: Brickhouse, 1982).

Lucas, Anthony J., *Nightmare: The Underside of the Nixon Years* (New York: Viking, 1976).

Lukas, Richard C., *Forgotten Holocaust: The Poles Under German Occupation 1939–1944* (Lexington: University of Kentucky Press, 1986).

Lumer, Hyman, *The Professional Informer* (New York: New Century, 1955).

Lumsden, Dr. Malvern, *Anti-Personnel Weapons* (Stockholm: International Peace Research Institute, 1975).

Lyon, Eugene, *The Enterprise of Florida: Pedro Menendez de Aviles and the Spanish Conquest, 1565–1568* (Gainsville: University of Florida Press, 1983).

McAlister, Lyle N., *Spain and Portugal in the New World, 1492–1700* (Minneapolis: University of Minnesota Press, 1984).

McCaffrey, James M., *Army of Manifest Destiny: The American Soldier in the Mexican War, 1846–1848* (New York: Oxford University Press, 1992).

McCardell, Lee, *Ill-Starred General: Braddock of the Coldstream Guards* (Pittsburg: University of Pittsburg Press, 1958).

McCarthy, Joseph R., *McCarthyism: The Fight for America* (New York: Davis-Adair, 1952).

McClain, Charles J., *In Search of Equality: The Chinese Struggle Against Discrimination in the Nineteenth Century* (Berkeley: University of California Press, 1994).

McDermott, John D., *Forlorn Hope: The Battle of Whitebird Canyon and the Beginning of the Nez Percé War* (Boise: Idaho State Historical Society, 1978).

McDonald, Dwight, *Discriminations: Essays and Afterthoughts* (New York: Grossman, 1974).

McDonnell, Janet A., *The Dispossession of the American Indian, 1887–1934* (Bloomington: Indiana University Press, 1991).

McGregor, James H., *The Wounded Knee Massacre from the Viewpoint of the Survivors* (Baltimore: Wirth Brothers, 1940).

McHugh, Tom, and Victoria Hobson, *The Time of the Buffalo* (New York: Alfred A. Knopf, 1972).

McKenzie, J.M., *The Partition of Africa, 1880–1900* (London: Metheun, 1983).

McMechen, Edgar Carlisle, *Life of Governor John Evans: Second Territorial Governor of Colorado* (Denver: Walgren, 1924).

McNeill, John Robert, *The Atlantic Empires of France and Spain: Louisbourg and Havana, 1700–1763* (Chapel Hill, NC: University of North Carolina Press, 1985).

McNeill, William, *Plagues and Peoples* (Garden City, NY: Doubleday, 1976).

McNitt, Frank, *Navajo Wars: Military Campaigns, Slave Raids, and Reprisals* (Alburquerque: University of New Mexico Press, 1990).

McWhorter, Lucius, *Crimes Agaainst the Yakimas* (North Yakima, WA: Republic, 1913).

Macy, Joanna Rogers, *Despair and Personal Power in the Nuclear Age* (Baltimore: New Society, 1983).

Madariaga, Salvador de, *The Rise of the Spanish American Empire* (London: Hollis & Carter Publishers, 1947).

Madaule, Jacques, *The Albigensian Crusade* (New York: Fordham University Press, 1967).

Madsen, Brigham M., *The Shoshoni Frontier and the Bear River Massacre* (Salt Lake City: University of Utah Press, 1985).

Mahon, John K., *History of the Second Seminole War, 1835–1842* (Gainesville: University of Florida Press, 1967).

Maier, Charles S., *The Unmasterable Past: History, Holocaust, and German National Identity* (Cambridge: Harvard University Press, 1988).

Makhijana, Arjun, and Scott Saleska, *High-Level Dollars, Low-Level Sense: A Critique of Present Policy for the Management of Long-Lived Radioactive Wastes and Discussion of an Alternative Approach* (Takoma Park, MD: Institute for Energy and Environmental Reserach, 1992).

Mander, Jerry, *In the Absence of the Sacred: The Failure of Technology and the Survival of the Indian Nations* (San Francisco: Sierra Club Books, 1991).

Manes, Christopher, *Green Rage: Radical Environmentalism and the Unmaking of Civilization* (Boston: Little, Brown, 1990).

Manley, Henry M., *The Treaty of Fort Stanwix, 1784* (Rome, NY: Rome Sentinel, 1932).

Manring, B.F., *The Conquest of the Coeur d'Alenes, Spokane and Palouses* (Spokane, WA: Inland, 1912).

Marrin, Albert, *Struggle for a Continent: The French and Indian Wars, 1690–1760* (New York: Anteneum, 1987).

Maria, Brother Nectario, *Juan Colón Was A Spanish Jew* (New York: Cedney 1971).

Marrus, Michael R., *The Holocaust in History* (Hanover, NH: Brandeis University Press & University Press of New England, 1987).

———, ed., *The Nazi Holocaust: Historical Articles on the Destruction of European Jews, Vol. 9* (Westport, CT: Meckler, 1989).

Marrus, Michael R., and Robert O. Paxton, *Vichy France and the Jews* (New York: Columbia University Press, 1981).

Marshall, Burke, and Jack Schwarz, *The My Lai Massacre and Cover-Up: Beyond the Reach of the Law?* (New York: Free Press, 1976).

Marszalek, John F., *Sherman: A Soldier's Passion for Order* (New York: Free Press, 1933).

Martin, Calvin, ed., *The American Indian and the Problem of History* (New York: Oxford University Press, 1987).

Martin, James Kirby, Randy Roberts, Steven Mintz, Linda O. McMurray and James H. Jones, *America and Its People, Vol. 1: To 1877* (New York: HarperCollins College, [2nd. ed.] 1993).

Martin, Joel W., *Sacred Revolt: The Muskogees' Struggle for a New World* (Boston: Beacon Press, 1991).

Martin, Paul S., and H.E. Wright, *Pleistocene Extinctions: The Search for a Cause* (New Haven, CT: Yale University Press, 1967).

Marx, Robert F., with Jenifer G. Marx, *In Quest of the Great White Gods: Contact Between the Old and New World from the Dawn of History* (New York: Crown, 1992).

Mason, Philip P., ed., *After Tippecanoe: Some Aspects of the War of 1812* (East Lansing, MI & Toronto: Michigan State University Press & Ryerson Press, 1963).

Matthiessen, Peter, *Indian Country* (New York: Viking, 1984).

Matusow, Harvey, *False Witness* (New York: Cameron & Kahn, 1955).

Mayhall, Milfred P., *The Kiowas* (Norman: University of Oklahoma Press, 1962).

Medvin, Norman, *The Energy Cartel* (New York: Vintage, 1974).

Melvoin, Richard I., *New England Outpost: War and Society in Colonial Deerfield* (New York: W.W. Norton, 1989).

Mendelsohn, John, and Donald S. Detwiler, eds., *The Holocaust: Selected Documents in Eighteen Volumes* (New York: Garland, 1982).

Menchú, Rigoberta, *I Rigoberta Menchú* (London: Verso, 1983).

Mendoza, Patrick J., *Song of Sorrow: Massacre at Sand Creek* (Denver: Willow Wind, 1993).

Meriam, Lewis, et al., *The Problem of Indian Administration* (Baltimore: John Hopkins University Press, 1928).

Merk, Frederick, *Manifest Destiny and Mission in American History: A Reinterpretation* (New York: Alfred A. Knopf, 1963).

Merwick, Donna, *Possessing Albany, 1630–1710: The Dutch and English Experiences* (Cambridge: Cambridge University Press, 1990).

Meyer, Arno J., *Why Did the Heavens Not Darken? The "Final Solution" in History* (New York: Pantheon, 1990).

Middleton, Richard, *Bells of Victory: The Pitt-Newcastle Ministry and the Conduct of the Seven Years' War, 1757–1762* (Cambridge: Cambridge University Press, 1985).

Milanich, Jerald T., and Samuel Proctor, eds., *Tacachule: Essays on the Indians of Florida and Southeastern Georgia During the Historic Period* (Gainesville: University of Florida Press, 1978).

Milibrand, Ralph, *The State in Capitalist Society: An Analysis of the Western System of Power* (New York: Basic Books, 1969).

Miller, J.R., *Sweet Promises* (Toronto: University of Toronto Press, 1991).

———, *Shingwauk's Vision: A History of Native Residential Schools* (Toronto: University of Toronto Press, 1996).

Miller, Richard, *Under the Cloud: The Decades of Nuclear Testing* (New York: Free Press, 1986).

Mills, C. Wright, *The Power Elite* (New York: Oxford University Press, 1956).

Miner, H. Craig, *The Corporation and the Indian: Tribal Sovereignty and Industrial Civilization in Indian Territory, 1865–1907* (Columbia: University of Missouri Press, 1976).

Misrach, Richard, and Myriam Weisang Misrach, *Bravo Twenty: The Bombing of the American West* (Baltiomore: Johns Hopkins University Press, 1990).

Mitchell, Annie, *Jim Savage and the Tulareno Indians* (Los Angeles, Westernlore Press, 1957).

Miquelon, Dale, *New France: "A Supplement to Europe"* (Toronto: McClellan & Stewart, 1987).

Montague, Ashley, *Man's Most Dangerous Myth: The Fallacy of Race* (Cleveland/New York: World, 1964).

Mooney, James M., *Historical Sketch of the Cherokee* (Chicago: Aldine, 1975 reprint of the 1900 edition).

———, *The Aboriginal Population of America North of Mexico* (Washington, D.C.: Smithsonian Miscellaneous Collections LXXX, No.7, Smithsonian Institution, 1928).

Moore, J.H., *The Cheyenne Nation: A Social and Demographic History* (Lincoln: University of Nebraska Press, 1987).

Moore, Louis R., *Mineral Development on Indian Lands: Cooperation and Conflict* (Denver: Rocky Mountain Mineral Law Foundation, 1983).

Moorhead, Max, *The Apache Frontier: Jacobo Ugarte and Spanish-Indian Relations in New Mexico, 1769–1791* (Norman: University of Oklahoma Press, 1968).

Morgan, Edmund S., *American Slavery-American Freedom: The Ordeal of Colonial Virginia* (New York: W.W. Norton, 1975).

Morgan, Ted, *Wilderness at Dawn: The Settling of the North American Continent* (New York: Simon & Schuster, 1993).

Morison, Samuel Elliot, *The European Discovery of America, Vol. 2: The Northern Voyages* (New York: Oxford University Press, 1971).

Morris, Donald R., *The Washing of Spears: The Rise and Fall of the Zulu Nation* (New York: Simon & Schuster, 1965).

Morrison, Kenneth M., *The Embattled Northeast: The Ellusive Ideal of Alliance in Abenaki-Euramerican Relations* (Berkeley: University of California Press, 1984).

Mörner, Magnus, *Race Mixture in the History of Latin America* (Boston: Little, Brown, 1967).

Morse, Arthur D., *While Six Million Died: A Chronicle of American Apathy* (New York: Random House, 1968).

Motolinia o Benavente, Torobio de, *Memoriales o libro de las cosas Nueva España y de los naturales dello* (Mexico City: UNAM, 1971).

Müller-Hill, Benno, *Murderous Science: Elimination by Scientific Selection of Jews, Gypsies, and Others, 1933–1945* (New York: Oxford University Press, 1988).

Mumey, Nolie, *History of the Early Settlements of Denver, 1859–1860* (Glendale, CA: Arthur H. Clark, 1942).

Murray, Keith A., *The Modocs and Their War* (Norman: University of Oklahoma Press, 1959).

Nadeau, Remi, *Fort Laramie and the Sioux* (Lincoln: University of Nebraska Press, 1967).

Nader, Ralph, and John Abbotts, *The Menace of Atomic Energy* (New York: W.W. Norton, 1977).

Naipaul, V.S., *The Return of Eva Perón* (New York: Alfred A. Knopf, 1980).

Nammack, Georgiana C., *Fraud, Politics, and the Dispossession of the Indians: The Iroquois Frontier and the Colonial Period* (Norman: University of Oklahoma Press, 1969).

Nankivell, J.H., *History of the Military Organization of Colorado, 1860–1935* (Denver: W.H. Kister, 1935).

Nash, George, *The Conservative Intellectual Movement in America Since 1945* (New York: Basic Books, 1975).

Nash, Gerald D. *The American West Transformed: The Impact of the Second World War* (Bloomington: University of Indiana Press, 1985).

Neckrich, Aleksandr M., *The Punished Peoples: The Deportation and Fate of Soviet Minorities at the End of the Second World War* (New York: W.W. Norton, 1978).

Neff, Andrew Love, *History of the Utah, 1847 to 1869* (Salt Lake City: University of Utah Press, 1940).

Neihardt, John G., *Black Elk Speaks* (Lincoln: University of Nebraska Press, 1961).

Neumann, Peter, *The Black March: The Personal Story of an SS Man* (New York: Bantam, 1958).

Neuser, Jacob, *Stranger at Home: "The Holocaust," Zionism, and American Judaism* (Chicago: University of Chicago Press, 1981).

Newcomb, Jr., W.W., *The Indians of Texas* (Austin: University of Texas Press, 1961).

Newson, Linda, *The Cost of Conquest: Indian Decline in Honduras Under Spanish Rule* (Boulder, CO: Westview Press, 1986).

Neyman, J., ed., *Proceedings of the Sixth Berkeley Symposium on Mathematical Statistics and Probability* (Berkeley: University of California Press, 1971).

Nichols, Edward J., *Zach Taylor's Little Army* (Garden City, NJ: Doubleday, 1963).

Nichols, David A., *Lincoln and the Indians* (Columbia: University of Missouri Press, 1978).

Nickerson, Hoffman, *The Inquisition: A Political and Military History of Its Establishment* (Port Washington, NY: Kennikat Press, 1968 reprint of 1932 original).

Nolan, Keith Wilson, *Into Laos: The Story of Dewey Canyon II/Lam Son 719* (Navato, CA: Presidio Press, 1986).

Nolte, Ernst, *Der Fascismus in seiner Epoche* (Munich: Piper, 1963); in translation as *Three Faces of Fascism: Action Française, Italian Fascism, National Socialism* (New York: Holt, Rinehart & Winston, 1966).

———, *Deutschland und der kalte Krieg* (Munich: Piper, 1976).

———, *Marxismus und Industrielle Revolution* (Stuttgart: Klett-Cotta, 1983).

———, *Der europäische Bürgerkrieg, 1917–1919* (Berlin: Corso bei Seidler, 1987).

Novak. S., *The Electric War* (San Francisco: Sierra Club Books, 1976).

Noyse, Stanley, *Los Comanches: The Horse People, 1715–1845* (Albuquerque: University of New Mexico Press, 1993).

Nurowski, Roman, ed., *1939–1945: War Losses in Poland* (Pozán: Wydawnictwo Zachodnie, 1960).

Nussbaum, Alfred, *A Concise History of the Laws of Nations* (New York: Macmillan, 1954).

Nye, Col. William Sturtevant, *Carbine and Lance: The Story of Old Fort Sill* (Norman: University of Oklahoma Press, 1937).

———, *Plains Indian Raiders; The Final Phases of Warfare from the Arkansas to the Red River* (Norman: University of Oklahoma Press, 1968).

O'Connell, Robert, *Of Arms and Men: A History of War, Weapons, and Aggression* (New York: Oxford University Press, 1989).

O'Donnell, James M. III, *Southern Indians in the American Revolution* (Knoxville: University of Tennessee Press, 1973).

O''Donnell, Terrance, *An Arrow in the Earth: General Joel Palmer and the Indians of Oregon* (Portland: Oregan Historical Society Press, 1991).

Ofer, Dalia, *Escaping the Holocaust* (New York: Oxford University Press, 1990).

Ogg, Austin, *The Old Northwest* (New Haven, CT: Yale University Press, 1921).

Oglesby, Carl, and Richard Shaull, *Containment and Change: Two Dissenting Views on American Foreign Policy* (New York: Macmillan, 1967).

Ohshinsky, David M., *A Conspiracy So Immense: The World of Joe McCarthy* (New York: Free Press, 1983).

Oldenbourg, Zoé, *Massacre at Montségur: A History of the Albigensian Crusade* (New York: Pantheon, 1961).

Olson, James C., *Red Cloud and the Sioux Problem* (Lincoln: University of Nebraska Press, 1965).

Olson, McKinley C., *Unacceptable Risk: The Nuclear Power Controversy* (New York: Bantam, 1976).

O'Neill, Dan, *The Firecracker Boys* (New York: St. Martin's Press, 1994).

Orfield, Gary, *A Study of Termination Policy* (Denver: National Congress of American Indians, 1965).

Ortiz, Simon J., *From Sand Creek* (New York: Thunder's Mouth Press, 1981).

———, *Woven Stone* (Tucson: University of Arizona Press, 1992).

Ostalaza, Margarita, *Política Sexual y Socialización Pólita de la Mujer Puertorriqueña la Consolidacion del Bloque Histórico Colonial de Puerto Rico* (Río Piedras, PR: Ediciones Huracan, 1989).

Ostling, Kristen, and Joanna Miller, *Taking Stock: The Impact of Militarism on the Environment* (New York: Science for Peace, 1992).

Otis, D.S., *The Dawes Act and the Allotment of American Indian Land* (Norman: University of Oklahoma Press, 1973).

Packenham, Thomas, *The Scramble for Africa: The White Man's Conquest of the Dark Continent from 1876 to 1912* (New York: Random House, 1991).

Packer, Herbert L., *Ex-Communist Witnesses* (Stanford, CA: Stanford University Press, 1962).

Padden, Ian, *The Fighting Elite: U.S. Rangers* (New York: Bantam, 1985).

Painter, James, *Guatemala: False Hope, False Freedom* (London: Catholic Institute for International Relations, 1987).

Palou, Fray Francisco, *Life and Apistolic Labors of the Venerable Father Junipero Serra* (Pasadena, CA: G.W. James, 1913).

———, *Historical Memoirs of New California* (New York: Russell & Russell, 1966).

Palumbo, Michael, *The Palestinian Catastrophe: The 1948 Expulsion of a People from their Homeland* (London: Faber & Faber, 1987).

Parenti, Michael, *Inventing Reality: The Politics of the News Media* (New York: St. Martin's Press, 1993).

Parker, Geoffrey, *The Thirty Years' War* (New York: Military Heritage Press, 1984).

Parker, Watson, *Gold in the Black Hills* (Norman: University of Oklahoma Press, 1966).

Parlow, Anita, *Cry, Sacred Ground: Big Mountain, U.S.A.* (Washington, D.C.: Christic Institute, 1988).

Parry, J.H., *The Age of Reconnaissance: Discovery, Exploration and Settlement, 1450–1650* (Berkeley: University of California Press, 1963).

Patai, R., and J. Patai-Wing, *The Myth of the Jewish Race* (Detroit: Wayne State University Press, 1989).

Paterson, Thomas G., ed., *The Origins of the Cold War* (Lexington, MA: Heath, 1974).

Patterson, William L., *The Man Who Cried Genocide: An Autobiography* (New York: International, 1971).

Pauling, Linus, *No More War* (New York: Dodd, Meade, 1958).

Pawells, Louis, and Jacques Bergier, *Le Matin des Magiciens* (Paris: Editions Gallimard, 1960); in translation as *The Morning of the Magicians* (New York: Stein & Day, 1965).

Payne, Robert, *The Dream and the Tomb: A History of the Crusades* (New York: Stein & Day, 1984).

Pearce, Jenny, *Under the Eagle: U.S. Intervention in Central America and the Caribbean* (Boston: South End Press, 1981).

Pearson, Jessica S., *A Sociological Analysis of the Reduction of Hazardous Radiation in Uranium Mines* (Washington, D.C.: National Institute for Occupational Safety and Health, 1975).

Peckham, Howard Henry, *The Colonial Wars, 1689–1762* (Chicago: University of Chicago Press, 1964).

———, *Pontiac and the Indian Uprising* (New York: Russell & Russell, 1970).

Peckham, Howard Henry, and Charles Gibson, eds., *The Attitudes of the Colonial Powers Towards the American Indian* (Salt Lake City: University of Utah Press, 1969).

Pelcher, David M., *The Diplomacy of Annexation: Texas, Oregon, and the Mexican War* (Columbia: University of Missouri Press, 1973).

Perkins, Bradford, *Prologue to War: England and the United States, 1805–1812* (Berkeley: University of California Press, 1961).

Peroff, Nicholas, *Menominee DRUMS: Tribal Termination and Restoration, 1954–1974* (Norman: University of Oklahoma Press, 1982).

Peters Cynthia, ed., *Collateral Damage: The "New World Order" At Home and Abroad* (Boston: South End Press, 1992).

Peterson, Merrill D., *Thomas Jefferson and the New Nation* (New York: Oxford University Press, 1973).

Perry, Richard J., *Apache Reservation: Indigenous Peoples and the American State* (Austin: University of Texas Press, 1993).

Pettitpas, Katherine, *Severing the Ties That Bind: Government Repression of Indigenous Religious Ceremonies on the Prairies* (Winnipeg: University of Manitoba Press, 1994).

Philp, Kenneth, *Assault on Assimilation: John Collier's Crusade for Indian Reform, 1920–1954* (Tucson: University of Arizona Press, 1977).

Pierce, Berton, *The Invasion of Canada, 1812–1813* (Boston: Little, Brown, 1980).

Pilat, Oliver, *The Atom Spies* (New York: Putnam, 1952).

Pinto, Constâncio, *East Timor's Unfinished Struggle: Inside the Timorese Resistance* (Boston: South End Press, 1996).

Plant, Richard, *The Pink Triangle: The Nazi War Against Homosexuals* (New York: New Republic/Henry Holt, 1986).

Plucknett, Thomas F.T., *A Concise History of the Common Law* (Rochester, NY: The Lawyers Co-operative, 1936).

Po-Chia Hsia, R., *The Myth of Ritual Murder: Jews and Magic in Reformation Germany* (New Haven, CT: Yale University Press, 1988).

Pohl, J. Frederick, *The Viking Settlements of North America* (New York: Clarkson N. Potter, 1972).

Poliakov, Léon, *Harvest of Hate: The Nazi Program for the Destruction of the Jews of Europe* (Syracuse, NY: Syracuse University Press, 1954).

Ponchaud, François, *Cambodia Year Zero* (New York: Penguin, 1978).

Prados, John, *The President's Secret Wars: CIA and the Pentagon Covert Operations from World War II through Iranscam* (New York: William Morrow, [2nd. ed.] 1986).

Prager, Dennis, and Joseph Telushkin, *Why the Jews? The Reason for Antisemitism* (New York: Simon & Schuster, 1983).

Pratt, Col. Richard H., *Battlefield and Classroom: Four Decades with the American Indian* (New Haven, CT: Yale University Press, 1964).

Pressac, Jean-Claude, *Auschwitz: Technique and Operation of the Gas Chambers* (New York: Holmes & Meier, 1989).

Prokosh, Eric, *The Simple Art of Murder: Anti Personnel Weapons and Their Developers* (Philadelphia: National Action/Research on the Military-Industrial Complex, 1972).

Prucha, Francis Paul, *American Indian Policy in the Formative Years: The Trade and Intercourse Acts, 1790–1834* (Lincoln: University of Nebraska Press, 1970).

———, *Americanizing the American Indian: Writings of the "Friends of the Indian," 1800–1900* (Lincoln: University of Nebraska Press, 1973).

————, *The Great Father: The United States Government and the American Indian* (Lincoln: University of Nebraska Press, 1984).

Prunier, Gérard, *The Rwanda Crisis: History of a Genocide* (New York: Columbia University Press, 1995).

Quattlebaum, Paul, *The Land Called Chicora: The Carolinas under the Spanish Rule with French Intrusions, 1520–1670* (Gainesville: University of Florida Press, 1956).

Quinn, David Beers, ed., *The Roanoak Voyages, 1584–1590* (Cambridge: Hakluyt Society, 1955).

————, *The Elizabethans and the Irish* (Ithaca, NY: Cornell University Press, 1966).

————, *England and the Discovery of America, 1481–1620* (New York: Alfred A. Knopf, 1974).

Radin, Paul, *The Winnebago Tribe* (Washington, D.C.: Bureau of American Ethnography, Smithsonian Institution, 37th Annual Report, 1923).

Radosh, Ronald, and Joyce Milton, *The Rosenberg File: A Search for the Truth* (New York: Holt, Rinehart & Winston, 1983).

Ramenofsky, Ann F., *Vectors of Death: The Archaeology of European Contact* (Albuquerque: University of New Mexico Press, 1987).

Randel, William Pierce, *The Ku Klux Klan: A Century of Infamy* (Philadelphia: Chilton, 1965).

Raneleigh, John, *The Agency: The Rise and Decline of the CIA* (New York: Touchstone, 1987).

Raper, Arthur F., *The Tragedy of Lynching* (Chapel Hill: University of North Carolina Press, 1933).

Rapaport, Roger, *The Great American Bomb Machine* (New York: E.P. Dutton, 1971).

Rassinier, Paul, *The Drama of the European Jews* (Silver Springs, MD: Steppingstones, 1975).

————, *Debunking the Holocaust Myth: A Study of the Nazi Concentration Camps and the Alleged Extermination of European Jewry* (Torrance CA: Institute for Historical Review, 1978).

Raunet, Daniel, *Without a Surrender of Consent: A History of the Nishga Land Claims* (Vancouver, B.C.: Douglas & McIntire, 1984).

Rauschning, Hermann, *The Voice of Destruction* (New York: G.P. Putnam's Sons, 1940).

Rawlyk, George A., *Nova Scotia's Massacusets: A Study of Massachusetts-Nova Scotia Relations, 1630 to 1784* (Montreal: McGill-Queens University Press, 1973).

Read, James Morgan, *Atrocity Propaganda, 1914–1919* (New York: Arno Press, 1972).

Reedstrom, E. Leslie, *Apache Wars: An Illustrated Battle History* (New York: Sterling, 1990).

Rees, David, *Harry Dexter White: A Study in Paradox* (New York: Coward, McCann & Geoghegan, 1973).

Reff, Daniel T., *Disease, Depopulation, and Culture Change in New Spain, 1518–1764* (Salt Lake City: University of Utah Press, 1991).

Regenstein, Lewis, *The Politics of Extinction* (New York: Macmillan, 1975).

Reinow, Robert, and Leona Train Reinow, *Our New Life with the Atom* (New York: Thomas Crowell, 1959).

Reith, Charles C., and Bruce M. Thompson, eds., *Deserts as Dumps? The Disposal of Hazardous Materials in Arid Ecosystems* (Albuquerque: University of New Mexico Press, 1992).

Reitlinger, Gerald, *The SS: Alibi of a Nation, 1922–1945* (New York: Viking, 1957).

————, *The Final Solution: The Attempt to Exterminate the Jews of Europe, 1939–1945* (New York: Beechhurst Press, 1953).

Reno, Phil, *Navajo Resources and Economic Development* (Albuquerque: University of New Mexico Press, 1981).

Reuben, William A., *The Honorable Mr. Nixon and the Alger Hiss Case* (New York: Action Books, 1956).

————, *The Atom Spy Hoax* (New York: Action Books, 1960).

Rhodes, Richard, *The Making of the Atomic Bomb* (New York: Simon & Schuster, 1986).

Rich, Norman, *Hitler's War Aims: Ideology, the Nazi State, and the Course of Expansion* (New York: W.W. Norton, 1973).

Richardson, Boyce, *People of Terra Nullius: Betrayal and Rebirth in Canada* (Seattle/Vancouver: University of Washington Press/Douglas McIntire, 1993).

Richardson, Leon B., *The History of Dartmouth College, 2 vols.* (Hanover, NH: Dartmouth College Pubs., 1932).

477

Richardson, Rupart Norval, *The Comanche Barrier to Southern Plains Settlement: A Century and a Half of Savage Resistance to Advancing White Settlement* (Glendale, CA: Arthur H. Clark, 1933).

Richie, Robert C., *The Duke's Province: A Study of New York Politics and Society, 1664–1691* (Chapel Hill, NC: University of North Carolina Press, 1977).

Richter, Daniel K., *The Ordeal of the Longhouse: The Peoples of the Iroquois Confederation in the Era of Colonization* (Chapel Hill: University of North Carolina Press, 1992).

Richter, Daniel K., and James H. Merrill, eds., *Beyond the Covenant Chain: The Iroquois and Their Neighbors in Indian North America 1600–1800* (Syracuse, NY: Syracuse University Press, 1987).

Riddell, Jeff C., *The Indian History of the Modoc War and the Causes That Led to It* (Medford, OR: Pine Cone, 1973).

Rieff, David, *Slaughterhouse: Bosnia and the Failure of the West* (New York: Touchstone, 1995).

Rifkin, Jeremy, *Entropy: A New World View* (New York: Viking, 1980).

Ringholz, Raye C., *Uranium Frenzy: Boom and Bust on the Colorado Plateau* (Albuquerque: University of New Mexico Press, 1989).

Riser, Carl C., *Oil! Titan of the Southwest* (Norman: University of Oklahoma Press, 1949).

Roberts, Adam, and Richard Guelff, eds., *Basic Documents on the Laws of War* (Oxford: Clarendon Press, 1981).

Robbins, Anothony, Arjun Makhijani and Katherine Yih, *Radioactive Heaven and Earth: The Health and Environmental Effects of Nuclear Weapons Testing In, On, and Above the Earth* (New York/London: Apex Press/Zed Books, 1991).

Roberts, Adam, and Richard Guelff, *Documents on the Laws of War* (Oxford: Clarendon Press, 1982).

Robertson, James, and John Lewallen, eds., *The Grass Roots Primer* (San Francisco: Sierra Club Books, 1975).

Robinson, Eric, *The American Revolution in Its Political and Military Aspects, 1763–1783* (New York: Oxford University Press, 1955).

Robinson, Jacob, *And the Crooked Shall Be Made Straight: The Eichmann Trial, the Jewish Catastrophe, and Hannah Arendt's Narrative* (New York: Macmillan, 1965).

Robinson, Nehemiah, *The Genocide Convention: A Commentary* (New York: Institute for Jewish Affairs, 1960).

Rochlin, Gene I., *Plutonium, Power, and Politics* (Berkeley: University of California Press, 1979).

Rock, David, *Argentina, 1516–1987* (Berkeley: University of California Press, 1987).

Roe, Frank Gilbert, *The Indian and His Horse* (Norman: University of Oklahoma Press, 1955).

Roessel, Ruth, ed., *Navajo Stories of the Long Walk* (Tsaile, AZ: Navajo Community College Press, 1973).

Rogin, Michael P., *Fathers and Children: Andrew Jackson and the Subjugation of the American Indian* (New York: Alfred A. Knopf, 1975).

Roosevelt, Theodore, *The Strenuous Life* (New York: Macmillan, 1901).

Rosenbaum, Alan S., *Is the Holocaust Unique? Perspectives in Comparative Genocide* (Boulder, CO: Westview Press, 1996).

Rosenberg, Alan, and Gerald E. Meyers, eds., *Echoes from the Holocaust: Philosophical Reflections on a Dark Time* (Philadelphia: Temple University Press, 1988).

Rosenberg, Howard I., *Atomic Soldiers: American Victims of Nuclear Experiments* (Boston: Beacon, 1980).

Rosenthal, Debra, *At the Heart of the Bomb: The Dangerous Allure of Weapons Work* (Menlo Park, CA: Addison-Wesley, 1990).

Roth, Cecil, *The Spanish Inquisition* (New York: W.W. Norton, 1964 reprint of 1937 original).

Roth, John, and Michael Berenbaum, *Holocaust: Religious and Philosophical Implications* (New York: Paragon House, 1989).

Rothfels, Hans, *The German Opposition to Hitler: An Appraisal* (Chicago: Henry Regnery, 1962).

Rothman, Hal, *On Rims and Ridges: The Los Alamos Area Since 1880* (Lincoln: University of Nebraska Press, 1992).

Rountree, Helen C., *The Powhatan Indians of Virginia: Their Traditional Culture* (Norman: University of Oklahoma Press, 1989).

Rubenstein, Richard, *The Cunning of History: The Holocaust and the American Future* (New York: Harper & Row, 1978).

———, *The Age of Triage: Fear and Hope in an Overcrowded World* (Boston: Beacon Press, 1983).

Ruby, Robert H., *The Spokane Indians: Children of the Sun* (Norman: University of Oklahoma Press, 1970).

———, *The Cayuse Indians: Imperial Tribesmen of Old Oregon* (Norman: University of Oklahoma Press, 1972).

Rushmore, Elsie M., *The Indian Policy During Grant's Administration* (New York: Marion Press, 1914).

Russell, Bertrand, *War Crimes in Vietnam* (New York: Monthly Review Press, 1967).

Russell, Philip, *El Salvador in Crisis* (Denver: Colorado River Press, 1984).

Russell Tribunal, *Report of the Fourth Russell Tribunal on the Rights of the Indians of the Americas* (Nottingham: Bertrand Russell Foundation, 1980).

Ryan, Lyndall, *The Aboriginal Tasmanians* (St Lucia: University of Queensland Press, 1981).

Sagan, Eli, *The Lust to Annihilate: A Psychoanalytic Study of Violence in Ancient Greek Culture* (New York: Psychohistory Press, 1979).

Sagi, Nana, *German Reparations: A History of the Negotiations* (Jerusalem: Hebrew University, 1980).

Said, Edward, *Orientalism* (New York, Pantheon, 1978).

———, *The Question of Palestine* (New York: Vintage, 1992).

———, *The Pen and the Sword: Conversations with David Barsamian* (Monroe, ME: Common Courage Press, 1994).

Sakai, J., *Settlers: The Myth of the White Proletariat* (Chicago: Morningstar Press, 1983).

Sale, Kirkpatrick, *The Conquest of Paradise: Christopher Columbus and the Columbian Legacy* (New York: Alfred A. Knopf Publishers, 1990).

———, *Dwellers in the Land: The Bioregional Vision* (Philadelphia: New Society, 1991).

Salisbury, Neal, *Manitou and Providence: Europeans, Indians and the Making of New England, 1500–1643* (New York: Oxford, 1982).

Sánchez-Alboronoz, Nicolás, *The Population of Latin America: A History* (Berkeley: University of California Press, 1974).

Sanders, R., *Project Plowshare: The Development of Peaceful Uses of Nuclear Explosives* (Washington, D.C.: Public Affairs Press, 1962).

Sanders, Ronald, *Lost Tribes and Promised Lands: The Origins of American Racism* (Boston: Little, Brown, 1978).

Sandoz, Mari, *Crazy Horse: Strange Man of the Oglalas* (New York Alfred A. Knopf, 1942).

———, *The Buffalo Hunters: The Story of the Hidesmen* (New York: Hasting House, 1954).

———, *Cheyenne Autumn* (New York: Avon, 1964).

———, *The Battle of the Little Big Horn* (New York: Curtis, 1966).

Sartre, Jean Paul, and Arlette El Kaim-Sartre, *On Genocide and a Summary of the Evidence and Judgements of the International War Crimes Tribunal* (Boston: Beacon Press, 1968).

Satz, Ronald, *American Indian Policy in the Jacksonian Era* (Lincoln: University of Nebraska Press, 1975).

Sauer, Carl Ortwin, *The Early Spanish Main* (Berkeley: University of California Press, 1966).

———, *Sixteenth Century North America* (Berkeley: University of California Press, 1971).

Schaaf, Gregory, *Wampum Belts and Peace Trees: George Morgan, Native Americans and Revolutionary Diplomacy* (Golden, CO: Fulcrum, 1990).

Schneir, Walter and Miriam, *Invitation to an Inquest* (New York: Pantheon, [3rd ed.] 1983).

Schilz, Thomas F., *The Lipan Apaches in Texas* (El Paso: Texas Western Press, 1987).

Schmalz, Peter S., *The Ojibwa of Southern Ontario* (Toronto: University of Toronto Press, 1991).

Schmidt, Carl, *Political Theology: Four Chapters on the Concept of Sovereignty* (Cambridge, MA: MIT Press, 1985 trans. of 1922 original).

Schmidt, Martin F., and Dee Brown, *Fighting Indians of the West* (New York: Scribner's, 1948).

Schmidt, Matthias, *Albert Speer: End of a Myth* (New York: St. Martin's Press, 1984).

Schmidt, Michael, *The New Reich: Violent Extremism in Germany and Beyond* (New York: Pantheon, 1993).

Schneir, William and Miriam, *Invitation to an Inquest* (New York: Pantheon, [3rd, ed.] 1983),.

Scholes, Frances V., *Church and State in New Mexico, 1610–1650* (Albuquerque: University of New Mexico Press, 1942).

Schubert, Jack, and Ralph E. Lapp, *Radiation: What It Is and How It Affects You* (New York: Viking, 1958).

Schultz, Duane, *Month of the Freezing Moon: The Sand Creek Masscare, November, 1864* (New York: St. Martin's Press, 1990).

————, *Over the Earth I Come: The Great Sioux Uprising of 1862* (New York: St. Martin's Press, 1992).

Schwab, Peter, ed., *Biafra* (New York: Facts on File, 1971).

Schwartz, Stewart B., *The Iberian Mediterranean and Atlantic Traditions in the Formation of Columbus as a Colonizer* (Minneapolis: University of Minnesota Press, 1986).

Scientists' Review Panel on the WIPP, *Evaluation of the Waste Isolation Pilot Plant (WIPP) as a Water Saturated Nuclear Waste Repository* (Albuquerque, NM: Concerned Citizens for Nuclear Safety, Jan. 1988).

Scott, David L., *Financing the Growth of the Electric Utilities* (New York: Praeger, 1976).

Scudder, Thayer, et al., *No Place To Go: Effectes of Compulsory Relocation on Navajos* (Philadelphia: Institute for the Study of Human Issues, 1982).

Seaborg, Glenn T., and William R. Corliss, *Man and Atom: Building a New World Through Nuclear Technology* (New York: E.P. Dutton, 1971).

Seaton-Watson, Hugh, *Nations and States: An Inquiry into the Origins of Nations and the Politics of Nationalism* (Boulder, CO: Westview Press, 1977).

Sereny, Gitta, *Albert Speer: His Battle with Truth* (New York: Alfred A. Knopf, 1995).

Severin, Tim, *The Brendan Voyage* (New York: McGraw-Hill, 1978).

Shannon, Albert Clement, *The Popes and Heresy in the Thirteenth Century* (New York: AMS Press, 1979).

Shapiro, Jacob, *Radiation Protection* (Cambridge, MA: Harvard University Press, [3rd ed.] 1990).

Shapiro, Shelly, ed., *Truth Prevails: The End of the "Leuchter Report"* (Albany, NY: Holocaust Education Project, 1990).

Sharp, Malcolm P., *Was Justice Done? The Rosenberg-Sobell Case* (New York: Monthly Review, 1956).

Shaw, David, *The Pleasure Police* (Garden City, NY: Doubleday, 1996).

Shawcross, William, *Sideshow: Kissinger, Nixon, and the Destruction of Cambodia* (New York: Simon & Schuster, 1979).

Shea, William L., *The Virginia Militia in the Seventeenth Century* (Baton Rouge: Louisiana State University Press, 1983).

Sheehan, Edward R.F., *Agony in the Garden: A Stranger in Guatemala* (New York: Houghton-Mifflin, 1989).

Sheehan, Bernard, *Savagism and Civility: Indians and Englishmen in Colonial Virginia* (Cambridge: Harvard University Press, 1980).

Sherill, Robert, *Gothic Politics in the Deep South: Stars of the New Confederacy* (New York: Grossman, 1968).

Sherman, William L., *Forced Native Labor in Sixteenth Century Central America* (Lincoln: University of Nebraska Press, 1979).

Sherwin, Martin, *A World Destroyed: The Atomic Bomb and the Grand Alliance* (New York: Alfred A. Knopf, 1975).

Shipeck, Florence Connolly, *Pushed into the Rocks: Southern California Indian Land Tenure, 1769–1986* (Lincoln: University of Nebraska Press, 1988).

Shiva, Vandana, *Staying Alive: Women, Ecology and Development* (London: Zed Books, 1989).

Shkilnyk, Anastasia M., *A Poison Stronger Than Love: The Destuction of an Ojibwa Community* (New Haven: Yale University Press, 1985).

Shrader-Frechette, K.S., *Buying Uncertainty* (Berkeley: University of California Press, 1993).

Sikov, Melvin R., and D. Dennis Mahlum, eds., *Radiation Biology of the Fetal and Juvenile Mammal: Proceedings of the Ninth Annual Hanford Biology Symposium at Richland, Washington, 5–8 May 1969* (Springfield, VA: Clearinghouse for Federal Scientific and Technical Information, 1969).

Silverberg, Robert, *The Pueblo Revolt* (New York: Weybright & Talley, 1970).

Simmons, Marc, *The Last Conquistador: Juan de Oñate and the Settling of the Far Southwest* (Norman: University of Oklahoma Press, 1991).

Simon, Jean-Marie, *Guatemala: Eternal Spring, Eternal Tyranny* (New York: W.W. Norton, 1987).

Simpson, Christopher, *Blowback: America's Recruitment of Nazis and its Effects on the Cold War* (New York: Collier Books, 1988).

Sinclair, Sir Ian, *The Vienna Convention on the Law of Treaties* (Manchester: Manchester Press, [2nd. ed.] 1984).

Singer, David, ed., *The American Jewish Yearbook, 1987* (New York: American Jewish Committee, 1987).

Skinner, Michael, *Red Flag* (Novato, CA: Presidio Press, 1983).

Sklar, Holly, ed., *Trilateralism: The Trilateral Commission and Elite Planning for Global Management* (Boston: South End Press, 1980).

———, *Washington's War on Nicaragua* (Boston: South End Press, 1988).

Slotkin, Richard, and James K. Folsom, eds., *So Dreadful a Judgement: Puritan Responses to King Philip's War, 1676–1677* (Middletown, CT: Wesleyan University Press, 1978).

Smead, Howard, *Blood Justice: The Lynching of Charles Mack Parker* (New York: Oxford University Press, 1986).

Smith, Bradley F., *Reaching Judgement at Nuremberg* (New York: Basic Books, 1977).

———, *The Road to Nuremberg* (New York: Basic Books, 1981).

Smith, Henry DeWolf, *Atomic Energy for Military Purposes: The Official Report on the Development of the Atomic Bomb Under the Auspices of the United States Government, 1940–1945* (Princeton, NJ: Princeton University Press, 1945).

Smith, John Chabot, *Alger Hiss: The True Story* (New York: Holt, Rinehart & Winston, 1976).

Smith, Joseph Burholder, *The Plot to Steal Florida: James Madison's Phoney War* (New York: Arbor House, 1983).

Smith, Marcus J., *Dachau: The Harrowing of Hell* (Albany: State University Press of New York, 1995).

Smith, Neil, *Uneven Development: Nature, Capital and the Production of Space* (Oxford: Basil Blackwell, 1984).

Smith, Page, *Killing the Spirit: Higher Education in America* (New York: Penguin, 1990).

———, *A New Age Now Begins: A People's History of the American Revolution, Vol. 2* (New York: McGraw-Hill, 1976).

Solnit, Rebecca, *Savage Dreams: A Journey Into the Hidden Wars of the American West* (San Francisco: Sierra Club, 1994).

Sonnichsen, C.L., *The Mescalero Apaches* (Norman: University of Oklahoma Press, 1958).

Sorenson, J.B., *Radiation Issues: Government Decision Making and Uranium Expansion in Northern New Mexico* (Albuquerque: San Juan Regional Uranium Study Working Paper No. 14, 1978).

Sorkin, Alan L., *The Urban American Indian* (Lexington, MA: Lexington Books, 1978).

Sosin, Jack M., *Whitehall and the Wilderness: The Middle West in British Colonial Policy, 1760–1775* (Lincoln: University of Nebraska Press, 1961).

Spector, Ronald H., *After Tet: The Bloodiest Year in Vietnam* (New York: Vintage, 1993).

Speer, Albert, *Inside the Third Reich: Memoirs* (New York: Macmillan, 1970).

———, *Spandau: The Secret Diaries* (New York: Macmillan, 1976).

———, *The Slave State: Heinrich Himmler's Master Plan for SS Supremacy* (London: Weidenfield and Nicholson, 1981).

Spicer, Edward H., *A Short History of the Indians of the United States* (New York: Van Nostrand Rinehold, 1969).

Sprague, Marshall, *Massacre: The Tragedy at White River* (Boston: Little, Brown, 1957).

Stacy, C.P., *Quebec 1759: The Siege and the Battle* (Toronto: McGill-Queens University Press, 1959).

Stagg, Jack, *Anglo-Indian Relations in North America to 1763 and an Analysis of the Royal Proclamation of 7 October 1763* (Ottawa: Carlton University Press, 1981).

Stanley, George F., *New France: The Last Phase, 1744–1760* (Toronto: McGill-Queens University Press, 1968).

Stannard, David E., *American Holocaust: Columbus and the Conquest of the New World* (New York: Oxford University Press, 1992).

————, *Before the Horror: The Population of Hawai'i on the Eve of Western Contact* (Honolulu: Social Science Research Institute of Hawai'i Press, 1989).

Stanton, William, *The Leopard's Spots: Scientific Attitudes Towards Race in America, 1815–1859* (Chicago: University of Chicago Press, 1960).

State Museum of Auschwitz-Birkenau, *Memorial Book: The Gypsies of Auschwitz-Birkenau* (Munich: K.G. Saur, 1993).

Stavins, Ralph, Richard J. Barnet and Marcus G. Raskin, *Washington Plans an Aggressive War* (New York: Random House, 1971).

Stearn, E. Wagner, and Allen E. Stearn, *The Effects of Smallpox on the Destiny of the American Indian* (Boston: Bruce Humphries, 1945).

Stegner, Wallace, *Beyond the Hundredth Meridian: John Wesley Powell and the Second Opening of the American West* (Boston: Houghton Mifflen, 1954).

Stein, George H., *The Waffen SS: Hitler's Elite Guard at War, 1939–1945* (Ithaca, NY: Cornel University Press, 1966).

Steinberg, *The Jews Against Hitler (Not Like a Lamb)* (London: Gordon & Creminosi, 1978).

Stern, Kenneth, *Holocaust Denial* (New York: American Jewish Committee, 1994).

Stern, Philip M., *The Oppenheimer Case: Security on Trial* (New York: Harper & Row, 1969).

Sternglass, Ernest J., *Low Level Radiation* (New York: Ballantine, 1972).

Steele, Ian K., *Betrayals: Fort William Henry and the "Massacre"* (New York: Oxford University Press, [rev. ed.] 1993).

————, *Warpaths: Invasions of North America* (New York: Oxford University Press, 1994).

Stevens, Frank E., *The Black Hawk War: Including a Review of Black Hawk's Life* (Chicago: Aldine, 1903).

Stewart, Edgar I., *Custer's Luck* (Norman: University of Oklahoma Press, 1955).

Stockholm International Peace Research Institute, *Incendiary Weapons* (Cambridge, MA: MIT Press, 1975).

Stodder, Lucy W., *Mechanisms and Trends in the Decline of the Costanoan Indian Population of Central California* (Salinas: Coyote Press, 1986).

Stone, Lawrence, *The Family, Sex and Marriage in England, 1500–1800* (New York: Harper & Row, 1977).

Stotz, Charles Morse, *Outposts of the War for Empire* (Pittsburg: University of Pittsburg Press, 1985).

Strong, Simon, *Shining Path: Terror and Revolution in Peru* (New York: Times Books, 1992).

Stroud, Harry A., *The Conquest of the Prairies* (Waco, TX: Texian Press, 1968).

Sugdon, John, *Tecumseh's Last Stand* (Norman: University of Oklahoma Press, 1985).

Supple, Carry, *From Prejudice to Genocide: Learning About the Holocaust* (Stoke-on-Trent: Tretham Books, 1993).

Sutton, Imre, ed., *Irredeemable America: The Indians' Estate and Land Tenure in America* (Albuquerque: University of New Mexico Press, 1985).

Svaldi, David, *Sand Creek and the Rhetoric of Extermination: A Case Study in Indian-White Relations* (Lanham, MD: University Press of America, 1989).

Swanton, John Reed, *Final Report of the United States De Soto Expedition Commission* (Washington, D.C.: Smithsonian Institution, 1939).

Sweet, David G., and Gary B. Nash, eds., *Struggle and Survival in Colonial America* (Berkeley: University of California Press, 1981).

————, *The Indian Tribes of North America* (Washington, D.C.: Bureau of American Ethnography, Smithsonian Institution, 1952).

Sweezy, Paul M., and Harry Magdoff, *The Dynamics of U.S. Capitalism: Corporate Structure, Inflation, Credit, Gold, and the Dollar* (New York: Monthly Review, 1972).

Sword, Wiley, *President Washington's Indian War* (Norman: University of Oklahoma Press, 1985).

Szasz, Andrew, *Ecopopulism: Toxic Waste and the Movement for Environmental Justice* (Minneapolis: University of Minnesota Press, 1994).

Takaki, Ronald T., *Iron Cages: Race and Culture in Nineteenth Century America* (New York: Alfred A. Knopf, 1979).

———, *Hiroshima: Why America Dropped the Atomic Bomb* (Boston: Little, Brown, 1995).

Taylor, Graham D., *The New Deal and American Indian Tribalism: The Administration of the Indian Reorganization Act, 1934–45* (Lincoln: University of Nebraska Press, 1980).

Taylor, John G., *Indonesia's Forgotten War: The Hidden History of East Timor* (London: Zed Books, 1991).

Taylor, Rose, *The Last Survivor* (San Francisco: Johnck & Seeger, 1932).

Taylor, Telford, *Nuremberg and Vietnam: An American Tragedy* (Chicago: Quadrangle, 1970).

Tebbel, John, and Keith Jemison, *The American Indian Wars* (New York: Harper & Row, 1960).

Teller, Edward, et al., *Constructive Uses of Nuclear Explosions* (New York: McGraw-Hill, 1968).

Terrell, John Upton, *The Plains Apache* (New York: Thomas Y. Crowell, 1975).

Tetlow, Edwin, *The United Nations: The First 25 Years* (New York: Peter Owen, 1970).

Thatcher, J.B., *Christopher Columbus, 2 vols.* (New York: Putnam's Sons Publishers, 1903–1904).

Theoharis, Athan, *The Yalta Myths* (Columbia: University of Missouri Press, 1970).

———, *Seeds of Repression: Harry S. Truman and the Origins of McCarthyism* (Chicago: Quadrangle, 1971).

Thomas, David Hurtz, ed., *Columbian Consequences, Vol. 3: The Spanish Borderlands in Pan-American Perspective* (Washington, D.C.: Smithsonian Institution, 1991).

Thomas William, *Scorched Earth: The Military Assault on the Environment* (Philadelphia: New Society, 1995).

Thompson, Gerald, *The Army and the Navajo: The Bosque Redondo Reservation Experiment, 1863–1868* (Tucson: University of Arizona Press, 1982).

Thompson, Thomas, ed., *The Schooling of Native America* (Washington, D.C.: American Association of Colleges for Teacher Education, 1978).

Thornton, Russell, *American Indian Holocaust and Survival: A Population History Since 1492* (Norman: University of Oklahoma Press, 1987).

———, *The Cherokees: A Population* History (Lincoln: University of Nebraska Press, 1990).

Thorpe, Dagamr, *Newe Segobia: The Western Shoshone People and Land* (Lee, NV: Western Shoshone Sacred Lands Association, 1982).

Thrapp, Dan, *The Conquest of Apacheria* (Norman: University of Oklahoma Press, 1967).

Tibbles, Thomas Henry, *The Ponca Chiefs: An Account of the Trial of Standing Bear* (Lincoln: University of Nebraska Press, 1972).

Tiffin, Chris, and Alan Lawson, eds., *De-Scribing Empire: Post-colonialism and Textuality* (London/New York: Routledge, 1994).

Tiger, Edith, ed., *In Re Alger Hiss: Petition for a Writ of Error Coram Nobis* (New York: Hill & Wang, 1979).

Tilghman, Zoe A., *Quannah: Eagle of the Comanches* (Oklahoma City: Harlow, 1958).

Tinker, George E., *Missionary Conquest: The Gospel and Native American Cultural Genocide* (Minneapolis: Fortress Press, 1993).

Tissier, Pierre, *The Government of Vichy* (London: Macmillan, 1942).

Titus, James, *The Old Dominion at War: Society, Politics and Warfare in Late Colonial Virginia* (Columbia: University of South Carolina Press, 1991).

Todorov, Tzvetan, *The Conquest of America: The Question of the Other* (New York: Harper & Row Publishers, 1984).

———, *Facing the Extreme: Moral Life in the Concentration Camps* (New York: Henry Holt, 1996).

Toledano, Ralph de, and Victor Lasky, *Spies, Dupes and Diplomats* (New Rochelle, NY: Arlington House, 1976).

Tolnay, Stewart E., and E.M. Beck, *A Festival of Violence: An Analysis of Southern Lynchings, 1882–1930* (Urbana: University of Illinois Press, 1955).

Toynbee, Arnold, *A Study of History* (New York: Oxford University Press, 1947).

Trafzer, Clifford E., *The Kit Carson Campaign: The Last Great Navajo War* (Norman: University of Oklahoma Press, 1982).

Trafzer, Clifford E., and Richard D. Scheuerman, *Renegade Tribe: The Palouse Indians and the Invasion of the Inland Pacific Northwest* (Pullman: Washington State University Press, 1986).

Trask, Haunani-Kay, *From a Native Daughter: Colonialism and Sovereignty in Hawai'i* (Monroe, ME: Common Courage Press, 1993).

Trelease, Allen W., *Indian Affairs in Colonial New York: The Seventeenth Century* (Ithaca, NY: Cornell University Press).

Trenholm, Virginia Cole, *The Arapahoes: Our People* (Norman: University of Oklahoma Press, 1970)

Trigger, Bruce, *The Huron: The Farmers of the North* (New York: Case Studies in Cultural Anthropology, 1969).

———, *The Children of Aataentsic*, 2 vols. (Montreal: McGill-Queens University Press, 1976).

———, ed., *Handbook of North American Indians, Vol. 15: The Northeast* (Washington, D.C.: Smithsonian Institution, 1978).

———, *Natives and Newcomers: Canada's "Heroic Age" Reconsidered* (Kingston & Montréal: McGill-Queens University Press, 1985).

Troper, Harold, *None Is Too Many: Canada and the Jews of Europe, 1933–1948* (New York: Random House, 1982).

Trudel, Marcel, *The Beginnings of New France, 1524–1663* (Toronto: University of Toronto Press, 1973).

Trumbo, Dalton, *The Time of the Toad: A Study of Inquisition in America* (New York: Harper & Row, 1973).

Trunk, Isaiah, *Jewish Responses to Nazi Persecution: Collective and Individual Behavior in Extremis* (New York: Stein & Day, 1979).

Tuchman, Barbara, *Stilwell and the American Experience in China, 1911–45* (New York: Macmillan, 1971).

Tucker, Glenn, *Tecumseh: Visions of Glory* (Indianapolis: Bobbs-Merrill, 1956).

Tucker, M. Belinda, Waddell M. Herron, Dan Nakasai, Luis Ortiz-Franco and Lenore Stiffarm, *Ethnic Groups in Los Angeles: Quality of Life Indicators* (Los Angeles: UCLA Ethnic Studies Centers, 1987).

Turner, Don, *Custer's First Massacre: The Battle of the Washita* (Amarillo, TX: Humbolt Gulch Press, 1968).

Uhl, Michael, and Tod Ensign, *G.I. Guinea Pigs: How the Pentagon Exposed Our Troops to Dangers More Deadly Than War* (New York: Playboy Press, 1980).

Ungar, Sanford J., *The Papers & The Papers: An Account of the Legal and Political Battle Over the Pentagon Papers* (New York: E.P. Dutton, 1972).

———, *FBI: An Uncensored Look Behind the Walls* (Boston: Atlantic-Little, Brown, 1976).

United Nations War Crimes Commission, *Law Reports of Trials of War Criminals*, 24 vols. (London: His Majesty's Stationery Office, 1948.

Unruh, John D., *The Plain Across: The Overland Immigrants and the Trans-Mississippi West, 1840–1860* (Urbana: University of Illinois Press, 1979).

———, *The White Man's Wicked Water: The Alcohol Trade and Prohibition in Indian Country, 1802–1892* (Lawrence: University Press of Kansas, 1996).

Upton, Helen M., *The Everett Report in Historical Perspective: The Indians of New York* (Albany: New York State Bicentennial Commission, 1980).

Urban, Greg, and Joel Sherzer, eds., *Nation-States and Indians in Latin America* (Austin: University of Texas Press, 1991).

Utley, Robert M., *The Last Days of the Sioux Nation* (New Haven, CT: Yale University Press, 1963).

Vabres, Donnebieu de, *Le Procès de Nuremberg* (Paris: Editions Monat Montchrestien, 1947).

Van de Water, Frederick F., *Glory Hunter: A Life of General Custer* (New York: Bobbs-Merrill, 1934).

Varner, John Grier, and Jeanette Johnson Varner, *The Dogs of Conquest* (Norman: University of

Oklahoma Press, 1983).

Vaughan, Alden T., *The New England Frontier: Puritans and Indians, 1620–1675* (Boston: Little, Brown, 1965).

Vaughn, J.W., *With Crook at the Rosebud* (Harrisburg, PA: Stackpole, 1956).

Vaugn, Robert, *Only Victims: A Study of Show Business Blacklisting* (New York: Putnam's, 1972).

Verano, John W., and Douglas H. Ubelaker, *Disease and Demography in the Americas* (Washington, D.C.: Smithsonian Institution, 1992).

Verney, Jack, *The Good Regiment: The Carignan-Salières Regiment in Canada, 1665–1668* (Montréal: McGill-Queens University Press, 1991).

Vescey, Christopher, and William Starna, eds., *Iroquois Land Claims* (Syracuse, NY: Syracuse University Press, 1988).

Vestal, Stanley, *Sitting Bull: Champion of the Sioux* (Norman University of Oklahoma Press, 1932).

———, *Warpath and Council Fire: The Plains Indian Struggle for Survival in War and Diplomacy, 1851–1891* (New York: Random House, 1948).

Vickery, Michael, *Cambodia, 1975–1982* (London: Allen & Unwin, 1984).

Vidal-Niquet, Pierre, *Assassins of Memory: Essays on the Denial of the Holocaust* (New York: Columbia University Press, 1992).

Villamarin, Juan A., and Judith E. Villamarin, *Indian Labor in Mainland Colonial Spanish America* (Newark: University of Delaware Press, 1975).

Viola, Herman J., *After Columbus: The Smithsonian Chronicle of the North American Indians* (Washington, D.C.: Smithsonian Books, 1990).

Virilio, Paul, *Popular Defense & Ecological Struggles* (New York: Semiotext[e], 1990).

Voorhis, Jerry, *The Strange Case of Richard Milhouse Nixon* (New York: Popular Library, 1973).

Wachtel, Nathan, *The Vision of the Vanquished: The Spanish Conquest of Peru Through Indian Eyes, 1530–1570* (Sussex: Harvester Press, 1977).

Waddell, Col. Dewey, and Maj. Norm Wood, *Air War-Vietnam* (New York: Arno Press, 1978).

Wade, Wyn Craig, *The Fiery Cross: The Ku Klux Klan in America* (New York: Simon & Schuster, 1987).

Walker, J. Samuel, *Containing the Atom: Nuclear Regulation in a Changing Environment, 1963–1971* (Berkeley: University of California Press, 1992).

Walker, M., *National Front* (London: Fontana, 1977).

Wallace, Anthony F.C., *King of the Delawares: Teedyuscung, 1700–1763* (Philadelphia: University of Pennsylvania Press, 1949).

———, *The Death and Rebirth of the Seneca* (New York: Alfred A. Knopf, 1970).

Wallace, Ernest, *Ranald S. Mackenzie on the Texas Frontier* (Lubbock: West Texas Museum Association, 1964).

Wallace, Ernest, and E. Adamson Hoebel, *The Comanches: Lords of the Southern Plains* (Norman: University of Oklahoma Press, 1952).

Walliman, Isador, and Michael N. Dobkowski, eds., *Genocide and the Modern Age: Etiology and Case Studies of Mass Death* (New York: Greenwood Press, 1987).

Walther, Juan Carlos, *La Conquista del Desierto* (Buenos Aires: Editorial Universitorio Buenos Aires, 1971).

Ward, Harry M., *The United Colonies of New England, 1643–1690* (New York: St. Martin's, 1961).

Ware, Captain Eugene F., *The Indian War of 1864* (New York: St. Martin's Press, 1960).

Warnock, D., and K. Bossong, ed., *Nuclear Power and Civil Liberties: Can We Have Both?* (Washington, D.C.: Citizens Energy Project, 1978).

Warren, Frank A., III, *Liberals and Communism* (Bloomington: Indiana University Press, 1946).

Washburn, Wilcomb E., *The Governor and the Rebel: A History of Bacon's Rebellion in Virginia* (Chapel Hill: University of North Carolina Press, 1957).

Webb, Walter P., *The Texas Rangers: A Century of Frontier Defense* (Austin: University of Texas Press, 1989 reprint of 1935 original).

Weber, David J., *New Spain's Far Northern Frontier: Essays on Spain in the American West* (Albuquerque: University of New Mexico Press, 1979).

————, *The Spanish Frontier in North America* (New Haven: Yale University Press, 1992).

Weddle, Robert S., *Spanish Sea: The Gulf of Mexico in North American Discovery, 1500–1685* (College Station: Texas A&M University Press, 1985).

Weems, John Edward, *Death Song: The Last of the Indian Wars* (Garden City, NY: Doubleday, 1976).

Weiman, Gabriel, and Conrad Winn, *Hate on Trial: The Zundel Affair, the Media, and Public Opinion in Canada* (Oakland, Ont.: Mosaic Press, 1986).

Weinberg, Albert K., *Manifest Destiny: A Study of Nationalist Expansion in American History* (Baltimore: Johns Hopkins University Press, 1935).

Weinstein, Allen, *Perjury: The Hiss-Chambers Case* (New York: Alfred A. Knopf, 1988).

Weisberg, Barry, *Ecocide in Indochina: The Ecology of War* (San Francisco: Canfield Press, 1970).

Weisbord, Robert, *Genocide? Birth Control and the Black American* (Westport, CT: Greenwood Press, 1975).

Weiss, John, *Ideology of Death: Why the Holocaust Happened in Germany* (New York: Ivan R. Dee, 1966).

Welch, James, *The Battle of The Little Big Horn and the Fate of the Plains Indians* (N.Y.: W.W. Norton, 1994).

Wells, Robert V., *The Population of the British Colonies in America Before 1776: A Survey of the Census Data* (Princeton, NJ: Princeton University Press, 1975).

Weston, Burns H., Richard A. Falk, and Anthony D'Amato, *Basic Documents in International Law and World Order* (St. Paul, MN: West, [2nd. ed.] 1990).

Wexley, John, *The Judgement of Julius and Ethel Rosenberg* (New York: Ballantine, 1977).

Weyler, Rex, *Blood of the Land: The U.S. Government and Corporate War Against the American Indian Movement* (Philadelphia: New Sociey, [2nd ed.] 1992).

Wharton, Clarece R., *Satanta: The Great Chief of the Kiowas and His People* (Dallas: B. Upshaw & Co., 1935).

Whitaker, Ben, *Revised and Updated Report on the Question of the Prevention and Punishment of the Crime of Genocide* (New York: United Nations Economic & Social Council, Commission on Human Rights, 1985).

White, Richard, *The Middle Ground: Indians, Empires, and Republics in the Great Lakes Region, 1650–1815* (Cambridge: Harvard University Press, 1991).

Widmer, Randolf J., *The Evolution of the Calusa: A Nonagricultural Chiefdom on the Southwest Florida Coast* (Tuscaloosa: University of Alabama Press, 1988).

Wiesel, Elie, *Legends of Our Time* (New York: Holt, Rinehart & Winston, 1968).

————, *Night* (New York: Hill & Wang, 1972).

Wiesenthal, Simon, *Sails of Hope* (New York: Macmillan, 1973).

————, *Justice, Not Vengeance: Recollections* (New York: Grove Weidenfeld, 1989).

Wilcox, Fred, *Waiting for an Army to Die: The Tragedy of Agent Orange* (New York: Random House, 1983).

Wilkins, Thurman, *Cherokee Tragedy: The Ridge Family and the Destruction of a People* (New York: Macmillan, 1970).

Williams, Davis Wallace, *Education for Extinction: American Indians and the Boarding School Experience, 1875–1928* (Lawrence: University Press of California, 1995).

Williams Jr., Robert A., *The American Indian in Western Legal Thought: The Discourses of Conquest* (New York: Oxford University Press, 1990).

Williams, T. Harry, *The History of American Wars from 1745 to 1918* (Baton Rouge: Louisiana State University Press, 1981).

Williams, William Appleman, *The Tragedy of American Diplomacy* (New York: Dell, [2nd. ed.] 1972).

Wills, Garry, *Nixon Agonistes: The Crisis of a Self-Made Man* (New York: New American Library, 1979).

Wilson, Dorothy Clarke, *Bright Eyes: The Story of Susette La Flesche* (New York: McGraw-Hill, 1974).

Wilson, Raymond, *Ohiyesa: Charles Eastman, Santee Sioux* (Urbana: University of Illinois Press, 1983).

Wilson, Terry P., *The Underground Reservation: Osage Oil* (Lincoln: University of Nebraska Press, 1985).

Wise, David, *The Politics of Lying: Government Deception, Secrecy and Power* (New York: Random House, 1973).

_____, *The American Police State: The Government Against the People* (New York: Random House, 1976).

Women of All Red Nations, *American Indian Women* (New York: International Indian Treaty Council, 1978).

Wood, Bryce, *Dismantling the Good Neighbor Policy* (Austin: University of Texas Press, 1985).

Wood, Peter H., Gregory A. Waselkov and M. Thomas Hatley, eds., *Powhatan's Mantle: Indians in the Colonial Southeast* (Lincoln: University of Nebraska Press, 1989).

Woods, Patricia D., *French-Indian Relations on the Southern Frontier, 1699–1762* (Ann Arbor: University of Michigan Press, 1980).

Woodward, C. Vann, *The Strange Career of Jim Crow* (New York: Oxford University Press, 3rd rev. ed., 1974).

Wright, J. Leight Jr., *The Anglo-Spanish Rivalry in North America* (Athens: University of Georgia Press, 1971).

————, *The Only Land They Knew: The Tragic Story of the Indians of the Old South* (New York: Free Press, 1981).

Wright, Ronald, *Time Among the Maya: Travels in Belize, Guatemala and Mexico* (New York: Viking, 1989).

Wrone, David R., and Russell S. Nelson, Jr., *Who's the Savage? A Documentary History of the Mistreatment of the North American Indians* (Greenwich, CT: Fawcett, 1973).

Wrong, George M., *The Rise and Fall of New France, 2 vols.* (New York: Macmillan, 1928).

Wyman, David S., *The Abandonment of the Jews: America and the Holocaust, 1941–1945* (New York: Pantheon, 1984).

Yahil, Leni, *The Holocaust: The Fate of the European Jewry, 1932–1945* (New York: Oxford University Press, 1990).

Yaroshinka, Alla, *Chernobyl: The Forbidden Truth* (Lincoln: University of Nebraska Press, 1995).

Yatindra, Kaylan, *Genocide in Bangladesh* (Bombay: Orient Longman, 1972).

Yitzak, Arad, *Belzec, Sobibór, Treblinka: The Operation Reinhart Death Camps* (Bloomington: Indiana University Press, 1987).

Yockey, Francis Parker, *Imperium: The Philosophy of History and Politics* (Los Angeles: Noontide Press, 1992).

Young, Robert, *White Mythologies: Writing History and the West* (London/New York: Routledge, 1990).

Zantwijk, Rudolph van, *The Aztec Arrangement: The Social History of Pre-Spanish Mexico* (Norman: University of Oklahoma Press, 1985).

Zaslow, Morris, and Wesley B. Turner, eds., *The Defended Border: Upper Canada and the War of 1812* (Toronto: Macmillan, 1964).

Zelinsky, Wilbur, *Cultural Geography of the United States* (Engelwood Cliffs, NJ: Prentice-Hall, 1973).

Zerzan, John, *Future Primitive and Other Essays* (Brooklyn, NY: Autonomedia/Anarchy, 1994).

Zinn, Howard, *A People's History of the United States* (New York: HarperCollins, 1990).

Zohra, Ranbir, ed., *The Chinese Revolution, 1900–1950* (Boston: Houghton Mifflin, 1974).

Zorita, Alonzo de, *Life and Labor in Ancient Mexico: The Brief and Summary Relation of the Lords of New Spain* (New Brunswick, NJ: Rutgers University Press, 1963).

Zundel, Ernst, *UFOs: Nazi Secret Weapons?* (Toronto: Samisdat, 1982).

Articles

Aldrich, Hope, "The Politics of Uranium," *Santa Fe Reporter*, Dec. 7, 1978.

———, "Problems Pile Up at the Uranium Mills," *Santa Fe Reporter*, Nov. 13, 1980.

Alexander, Edward, "Stealing the Holocaust," *Midstream*, November 1980.

Allen, Charles R. Jr., "The Role of the Media in the Leuchter Matter: Hyping a Holocaust Denier," in Shelly Shapito, ed., *Truth Prevails: The End of the "Leuchter Report"* (Albany, NY: Holocaust Education Project, 1990).

Ambler, Marjane, "Uranium Millworkers Seek Compensation," *APF Reporter*, Sept. 1980.

———, "Mine Dewatering Operation in New Mexico Seen Violating Arizona Water Standards," *Nuclear Fuel*, Mar. 1, 1982.

———, "Wyoming to Study Tailings Issue," *Denver Post*, Feb. 5, 1984.

———, "Lagunas Face Fifth Delay in Uranium Cleanup," *Navajo Times Today*, Feb. 5, 1986.

Anaya, S. James, "The Rights of Indigenous People and International Law in Historical and Contemporary Perspective," In Robert N. Clinton, Nell Jessup Newton and Monroe E. Price, eds., *American Indian Law: Cases and Materials* (Charlottesville, VA: Michie, 1991).

Anonymous, "The Liquidation of Dull Knife," *Nebraska History*, No. 22, 1941.

Appleby, Andrew B., "Disease or Famine? Mortality in Cumberland and Westmoreland," *Economic History Review*, 2nd Ser., No. 26, 1973.

Archer, V.E., J.K. Wagoner and F.E. Lundin, "Lung Cancer Among Uranium Miners in the United States," *Health Physics*, No 25, 1973.

Archer, V.E., J.D. Gillan and J.K. Wagoner, "Respiratory Disease Mortality Among Uranium Miners," *Annals of the New York Academy of Sciences*, No. 271, 1976.

Axtell, James, "The White Indians of North America," in his *The European and the Indian: Essays in the Ethnohistory of North America* (New York: Oxford University Press, 1981).

———, "The Scholastic Philosophy of the Wilderness," in Axtell's edited *The European and the Indian: Essays in the Ethnohistory of North America* (New York: Oxford University Press, 1992).

———, "The Rise and Fall of the Powhatan Empire," in his *After Columbus: Essays in the Ethnohistory of North America* (New York: Oxford University Press, 1988).

Baker, James N., "Keeping a Deadly Secret: The Feds Knew the Mines Were Radioactive," *Newsweek*, June 18, 1990.

Balogh, Sangor, "Following in the Footsteps of the Ku Klux Klan: Anti-Gypsy Organization in Romania," *Nemzetközi Cigány Szövetseg Bulletin*, No. 5, 1993.

Barnes, Harry Elmer, "Revisionism: A Key to Peace," *Rampart Journal*, Spring 1966.

———, "Zionist Fraud," *American Mercury*, Fall 1968.

———, "Revisionism and the Promotion of Peace," *Journal of Historical Review*, Spring 1982.

Barnes, Ralph W., "The Shame of Nuremberg," *New York Times*, Sept. 15, 1935.

Barry, Tom, "Bury My Lungs at Red Rock: Uranium Mining Brings New Peril to the Reservation," *The Progressive*, Oct. 1976.

Barsh, Russel, "Indian Land Claims Policy in the United States," *North Dakota Law Review*, No. 58, 1982.

Bauer, Yehuda, "Whose Holocaust?" *Mainstream*, Vol. 26, No. 9, Nov. 1980.

———, "The Place of the Holocaust in Contemporary History," in Jonathan Frankel, ed., *Studies in Contemporary Jewry, Vol. 1* (Bloomington: Indiana University Press, 1984).

———, "Revisionism—The Repudiation of the Holocaust and Its Historical Significance," in Yisrael Gutman and Gideon Grief, eds., *The Historiography of the Holocaust Period* (Jerusalem: Hebrew University Monographs, 1988).

———, "The Death-Marches, January-May, 1945," in Michael R. Marrus, ed., *The Nazi Holocaust: Historical Articles on the Destruction of European Jews*, Vol. 9 (Westport, CT: Meckler, 1989).

———, "Jewish Resistance and Passivity in the Face of the Holocaust," in François Furet, ed., *Unanswered Questions: Nazi Germany and the Genocide of the Jews* (New York: Schocken Books, 1989).

———, "Is the Holocaust Explicable?" in Yehuda Bauer, et al., *Remembering for the Future: Working Papers and Addenda*, 2 vols. (Oxford: Pergamon Press, 1989).

———, "Gypsies," in Yisrael Gutman, ed., *Encyclopedia of the Holocaust* (New York: Macmillan, 1990).

————, "Continuing Ferment in Eastern Europe," *SICSA Report*, Vol. 4, Nos. 1/2, 1990.

————, "Holocaust and Genocide: Some Comparisons," in Peter Hayes, ed., *Lessons and Legacies: The Meaning of the Holocaust in a Changing World* (Evanston, IL: Northwestern University Press, 1991).

Baydo, Gerald, "Overland from Missouri to Washington Territory in 1854," *Nebraska History*, Vol. 52, No. 1, 1971.

Beard, Charles, "Heroes and Villains of the World War," *Current History*, Vol. 24, 1926.

Beardsley, Monroe C., "Reflections on Genocide and Ethnocide," in Richard Arens, ed., *Genocide in Paraguay* (Philadelphia: Temple University Press, 1976).

Bearss, Edwin C., "The Battle of Pea Ridge," *Arkansas Historical Quarterly*, Vol. 20, no. 1, 1961.

Bertell, Rosalie, "Nuclear Suicide," *America,* No. 131, 1974.

————, "More About Nuclear Suicide," *Nuclear Opponents,* May-June 1975.

————, "Radiation Exposure and Human Species Survival," in Committee on Federal Research into the Biological Effects of Ionizing Radiation, *Issue Papers: Working Documents of 10 March 1980 Public Meeting* (Bethesda, MD: National Institutes of Health,1980).

Berry, Jason, "Duke's Disguise," *New York Times*, Oct. 16, 1991.

Black, Peter, "Forced Labor in the Concentration Camps, 1942–1944," in Michael Berenbaum, ed., *A Mosiac of Victims: Non-Jews Persecuted and Murdered by the Nazis* (New York: New York University Press, 1990).

Block, Fred, "Economic Instability and Military Strength: The Paradoxes of the 1950 Rearmament Decision," *Politics and Society*, Vol. 10, No. 1, 1980.

Bolt, Menno, "Social Correlates of Nationalism: A Study of Native American Leaders in a Canadian Internal Colony," *Comparative Political Studies*, Vol. 14, No. 2, Summer 1981.

Bolté, Philip L., "The Tank Killers: Tungsten vs. Depleted Uranium," *National Defense*, May/June 1983.

Borah, Woodrow W., "America as Model: The Impact of European Expansion on the Non-European World," *Actas y Memorias, XXXV Congreso Internacional de Americanistas, Mexico, 1962: Vol.III* (Mexico City: Editorial Libros de Mexico, 1964).

————, "Conquest and Population: A Demographic Approach to Mexican History," *Proceedings of the American Philosophical Society*, No. 113, 1968.

————, "New Demographic Research on the Sixteenth Century in Mexico," in Howard F. Cline, ed., *Latin American History, Vol. II: Essays on Its Study and Teaching, 1898–1965* (Berkeley: University of California Press, 1966).

Borah, Woodrow W. and Sherburne F. Cook, "Conquest and Population: A Demographic Approach to Mexican History," *Proceedings of the American Philosophical Society*, CXIII, 1969.

Boyce, Douglas W., "'As the Wind Scatters the Smoke': The Tuscarora in the Eighteenth Century," in Daniel K. Richter and James H. Merrill, eds., *Beyond the Covenant Chain: The Iroquois and Their Neighbors in Indian North America 1600–1800* (Syracuse, NY: Syracuse University Press, 1987).

Boyce, William J., "The Plutonium Predicament," *New York Times*, May 2, 1995.

Branson, Louise, "Romanian Gypsies Being Terrorized," *San Francisco Chronicle*, Dec. 19, 1993.

Brown, Frederick, "French Amnesia," *Harpers*, Dec. 1981.

Buckley, William F. Jr., "The Liberty Lobby and the Carto Network of Hate," *ADL Facts*, Vol. 27, No. 2, Winter 1982.

Buntin, Martha, "The Removal of the Wichitas, Kiowas, Comanches and Apaches to the Present Agency," *Panhandle-Plains Historical Review*, No. 4, 1931.

Burnham, David, "Rise in Cancer Death Rate Tied in Study to Plutonium," *New York Times*, June 6, 1976.

————, "Study of Atom Workers' Death Raises Question About Radiation," *New York Times*, Oct. 25, 1976.

————, "Gulf Aids Admit Cartel Increased Price of Uranium," *New York Times*, June 17, 1977.

————, "8000 pounds of Atom Materials Unaccounted for by Plants in U.S.," *New York Times*, Aug. 5, 1977.

————, "House Aid Tells of Suspicion U.S. Uranium Was Stolen 10 Years Ago," *New York Times*, Aug. 9, 1977.

————, "C.I.A. Said in 1974 Israel Had A-bombs," *New York Times,* Jan. 27, 1978.

————, "The Case of the Missing Uranium," *Atlantic Monthly,* Jan. 1979.

Cambell, Walter S., "The Cheyenne Dog Soldiers," *Chronicles of Oklahoma,* Vol. 1, No. 1, 1923.

Campisi, Jack, "From Stanwix to Canadaigua: National Policy, States' Rights and Indian Land," in Christopher Vescey and William Starna, eds., *Iroquois Land Claims* (Syracuse, NY: Syracuse University Press, 1988).

Canny, Nicholas P., "The Ideology of English Colonization: From Ireland to America," *William and Mary Quarterly,* 3d. ser., XXX, 1973.

Carter, Luther J., "Uranium Mill Tailings: Congress Addresses a Long Neglected Problem," *Science,* Oct. 13, 1978.

Cave, Alfred A., "Who Killed John Stone? A Note on the Origins of the Pequot War," *William and Mary Quarterly,* No. 49, 1992.

Cerio, Gregory, "The Black Legend: Were the Spaniards *That* Cruel?" *Newsweek: Columbus Special Issue,* Fall/Winter 1992.

Champaign, Duane, "The Delaware Revitalization Movement of the Early 1760s: A Suggested Reinterpretation," *American Indian Quarterly,* No. 12, 1988.

Chomsky, Noam, "Objectivity and Liberal Scholarship," in his *American Power and the New Mandarins* (New York: Pantheon, 1969).

————, "The Faurisson Affair: His Right to Say It," *The Nation,* Feb. 28, 1981.

————, "Freedom of Expression? Absolutely," *Village Voice,* July 1, 1981.

————, "The Commissars of Literature," *The New Statesman,* Aug. 14, 1981.

Churchill, Ward, "The Same Old Song," in his *Marxism and Native Americans* (South End Press, 1983).

————, "Indigenous Peoples of the U.S.: A Struggle Against Internal Colonialism," *The Black Scholar,* Vol. 16, No. 1, Feb. 1985.

————, "To Serve and Protect? Police Armaments in the United States," *New Studies on the Left,* Vol. XIV, Nos. 1–2, 1989.

————, "It Did Happen Here: Sand Creek, Scholarship and the American Character," in his *Fantasies of the Master Race: Literature, Cinema and the Colonization of American Indians* (Monroe, ME: Common Courage Press, 1992).

————, "The New Racism: A Critique of James A. Clifton's The Invented Indian," in his *Fantasies of the Master Race: Literature, Cinema and the Colonization of American Indians* (Monroe, ME: Common Courage Press, 1992).

————, "American Indian Self-Governance: Fact, Fantasy and Prospects for the Future," in his *Struggle for the Land: Indigenous Resistance to Genocide, Ecocide and Expropriation in Contemporary North America* (Monroe, ME: Common Courage Press, 1993).

————, "Naming Our Destiny: Toward a Language of American Indian Liberation," in his *Indians Are Us? Culture and Genocide in North America* (Monroe, ME: Common Courage Press, 1994).

————, "Perversions of Justice: Examining the Doctrine of U.S. Rights to Occupany in North America," in David S. Caudill and Steven Jay Gould, *Radical Philosophy of Law: Contemporary Challenges to Mainstream Legal Theory and Practice* (Atlantic Highlands, NJ: Humanities Press, 1995).

————, "Genocide: Toward A Functional Definition," in his *Since Predator Came: Notes on the Struggle for American Indian Liberation* (Littleton, CO: Aigis, 1995).

————, "Like Sand in the Wind: The Making of an American Indian Diaspora," in his *Since Predator Came: Notes on the Struggle for American Indian Liberation* (Littleton, CO: Aigis, 1995).

————, "The Earth Is Our Mother: Struggles for American Indian Land and Liberation in the Contemporary United States," in his *Since Predator Came: Notes on the Struggle for American Indian Liberation* (Littleton, CO: Aigis, 1995).

————, "Genocide in Arizona? The Navajo–Hopi Land Dispute in Perspective," in his *Notes From a Native Son: Selected Essays on Indigenism, 1985–1995* (Boston: South End Press, 1996).

Clastres, Pierre, "De l'Ethnocide," *L'Homme,* July–Dec. 1974.

Clemmer, Richard O., "The Energy Economy and Pueblo Peoples, in Joseph Jorgenson, ed., *American Indians and Energy Development* (Cambridge, MA: Anthropological Resource Center, 1978).

Coffin, Tristan, "The MX: America's $100 Billion 'Edsel'," *Washington Spectator*, Oct. 15, 1980.

Cohen, Felix S., "The Erosion of Indian Rights, 1950–53: A Case-Study in Bureaucracy," *Yale Law Journal*, No. 62, 1953.

Collier, John, "The Vanishing American," *The Nation*, Jan.11, 1928.

Comey, David Densmore, "The Legacy of Uranium Tailings," *Bulletin of Atomic Scientists*, Sept. 1975.

Concerned Citizens for Nuclear Safety, "What Is WIPP?" *The Radioactive Rag,* Winter/Spring 1992.

Connelley, William E., "The Treaty Held at Medicine Lodge," *Collections of the Kansas State Historical Society*, Vol. XVII, 1928.

Cook, Blanche Weisen, "Cold War Fallout," *The Nation*, Dec. 9, 1996.

Cook, Sherburne F., "Historical Demography," in Robert F. Heizer, ed., *Handbook of the North American Indians, Vol. 3: California* (Washington, D.C.: Smithsonian Institution, 1978).

Cox, Jack, "Casualties Mounting from U-Rush of '49," *Denver Post*, Sept. 2, 1979.

———, "Effects of Radiation on Early Miners Comes to Light," *Denver Post*, Sept. 3, 1979.

———, "Studies Show Radon Guidelines May Be Weak," *Denver Post*, Sept. 4, 1979.

Cox, Jeff, "Nuclear Waste Recycling," *Environmental Action Bulletin*, No. 29, May 1976.

Crosby, Alfred W. Jr., "Virgin Soil Epidemics as a Factor in Aboriginal Depopulation in America," *William and Mary Quarterly*, No. 33, 1976.

Cuddahy, John Murray, "The Holocaust: The Latent Issue in the Uniqueness Debate," in Philip F. Gallagher, ed., *Christians, Jews, and Other Worlds: Patterns of Conflict and Accommodation* (Lanham, MD: University Press of America, 1988).

Curry, Bill, "A-Test Officials Feared Outcry After Health Study," *Washington Post*, Apr. 14, 1979.

Curtis, E.S., "Vanishing Indian Types: The Tribes of the Northwest Plains," *Scribner's*, June 1906.

Czech, Danuta, "The Auschwitz Prisoner Administration," in Yisrael Gutman and Michael Berenbaum, eds., *Anatomy of the Auschwitz Death Camp* (Bloomington/Washington, D.C.: Indiana University Press/U.S. Holocaust Memorial Museum, 1994).

Dadrian, Vahakn N., "The Structural-Functional Components of Genocide," in Israel Drapkin and Emilio Viano, eds., *Victimology: A New Focus* (Lexington, MA: C.C. Heath, 1974).

———, "A Typology of Genocide," *International Review of Modern Sociology*, No. 5, Fall 1975.

Darby, Creg, "Beware the Fast Flux: Industry is Readying a New Kind Of Nuke," *The Progressive*, Sept. 1980.

Davies, Alan T., "The Queen Versus James Keegstra: Reflections on Christian Antisemitism in Canada," *American Journal of Theology and Philosophy*, Vol. 9, Nos. 1–2, Jan.-May 1988.

———, "A Tale of Two Trials: Antisemitism in Canada," *Holocaust and Genocide Studies*, Vol. 4, 1989.

Dawidowicz, Lucy S., "The Holocaust Was Unique in Intent, Scope, and Effect," *Center Magazine*, July-August, 1981.

Dawson, Thomas F., "Colonel Boone's Treaty with the Plains Indians," *The Trail*, Vol. XIV, 1921.

Day, Gordon G., "Rogers' Raid in the Indian Tradition," *Historical New Hampshire*, No. 17, 1962.

———, "The Ouragie War: A Case History in Iroquois-New England Indian Relations," in Michael K. Foster, Jack Campisi and Marianne Mithun, eds., *Extending the Rafters: Interdisciplinary Approaches to Iroquoian Studies* (Albany: State University Press of New York, 1984).

Deegan, Kathleen A., "Cultures in Transition: Fusion and Assimilation Among the Eastern Timucua," in Jerald T. Milanich and Samuel Proctor, eds., *Tacachule: Essays on the Indians of Florida and Southeastern Georgia During the Historic Period* (Gainesville: University of Florida Press, 1978).

Degler, Carl N., "Bad History," *Commentary*, June 1981.

Deloria, Philip S., "CERT: It's Time for an Evaluation," *American Indian Law Newsletter*, Sept./Oct. 1982.

Dickinson, John A., "The Pre-Contact Huron Population: A Reappraisal," *Ontario History*, No. 72, 1980.

Dillingham, Brint, "Indian Women and IHS Sterilization Practices," *American Indian Journal*, Vol. 3, Jan. 1977.

Dobyns, Henry F., "Estimating American Aboriginal Population: An Appraisal of Techniques with a New Hemispheric Estimate," *Current Anthropology*, No, 7.

———, "More Methodological Perspectives on Historical Demography," *Ethnohistory*, No.36, 1989.

Doenecke, Justus D., "Harry Elmer Barnes: Prophet of a Usable Past," *History Teacher*, Feb. 1975.

Dowd, Gregory Evans, "The French King Wakes Up in Detroit: 'Pontiac's War' in Rumor and History," *Ethnohistory*, No. 37, 1990.

———, "Thinking and Believing: Nativism and Unity in the Ages of Pontiac and Tecumseh," *American Indian Quarterly*, No. 16, 1992.

Downs, Ernest, "How the East Was Lost," *American Indian Journal*, Vol. 1, No. 2, 1975.

Draper, William R., "The Last of the Red Race," *Cosmopolitan*, Jan 1902.

Dreeson, D.R., "Uranium Mill Tailings: Environmental Implications," *Los Alamos Scientific Laboratory Mini-Report*, Feb. 1978.

Duffy, John, "Smallpox and the Indians in the American Colonies," *Bulletin of the History of Medicine,* No. 25, 1951.

Dutt, R. Palme, "India, Pakistan, Bangledesh," *Labour Monthly*, No. 54, 1972.

Eckhardt, Alice, and A. Roy Eckhardt, "The Holocaust and the Enigma of Uniqueness: A Philosophical Effort at Practical Clarification," *Annals of the American Academy of Political and Social Science*, No. 45, July 1980.

Editors, "The Native American Connection," *Up Against the Wall Street Journal*, Oct. 29, 1979.

Eid, Leroy V., " 'National' War Among Indians of Northeastern North America," *Canadian Review of American Studies*, No. 16, 1985.

———, " 'A Kind of Running Fight': Indian Battlefield Tactics in the Late Eighteenth Century," *Western Pennsylvania Historical Magazine*, No. 71, 1988.

Elliot, Stanton, "The End of the Trail," *Overland Monthly*, July 1915.

Estin, Ann Laque, "*Lonewolf v. Hitchcock*: The Long Shadow," in Sandra L. Cadwalader and Vine Deloria, Jr., eds., *The Aggressions of Civilization: Federal Indian Policy Since the 1880s* (Philadelphia: Temple University Press, 1984).

Fackenheim, Emil, "Foreword" in Yehuda Bauer, ed., *The Jewish Emergence from Powerlessness* (London: Macmillan, 1979).

Fadiman, Anne, "The Downwind People: A Thousand Americans Sue for Damage Brought on by Atomic Fallout," *Life*, June 1980.

Falk, Richard, "Ethnocide, Genocide, and the Nuremberg Tradition of Moral Responsibility," in Virginia Held, Sidney Morganbesser and Thomas Nagel, eds., *Philosophy, Morality, and International Affairs* (New York: Oxford University Press, 1974).

Farmer, John, "Piñeda's Sketch," *Southwestern Historical Quarterly*, No. 63, 1959.

Faurisson, Robert, "The Problem of Gas Chambers," *Journal of Historical Review*, Summer, 1980.

Fausz, J. Frederick, " 'The Barbarous Massacre' Reconsidered: The Powhatan Uprising of 1622 and the Historians," *Explorations in Ethnic Studies*, No. 1, 1978.

———, "George Thorpe, Nemattanew, and the Powhatan Uprising of 1622," *Virginia Cavalcade*, No. 28, 1979.

———, "Opechancanough: Indian Resistance Leader," in David G. Sweet and Gary B. Nash, eds., *Struggle and Survival in Colonial America* (Berkeley: University of California Press, 1981).

———, "An 'Abundance of Blood Shed on Both Sides': England's First Indian War, 1609–1614," *Virginia Magazine of History and Biography*, No. 98, 1990.

Fay, Sidney B., "New Light on the Origins of the World War," *American Historical Review*, Vol. 25, 1920.

Feest, Christian F., "Powhatan: A Study in Political Organization," *Weiner Volkerkundliche Mitteilungen*, No. 13, 1966.

Feingold, Henry, "How Unique Is the Holocaust?" in Alex Grobman and Daniel Landes, eds., *Genocide: Critical Issues of the Holocaust* (Los Angeles: Rossell, 1983).

Finkle, Miriam P., and Birute O. Briskis, "Pathological Consequences of Radiostrontium Administered to Fetal and Infant Dogs," in Melvin R. Sikov and D. Dennis Mahlum, eds., *Radiation Biology of the Fetal and Juvenile Mammal: Proceedings of the Ninth Annual Hanford Biology Symposium at Richland, Washington, 5–8 May 1969* (Springfield, VA: Clearinghouse for Federal Scientific & Technical Information, 1969).

Flower, B.O., "An Interesting Representative of a Vanishing Race," *Arena*, July 1896.

Foot, Kristine L., "*U.S. v. Dann*: What It Portends for Millions of Acres in the Western United States," *Public Land Law Review*, No. 5, 1984.

Forster, Arnold, "The Ultimate Cruelty," *ADL Bulletin*, June 1959.

Frederickson, John C., "Kentucky at the Thames, 1813," *Register of Kentucky History*, Spring 1985.

Freedberg, Louis, "Livermore: Panel Recommends Ending Nuclear Arms Work," *San Francisco Chronicle*, Feb. 2, 1995.

Frick, Winifred E., "Native Americans Approve Nuclear Waste on Tribal Lands," *Santa Cruz on a Hill Press*, Mar. 16, 1995.

Friedländer, Saul, "On the Possibility of the Holocaust: An Approach to Historical Synthesis," in Yehuda Bauer and Nathan Rosenstreich, eds., *The Holocaust as Historical Experience* (New York: Quadrangle, 1981).

Friedman, Philip, "The Lublin Reservation and the Madagascar Plan: Two Aspects of Nazi Jewish Policy During the Second World War," *YIVO Annual of Jewish Social Studies*, 1953.

Garber, Zev, and Bruce Zuckerman, "Why Do We Call the Holocaust 'The Holocaust'? An Inquiry into the Psychology of Labels," *Modern Judaism*, Vol. 9, No. 2, 1989.

Garrity, Michael, "The U.S., Colonial Empire is as Close as the Nearest Reservation," in Holly Sklar, ed., *Trilateralism: The Trilateral Commission and Elite Planning for Global Management* (Boston: South End Press, 1980).

———, "The Pending Energy Wars: America's Final Act of Genocide," *Akwesasne Notes*, Early Spring 1980.

Gayner, Jeffrey, "The Genocide Treaty," *Journal of Social and Political Studies*, No. 2, Winter 1977.

Gilbert, Madonna, "Radioactive Water Contamination on the Redshirt Table, Pine Ridge Reservation, South Dakota" (Porcupine, SD: WARN Reports, Mar. 1980).

Gillette, Robert, "Radiation Spill at Hanford: The Anatomy of an Accident," *Science*, No. 181, Aug. 1973.

Givens, Bruce J., "The Iroquois Wars and Native Firearms," in Bruce A. Cox, ed., *Native People, Native Lands* (Ottawa: Carlton University Press, 1988).

Gofman, John W., "The Question of Radioactive Causation of Cancer in Hanford Workers," *Health Physics*, No. 37, 1979.

Gofman, John W., and Arthur R. Tamplin, "Epidemiologic Studies of Carcingogenesis by Ionizing Radiation," in J. Neyman, ed., *Procedings of the Sixth Berkeley Symposium on Mathematical Statistics and Probability* (Berkeley: University of California Press, 1971).

Goldenberg, Sydney L., "Crimes Against Humanity, 1945–1970," *Western Ontario Law Review*, No. X, 1971.

Gorz, Andre, "From Nuclear Energy to Electric Fascism," in his *Ecology as Politics* (Boston: South End Press, 1980).

Gouldner, Alvin W., "Stalinism: A Study in Internal Colonialism," *Telos*, No. 34, Winter 1977–78.

Greene, Jack P., "The Seven Years' War and the American Revolution: The Casual Relationship Reconsidered," *Journal of Imperial and Commonwealth History*, No. 8, 1980.

Grossman, P.Z., and E.S. Cassedy, "Cost Benefit Analysis of Nuclear Waste Disposal," Science, *Technology and Human Values*, Vol. 10, No. 4, 1985.

Groundwork Collective, "The Illusion of Cleanup: A Case Study at Hanford," *Groundwork*, No. 4, Mar. 1994.

Grove, Lloyd, "Lament the Gypsies: 40 Years After Auschwitz, Petitioning for a Place," *Washington Post*, July 21, 1984.

Guerra, Francisco, "La epidemia americana de influenza en 1493," *Revista de Indias*, No. 45, 1985.

Guthrie, John, "The Fetterman Massacre," *Annals of Wyoming*, No. 9, 1932.

Gutman, Yisrael, "The Armed Struggle of the Jews in Nazi-Occupied Countries," in Leni Yahil, *The Holocaust: The Fate of the European Jewry, 1932–1945* (New York: Oxford University Press, 1990).

Habermas, Jürgen, "Neoconservative Cultural Criticism in the United States and West Germany: An Intellectual Movement in Two Popular Cultures," *Telos*, No. 56, 1983.

Hadi, Rabab, "The Gulf Crisis: How We Got There," in Gregg Bates, ed., *Mobilizing Democracy: Changing the U.S. Role in the Middle East* (Monroe, ME: Common Courage Press, 1991).

Hammond, George P., "The Search for the Fabulous in the Settlement of the Southwest," in David J. Weber, ed., *New Spain's Far Northern Frontier: Essays on Spain in the American West* (Albuquerque: University of New Mexico Press, 1979).

Hancock, Ian. " 'Uniqueness' of the Victims: Gypsies, Jews and the Holocaust," *Without Prejudice*, Vol. 1, No. 2, 1988.

———, "Uniqueness, Gypsies and Jews," in Yehuda Bauer, et al., *Remembering for the Future: Working Papers and Addenda* (Oxford: Pergamon Press, 1989).

———, "Responses to the *Porrajmos:* The Romani Holocaust," in Alan S. Rosenbaum, ed., *Is the Holocaust Unique? Perspectives on Comparative Genocide* (Boulder, CO: Westview Press, 1996).

Hanson, Randel D., "Mescalaro Apache: Nuclear Waste and the Privatization of Genocide," *The Circle*, Aug. 1994.

———, "Nuclear Agreement Continues U.S. Policy of Dumping on Goshutes," *The Circle*, Oct. 1995.

Harff, Barbara, and Ted Gurr, "Towards an Empirical Theory of Genocide and Politicide: Identification and Measurement of Cases Since 1945," *International Studies Quarterly*, Vol. 32, No. 3, Sept. 1988.

Harner, Michael, "The Ecological Basis of Aztec Sacrifice," *American Ethnologist*, No. 4, 1977).

———, "The Enigma of Aztec Sacrifice," *Natural History*, No. 76, 1977.

Hart, Jeffrey, "Discovering Columbus," *National Review*, October 15, 1990, 56–7.

Harvey, Charles M., "The Last Race Rally of Indians," *World's Work*, May 1904.

Harvey, C., "Congressional Plenary Power Over Indian Affairs: A Doctrine Rooted in Prejudice," *American Indian Law Review*, No. 10, 1982.

Hassler, Peter, "The Lies of the Conquistadors: Cutting Through the Myth of Human Sacrifice," *World Press Review*, Dec. 1992.

Haynes, Vance, "Elephant-hunting in North America," *Scientific American*, Vol. 214, No.6, 1966.

Hayter, Earl W., "The Ponca Removal," *North Dakota Historical Review*, No. 6, 1932.

Henig, Gerald T., "A Neglegcted Cause of the Sioux Uprising," *Minnesota History*, Vol. 45, No. 3, Fall 1976.

Henige, David, "If Pigs Could Fly: Timicuan Population and Native American Historical Demography," *Journal of Interdisciplinary History*, No. 16, 1985–1986.

———, "On the Current Devaluation on the Notion of Evidence: A Rejoinder to Dobyns," *Ethnohistory*, No. 36, 1989.

———, "Their Numbers Become Thick: Native American Historical Demography as Expiation," in James A. Clifford, ed., *The Invented Indian: Cultural Fictions and Government Policies* (New Brunswick, NJ: Transaction Books, 1990).

Hentoff, Nat, "An Ad That Offends: Who's On First?" *The Progressive*, May 12, 1992.

Higginson, Ella, "The Vanishing Race," *Red Man*, Feb. 1916.

Hill, Burton S., "The Great Indian Treaty Council of 1851," *Nebraska History*, Vol. 47, No. 1, 1966.

Hill, Leonidas E., "The Trial of Ernst Zundel: Revisionism and the Law in Canada," *Simon Wiesenthal Annual*, 1989.

Hines, William, "Cancer Risk at Nuclear Plant? Government Hushes Up Alarming Study," *Chicago Sun-Times*, Nov. 13, 1977.

Hinschman, Steve, "Rebottling the Nuclear Genie," *High Country News*, Jan. 19, 1987.

Hirsch, Adam J., "The Collision of Military Cultures in Seventeenth Century New England," *Journal of American History*, No. 74, 1987–1988.

Hoffman, Fred, "Inside the L.A. Secret Police," *Covert Action Quarterly*, No. 42, Fall 1992.

Hoffman, Paul E., "A New Voyage of North American Discovery: Pedro de Salazar's Visit to the 'Island of Giants'," *Florida Historical Quarterly*, No. 58, Apr. 1980.

———, "Nature and Sequence of the Spanish Borderlands, 1500–1566," *South Carolina Historical Magazine*, No. 84, 1983.

Hohenberg, John, "The Crusade that Changed the U.N.," *Saturday Review*, Nov. 9, 1968.

Hollingsworth, J.W., "Delayed Effects on Survivors of the Atomic Bomb Casualty Commission, 1947–1950." *New England Journal of Medicine*, No. 263, Sept. 1960.

Homze, Edward L., "Nazi Germany's Forced Labor Program," in Michael Berenbaum, ed., *A Mosaic of Victems: Non-Jews Persecuted and Murdered by the Nazis* (New York: New York University Press, 1990).

Hoppe, Richard, "A Stretch of Desert Along Route 66—the Grants Belt—Is Chief Locale for U.S. Uranium," *Engineering and Mining Journal*, Vol. 79, No. 11, 1978.

Horowitz, Irving Louis, "Genocide and the Reconstruction of Social Theory: Observations on the Exclusivity of Collective Death," *Armenian Review*, No. 37, 1984.

Hrdlicka, Ales, "The Vanishing Indian," *Science*, No. 46, 1917.

Huerta, Carlos C., "Revisionism, Free Speech and the Campus," *Midstream*, Apr. 1992.

Huey, Chris, "The Río Puerco River: Where Did the Water Go?" *The Workbook*, No. 11, 1988.

Hulen, David, " 'After the Bombs' " Questions Linger about Amchitka Nuclear Tests," *Anchorage Daily News*, Feb. 7, 1994.

Hunt, F.A., "Adobe Walls Argument: An Indian Attack on a Party of Buffalo Hunters," *Overland Monthly*, May 1909.

Hunter, Sr., J. Marvin, "The Battle of Palo Duro Canyon," *Frontier Times*, Vol. XXI, No. 4, 1944.

Hunczak, Taras, "Ukrainian Losses During World War II," in Michael Berenbaum, ed., *A Mosaic of Victims: Non-Jews Persecuted and Murdered by the Nazis* (New York: New York University Press, 1990).

Huttenbach, Henry, "Locating the Holocaust on the Genocide Spectrum: Towards a Methodology of Definition and Categorization," *Holocaust and Genocide Studies*, Vol. 3, No. 3, 1988.

Huyghe, Patrick, and David Konigsberg, "The Grim Legacy of Nuclear Testing," *New York Times Magazine*, Apr. 22, 1979.

Inouye, Daniel, "1986 Black Hills Hearings on S. 1453, Introduction," *Wicazo Sa Review*, Vol. IV, No. 1, Spring 1988.

Irvin, Amelia, "Energy Development and the Effects of Mining on the Lakota Nation," *Journal of Ethnic Studies*, Vol. 10, No. 2, Spring 1982.

Ivins, Molly, "100 Navjo Families Sue on Radioactive Waste Spill," *New York Times*, Aug. 15, 1980.

Jackovitch, Karen G., and Mark Sennet, "The Children of John Wayne, Susan Hayward and Dick Powell Fear That Fallout Killed Their Parents," *People*, Nov. 10, 1980.

Jackson, Dan, "Mine Devlopment on U.S. Indian Lands," *Engineering and Mining Journal*, Jan. 1980.

Jackson, Robert H., "Opening Statement," in *The Nuremberg Case as Presented by Robert H. Jackson, Chief of Counsel for the United States* (New York: Alfred A. Knopf, 1947).

Jacobs, Wilber R., "The Tip of the Iceberg: Precolumbian Demography and Some Implications for Revisionism," *William and Mary Quarterly*, 3rd Ser., No. 31, 1974.

Jaffe, Susan, "Repression: The New Nuclear Danger," *Village Voice*, Mar. 31, 1980.

Jane, Cecil, "The Question of the Literacy of Christopher Columbus," *Hispanic American Historical Review*, Vol. 10, 1930.

Jennings, Francis, "Glory, Death and Transfiguration: The Susquehannock Indians in the Seventeenth Century," *Proceedings of the American Philosophical Society*, No. 112, 1968.

————, "Susquahannocks," in Bruce Trigger, ed., *Handbook of North American Indians, Vol. 15: The Northeast* (Washington, D.C.: Smithsonian Institution, 1978).

Johansen, Bruce E., "The Great Uranium Rush," *Baltimore Sun*, May 13, 1979.

Johansson, S. Ryan, and S.H. Preston, "Tribal Demography: The Navajo and Hopi Populations as Seen Through Manuscripts from the 1900 Census," *Social Science History*, No. 3, 1978.

Johnson, Giff, "Bikinians Facing Radiation Horrors Once More," *Micronesia Support Committee Bulletin*, May-June 1978.

————, "Nuclear Legacy: Islands Laid Waste," *Oceans*, January 1980.

————, "Nuclear Clouds Over the Marshalls," *Glimpse*, Vol. 21, No. 4, 1981.

————, "Another Nuclear Cover-Up," *Micronesia Support Committee Bulletin*, Vol. 6, No. 2, Summer 1981.

Johnson, Richard R., "The Search for a Usable Indian: An Aspect of the Defense of New England," *Journal of American History*, No. 64, 1977.

Johnson, Susan, "Epidemics: The Forgotten Factor in Seventeenth Century Native Warfare in the St. Lawrence Region," in Bruce A. Cox, ed., *Native People, Native Lands* (Ottawa: Carlton University Press, 1988).

Jorgenson, Bud, "Easing of Uranium Export Rules Urged for Canada," *Ottawa Globe and Mail*, May 4, 1986.

Josephy, Jr., Alvin M., "The Murder of the Southwest," *Audubon Magazine*, July 1971.

Judge, Bill, "The Battle of Bear River," *True West,* Jan.-Feb. 1961.

Katz, Steven T., "Language, Epistemology and Mystical Pluralism," in Steven T. Katz, ed., *Mysticism and Philosophical Analysis* (New York: New York University Press, 1978).

————, "The 'Unique' Intentionality of the Holocaust," *Modern Judaism*, Vol. 1, No.2, September 1981.

————, "The Unique Intentionality of the Holocaust," in Steven T. Katz, ed., *Post-Holocaust Dialogues: Critical Studies in Modern Jewish Thought* (New York: New York University Press, 1983).

————, "The 'Conservative' Character of Mystical Experience," in Steven T. Katz, ed., *Mystical and Religious Traditions* (New York: Oxford University Press, 1983).

————, "Organizing Genocide: Reflections on the Role of Technology and Bureaucracy in the Holocaust," in Alan Rosenberg and Gerald E. Meyers, eds., *Echoes from the Holocaust: Philosophical Reflections on a Dark Time* (Philadelphia: Temple University Press, 1988).

————, "The Pequot War Reconsidered," *New England Quarterly*, No. 64, 1991.

————, "Defining the Uniqueness of the Holocaust: Preliminary Clarifications," in Dan Cohn-Sherbok, ed., *A Traditional Quest: Essays in Honor of Louis Jacobs* (London: Routledge, 1991).

————, "Mystical Speech and Mystical Meaning," in Steven T. Katz, ed., *Mysticism and Language* (New York: Oxford University Press, 1992).

————, "The Uniqueness of the Holocaust: The Historical Dimension," in Alan S. Rosenbaum, ed., *Is the Holocaust Unique? Perspectives on Comparitive Genocide* (Boulder, CO: Westview Press, 1996).

Kaufman, Natalie Hevener, and David Whiteman, "Opposition to Human Rights Treaties in the United States Senate: The Legacy of the Bricker Amendment," *Human Rights Quarterly,* No. 10, 1988.

Kelly, John, "We Are All Part of the Ojibway Circle," in Michael Ondaatje, ed., *From Ink Lake* (Toronto: Lester & Orpen Dennys, 1990).

Kinlicheel, Hosteen, "An Overview of Uranium and Nuclear Development on Indian Lands in the Southwest," *Southwest Indigenous Uranium Forum Newsletter*, Sept. 1993.

Kinzer, Steven, "Germany Cracks Down: Gypsies Come First," *New York Times*, Sept. 27, 1992.

Kirby, Leo P., "Patrick Edward Connor: First Gentile in Utah," *Journal of the West*, Vol. 2, No. 3, 1963.

Klasky, Philip M., "The Eagle's Eye View of Ward Valley: Environmentalists and Native Americans Fight Proposed Waste Dump in the Mojave Desert," *Wild Earth*, Spring 1994.

Knack, Martha C., "MX Issues for Native American Communities," in Francis Hartigan, ed., *MX in Nevada: A Humanistic Perspective* (Reno: Nevada Humanities Press, 1980).

Korman, Gerd, "The Holocaust in Historical Writing," *Societas*, Vol. 2, No. 3, 1972.

Kohn, Howard, and Barbara Newman, "How Isreal Got the Bomb," *Rolling Stone*, No. 252, Jan. 12, 1977.

Kohn, J., "Reservations to Multilateral Treaties: How International Legal Doctrine Reflects World Vision," *Harvard International Law Journal*, No. 71, 1982.

Korman, Gerd, "The Holocaust in Historical Writing," *Societas*, Vol. 2, No. 3, 1972.

Krakowski, Samuel, "The Death Marches in the Evacuation of the Camps," in *The Nazi Concentration Camps* (Jerusalem: Yad Vashim, 1984).

Krawchenko, Bodhan, "Soviet Ukraine Under Nazi Ocupation, 1941–1945," in Y. Boshyk, ed., *Ukraine During World War II: History and Aftermath* (Edmunton: Canadian Institute for Ukrainian Studies, University of Alberta, 1986).

Kroeber, A.L., "Native American Population," *American Anthropologist*, N.S., XXXVI, 1934.

————, "Evolution, History and Culture," in Theodora Kroeber, ed., *An Anthropologist Looks at History* (Berkeley: University of California Press, 1971).

Krugman, Hartmut, and Frank von Hippel, "Radioactive Wastes: A Comparison of U.S. Military and Civilian Inventories," *Science*, No. 1977.

Kumanev, Georgily A., "The German Occupation Regime on Occupied Territory in the

U.S.S.R. (1941–1944)," in Michael Berenbaum, ed., *A Mosaic of Victims: Non-Jews Persecuted and Murdered by the Nazis* (New York: New York University Press, 1990).

LaDuc, Thomas, "The Work of the Indian Claims Commission Under the Act of 1948," *Pacific Historical Review*, No. 26, 1957.

LaDuke, Winona, "Native Environmentalism," *Earth Island Journal*, Summer 1993.

———, "CERT: An Outsider's View In," *Akwesasne Notes*, Summer 1980.

LaFarge, Oliver, "Termination of Federal Supervision: Disintegration and the American Indian," *Annals of the American Academy of Political and Social Science*, No. 311, May 1975.

Lang, Larry, "Missing Hanford Documents Probed by Energy Department," *Seattle Post-Intelligencer*, Sept. 20, 1991.

Langham, Charles H., "From Condemnation to Praise: Shifting Perspectives on Hispanic California," *California Historical Society Quarterly*, No. 61, Winter 1983.

Larson, Janet, "And Then There Were None," *Christian Century*, Jan. 26, 1977.

Larson, Lewis H. Jr., "Historic Guale Indians of the Georgia Coast and the Impact of the Spanish Mission Effort," in Jerald T. Milanich and Samuel Proctor, eds., *Tacachule: Essays on the Indians of Florida and Southeastern Georgia During the Historic Period* (Gainesville: University of Florida Press, 1978).

Lauriston, Victor, "The Case for General Proctor," in Morris Zaslow and Wesley B. Turner, eds., *The Defended Border: Upper Canada and the War of 1812* (Toronto: Macmillan, 1964).

Legters, Lyman H., "The Soviet Gulag: Is It Genocidal?" in Israel W. Charny, ed., *Toward the Understanding and Prevention of Genocide: Proceedings of the International Conference on the Holocaust and Genocide* (Boulder, CO: Westview Press, 1984).

Lemkin, Raphaël, "Genocide: A Modern Crime," *Free World*, Apr. 1945.

———, "Genocide," *American Scholar*, Vol. 15, No. 2, 1946.

———, "Genocide as a Crime Under International Law," *American Journal of International Law*, No. XLI, 1947.

Leuchter, Frederick A., "Inside the Auschwitz 'Gas Chambers'," *Journal of Historical Review*, Summer 1989.

Lewis, Norman, "The Camp at Ceclio Baez," in Richard Arens, ed., *Genocide in Paraguay* (Philadelphia: Temple University Press, 1976).

Liefgree, Dan, "Church Rock Upset at UNC," *Navajo Times*, May 8, 1980.

Lípam, Jìrí, "The Fate of the Gypsies in Czechoslavakia Under Nazi Occupation," in Michael Berenbaum, ed., *A Mosaic of Victims: Non-Jews Persecuted and Murdered by the Nazis* (New York: New York University Press, 1990).

Lippman, M., "The Drafting of the 1948 Convention on the Punishment and Prevention of Genocide," *Boston University International Law Journal*, No. 3, 1984.

Lipstadt, Deborah E., "The Bitburg Controversy," in David Singer, ed., *The American Jewish Yearbook, 1987* (New York: American Jewish Committee, 1987).

Locklear, Arlinda, "The Oneida Land Claims: A Legal Overview," in Christopher Vescey and William Starna, eds., *Iroquois Land Claims* (Syracuse, NY: Syracuse University Press, 1988).

Lowry, Joan, and Janet Day, "Flats Water Threat Cited," *Rocky Mountain News*, Dec. 7, 1988.

Lutz, Brenda Davis, and James Lutz, "Gypsies as Victims of the Holocaust," *Holocaust and Genocide Studies*, No. 9, 1995.

Lyons, Richard D., "Carter Favors Ban on Atomic Reactors in Earth Satellites," *New York Times*, Jan. 31, 1978.

———, "Public Fears over Nuclear Hazards Are Increasing," *New York Times*, July 1, 1979.

McCleod, Christopher, "Kerr-McGee's Last Stand," *Mother Jones*, Dec. 1980.

———, "Uranium Mines and Mills May Have Caused Birth Defects Among Navajo Indians," *High Country News*, Feb. 4, 1985.

McCartney, Martha M., "Cockacoeske, Queen of the Pamunkey: Diplomat and Suzeraine," in Peter H. Wood, Gregory A. Waselkov and M. Thomas Hatley, eds., *Powhatan's Mantle: Indians in the Colonial Southeast* (Lincoln: University of Nebraska Press, 1989).

McDonald, Dwight, "Hannah Arendt and the Jewish Establishment," in his *Discrimination: Essays and Afterthoughts* (New York: Grossman, 1974).

McMillen, Liz, "The Uniqueness of the Holocaust," *Chronicle of Higher Education*, June 22, 1994.

Madsden, Reed, "Cancer Deaths Linked to Uranium Mining," *Deseret News*, June 4, 1979.

Makin, Kirk, "Douglas Christie: Counsel for the Defense," *Ontario Lawyers' Weekly*, Mar. 29, 1985.

Mancuso, Thomas F., Alice Stewart and George Kneale, "Radiation Exposures of Hanford Workers Dying of Various Causes," *Health Physics*, No.33, 1977.

Manley, Michael S., "Red Jacket's Last Campaign," *New York History*, No. 21, April 1950.

Manning, Patrick, "The Slave Trade: The Formal Demography of a Global System," in J.I. Inikori and S.L. Engerman, eds., *The Atlantic Slave Trade: Effects on Economics, Societies and Peoples in Africa, the Americas and Europe* (Durham, NC: Duke University Press, 1992).

Marshall, Peter, "Colonial Protest and Imperial Retrenchment: Indian Policy, 1764–1768," *Journal of American Studies*, No. 5, 1971.

Martin Paul S., and J.E. Moisiman, "Stimulating Overkill by PaleoIndians," *American Scientist*, Vol. 63, No. 3, May-June 1975.

Mason, Carol I., "A Reconsideration of Westo-Yuchi Identification," *American Anthropologist*, No. 65, 1963.

Matter, Robert Allen, "Missions in the Defense of Spanish Florida," *Florida Historical Quarterly*, No. 54, 1975.

Mayo, Anna, "The Nuclear State in Ascendancy," *Village Voice*, Oct. 22, 1980.

Mead, James R., "The Little Arkansas," *Transactions of the Kansas State Historical Society*, Vol. 10, 1908.

Merrell, James H., "Cultural Continuity Among the Piscataway Indians of Colonial Maryland," *William and Mary Quarterly*, No. 36, 1979.

Meinhart, Nick, "The Four Corners Today, the Black Hills Tomorrow?" *Black Hills/Paha Sapa Report*, Aug. 1979.

Melson, Robert, "Provocation or Nationalism: A Critical Inquiry into the Armenian Genocide of 1915," in Richard Hovannisian, ed., *The Armenian Genocide in Perspective* (New Brunswick, NJ: Transaction, 1986).

Mesler, Bill, "The Pentagon's Radioactive Bullet," *The Nation*, Oct. 21, 1996.

Meyerhoff, Harvey, "Council Decries Germany's Treatment of Gypsies," *U.S. Holocaust Memorial Council Newsletter*, Winter 1992–1993.

Milani, V.I., "The Written Language of Christopher Columbus," *Forum Italicum*, 1973.

Miller, Virginia P., "Whatever Happened to the Yuki?" *Indian Historian*, No. 8, 1975.

Milton, Sybil, "The Context of the Holocaust," *German Studies Review*, Vol. 13, No. 2, 1990.

———, "The Racial Context of the Holocaust," *Social Education*, Feb. 1991.

———, "Nazi Policies Towards the Roma and Sinti, 1933–1945," *Journal of the Gypsy Lore Society*, Vol. 2, No. 1, 5th Series, 1992.

Mooney, James, "The Passing of the Indian," *Proceedings of the Second Pan American Scientific Congress, Sec. 1: Anthropology* (Washington, D. C.: Smithsonian Institution, 1909–1910).

Morison, Kenneth M., "The Bias of Colonial Law: English Paranoia and the Abenaki Arena of King Philip's War," *New England Quarterly*, No. 53, 1980.

Morris, Glenn T., and Ward Churchill, "Between a Rock and a Hard Place: Left-Wing Revolution, Right-Wing Reaction and the Destruction of Indigenous Peoples," *Cultural Survival Quarterly*, Fall 1988.

Morris, James, "The Final Solution, Down Under," *Horizon*, Vol. 14, No. 1, Winter 1972.

Muckleroy, Anna, "The Indian Policy of the Republic of Texas," (4 pts.) *Southwestern Historical Quarterly*, Apr., July, Oct. 1922; Jan. 1923.

Muldoon, James, "The Indian as Irishman," *Essex Institute Historical Collections*, No. 111, 1975.

Myers, Robert A., "Island Carib Cannibalism," *New West Indies Guide*, 1984 edition.

Nafzinger, E.W., and W.L. Richter, "Biafra and Bangladesh: The Political Economy of a Secessionist Conflict," *Peace Research Journal*, Vol. 13, No. 2, 1976.

Nafziger, Richard, "Uranium Profits and Perils," in LaDonna Harris, ed., *Red Paper* (Albuquerque: Americans for Indian Opportunity, 1976).

Navasky, Victor, "Alger Hiss," *The Nation*, Dec. 9, 1996.

Neel, J.V., "Health and Disease in Unacculturated Amerindian Populations," in Ciba Foundation, *Health and Disease in Tribal Societies* (Amsterdam: Elsevier/Excerpta Medica, 1977).

Neitschmann, Bernard, and William Le Bon, "Nuclear Weapons States and Fourth World Nations," *Cultural Survival Quarterly*, Vol, No. 4, 1987.

Nielson, Richard A., "American Indian Land Claims: Land versus Money as a Remedy," *University of Florida Law Review*, Vol. 19, No. 3, 1973.

Nixon, Charles R., "Self-Determination: The Nigeria/Biafra Case," *World Politics*, No. 24, 1972.

Noble, Kenneth B., "The U.S. for Decades Let Uranium Leak at Weapons Plant," *New York Times*, Oct. 15, 1988.

Nolte, Ernst, "Between Myth and Revisionism," in H.W. Koch, ed., *Aspects of the Third Reich* (London: Allen & Unwin, 1985).

Odom, Martha, "Tanks That Leak, Tanks That Explode... Tanks Alot DOE," *Portland Free Press*, May 1989.

O'Gara, Geoffrey, "Canny CERT Gets Money, Respect, Problems," *High Country News*, Dec. 14, 1979.

O'Guin, Becky, "DOE: Nation to Burn and Vitrify Plutonium Stores," *Colorado Daily*, Dec. 10, 1996.

Olbert, John C., "Yocket: Profile of an American Hitler," *The Investigator*, Oct. 1984.

Ortiz, Simon J., "Our Homeland: A National Sacrifice Area," in his *Woven Stone* (Tucson: University of Arizona Press, 1992).

Owen, A.D., "The World Uranium Industry," *Raw Materials Report*, Vol. 2, No. 1, Spring 1983.

Papazian, Pierre, "A 'Unique Uniqueness'?" *Midstream*, Vol. 30, No. 4, April 1984.

Pargellis, Stanley G., "Braddock's Defeat," *American History Review*, No. 41, 1936.

Parry, John H., "The Navigators of the Conquista," *Terra Incognitae*, No. 10, 1978.

Pearce, Susan, and Karen Navarro, "The Legacy of Uranium Mining for Nuclear Weapons," *Earth Island Journal*, Summer 1993.

Percy, George, "'A Trewe Relacyon': Virginia from 1609 to 1612," *Tyler's Quarterly Historical and Genealogical Magazine*, No. 3, 1922.

Peres, Ken, and Fran Swan, "The New Indian Elite: Bureaucratic Entrepreneurs," *Akwesasne Notes*, Late spring 1980.

Perry, "Denying the Holocaust," *Encore American and Worldwide News*, Sept. 1981.

Peterson, H.L., "The Military Equipment of the Plymouth and Bay Colonies, 1620–1690," *New England Quarterly*, No. 20, 1947.

Peyser, Joseph L., "The 1730 Siege of the Foxes," *Illinois Historical Journal*, Vol. LXXX, No. 3, 1967.

———, "The Chickasaw Wars of 1736 and 1740," *Journal of Mississippi History*, February 1982.

———, "The Fate of the Fox Survivors: A Dark Chapter in the History of the French in the Upper Country, 1726–1737," *Wisconsin Magazine of History*, Vol. 73, No. 2, 1990.

Pike, Sumner T., "Witch-Hunting Then and Now," *Atlantic Monthly*, Nov. 1947.

Pinsky, Mark Alan, "New Mexico Spill Ruins a River: The Worst Radiation Accident in History Gets Little Attention," *Critical Mass*, Dec. 1979.

Pitman, Frank, "Navajos–UNC Settle Tailings Spill Lawsuits," *Navajo Times*, Apr. 22, 1985.

Pohl, Robert O., "Health Effects of Radon-222 from Uranium Mining," *Science,* Aug. 1979.

Pokagon, Simon, "The Future of the Red Man," *Forum*, Aug 1987.

Polonsky, Anthony, "Introduction" to Michael Burleigh and Wolfgang Wipperman, *The Racial State: Germany, 1933–45* (Cambridge: Cambridge University Press, 1991).

Pommershein, Frank, "The Black Hills Case: On the Cusp of History," *Wicazo Sa Review*, Vol. 4, No. 1, 1988.

Pope, Charles, "Nuclear Arms Cleanup Bill: A Tidy $230 Billion," *San Jose Mercury News*, Apr. 4, 1995.

Post, John D., "The Mortality Crisis of the Early 1770s and European Demographic Trends," *Journal of Interdisciplinary History*, No. 21, 1990.

Powell, William S., "Aftermath of the Masscre: The First Indian War, 1622–1632," *Virginia Magazine of History and Biography*, No. 66, 1958.

Pressac, Jean-Claude, "The Deficiencies and Inconsistencies of the 'Leuchter Report'," in Shelly Shapiro, ed., *Truth Prevails: The End of the "Leuchter Report"* (Albany, NY: Holocaust Education Project, 1990).

Prutschi, Manuel, "The Zundel Affairs," in Alan Davies, ed., *Antisemitism in Canada* (Rexdale, Ont.: John Wiley & Sons, 1992).

Quirk, Robert E., "Notes on a Controversial Controversy: Juan Gines de Sepúlveda and Natural Servitude," *Hispanic American Historical Review*, XXXIV, 1954.

Randall, David R., "The Indian Slave Trade and Population of Nicaragua During the Sixteenth Century," in William Denevan, ed., *The Native Population of the Americas in 1492* (Madison: University of Wisconsin Press, 1976).

Randolph, E.O., "The Dunmore War," *Ohio Archaelogical and Historical Publications*, No. 11, 1931.

Ranlet, Philip, "Another Look at the Causes of King Philip's War," *New England Quarterly*, No. 61, 1988.

Revolutionary Communist Party, U.S.A., "Searching for the Second Harvest," in Ward Churchill, ed., *Marxism and Native Americans* (Boston: South End Press, 1983).

Richardson, Rupert N., "The Comanche Reservation in Texas," *West Texas Historical Association Yearbook*, Vol. V, 1929.

————, "The Comanche Indians at the Adobe Walls Fight," *Panhandle-Plains Historical Review*, No. 4, 1931.

Risely, Mary, "LANCL Gropes to Find a New Way," *Enchanted Times*, Fall/Winter 1993.

Rister, Carl Coke, "The Significance of the Destruction of the Buffalo in the Southwest," *Southwestern Historical Quarterly*, Vol. 33, No. 1, 1929.

Robbins, Lynn A., "Energy Development and the Navjo Nation: An Update," in Joseph Jorgenson, ed., *American Indians and Energy Development* (Cambridge, MA: Anthropological Resource Center, 1978).

Rosenberg, Alan, "Was The Holocaust Unique? A Peculiar Question," in Isador Walliman and Michael N. Dobkowski, eds., *Genocide and the Modern Age: Etiology and Case Studies of Mass Death* (New York: Greenwood Press, 1987).

————, "An Assault on Western Values," *Dimension*, Spring, 1985.

Rosenberg, David Alan, "The U.S. Nuclear Stockpile, 1945 to 1950," *Bulletin of Atomic Scientists*, Mat 1980.

Rosensaft, Menachem, "The Holocaust: History as Aberration," *Midstream*, May, 1977.

Russell, Don, "How Many Indians Were Killed? White Man Versus Red Man: Facts and Legend," *American West*, July 1973.

Russell, Peter E., "Redcoats in the Wilderness: British Officers and Irregular Warfare, 1740 to 1769," *William and Mary Quarterly*, No. 35, 1978.

Ruta, Suzanne, "Fear and Silence at Los Alamos," *The Nation*, Jan. 11, 1993.

Salaff, Steven, "The Cigar Lake Mine: The Real Drilling Begins at Saskatchewan's Prize Uranium Deposit," *Sakatchewan Business*, Mar. 1985.

Salisbury, Neal, "Indians and Colonists in Southern New England after the Pequot War: An Uneasy Balance," in Laurence M. Hauptman and James D. Wherry, eds., *The Pequots in Southern New England: The Fall and Rise of an American Indian Nation* (Norman: University of Oklahoma Press, 1990).

————, "Towards the Covenant Chain: Iroquois and Southern New England Algonkians, 1637–1685," in Daniel K. Richter and James H Merrill, eds., *Beyond the Covenant Chain: The Iroquois and their Neighbors in Indian North America, 1600–1800* (Syracuse, NY: Syracuse University Press, 1987).

Salmon, Roberto Mario, "The Disease Complaint at Bosque Redondo (1864–1868)," *The Indian Historian*, No. 9, 1976.

Samet, M.J., et al., "Uranium Mining and Lung Cancer Among Navajo Men," *New England Journal of Medicine*, No. 310, 1984.

Sandos, James A., "Junipero Serra's Canonization and the Historical Record," *American Historical Review*, No. 93, 1988.

Sartre, Jean Paul, "On Genocide," *Ramparts*, Feb. 1968.

Sauer, Carl O., "The Road to Cibola," in John Leighy, ed., *Land and Life* (Berkeley: University of California Press, 1963).

Schneider, Keith, "Seeking Victims of Radiation Near Weapons Plant," *New York Times*, Oct. 17, 1988.

Schneider, Peter, "Hitler's Shadow: On Being a Self-Conscious German," *Harper's*, Sept. 1987.

Scoles, Francis V., "The Spanish Conqueror as Businessman: A Chapter in the History of Fernando Cortés," *New Mexico Quarterly*, No. 28, 1958.

Schomish, J.W., "Eid Lifts the Ban on Eating Church Rock Cattle," *Gallup Independent*, May 22, 1980.

Schumacher, Elouise, "440 Billion Gallons: Hanford Wastes Could Fill 900 King Domes," *Seattle Times*, Apr. 13, 1991.

Schwagen, Anthony S., and Thomas Hollbacher, "Lung Cancer Among Uranium Miners," in *The Nuclear Fuel Cycle* (Cambridge, MA: Union of Concerned Scientists & Friends of the Earth, 1973).

Schwarz, Loretta, "Uranium Deaths at Crown Point," *Ms. Magazine*, Oct. 1979.

Schwelb, Egon, "Crimes Against Humanity," *The British Yearbook of International Law*, No. 23, 1946.

Seideman, Paul, "DU: Material with a Future," *National Defense*, Jan. 1984.

Sereny, Gita, "The Men Who Whitewash Hitler," *The New Statesman*, Nov. 1979.

Severo, Richard, "Too Hot to Handle," *New York Times Magazine*, Apr. 10, 1977.

Shapiro, Edward S., "Antisemitism, Mississippi Style," in David Gerber, ed., *Antisemitism in American History* (Urbana: University of Illinois Press, 1986).

Shea, Christopher, "Debating the Uniqueness of the Holocaust," *Chronicle of Higher Education*, May 31, 1996.

Shields, Lilian B., "Relations with the Cheyennes and Arapahoes in Colorado to 1861," *Colorado Magazine*, Aug. 1927.

Shields, Laura Magnum, and Alan B. Goodman, "Outcome of 13,300 Navajo Births from 1964–1981 in the Shiprock Uranium Mining Area," (New York: unpublished paper presented at the American Association of Atomic Scientists Symposium, May 25, 1984).

Shields, Laura Magnum, et al., "Navajo Birth Outcomes in the Shiprock Uranium Mining Area," *Health Physics*, Vol. 63, No. 5, 1992.

Shuey, Chris, "The Widows of Red Rock," *Scottsdale Daily Progress Saturday Magazine,* June 2, 1979.

Sievers, M.A., "The Shifting Sands of Sand Creek Historiography," *Colorado Magazine*, No. 49, 1972.

Siskind, Janet, "A Beautiful River That Turned Sour," *Mine Talk*, Summer/Fall 1982.

Smillie, John D., "Whatever Happened to the Energy Crisis?" *The Plains Truth*, Apr. 1986.

Smith, Andrea, "The HIV-Correlation to Hepatitis-A and B Vaccines," *WARN Newsletter*, Summer 1992.

Smith, Randall, "Charge Ike Misled Public on N-Tests," *New York Daily News*, Apr. 20, 1979.

Smith, R., "Radon Emissions: Open Pit Uranium Mines Said to Be Big Contributor," *Nucleonics Week*, May 25, 1978.

Smith, Roger W., "Human Destructiveness and Politics: The Twentieth Century as an Age of Genocide," in Isador Walliman and Michael N. Dobkowski, eds., *Genocide and the Modern Age: Etiology and Case Studies of Mass Death* (New York: Greenwood Press, 1987).

Smith, Roger W., Eric Markusen, and Robert Jay Lifton, "Professional Ethics and the Denial of the Armenian Genocide," *Holocaust and Genocide Studies*, No. 9, 1995.

Snow, Dean R., and Kim M. Lamphear, "European Contact and Depopulation in the Northeast: The Timings of the First Epidemics," *Ethnohistory*, No. 35, 1988.

Sokolov, Raymond, "Stop Hating Columbus," *Newsweek: Columbus Special Issue*, Fall/Winter 1992.

Spinden, J.H., "The Population of Ancient America," *Geographical Review*, No. 18, 1928.

———, "Population of Ancient America," in *Anthropological Report* (Washington, D.C.: Smithsonian Institution, 1929).

Stannard, David E., "The Consequences of Contact: Toward an Interdiscplinary Theory of Native Responses to Biological and Cultural Invasion," in Havid Hurtz Thomas, ed., *Columbian Consequences, Vol. 3: The Spanish Borderlands in Pan-American Perspective* (Washington, D.C.: Smithsonian Institution, 1991).

———, "Disease and Infertility: A New Look at the Collapse of Native Populations in the Wake of Contact," *Journal of American Studies*, No. 24, 1990.

————, "The Politics of Holocaust Scholarship: Uniqueness as Denial," in Alan S. Rosenbaum, *Is the Holocaust Unique? Perspectives in Comparative Genocide* (Boulder, CO: Westview Press, 1996).

Stapinska, "Stateless, Faceless, Endless Victims," *Yorkshire Post*, Jan. 28, 1995.

Starna, William A., "The Pequots in the Early Seventeenth Century," in Laurence M. Hauptman and James D. Wherry, eds., *The Pequots in Southern New England: The Fall and Rise of an American Indian Nation* (Norman: University of Oklahoma Press, 1990).

Steele, Janet, "Uranium Development in the San Juan Basin," in Leslie J. Freeman's *Nuclear Witnesses: Insiders Speak Out* (New York: W.W. Norton, 1982).

Steiner, George, "The Long Life of Metaphor: A Theological-Metaphysical Approach to the *Shoah*," in Asher Cohen, et al., eds., *Comprehending the Holocaust: Historical Research* (New York: Peter Lang, 1988).

Sternglass, Ernest J., "Cancer:Relation of Prenatal Radiation to Development of the Disease in Childhood," *Science*, June 7, 1963.

————, "Infant Mortality and Nuclear Tests," *Bulletin of Atomic Scientists*, Apr. 1969.

————, "Can the Infants Survive?" *Bulletin of Atomic Scientists*, June 1969.

————, "The Death of All Children," *Esquire*, Sept. 1969.

Strandberg, Susan, "Researcher Claims Thousands of Gypsies Exterminated by Czechs," *Decorah Journal*, May 5, 1994.

Street, William D., "Cheyenne Indian Massacre on the Middle Fork of the Sappa," *Transactions of the Kansas State Historical Society*, Vol. X, 1907–1908.

Streit, Christian, "The Fate of Soviet Prisoners of War," in Michael Berenbaum, ed., *A Mosaic of Victims: Non-Jews Persecuted and Murdered by the Nazis* (New York: New York University Press, 1990).

Stürmer, Michael, "Weder verdrängen noch bewälten. Geschte und Gegenwartsbewusstein der Deutschen," *Schweizer Monatschefte*, No. 66, Sept. 1986.

Sullivan, Kathleen M., "The First Amendment Wars," *The New Republic*, Sept. 28, 1991.

Sutch, Richard, "The Care and Feeding of Slaves," in Paul A. David, Herbert G. Gutman, Richard Sutch, Peter Temin and Gavin Wright, *Reckoning with Slavery: A Critical Study in the Quantitive History of American Negro Slavery* (New York: Oxford University Press, 1976).

Szafranski, Jan, "Poland's Losses in World War II," in Roman Nurowski, ed., *1939–1945: War Losses in Poland* (Pozán: Wydawnictwo Zachodnie, 1960).

Taft, Sen. Robert A., "Equal Justice Under the law: The Heritage of English-Speaking Peoples and Their Responsibility," *Vital Speeches*, Vol. 13, No. 2, Nov. 1, 1946.

Taliman, Valerie, "Nine Tribes Look at Storage: Signs Point to Nuclear Dump on Native Land," *Smoke Signals*, Aug. 1993.

————, "Nuclear Guinea Pigs: Native People Were on the Front Lines of Exploitation," *Native American Smoke Signals*, Jan. 1994.

Taylor, Telford, "The Nuremberg War Crimes Trials," *International Conciliation*, No. 450, Apr. 1949.

Tessier, Denise, "Uranium Mine Gas Causes Lung Cancer, UNM Group Told," *Albuquerque Journal*, Mar. 11, 1980.

Thomas, Robert K., "Colonialism: Classic and Internal," *New University Thought*, Winter 1966–1967.

Thornton, Russell, "Implications of Catlin's American Indian Population Estimates for Revisionism of Mooney's Estimate," *American Journal of Physical Anthropology*, No. 49, 1978.

————, "American Indian Historical Demography: A Review Essay with Suggestions for the Future," *American Indian Culture and Research Journal*, No. 3, 1979.

————, "But How Thick Were They? A Review Essay of *Their Number Become Thinned*," *Contemporary Sociology*, No. 13, 1984.

————, "Cherokee Population Losses During the Trail of Tears: A New Perspective and a New Estimate," *Ethnohistory*, No. 31, 1984; included in William L. Anderson, ed., *Cherokee Removal, Before and After* (Athens: University of Georgia Press, 1991).

Thorpe, Grace, "Radioactive Racism? Native Americans and the Nuclear Waste Legacy," *The Circle*, Apr. 1995.

Trennerry, Walter N., "The Shooting of Little Crow: Heroism or Murder?" *Minnesota History*, Vol. 38, 1962.

Trigger, Bruce, "The Destruction of Huronia: A Study in Economic and Cultural Change, 1609–1650," *Transactions of the Royal Canadian Institute*, XXXIII, 1960.

———, "The Mohawk-Mahican War (1624–28): The Establishment of a Pattern," *Canadian Historical Review*, No. 52, 1971.

Tso, Harold, and Laura Mangum Shields, "Navajo Mining Operations: Early Hazards and Recent Innovations," *New Mexico Journal of Science*, Vol. 12, No. 1, Spring 1980.

Trosper Ronald L., "Appendix I: Indian Minerals," in American Indian Policy Review Commission, *Task Force 7 Final Report: Reservation and Resource Development and Protection* (Washington, D.C.: 95th Cong., 1st Sess., U.S. Government Printing Office, 1977).

Ubelaker, Douglas H., "Prehistoric New World Population Size: Historic Review and Currrent Appraisal of North American Estimates," *American Journal of Physical Anthropology*, No. 45, 1976.

———, "The Sources and Methods for Mooney's Estimates of North American Indian Populations," in William H. Deneven, ed., *The Native Population of the Americas in 1492* (Madison: University of Wisconsin Press, 1976).

———, "North American Indian Population Size: Changing Perspectives," in John W. Verano and Douglas H. Ubelaker, eds., *Disease and Demography in the Americas* (Washington, D.C.: Smithsonian Institution, 1992).

Upton, L.F.S., "The Extermination of the Beothuks of Newfoundland," *Canadian Historical Review*, No. 58, 1977.

Uriel, Tal, "On the Study of the Holocaust and Genocide," *Yad Vashem Studies*, No. 13, 1979.

Valentine, Paul, "Dancing with Myths," *Washington Post*, Apr. 7, 1991.

Vance, John T., "The Congressional Mandate and the Indian Claims Cimmission," *North Dakota Law Review*, No. 45, 1969.

Vaughan, Alden T., "Pequots and Puritans: The Causes of the War of 1637," *William and Mary Quarterly*, 3d Ser. XXI, 1964.

———, "Frontier Banditti and the Indians: The Paxton Boys' Legacy, 1763–1775," *Pennsylvania History*, No. 51, 1984.

Vignaud, Henry, "Columbus a Spaniard and a Jew?" *American History Review*, Vol. 18, 1913.

Vulliamy, Ed, "Middle Managers of Genocide," *The Nation*, June 10, 1996.

Wagoner, Joseph K., et al., "Radiation as the Cause of Lung Cancer in Uranium Miners," *New England Journal of Medicine*, No. 273, 1965.

Wald, Mathew L., "Wider Peril Seen in Nuclear Waste from Bomb Making," *New York Times*, Mar. 28, 1991.

Wallace, Edward S., and Adrian S. Anderson, "R.S. Mackenzie and the Kickapoos: The Raid into Mexico in 1873," *Arizona and the West*, Vol. II, 1965.

Washburn, Wilcomb E., "A Moral History of Indian-White Relations: Needs and Opportunities for Study," *Ethnohistory*, No. 4, 1957.

———, "Distinguishing History from Moral Philosophy and Public Advocacy," in Calvin Martin, ed., *The American Indian and the Problem of History* (New York: Oxford University Press, 1987).

Wasserman, Harvey, "The Sioux's Last Fight for the Black Hills," *Rocky Mountain News*, Aug. 24, 1980.

Wechsler, Herbert,, "The Issues of the Nuremberg Trial," *Political Science Quarterly*, No. 62, Mar. 1947.

Weisberg, Jacob, "The Heresies of Pat Buchanan," *The New Republic*, Oct. 22, 1990.

West, Elizabeth Howard, "The Indian Policy of Bernardo de Galvez," *Proceedings of the Mississippi Valley Historical Association*, No. 8, 1914–1915.

West, G. Derek, "The Battle of Sappa Creek, 1875," *Kansas Historical Quarterly*, Vol. 34, No. 2, 1968.

Weurthner, George, "An Ecological View of the Indian," *Earth First!*, Vol. 7, No. 7, Aug. 1987.

Wiesel, Elie, "Now We Know," in Richard Arens, ed., *Genocide in Paraguay* (Philadelphia: Temple University Press, 1976).

Williams, Ethel J., "To Little Land, Too Many Heirs: The Indian Heirship Land Problem," *Washington Law Review*, No. 46, 1971.

Wilson, Wesley C., "The Army and the Piegans: The Baker Massacre on the Marias, 1870," *North Dakota History*, No. 32, 1965).

Winks, Robin W., "The British North American West and the Civil War," *North Dakota History*, Vol. 24, 1957.

Winston, Sanford, "Indian Slavery in the Carolina Region," *Journal of Negro History*, No. 19, 1934.

Winthrop, Patricia J., and J. Rothblat, "Radiation Pollution in the Environment," *Bulletin of Atomic Scientists*, Sept. 1981.

Women of All Red Nations, "Radiation: Dangerous to Pine Ridge Women," *Akwesasne Notes*, Spring, 1980.

Wood, Peter H., "The Changing Population of the Colonial South: An Overview by Race and Region, 1685–1790," in Peter H. Wood, Gregory A. Waselkov and M. Thomas Hatley, eds., *Powhatan's Mantle: Indians in the Colonial Southeast* (Lincoln: University of Nebraska Press, 1989).

Woods, Patricia D., "The French and the Natchez Indians in Louisiana, 1700–1732," *Louisiana History*, No. 19, 1978.

Worrall, Arthur J., "Persecution, Politics and War: Roger Williams, Quaker, and King Philip's War," *Quaker History*, No. 66, 1977.

Wright, Peter M., "The Pursuit of Dull Knife from Fort Reno, 1878–1879," *Chronicles of Oklahoma*, No. 46, 1968.

Wright, Quincy, "The Law of the Nuremberg Trial," *American Journal of International Law*, No 41, Jan. 1947.

Wyndham, Susan, "Death in the Air," *Australian Magazine*, Sept. 29–30, 1990.

Young, Henry J., "A Note on Scalp Bounties in Pennsylvania," *Pennsylvanian History*, No. 24, 1957.

Zielinski, Mike, "Armed and Dangerous: Private Police Forces on the March," *Covert Action Quarterly*, No. 54, Fall 1995.

U.S. Government Documents

Commission on the Ukrainian Famine, *Investigation of the Ukrainian Famine, 1932–1933: Report to Congress* (Washington, D.C.: U.S. Government Printing Office, 1988).

Gofman, John W., "Federal Radiation Council Guidelines for Radiation Exposure of the Population at Large—Protection or Disaster?" U.S. Congress, Joint Committee on Atomic Energy, *Environmental Effects of Producing Electric Power* (Washington, D.C.: 91st Cong., 1st Sess., U.S. Government Printing Office, 1969).

National Academy of Sciences, Division of Earth Science, Committee on Waste Disposal, *The Disposal of Radioactive Waste on Land* (Washington, D.C.: NAS-NRC Pub. 519, 1957).

Office of United States Chief Counsel for Prosecution of Axis Criminality, *Trials of War Criminals Before the Nuremberg Military Tribunals Under Control Council Law N. 10, Vols. 1–15* (Washington, D.C.: U.S. Government Printing Office, 1951–53).

Trosper, Ronald L., "Appendix I: Indian Minerals," in American Indian Policy Review Commission, *Task Force 7 Final Report: Reservation and Resource Development and Protection* (Washington, D.C.: U.S. Government Printing Office, 1977).

U.S. Bureau of the Census, *Fifteenth Census of the United States, 1930: The Indian Population of the United States and Alaska* (Washington, D.C.: U.S. Government Printing Office, 1937).

———, *General Social and Economic Characteristics: United States Summary* (Washington, D.C.: U.S. Government Printing Office, 1983).

———, Population Division, Racial Statistics Branch, *A Statistical Profile of the American Indian Population* (Washington, D.C.: U.S. Government Printing Office, 1988).

U.S. Congress, Joint Committee on Atomic Energy, *Environmental Effects of Producing Electric Power* (Washington, D.C.: 91st Cong., 1st Sess., U.S. Government Printing Office, 1969).

U.S. Congress, Office of Technology Assessment, *Complex Cleanup: The Environmental Legacy of Nuclear Weapons Production* (Washington, D.C.: Government Printing Office, 1991).

U.S. Department of Energy, Federal Energy Administration, Office of Strategic Analysis, *Project Independence: A Summary* (Washington, D.C.: U.S. Government Printing Office, 1974).

———, *Environmental Assessment on Remedial Action at the Riverton Uranium Mill Tailings Site, Riverton, Wyoming* (Albuquerque: DOE Western Regional Office, June 1987).

———, Monitored Retrievable Storage Commission, "Nuclear Waste: Is There a Need for

Federal Interim Storage?" in *Report of the Monitored Retrievable Storage Commission* (Washington, D.C.: U.S. Government Printing Office, 1989).

————, Nuclear Information and Resource Service, *Nuclear Power and National Energy Strategy* (Washington, D.C.: U.S. Government Printing Office, 1991).

————, *Announced United States Nuclear Tests July 1945 Through December 1991* (Washington, D.C.: U.S. Government Printing Office, 1992).

————, Office of Environmental Management, *Closing the Circle of the Atom: The Environmental Legacy of Nuclear Weapons Production in the United States and What the Department of Energy Is Doing About It* (Washington, D.C.: DOE/EM-0228, Jan. 1995).

————, Office of Environmental Management, *Environmental Management 1995* (Washington, D.C.: DOE.EM-0228, Feb. 1995).

————, Office of Environmental Management, *Estimating the Cold War Mortgage: The 1995 Baseline Environmental Management Report* (Washington, D.C.: DOE/EM-0232, Mar. 1995).

U.S. Department of Health and Human Services, Indian Health Services, *Health Hazards Related to Nuclear Resources Development on Indian Land* (Washington, D.C: 97th Cong. 2nd. Sess., U.S. Government Printing Office, 1983).

————, Public Health Service, *Chart Series Book* (Washington, D.C.: U.S. Government Printing Office, 1988).

U.S. Department of Interior, American Indian Policy Review Commission, *Task Force 7 Final Report: Reservation and Resource Development and Protection* (Washington, D.C.: 95th Cong., 1st Sess., U.S. Government Printing Office, 1977).

————, Bureau of the Census, "Indian Population by Divisions and States, 1890–1930," *Fifteenth Census of the United States, 1930: The Indian Population of the United States and Alaska* (Washington, D.C.: U.S. Government Printing Office, 1937).

————, Bureau of the Census, 1980 Census of Population, *Supplementary Reports: Race of the Population of the States by Race, 1980* (Washington, D.C.: U.S. Government Printing Office, 1981).

————, Bureau of Indian Affairs, *Indian Lands Map: Oil, Gas and Minerals on Indian Reservations* (Washington, D.C.: U.S. Government Printing Office, 1978).

————, Bureau of Land Management, *Final Environmental Impact Statement for the Jackpile Uranium Mine Reclamation Project, 2 vols.* (Albuquerque: BLM New Mexico Area Office, 1986).

————, Environmental Protection Agency, *Potential Health and Environmental Hazards of Nuclear Mine Wastes* (Washington, D.C.: U.S Government Printing Office, 1983).

————, Indian Claims Commission, *Final Report* (Washington, D.C.: 96th Cong., 1st Sess., U.S. Government Printing Office, 1979).

————, Public Land Review Commission, *One-Third of the Nation's Land* (Washington, D.C.: 91st Cong., 2nd Sess., U.S. Government Printing Office, 1970).

U.S. Department of Justice, Commission on Civil Rights, *The Navajo Nation: An American Colony* (Washington, D.C.: U.S. Government Printing Office, 1976).

U.S. Department of War, *The War of Rebellion: A Compilation of the Official Records of the Union and Confederated Armies,* four series, 128 vols. (Washington, D.C.: U.S. Government Printing Office, 1880–1901) Series I, Vol. XXII, Pt. 2.

U.S. House of Representatives, *The Indian Problem: Resolution of the Committee of One Hundred by the Secretary of Interior and Review of the Indian Problem* (Washington, D.C.: 68th Cong., 1st Sess., U.S. Government Printing Office, 1925).

————, *Resolution of the Committee of One-Hundred by the Secretary of Interior and Review of the Indian Problem* (Washington, D.C.: 68th Cong., 1st Sess., U.S. Government Printing Office, 1928).

————, Committee on Interstate and Foreign Commerce, Subcommittee on Health and Environment, *Effects of Radiation on Human Health, Vol. 1: Effects of Ionizing Radiation* (Washington, D. C.: 95th Cong., 2d Sess., U.S. Government Printing Office, 1978).

————, Committee on Interior and Insular Affairs, Subcommittee on Energy and the Environment, *Hearings on the Nuclear Waste Policy Act* (Washington, D.C.: 100th Cong., Ist Sess., U.S. Government Printing Office, 1988).

U.S. Navy, *Naval Weapons Center Silver Anniversary* (China Lake Naval Weapons Center: Technical

Information Dept. Publishing Division, Oct. 1968).

    U.S. Senate, *Hearings on the Genocide Convention Before the Senate Committee on Foreign Relations* (Washington, D.C.: 98th Cong., 2nd. Sess., U.S. Government Printing Office, 1984).

    ———, *Hearings on the Genocide Convention Before a Subcommittee of the Senate Committee on Foreign Relations* (Washington, D.C.: 99th Cong., 1st Sess., U.S. Government Printing Offices, 1985).

    ———, *Executive Report Number 2* (Washington, D.C.: 99th Cong., 1st Sess., U.S. Government Printing Office, 1985).

INDEX

A

Abenakis: 148, 183, 191, 201, 202, 272n366, 373; attrition of: 201n, 205n; eastern division of: 169, 170, 201n, 202n, 204; St. François massacre of: 205; western division of: 201n

Aberdeen Saturday Pioneer. 244

Adams, John: 210n

Adobe Walls, battle of: 237

AEC, see Atomic Energy Commission

Aerojet Ordnance Corp., depleted uranium ammunition of: 301n

Affirmation of the Principles of International Law Recognized by the Charter of the Nuremberg Tribunal (1946): 435n

Agent Orange: 333n

Aggressive War, concept of: 379n, 380

Aguirre, Anselmo: 111

Ajuricaba (Manau): 108

Alamagordo, *see* White Sands Missile Test Range

Albigensian Crusades: 402

Alcan Corp.: 112

alcohol/alcoholism: 247n, 293; as mechanism of genocide: 405

Alexander, Edward: 36

Alfred University: 81

Algeria, French colonization of: 92, 404n, 441n68

Algiers Declaration (1976): 444n122

Alvars Cabral, Pedro: 99

Alperovitz, Gar: 295n

Alvarado, Pedro de: 99, 102, 109, 139-40n

Amchitka Island, "Long Shot" nuclear test on: 330n

Amerasia spy case: 369n

Americal Division: 382n

American Bar Association (ABA): 373, 378, 381, 391n50; obstruction of Genocide Convention by: 376n

American Civil Rights Congress (CRC): 376

American Civil War: 225; American Indian participation in: 280n513; Pea Ridge campaign of: 280n513

American Communist Party: 370n

American Community Behavior. 414

American Convention on Human Rights (1964): 371

American Historical Association: 283n562

American History Review: 91

American Indian Movement (AIM): 7, 9, 11, 43, 117, 318; "Cable Splicer" counterinsurgency scenario tested against: 341n; Colorado chapter of: 2n, 127n100; "Garden Plot" counterinsurgency scenario tested against: 341n

American Jewish Congress: 69

American Museum, the: 185n

American Nazi Party: 56n38

American Telephone and Telegraph Co. (AT&T): 302n, 303

American War of Independence: 185, 189, 207-9

AMEX: 307

Amherst, Jeffrey: and bacteriological genocide: 2, 64, 92, 154, 196n, 206, 261n132

Amnesty International: 116

Anaconda Copper Corp.: 311n, 315; Bluewater uranium mill of: 315; denies environmental/health effects of uranium mining: 312n, 315n; Jackpile-Paguate uranium mining complex of: 309, 310n

anarchy/anarchism: 6

Anarchy magazine: 6

Anderson, E.L.: 21

Anthony, Scott J.: 279n506

antisemites/antisemitism: xi, 20, 27, 32, 37, 43, 50, 63, 73, 82-4

Apalachees: 134, 159, 160, 189, 200, 201; absorb Yamasee survivors: 201; become Seminoles: 201; English extermination of: 203-4

App, Austin J.: 20-1, 25-6, 49, 50, 56n26, 62n138

Arabs, British wars against: 92

Arapahos: 228-38, 282n538; and 1851 Ft. Laramie Treaty: 223; and 1862 Treaty of Ft. Wise: 224n; massacred at Sand Creek: 232-3; smallpox among: 155n; U.S. extermination of: 64

Arbenz, Jacobo: 114

Archer, Victor: 306, 307, 353n49

Arendt, Hannah: xiii, 66, 79n47, 414, 443n90

Argall, Thomas: 165

Argonne National Scientific Laboratory: 299-300; *also see* Westinghouse Corp.

Argentina: anti-Indian policies of: 103; conquest of: 109

Arkansas Territory, creation of: 218

Armenia/Armenians: Kishniev pogrom against: 405; Turkish genocide of: xiv, xvi, 30, 31, 32-3, 34, 36, 64, 406, 421

Armantrout, William: 54n9

Arnold of Cîtreaux: 402

Arrow Cross, the: 43

Carranco, Lynwood: 8
Carson, Christopher "Kit": 144-5, 149, 235n, 251n
Carter, Jimmy: 37n
Carthage, Roman genocide in: 401
Cartier, Jacques: 190
Carto, Elizabeth: 22n
Carto, Willis: 21, 22, 383; apologizes to Mel Mermelstein: 22-3n
Case of the Mormon Cow, the: 223n
Castillo, Bobby: 258n78
Caterpillar Corp.: 112
Cathars, genocide of: 402
Ceanese Corp.: 111
Cebolla land grant: 289
Central Intelligence Agency (CIA): 114, 115n, 297n, 383n, 392
Ceremony: 289
Cesar Tabay, Julio: 111
Chalk, Frank: 12, 251, 399, 408n, 420n, 422n, 423-4, 425n, 428n, 429, 431, 443n92; endorsed by Katz: 428n; endorses notion of "ethnocide": 424n
Chambers, Whitaker: 370n
Champlain, Samuel de: 190-1, 192, 270n304; evicted from Québec: 191; founds Québec: 191
Charney, Israel: xiv, 31, 51; denounces exclusivism: 51-2
Chelmno, see death camps
Chemehuavi Valley Indian Reservation: 340
Chemical Nuclear Corp.: 336n
Cheney, Lynne: 4, 66
Cherokee Cases, the: 275n425
Cherokees: 149, 183, 196n, 200-2, 204, 212, 280n513; and Tecumseh: 215; and Trail of Tears: 144; and Red Stick War: 216; encounter with de Soto of: 161; English war against: 205, 260n113
Chesapeake Confederation: 166n; Accohannocks: 166n; Accomacs: 166n; Monacans: 166n; Patatwomacs (Potomacs): 166n, 167; Piscataways: 167, 168, 175, 200, 264n192
Cheyennes: 224, 228-38, 280n506, 282n538, 283n556, 318; and 1851 Ft. Laramie Treaty: 223; and 1861 Treaty of Ft. Wise: 224n; Camp Weld meeting of: 231, 281n529; deported to Oklahoma: 242; Dog Soldiers of: 234-5, 236, 244n; Mackenzie campaign against: 240-2; massacred at Buffalo Springs: 231; massacred at Camp Robinson: 243; massacred at Sand Creek: 232-3; massacred at the Washita: 236; smallpox among: 155n;

U.S. extermination of: 64, 92; 1878 "breakout" of: 243
Chickasaws: 183, 202, 203, 208; and Tecumseh: 215; and Trail of Tears: 144; encounter with de Soto of: 161; wars with the French: 195-6
Chilam Balam: 104
Chile, conquest of: 99, 108; reduccione policy in: 108, 112-3
China Lake Naval Weapons Center (Cal.): 330, 358n122, 358n134; Military Target Range of: 330n
Chinese immigrants, violence against: 374
Chivington, John M.: 13n3, 92, 129, 229-32, 233n, 234, 235n, 281n526, 281n529, 281n537; and Sand Creek Massacre: 232-3; as Methodist minister: 229; "nits make lice" statement of: 229; personal cowardice of: 281n537
Choctaws: 195, 196, 202; and Trail of Tears: 144; encounter with de Soto of: 161; smallpox among: 161
Chomsky, Noam: xv, 10, 22n, 442n86
Christian, William: 274n410
Christie, Douglas: 23
Christopher Columbus: Documents and Proofs of His Genoese Origin: 89-90
Chronicle of Higher Education: 65-6
Chronicle of the Lodz Ghetto, The: 41
Church, Benjamin: 177
Church, Frank: 377-8
Church Rock nuclear spill, see United Nuclear Corp.
Churchill, Ward: xi, xii, xiv, xv, xvi, 43, 81-3, 97-8, 399n
Churchill, Winston: 405, 410n; advocates use of poison gas against Kurds: 405n
Cieza de Léon, Pedro de: 103, 105
cigarettes, see tobacco smoking
Clark, George Rogers: 149, 185, 209, 275n418, 276n432
Clean Water Act of 1972: 353n54
Climax Uranium Corp.: 307
Clinton, Bill: 326, 345, 390n; and neutron bomb development: 345n
Clinton, James: 212
Cockacoeske (Tsenacommacah): 167n
Cohen, Felix S.: 340-1, 361n164
Cohn, Norman: 419, 434n, 442n76
Cold War, the: 289, 304, 318, 320, 326n, 334, 340, 341, 343, 346, 349, 371n, 411; causes of: 371
Collier, John: 286n592
Colorado River Tribes Indian Reservation: 340

Fort Kearny, Neb.: 223n
Fort Laramie, Wyo.: 223, 224n, 238, 239n
Fort Laramie Treaty (1851): 223
Fort Laramie Treaty (1868): 238-9, 242n
Fort Lyon, Colo.: 231, 232, 233
Fort Madison, Ill.: 214
Fort Marion, Fla.: 237
Fort McDermitt Reservation, Utah: 338
Fort Michilimackinac, Mich.: 195n, 205
Fort Mimms, Ala.: 215
Fort Mojave Indian Reservation: 340
Fort Niagara, NY: 205
Fort of Castillo de San Marcos (San Augustín),
     Fla.: 188, 262n167
Fort Orange (Albany), NY: 192
Fort Phil Kearny, Wyo.: 238, 283n556
Fort Pitt, Penn.: 268n276
Fort Reno, Wyo.: 283n556
Fort Rosalie, Miss.: 196
Fort Sill, Okla.: 237
Fort Snelling, Minn.: 226
Fort Sumner, NM: 145
Fort William Henry, NY: 204, 273n383
Four Corners region: as National Sacrifice Area:
     287n603, 318; uranium discovered in: 293-
     4; uranium mined in: 306-11, 317
Four Power Agreement (1945): 407
Fourth International Russell Tribunal: 111-2
French and Indian War, see Seven Years' War
Frenchtown, battle of: 215
Freire, Paulo/Freirian pedagogy: 11
Frobisher, Martin: 162
From Time Immemorial: xvii n 8

G

Galeano, Eduardo: 8, 120, 293
Gall (Lakota): 242
Gallup polls: 25
Gandia, Enrique de: 90
Garcia, Herman: 315n
Gates, Thomas: 263n181
Gehlen, Reinhard: 297n
General Allotment Act (1887): 245-6, 284n573,
     292, 366n; impacts of: 292n
General Electric Corp. (GE), Hanford nuclear
     facility of: 300
General Motors Corp. (GM): 302n
Geneva Convention (1949), 1977 Protocols
     Additional to: 372
Genghis Khan: 401, 421, 442n83
genocide, definition of: xi-xiii, 10, 12, 19, 68, 69-
     70, 248, 250-1, 290, 368, 388n; according to
     Axtell: 51n, 74; according to Bauer: 425;

according to Chalk and Jonassohn: 424;
     according to Churchill: 432-3; according
     to Dadrian: 419-20; according to Drost:
     414-5; according to Fein: 420; according to
     Horowitz: 423; according to Katz: 67, 70,
     72, 428; according to Kuper: 418-9;
     according to Legters: 421; according to
     Lemkin: 68-70, 290n, 366n, 407-8, 412n;
     according to Melson: 421-2; according to
     Sartre: 416; according to Savon: 422;
     according to Smith: 421; according to the
     U.N.: 71-2, 290n, 367-8, 409, 412;
     confusion about: 399-400; popular
     vulgarization of: 70
Genocide Convention, see Convention on
     Prevention and Punishment of the Crime
     of Genocide
Genocide Convention Implementation Act
     ("Proxmire Act"): 306
Georgia Colony: 208, 274n410; as Chicora: 188
Georgia Pacific Corp.: 112
Geshichte der Deutschen: 28
Gestapo, see SS
Getty Oil Corp.: 336n
Ghost Dance, the: 243-4, 284n574
Gilbert, Humphrey: 180
Gilbert, Martin: 14n18, 37n
Gilbert, Raleigh: 169
Gingrich, Newt: 430n
Girodet, Jean: 414n
Giufrida, Louis: 341n
Goebbels, Josef: 229n
Gofman, John W.: 329n, 336, 343
Goldfarb, Michael: 42
Golovin, V.M.: 141
Gomez, Esteban: 161n
Goodyear Atomic Corp., Portsmouth, Ohio,
     nuclear facility of: 320n
Gore, Al: 348
Gough, Mike: 344n
Gould, Jay M.: 346; correlates AIDS and nuclear
     contamination: 342-3
Gould, Stephen Jay: 49
Gramsci, Antonio: 15n22, 73
Grant, Ulysses S.: 245
Grants Uranium Belt: 294, 307-10, 312, 314,
     319n, 345
Grattan, John L.: 223n
Great Sioux Reservation: 145, 239n
Greenpeace: 328n
Greenville Treaty (1794): 214
Grey Beard (Cheyenne): 238
Grinde, Donald A., Jr.: 120, 121, 261n132

44-5, 52, 85, 147, 421; racial doctrine of: 44, 64, 421n; 1940 "Commissar Order" of: 39

Hoax of the Twentieth Century, The: 21, 50, 66

Hoggan, David Leslie: 21

Hollywood: 3, 180, 298; and McCarthyism: 298n

Holocaust, the (*Shoah*): xi, xii, xiii, xv-xvi, 8, 9, 12, 19, 29, 64, 110, 137, 156, 229n, 405n, 414n, 417n, 421, 424, 425, 427, 428n, 430n; denial of: xi, xiii, 7, 11, 19-29, 63, 66, 383; disease attrition within: 156, 258n82, 261n141; Jewish resistance to: 424-5n; mystification of: xi-xii, xiii, 73-4; penalties for denial of: xiii, 63; perpetration by "ordinary men": 186-7n; scope of: 49

Holocaust and the Historians, The: 50

Holocaust exclusivism (Jewish exclusivism), school of: xi, xiii-xiv, xv, 7, 9, 31-6, 38, 39-40, 41-3, 49-50, 52, 63, 64, 66, 69-70, 73, 74-5, 83, 110; underlying motivations of: xiii-xiv, 36n, 73-4

Holocaust in Historical Context, The: 50, 66, 67, 433n

Holocaust in Historical Perspective, The: 50

Holocaust in History, The: 34

Homestead Act (1865): 284n573

homosexuals, nazi persecution of: 72n

Honduras, conquest of: 99

Hoover, J. Edgar: 58n63

Horowitz, Irving Louis: 422-3, 431, 443n90

Hössbach, Friedrich/Hössbach Memorandum: 61n118

House Resolution 108 (1953): 287n602, 367n

House Un-American Activities Committee: 369n

Hubbard, William: 171n, 173n

Hudson, Henry: 169n, 197

Hudson's Bay Co.: 192, 195n, 271n328

Huguenots, persecution of: 188, 270n33, 403

Hurons: 119, 270n325; align with French: 192; "anthropological extermination" of: 193; merge with other peoples: 193; missionaries and: 192-3

Hurt, R. Douglas: 135

Hussites, expungement of: 402

I

Ibarra, Francisco de: 99

I.G. Farben Corp.: 303n

Illuminati, the: 23n, 191

Indian Citizenship Act (1924): 246, 366n

Indian Claims Commission: 290-1n, 357n116, 379n; final report of: 291

Indian Health Service (IHS), *see* U.S. Bureau of Indian Affairs

"Indian Problem" ("Indian Question"), the: 156, 174

Indian Removal Act (1830): 144

Indian Reorganization Act (IRA; 1934): 247, 292, 366n

Indian Wars: 3, 13n5, 130, 147, 158-9, 245; Apache Wars: 220; Beaver Wars: 181, 194; Black Hawk's War: 217-8; Buffalo War: 236-7, 239; Centennial Campaign: 239-42; Cherokee War: 205; Chickasaw Wars: 195-6; Couer d'Alene War: 222; Drummer's War: 201, 204; Esopus War: 199; Fox War: 195; French and Indian Wars: 154, 183; George Washington's War: 212-3; Geronimo Campaign: 220; Indian War of 1864: 230-4; Kickapoo Campaign: 237; King Philip's War: 152, 174-8, 180; Kit Carson Campaign: 144-5; Little Crow's War: 145, 229n; Lord Dunmore's War: 207; Mariposa War: 221; Modoc War: 145, 221; Nez Percé Campaign: 222; overall attrition caused by: 157-9; Peach War: 199; Pequot War: 152, 154n, 171-3, 198; Red Cloud's War: 238; Red Sticks War: 215-6; Rogue River War: 221; Round Valley Wars: 217, 277n462; Seminole Wars: 217, 277n462; Sheepeater War: 222; Snake War: 222; Sullivan Campaign: 208; Tuscarora War: 148, 200, 204; Victorio Campaign: 220; Wichita Campaign: 225n; Yakima War: 221-2; Yamasee War: 148, 200-1, 204

indigenous health data: 247-8, 293; infant mortality: 293; life expectancies: 293

indigenous mineral resources, expropriation of: 246-7, 292

indigenous population declines (general): 1, 97, 106, 137, 157-9; in Brazil: 104; in California: 257n68; in Caribbean Basin: 86; in Guatemala: 102; in Española: 86; in Mexico: 98, 101-2; in Nicaragua: 102; in Paraguay: 110; in Peru: 102-3; in U.S.: 129, 130-1, 156, 188, 245

indigenous population declines (particular): Abenakis: 149n, 170, 205n; Absarokes: 155n; Androscoggins: 148n; Appalachees: 204; Arapahos: 155n; Arikara: 155n; Assiniboins: 155n; Bloods: 155n; Blackfeet: 155n; Cahuillas: 221; Cherokees: 144; Chickamaugas: 208; Choctaws: 144, 155n; Cheyennes: 243, 155n; Cocopahs: 221; Cofitachiquis: 201; Comanches: 238, 155n; Creeks: 144, 216; Diné: 145; Doegs: 168; Eries: 194n; Esopus: 199; Gros Ventres:

J

Jackson, Andrew: 186, 216, 219, 251n, 260n119, 275n426; and Indian Removal: 216, 277n460; and Red Stick War: 186, 216, 277n456; 457
Jackson, Robert H.: 365n
Jamestown Plantation: 147, 163–7, 175, 179, 188, 210; founding of: 163, 263n181
Japanese Americans, internment of: 31–2, 58n63
Jefferson, Thomas: 150n, 211, 219; Louisiana Purchase of: 219
Jennings, Francis: 8, 131–2, 134, 135, 139, 178, 253n10; on European origins of scalping: 178
Jenny Expedition, the: 283n559
Jewish Defense League (JDL): 82
Jewish exclusivism, *see* Holocaust exclusivism, school of
Jewish Information Bulletin: 22n
Jewish ritual murder, myth of: 118, 136n
Jim Crow segregation: 378
Jiménez, Marcelo: 111
John Birch Society: 383
Johnson, Hiram W.: 27
Johnson, Lyndon B.: 336n, 380
Johnson, William: 202n, 204, 206n
Johnson Varner, Jeanette: 8
Joint Congressional Committee on Atomic Energy: 298n
Jonassohn, Kurt: 12, 251, 399, 408n, 420n, 422n, 423–4, 425n, 428n, 429, 431; endorsed by Katz: 428n; endorses notion of "ethnocide": 424n
Journal of Historical Review, The: 22
Juan Colón Was A Spanish Jew: 91

K

Kampuchea, *see* Cambodia
Karait Jews, exemption from the Holocaust of: 40
Katanga, genocide in: 53, 64
Katson, Trisha: 396n67
Katz, Steven T.: 14n18, 34–5, 49, 65–6, 67, 71, 138, 157–9, 427–9, 430n, 431, 433n; definition of genocide of: 67, 70, 72, 428; denies Armenian genocide: 33n; denies bacteriological genocide: 155n; denies Bosnian genocide: 53n; denies genocide of American Indians: 138, 157–9; denies genocide against homosexuals: 72n; denies nazi genocide against homosexuals: 72n; denies Pequot genocide: 73n, 173n, 265n220, 429; distorts Genocide Convention: 71–3; distorts Lemkin: 51n, 67–70; distorts

Thornton: 157–9; Jewish exclusivism of: 50, 427–9; mysticism of: 428n; on Chalk and Jonassohn: 428n; on cultural genocide: 428n; revisionist sources of: 33n
Kaufman, Irving R.: 299n
Keegstra, Jim: 23n
Kellogg-Briand Pact (1928): 372n
Kennedy, John F.: 303, 304n
Kerr-McGee Corp.: 311, 314, 320n, 353n54, 354n65; Ambrosia Lake uranium mill of: 312–4; Church Rock uranium mine of: 308; Cimarron nuclear plant of: 320n; job training pgm. of: 310; Grants uranium mine/mill of: 307, 314; Red Rock uranium mine of: Shiprock uranium mine/mill of: 307, 304
Kelly, James: 222
Kendrick, Donald: 37n
Kennekuk (Kickapoo): 217n
Kerry, John: 397n76
Khmer Rouge: 57n54, 64, 390
Kickapoos: 213, 217; decimation at the Thames: 215; flight to Mexico of: 217n; Mackenzie's campaign against: 237
Kieft, Willem: 181, 197–8, 199
King, Matthew: 120
King Charles I of England: 167n, 169n
King George II of England: 204
King George III of England, 1763 Proclamation of: 206, 209, 274n401
King George's War (War of the Austrian Succession): 202, 204
King Hendrick (Mohawk): 184
King James I of England: 263n174
King Philip of Spain: 103
King William's War (War of the League of Augsburg): 202, 203; Treaty of Ryswick ends: 203
Kiowas: 225, 237, 240; and 1851 Ft. Laramie Treaty: 223; smallpox among; surrender of: 237–8
Kirtland Air Force Base (NM): 321
Kitchener, Horatio Herbert: 404n
Kleist, Peter: 56n26
Knox, Henry: 213, 276n435
Kohl, Helmut: 29, 57n43
Komatsu Corp.: 112
Korean War: 296, 299n, 371n
Krauthammer, Charles: 5, 6
Kroeber, Alfred L.: 117, 118, 132–3, 134, 254n22; racism of: 132; statistical manipulations of: 117, 132–3
Ku Klux Klan: 42, 56n38, 374–5; in Colorado:

375n; in Indiana: 375n; in New Jersey: 375n; lynchings by: 374
Kuhnrich, H.: 46
Kuper, Leo: 401, 403, 416-8, 419, 420, 434n, 441n68, 442n73; definition of genocide of: 418, 419; differs with Sartre: 416-7, 441n69
Kurds: 405n

L

La Flesche, Susette: 181
la Florida (Pascua Florida): 129, 159, 188, 200, 208; Everglades area of: 217, 218, 277n462; taken by U.S.: 189; transferred between Spain and Britain: 189
La Salle College: 20
LaBlanc, Lawrence J.: 387, 413n
Lakotas ("Sioux"): 224, 238-44, 282n538, 283n556, 284n573, 317n; and "Red Cloud's War": 238; Black Hills taken from: 242n; Blue Water massacre of: 233n; Bohinupa Band of: 284n574; defense of Powder River by: 239-42; Hunkpapa Band of: 242, 284n574; Ituzipco Band of: 284n574; Little Big Horn victory of: 240; Minneconjou Band of: 243, 284n574; Oglala Band of: 284n574; Sicungu (Brûlé) Band of: 284n574; Sihasapa (Blackfeet) Band of: 284n574; smallpox among: 155n; starvation of: 284n573; reservations of: 317n, 318; Wounded Knee massacre of: xiv, 2-3, 92, 244; 1851 Ft. Laramie Treaty and: 223
Lamdan, Yitzak: xii
Lansky, Meyer: 83
LaRouche, Lyndon: 23n
Las Casas, Bartolomé de: 87-8, 98, 99, 133, 257n71
Lawrence Livermore Laboratories: 299, 321, 329n
Laylock, Dryden: 187
Le Fevre, Robert: 26n
Le Passage de la Ligne: 19
League of Nations: 406; preliminary peace conference of: 406; International Conference for the unification of Criminal Law of: 407
Lector, Hannibal: 93-4
Legion for the Survival of Freedom: 22n
Legters, Lyman: 421, 442n84
Lemkin, Raphaël: 10, 51n, 67, 71, 363, 373n, 407-8, 411, 413n, 414, 416, 426, 431, 432n, 433n, 444n118; and League of Nations: 407; coins term ethnocide: 414n; coins term genocide: 7, 59n82, 67; definition of genocide of: 68-70, 377n, 388, 407-8, 425;

drafts Genocide Convention: 10, 363, 409; official U.S. abuse of: 373n, 410n
Lenni Lenâpés: 184, 199, 203-8, 213, 214; decimation of: 215; Moravian faction massacred: 207; "named" after de la Warr: 163m; smallpox among: 154, 206
Lepke (Louis Buchalter): 83
Leuchter, Fred A.: 24, 26, 54n9
Leupp, Francis: 245, 292n, 366n
Lewis and Clark expedition: 185n
Liberty Lobby: 21, 22n, 23n, 383, 396n67
Libyans, Italian atrocities against: 89
Lieber Code (1863): 146n
Lieber, Francis: 146n
Líevano, Pedro: 139
Lifton, Robert Jay: 11, 19
Lincoln, Abraham: 218, 226n
Lindbergh, Charles A.: 27, 28
Lindquist, Sven: 404n
Lipán Apaches: 108, 189, 269n, 298; Lipanjennes Band of: 219n; Lipanes Abejo Band of: 219n; Lipanes de Arriba Band of: 219n; scalp bounty on: 219; smallpox among: 155n; survivors absorbed by Mescaleros: 219n
Lipstadt, Deborah: xvii n 1, 11, 14n18, 25, 49, 57n57, 73; academic stature of: 25; denies Cambodian genocide: 33; denies genocide of American Indians: 11; denies stalinist genocide: 33; ignores Gypsy holocaust: 36, 49; Jewish exclusivism of: 31-6, 51n; on "Armenian tragedy of 1918": 32; on "Japanese" internment: 31-2; on uniqueness of the Holocaust: 33-4; rejoins Nolte: 29-30, 31, 58n61; rebuts Holocaust deniers: 25-9
Little Big Horn River, battle of: 236n, 240n
Little Crow (Santee Dakota): 227; scalp and skull of displayed: 227
Little Matter of Genocide, A: xi, xii, xvi, 8, 11, 12
Little Thunder (Lakota): 223n
Little Turtle (Miami): 213, 276n434
Little Wolf (Cheyenne): 243, 284n572
Litton Industries: 112, 303
Loaisa, Rodrigo de: 103
Lockheed Aerospace Corp.: 303
Logan, Benjamin: 212
Lonewolf v. Hitchcock (1903): 286n595, 291
Looking Elk, Stanley: 317n
López de Cárdenas, García: 160n
Lord Dunmore: 207, 2309n, 274n401
Los Alamos National Scientific Laboratory: 294, 299, 317, 319, 321, 324, 335; Area G of:

320-1
"Lost Colony," *see* Roanoak Plantation
Louisiana Purchase (1803): 219
Lovewell, John: 186n
Low-Level Radioactive Waste Policy Act (1980): 360n161
Lucas Garcia, Fernando: 114
Luciano de Silva, Manuel: 90
Lugar, Richard: 384
Lugar-Helms-Hatch Sovereignty Package: 385-7
Lukács, Georg: 15n22
Luke Air Force Base, Ariz.: 358n134
Luxembourg, nazi genocide in: 67-8
lynching: 374-5

M

Mabachi, siege of: 195
MacArthur, Douglas: 371n
Mackenzie, Ranald S.: 237, 240-2; at Palo Duro Canyon: 237; Kickapoo campaign of: 237; northern campaign of: 240-2; suspends Lakota rations: 242n
Madagascar Plan, the: 34n, 35n, 44n
Madariaga, Salvador: 91
Madole, James: 20
Majdanek, *see* death camps
Maine Colony, scalp bounty of: 182, 183, 202n
Maktos, John: 365
Malcolm X: 346
Mallery, Garrick: 253n10
Mancuso, Thomas F.: 323n, 329n
Mangus (Narragansett): 174n
Manhattan Project: 294, 298; Enrico Fermi's team in: 333n; Trinity Project of: 294, 298n, 299
Manifest Destiny, doctrine of: 211, 219, 221n; compared to nazi *Lebensraumpolitik*: 147
Manson Family: 427n
Manufacturing Consent: xv
Manzanar, *see* concentration camps
Mao Tse Tung: 370
Marcellus, Tom: 21n
María, Nectario: 91
Marks, Sidney: 329n
Markusen, Erik: 11, 19
Marrus, Robert: 14n18, 34
Marshall Islands: 324, 327; Bikini Island nuclear test: 324n, 342n; Enewetak nuclear test: 324n, 342m; Kili Island: 324n; overall nuclear testing in: 324n, 328n; radiation effects on population of: 324-5n, 328n; Rongelap Atoll: 328n, 342n, 357n113; Utirik Atoll: 328n, 342n, 357n113
Marshall, George: 295n

Marshall, John: 125n60, 211, 275n425
Martin, John: 164
Martin, Paul S.: 135
Martin, Roque: 105
Martineau: James H.: 227n
Marquand, Leo: 418
Marqués de Rubí: 189
Marx, Karl: 250
marxists/marxism: 119, 418
Maryland Colony, scalp bounty of: 184, 268n276
"Masada" (poem): xii
Masada, siege of: xiii
Mason, John: 171-2, 260n120
Masonic Orders: 91
Massachusetts Bay Colony: 139, 140, 152, 154n, 170-3, 174n, 259n100; campaign against the Pequots of: 171-2; founding of: 170; King Philip's War and: 175-8; scalp bounty of: 180, 182
Massachusetts Institute of Technology (MIT): 21
Massacre of St. Bartholomew: 403
massacres of American Indians: Acoma: 189; Bad Axe River: 217; Bear river: 224n, 227; Blue Water: 223n; Buffalo Springs: 231; Camp Robinson: 243; Conestoga: 206; Crooked Creek: 225n; El Mozote: 116; La Cayentana: 115; Humbolt County massacres: 220; Kittanning: 185n; Las Vueltas: 116, 127n98; Los Llanitos: 116, 127n98; Marias River: 240n; Moravian: 207; Mystic: 92, 171-2, 175, 185n, 265n210; Neoheroka: 200; of Narragansetts: 175-6; Peskeompscut River: 176; Río Gualsinga: 116, 127n98; Río Sampul: 116; Sand Creek: xv, 2n, 3, 92, 186, 232-3, 234, 236n, 238, 268n280, 281; Sappa Creek: 237; Slaughter of the Innocents: 198; St. François: 205; Washita: 150n, 236, 240; Weaverville: 220; Wounded Knee: xiv, 2-3, 92, 244; Yreka: 221n
Massasoit (Wampanoag): 170n, 175, 265n222
Matabele, British decimation of: 403, 439n28
Mather, Cotton: 139, 266n249
Mather, Increase: 177, 266n149
Mathew, Thomas: 168
Mathias, Charles: 387, 397n76
Mayans: 106, 108, 118; contemporary genocide of: 92; historical genocide of: 99, 102; impact of disease upon: 139; Ixil division of: 114; Kekchi division of: 114
Mayer, Arno J.: 43, 47n
McCalden, William David: 20n, 21
McCarthy, Joseph R.: 298-9, 369n

Norse, *see* Vikings
North American bison (buffalo), extermination of: 150, 282n546
North American Free Trade Agreement (NAFTA): 345
North Atlantic Treaty Organization (NATO): 300n
Northwest Ordinance (1787): 211
Northwest Territory, the: 154, 213-4; Greenville Boundary of: 214
Northwestern University: 55n14
Notre Dame Law School: 21n
Nuclear Fuel Service Corp.: 320n; West Valley, NY, nuclear waste storage facility of: 335, 336n, 340n
Nuclear Materials and Engineering Corp.: 320n
nuclear waste disposal: 332-40; at Yucca Mountain: 230, 339, 360n158; increasing need of: 334; monitored retrievable site (MRS) concept of: 335-7, 359n145, 360n150; permanent repository concept of: 335-6; toxicity of: 334n; quantities of: 334-5; Waste Isolation Pilot Project (WIPP) of: 338
Nuclear Waste Policy Act (1982): 304n, 359n141; 1987 revision of: 359n143
Nuremberg defense, the: 372
Nuremberg Doctrine, the: 380, 382
Nuremberg Laws, the: 40, 79n29, 163n403; "Blood Protection" provision of: 79n29, 163n
Nuremberg rallies, the: 94
Nuremberg Trials, the: 21, 290n, 343, 363, 364, 365n, 367n, 379n, 380, 409, 441n76
Nuremberg Tribunal (International Military Tribunal): 143, 385, 390, 407, 408; charter of: 380, 413n, 415
Nye, Gerald P.: 27

O

O'Connell, Robert: 154
Of Arms and Men: 154
Office of Strategic Services (OSS): 297n
Ohio Company of Virginia/Ohio Land Co.: 204, 209; Washington's involvement in: 209
Oklahoma Territory ("Permanent Indian Territory"): 217
O'Leary, Hazel: 339
Olin Corp., depleted uranium ammunition of: 301n, 302n
Oldham, John: 152
Oñate, Juan de: 189, 263n168, 269n294
Ortiz, Simon J.: 294n, 312-4

Opechancanough (Tsenacommacah): 165-7, 264n185
Operation Plowshare: 326n, 331, 332n, 339, 358n126; contamination by: 358n129; Operation Ketch of: 331; Palenquin device of: 358n132; Panama Canal plan of: 331; Project Gasbuggy of: 331, 358n131; Project Rio Blanco of: 331; Project Ruleson of: 331
Opium Wars, the: 92, 405
Oppenheimer, J. Robert: 299n, 358n126
ORDEN: 115-6
Oregon Territory: 220, 221-2, 223; Couer d'Alene War in: 222; Rogue River War in: 221; Sheepeater campaign in: 222; Snake War in: 222; U.S. acquisition of: 218; Yakima War in: 222
Origins of Totalitarianism, The: 414
Oriskiny, battle of: 208
Ottawas: 203, 206, 208, 213, 214; Amherst's bacteriological extermination of: 64, 154, 196n, 206; decimation at the Thames: 215
Ottoman Empire: xvii n 8
Oxford University Press: 429

P

Paiutes ("Snakes"): 222, 279n496, 342n; cancer rate among: 327; Gahrump Band of: 327; Las Vegas Colony of: 327; Walpapi Band of: 222; Yahuskin Band of: 222
Palestine/Palestinians: xii, xvii n 8, 34n, 50n, 73n, 74, 84; Israeli genocide of: 74, 398n89
Palfrey, John Gorham: 131-2, 173n, 254n12, 266n249; statistical manipulations of: 131-2
Palo Duro Canyon, battle of: 237
Panama: anti-Indian policies of: 113; conquest of: 99, 105; U.S. invasion of: 389
Papazian, Pierce: 63
Paraguay: 424n; denial of genocide by: 412n; genocide of the Achés by: 421
Parker, Quannah (Comanche): 237, 283n550
Parkman, Francis: xiv-xv, 173n, 266n249
Patterson, William L.: 376, 434n
Paxton Boys, the: 206
Peabody Coal Co.: 249, 317
Peckham, Howard: 261n132
Pell, Claiborne: 397n76
Penn, Thomas: 185n
Pennsylvania Colony, scalp bounty of: 184
Pentagon, the: 325; Hanford cover-up of: 323; recruitment of nazis by: 302n; weapons development pgms. of: 302-3
Pequots: 148, 150n, 174, 178n, 196n, 198, 200,

Rassinier, Paul: 19-20, 25, 29, 30, 36, 49
Reagan, Ronald: 28, 29, 341n, 364, 390n; and the
    Genocide Convention: 364, 384, 396n70,
    397n72; and NSC 68: 297n; and U.S.
    conflict with Libya: 383, 396n71; and U.S.
    invasion of Grenada: 383, 396n71; and low
    intensity warfare: 383; economic policies of:
    297n
"Recovery of Masada, The" (essay): xiii
Red Cloud (Lakota): 238
Red Jacket (Seneca): 276n430
Red Sticks (Batón Rouge), see Creeks
Rehnquist, William: 377-8
Reichstag fire, the: 369
Reid v. Covert (1957): 394n30
Reno, Marcus: 240n
Reuters News Service: 112
Reuther, Walter: 301n
Revolutionary Communist Party, USA (RCP): 6,
    7, 118, 136n
Reynolds, John: 217
Reynolds, "Lonesome Charlie": 239n
Rhode Island Colony: 174n, 175, 177
Richmond, Harry: 232n
Riél, Louis: 211n
Rio Tinto Zinc Corp.: 112, 310n
Rios Mott, Efrain: 114
Roanoak Plantation ("Lost Colony"): 148, 161,
    162n, 259n100
Rockefeller, Nelson: 336n
Rockwell International Corp.: 307
Rockwell, George Lincoln: 20
Rocky Flats nuclear weapons facility (Colo.):
    299, 335; breast cancer rates around: 335n;
    closure of: 320; illegal plutonium burning
    at: 335n; nuclear waste storage at: 335n
Rocky Mountain News: 187, 228, 229n, 231n,
    281n526; exterminationist rhetoric of: 228-
    9; praises Sand Creek Massacre: 234-5,
    268n281; 1995 apology of: 234n
Roco, Julio: 109
Rogers, Robert: 205
Roman Catholic Church: 402; Dominican Order
    of: 403; Franciscan Order of: 140, 189; Jesuit
    Order of: 138, 140, 192, 283n557
Roman Nose (Cheyenne): 244n
Romani (Roma), see Gypsies
Romania, persecution of Gypsies in: 41-2
Roosevelt, Franklin Delano (FDR): 28, 286n592,
    325, 368
Roosevelt, Theodore: xv, 151n, 406
Rosebud Creek, battle of: 240
Rosenbaum, Alan S.: 65, 430n

Rosenberg, Alfried: 88
Rosenberg, Ethel: 298n, 299n, 369n
Rosenberg, Julius: 298, 299n, 369n
Rothfels, Hans: 51
Rowlandson, Mary: 176n
Royal Dutch Shell Corp.: 112
Rubenstein, Richard L.: xii, 31
Rusk, Dean: 375-6
Russell, Bertrand: 379, 415, 416
Russell Tribunal, the: 380, 382, 415n
Rutgers University: 422
Rutherford, Griffith: 274n410
Rwanda, genocide in: 12, 53, 64, 250n, 390,
    391n; Hutus and: 426; tribunal convened
    on: 400n

S

Sacs (Sac and Fox): 214; adopt Mesquakies: 214;
    in Black Hawk's War: 217-8; Iowa
    reservation of: 218; massacred at Bad Axe
    River: 218; Nebraska reservation of: 217n
Sagadohoc Colony: 169
Said, Edward: 120
Sails of Hope: 90
Salazar, Pedro de: 262n152
Sale, Kirkpatrick: 8, 87, 88, 120, 121
Samisdat Publications: 23n
Sandia National Scientific Laboratories (NM):
    320, 324
SANE: 361n167
San Francisco Bulletin: 156
Sandinistas, see Nicaragua
Sandusky, battle of: 208
Santo Tomás, Domingo de: 103, 106
Sarbanes, Paul: 397n76
Sartre, Jean Paul: 379, 416, 417, 419, 429, 434n,;
    441n68; "colonialism equals genocide"
    thesis of: 416, 433n, 441n69;
    "intentionalist/function–alist controversy"
    and: 441n67
Sassacus (Pequot): 171-3
Satank (Kiowa): 237
Saturday Review: 404
Sauer, Carl O.: 8, 120, 133
Savon, Henri: 422-3, 431
Sayr, Hal: 232n, 234n
scalps/scalping, origins and practice of: 1, 2, 129,
    180-8, 198, 219, 227; display of: 185n, 186,
    187n; European origins of: 178, 188, 267,
    256; for bounty: 1, 176, 180-8, 219, 220,
    227, 268n276
Schindler's List (movie): 41
Schlafly, Phyllis: 383

Winslow, Josiah: 175
Winthrop, John: 152
Wirth, Tim: 391n
Wirz, Henry: 146
witches/witchburning: 71n, 402
Wituwamat (Wampanoag), head of displayed: 267n254
Wizard of Oz, The: 244
Wolfe, James: 184
Women Strike for Peace: 361n167
Wood, William: 255n28
World Communist Conspiracy, myth of: 369
World Court, *see* International Court of Justice
World Health Organization (WHO): 249, 361n165
W.R. Grace Co.: 112
Wright, Ben: 221n
Wyandots: 206, 207, 208, 213, 214; absorb Huron survivors: 193n; decimation at the Thames: 215; smallpox among: 215
Wyatt, Francis: 166
Wynkoop, Edward: 231, 232n, 235n, 281n529

Y

Yahil, Leni: 14n18
Yakimas: 221-2; and Hanford nuclear facility: 323; and MRS: 337; reservation of: 300; U.S. wars against: 221-2
Yale University: 344n, 407; press of: 429
Yalta Conference (1945): 370
Yankee Atomic Electric Co.: 301
Yeardley, George: 165-6
Yockey, Francis Parker: 21n
Yugoslavia, nazi genocide in: 38n48
Yuma Proving Grounds (Ariz.): 358n134

Z

Zannis, Mark: 8
Zeiss Optics Corp.: 303n
Zerubavel, Yael: xiii
zionists/zionism: xiii, xvii n 8, 7, 21n, 32n, 55n23, 83, 117; and German reparations to Israel: 26; German antipartisan operations against: 46-7; "Fifth Column" of: 32
Zorito, Alonzo de: 102
Zulu War: 92, 403
Zundel, Ernst: 23-4, 26, 54n13
Zweier lei Untergang: 29

1st Colorado Volunteer Cavalry Regiment.: 234n, 281n531
3rd Colorado Volunteer Cavalry Regiment.: 13n3, 186, 228-5, 268n281, 281n531; and Sand Creek Massacre: 232-4; becomes "Bloody Third": 234; formation of: 228, 229; known as "Bloodless Third": 232
4th U.S. Cavalry Regiment.: 237
7th U.S. Cavalry Regiment.: 92, 150, 235n; and Washita massacre: 236; and Wounded Knee massacre; destroyed at the Little Big Horn: 240
10th U.S. Cavalry Regiment.: 244n